Principles of
Object-Oriented
Software
Development

INTERNATIONAL COMPUTER SCIENCE SERIES

Consulting Editor   **A D McGettrick**   University of Strathclyde

SELECTED TITLES IN THE SERIES

Principles of
Object-Oriented
Software
Development

Anton Eliëns

Vrije Universiteit, Amsterdam

ADDISON-WESLEY
PUBLISHING
COMPANY

Wokingham, England • Reading, Massachusetts • Menlo Park, California • New York
Don Mills, Ontario • Amsterdam • Bonn • Sydney • Singapore
Tokyo • Madrid • San Juan • Milan • Paris • Mexico City • Seoul • Taipei

Cover designed by Chris Eley
and printed by the Riverside Printing Co. (Reading) Ltd
Typeset by the author
Printed and bound by the University Press, Cambridge

First printed 1994

ISBN 0-201-62444-3

British Library Cataloguing-in-Publication Data
A catalogue record for this book is available from the British Library.

Library of Congress Cataloging-in-Publication Data is available

Foreword

This book is an important contribution to object-oriented literature, bridging the gap between the language and software engineering communities. It covers language design issues relating to inheritance, types, polymorphism, and active objects as well as software design paradigms such as the object modeling technique (OMT), the model-view-controller paradigm (MVC) and responsibility-driven design. Its four-part subdivision of the subject matter into design, languages and systems, foundations, and application frameworks nicely balances practice and theory, covering both practical design techniques and foundational models. Its use of C++ as the primary application language, with Smalltalk and Eiffel as additional languages, allows the book to be used in courses with programming assignments in mainstream object-oriented languages.

The overall sense of balance and perspective is matched by an engaging style and a modern treatment of an exceptionally broad range of topics in the body of the book. The conceptually challenging questions at the end of each chapter (with answers in an appendix) are sometimes humorous. For example, the question "Why do you need friends?", which invites the reader to examine the value of this C++ language construct, is nicely answered by pointing out tradeoffs between efficiency and safety, ending with the admonition "treat friends with care".

Object-oriented programming started as a language framework for single-user systems, but is maturing into a technology for heterogeneous, distributed network systems that focus on interoperability and glue for the composition of heterogeneous modules. The notion of structure in object-oriented programming is analogous to, but more complex than, the structure of structured programming. This book reflects the maturation process from single-user to distributed systems technology and provides a bridge from object-oriented concepts of single-user programming to distributed software design concepts.

Basic object-oriented concepts are introduced from the viewpoint of design, thereby motivating language concepts by their role in the software life cycle. The first four chapters provide a gentle introduction to fundamental concepts that yields unexpected insights for the seasoned reader. Chapter 1 examines paradigms of programming and provides a distinctive object-oriented view of the software life cycle, while chapter 2 presents C++, examines its benefits and pitfalls, and compares it to Smalltalk and Eiffel. Chapter 3 on object-oriented design includes an insightful discussion of models, contracts, and specifications that provides a comparative overview and synthesis of alternative approaches to the conceptual foundations of design. Chapter 4 rounds out the section on design with a discussion of testing and metrics for software validation that provides a practical counterpoint to the conceptual focus of earlier chapters.

The topics in the first four chapters are well chosen to provide a foundation for later topics. The chapter on language design principles includes an up-to-date review of models of inheritance and delegation, the chapter on concurrency examines inheritance anomalies, concurrent object models, and principles of distributed programming, while the chapter on composition and collaboration explains callbacks, window management, and event-driven computation. The three chapters on foundations examine, in a substantive but relaxed way, algebraic models for abstract data types, calculi for type polymorphism, and behavioral refinement through subtyping. The two final chapters provide an account of interoperability, standards, library design, requirements engineering, hypermedia links, and heterogeneous systems.

This book covers an unusually broad range of topics in an eminently readable fashion and is unique in its balance between theory and practice and its multifaceted approach. Anton Eliëns demonstrates an up-to-date mastery of the literature and the rare ability to compare, evaluate, and synthesize the work of different software research and development communities. He is to be commended on his skill and versatility in weaving a sequential expository thread through a heterogeneous, distributed domain of subject matter.

Peter Wegner

Preface

This is a book about object-oriented software development. It reflects the contents of an upper-level undergraduate course on Object-Oriented Programming, given at the Vrije Universiteit Amsterdam.

Features of this book

- It provides an introduction to object-oriented programming, covering design, languages, and foundational issues concerning *abstract data types* and *inheritance*. It also pays attention to environments, library support and application frameworks for OOP, in particular for graphical user interfaces and hypermedia.

- It contains an exposition of the conceptual issues underlying the design of object-oriented languages, and in particular the notion of *active objects* (that is, the extension of object-oriented languages with concurrency) is covered in detail.

- Foundational issues and formal aspects of object-oriented programming are examined extensively. A major theme of the book is to establish precisely the relation between the guidelines and prescriptions emerging from software engineering practice on the one hand, and the constraints and insights originating out of a type theoretical analysis of abstract data types and polymorphism on the other.

- Many of the notions introduced and problems discussed are clarified by short programs, most of which are in C++. However, no prior knowledge of C++ is required since a brief tutorial on C++, as well as on Smalltalk and Eiffel, is included in the appendix.

- The material is organized around *slides*. The slides occur in the text in reduced format, but are also available for use on an overhead projector. Each slide captures some important notion or concept which is explained and commented upon in the accompanying text. A separate *Instructor's Guide* is available, which provides hints for presenting the slides and answers to the questions posed at the end of each chapter.

Intended readers This book may be used as the primary text for a course on OOP or independently as study or reference material. It may be used by the following categories of readers:

- *students* – as a textbook or as supplementary reading for research or project papers.

- *software engineers* – as (another) text on object-oriented programming.

- *professional teachers* – as ready-made material for a course on object-oriented programming.

Naturally, this is not meant to exclude other readers. For instance, researchers may find the book useful for its treatment of the foundational aspects of OOP, or programmers may benefit from the hints and example programs in C++. Another reason for using this book may be its compact representation of already familiar material and the references to other (often research) literature.

The book is meant to be self-contained. As prior knowledge, however, a general background in computer science (that is, computer languages and data structures as a minimum) is required. To fully understand the sections that deal with foundational issues or formal aspects, the reader must also have some knowledge of elementary mathematical logic.

Organization The book is divided into four parts. Each part presents the issues involved in object-oriented programming from a different perspective, which may be characterized respectively as *design, languages, foundations* and *applications*.

Part I: Designing Object-Oriented Systems

1. *Introduction:* This chapter gives an introduction to the area of object-oriented programming. It presents some background and summarizes the viewpoints adhered to in the rest of the book. It also gives a global view on the object-oriented life cycle and discusses object-orientation as a paradigm of programming. It further presents an overview of the material covered with reference to the literature used and suggestions for further reading.

2. *Object-oriented programming constructs:* This chapter explains the basic notions underlying object-oriented programming, notably encapsulation and inheritance. Also, it introduces the programming language C++. A canonical approach to developing concrete data types is presented and some of the benefits and pitfalls of object-oriented programming in C++ are discussed.

3. *Object-oriented design:* This chapter discusses the process of software development and the various modeling perspectives involved in analysis and design. It further explains the issues involved in arriving at a proper object model, introduces the notion of *contract* as an instrument to capture the relationships between object classes, and discusses the transition from specification to design.

4. *Software engineering perspectives:* In this chapter the notion of robust software is taken as a starting point to explore the relevance of test methods for the validation of object-oriented software. In particular, we discuss the notion of runtime consistency as enforced by behavioral contracts. Also, we take a look at a number of metrics for object-oriented software and discuss some guidelines for class design.

Part II: Object-Oriented Languages and Systems

5. *Object-oriented language design:* This chapter explains concepts underlying the design of object-oriented languages and gives a characterization of a number of them, in particular Smalltalk, Eiffel and C++. It further presents some alternative object models and discusses dynamic inheritance by delegation. It also analyses issues involved in meta-level architectures for class-based languages.

6. *Distribution and concurrency:* This chapter discusses the relevance of distribution and concurrency for object-oriented modeling. It analyses the relation between objects and processes and presents the notion of *active objects* as a means of introducing concurrency in object-oriented languages. It deals with a number of concurrent extensions of C++ and discusses problems involved in combining processes by inheritance. Finally, the chapter explores some of the requirements for distribution.

7. *Composition mechanisms:* This chapter explores a number of composition techniques that may be employed in the development of object-oriented systems. These composition mechanisms include inheritance and interaction through delegation. Further, it explores cooperation schemes, such as the MVC paradigm, which are employed in window-based applications, and it gives an example of employing an event-driven computation model to guarantee global consistency.

Part III: Foundations of Object-Oriented Modeling

8. *Abstract data types:* This chapter considers the notion of abstract data types from the perspective of *types as constraints*. It presents an algebraic approach in which objects may be characterized as algebras. Further, it explains the difference between the classical approach of realizing abstract data types in procedural languages and the realization of abstract data types in object-oriented languages. The implications of a more pragmatic conception of types is also discussed.

9. *Polymorphism:* This chapter discusses inheritance from a declarative perspective, and gives a precise characterization of the subtype relation. It further discusses the various flavors of polymorphism and presents a type theoretical treatment of genericity and overloading. Also, type calculi that capture data hiding and self-reference are given. These insights will be related to the realization of polymorphism in Eiffel and C++.

10. *Behavioral refinement:* This chapter extends the notion of types as constraints to include behavioral properties. It presents an assertion logic for the verification of programs and discusses the operational model underlying the verification of object behavior based on traces. It further gives precise guidelines to determine whether classes that are syntactical subtypes satisfy the behavioral refinement relation. Finally, an overview is given of formal approaches to characterize the behavior of collections of objects.

Part IV: Object-Oriented Application Frameworks

11. *Libraries and environments:* This chapter discusses the problems involved in application development and raises the issue of standards. It discusses some of the design choices that may arise in developing libraries, presents a number of methods and tools that may be used in software development, and discusses the criteria for evaluating class libraries, mentioning a number of libraries for C++. Included is a list of *ftp* sites where these libraries may be obtained by those having access to the Internet.

12. *Hypermedia frameworks:* This chapter asserts the relevance of object-oriented technology for the development of hypermedia. It discusses the notions underlying hypermedia and presents a model allowing for the inclusion of timing constraints. Further, it discusses a multi-paradigm approach to programming multi-media interfaces, and explores some of the problems involved in developing heterogeneous systems. The chapter concludes with some reflections on the future of object-oriented programming.

Tracks For those developing a course on object-oriented programming, the book offers a choice between various tracks, for which the ingredients are sketched below. Also, an indication is given of the sections that contain more advanced material.

	regular	extended	advanced
programming	2, 5, 7, 12	6, 8, 11	7,8
software engineering	1, 3, 4, 11	8.1, 8.2, 10.1, 10.2, 10.4	8, 10
theoretical	8, 9, 10	1, 3, 4, 5	9.5, 9.6, 10.3

The *programming track*, consisting of chapters 2, 5, 7 and 12, may be augmented with material from the appendices and chapters 6, 8 and 11. The *software engineering track*, consisting of chapters 1, 3, 4 and 11, may be augmented with material from the theoretical track as indicated. The *theoretical track*, consisting of chapters 8, 9 and 10, may need to be augmented with more general information concerning OOP provided in the other tracks.

Background and motivations My own interest in OOP stems from my research on the language DLP, a language integrating logic programming with object-oriented features and parallelism (Eliëns, 1992). When looking for material for a course on object-oriented programming, I could not find a book that paid sufficient attention to foundational and formal aspects. Most of the books were written from a perspective on OOP that did not quite suit my purposes. What I was looking for could to some extent only be found in research papers. As a consequence, I organized my OOP course around a small number of papers, selecting the papers that, to my mind, can be considered as *landmark papers*, papers that have become known as originally presenting some significant notion or insight. The apparent disadvantage of basing a course on OOP on papers is the obvious lack of a unified view, and of a consistent use of terminology. The advantage of such an approach, however, is that students are encouraged to assess the contribution of each paper and to form their own view by comparing critically the different viewpoints expressed in the papers. Personally, I favor the use of original papers, since these somehow show more clearly how the ideas put forward originated. Later, more polished, renderings of these same ideas often lack this quality of 'discovery'.

The idea of organizing a book around slides came quite naturally, as the result of structuring the growing collection of slides, and the wish to maintain the compact representation offered by the slides.

The choice of material reflects my personal prefence for foundational issues, in other words, papers that are focused on concepts rather than (mal)practice. The choice of material has also been colored by my interest for (distributed) hypermedia systems and (to some extent) by my previous work on distributed logic programming. Although the book is certainly not focused on language constructs, modeling issues as well as foundational issues are generally related to existing or conceivable language constructs, and (whenever possible) illustrated by working examples developed for that purpose.

The choice for C++ to present the examples reflects my belief that C++ is a valid programming language for object-oriented programming. However, I also believe that in the (near) future multi-paradigm approaches (extending C++) will play a significant role.

The approach taken in this book may be characterized as *abstract*, in the sense that attention is paid primarily to concepts rather than particular details of a solution or implementation language. By chance, in response to a discussion in my class, I looked up the meaning of *abstract* in a dictionary, where to my surprise I learned that one of its meanings is *to steal, to take away dishonestly*. Jokingly, I remarked that this meaning sheds a different light on the notion of *abstract data types*, but at a deeper level I recognized the extent to which the ideas presented in this book have profited from the ideas originally developed by others. My rendering of these ideas in a more abstract form is, however, not meant to appropriate them in a dishonest way, but rather to give these ideas the credit they deserve by fitting them in a context, a framework encompassing both theoretical and pragmatical aspects of object-oriented computing. As one of the meanings of the adjective *abstract*, the dictionary also lists the word *abstruse* (not easy to understand). There is no need to say that, within the limits of my capabilities, I have tried to avoid becoming abstruse.

Finally, in presenting the material, I have tried to retain a sufficient degree of objectivity. Nevertheless, whenever personal judgments have slipped in, they are rather meant to provoke a discussion than provide a final answer.

Information For any questions or comments you may contact the author at `eliens@cs.vu.nl` by electronic mail, or at Dr A. Eliëns, Vrije Universiteit, Department of Mathematics and Computer Science, De Boelelaan 1081, 1081 HV Amsterdam, The Netherlands.

Acknowledgements In writing this book, I have profited from the enthusiasm and criticism of numerous students and colleagues. In particular I should like to thank, in arbitrary order, Hans van Vliet, Henri Bal, Dick Grune, Cees Visser, Ira Pohl, John Caspers, Jacco van Ossenbruggen and Matthijs van Doorn. Also, I should like to thank Chris Dollin for his detailed and constructive comments. Finally, thanks to Simon Plumtree and Andrew McGettrick for, as they will surely understand, 'playing it by ear'.

The short musical phrases appearing at the beginning of each chapter are taken from *The Notebook for Anna Magdalena Bach* (which are intended primarily for young players). Despite their apparent simplicity, however, they are acknowledged by experienced pianists as being hard to play properly, yet they are among the standard exercises for learner pianists. In a way this reflects the problem of teaching object-oriented programming. The concepts underlying object-oriented programming may at first seem deceptively simple (and not require the complexity of C++ or a type theoretical analysis). However, in developing object-oriented models some intrinsically difficult questions remain, for which we have no definite answer and which may even require extensive expertise and technology to come up with a partial solution. Returning to the music, I often find myself improvising, leaving the written music for what it is, a starting point.

Anton Eliëns
Amsterdam
October 1994

Contents

Part I

Designing Object-Oriented Systems

1

Introduction

To gain an understanding of some new area, it is virtually unavoidable to be immersed in the material for a while without exactly understanding where it will lead.

Introduction – *Principles of Object-Oriented Software Development*   1

- history – *object speak*
- abstraction – *responsibilities in OOP*
- software development – *the OO life-cycle*
- paradigms of programming
- additional literature

Additional keywords and phrases: *client-server model, behavioral refinement, analysis, design, implementation, features and benefits*

Slide 1-1: Introduction

This first chapter will give a preliminary characterization of object-oriented programming, sketch some of its history and give an outline of the theme of this book, which may be summarized by the phrase that *OOP provides a new means for abstraction in both programming and design*. However, as will become clear later on, what OOP offers is not altogether new. One of the goals set for this book is to relate the mechanisms offered by OOP to their precedents in the history of computer programming and design languages. The reader may then establish whether OOP is just another toy for software developers or a significant contribution to both software engineering and programming. At the end of this introductory chapter, references are provided to the other literature in the field.

1.1   What is object-orientation?

Prior to any other characterization, it must be stressed that object-oriented programming does not deal with programming in the sense of developing algorithms or data structures, but must be studied as a (collection of) means for the organization of programs and, more generally, techniques for designing programs. From this perspective, OOP may be regarded as an emerging methodology. See slide 1-2.

As the primary means for structuring a program or design, OOP provides *objects*. Objects may model real life entities, may function to capture abstractions of arbitrary complex phenomena, or may represent system artifacts such as stacks or graphics.

Operationally, objects control the computation. From the perspective of program development, however, the most important characteristic of objects is not their behavior as such, but the fact that the behavior of an object may be described by an abstract characterization of its interface. Having such an abstract characterization suffices for design. The actual behavior of the object may be implemented later and refined according to need.

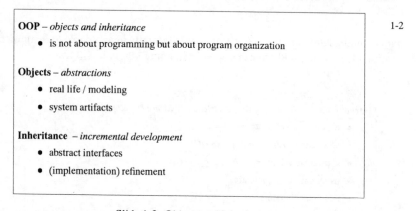

Slide 1-2: Objects and inheritance

Perhaps the most important contribution of object orientation to the practice of programming is the use of inheritance to specify relations between (classes of) objects. Inheritance provides a means to add functionality to a specification incrementally. Inheritance thus enables better conceptual modeling, since it allows a factoring out of the common parts of a specification and the reuse of specifications. When used in a disciplined fashion, inheritance allows stepwise refinement of the specification of the type of a class of objects, and it allows us to view different objects of different types as belonging to a common (super) type.

Some history In the last few decades, we have been able to witness a rapid change in the technology underlying our computer systems. Simultaneously, our ideas of how to program these machines have changed radically as well.

The history of programming languages may be regarded as a progression from low level constructs towards high level abstractions, that enable the programmer to specify programs in a more abstract manner and hence allow problem related abstractions to be captured more directly in a program. This development towards high level languages was partly motivated by the need to be able to verify that a program adequately implemented a specification (given in terms of a formal description of the requirements of an application). Regarded from this perspective, it is then perhaps more appropriate to speak of a progression of *paradigms of programming*, where a paradigm must be understood as a set of mechanisms and guidelines telling us how to employ these mechanisms.

The first abstraction mechanism beyond the level of assembler language and macros is provided by *procedures*. Procedures play an important role in the method of *stepwise refinement* introduced by the school of *structured programming*. Stepwise refinement allows the specification of a complex algorithm gradually in more and more detail.

Program verification amounts to establishing whether the implementation of an algorithm in a programming language meets its specification given in mathematical or logical terms. Associated with the school of structured programming is a method of verification based on what has become known as *Hoare logic*, which proceeds by introducing *assertions* and establishing that procedures meet particular pre- and post-conditions.

Other developments in programming language research aimed at providing ways in which to capture the mathematical or logical meaning of a program more directly. These developments resulted in a number of functional programming languages (e.g. ML, Miranda) and logic programming languages, of which Prolog is the most well-known. The programming language Lisp may in this respect also be regarded as a functional language.

The history of object-oriented programming may be traced back to a concern for *data abstraction*, which was needed to deal with algorithms that involved complex data structures. The notion of *objects*, originally introduced in Simula (Dahl and Nygaard, 1966), has significantly influenced the design of many subsequent languages,(eg. CLU, Modula and Ada). The first well-known *object-oriented language* was Smalltalk, originally developed to program the *Dynabook*, a kind of machine that is now familiar to us as a laptop or notebook computer. In Smalltalk, the data hiding aspect of objects has been combined with the mechanism of inheritance, allowing the reuse of code defining the behavior of objects. The primary motivation behind Smalltalk's notion of *objects*, as a mechanism to manage the complexity of graphic user interfaces, has now proven its worth, since it has been followed by most of the manufacturers of graphic user interfaces and window systems. Summarizing, from a historical perspective, the introduction of the object-oriented approach may be regarded as a natural extension to previous developments in programming practice, motivated by the need to cope with the complexity of new applications. History doesn't stop here. Later developments, represented by Eiffel and to a certain extent C++, more clearly reflected the concern with abstraction and verification, which intrinsically belongs to the notion of *abstract data types* as supported by these languages.

1.1.1   Object speak

Smalltalk may be held responsible for the initial popularity of the object-oriented approach. However, the terminology it introduced was somewhat unfamiliar, and for many evidently hard to grasp. See slide 1-3.

Perhaps unfortunately, it is not true that currently every programmer uses an object-oriented language. Nor is it true that everybody is in favor of object orientation. To study

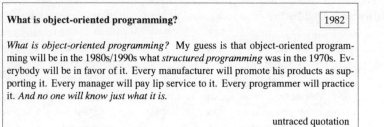

Slide 1-3: Object Oriented Programming

object-oriented programming, however, the least one can do is to become familiar with the terminology employed.

In this section, we will discuss the terminology associated with object orientation, and look at what features and benefits are generally acclaimed by proponents of an object-oriented approach.

Object terminology Objects provide the means by which to structure a system.   In Smalltalk (and most other object-oriented languages) objects are considered to be grouped in classes. A *class* specifies the behavior of the objects that are its instances. Also, classes act as templates from which actual objects may be created. Inheritance is defined for classes only. From the perspective of design, inheritance is primarily meant to promote the reuse of specifications. See slide 1-4.

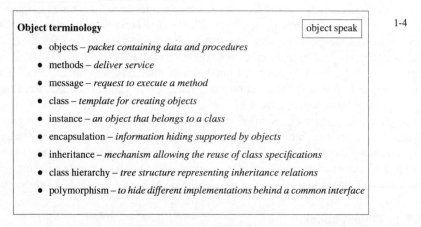

Slide 1-4: Object terminology

The use of inheritance results in a class hierarchy that, from an operational point of view, determines the dispatching behavior of objects, that is what method will be selected in response to a message. If certain restrictions are met (see sections 3.3, 9.2 and 10.4), the class hierarchy corresponds to a type hierarchy, specifying the subtype relation between classes of objects.

Finally, an important feature of object-oriented languages is their support for poly-morphism. Polymorphism is often incorrectly identified with inheritance. Polymorphism by inheritance makes it possible to hide different implementations behind a common in-terface. However, other forms of polymorphism may arise by overloading functions and the use of generic (template) classes or functions. See sections 1.1.2 and 9.3.

Features and benefits of OOP Having become acquainted with the terminology of OOP, we will briefly review what are generally considered features and benefits from a prag-matic point of view. This summary is based on Pokkunuri (1989). I do expect, however, that the reader will take the necessary caution with respect to these claims. See slide 1-5.

Both *information hiding* and *data abstraction* relieve the task of the programmer using existing code, since these mechanisms mean that the programmer's attention is no longer distracted by irrelevant implementation details. On the other hand, the developer of the code (i.e. objects) may profit from information hiding as well since it gives the pro-grammer the freedom to optimize the implementation without interfering with the client code. Sealing off the object's implementation by means of a well-defined message inter-face moreover offers the opportunity to endow an object with (possibly concurrent) au-tonomous behavior.

Features of OOP   1-5

information hiding: state, autonomous behavior

data abstraction: emphasis on *what* rather than *how*

dynamic binding: binding at runtime, polymorphism

inheritance: incremental changes (specialization), reusability

---

Slide 1-5: Features of OOP

The flexible dispatching behavior of objects that lends objects their polymorphic behavior is due to the dynamic binding of methods to messages. For the language C++, polymorphic object behavior is effected by using virtual functions, for which, in contrast to ordinary functions, the binding to an actual function takes place at runtime and not at compile-time. In this way, inheritance provides a flexible mechanism by which to reuse code since a derived class may specialize or override parts of the inherited specification.

Apparently, at the current stage of OOP, it is still difficult to distinguish clearly between what are just features and what must be regarded as actual benefits. From a pragmatic viewpoint, OOP offers *encapsulation* and *inheritance* as the major abstraction mechanisms to be used in program development. See slide 1-6.

Encapsulation promotes *modularity*, meaning that objects must be regarded as the building blocks of a complex system. Once a proper modularization has been achieved, the implementor of the object may postpone any final decisions concerning the imple-mentation at will. This feature allows for quick prototyping, with the risk that the 'quick and dirty' implementations will never be cleaned up. However, experience with con-structing object-oriented libraries has shown that the modularization achieved with ob-jects may not be very stable. See chapter 11.

Another advantage of an object oriented approach, often considered as the main advantage, is the reuse of code. Inheritance is an invaluable mechanism in this respect, since the code that is reused seldom offers all that is needed. The inheritance mechanism enables the programmer to modify the behavior of a class of objects without requiring access to the source code.

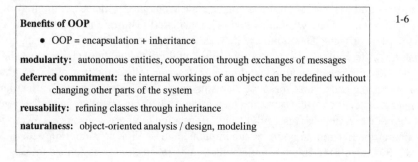

Slide 1-6: Benefits of OOP

Although an object-oriented approach to program development indeed offers great flexibility, some of the problems it addresses are intrinsically difficult and cannot really be solved by mechanisms alone. For instance, modularization is recognized to be a notoriously difficult problem in the software engineering literature. Hence, since some of the promises of OOP depend upon the stability of the chosen modularization, the real advantage of OOP may be rather short-lived. Moreover, despite the optimistic claims about 'tuning' reused code by means of inheritance, experience shows that often more understanding of the inherited classes is needed than is available in their specification.

The probability of arriving at a stable modularization may increase when shifting focus from programming to design. The mechanisms supported by OOP allow for modeling application oriented concepts in a direct, natural way. But this benefit of OOP will only be gained at the price of increasing the design effort.

1.1.2 Polymorphism

Polymorphism essentially characterizes the type of a variable, function or object. Polymorphism may be due to overloading, parametrized types or inheritance. Polymorphism due to inheritance is often considered as the greatest contribution of object-oriented languages. This may be true, but the importance of generic (template) types and overloading should not be overlooked.

In slide 1-7 some examples are given of declarations involving polymorphic types. The function *print* is separately defined for *int* and *float*. Also, a generic *list* class is defined by means by employing *templates*. The list may be used for any kind of objects, for example integers. Finally, a *shape* class is defined from which a *circle* class is derived. An instance of the *circle* may be referred to by using a *shape* pointer, because the type *shape* encompasses *circle* objects.

Overloading

> *extern* void print(int);   `print`
>
> *extern* void print(float);

Generic class – *templates*

> *template< class* T > *class* list { ... }   `list<T>`
>
> list<int>* alist;

Polymorphism by inheritance

> *class* shape { ... };   `shape`
>
> *class* circle : *public* shape { ... }
>
> shape* s = new circle;

Slide 1-7: Polymorphic type declarations

Inheritance and virtual functions The power of inheritance in C++ comes from virtual functions and dynamic binding. Dynamic binding realizes the polymorphism inherent in the static type structure of the inheritance hierarchy in a dynamic way. Dynamic binding is illustrated by the example shown in slide 1-8.

Virtual functions – *dispatching*

> *class* A {   `A`
>
> *public*:
>
> *virtual* void *operator*()() { cout ≪ "A"; }
>
> };
>
> *class* B : *public* A {   `B`
>
> *public*:
>
> *virtual* void *operator*()() { cout ≪ "B"; }
>
> };

Slide 1-8: Virtual functions – dispatching

The class A defines a virtual member function (that results in printing A) which is redefined by a similar function in class B (which results in printing B). As an example of using the classes defined above, look at the following program fragment:

> A* a = new B(); (* a)();

In case the function would not have been defined as virtual, the outcome of applying it to (a pointer to) a B object would have been A, instead of B.

Virtual functions that are redefined in derived classes may still access the original version defined in the base class, as illustrated in slide 1-9.

```
Scoping – explicit                                              1-9

    class B : public A {                          B′
    public:
    virtual void operator()() {
        cout ≪ "B"; A::operator()();
        }
    };
```

Slide 1-9: Virtual functions – scoping

Scoping may be used within a member function of the class as well as by a client (when invoking a member function) as illustrated below.

A∗ a = new B(); a→ A::*operator*()(); (∗ a)();

The outcome of this statement is *ABA*.

Such a scoping mechanism is certainly not unique to C++, although the notation for it is. In Smalltalk, the expression *super* may be used to access methods defined in the ancestor class, and in Eiffel one must use a combination of redefining and renaming to achieve this. As a remark, I prefer the use of *operator*()() when any other method name would be arbitrary. The attractiveness of *operator*()() is that it is used as a function application operator, as in (∗*a*)().

1.1.3 Responsibilities in OOP

After this first glance at the terminology and mechanisms employed in OOP, we will look at what I consider to be the contribution of OOP (and the theme of this book) in a more thematic way. The term 'responsibilities' in the title of this section is meant to refer to an approach to design that has become known as *responsibility driven design* (see Wirfs-Brock, 1989). Of course, the reader is encouraged to reflect on alternative interpretations of the phrase *responsibilities in OOP*.

The approach captured by the term *responsibilities* stresses the importance of an abstract characterization of what services an object delivers, in other words what responsibilities an object carries with respect to the system as a whole. This notion of responsibilities may also be regarded as the background of *contracts* as introduced in Meyer (1988), which specify in a precise manner the relation between an object and its 'clients'.

Objects allow one to modularize a system in distinct units, and to hide the implementation details of these units, by packaging data and procedures in a record-like structure and defining a message interface to which users of these units must comply. *Encapsulation* refers to the combination of packaging and hiding. The formal counterpart of encapsulation is to be found in the theory of *abstract data types*. An abstract data type (ADT) specifies the behavior of an entity in an abstract way by means of what are called *operations* and *observations*, which operationally amount to procedures and functions to change or observe the state of the entity. See also section 8.3.

Abstract data types, that is elements thereof, are generally realized by employing a hidden *state*. The state itself is invisible, but may be accessed and modified by means of the observations and operations specified by the type. See slide 1-10.

Encapsulation   1-10

   • Abstract Data Types

                                             ADT

       ADT = state + behavior

Object-Oriented Modeling

   • data oriented

Slide 1-10: Abstract Data Types – encapsulation

Complex applications involve usually complex data. As observed by Wirfs-Brock (1989), software developers have reacted to this situation by adopting more data oriented solutions. Methods such as semantic information modeling and object-oriented modeling were developed to accommodate this need. See also sections 3.4.1 and 11.3.

Objects may be regarded as embodying an (element of an) abstract data type. To use an object, the client only needs to know *what* an object does, not (generally speaking) *how* the behavior of the object is implemented. However, for a client to profit from the data hiding facilities offered by objects, the developer of the object must provide an interface that captures the behavior of the object in a sufficiently abstract way. The (implicit) design guideline in this respect must be to regard an object as a *server* that provides high level services on request and to determine what services the application requires of that particular (class of) objects(s). See slide 1-11.

Naturally, the responsibilities of an object cannot be determined by viewing the object in isolation. In actual systems, the functionality required is often dependent on complex interactions between a collection of objects that must cooperate in order to achieve the desired effect. However, before trying to specify these interactions, we must indicate more precisely how the communication between a server and a single client proceeds.

From a language implementation perspective, an object is nothing but an advanced data structure, even when we fit it in a client-server model. For design, however, we must shift our perspective to viewing the object as a collection of high level, application oriented services. Specifying the behavior of an object from this perspective, then, means to define what specific information the object is responsible for and how it maintains the integrity of that information. See slide 1-12.

The notion of *contracts* was introduced by Meyer (1988) to characterize in a precise manner what services an object must provide and what requirements clients of an object must meet in order to request a service (and expect to get a good result). A contract

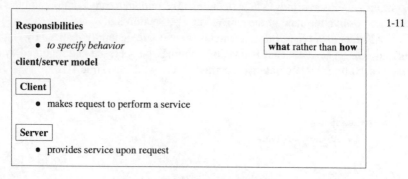

Slide 1-11: Responsibilities in OOP

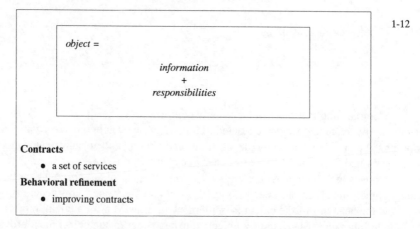

Slide 1-12: Contracts and behavioral refinement

specifies both the requirements imposed on a client and the obligations the server has, provided the requirements are met. When viewed from the position of a client, a contract reveals what the client can count on when the requirements are fulfilled. From the position of the server, on the other hand, when a client does not fulfill the requirements imposed, the server has no obligation whatsoever.

Formally, the requirements imposed on the client and the obligations of the server can be specified by means of pre- and post-conditions surrounding a method. Nevertheless, despite the possibility of formally verifying these conditions, the designer must specify the right contract for this approach to work at all. A problem of a more technical nature the designer of object-oriented systems faces is how to deal with inheritance.

Inheritance, as a mechanism of code reuse, supports the refinement of the specification of a server. From the perspective of abstract data types, we must require that the derived specification refines the behavior of the original server. We must answer the following two questions here. What restrictions apply, when we try to refine the behavior of a server object? And, ultimately, what does it mean to improve a contract?

Behavioral refinement Inheritance provides a very general and powerful mechanism for reusing code. In fact, the inheritance mechanism is more powerful than is desirable from a type-theoretical perspective.

Conformance – *behavioral refinement*

1-13

$$\textbf{if } B <_{refines} A$$
then
B **may be used**
wherever A **is allowed**

Slide 1-13: Behavioral refinement

An abstract data type specifies the behavior of a collection of entities. When we use inheritance to augment the definition of a given type, we either specify new behavior in addition to what was given, or we modify the inherited behavior, or both. The restriction that must be met when modifying behavior is that the objects defined in this way are allowed to be used at all places where objects of the given type were allowed. This restriction is expressed in the so-called *conformance rule* that states that *if* $B <_{refines} A$ *then B may be used wherever A is allowed.* Naturally, when behavior is added, this condition is automatically fulfilled. See slide 1-13.

The conformance rule gives a very useful heuristic for applying inheritance safely. This form of inheritance is often called 'strict' inheritance. However, it is not all that easy to verify that a class derived by inheritance actually refines the behavior specified in a given class. Partly, we can check for syntactic criteria such as the signature (that is, type) of the individual methods, but this is definitely not sufficient. We need a way in which to establish that the behavior (in relation to a possible) client is refined according to the standard introduced above. In other words we need to know how to improve a *contract*.

Recall that from an operational point of view an object may be regarded as containing data attributes storing information and procedures or methods representing services. The question *"how to improve a contract?"* then boils down to two separate questions, namely: (1) *"how to improve the information?"* and (2) *"how to improve a service?"*. To provide better *information* is, technically speaking, simply to provide more information, that is more specific information. Type-theoretically, this corresponds to narrowing down the possible elements of the set that represents the (sub) type. To provide a better *service* requires either relieving the restrictions imposed on the client or improving the result, that is tighten the obligations of the server. Naturally, the *or* must be taken as non-exclusive. See slide 1-14.

To improve a *contract* thus simply means adding more services or improving the services that are already present. As a remark, Meyer (1988) inadvertently uses the term *subcontract* for this kind of refinement. However, in my understanding, subcontracting is more a process of delegating parts of a contract to other contractors whereas refinement, in the sense of improving contracts, deals with the contract as a whole, and as such has a more competitive edge.

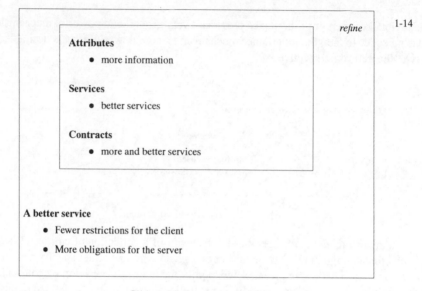

Slide 1-14: Improving services

Summarizing, at a very high level we may think of objects as embodying a *contract*. The contract is specified in the definition of the class of which that object is an instance. Moreover, we may think of inheritance as a mechanism to effect *behavioral refinement*, which ultimately means to improve the contract defining the relation between the object as a server and a potential client.

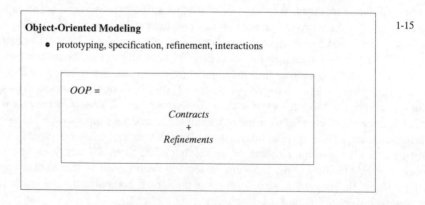

Slide 1-15: Object-oriented modeling

To warrant the phrase *contract*, however, the designer of an object must specify the functionality of an object in a sufficiently abstract, application oriented way. The (implicit) guideline in this respect is to construct a *model* of the application domain. See slide 1-15.

The opportunity offered by an object-oriented approach to model concepts of the application domain in a direct way makes an object-oriented style suitable for incremental prototyping (provided that the low-level support is available).

The metaphor of contracts provides valid guidelines for the design of objects. Because of its foundation in the theory of abstract data types, contracts may be specified (and verified) in a formal way, although in practice this is not really likely to occur.

Before closing this section, I wish to mention a somewhat different interpretation of the notion of *contracts* which is proposed by Helm *et al.* (1990). There contracts are introduced to specify the behavior of collections of cooperating objects. See section 10.5.

1.2   The object-oriented software life-cycle

No approach to software development is likely to survive unless it solves some of the real problems encountered in software engineering practice. In this section we will examine how the object-oriented approach is related to the conceptions of the life-cycle of software and what factors may motivate the adoption of an object-oriented approach to software development.

Despite some variations in terminology, there is a generally agreed-on conception of the various phases in the development of a software product. Roughly, a distinction can be made between a phase of *analysis*, which aims at specifying the requirements a product must meet, a phase of *design*, which must result in a conceptual view of the architecture of the intended system, and a phase of *implementation*, covering coding, testing and, to some extent, also maintenance activities. See slide 1-16.

No such consensus exists with respect to the exact relation between these phases. More specifically, there is a considerable variation in methods and guidelines describing how to make the transition from one phase to another. Another important issue is to determine what the products are exactly, in terms of software and documentation, that must result from each phase.

The traditional conception of the software life-cycle is known as the *waterfall model*, which prescribes a strictly sequential transition between the successive phases, possibly in an iterative manner. Strict regulations with respect to validation of the products resulting from each phase may be imposed to avoid the risk of backtracking. Such a rigid approach, however, may cause severe problems, since it does not easily allow for modifying decisions taken earlier.

One important problem in this respect is that the needs of the users of a system may change over time, invalidating the requirements laid down in an earlier phase. To some extent this problem may be avoided by better techniques of evoking the user requirements in the analysis phase, for instance by developing a prototype. Unfortunately, the problem of accommodating changing user needs and adapting to changing circumstances (such as hardware) seems to be of a more persistent nature, which provides good reason to look at alternative software development models.

Software development models The software engineering literature abounds with descriptions of failing software projects and remedies proposed to solve the problem of software not meeting user expectations.

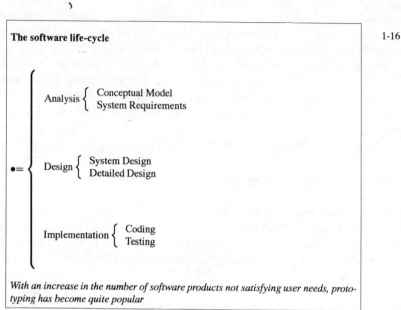

Slide 1-16: The software life-cycle

User expectations may be succinctly characterized by the RAMP requirements listed in slide 1-17. Reliability, adaptability, maintainability and performance are not unreasonable demands in themselves. However, opinions on how to satisfy these criteria clearly diverge.

Requirements – user needs are constantly evolving   1-17

       Reliability – *incremental development, reuse, synthesis*

       Adaptability – *evolutionary prototyping*

       Maintainability – *incremental development, synthesis*

       Performance – *incremental development, reuse*

Slide 1-17: Requirements – RAMP

Bersoff and Davis, 1991 and Davis *et al.* (1988) explain how the choice of a particular software development model may influence the chances of successfully completing a software project. As already mentioned, *rapid throwaway prototyping* may help to evoke user needs at an early stage, but does not help much in adapting to evolving user requirements. A better solution in this respect is to adopt a method of *evolutionary prototyping*. Dependent on the technology used, however, this may cause severe problems in maintaining the integrity and robustness of the system. Less flexible, but more reliable is an approach of *incremental development*, which proceeds by realizing those parts of a system for which the user requirements can be clearly specified.

Another means of adapting to changing user requirements is to use a technique of *automated software synthesis*. However, such an approach works only if the user requirements can be formalized easily. This is not always very likely, unless the application domain is sufficiently restricted. A similar constraint adheres to the *reuse of software*. Only in familiar application domains is it possible to anticipate how user requirements may change and how to adapt the system appropriately. Nevertheless, the reuse of software seems a very promising technique with which to reduce the cost and time involved in software products without (in principle) sacrificing reliability and performance. See slide 1-18.

Software Development Models   1-18

- rapid throwaway prototyping – *quick and dirty*
- incremental development – *slowly evolving*
- evolutionary prototyping – *evolving requirements*
- reusable software – *reduces cost and time*
- automated software synthesis – *one level of abstraction higher*

Slide 1-18: Software development models

Two of the principal advocates of object-oriented technology, Cox and Meyer, regard the reuse of software as the ultimate solution to the software crisis. However, the true solution is in my opinion not so straightforward. One problem is that tools and technologies are needed to store and retrieve reusable components. That simple solutions do not suffice is illustrated by an anecdote reported by Alan Kay telling how difficult it was to find his way in the Smalltalk class structure after a significant change, despite the browsing facilities offered by the Smalltalk system.

Another problem lies in the area of human factors. The incentives for programmer productivity have too long been directed at the number of lines of code to make software reuse attractive. This attitude is also encouraged in universities. Moreover, the reuse of other student's work is usually (not unjustifiably) punished instead of encouraged.

However, having a sufficiently large store of reusable software at our disposal will allow us to build software meeting the RAMP requirements stated above, only if we have arrived at sufficiently stable abstractions of the application domain.

In the following, we will explore how object-oriented technology is motivated by problems occurring in the respective phases of the software life-cycle and how it contributes to solving these problems.

1.2.1 Analysis

In academic environments software often seems to grow, without a clear plan or explicit intention of fulfilling some need or purpose, except perhaps as a vehicle for research. In contrast, industrial and business software projects are usually undertaken to meet some explicit goal or to satisfy some need.

One of the main problems in such situations, from the point of view of the developers of the software, is to extract the needs from the future users of the system and later to negotiate the solutions proposed by the team. The problem is primarily a problem of *communication*, of bridging the gap between two worlds, the world of domain expertise on the one hand and that of expertise in the craft of software development on the other.

In a number of publications (Coad and Yourdon, 1991a; Wirfs-Brock *et al.*, 1990; and Meyer, 1988) object-oriented analysis has been proposed as providing a solution to this problem of communication. According to Coad and Yourdon (1991a), object-oriented techniques allow us to capture the system requirements in a model that directly corresponds with a conceptual model of the problem domain. See slide 1-19.

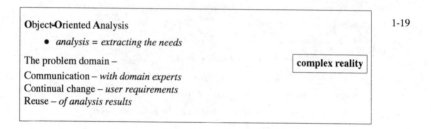

Slide 1-19: Object-Oriented Analysis

Another claim made by proponents of OOP is that an object-oriented approach enables a more seamless transition between the respective phases of the software life-cycle. If this claim is really met, this would mean that changing user requirements could be more easily discussed in terms of the consequences of these changes for the system, and if accepted could in principle be more easily propagated to the successive phases of development.

One of the basic ideas underlying object-oriented analysis is that the abstractions arrived at in developing a conceptual model of the problem domain will remain stable over time. Hence, rather than focusing on specific functional requirements, attention should be given to modeling the problem domain by means of high level abstractions. Due to the stability of these abstractions, the results of analysis are likely candidates for reuse.

The reality to be modeled in analysis is usually very complex. Coad and Yourdon (1991a) mention a number of principles or mechanisms with which to manage complexity. These show a great similarity to the abstraction mechanisms mentioned earlier. See slide 1-20.

Personally, I do not feel entirely comfortable with the characterization of the analysis phase given by Coad and Yourdon (1991a), since to my mind user needs and system requirements are perhaps more conveniently phrased in terms of functionality and constraints than in terms of a model that may simultaneously act as an architectural sketch of the system that is to be developed.

However, I do agree with Coad and Yourdon (1991a), and others, that the products of analysis, that is the documents describing user needs and system requirements, should as far as possible provide a conceptual model of the domain to which these needs and requirements are related.

Principles for managing complexity   1-20

Abstraction – procedural / data
Encapsulation – information hiding
Inheritance – expression of commonality
Message passing – consistent interface
Organization – object / attributes
Scale – components, frameworks
Behavior – actors, servers, agents

Slide 1-20: Managing complexity

Actually, I do consider the blurring of the distinction between analysis and design, and as we will see later, between design and implementation, as one of the attractive features of an object-oriented approach.

Analysis methods The phases of *analysis* and *design* differ primarily in orientation: during analysis the focus is on aspects of the problem domain and the goal is to arrive at a description of that domain to which the user and system requirements can be related. On the other hand, the design phase must result in an architectural model of the system, for which we can demonstrate that it fulfills the user needs and the additional requirements expressed as the result of analysis.

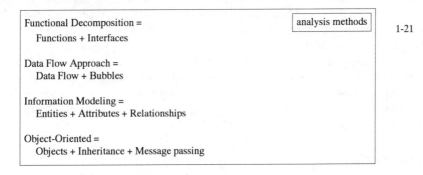

Functional Decomposition =   analysis methods   1-21
    Functions + Interfaces

Data Flow Approach =
    Data Flow + Bubbles

Information Modeling =
    Entities + Attributes + Relationships

Object-Oriented =
    Objects + Inheritance + Message passing

Slide 1-21: Analysis methods

Coad and Yourdon (1991a) discuss a number of methods that are commonly used in analysis (see slide 1-21). The choice of a particular method will often depend upon circumstances of a more sociological nature. For instance, the experience of a team with a particular method is often a crucial factor for success. For this reason, perhaps, an eclectic method combining the various approaches may be preferable (see, for instance, Rumbaugh *et al.*, 1991). However, it is doubtful whether such an approach will have the same benefits as a purely object-oriented approach. See also section 11.3.

I will briefly characterize the various methods mentioned by Coad and Yourdon (1991a). For a more extensive description and evaluation the reader is referred to, for example, Jones (1990).

The method of *Functional Decomposition* aims at characterizing the steps that must be taken to reach a particular goal. These steps may be represented by functions that may take arguments in order to deal with data that is shared between the successive steps of the computation. In general, one can say that this method is not very good for data hiding. Another problem is that non-expert users may not be familiar with viewing their problem in terms of computation steps. Also, the method does not result in descriptions that are easily amenable to change.

The method indicated as the *Data Flow Approach* aims at depicting the information flow in a particular domain by means of arrows that represent data and bubbles that represent processes acting on these data.

Information Modeling is a method that has become popular primarily for developing information systems and applications involving databases. As a method, it aims at modeling the application domain in terms of *entities*, that may have attributes, and relations between entities.

An *object-oriented* approach to analysis is very similar in nature to the information modeling approach, at least with respect to its aim of developing a conceptual model of the application domain. However, in terms of their means, both methods differ significantly. The most important distinction between *objects*, in the sense of OOP, and *entities*, as used in information modeling, to my mind lies in the capacity of objects to embody actual behavior, whereas entities are of a more passive nature.

Discussion At this stage it is very difficult to draw any final conclusions with respect to object-oriented analysis. Currently methods are proposed that integrate the various techniques, such as for example the Object Modeling Technique (Rumbaugh *et al.*, 1991), which integrates information modeling, data flow analysis and a technique for modeling the dynamic behavior of objects.

Returning to my initial remarks, I think we may safely set as the goal for every method of analysis to aim at *stable abstractions*, that is a conceptual model that is robust with respect to evolving user requirements. Also, we may state a preference for methods which result in models that have a close correspondence to the concepts and notions used by the experts operating in the application domain.

1.2.2 Design

In an object-oriented approach, the distinction between *analysis* and *design* is primarily one of emphasis; emphasis on modeling the reality of the problem domain versus emphasis on providing an architectural model of a system that lends itself to implementation.

One of the attractive features of such an approach is the opportunity of a seamless transition between the respective phases of the software product in development. The classical waterfall model can no longer be considered as appropriate for such an approach. An alternative model, the *fountain model*, is proposed by Henderson-Sellers (1992). This model allows for a more autonomous development of software components, within the constraints of a unifying framework. The end goal of such a development process may be viewed as a repository of reusable components. A similar viewpoint has originally been proposed by Cox (1986) and Meyer (1988).

In examining the primary goals of design, Meyer (1988) distinguishes between *reusability*, *quality* and *ease of maintenance*. Naturally, reusable software presupposes quality, hence both quality and maintainability are important design goals. See slide 1-22.

1-22

Object-Oriented Design

  • *reuse, quality, maintenance*

The software life-cycle

	Traditional	Object Oriented
Requirements	20	20
Design	30	50
Implementation	35	20
Testing	15	10

Slide 1-22: Object-oriented design

In Meyer (1988) a rough estimate is given of the shift in effort between the phases of the software life-cycle, brought about by an object-oriented approach. Essentially, these figures show an increase in the effort needed for design. This is an immediate consequence of the observation that the development of reusable code is intrinsically more difficult.

To my mind, there is yet another reason for the extra effort involved in design. In practice it appears to be difficult and time consuming to arrive at the appropriate abstract data types for a given application. The implementation of these structures, on the other hand, is usually straightforward.

This is another indication that the unit of reuse should perhaps not be small pieces of code, but rather (the design of) components that fit into a larger framework.

Software quality From the perspective of software quality and maintenance, these mechanisms of *encapsulation* and *inheritance* may be characterized as powerful means to control the complexity of the code needed to realize a system. See slide 1-23.

In Meyer (1988) it is estimated that maintenance accounts for 70% of the actual cost of software. Moreover, *adaptive maintenance*, which is the adaptation to changing requirements, accounts for a disproportionately large part of the cost. Of primary importance for maintenance, in the sense of the correction of errors, is the *principle of locality* supported by encapsulation, data abstraction and hiding. In contrast, inheritance is a feature that may interfere with maintenance, since it often breaks down the protection offered by encapsulation. However, to cope with changing requirements, inheritance provides both a convenient and relatively safe mechanism.

1.2.3 Implementation

In principle, the phase of implementation follows on from the design phase. In practice, however, the products of design may often only be regarded as providing a *post hoc* justification of the actual system. As noted, for instance, in Halbert and O'Brien (1987), an object-oriented approach may blur the distinction between design and implementation, even to the extent of reversing their actual order. The most important distinction be-

```
┌─────────────────────────────────────────────────────────────────────────┐
│ Software quality                                                    1-23  │
│                                                                           │
│   • correctness, robustness, extendibility, reusability, compatibility    │
│                                                                           │
│ Maintenance 70% of costs                                                  │
│                                                                           │
│     Requirements change       41.8%                                       │
│     Data format change        17.4%                                       │
│     Emergency fixes           12.4%                                       │
│     Routine debugging           9%                                        │
│     Hardware changes          6.2%                                        │
│     Documentation             5.5%                                        │
│     Efficiency improvements     4%                                        │
│                                                                           │
└─────────────────────────────────────────────────────────────────────────┘
```

Slide 1-23: Software quality

tween design and implementation is hence the level of abstraction at which the structure of the system is described. Design is meant to clarify the conceptual structure of a system, whereas the implementation must include all the details needed for the system to run. Whatever approach is followed, in the end the design must serve both as a *justification* and *clarification* of the actual implementation.

This role of design is of particular importance in projects that require long-term maintenance. Correcting errors or adapting the functionality of the system on the basis of code alone is not likely to succeed. What may help, though, are tools that extract explanatory information from the code. See, for example, sections 11.2.1 and 11.3.3.

Testing and maintenance Errors may (and will) occur during the implementation as well as later when the system is in operation. Apart from the correction of errors, other maintenance activities may be required, as we have seen previously.

In Knuth (1992), an amusing account is given of the errors Knuth detected in the TEX program over a period of time. These errors range from trivial typos to errors on an algorithmic level. See slide 1-24.

An interesting and important question is to what extent an object-oriented approach, and more specifically an object-oriented implementation language, is of help in avoiding and correcting such errors. The reader is encouraged to make a first guess, and to verify that guess later.

As an interesting aside, the TEX system has been implemented in a language system called Web. The Web system allows one to merge code and explanatory text in a single document, and to process that document as either code or text. In itself, this has nothing to do with object orientation, but the technique of documentation supported by the Web system is also suitable for object-oriented programs. We will mention a Web-like system for C++ in chapter 11.

Object-oriented language support Operationally, *encapsulation* and *inheritance* are considered to be the basic mechanisms underlying the object-oriented approach. These

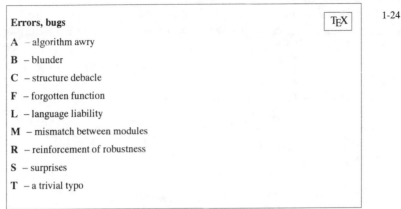

Slide 1-24: TEX errors and bugs – Knuth (1992)

mechanisms have been realized in a number of languages. (See slide 1-25. See also chapter 5 for a more complete overview.)

Historically, Smalltalk is often considered to be the most important object-oriented language. It has served as an implementation vehicle for a variety of applications (see, for instance, Pope, 1991). No doubt, Smalltalk has contributed greatly to the initial popularity of the object-oriented approach, yet its role is being taken over by C++, which now has the largest community of users. Smalltalk is a purely object-oriented language, which means that every entity, including integers, expressions and classes, is regarded as an object.

The popularity of the Smalltalk language may be attributed partly to the Smalltalk environment, which allows the user to inspect the properties of all the objects in the system and which, moreover, contains a large collection of reusable classes. Together with the environment, Smalltalk provides excellent support for fast prototyping.

The language Eiffel, described by Meyer (1988), may also be considered as a pure object-oriented language, pure in the sense that it provides classes and inheritance as the main device with which to structure a program. The major contribution of Eiffel is its support for correctness constructs. These include the possibility to specify pre- and post-conditions for methods, as well as to specify a *class invariant*, that may be checked before and after each method invocation.

The Eiffel system comes with a number of libraries, including libraries for graphics and window support, and a collection of tools for browsing and the extraction of documentation. See also chapter 11.

The C++ language (Stroustrup, 1991) has a somewhat different history. It was originally developed as an extension of C with classes. A primary design goal of C++ has been to develop a powerful but efficient language. In contrast to Smalltalk and Eiffel, C++ is not a pure object-oriented language; it is a *hybrid* language in the sense that it allows us to use functions in C-style as well as object-oriented constructs involving classes and inheritance.

Much of the support that comes with Smalltalk and Eiffel may be acquired for C++ in the form of third party libraries or toolkits. A number of these libraries and toolkits are discussed in chapter 11 and 12.

Currently, a number of research groups (including my own) are working on extending C++ with concurrency. An overview of these efforts and the conceptual issues involved is given in chapter 6.

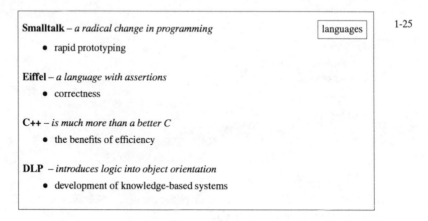

Slide 1-25: Object-oriented languages

As the final language in this brief overview, I wish to mention the distributed logic programming language DLP (see Eliëns, 1992). The DLP language combines logic programming with object-oriented features and parallelism. I mention it, partly because the development of this language was my first involvement with OOP. And further, because it demonstrates that other paradigms of programming, in particular logic programming, may be fruitfully combined with OOP. The language DLP provides a high level vehicle for modeling knowledge-based systems in an object-oriented way.

A more extensive introduction to the Smalltalk, Eiffel, C++ and DLP languages is given in the appendix.

1.3   Paradigms of programming

Since the introduction of programmable devices, our conception of programming has undergone radical changes. New insights with respect to programming have been reflected in a succession of high level programming languages, such as Algol-60, Algol-68, Simula, Pascal, C, Modula-2, Modula-3, CLU, Ada, Ada9X and numerous others.

These programming languages were all introduced to support some specific style of programming. All of them have in some way set an example of a *good* programming style. This is exactly what we mean by the phrase *paradigm of programming*, a style of programming that may somehow be considered mandatory for developing (a particular category of) applications. As an example, consider the use of Pascal as a vehicle for teaching structured programming, or the use of Modula-2 as a vehicle for teaching the employment of abstract data types.

In a landmark paper with the title *"What is object-oriented programming?"*

Object-Oriented Programming

- *high tech synonym for good*

Styles of programming

- A language *supports* a style of programming if it provides facilities that make it convenient (easy, safe and efficient) to use that style

- compile/runtime checks

- clean interpretation/ orthogonal / efficient / minimal

1-26

Slide 1-26: Styles of programming

(Stroustrup, 1988), Stroustrup raises the question of when a language may be considered to support a particular style of programming. See slide 1-26.

In general, one can say that a language supports a particular style of programming if it provides facilities, both syntactic and semantic, that makes it convenient (that is easy, safe and efficient) to use that style. The crucial distinction that must be made in this context is that between allowing a certain style and providing support for that style. Allowing means that it is possible to program in that style. To support a given style, however, requires in addition that suitable compile and runtime checks are provided to enforce a proper use of the relevant language constructs. With these considerations in mind, one could question the assertion that *Ada is object-oriented* or that *Modula supports abstract data types*. Naturally, this attitude backfires with C++. Does C++ support abstract data types and is it really object-oriented?

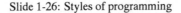

Procedural programming

- procedures, use the optimal algorithms

Modules

- hide the data, provide functional abstractions

Data abstraction

- types, provide a sufficiently complete set of operations

Object-oriented programming – *organize your types*

- make commonality explicit by using inheritance

1-27

Slide 1-27: Paradigms of programming

It is equally important to establish whether a language allows a clean interpretation of the constructs introduced, whether the constructs supporting object orientation are *orthogonal* to (that is independent of) the other constructs of the language, whether an *efficient* implementation of these constructs is possible, and whether the language is kept *minimal*, that is without superfluous constructs.

Before establishing in more detail what the main ingredients of object-orientation are, let us briefly look at some of the styles of programming that may be considered as leading to an object-oriented style. See slide 1-27.

In his article, Stroustrup (1988) stresses the continuity between the respective styles of programming pictured in slide 1-27. Each style is captured by a short phrase stating its principal concern, that is guidelines for developing *good* programs.

1.3.1 Procedural programming

The procedural style of programming is most closely related to the school of structured programming, of which for instance Dijkstra (1976) and Gries (1981) are important proponents. The procedural style supports a method of program development that is known as *stepwise refinement*. Stepwise refinement is an important heuristic for developing complex algorithms. Instead of writing out a complex algorithm in all its detail, the method allows for refining the elementary steps of the basic algorithm by means of increasingly detailed procedures.

1-28

```
while ( programming == art ) {
        incr( pleasure );
        decr( bugs );
        incr( portability );
        incr( maintainability );
        incr( quality );
        incr( salary );
} // live happily ever after
```

Slide 1-28: Programming as an art

As a playful example of this style of programming, consider the fragment that may be found on the cover of Knuth (1992). See slide 1-28. Ignoring the contents, clearly the structure shows an algorithm that is conceived as the repeated execution of a number of less complex steps.

1.3.2 Data abstraction

When programs became larger and data more complex, the design of correct algorithms was no longer the primary concern. Rather, it became important to provide access to data in a representation independent manner. One of the early proponents of data hiding was Parnas (1972a,b), who introduced a precursor to the notion of *data abstraction* as it has become popular in object-oriented languages such as Smalltalk or C++.

As a language that supports data hiding, we may think of Modula-2 that offers strong support for modules and the specification of import and export relations between modules. Also the *package construct* of Ada provides support for data hiding. See slide 1-29.

Modules as provided by Modula-2 and Ada give a syntactic means for decomposing a program into more or less independent components. It is precisely the purely syntactic nature of modules that may be considered the principal defect of this approach to data hiding. Semantically, modules provide no guideline with respect to how to decompose a program into meaningful components.

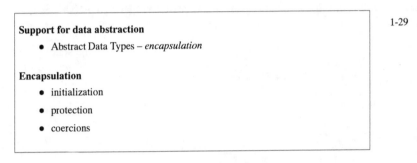

Slide 1-29: Data abstraction

To express the meaning of a module, we need the stronger notion of *types*, in the sense of *abstract data types* which are characterized by a set of operations. The notion of types, as for example supported in CLU (Liskov and Zilles, 1974, 1974), enables us to determine whether our decomposition satisfies certain formal criteria. For instance, we may ask whether we have defined sufficiently many operations for a given type and whether we have correctly done so. An important advantage of using abstract data types is that we can often find a mathematical model that formally characterizes the behavior of that type. From the perspective of formal methods, data abstraction by means of abstract data types may be considered as one of the principal means for the specification and verification of complex software systems. See also sections 8.3 and 10.5.

From an implementation perspective, to support data abstraction a language must provide constructs to implement *concrete realizations* of abstract data types. Such support requires that means are provided to create and initialize elements of a concrete type in a safe way, and that vulnerable data is effectively protected.

Very important is the possibility of defining generic types, that is types which take a (type) parameter with which they are instantiated. For example, the definition of a *stack* does not differ for a stack of integers, a stack of strings or a stack of elements from an arbitrary user-defined type.

1.3.3   Object-oriented programming

There is a close similarity between the object model as presented earlier and the notion of abstract data types just described. Both objects and abstract data types define a set of applicable operations that completely determine the behavior of an object or an element of the data type. To relate an object to an abstract data type we need the notion of *class*, that serves as the description on an abstract level of the behavior of (a collection of) objects. (The objects are called the *instances* of the class.)

As noted in Stroustrup (1988), abstract data types as such, although mathematically satisfying, are rather inflexible and inconvenient for specifying complex software systems. To attain such flexibility, we need to be able to organize our types and express the commonality between them. The notion of class supports this by a mechanism called *inheritance*. When regarding classes as types, inheritance may be seen as introducing polymorphic types. A class that is derived from a particular class (the base class) may be treated by the compiler as a subtype of (the type of) that particular class. See slide 1-30.

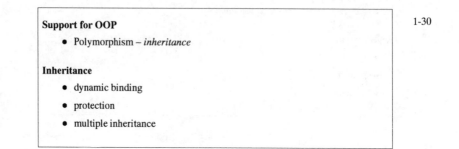

Slide 1-30: Support for OOP

Operationally, the power of inheritance comes from message dispatching. For C++, this mechanism is called *dynamic binding*. Message dispatching takes care of selecting the right method in response to a message or method call. In a hierarchy of (derived) classes, a method for an object may be either defined within the class of the object itself or by one of the classes from which that class is (directly or indirectly) derived. Message dispatching is an essential mechanism for supporting polymorphism, since it allows to choose the most appropriate behavior for an object of a given type. This must occur at runtime, since the type of an object as determined at compile-time may be too general.

An important issue in determining whether a language supports object-oriented programming is whether it offers a protection mechanism to shield the vulnerable parts of a base class from the classes that derived from that class.

Another question of interest is whether a language must support multiple inheritance. Clearly, there is some disagreement on this issue. For example, Smalltalk-80 does not support multiple inheritance. The Eiffel language, on the other hand supported multiple inheritance from its first days. For C++, multiple inheritance was introduced at a later stage. At first, it was thought to be expensive and not really necessary. Closer analysis, however, revealed that the cost was not excessive. (See Ellis and Stroustrup, 1990.) The issue of multiple inheritance is still not resolved completely. Generally, it is acknowledged to be a powerful and at the same time natural extension of single inheritance. However, the inheritance mechanism itself seems to be under attack. Some doubt remains as to whether inheritance is a suitable composition mechanism when regarded from the perspective of reuse and reliability.

1.4   Landmark papers

The material presented in this book was originally based on a number of *landmark papers*. I consider these papers still as being important, since they originally expressed some important notion or concept. Moreover, most of these papers are often referred to in other papers and literature on OOP. Naturally, other material has been used as well.

Part I: Designing Object-Oriented Systems In this part an introduction is given to object-oriented programming in C++ based on Stroustrup (1988). An updated version of this paper can be found in Stroustrup (1991). As additional literature on C++ I have also consulted Coplien (1992), which provides an excellent motivation for the use of particular idioms in C++. Snyder (1986) contributes to the field of OOP by showing the importance of protection mechanisms, especially in the context of inheritance. Object-oriented design is treated on the basis of Beck and Cunningham (1989) and Booch (1986). Many of the insights with respect to types and inheritance can be found in Halbert and O 'Brien (1987), which also presents valid arguments for using types as the principle for structuring a design. See slide 1-31.

Part I: Designing Object-Oriented Systems   1-31

- B. Stroustrup – *What is "Object-Oriented Programming"?*

- A. Snyder – *Encapsulation and inheritance in object-oriented programming languages*

- K. Beck and W. Cunningham – *A Laboratory for Teaching Object-Oriented Thinking*

- G. Booch – *Object-Oriented Development*

- D. Halbert and P. O 'Brien – *Using Types and Inheritance in Object-Oriented Programming*

Slide 1-31: Part I: Designing Object-Oriented Systems

Also, we will discuss *contract theory* proposed originally by Meyer (1988). In this section the focus will be primarily on the software engineering implications of contract theory. A treatment of the formal aspects is postponed until part III. In addition, I will look at the validation and testing of object-oriented programs, and explore some possible metrics for OOP.

Part II: Object-Oriented Languages and Systems Our discussion of object-oriented languages will take the well-known paper by Wegner (1987) as its starting point. An overview will be given of currently existing object-oriented programming languages and their major design goals. Next, I will explain the distinction between delegation and inheritance, and discuss the notion of classless languages as, for example, exemplified in Ungar and Smith (1987). Further, I will discuss an alternative to the meta-programming facilities offered by Smalltalk, and describe a general meta-level reflective architecture of object-oriented languages based on Cointe (1987). See slide 1-32.

Slide 1-32: Part II: Object-Oriented Languages and Systems

I will also discuss in detail the problems encountered when extending an object-oriented language with concurrency. An overview will be given of a number of concurrent extensions of C++.

Finally, the issues involved in specifying the cooperation between a collection of objects are explored. This discussion has been inspired by Helm *et al.* (1990), who present a formalism (also called *contracts*) to describe the interaction between objects. However, I will concentrate primarily on techniques with which to model the interaction and dependencies between objects. Of particular relevance in this respect is the event-driven computation model presented by Henderson (1993), which will be illustrated by an example.

Part III: Foundations of Object-Oriented Modeling In part III we study the theoretical foundations of object-oriented modeling. Our starting point will be the treatment of an algebraic approach to abstract data types and a discussion of the divergence between the realization of abstract data types in modular and object-oriented languages, based on Cook (1990).

Slide 1-33: Part III: Foundations of Object-Oriented Modeling

Then, I will clarify the distinction between *classes* and *types*, following Wegner and Zdonik (1988) and, following the same source, we will investigate the implication of this distinction on the use of inheritance. Further, a type calculus derived from Pierce (1993), but originally based on Cardelli and Wegner (1985), is presented to explain in a formal setting the mechanisms of encapsulation and inheritance. See slide 1-33.

In addition, I will sketch an outline of the proof-theory needed to establish the correctness of specifications obtained by the modification of a given type by means of inheritance.

Part IV: Object-Oriented Application Frameworks Taking Meyer (1990) as a starting point, we will discuss the issues involved in the development of object-oriented libraries. Further, I will briefly describe a number of the libraries and toolkits available for C++. See slide 1-34.

Part IV: Object-Oriented Application Frameworks   1-34

- B. Meyer – *Lessons from the design of the Eiffel Libraries*
- N. Meyrowitz – *Intermedia: The Architecture and Construction of an Object-Oriented Hypermedia System and Applications Framework*

Slide 1-34: Part IV: Object-Oriented Application Frameworks

Hypermedia systems represent an area in which OOP has very successfully been applied. Also, it has induced interesting research topics for OOP. To conclude the book, I will discuss some of the recent (OOP-related) developments in hypermedia research, and attempt some reflections on the future of OOP.

1.5   Further reading in OOP

The papers listed in the previous section provide a starting point for studying the various areas and applications of object-oriented technology presented in the book. Recommendations for further reading are given below.

Object-Oriented Programming An exhaustive, yet excellent description of C++ is given in Stroustrup (1991). An excellent introduction to C++ is given in Lippman (1991). In Coplien (1992) a number of advanced idioms and styles for using C++ are treated. An introduction to object-oriented programming is given in Budd (1991), which covers a variety of languages. The language Eiffel is introduced in Meyer (1988). The original introduction to Smalltalk is by Goldberg and Robson (1983). Data abstraction and object-oriented programming in C++ is dealt with in Gorlen *et al.* (1990). Another introduction to object-oriented programming and C++ is given in Wiener and Pinson (1988). An early book on OOP is Cox (1986). Graham (1991) gives a very readable overview of object-oriented methods. Winblad *et al.* (1990) survey a number of important issues in object-oriented software development. An overview of applications of object-oriented programming is given by Pinson and Wiener (1990) and Harmon and Tayler (1993).

Data abstraction and algorithms in C++ The number of books providing a university course level introduction to the use of C++ for the development of abstract data types and algorithms is steadily increasing. We have, among others, Headington and Riley (1994),

Sedgewick (1992), Budd (1994), Bergin (1994) and Weiss (1993) (of which nearly identical texts are available for C and Ada).

Object-Oriented Programming and Software Engineering Object-oriented design with applications is covered in Booch (1994). Object-oriented analysis is the subject of Coad and Yourdon (1991a). A very readable account of object-oriented design is given in Wirfs-Brock *et al.* (1990). Ince (1991) gives an introduction to software engineering with C++. McGregor and Sykes (1992) deal with the advantages of an object-oriented approach from the perspective of reuse. In Jacobson *et al.* (1992) a method for object-oriented development is described together with an accompanying case tool. Henderson-Sellers (1992) gives a concise overview of the issues in object-oriented analysis and design. Further, we have Champeaux *et al.* (1993), which covers analysis and design, and Wilkie (1993), which provides a professional guide to object-oriented software engineering. In Rumbaugh *et al.* (1991) a method for modeling object-oriented systems is introduced. Also worth mentioning is Henderson (1993), which presents a canonical approach to map formal designs to C++ code, and Coleman *et al.* (1994) which presents a promising synthesis of a number of object-oriented development methods.

Object-Oriented Programming and Artificial Intelligence The role of object-oriented programming in artificial intelligence is exhaustively treated in Tello (1989). Apart from describing numerous AI systems embodying object-oriented notions, a number of research issues concerning the relation of object-oriented programming to AI are discussed. The CLOS perspective on OOP is presented in Paepcke (1993). Also worth mentioning is Blum (1992), which presents an object-oriented framework for developing connectionist systems and neural networks in C++.

Theoretical Issues of Object-Oriented Programming In Danforth and Tomlinson (1988) an overview is given of theoretical work on type-systems for object-oriented programming languages. In de Bakker *et al.* (1990) a number of research papers are collected together dealing with the foundations of object-oriented programming languages. Specification and verification techniques for abstract data types are covered in Dahl (1992). Also worth mentioning is Palsberg and Schwartzback (1994), which presents an encompassing study (including tools) of the type theoretical aspects of OOP.

Object-oriented databases A collection of research papers concerning object-oriented notions in databases and expert systems is contained in Kim and Lochovsky (1989). A more systematic discussion of the problems in combining object-oriented, deductive and hypermedia technologies is given in Parsay *et al.* (1989).

Additional literature Object-oriented programming and concurrency is the subject of the majority of papers in Yonezawa and Tokoro (1987) and Agha *et al.* (1993). A variety of research papers may further be found in Shriver and Wegner (1987). Of particular interest are the standardization efforts reported in OMG (1991) and Cattell (1994). Finally, an invaluable source of material is provided by the various conference proceedings, including those of OOPSLA, ECOOP and TOOLS, and the numerous magazines concerning object-oriented programming, such as *JOOP*, the *C++Report*, *IEEE Computer*, *IEEE Software* and the *ACM SIGPLAN Notices*.

Summary

This chapter has given an outline of the major theme of this book, which may be characterized as the unification of a software engineering perspective and a foundational approach. The minor theme may be characterized by saying that a considerable amount of technology is involved.

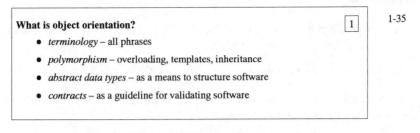

Slide 1-35: Section 1.1: What is object orientation?

In section 1 we looked at the terminology associated with OOP, the notion of *polymorphism* and we discussed an approach to the development of software that centers around the identification of responsibilities and the definition of abstract data types embodying the mutual responsibilities of a client and a server object in terms of a *contract*. See slide 1-35.

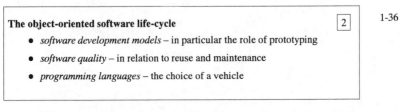

Slide 1-36: Section 1.2: The object-oriented software life-cycle

In section 2 we looked at the object-oriented software life-cycle, consisting of the phases of analysis, design and implementation. We discussed software development models and the role of prototyping, how an object-oriented approach may promote software quality and facilitate maintenance, and we looked at some programming languages as vehicles for the implementation of object-oriented code. See slide 1-36.

Then, in section 3, we looked at object-orientation as a paradigm of programming, extending an abstract data type approach with support for the organization of object types in a polymorphic type structure. See slide 1-37. Further, an overview was given of the literature available on OOP, including a number of landmark papers on which this book was originally based.

Paradigms of programming ⬚3 1-37

- *styles of programming* – as a family of conventions
- *data abstraction* – and its possible realizations
- *polymorphism* – and the features of inheritance

Slide 1-37: Section 1.3: Paradigms of programming

Questions

(1) How would you characterize OOP and what, in your opinion, is the motivation underlying the introduction of OOP?

(2) Characterize the most important features of OOP.

(3) What influence is an object-oriented approach said to have on the software life-cycle? What is your own opinion?

(4) How would you characterize *software quality*? Discuss the problem of maintenance.

(5) Mention a number of object-oriented programming languages, and give a brief characterization.

(6) How is OOP related to programming languages?

(7) What classes of languages support OOP features? Explain.

2

Object-oriented programming constructs

Object orientation has brought about a radical shift in our notion of computation and how we look at programming. This chapter introduces the basic mechanisms of object-oriented programming.

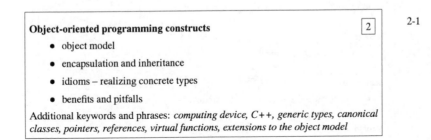

Slide 2-1: Object-oriented programming constructs

First, however, we will explore the relation between the object model of computation and our traditional notion of computation, based on the Von Neumann machine model. In particular, we will be concerned with delineating the possible meanings of the claim that an object-oriented approach is instrumental in managing the *complexity* of software products. Then, after explaining the two major constituents of object-oriented programming, *encapsulation* and *inheritance*, we will discuss some idioms for using these mechanisms as well as the potential benefits and pitfalls of an object-oriented approach.

Also, we will briefly look at some extensions to the basic object model and their relevance to the practice of object-oriented programming.

2.1 The object model

Programming is, put briefly, to provide a computing device with the instructions it needs to do a particular computation. In the words of Dijkstra: *"Programming is the combination of human reasoning and symbol manipulation skills used to develop symbol manipulators (programs). By supplying a computer to such a symbol manipulator it becomes a* concrete *one."* Although we are by now used to quite fashionable computing devices, including graphic interfaces and multimedia peripherals, the abstract meaning of a computing device has not essentially altered since the original conception of the mathematical model that we know as the Turing machine (see below).

Despite the fact that our basic mathematical model of a computing device (and hence our notion of computability) has not altered significantly, the development of high level programming languages has meant a drastic change in our conception of programming. Within the tradition of imperative programming, the introduction of objects, and object-oriented programming, may be thought of as the most radical change of all. Indeed, at the time of the introduction of Smalltalk, one spoke of a true revolution in the practice of programming.

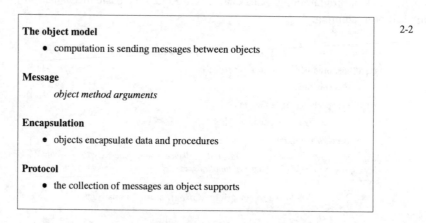

Slide 2-2: The object model

The object model introduced by Smalltalk somehow breaks radically with our traditional notion of computation. Instead of regarding a computation as the execution of a sequence of instructions (changing the state of the machine), object-based computation must be viewed as sending messages between objects. Such a notion of computation had already been introduced in the late 1960s in the programming language Simula (see Dahl and Nygaard, 1966). Objects were introduced in Simula to simulate complex real world events, and to model the interactions between real world entities.

In the (ordinary) sequential machine model, the result of a computation is (represented by) the state of the machine at the end of the computation. In contrast, computation in the object model is best characterized as cooperation between objects. The end result then consists, so to speak, of the collective state of the objects that participated in the computation. See slide 2-2.

Operationally, an object may be regarded as an abstract machine capable of answering messages. The collection of messages that may be handled by an object is often referred to as the *protocol* obeyed by the object. This notion was introduced in the Smalltalk programming environment originally to provide the means to group the messages to which an object may respond. For instance, the distinction between methods for initialization and methods for modification or processing may be convenient in developing or using a program. The notion of *protocol* may also be given a more formal interpretation, as has been done for instance in the notion of *contracts* (introduced in Eiffel) stating the requirements that must be adhered to in communicating with an object.

Structurally, an object may be regarded as a collection of data and procedures. In principle, the data are invisible from the outside and may be manipulated only by invoking the right procedure. In a pure object-oriented language such as Smalltalk and Eiffel, sending a message to an object is the only way of invoking such a procedure. Combined, *data-hiding* and *message interface abstraction* will be referred to as *encapsulation*. Actually, object-oriented languages, while in some way supporting objects as collections of data and procedures, may differ subtly in the degree and way in which they support data-hiding and abstraction.

In the next section we will introduce C++, which unlike the purely object-oriented languages Smalltalk and Eiffel may be called a hybrid language. Apart from the support of object-oriented features, C++ also supports ordinary functions and procedures. Consequently, it does not impose a strictly object-oriented computation model, but leaves the programmer the choice of what means are used to express a computation. Some do consider this freedom to be a disadvantage.

Computability and complexity Mathematically, a computing device consists of a finite table of instructions and a possible infinite memory in which to store intermediate results. In order to perform a computation the device also needs an input and some means by which to display the results.

For now, we need not be concerned with the precise mathematical details of our model of a computing device. For a very much more precise and elaborate description of the Turing machine, the interested reader is referred to Hopcroft (1979). What is important, however, is that this model captures in a very precise sense the notion of computation, in that it allows us to characterize what can be computed, and also what a computation will cost, in terms of computing time and memory usage.

An interesting, but perhaps somewhat distressing, feature of the Turing machine model is that it is the strongest model we have, which means that any other model of computation is at best equivalent to it. Parallel computation models in effect do extend the power of (sequential) Turing machines, but only in a linear relation with the number of processors. In other words, the Turing machine defines what we may regard as *computable* and establishes a measure of the complexity of a computation, in space and time. The awareness of the intrinsic limitations imposed by a precise mathematical notion of computability has, for example, led to regard the claims of artificial intelligence with some caution (see Rabin, 1974). However, the theoretical insight that a problem may in the worst case not be solved in finite time or space should not hinder us in looking for an optimal, approximate solution that is reachable with bounded resources.

An equally important feature of the Turing machine model is that it gives us an illustration of what it means to program a computing device, that is to instruct the machine to perform actions dependent on its input and state. As an extension to the model, we can easily build a *universal* computing device, into which we may feed the description of some particular machine, in order to mimic the computation of that machine. Apparently, this gives us a more powerful machine. However, this has proven not to be the case. Neither does this universal device enlarge the class of computable problems, nor does it affect in any significant sense the computational complexity of what we know to be computable. See slide 2-3.

Computing devices   2-3

- mathematical model – *Turing machine*
- universal machine – machines as programs
- computability & complexity – time/space bounded

Object-oriented programming does not enlarge the class of computable problems, nor does it reduce the computational complexity of the problems we can handle.

Slide 2-3: Computing devices

Interestingly, there is an extension of the (basic and universal) Turing machine model that allows us to extend the narrow boundaries imposed by a mathematical characterization of computability. This extension is known as an *oracle* machine, and as the name suggests, the solution to an (otherwise) intractable problem must come from some external source, be it human, machine-like or divine (which is unlikely). Partly, this explains why *intelligent* systems (such as automatic translation systems) are, to a certain extent, intrinsically interactive, since only the human user can provide the (oracle) information needed to arrive at a solution.

Our model of a computing device does quite precisely delimit the domain of computable problems, and gives us an indication of what we can expect the machine to do for us, and what not. Also, it illustrates what means we have available to program such a device, in order to let it act in the way we want. Historically, the Turing machine model may be regarded as a mathematical description of what is called the Von Neumann machine architecture, on which most of our present day computers are based. The Von Neumann machine consists of a memory and a processor that fetches data from the memory, does some computation and stores the data back in memory. This architecture has been heavily criticized, but no other model has yet taken its place. This criticism has been motivated strongly by its influence on the practice of programming. Traditionally, programs for the Von Neumann architecture are conceived as sequences of instructions that may modify the state of the machine. In opposition to this limited, machine oriented view of programming a number of proposals have been made that intended to arrive at a more abstract notion of programming, where the machine is truly at the service of the programmer and not the other way around.

One of these proposals to arrive at a more abstract notion of programming is advocated as the *object-oriented approach*. Before studying the intrinsics of the object-oriented approach, however, it may be useful to reflect on what we may expect from it. Do we hope to be able to solve more problems, or to solve known problems better? In other words, what precisely is the contribution of an object-oriented approach?

Based on the characterization of a computing device, some answers are quite straightforward. We cannot expect to be able to solve more problems, nor can we expect to reduce the computational complexity of the problems that we can solve. What an object-oriented approach can contribute to, however, is simply in providing better means with which to program the machine. Better means, to reduce the chance of (human) errors, better means, also, to manage the complexity of the task of programming (but not to reduce the computational complexity of the problem itself). In other words, by providing abstractions that are less machine oriented and more human oriented, we may enlarge the class of problems that we can tackle in the reality of software engineering. However, we simply cannot expect that an object-oriented approach may in any sense enlarge our notion of what is computable.

2.2   Encapsulation and inheritance in C++

Operationally, the basic features of object-oriented programming may be characterized as *encapsulation* and *inheritance*. Encapsulation means primarily support for the realization of abstract data types, and inheritance provides a mechanism for sharing code which ultimately is a means of defining polymorphic (sub)types. Additional requirements were mentioned: support for type conversion and protection (both for clients and derived classes). In this section we will introduce the features of C++ supporting OOP, and we will (try to) establish to what extent these features satisfy the requirements stated previously. A complementary introduction to C++ is given in appendix C. This section only intends to highlight the more specifically object-oriented features of C++.

2.2.1   Encapsulation

The C++ language is a direct descendant of the popular systems programming language C. The principal difference to C, apart from the introduction of classes and the mechanism of inheritance, is that C++ fully supports static type checking. This allows a programmer to write *type safe* programs. An important distinction here is between *type safe* programs and *type secure* programs. *Type secure* means that no runtime error can occur due to type errors. By incorporating the mechanism of explicit type conversions (casts), C++ allows the programmer to explicitly deviate from the strict typing scheme. In some cases this may be necessary. Personally, I find that this not a disadvantage, but I am sure not everyone will agree on that. Ultimately, good programming requires a disciplined use of the constructs provided by a language, including the low level constructs which may be necessary for special purposes.

Classes Classes are the primary construct for realizing abstract data types in C++. As stated before, the ultimate goal in realizing a data type is to provide the elements of that type with behavior such that they conform to our expectations and (equally important) such that they cooperate fluently with objects that already exist, including the objects (of types) predefined by the language. In the following, we will take a simple example (of a *counter*) to illustrate the various features available for defining the behavior of a class of objects. See slide 2-4.

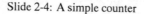

```
class counter {                                                    2-4
int n;
public:
counter() { n = 0; }
void operator++() { n = n + 1; }
int value() { return n; }
};
```

Slide 2-4: A simple counter

The *counter* as defined above maintains an integer n to record its state. The variable n is a *private* data member of the class *counter*. In more traditional object-oriented terminology, we may call n an instance variable. In the public section of the *counter* we encounter a number of methods, or *function members* as they are called for C++. First, we have a function member with the same name as the class, namely *counter*. This member is called the *constructor* and is invoked when creating a *counter* object. The definition of the function body of the constructor immediately follows the declaration of the constructor. This is done primarily because it is convenient for the exposition. However, in practice this may also be done for reasons of efficiency, since function bodies that are directly defined are, whenever possible, expanded inline in the program text during compilation.

When looking at the use of a *counter* object, as in the example below,

```
counter c; c++;
cout << c.value();
```

the first thing to note is that a counter is created by declaring the variable c to be of type *counter*. Next, we see that the counter c is incremented (by one), and finally, the value of the counter is written to standard output.

Constructors and destructors Many errors in programming occur due to improperly initialized data values. The proper initialization of elements of a data type often requires conformance with some informally stated protocol. To take care of the creation and initialization of objects, C++ classes support *constructors* as special member functions. The *constructor* of a class is called when an object (instance) of that class is created.

To illustrate the use of constructors, the simple *counter* of the previous section is extended to contain a string (that is a *char** pointer to a sequence of characters) as an additional data member. See slide 2-5. This pointer, called *id*, contains the name of the counter.

Instead of one constructor, as in the previous version, the current *counter* class contains two constructors. The first constructor, that is defined as

```
counter(int v = 0 ) : n(v) { init("default"); }
```

2-5

```
class counter {
public:
counter(int v = 0 ) : n(v) { init("default"); }
counter(char* s, int v=0) : n(v) { init(s); }
~counter() { delete[] id; }

char* name() { return id; }

void operator++() { n = n + 1; }
int value() { return n; }
private:
int n; char* id;
void init(char* s) {
    id = new char[strlen(s)+1];
    strcpy(id, s);
    }
};
```

Slide 2-5: A named counter

functions as the default constructor. First note that the integer parameter of the constructor is given a default value of zero. Before evaluating the function body, which initializes the *id* string to a default value, the initialization stated after the colon is performed.
This results in initializing the data member n to its appropriate value. The initialization
of data members (which may be objects of user-defined classes) directly after the colon
is often more efficient than an initialization by explicit assignment.

The function *init*, which takes care of allocating resources for the name of the
counter, is defined outside the scope of the class definition for the counter. That the function belongs to the counter is indicated with the scoping operator, which is written as two
colons.

Constructors may be overloaded. The second constructor is chosen when a string
(*char*) is given as an argument at creation time. Also this constructor declares a default
value of zero for its integer parameter. In its function body *init* is called to create a new
(*char*) string containing the contents of the argument string. An example of its use is:

```
counter c("ctr-1"); c++;
cout ≪ c.name() ≪ " = " ≪ c.value();
```

Apart from a member function *name* which returns the *id* of the counter, we also
encounter a *destructor* for a counter object, defined as

```
~counter() { delete[] id; }
```

This destructor deletes the (*char*) string *id*. The destructor is called either when an object of type *counter* ends its lifetime by a change of scope or, in the case of a pointer to
a *counter* object, when the programmer explicitly disposes of the object. Both *new* and
delete are keywords of C++, introduced to manage dynamic memory allocation. In the

absence of garbage collection, these are the only means the programmer has of dynamically creating and destroying objects. In C++ it is possible to bypass the memory allocation scheme provided by the language, but this requires much programmer expertise.

Protection Classes provide encapsulation in the sense of data hiding by allowing both private and public sections. Usually, the private section contains data members that may not be directly accessed by clients of the object, and the public section contains methods or function members to inspect or modify the (hidden) data members. However, despite the explicit definition of a private section, illegal access may still be possible.

The type modifier *const* may be employed to indicate that a particular data item is constant or that some operation does not modify an object. See slide 2-6.

2-6

```
class counter {
public:
counter(int v = 0 );
counter( char* s, int v = 0 );
~counter() { delete[] id; }
const char*  name() const { return id; }
void operator++() { n = n + 1; }
int value() const { return n; }
private:
int n; char*  id;
void init(char* s);
};
```

Slide 2-6: Using *const* to protect access

First look at the use of *const* in

const char* name() const { return id; }

Without the first *const* the (*char**) string that is returned by the function *counter::name* may be modified as in the example. This is allowed since the function just returns a pointer to the data member *id*. When declaring the result of the function to be *const*, the (*char**) string returned may no longer be modified since it is considered to be a constant. The example below then results in a compile-time error

```
counter c("ctr-2"); c++;
c.name()[4]='1';
cout « c.name() « " = " « c.value();
```

The other use of *const* is illustrated by the second occurrence of *const* in the definition of the member function *name*. In this way, the programmer may state that the member function does not modify any of the data members of the object. This use of *const* may be regarded as a means of documenting the role of a member function, namely as one that merely inspects the object instead of modifying its state. In a similar way, the member function *value* may be documented as being a safe operation.

Type conversion When defining a class as the realization of some (abstract) type, the programmer must be well aware of the relation of an object to elements of other data types, including built-in types. For example, when defining the constructors for a counter we have allowed for constructing a counter from an integer as well as a (*char**) string. The C++ language provides facilities for automatic type conversion based on the one-argument constructors defined for a class. Complementary to type conversion based on constructors, C++ allows the programmer to define type conversion operators that map the object to the specified type by means of a user-defined mapping function. See slide 2-7.

2-7

```
class counter {
public:
    counter(int v = 0 ) : n(v), id("default") { }
    counter( char*  s, int v = 0 );
    ~counter() { delete[] id; }
    const char*  name() { return id; }
    void operator++() { n = n + 1; }
    operator int() { return n; }
    operator char* () { return id; }
private:
    int n; char*  id;
};
```

Slide 2-7: Widening and narrowing conversions

In the example below, the function *fun* is defined with a reference to a counter as a parameter. When calling this function with a (*char**) string, the compiler automatically takes care of calling the appropriate constructor in order to convert the (*char**) string to a *counter* object. For example, when defining

```
void fun( counter& c ) {
    cout << (char* ) c << " = " << (int) c;
}
```

then the call

```
fun("ctr-3");
```

results in the creation of a new counter (initialized to zero) and displaying of the name of the counter and its value.

Conversely, as shown in the example, it is possible to make use of the opposite conversions, from a *counter* to either a (*char**) string or integer. In the example, the name and the value of the counter are printed not by calling the appropriate member functions, but by an explicit conversion of the counter to, respectively, a (*char**) string and an integer. Conversion to a (*char**) string is defined by the member function

    operator char* () { *return* id; }

and conversion to an *int* is defined similarly. The effect of these conversions may also be achieved by explicit field selection, which is to be preferred whenever the value of the conversion is not immediately obvious. Indeed, returning a (*char**) from a counter is dubious, whereas it would be perfectly natural for a *token* consisting of an integer identifier and the string representation of the token.

    Potentially, type conversions are dangerous operations since, inevitably, information will be lost during the conversion. Moreover, the use of both a constructor for (*char**) and a type conversion operator to (*char**) may lead to ambiguities when the compiler tries to resolve an overloaded function call.

Overloading and friends Type conversions enable the programmer to overload a function implicitly. Explicit overloading of functions and operators is also possible. Both overloading and type conversions contribute to the polymorphic behavior of objects. Widening and narrowing conversions (also called *promotions* and *coercions*) are defined classwise. Explicit function overloading, in contrast, is of a more global nature, since it may define an arbitrary functional relation between between user-defined and/or built-in types.

2-8

```
class counter {
friend int operator< (counter&, int);
public:

counter(int v = 0 );
counter( char*  s, int v = 0 );
~counter() { delete[] id; }

const char*  name() { return id; }
int value() const { return n; }
void operator++() { n = n + 1; }

private: int n; char*  id;
void init(char*  s);
};

int operator< (counter& c, int i) { return c.n < i; }
```

Slide 2-8: Overloading and friends

    In the *counter* defined in slide 2-8, one of the familiar comparison operators has been overloaded to allow for a comparison of the value of a *counter* object with an integer value. In the example, the comparison operator has been declared to be a *friend* of the class *counter*. Declaring a function (or a class) to be a *friend* grants that function (or the member functions of the class) access to the private parts of the object. For the example given, it would not have been necessary to declare the operator as a *friend*, but, as for instance in the case of matrix multiplications, reasons of efficiency often will cause the programmer to break encapsulation of the class by means of a *friend* declaration.

The use of the operator is illustrated by the following code fragment:

```
counter c("ctr-4"); c++;
if ( c < 2 )
        cout ≪ c.name() ≪ " = " ≪ c.value();
```

Overloading and type conversion exemplify the flexibility of a polymorphic type system. However, both techniques may be considered to provide an *ad hoc* solution to the problem of incorporating polymorphism in the language when compared with the polymorphism introduced by inheritance and generic (template) types. These will be studied in the following sections.

2.2.2 Inheritance

Inheritance is perhaps the most distinct feature of object-oriented programming. Pragmatically, from a software engineering perspective, inheritance provides a mechanism for *code sharing* and *code reuse*. From a type theoretical point of view, inheritance is one of the mechanisms supporting polymorphism. Operationally, the power of inheritance in C++ comes from the use of *virtual functions* and *dynamic binding*.

Abstract classes The classical example to demonstrate the use of inheritance and the virtues of dynamic binding is a hierarchy of shapes. The hierarchy of shapes consists of an abstract shape from which concrete shapes, such as a circle and a rectangle, may be derived. When deriving concrete shapes, the programmer merely has to provide the appropriate constructors and define the actual method for displaying the shape. An abstract shape is defined as in slide 2-9.

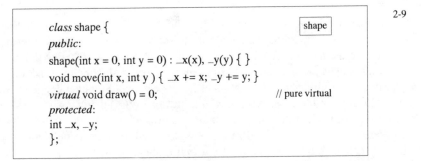

2-9

```
class shape {                                    shape
public:
shape(int x = 0, int y = 0) : _x(x), _y(y) { }
void move(int x, int y ) { _x += x; _y += y; }
virtual void draw() = 0;                     // pure virtual
protected:
int _x, _y;
};
```

Slide 2-9: Abstract shape

A shape, viewed as an abstract entity, contains data members for its origin, and further must provide, apart from a constructor, the methods for moving and drawing a shape. The abstract class *shape* defines a constructor which sets the origin to $(0, 0)$, unless other values have been provided. The member function *move* may be implemented for all shapes as simply changing the origin in an appropriate way. On the other hand, drawing a shape is undefined for an abstract shape. For this reason the member function *draw* is declared as *pure virtual*, meaning that it must be redefined by a class derived from the class *shape*. A class with pure virtual functions is an abstract class. An abstract class can have no instances. For example

> shape s;   // error: abstract class

would result in a compiler error.

Having an abstract class *shape* available, we may define concrete shapes, such as *circle* and *rectangle*, as in slide 2-10.

2-10

```
class circle : public shape {                              circle
public:
circle( int x, int y, int r) : shape(x,y), _radius(r) { }
void draw() { cout ≪ "C:" ≪ _x ≪ _y ≪ _radius; }
protected:
int _radius;
};
class rectangle : public shape {                           rectangle
public:
rectangle( int x, int y, int l, int r ) : shape(x,y), _l(l), _r(r) { }
void draw() { cout ≪ "R:" ≪ _x ≪ _y ≪ _l ≪ _r; }
protected:
int _l,_r;
};
```

Slide 2-10: Concrete shapes

For a *circle* we need to define, apart from its origin, a *radius*. And, similarly, for a rectangle we need to define the length of the sides. Both *circle* and *rectangle* inherit the origin and the member function *move* from the *shape* class. Instantiating the inherited part takes place, as indicated after the colon, before evaluating the function body of the constructor. Unlike the initialization of instance variables, which may be assigned a value in the body of the constructor, the initialization of the inherited parts must be done in this way. An explicit initializer is required unless a default constructor is available. The difference between the initialization of a data member immediately after the colon or in the function body of the constructor is quite subtle. In the latter case, a default constructor will be applied to create the data member and the subsequent assignment in the function body may lead to the creation of another instance. Generally, it is safer and more efficient to initialize data members immediately after the colon. Unfortunately, it is not always possible to initialize data in the colon-list. Also, there is no way in which to communicate between the initializers, which may result in repeated computations when there is a dependency between the initial values of the data members.

A concrete shape class must necessarily (re)define the member function draw, since an abstract shape cannot possibly know how to draw itself.

A code fragment illustrating the use of concrete shapes looks as follows:

```
circle c(1,1,2); rectangle r(2,2,1,1);
c.draw(); r.draw();
```

Note that calling *draw* is for both kinds of shapes the same. The difference between the two distinct shapes, however, becomes visible when calling the function *draw*. The function *draw* specified for *circle* overrides the specification given for the abstract *shape*, and similarly for *rectangle*.

Dynamic binding The reuse of code is one of the most important aspects of inheritance. The principle underlying the efficient reuse of code (by employing inheritance) may be characterized as *"programming by stating the difference,"* which means that one has to (re)define the features of the derived class that are added to or different from what is provided by the base class. To fully exploit this principle we need *virtual* functions, that is functions for which dynamic binding applies.

Operationally, dynamic binding may be regarded as a *dispatching mechanism* that acts like a *case statement* to select (dynamically) the appropriate procedure in response to a message. In many procedural programs, such a case statement often occurs (explicitly) when a kind of polymorphism is introduced by means of an explicit tag (as, for example, in combination with a union or a variant-record). The use of such tags may become a nightmare when modifying the informal type system, since each case statement then needs to be updated. Using inheritance with dynamic binding, such case statements are, so to speak, implicitly inserted by the compiler or interpreter. The obvious advantage of such a feature, apart from reducing the amount of code that must be written, is that maintenance is greatly facilitated. A possible disadvantage, however, might be that *program understanding* becomes more difficult since many of the choices are now implicitly made by the dispatching mechanism instead of being written out explicitly.

To illustrate the power of virtual functions (and dynamic binding) we will add a compound shape to our hierarchy of shapes. See slide 2-11.

A compound shape is actually a linked list of shapes. To add shapes to the list, the class *compound* extends the class *shape* with a member function *add*. Both the member functions *move* and *draw* are redefined in order to manipulate the list of shapes in the appropriate way. The list is traversed by recursively invoking the function for the objects stored in the *next* pointer unless *next* is empty, which indicates the end of the list. The class *compound* is made a subclass of *shape* to allow a *compound* shape to be treated as a *shape*.

As an example of the use of a compound shape, consider the following fragment:

```
compound s;
s.add( new circle(1,1,2) );
s.add( new rectangle(2,2,3,5) );
s.draw(); s.move(7,7); s.draw();
```

After creating an empty compound shape, two shapes, respectively a circle and a rectangle, are added. The compound shape is asked to draw itself, it is moved, and then asked

```
class compound : public shape {                    compound
public:
compound( shape* s = 0 ) : fig(s) { next = 0; }
void add( shape* s ) {
if (next) next→ add(s); else next = new compound(s);
}
void move(int x, int y) {
  if (fig) fig→ move(x,y);
  if (next) next→ move(x,y);
}
void draw() {
  if (fig)  fig→ draw();
  if (next) next→ draw();
}
private:
shape* fig; compound* next;
};
```

2-11

Slide 2-11: Compound shapes

to draw itself again. The compound shape object, when moving and drawing the list of shapes, has no knowledge of what actual shapes are contained in the list, which may be compound shapes themselves. This illustrates how we may achieve polymorphic behavior by using inheritance.

A more explicit example of the polymorphic behavior of shapes is given by the following code fragment.

```
shape* fig[3];
fig[0] = &s;                                    // the compound shape
fig[1] = new circle(3,3,5);
fig[2] = new rectangle(4,4,5,5);

for( int i = 0; i <  3; i++ )
        fig[i]→ draw();
```

After storing some actual shapes, including a compound shape, in an array of (pointers to) shapes, a simple loop with a uniform request for drawing is sufficient to display all the shapes contained in the array, independent of their actual type.

This example is often used to demonstrate that when adopting an object-oriented approach the programmer no longer needs to include lengthy case statements to choose between the various drawing operations on the basis of an explicit type tag.

The careful reader may have noted that the absence of the declaration *virtual* for the member function *move* may lead to problems. Indeed, this leads to erroneous behavior since moving only the origin of the compound shape will not do. In our slightly wasteful implementation of a compound shape, the member variables inherited from *shape* play no role. Instead, each shape in the list must be moved. This could be repaired either by declaring the function *shape* :: *move* as virtual or by redefining *compound* :: *draw* and eliminating *compound* :: *move*. This illustrates that it takes careful consideration to decide whether or not to make a member function virtual. Some even suggest making member functions virtual by default, unless it is clear that they may be declared non-virtual.

Multiple inheritance Graphical shapes are a typical example of objects allowing for a tree-shaped taxonomy. Sometimes, however, we wish to define a class not from a single base class, but by deriving it from multiple base classes, by employing multiple inheritance.

2-12

```
class student { ... };
class assistant { ... };
class student_assistant
          : public student, public assistant {
public:
student_assistant( int id, int sal )
          : student(id), assistant(sal) {}
};
```

Slide 2-12: Multiple inheritance

In slide 2-12, one of the classical examples of multiple inheritance is depicted, defining a *student_assistant* by inheriting from *student* and *assistant*.

Dynamic binding for instances of a class derived by multiple inheritance works in the same way as in the case of single inheritance. However, ambiguities between member function names must be resolved by the programmer.

2-13

```
class person { };
class student : virtual public person { ... }
class assistant : virtual public person { ... }
class student_assistant
      : public student, public assistant { ... };
```

Slide 2-13: Virtual base classes

When using multiple inheritance, one may encounter situations where the classes involved are derived from a common base class, as illustrated in slide 2-13.

To ensure that *student_assistant* contains only one copy of the *person* class, both the *student* and *assistant* classes must indicate that the *person* is inherited in a virtual manner. Otherwise, we may not have a declaration of the form

person* p = new student_assistant(20,6777,300);

since the compiler would not know which *person* was meant (that is, how to apply the conversion from *student_assistant* to *person*).

2.2.3 Using assertions

Whatever support a language may offer, reliable software is to a large extent the result of a disciplined approach to programming. The use of assertions has long since been recognized as a powerful way in which to check whether the functional behavior of a program corresponds with its intended behavior. In effect, many programming language environments support the use of assertions in some way. For example, both C and C++ define a macro *assert* which checks for the result of a boolean expression and stops the execution if the expression is false.

In the example in slide 2-14, assertions are used to check for the satisfaction of both the pre- and post-conditions of a function that computes the square root of its argument, employing a method known as Newton iteration.

2-14

```
double sqrt( double arg ) {                              sqrt
require ( arg ≥ 0 );
double r=arg, x=1, eps=0.0001;
while( fabs(r− x) > eps ) {
  r=x; x=r-((r∗ r-arg)/(2∗ r));
  }
promise ( r− arg ∗ arg ≤ eps );
return r;
}
```

Slide 2-14: Using assertions in C++

In the example, the macro *assert* has been renamed *require* and *promise* to indicate whether the assertion serves as, respectively, a pre- or post-condition. As the example in slide 2-14 shows, assertions provide a powerful means by which to characterize the behavior of functions, especially in those cases where the algorithmic structure itself does not give a good clue as to what the function is meant to do.

Object design The use of assertions has been promoted in Meyer (1988) as a design method for object-oriented programming in Eiffel. The idea is to define the functionality of the various methods by means of pre- and post-conditions stating in a precise manner the requirements that clients of an object must meet and the obligations an object has when executing a method. Together, the collection of methods annotated with pre- and post-conditions may be regarded as a *contract* between the object and its potential clients. See section 3.3.

Whereas Eiffel directly supports the use of assertions by allowing access to the value of an instance variable before the execution of a method through the keyword *old*, the C++ programmer must rely on explicit programming to be able to compare the state before an operation with the state after the operation.

2-15

```
class counter {                                          counter
public:
counter(int n = 0) : _n(n) {
    require( n ≥ 0 );
    promise( invariant() );              // check initial state
    }
virtual void operator++() {
    require( true );                     // empty pre-condition
    hold();                              // save the previous state
    _n += 1;
    promise( _n == old_n + 1 && invariant() );
    }
int value() const { return _n; }         // no side effects
virtual bool invariant() { return value() ≥ 0; }
protected:
int _n;
int old_n;
virtual void hold() { old_n = n; }
};
```

Slide 2-15: The *counter* contract

As an example, the annotated *counter* in slide 2-15 includes a member function *hold* to store the value of its instance variable. It is used in the *operator++* function to check whether the new value of the counter is indeed the result of incrementing the old value.

Assertions may also be used to check whether the object is correctly initialized. The pre-condition stated in the constructor requires that the counter must start with a value not less than zero. In addition, the constructor checks whether the class invariant, stated in the (virtual) member function *invariant*, is satisfied. Similarly, after checking whether the post-condition of the *operator* + + function is true, the invariant is checked as well.

When employing inheritance, care must be taken that the invariance requirements of the base class are not violated.

The class *bounded*, defined in slide 2-16, refines the class *counter* by imposing an additional constraint that the value of the (bounded) counter must not exceed some user-defined maximum. This constraint is checked in the *invariant* function, together with the original *counter* :: *invariant*(), which was declared virtual to allow for overriding by inheritance.

In addition, the increment *operator++* function contains an extra pre-condition to check whether the state of the (bounded) counter allows it to perform the operation.

From a formal perspective, the use of assertions may be regarded as a way of augmenting the type system supported by object-oriented languages. More importantly, from a software engineering perspective, the use of assertions provides a guideline for the design of classes and the use of inheritance. In the next chapter we will discuss the use of assertions and the notion of contracts in more detail.

```
class bounded : public counter {                    [bounded]        2-16
public:
bounded(int b = MAXINT) : counter(0), max(b) {}
void operator++() {
    require( value() < max() );          // to prevent overflow
    counter::operator++();
    }
bool invariant() {
    return value() ≤ max && counter::invariant();
    }
private:
int max;
};
```

Slide 2-16: Refining the *counter* contract

2.3 Canonical class definitions

The multitude of constructs available in C++ to support object-oriented programming may lead the reader to think that object-oriented programming is not at all meant to reduce the complexity of programming but rather to increase it, for the joy of programming so to speak. This impression is partly justified, since the number and complexity of constructs is at first sight indeed slightly bewildering. However, it is necessary to realize that each of the constructs introduced (classes, constructors and destructors, protection mechanisms, type conversion, overloading, virtual functions and dynamic binding) are in some way essential to support object-oriented programming in a type safe, and yet convenient, way.

Having studied the mechanisms, the next step is to find proper ways, recipes as it were, to use these mechanisms. What we need, in the terminology of Coplien (1992), are *idioms*, that is established ways of solving particular problems with the mechanisms we have available. In his excellent book, Coplien discusses a number of advanced idioms for a variety of problem domains, including signal processing and symbolic computing.

In this section, we will look at two basic idioms, idioms that every C++ programmer needs to master or at least understand. These idioms concern the definition of concrete data types or *representation types* and their efficient implementation. It is not immediately obvious what lessons can be drawn for the realization of abstract data types in other languages.

2.3.1 Concrete data types

A concrete data type is the realization of an abstract data type. When a concrete data type is correctly implemented it must satisfy the requirements imposed by the definition of the abstract data type it realizes. These requirements specify what operations are defined for that type, and also their effects. In principle, these requirements may be formally specified, but in practice just an informal description is usually given. Apart from the demands imposed by a more abstract view of the functionality of the type, a programmer usually also wishes to meet other requirements, such as speed, efficiency in terms of storage and error conditions, to prevent the removal of an item from an empty stack, for example. The latter requirements may be characterized as requirements imposed by implementation concerns, whereas the former generally result from design considerations.

To verify whether a concrete data type meets the requirements imposed by the specification of the abstract data type is quite straightforward, although not always easy. However, the task of verifying whether a concrete data type is optimally implemented is rather less well defined. To arrive at an optimal implementation may involve a lot of skill and ingenuity, and in general it is hard to decide whether the right choices have been made. Establishing trade-offs and making choices, for better or worse, is a matter of experience, and crucially depends upon the skill in handling the tools and mechanisms available.

Canonical class   2-17

  ● default constructor

  ● copy constructor

  ● destructor

  ● assignment

  ● operators

Abstract data types must be indistinguishable from built-in types

---

Slide 2-17: Canonical class

When defining concrete data types, the list of requirements defining the *canonical class* idiom given in slide 2-17 may be used as a check list to determine whether all the necessary features of a class have been defined. Ultimately, the programmer should strive to realize abstract data types in such a way that their behavior is in some sense indistinguishable from the behavior of the built-in data types. Since this may involve a lot of work, this need not be a primary aim in the first stages of a software development project. But for class libraries to work properly, it is simply essential.

Following Coplien (1992), we will illustrate the notion of *concrete data types* by a *string* class. Strings are a well-understood data type, for which many libraries exist, such as the C-library represented by the *strings.h* include file. Strings support operations such as copying, concatenation and asking for the length of the string. In the example in slide 2-18, the C-string package is used to implement a *string* class.

As may be expected, there is a constructor for creating a *string* from a pointer to *char*, which is the low-level C representation of a string. The result of evaluating this constructor is to store the argument string in the private *char** data member.

The definition of a *default constructor* is mandatory. The default constructor of the *string* class is easily obtained by employing a default argument for the *char** constructor. When no argument is provided the private (low-level) string pointer is set to the empty string. A default constructor is required, since, for instance when creating an array of strings, the user is not allowed to initialize the individual (*string*) objects created. In such cases, the compiler uses a default constructor, which may be (re)defined by the implementor of the class. The other mandatory constructor is a so-called *copy constructor*. This constructor is used when creating a string by copying another *string* object. Copying occurs for example when passing an object by value to a function or when returning an object by value as the result of a function. By default, the compiler defines a standard copy constructor, which makes a shallow copy of the object, that is a copy of only the data members of the object, not what they refer to if they are pointers. However, a shallow copy is not in all cases satisfactory. For instance, in our *string* example, a shallow copy may cause the object to refer to the same *char** string. When deleting the objects, the shared *char** string pointer will be deleted twice, which on some systems may lead to a core dump. The copy constructor, as defined in the example, takes care of creating an actual copy of the *char** string. Similar considerations apply to the use of the assignment operator and hence this operator needs to be redefined as well.

String class | canonical | 2-18

```
class string {
public:
string(char* s="") { init(s); }
string(string& a) { init((char* )a); }
~string() { delete p; }
string& operator=( string& a ) {
  init((char* )a); return * this;
  }

string operator+( string& a );
int length() { return strlen(p); }
operator char* () { return p; }
private:
void init(char* s) {
  p = new char[strlen(s)+1]; strcpy(p,s);
  }
char* p;
};
```

Slide 2-18: A *string* class

In addition to the usual string operations, such as concatenation (for which the addition operator is used) and *length* (to determine the number of characters a string contains), there is also a *type conversion* operator that deserves special attention. Together, the constructor for creating a string from a *char** string and the type conversion operator for converting a string to a low level (*char**) string define a cyclic relation between *char** pointers and strings. This may lead to ambiguities with which the compiler cannot cope.

An example of the use of the *string* class is given below

```
string s1("hello"), s2("world");
cout << (char* ) s1 << (char* ) s2 ;
string s3(s1); string s4 = s2;
```

```
cout ≪ (char∗ ) s3 ≪ (char∗ ) s4;
string s5; s5 = s3 + " " + s4;
cout ≪ (char∗ ) s5;
```

The example shows the creation of two strings from *char*∗ pointers. These strings are written to standard output by using an explicit cast. Alternatively, the output operator might have been overloaded for *string*. Next, two strings are created as a copy from the previously created strings. Note that in both cases the *copy constructor* is called. The assignment operator is only used to store the result of concatenating the strings just created.

Evidently, the implementation of the *string* class is far from optimal. Both in performance and storage there is a lot of unnecessary overhead. In the next section, we will look at how to improve the actual behavior of *string* objects.

2.3.2 Envelope and letter classes

The *string* class defined previously is *correct* in the sense that it satisfies the requirements imposed by (the informal specification of) our notion of strings. Moreover it is *safe*, in the sense that it does not carry the danger of potential core dumps.

String handler | envelope | 2-19

```
class string {
public:
string(char∗  s = "") { rep = new stringrep(s); }
string(string& a) { rep = a.rep; rep→ count++; }
string& operator=( string& a ) {
        a.rep→ count++;
        if (--rep→ count ≤  0 ) delete rep;
        rep = a.rep;
        return ∗ this;
        }
string operator+( string& a );
int length() { return strlen(rep→ rep); }
operator char∗ () { return rep→ rep; }
private:
stringrep∗  rep;
};
```

Slide 2-19: A *string* handler class

However, although it is a *correct* and *safe* realization of the abstract data type *string* (partially, that is), it is not an *efficient* nor in any sense *optimal* implementation. To illustrate the second basic idiom, that of *envelope/letter* pairs, the string example will be extended to include reference counting as a means by which to reduce the storage required and the overhead of creating and deleting strings.

The idea of the *envelope/letter* idiom is that the program manipulates objects (*letters*) through special wrappers (*envelopes*) which contain a pointer to the associated letter. The envelope can deal with some general issues (for example, ensuring that store is managed correctly on assignment), while deferring other operations to the letter. This separation of concerns makes developing a suitable class interface easier. We will also refer to the *envelope/letter* idiom as the *handler/body* idiom. A string handler (*envelope*) class may be defined as in slide 2-19.

String body | letter | 2-20

```
class stringrep {
friend string;
private:
stringrep(char* s) {
      rep = new char[strlen(s)+1]; strcpy(rep,s);
      count = 1;
      }
~stringrep() { delete[] rep; }
char* rep;
int count;
};
```

Slide 2-20: A *string* body class

Both the *copy constructor* and the *assignment operator* are defined to make use of the reference counting scheme. For instance, after decrementing the reference counter, when this counter is zero the object representing the actual string is deleted. The details of creating and deleting the storage needed to represent the actual string are hidden by the (body) *stringrep* class. The body (*letter*) class may be defined as in slide 2-20.

The class *string* is declared to be a *friend* of the *stringrep* class, to allow the *string* direct access to the data members. Notice that the class *stringrep* has no *public* constructors. It is not intended to be used by others. Only *friend* classes are allowed to create actual instances of it.

In later versions of C++ it is possible to nest class definitions. This may be convenient for keeping the class name space from being polluted by auxiliary classes. Evidently, our *stringrep* class may be defined within the scope of the class *string*. This is left as an exercise for the reader.

2.4 Generic types

Reuse of software is one of the ways in which to produce reliable systems, that is, the reuse of reliable software. Many of the data types that are used to specify software systems have a lot in common. For instance, there is little difference between a stack of integers or a stack of strings, or a stack for any other data type. So it would be more convenient to have a generic stack, which may be used as or instantiated to a stack of integers, strings or whatever. Evidently, the various container types such as *stack, list, bag* and *set* are likely candidates for being realized by generic types.

Generic types   2-21

  • *polymorphic types* – pointers, *void*∗

  • *parametrized types* – template classes

Generic types are essential for *programming in the large*

Slide 2-21: Generic types

The C++ language supports two kinds of generic types, *polymorphic* (pointer) and *parametrized.* See slide 2-21. In section 2.2.2 we have already seen that an abstract or generic shape type may be specified and later refined into concrete types, giving rise to a polymorphic hierarchy. The base class from which this hierarchy is derived may be regarded as a constraint with respect to the possible element types of a generic container. A similar notion of type hierarchy is exploited in the solution of generic types involving *void* pointers. The use of *void*∗ was one of the two ways to deal with unconstrained generic types in C++ before templates were introduced in version 3.0. The other way was the use of equally error-prone macro definitions. The use of *void*∗ will be illustrated as a warning; this is how it should *not* be done. The preferred way in which to specify generic types in C++ is to employ the template construct, which allows the programmer to parametrize a class or function definition with a type parameter.

2.4.1 Base class hierarchies

Inheritance allows the programmer to define a class hierarchy which corresponds to a hierarchy of (polymorphic) pointer types. In particular, the root class (at the top of the hierarchy) corresponds to a pointer type that acts as a generic type with respect to the pointer types corresponding with the other classes in the hierarchy. In addition, the root class specifies an interface common to all classes lower in the hierarchy.

The polymorphic property of (base class) pointers allows for the definition of a generic container for element types ranging over the pointer types corresponding to the descendants of the base class.

As an example, look at the *shapelist* defined in slide 2-22. The class *shapelist* declares instance variables *hd* (of type *shape*∗) and *tl* (of type *shapelist*∗). The insertion of a new element results in the creation of a new *shapelist* which has the element as a head and the original list as its tail. Note that the head of each list is a pointer to an instance of *shape* or one of its derived classes. A pointer is needed since the size of the actual object will vary depending on the actual type of the object inserted. For example, a *circle* extends a *shape* by including an additional instance variable giving its radius.

Employing base class hierarchies offers a safe, yet limited, means by which to define generic (container) types. (Limited, because the base class imposes constraints on the actual types for which the generic data type may be used.)

```
Class hierarchies                                    2-22

    class shapelist {                      shapelist
    public:
    shapelist(shape* el=0, shapelist* sl=0)
                    : hd(el), tl(sl) { }
    shapelist* insert(shape* el) {
         require( el );                  // el must exist
         if (!hd) hd = el;
         else return new shapelist(el,this);
         }
    shape* head() { return hd; }
    shapelist* tail() { return tl; }
    private:
    shape* hd;
    shapelist* tl;
    }
```

Slide 2-22: Base class polymorphism

The *void* pointer Employing *void* pointers allows for the definition of unconstrained generic types, although in a rather crude way. To understand how that works, it is necessary to reflect on the meaning of a type system. One important aspect of a type system is that it may protect the programmer from a number of common errors, ranging from trivial typos to inconsistent structures. In particular, when the type system supports subtyping, the compiler may check whether the actual relation satisfies the subtyping relation. A type gives information concerning the object to which a variable or expression refers. The more specific a type, the more a compiler needs to know in order to assist the programmer in specifying correct programs. From this perspective, the *void* pointer figures as the top of the type hierarchy, since the compiler cannot be assumed to have any knowledge concerning its (correct) use. Consequently, the compiler leaves the responsibility entirely to the user, who may convert the *void* pointer to any type at will. Because of this absence of type information, the *void* pointer may indeed be called a *generic* type.

An example of employing the *void* pointer to define a generic stack is given in slide 2-23.

For storing the contents of the stack, an array of *void* pointers is created when evaluating the constructor, which is deleted when the destructor is called. Provisions for dynamically enlarging the size of the stack and for testing its bounds have been omitted, but this is easily provided for.

An example of using the stack may look as follows:

```
stack s(100);
char plus = '+'; char c = 'c ';
s.push(&plus); s.push(&plus); s.push(&c);
while ( !s.empty() ) {
```

```
typedef void* type;                          generic void*
class stack {                                      stack
public:
stack( int n = 12 ) {
      top = -1;
      impl = new type[n];
      }
~stack() { delete[] impl; }
bool empty() { return top == -1; }
void push( type it ) { impl[++top] = it; }
type pop() { return impl[top--]; }
private:
int top; type*  impl;
};
```

2-23

Slide 2-23: Using the *void* pointer

```
cout ≪ * (char* ) s.pop();
}
```

To retrieve a value, first the pointer must be cast to a pointer of the appropriate type, and then it may be de-referenced to deliver the actual value. This code clearly illustrates that the user is entirely responsible for correctly using the stack. Now when we look at the code, to push elements on the stack, it is sufficient to take the address of the value inserted. However, when removing elements from the stack, the user must know precisely what the type of the element popped is. In the example, this first requires the conversion of the *void* pointer to a *char* pointer, and then a de-reference with an explicit cast to *char*. Evidently, generic types of this kind are error-prone, not to say ugly.

2.4.2 Template classes

Template classes are supported only in the later releases of C++ (AT&T 3.0, Zortech 3.1). Before the actual support of template classes, and even with the support for template classes available, programmers have extensively used the macro preprocessor to define generic classes. A disadvantage of such an approach is that it easily leads to deviant notation and the use of non-standard constructs or preprocessor facilities. Another important disadvantage of using the preprocessor is that there is no direct compiler support for checking whether a template has correctly been defined and instantiated. And similar objections hold equally as strong for defining constants, inline functions or template functions as macros. In slide 2-24, the example of a generic stack has been rewritten to employ template classes.

One (subtle) difference between the previous definition, using *void* pointers, and the current definition that uses templates is that an instantiated template stack may hold objects (or references to objects), whereas the other version only allows the storage of

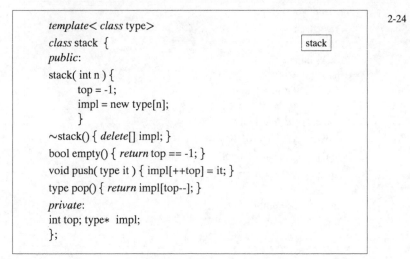

Slide 2-24: Template class

pointers to objects. See section 2.5.1 for a discussion on the difference between objects, references and pointers.

Another, very important, difference is illustrated by the code fragment showing the use of a (template) stack

```
stack<char> s(100);
s.push('+'); s.push('+'); s.push('c ');
while ( !s.empty() ) {
        cout ≪ s.pop();
        }
```

When creating the stack, the user must explicitly indicate what type of elements the stack contains. Other uses of the stack do not require any explicit type conversions and are completely type checked by the compiler. Note that the template construct actually adds to the power of the language, since a stack of *void* pointers may easily be defined by giving the right instantiation parameters.

Using templates A practical disadvantage of template classes is that they may result in generating lots of (instantiation) code. To avoid excessive code generation, we may employ generically typed wrapper classes providing safe access to an implementation employing *void**. The rationale underlying such an approach is that we may use any implementation technique as long as we provide the user with a type-safe interface.

We will conclude this section on generic types by looking at a type-safe generic list class, employing *void* to represent the actual list structure. (This example involves some rather complex features of C++.)

An unconstrained, yet unsafe, implementation of a list is given by the definition of a *cell*, as depicted in slide 2-25.

2-25

```
struct cell {                                            cell
cell(void* hd=0, cell* tl=0) : el(hd), next(tl) {}
~cell() { if(next) delete next; }
void insert(void* e);
void* el;
cell* next;
};
void cell::insert(void* e) {                             insert
    if (!el) el = e;
    else if (!next) next = new cell(e);
    else next→ insert(e);
}
```

Slide 2-25: The *cell* representation of a list

As an example of a generic type-safe wrapper class that may be used to access the list structure, look at the definition of the template list class given in slide 2-26. Apart from a constructor which initializes the inner cell to zero and a destructor which destroys the inner cell, the class interface for list defines the function *insert*, which is used to insert references to objects of type E, and a conversion operator that delivers an instance of class *iter<E>*, where E is the instantiation parameter type of the list. Instances of *iter<E>* may be used as an iterator giving access to the elements of the list (see below).

For inserting an element, we must convert the typed reference into a *void* pointer by taking the address of the argument of *insert*. We then create a new cell if the inner cell is still zero and employ *cell* :: *insert* otherwise.

Iterators provide a convenient method to access a variety of structures in a uniform way. In the literature various styles of iterators are employed, some using explicit *first*, *next* and *exist* functions and others using the more concise applicative notation, as used for defining the class *iter* given in slide 2-27.

Below, an example is given of how an iterator may be used to traverse the list

```
void main() {
list<int> lst;
lst.insert(1); lst.insert(2);
iter<int> it = lst;                                  // get the iterator
int* p = 0;                                          // start
while ( p = it() ) {
    cout ≪ "item;" ≪ * p ≪ endl;                     // take the value
    }
}
```

Note that to obtain an iterator, that is an instance of *iter<int>*, we simply employ the conversion operator for *iter<E>*, which is automatically applied when assigning the list to *it*.

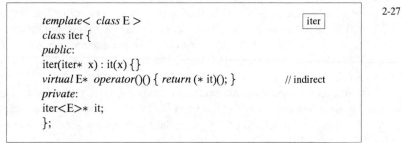

2-26

```
template< class E >                                    list<E>
class list {
friend class listiter<E>;
public:
list() { c = 0; }
~list() { if(c) delete c; }
void insert(const E& el);
operator iter<E>() { return listiter<E>(c); }          //(*)
private:
cell* c;
};
template< class E >                              list<E> :: insert
void list<E>::insert(const E& el) {
void* x = (void* ) &el;
if (!c) c = new cell(x);
else c→ insert(x);
}
```

Slide 2-26: A template *list* wrapper

```
template< class E >                                         iter
class iter {
public:
iter(iter* x) : it(x) {}
virtual E* operator()() { return (* it)(); }             // indirect
private:
iter<E>* it;
};
```

Slide 2-27: The definition of iterators

To obtain the elements of the list, a pointer to *int* is initialized to zero. As long as invoking *iter<int> :: operator()* for *it* (which may concisely be written as *it()*) results in a non-zero (pointer) value, the (de-referenced) result will be written to standard output. When *it()* produces a zero pointer value, we have reached the end of the list.

The actual definition of both *iter<E>* and *listiter<E>* is somewhat complicated due to the fact that C++ employs dynamic binding only when virtual members are invoked through pointers or references.

The constructor for *iter* expects an instance of *iter* as a parameter. The *iter :: operator()* function in its turn invokes the *operator()* function for the *iter** instance variable *it*.

The actual work is done by *listiter*. Its constructor takes a cell pointer, which is given to it when invoking the *list<E> :: operator iter<E>* conversion function. To redi-

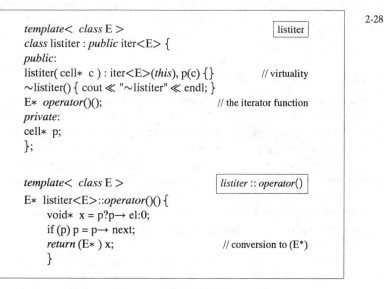

2-28

```
template< class E >                              listiter
class listiter : public iter<E> {
public:
listiter( cell* c ) : iter<E>(this), p(c) {}              // virtuality
~listiter() { cout ≪ "~listiter" ≪ endl; }
E* operator()();                         // the iterator function
private:
cell* p;
};


template< class E >                         listiter :: operator()
E* listiter<E>::operator()() {
    void* x = p?p→ el:0;
    if (p) p = p→ next;
    return (E* ) x;                      // conversion to (E*)
}
```

Slide 2-28: The *listiter* class

rect the invocation of *iter* :: *operator*() to the *operator*() function of the instance of *listiter*, the *this* pointer is given to *iter<E>* when initializing *iter<E>* as the base class.

The implementation of the *listiter<E>* :: *operator*() function itself is straightforward. It delivers zero whenever the *cell*∗ instance variable is zero. Otherwise it delivers the element of the cell, which is converted to the proper type and sets the cell pointer to the next element in the list.

2.5   Benefits and pitfalls

Having looked at a number of language constructs supporting object-oriented programming, and some of the idioms that apply to them, it is time to establish the potential benefits and pitfalls of the approach supported by these constructs. More particularly, since we have concentrated mostly on C++, we need to explore what advantages C++ offers when we adopt an object-oriented approach, and what disadvantages may adhere to choosing C++ instead of, say, Smalltalk or Eiffel.

Before examining the various language features (or absence thereof) in more detail, we may observe that C++ has a number of weaknesses that are directly due to the need to remain compatible with C. C offers many built-in types, such as *char*, *short*, *unsigned* and *int* for which the language defines implicit yet unsafe conversions. One of the awkward features of C, inherited by C++, is the equation of arrays with pointers. This equation causes the language to be non-orthogonal when dealing with pointers to arrays. For example

```
typedef int intarray[10];

intarray a, * p;
```

```
p = &a;                                          // warning: illegal pointer combination
```

results in a warning, whereas

```
typedef int Int;
Int i, * pi;
pi = &i;
```

is accepted. The fact that arrays are treated as pointers is also one of the obstacles to developing distributed extensions of C++, since it is impossible to know whether we are dealing with simply a pointer or an array. Another problem that may be attributed to the wish to maintain C compatibility is that the choice for defaults is often contrary to what one would expect. For example, the default for member functions is to be non-virtual, whereas from the perspective of object orientation the default should be virtual, as in Eiffel and Smalltalk. Similarly, in the case of multiple inheritance the default should be virtual inheritance, allowing derived classes to share common base classes. For a detailed account of the history of C++ and the motivations underlying its design, the reader is referred to Stroustrup (1994).

Choosing C++ means choosing a language with compile-time type checking. As an immediate advantage we then have compiler support for detecting errors, and (in the case of C++) *efficiency*. However, one of the drawbacks of this choice is a loss of *flexibility* (when compared with, for example, Smalltalk), and since C++ is a hybrid language, little enforcement of a purely object-oriented approach. In this respect, the language Eiffel, which also offers compile-time type checking, may be regarded as much more strongly enforcing of an object-oriented approach as well as a specific method of developing software based on the notion of *contracts* as a means of formalizing the dependencies between objects and their clients. See section 3.3.

An issue raised by Snyder (1986) is whether the principle of *encapsulation* as employed in data abstraction also applies to derived types or classes, considered as clients. More specifically, what language features support the definition of an interface that protect against illegal access by both regular clients and instances of derived classes?

Visibility and protection Evidently, unlimited access to inherited instance variables compromises encapsulation. Just imagine that, for example, we decided to change the representation of the origin of our abstract shape in section 2.2.2. The entire hierarchy of concrete shapes would then collapse, since instances of circles or rectangles would illegally refer to the origin coordinates when drawing themselves.

Rather surprisingly, of the three languages mentioned, Smalltalk, Eiffel and C++, only C++ allows us to differentiate between access by instances of the class itself and access by instances of derived classes. For both Smalltalk and Eiffel, instance variables are also freely accessible by instances of derived classes. Protection in C++ is enforced by the access specifiers *private*, *protected* and *public*. Declaring a section to be *private* means that it is only accessible for instances of the class itself. The declaration *protected* on the other hand also allows instances of derived classes access to that section. Naturally, the declaration *public* offers no protection since it is accessible by anyone.

A similar distinction plays a role with respect to the visibility of derived classes when regarded as (polymorphic) types. As a programmer, we sometimes like to use inheritance for the purpose of code sharing only, with no intention to declare a subtyping

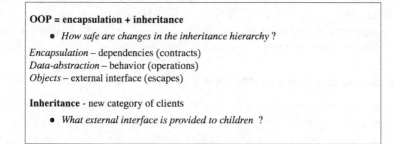

OOP = encapsulation + inheritance   2-29

- *How safe are changes in the inheritance hierarchy ?*

Encapsulation – dependencies (contracts)
Data-abstraction – behavior (operations)
Objects – external interface (escapes)

Inheritance - new category of clients

- *What external interface is provided to children ?*

Slide 2-29: Encapsulation and inheritance

relation between the two classes. In C++ one can declare a class to be either publicly inherited or privately inherited. The latter is intended to be used when only code sharing is intended and does not affect the type system, whereas the former is only to be used when a subtype relation is explicitly intended, as demonstrated in the shape hierarchy.

The C++ compiler offers only protection from mistakes, not from abuse. For example, we may access the private base class by employing casts, as illustrated in slide 2-30.

```
class A {                                              2-30
public:
A() { s = "XAX"; }
void print() { cout ≪ s; }
private:
char* s;
};
class B : private A {  }
```

Slide 2-30: Casting to private base classes

In slide 2-30 we have defined a class A, and a class B that privately inherits from A. As illustrated in the program fragment

```
A*  a = new B;                                      // error
A*  b = (A* ) new B;                                // accepted
b→ print();                                        // XAX
```

we can access the B part of A by using a cast. However, we can also gain access by completely bypassing the public interface of a class, as illustrated by the fragment below

```
char*  p = (char* ) b;
while( * p != 'X' ) p++;
cout ≪ p ≪ endl;                                   // XAX
```

The trick is to cast the object pointer to an array of *char*, which allows us to inspect each byte of the object.

Casting is the most dangerous feature offered by C and C++. It allows programmers to circumvent the type system in completely arbitrary ways.

2.5.1   Objects, pointers and references

Perhaps one of the most demanding aspects of C++, when compared to Smalltalk and Eiffel, is the existence of pointers and references to objects. Both in Smalltalk and Eiffel, the programmer needs to handle only a single kind of variable, whereas C++ requires the programmer to indicate explicitly what a variable stands for, a value, a pointer or a reference.

Notationally, the difference between values, references and pointers is reflected in the following declaration:

```
int n = 7;                                      // value
int& r = n;                             // reference to value n
int* p = &n;                               // pointer to n
```

When initializing a pointer, the address of the value must be given, whereas for a reference the value suffices.

An object (in C++) is a value. Because of the typing rules, the compiler knows what operations an object allows. The representation of a value is just a sequence of bits or bytes. Due to the type information, we may regard that sequence as, say, an integer or an object with structure. A reference is an implicit pointer to a value. The distinction between a pointer and a reference is that the programmer may treat a reference just as an ordinary object, whereas the use of a pointer requires explicit dereferencing.

```
class sneaky {                                        sneaky          2-31
private:
   int safe;
public:
   sneaky() { safe = 12; }
   int& sorry() { return safe; }
   int value() { return safe; }
};
```

Slide 2-31: Sneaky references

References and pointers are often used for reasons of efficiency. However, the use of pointers is known to be error-prone. Familiar problems that may occur when using pointers are for instance the existence of dangling references and unintended aliasing. References are less error-prone, since they do not require any explicit pointer manipulation. However, the class given in slide 2-31 illustrates a problem that is easily overlooked by many programmers.

Since a reference is actually an implicit pointer to a value, manipulating a reference may have unexpected results. In the example, the member function *sorry* returns a reference to a data member *safe*, instead of its value as the member function *value* does. The following code fragment illustrates what this means:

```
sneaky x;

cout ≪ x.value() ≪ endl;
x.sorry() = 17;
cout ≪ x.value() ≪ endl;
```

Since a reference may occur on the left-hand side of an assignment, in contrast to a value, the data member *safe* may be assigned an arbitrary value, despite the fact that it occurs in the *private* section of the class *sneaky*. The remedy to this abuse would have been to declare that the member function *sorry* returns a *const* int& instead of an int&, as in the example in section 2.2.1.

2.5.2   Virtual functions versus non-virtual functions

Another important difference between C++ on the one hand and Smalltalk and Eiffel on the other, is that *dynamic binding* is *not* the default, as it is for Smalltalk and Eiffel. In C++, a member function has to be declared *virtual* (higher up in the inheritance hierarchy) in order to profit from the polymorphic behavior that results from dynamic binding. The choice not to make dynamic binding the default is motivated by the philosophy underlying C++ not to affect the performance of a program if not needed.

Dynamic binding may be explained as searching for the appropriate method. If the method is not found in the object (class) itself it is searched for in the classes from which the object class has been derived. This search can be eliminated by associating with each object a virtual table that contains the actual functions to be called. The actual cost of this is only the storage required for a pointer and one additional indirection. In the case of multiple inheritance, only two indirections are required (see Ellis and Stroustrup, 1990). Given the fact that dynamic binding is not all that costly, what are the pros and cons of virtual functions?

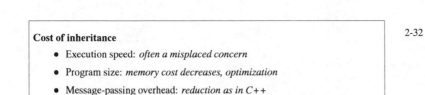

2-32

Cost of inheritance

- Execution speed: *often a misplaced concern*
- Program size: *memory cost decreases, optimization*
- Message-passing overhead: *reduction as in C++*
- Program complexity: *yo-yo problem: up and down the inheritance graph*

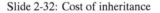

Slide 2-32: Cost of inheritance

As a first observation, execution speed is almost always a misplaced concern. More important usually is to find the proper structure for a program. After profiling its behavior, it usually suffices to optimize only selected parts to obtain the required execution speed.

Another important aspect, from the perspective of program development, is that the actual code size may dramatically decrease when using inheritance with dynamic binding. This allows maintenance and optimizations to be more easily done, since important parts of the code may be localized in a few (shared) ancestor classes.

However, when efficiency is of crucial concern, can we still use an object-oriented language? Actually, this is an area of active research. For interpreted languages, still better optimization strategies (involving caching and partial evaluation) are being developed. Adherents of this approach claim to reach an efficiency comparable to the efficiency of C++. On the other hand, for time critical applications each indirection may be one too many. To save on the cost of (member) function invocation, C++ allows the definition of *inline* functions, which are expanded by the compiler, similar to macro definitions. Also, member functions may be declared *inline*. However, virtual member functions may, obviously, not be inline expanded at compile time. Therefore it seems reasonable to have a choice between declaring a function as being virtual or non-virtual. However, in contrast to what C++ offers, the default (unmarked) case should probably be *virtual*.

Although the use of inheritance may result in decreasing the size of the code, it may also introduce an additional level of complexity. The problem that adheres to an (excessive) use of inheritance is known as the *yo-yo problem*. To find what function is actually called during the execution of a program may require an inspection of the entire inheritance graph. Having both virtual and non-virtual functions only adds to the complexity of understanding program behavior. What is required to tackle these problems is adequate browsing tools and tools to monitor the (dynamic) behavior of the program.

2.5.3   Memory management

Perhaps the most annoying feature of C++ (or rather absence of it) is memory management. Whereas both Smalltalk and Eiffel offer automatic garbage collection, the C++ programmer is required to rely on hand-crafted memory management.

2-33

```
class A {                                          A
public:
A() { cout ≪ "A"; }
~A() { cout ≪ "A"; }
};

class B : public A {                               B
public:
B() { cout ≪ "B"; }
~B() { cout ≪ "B"; }
};
```

Slide 2-33: Constructors and destructors

Memory management in C++ involves the use of constructors and destructors. In the following, we will look at some examples illustrating the order of invocation of constructors and destructors in relation to single and multiple inheritance.

The first example, given in slide 2-33, defines two classes (*A* and *B*, with *B* derived from *A*), each having a constructor and destructor writing the name of the class to standard output. An example of their use is:

A∗ a = new B; *delete* a;   // ABA
B∗ b = new B; *delete* b;   // ABBA

Recall that when creating an instance of a class, the constructors of the base classes (if any) are called first. This is exactly what happens above. However, contrary to what is expected, when deleting *a*, the destructor for *B* is not called, whereas it is invoked when deleting *b*.

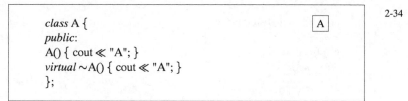

```
class A {                                                    A
public:
A() { cout ≪ "A"; }
virtual ∼A() { cout ≪ "A"; }
};
```

2-34

Slide 2-34: Virtual destructors

The remedy to this is to declare the destructor of *A* virtual, as in slide 2-34, since it dynamically invokes the destructor declared for the actual class type (*B*) of the object referenced. The program fragment

A∗ a = new B; *delete* a;   // ABBA
B∗ b = new B; *delete* b;   // ABBA

now behaves as desired.

```
class C: public A {                                          C
public:
C() { cout ≪ "C"; }
∼C() { cout ≪ "C"; }
};
class D : public B, public C {                               D
public:
D() { cout ≪ "D"; }
∼D() { cout ≪ "D"; }
};
```

2-35

Slide 2-35: Multiple inheritance

Multiple inheritance When employing multiple inheritance, similar rules are followed, as depicted in slide 2-35.

However, one problem we may encounter here is that classes may have a common base class. Look at the following program fragment:

D* a = new D(); *delete* a;   // ABACDDCABA

The outcome of creating and deleting *a* indicates that an instance of *D* contains two copies of *A*.

2-36

class B: *virtual public* A {   B
public:
B() { cout ≪ "B"; }
~B() { cout ≪ "B"; }
};

class C: *virtual public* A {   C
public:
C() { cout ≪ "C"; }
~C() { cout ≪ "C"; }
};

Slide 2-36: Virtual inheritance

Again, the remedy is to declare *A* to be virtually inherited by *B* and *C*, as depicted in slide 2-36. As reflected in the outcome of

A* a = new D(); *delete* a;   // ABCDDCBA

instances of the derived class *D* then have only one copy of *A*.

2.6 **Extensions to the object model** – *abnormal events*

When studying the literature on OOP, one can discern a tendency of convergence between the distinct (language) camps. For instance, as already noted, interpreted languages are being optimized to compete with C/C++, and on the other hand, proposals are being made to extend C++ with some of the more exotic features found in, for instance, Smalltalk or Flavors, features such as dynamic typing and meta classes. Also, there is an interesting convergence and mutual influence between Eiffel and C++. For instance, the newer version of Eiffel also supports constructors and overloading, whereas rumors have it that multiple inheritance in C++ has primarily been inspired by its use in Eiffel.

In the following we will briefly explore some extensions to the basic object model, and try to establish why they may be considered useful. See slide 2-37.

Meta classes are a feature of Smalltalk supporting the definition of class-wide variables and so-called class methods. Class methods must be used to create new instances of the class. Neither Eiffel nor C++ support meta classes, although C++ supports so-called *static* data and function members, which are accessible by all instances of a class. The action of creating objects (as instances of classes) is for both languages taken care of by special creation functions or *constructors*. A feature that is felt to be lacking in C++ is the possibility of obtaining type information during runtime. Although libraries exist that provide the required functionality (to some extent), it seems likely that the language will

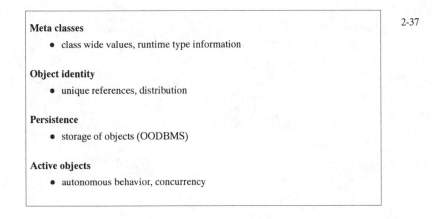

Slide 2-37: Extensions to the object model

be extended by constructs supporting this directly. (Currently, the ANSI standardization committee for C++ is studying proposals to introduce features supporting dynamic type information in C++.) See also section 11.1.2.

In most object-oriented systems, references to objects are system dependent (addresses in some memory space) and are usually lost when program execution stops. To facilitate debugging it would be convenient to be able to deal with (unique) symbolic references to objects. A more flexible scheme of object naming may also be important for distributed systems, since symbolic identities may also have meaning outside the program's execution space. See section 6.5.

Object identity also plays an important role in object-oriented data bases, since the persistent storage of objects requires a naming scheme that allows objects to be written to stable storage and retrieved independently from the current execution.

To my mind, one of the most interesting extensions to the basic object model is the notion of *active* objects, objects with autonomous behavior. Important issues that relate to this extension are, what concurrency model must be supported and what to do with distribution. See chapter 6. Moreover, from the perspective of design we must ask, are active objects useful and how do they fit in with the design of sequential systems?

Abnormal events In case the computation proceeds as required, everything is fine. But what should be done when a failure occurs due to memory exhaustion, arithmetical overflow or the violation of an assertion? Must we check for all possible errors or must we rely on separate exception handling mechanisms? In general, an abnormal event occurs when an operation cannot perform its desired computation. See slide 2-38.

When an abnormal event occurs, two possible courses of action can be taken. Either the operation can fail and raise an exception (thereby transferring the flow of control to an exception handler) or the operation can invoke a correction routine (that tries to correct the situation that caused the abnormal event) and continue the computation. The latter solution is called an *intervention*. In contrast to an exception, an intervention does not change the flow of control; it performs the correction and then resumes the operation.

Abnormal events   2-38

- *exceptions* – to indicate failure

- *intervention* – invocation of a correction routine

Exceptions in C++ | *try & catch* |

```
class Matherr { }
class Overflow : public Matherr {}
try {
    f();                              // do some arithmetic
}
catch (Overflow) {
                                      // handle Overflow
}
catch (Matherr) {
                             // handle non-Overflow Matherr
}
```

Assertions | *throw* |

```
template< class T, class X >
inline void Assert(T expr, X x) {
    if (!NDEBUG) if (!expr) throw x;
}
```

Slide 2-38: Abnormal events

Interventions are familiar from daily computing practice in the form of interrupts, such as are used to kill a process. Under Unix, an interrupt is implemented as a signal that may be associated with a handler. The interrupt handler usually invokes the exit function.

Exceptions, on the other hand, are not (yet) familiar to most programmers and are only supported by a few languages.

One of the languages supporting exceptions is Eiffel. In Eiffel, exceptions are closely linked with the notion of *contracts*. Abnormal events occur whenever a contract is violated, that is when either a pre-condition, post-condition or invariant is not satisfied. For each of these cases an exception handler may be specified in the class defining the object for which an exception is raised. The way in which abnormal events are dealt with in Eiffel conforms to what is called the *resumption model* in Buhr and MacDonald (1992). The resumption model allows a handler invoked for an exception to resume the computation after correcting the faulty situation. In Eiffel, the *retry* statement may be used to try the operation that resulted in raising an exception again.

Exceptions are part of the language definition of C++, but not many of the available compilers provide support for exceptions. The declaration of exceptions conforms to the definition of classes. For example, slide 2-38 declares a *Matherr* and an *Overflow* exception, which is publicly derived from *Matherr*. Obviously, the advantage of employing the class mechanism is that inheritance may be used to organize exceptions in groups.

The most specific exception may then be tested for first, as in the *catch* statements following the *try* block in slide 2-38. As the example shows, exception handling is activated by wrapping a group of statements or function calls in a *try* block. Whenever a failure occurs, the exception handlers declared by the subsequent *catch* statements will be tried to do something about it.

An exception may be raised by means of a *throw* statement as illustrated for the *Assert* function. The *Assert* function mimics the behavior of the *assert* macro, but in addition allows us to raise an explicit exception such as *BadArgs* or *Invariant* (provided these are defined as exceptions).

In contrast to Eiffel, which allows for resuming the computation after the occurrence of an exception, C++ supports only *termination* semantics for exceptions, which results in terminating the function call that caused the exception. The main reason to adopt termination semantics is (according to Stroustrup (1994)) that resumption semantics invites programmers to employ exceptions for things other than that for which they are meant, such as debugging and the like, or allocating new resources. However, such tasks are often better performed by an explicit *handler* function as may, for example, be defined to handle allocation problems when calling the *new* operator. Exceptions, on the other hand, are primarily meant to be used to handle errors for which no such remedies exist.

Lacking adequate language support, both exceptions and interventions may be simulated, respectively by setting a global flag which is tested after the operation and by adding intervention routine parameters to function definitions. However, such simulations are tedious and error-prone to implement and, moreover, violate encapsulation and endanger extensibility.

Summary

This chapter has introduced the basic mechanisms of object-oriented programming. We looked at a general characterization of the object model, supporting encapsulation and message passing, and observed that an object-oriented approach may reduce the complexity of the programming task but does not reduce the space and time needed to solve a problem.

The object model   1   2-39

- *object model* – encapsulation, message protocols
- *complexity* – what is the contribution of object orientation

---

Slide 2-39: Section 2.1: The object model

In section 2, we proceeded with a fairly detailed discussion of the language constructs provided by C++, including constructors, destructors, the type modifier *const* and *friend*s.

Further, we looked at a simple example demonstrating how to use inheritance for defining a type hierarchy of graphical shapes. In addition, it was shown how to develop robust code by using assertions.

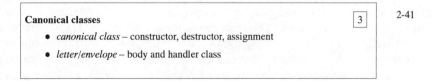

> **Encapsulation and inheritance in C++**   2   2-40
>
> - *encapsulation* – constructors, *const*, conversions, friends
> - *inheritance* – abstract and concrete shapes
> - *assertions* – pre- and post-conditions

Slide 2-40: Section 2.2: Encapsulation and inheritance in C++

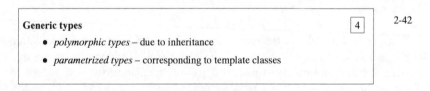

> **Canonical classes**   3   2-41
>
> - *canonical class* – constructor, destructor, assignment
> - *letter/envelope* – body and handler class

Slide 2-41: Section 2.3: Canonical classes

In section 3, some idioms were presented which may be taken as guidelines for the implementation of concrete data types. An instance of a canonical class behaves as if it is a built-in type. To provide an efficient implementation of a concrete data type, the *envelope/letter* idiom may be used, in which a distinction is made between an interface handler class and an implementation body class.

> **Generic types**   4   2-42
>
> - *polymorphic types* – due to inheritance
> - *parametrized types* – corresponding to template classes

Slide 2-42: Section 2.4: Generic types

In section 4, we discussed the realization of generic types in C++. Both base class hierarchies and template classes were discussed and illustrated with examples.

In section 5, we discussed some of the benefits and pitfalls of employing C++ for object-oriented programming. In particular, we discussed issues of protection, the distinction between objects, references and pointers and the pros and cons of inheritance. Further, we discussed the role of constructors and destructors in memory management.

Finally, we discussed a number of extensions of the basic object model, such as meta classes, carrying dynamic type information and features that are relevant for distribution, including persistence and active objects. We also discussed the issues that arise in dealing with abnormal events, which may for example occur when a pre-condition is violated.

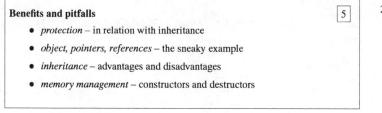

Slide 2-43: Section 2.5: Benefits and pitfalls

Slide 2-44: Section 2.6: Extensions to the object model

Questions

(1) Explain the meaning of the phrase *"object orientation reduces the complexity of programming."*

(2) Explain the role of constructors. What role do destructors play?

(3) What is the meaning of *const*? Give some examples.

(4) Characterize the two kinds of type conversions supported by C++.

(5) Why do you need `friends`?

(6) What is a canonical class? Characterize its ingredients and give an example.

(7) Explain the handler/body idiom. Give an example.

(8) What are generic types? Why are they useful? Explain how C++ supports generic types. Give an example.

(9) Explain how inheritance may jeopardize encapsulation. Can you think of a solution?

(10) Give an example of a class allowing external clients access to private data.

(11) Discuss the advantages and disadvantages of inheritance.

(12) What extensions to the classical object model can you think of? Why are these extensions needed?

Further reading

As textbooks on C++ I recommend Lippman (1991), Stroustrup (1991) and, for more advanced topics, Coplien (1992).

3

Object-oriented design

In the previous chapter we looked at the mechanisms that are available to define (classes of) objects and their relations at an implementation level. In this chapter we will focus on the design of object oriented systems and the role of the design document.

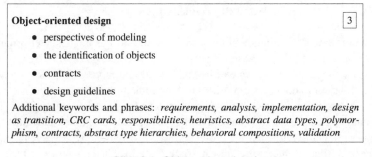

Object-oriented design | 3 | 3-1

- perspectives of modeling
- the identification of objects
- contracts
- design guidelines

Additional keywords and phrases: *requirements, analysis, implementation, design as transition, CRC cards, responsibilities, heuristics, abstract data types, polymorphism, contracts, abstract type hierarchies, behavioral compositions, validation*

Slide 3-1: Object-oriented design

Design involves the identification of objects and the description of their attributes and relations at a (higher) conceptual level, since the product of design is (usually) not meant to be executed by a machine but to be inspected and criticized by a human reader. Before discussing actual design issues, concerning class design and guidelines for good design, we will briefly reflect on the process of design and the notion of modeling, which occupies a central role in the object-oriented approach. Also, we will explore the notion of *contracts* and their possible role in the development of type hierarchies and behavioral compositions.

3.1 **The process of design**

Initially, object-oriented software development was language-driven. The motivation to adopt an object-oriented approach came first from the need to cope with increasingly complex software systems. Research in object-oriented programming was primarily concerned with the development of language mechanisms to support the new approach.

Only recently, has the attention shifted from language support mechanisms and the pragmatics of program development to issues of analysis and design. Research concerning language mechanisms, however, is still important, for example in the area of concurrent/distributed programming and the support of persistent objects. See part II.

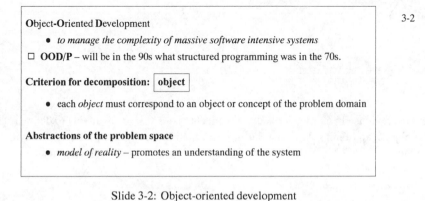

Slide 3-2: Object-oriented development

The common denominator in both analysis and design in an object-oriented approach may be characterized as a *decomposition into objects*. See slide 3-2. Objects, according to Booch (1986), are *crisp* entities, that *suffer* and *require* actions, which (must) have a clear relation to concepts or entities of the problem domain.

Ideally, we have a seamless transition between the phases of analysis, design and implementation. Seamless in the sense that the various phases employ a common object model, that is gradually refined as the project progresses. In other words, such a transition presupposes a notion of objects that may unify the activities in the respective phases. The central imperative of the object-oriented movement, namely to provide a *model of reality*, still betrays the conception of object-oriented programming as *simulation*, as originally expressed by Dahl and Nygaard (1966). The initial motivation underlying this approach is the idea that a natural representation of the problem domain in a software system may reduce the complexity of understanding the system implementing a solution. The presupposition here is that *modeling* involves the use of objects to represent the entities in the problem domain. Assuming the presupposition to hold, our task then reduces to identifying the right objects and showing that that particular decomposition is valid with respect to the original problem. The goal of design may then be stated as arriving at an architectural structure that adequately reflects the relevant properties of the problem domain.

3.1.1   The architecture of object-oriented systems

The process of software development has often been compared to the process of constructing buildings, usually in the context of defending a traditional software development method. The argument comes down to the statement that it takes a solid plan and sufficient time to lay the foundations and erect the building. The conclusion, generally, is a plea for a *science of software engineering/programming,* or an engineering discipline of software design. See for example Gries (1981) or Potter *et al.* (1991) for a similar argument in defense of formal specification methods. The line of reasoning exemplified by the building metaphor is defective in two respects. Firstly, the presupposition of a rigid ordering in time is clearly contradicted by the many attractive old city centers, which have often evolved over time without a plan. Secondly, the presupposition of a fixed method of development is clearly demonstrated to be false by modern building techniques, employing prefabricated components. Hence, neither temporal order nor procedures of construction are as fixed as they at first seem. The view expressed in the building metaphor also fails for the software life-cycle. Both throwaway and incremental prototyping have come to be accepted as viable methods for developing software. Nevertheless, when we speak of design, we think of some architectural blueprint of the system, the layout of its structure. What, we may ask, is the role of the design in the software life-cycle? And what is the function of its product, *the design document?*

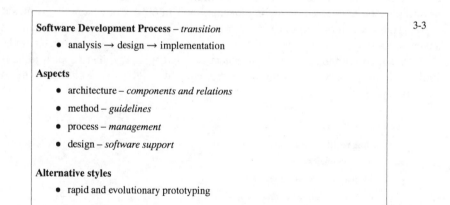

Slide 3-3: Software development process

In Jacobson *et al.* (1992), a detailed account is given of a method of object-oriented software engineering based on elementary architectural notions, such as (object) components and (use) relations, and strong convictions with respect to design guidelines and process management issues. See slide 3-3. An explicit distinction is made between the *architectural concepts,* which provide the means with which to construct various models, the *method,* which is a bag of guidelines telling us how to employ the architectural notions, the *process,* which details what steps to take to complete the software life-cycle, and the *tools,* which provide the software support either for the construction of models or for managing the actual process of software development, or both.

In Jacobson *et al.* (1992), both the method and issues of process development are spelled out in great detail, illustrated by a number of examples. These issues are clearly important in actual production environments (business or industrial), but seem to be dependent to a large extent on non-technological factors. From the perspective of software technology, we are primarily interested in the architectural notions underlying the various methods and, to a lesser extent, in the tool support for these methods. Also, apart from the architectural structure *per se*, we are interested in what properties a design model must have in order that we may verify that a model satisfies its initial requirements.

3.1.2 Perspectives of modeling

Understanding a problem domain may be quite demanding. Understanding is even more difficult when the description of the domain is cast in some representation pertaining to the solution domain. An object-oriented approach is said to require less translation from the problem domain to the (software) solution domain, thus making understanding easier. Many proponents of an object-oriented approach, however, seem to be overly optimistic in their conception of the modeling task. From an epistemological point of view, modeling may be regarded as being essentially colored by the mechanisms that are available to express the model. Hence, rather than opposing the functional and object-oriented approach by claiming that an object-oriented approach aims at *modeling reality*, I would prefer to characterize the distinction in terms of (modeling from) a different vernacular, a different perspective due to different modeling mechanisms. In other words, a model is meant to capture some salient aspects of a system or problem domain. Dependent on what features are considered as most important, different means will be chosen to construct a model.

Even within the confines of an object-oriented approach, there appear to be radically different perspectives of the modeling required in the various phases of the software life-cycle.

Modeling reality – *vernacular*
- requirements – *use cases*
- analysis – *domain concepts*
- design – *system architecture*
- implementation – *language support*

Design model – *system oriented*
- provides a justification of the architecture

3-4

Slide 3-4: Perspectives of modeling

An important contribution of Jacobson *et al.* (1992) is the notion of *use cases* that describe the situations in which a user actually interacts with the system. Such a (use case) model is an important constituent of the *requirements* document, since it precisely describes what the system is intended for. For the purpose of analysis, it may be helpful to develop a more encompassing (conceptual) model of the problem domain. The advantage of such an approach is that the actual system may later easily be extended due to the generality of the underlying analysis model.

In contrast to the model used in analysis, both the design model and the implementation model are more *solution oriented* than *domain oriented*. The *implementation* model is clearly dependent on the available language support. Within a traditional life-cycle, the *design* model may be seen as a transition from analysis to implementation. The notion of *objects* may act as a unifying factor, relating the concepts described in the analysis document to the components around which the design model is built. However, as we have noted, object-oriented development does not necessarily follow the course of a traditional software life-cycle. Alternatively, we may characterize the function of the design document as a *justification* of the choices made in deciding on the final architecture of the system. This remark holds in so far as an object-oriented approach is adopted for both design and implementation. However, see Henderson-Sellers and Edwards (1990) for a variety of combinations of structured, functional and object-oriented techniques.

Dimensions of modeling When restricting ourselves to *design models*, we may again distinguish between different modeling perspectives or, which is perhaps more adequate in this context, *dimensions of modeling*.

In Rumbaugh *et al.* (1991), it is proposed to use three complementary models for describing the architecture and functionality of a system. See slide 3-5.

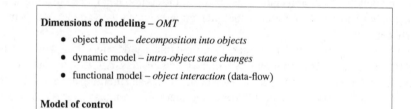

Slide 3-5: The OMT method

The OMT method distinguishes between an *object model*, for describing the (static) structure of object classes and their relations, a *dynamic model*, that describes for each object class the state changes resulting from performing operations, and a *functional model*, that describes the interaction between objects in terms of a *data-flow* graph.

An important contribution of Rumbaugh *et al.* (1991) is that it identifies a number of commonly used *control models*, including *procedure-driven* control, *event-driven* control and *concurrent* control. The choice for a particular control model may deeply affect the design of the system. See section 11.1.4 for a further discussion.

The OMT approach may be called a *hybrid method* since it employs non object-oriented techniques for describing intra-object dynamics, namely state-charts, and a functional approach involving data-flow diagrams, for describing inter-object communication.

Coherent models The OMT *object model*, however, only captures the static structure of the system. To model the dynamic and functional aspects, the object model is augmented with a *dynamic model*, which is given by state diagrams, and a *functional model*, which is handled by data flow diagrams. From a formal point of view this solution is rather unsatisfactory since, as argued in Hayes and Coleman (1991), it is hard to establish the consistency of the combined model, consisting of an object, dynamic and functional model.

Model criteria – *formal approach*   3-6

- *unambiguous* – single meaning
- *abstract* – no unnecessary detail
- *consistent* – absence of conflict

Slide 3-6: Coherent models – criteria

Consistency checking, or at least the possibility to do so, is important to increase our belief in the reliability (and reusability) of a model. To be able to determine whether a model is consistent, the model should be phrased in an unambiguous way, that is, in a notation with a clear and precise meaning. See slide 3-6. Also, to make the task of consistency checking manageable, a model should be as abstract as possible, by leaving out all irrelevant details. To establish the consistency of the combined model, covering structural, functional and dynamic aspects, the interaction between the various models must be clearly defined.

Currently, to my knowledge, there is no completely developed method encompassing the structural, functional and dynamic aspects of a system in a manner that is amenable to a rigorous formal approach. However, there is an emerging understanding of how to deal with these various aspects. Moreover, there are attempts towards a standardization of the notions employed in the various methods. See sections 11.1.2 and 11.3.

3.1.3   Functional versus object-oriented development

The functional approach is a relatively well-established method of software development. In essence, a functional approach amounts to decomposing a task into the steps that must be taken to complete it. For instance, when describing a compiler in a functional manner, a first decomposition can be made as follows:

lexical scan → parser → code generation

Each of these steps can be regarded as transforming its input to a representation suitable for the next step, finally resulting in an executable program. See slide 3-7. Obviously, the method of functional decomposition lends itself to a structured approach, since each step (in the example above) may be decomposed into a number of smaller steps. Graphically, a functional decomposition may be pictured as a tree with the elementary steps as its leaves. A functional decomposition may be augmented by a *data flow* diagram that depicts the nature of the data transformations effected by each step. Basically, a data flow diagram is a graph with nodes labeled by the (intermediate) data representations and edges that are labeled by the functional components identified in the function decomposition tree.

Functional development methods   3-7

- *each module represents a major step in the process*

Disadvantages

- no data abstraction / information hiding
- not responsive to changes
- inadequate for natural concurrency

Slide 3-7: Functional development methods

In contrast, the components that result from an object-oriented approach do not represent actual steps toward a solution, but rather may be seen as (abstract) entities that contribute to the solution on the basis of their assigned responsibilities. Correspondingly, the flow of control is far less regular than in a functional decomposition. The equivalent of the combined data flow and functional decomposition diagram for an object-oriented system is a message-passing diagram depicting the actual interaction between objects. This diagram is a graph with objects as nodes, and edges labeled by requests to execute a method. In general, this graph will be too complex to be represented pictorially. It is possible, however, to divide up an object interaction graph into meaningful related pieces, which is the approach taken for Fusion, for example. See section 11.3.1. Moreover, the complexity of object-interaction is compensated for by the opportunities for a more tight definition of the semantics, that is the responsibilities and obligations, of each (object) component participating in the computation.

The major drawback of a functional approach, as observed in Booch (1986), is the absence of *data abstraction* and information hiding. Typically, the functional approach is not concerned with issues of data representation, although it does allow additional procedural abstractions to access and modify the data. However, the functional approach does not in itself provide any support for a tight coupling between the functional components and data representations or the procedural abstractions that are used for the purpose of information hiding. Hence, changes in the data representation or the structure of the algorithm may ripple across the system in an unforeseen manner.

In contrast, object-oriented development is neither data nor procedure oriented, but strives to encapsulate both data and procedures acting on these data in objects. Instead of a detailed description of the steps that need to be taken to solve a problem or complete a task, the required functionality is distributed among the objects that may later be assembled (in a rather straightforward way) to actually perform the task.

Perhaps the most important advantage of encapsulating data and procedures, from the perspective of design, is that (in many cases) changes may be kept strictly *local* to the classes defining the relevant objects. See slide 3-8. Ideally, object-oriented design is *design for change*, in other words the development of an architecture that is adaptable to changing requirements or changes in the underlying software and hardware sup-

---

Object-oriented development – *design for change*   3-8
  • *localized changes*

Advantages
  • improved *maintainability*
  • improved *understandability*

Support for concurrency – *active objects*
  • no modifications needed for concurrency

Slide 3-8: Support for change

port. However, to achieve this adaptability generally requires a non-trivial effort during design, in order to find *stable abstractions* with a well-defined semantics that determines their role in the system.

Obvious potential spin-offs from the effort to design for change are improved maintainability of the system and a better understanding of its architectural structure. Another benefit of an object-oriented approach, mentioned in Booch (1986), is the possibility of introducing concurrency in a later stage. Starting from a functional decomposition, the introduction of concurrency would generally incur a total restructuring of the algorithm. With an object-oriented approach, however, concurrency may be introduced by employing *active objects*. In principle, clients of an object need not be aware of whether the object is *passive*, that is merely responding to messages, or *active*, which means that the object in addition to answering messages has (autonomous) behavior of its own. However, employing active objects imposes a number of additional constraints, on an implementation level but also on a design level. We will explore these issues in chapter 6.

3.2   Identifying objects

Object-oriented design aims at describing a system in terms of objects (as the primary components) and the interaction between them. Motivated by the wish to arrive at stable abstractions, object-oriented design is often characterized as *modeling reality*, that is the application domain. However, many applications require, at least partly, a *system oriented* view towards design, since they involve system artifacts for which there exist no clearly identifiable counterparts in the application domain. As an example, think of a window-based system. Many of the items (widgets) introduced in such a system belong to an artificial reality, which at best is only vaguely analogous with reality as we normally understand it.

Irrespective of whether the design is intended as a preliminary study before the implementation or as a *post hoc* justification of the actual system, the most important and difficult part of design is the *identification of objects* and the characterization of their role in the system and interaction with other objects.

As observed in McGregor and Sykes (1992), object-oriented design is best seen as *class oriented*, that is directed towards the *static* description of (classes of) objects, rather than a description of the dynamic interaction between actual objects. In section 5.4, we will discuss *class-less* languages which are well suited for exploratory programming. However, from the perspective of design, we are more interested in a (static) abstract specification of the components that constitute the system.

Object-Oriented Design – *decomposition into objects*   3-9
   • application/system/class oriented

Identifying objects – *responsibilities*
   • data/procedure oriented

Layers of abstraction
   • components, subsystems, frameworks

Slide 3-9: Object-oriented design

In comparison with a functional approach, object-oriented design is clearly *data oriented*. However, although a data oriented approach may provide a first guideline in developing the system, the primary concern in object-oriented design should be the *responsibilities* of an object rather than how it acts as a *data manager*, so to speak.

For larger systems, the complexity of the design may necessitate the introduction of additional layers of abstraction. Apart from objects, which must be regarded as the basic components of a system, we may need to isolate subsystems, consisting of a number of related object classes. When we have developed a subsystem that can be used in a variety of contexts, such a subsystem may be used as a *framework*. A framework is generally not only a collection of classes but must also be seen as an approach or method in its own way, since it usually imposes additional constraints on the development. For example, most development environments for window-based applications provide a framework consisting of a number of predefined classes and functions, and guidelines or recipes that prescribe how to use or adapt these classes and functions. Also, most frameworks impose a specific control model, such as the *event-driven* control model imposed by window programming environments. See chapter 7.

3.2.1   Modeling heuristics

Following Booch (1986), we have characterized objects as 'crisp' *entities* that *suffer* and *require* actions. From the perspective of system development, *objects* must primarily be regarded as *computational entities*, embodying the means by which we may express a computation. Modeling a particular problem domain, then, means defining abstractions in terms of *objects*, capturing the functional characteristics of that domain. The question is, how do we arrive at such a model? See slide 3-10.

In Booch (1986), a straightforward method of object oriented development is proposed, which consists of the successive identification of objects and their attributes, fol-

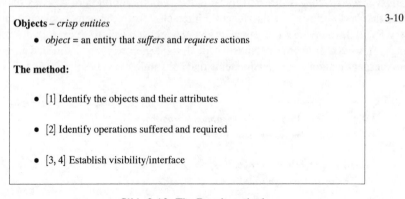

Slide 3-10: The Booch method

lowed by a precise characterization of the interobject visibility relations. In Booch (1991), a shift of emphasis has occurred towards determining the semantics of an individual object and the interaction between collections of objects. Booch (1991) provides extensive examples to illustrate the method, of which perhaps the most notable aspect is a graphic notation for describing the modular structure of a system.

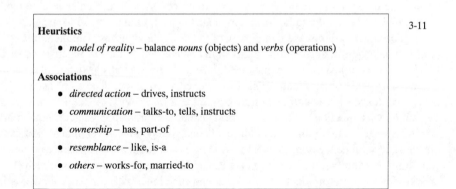

Slide 3-11: Heuristics for modeling

As a heuristic to arrive at the proper abstractions of the problem domain (in terms of object classes), Booch (1986) proposes scanning the requirements document for *nouns*, *verbs* and *adjectives*, and using these as initial suggestions for respectively *objects*, and *operations* and *attributes* belonging to objects (see slide 3-11). This technique has been adopted and augmented by a number of other authors, among which are Wirfs-Brock *et al.* (1990) and Rumbaugh *et al.* (1991). For example Wirfs-Brock *et al.* (1990) illustrate the technique in fine detail in several examples, including the design of an automated teller machine and a document processing system.

In addition to the interpretation of nouns as possible objects, verbs as possible operations on objects, and adjectives as possible attributes of objects, Rumbaugh *et al.*

(1991) suggest this technique to determine other relations and associations between object classes as well. For instance, a model of control and object interaction may be suggested by phrases indicating directed action or communication. Similarly, structural issues, such as whether an object owns another object or whether inheritance should be used, may be decided on the basis of resemblance or subordination relations.

Example – ATM (1) The example of an automated teller machine discussed in Wirfs-Brock *et al.* (1990) nicely illustrates a number of the notions that we have thus far looked at only in a very abstract way. A *teller* machine is a device, presumably familiar to everyone, that allows you to get money from your account at any time of the day. Obviously, there are a number of constraints that such a machine must satisfy. For instance, other people should not be allowed to withdraw money from your account. Another reasonable constraint is that a user cannot overdraw more than a designated amount of money. Moreover, each transaction must be correctly reflected by the state of the user's account.

Candidate classes   ATM   3-12

  - *account* – represents the customer's account in the banks database

  - *atm* – performs financial services for a customer

  - *cardreader* – reads and validates a customer's bankcard

  - *cashdispenser* – gives cash to the customer

  - *screen* – presents text and visual information

  - *keypad* – the keys a customer can press

  - *pin* – the authorization code

  - *transaction* – performs financial services and updates the database

---

Slide 3-12: The ATM example (1)

An initial decomposition into objects based on these requirements is shown in slide 3-12. In Wirfs-Brock *et al.* (1990), a fully detailed account is given of how one may arrive at such a decomposition by carefully reading (and re-reading) the requirements document. What we are interested in here, however, is how we may establish that we have not overlooked anything when proposing a design, and how we may verify that our design correctly reflects the requirements.

This particular example nicely illustrates the need for an analysis of the *use cases*. To develop a proper interface, we must precisely know what a user is expected to do (for instance, insert a bank card, key in a PIN code) and how the system must respond (what messages must be displayed, how to react to a wrong PIN code, etc.). Another decision that must be made is when the account will be changed as the result of a transaction. Also, we must decide what to do when a user overdraws.

A very important issue that we will look at in more detail in the next sections is how the collection of objects suggested above will interact. What means do we have to describe the cooperation between the objects, and how do we show that the proposed system meets all the requirements listed above? Moreover can we verify that the system satisfies all the constraints mentioned in the requirements document?

Validation However, before examining these questions and trying out different scenarios, we may as well try to eliminate the spurious classes that came up in our initial attempt. In Rumbaugh *et al.* (1991), a number of reasons are summarized that may be a ground on which to reject a candidate class. See slide 3-13.

3-13

Eliminating spurious classes

- *vague* – system, security-provision, record-keeping
- *attribute* – account-data, receipt, cash
- *redundant* – user
- *irrelevant* – cost
- *implementation* – transaction-log, access, communication

Good classes

- our candidate classes

Slide 3-13: Eliminating spurious classes

For example, the notion underlying the candidate class may be too *vague* to be represented by a class, such as the notion of *system* or *record-keeping*. Another reason for rejecting a suggested class may be that the notion represents not so much a class, but rather a possible attribute of a class. Further, a proposed class may either be *redundant*, for example the class *user*, or simply *irrelevant*, as is the class *cost*. And finally, a class may be too *implementation* oriented, such as the class *transaction-log* or classes that represent the actual communication or access to the account.

Looking back, our choice of candidate classes seems to have been quite fortunate, but generally this will not be the case, and we may use the checklist above to prune the list of candidate classes.

An interesting architectural issue is, how may we provide for future extensions of the system. How easily can we reuse the design and the code for a system supporting different kinds of accounts, or different input or output devices?

As illustrated by the example, a linguistic approach, despite its apparent naivité, may be a valuable heuristic in a first attempt at finding a decomposition into objects. However, the example also illustrates the need for additional heuristics to establish that the objects, as identified, interact as desired.

3.2.2 Responsibilities and collaborations

Design is to a large extent a matter of creative thinking. Heuristics such as performing a linguistic scan on the requirements document for finding objects (nouns), methods (verbs) and attributes (adjectives) may be helpful, but will hopelessly fail when not applied with good taste and judgement. Not surprisingly, one of the classical techniques of creative writing, namely the *shoe-box method*, has reappeared in the guise of an object-oriented development method. The shoe-box method consists of writing fragments and ideas on note cards and storing them in a (shoe) box, so that they may later be retrieved and manipulated to find a suitable ordering for the presentation of the material. To find a proper decomposition into objects, the method creates for each potential (object) class a so-called CRC card, which lists the *Class* name, the *Responsibilities* and the possible *Collaborators* of the proposed class. In a number of iterations, a collection of cards will result that more or less reflects the structure of the intended system.

According to the authors (see Beck and Cunningham, 1989), the method effectively supports the early stages of design, especially when working in small groups. An intrinsic part of the method consists of what the authors call *dynamic simulation*. To test whether a given collection of cards adequately characterizes the functionality of the intended system, the cards may be used to simulate the behavior of the system. When working in a group, the cards may be distributed among the members of the group, who participate in the simulation game according to their cards. See slide 3-14.

Object-Oriented Thinking | CRC | 3-14

Perspective: *immerse the reader in the* object-ness *of the material.*

☐ Give up global knowledge of control.
☐ Rely on the local knowledge of objects.

OO-Design with CRC cards

- Class, Responsibility, Collaborators.

Classname	*Collaborators*
Responsibilities	

Regressions: global variables, pointers, reliance on the implementation of objects.

Slide 3-14: The CRC method

A number of authors have adopted the method, or developed a method very similar, for identifying objects and characterizing their functionality in an abstract way. It is doubtful, however, whether the method has any significance beyond the early stages of analysis and design. Without any more formal means to verify whether the responsibilities listed adequately characterize the intended functionality of the system, the method amounts to not much more than brainstorming. Clearly, the method needs to be complemented by more formal means to establish whether the (implicit) protocols of interaction between the objects satisfy the behavioral requirements of the system.

Nevertheless, the elegant simplicity of the method is appealing, and the card format lends itself to easy incorporation in an on-line documentation system. Moreover, since the method imposes no strict order, and has relatively little overhead, it is indeed a good way in which to get an initial idea of what objects the system will comprise.

Example – ATM (2) Actually, the ATM example is an interesting example for comparing the various approaches, since it is used by many authors to illustrate their methods. In Wirfs-Brock *et al.* (1990) the example is used for spelling out all the steps that must be taken. In Rumbaugh *et al.* (1991) it is also extensively described to illustrate the various modeling techniques employed by the method. Also, in Beck and Cunningham (1989) the CRC cards method is illustrated by sketching the design of an automated teller machine.

The approaches presented in Beck and Cunningham (1989) and Wirfs-Brock *et al.* (1990) are actually very closely related. Both may be characterized as *responsibility-driven*, in that they concentrate on *responsibilities* and *collaboration* relations to model the interaction between objects. However, the method described in Wirfs-Brock *et al.* (1990) is much more detailed, and to some extent includes means to formally characterize the behavior of an object and its interaction with other objects. To this end it employs an informal notion of *contracts* as originally introduced by Meyer (1988).

In section 3.2.1 a number of candidate classes have been suggested for our ATM. Now, with the use of CRC cards, we will delineate the functionality of (a number of) these classes more precisely. Also we will establish how the various object classes must collaborate to perform their duties. At the highest level of the design, we may distinguish between two groups of classes: the classes representing the *banking model* (comprising the class *account* and the class *transaction*), and the classes that model the interaction with the user (comprising the class *card-reader* and the class *cash-dispenser*, very important indeed). At a lower level, we also need a class modeling the *database* that provides persistent storage for the user's account and the information needed for authorization. For each of these classes we will use a CRC card to indicate their responsibilities and the classes with which they need to collaborate.

The *banking model* consists of the classes *account* and *transaction*. The class *account* keeps a record of the actual *balance* of the *account* and must allow a user to *deposit* or *withdraw* money. However, for safety reasons, these operations are never carried out directly, but are performed by an intermediary *transaction* object. See slide 3-15.

The responsibilities of the *transaction* class may be summarized as: the validation of user requests and the execution of money transfers. The responsibility for maintaining audit information is also assigned to the *transaction* class. To act as required, a *transaction* object needs to communicate with a number of other objects. It must acquire information from both the *card-reader* and the *database* to check, for example, whether the user has entered the right PIN code. To validate a request, it must check whether the account will be overdrawn or not. To pay the requested money, it must instruct the *cash-dispenser* to do so. And it must contact the database to log the appropriate audit information. In contrast, an *account* only needs to respond to the requests it receives from a *transaction*. Apart from that, it must participate in committing the transaction to the bank's *database*. Note that the CRC method is non-specific about how the collaborations are actually realized; it is unclear which object will take the initiative. To model these aspects we will need a more precise notion of *control* that tells us how the potential behavior (or responsibility) of an object is activated.

The second group of classes may be called *interaction classes*, since these are

```
Banking model                                      ATM        3-15

        account                    transaction

        keeps balance              database

        deposit money

        withdraw money

        transaction                card-reader

        validation                 cash-dispenser

        performs transfer          account

        keeps audit info           database
```

Slide 3-15: The ATM example (2a)

meant to communicate with entities in the outside world, outside from the perspective of the system. Also the bank's *database* may be considered as belonging to the outside world, since it stores the information concerning the account and the authorization of customers in a system-independent manner. See slide 3-16.

```
Interaction classes                               ATM         3-16

        cardreader                 event

        signals insertion          transaction

        decodes strip

        cashdispenser              event

        emits cash                 transaction

        database                   event

        retrieves account          transaction

        records transaction        account

        authorization              database
```

Slide 3-16: The ATM example (2b)

Both the *card-reader* and the *cash-dispenser* rely on a class called *event*, which is needed to model the actions of the user. For example, when a user inserts a bankcard, we expect a transaction to start. For this to happen, we must presuppose an underlying system that dispatches the event to the *card-reader*, which in turn notifies the *teller machine* that a new transaction is to take place. See also section 7.3 for a comparative study of such mechanisms. The flow of control between a *transaction* object and the *cash-dispenser* is far more straightforward, since a *transaction* object only needs to issue the appropriate instruction. However, the actual interaction between the *cash-dispenser* and the underlying hardware, that turns out the money, may be quite intricate.

The *database* may either respond directly to the request coming from the *account* or *transaction* object or it may respond to *events* by taking the initiative to call the appropriate methods of the *account* and *transaction* objects. Whether the *database* may be accessed directly or will only react to events is actually dependent on the control model we assume when developing the system model.

3.2.3 Object roles and interaction

Objects rarely live in isolation. In a system of some complexity, a number of different kinds of object classes may usually be distinguished. Each kind of class may be regarded as playing a specific role in the system. For example, when considering our ATM, classes such as *card-reader* and *cash-dispenser* are of a completely different kind, and play a completely different role, than the classes *account* and *database* for instance, or the classes *event* and *transaction*. Often it will take some experimentation to decide how control must be distributed among the objects comprising the system. Although the framework chosen for the development of the system may partly determine the control model, there will usually be ample choice left for the designer of the system to define the interactions between objects.

Object roles   3-17

- *actor* – operates, (suffers no operations)
- *server* – suffers operations
- *agent* – suffers and operates (*actor & server*)

Slide 3-17: Object roles

An important function of the design document is to elucidate the role of each object class in the system, and to point out how the objects cooperate to complete the task. In Booch (1986), a distinction is made between objects that suffer no operations (actors), objects that only suffer operations (servers) and objects that both suffer and require operations (agents). Such a characterization in terms of *initiative* may give a first indication of the role an object plays in the system. For example, the *account* class in our ATM example is best characterized as a *server* class, whereas the *transaction class* may be regarded, in the terminology of Booch (1986), as an actor class, since it actively controls the computation. In many cases, the software control model adopted will also influence the way in which individual objects are supposed to behave. See slide 3-17.

With respect to a global view of the system, it is necessary to ensure that each object class is completely defined, that is to establish that each class provides a sufficiently complete method interface. In Booch (1986), a characterization is given of the kinds of methods that may occur in an interface. These include methods to create or destroy an object, methods to modify the state of an object and methods that only provide information on the state of an object, or parts thereof.

Class design – *round trip gestalt*

     analyze a little,
     design a little,
     implement a little,
     test a little...

3-18

Slide 3-18: Round trip gestalt class design

Before being able to make final decisions with respect to the functionality of a class, however, it is generally necessary to get a clear overall picture of the system first. This requires what Booch (1986) characterizes as *round trip gestalt* design, which in other words expresses the need to *analyze a little, design a little, implement a little, test a little...* (The notion of *gestalt* comes from perception psychology, where it means a global perceptual configuration emerging from the background.)

In the next section we will consider formal means to verify the correctness of our design. However, before that we will look at an example of a design paradigm that allows us to assign specific roles to object classes and to specify (in an implicit manner) the protocol of interaction between instances of these classes.

Example – the MVC paradigm A significant part of the effort of system development often goes into the design and implementation of the user interface. The general feeling with respect to user interface components is that these clutter up the design. Nevertheless, as the example of the automated teller machine shows, interaction with the user may be an intrinsic part of the system.

In Beck and Cunningham (1989), the CRC cards method has also been used to characterize the so-called *Model-View-Controller* paradigm, which has become popular as an architectural device for developing user interfaces. The *MVC* paradigm allows us to develop a user interface in a non-intrusive manner, that is without cluttering the application code. The idea is to provide standard (base) classes from which application-specific classes, that implement the particular details, may be derived. See slide 3-19.

The class derived from the *Model* class is intended to maintain the problem-related information. The only thing a *model* object needs to do is notify the other (dependent) objects when some of the information it carries has changed. In response to being notified of a change, the *view* object (an instance of the class which is derived from *View*) may request what it needs to know to refresh the display of the contents of the *model* object. A *controller* object is employed to interact with the user. Any relevant input is transferred to the *model* object, that may in its turn notify the *view* object of a change.

For the automated teller machine, the *account* class will be the obvious choice for being derived from the *Model* class. Clearly, the *card-reader* class will have *Controller*

Slide 3-19: The Model-View-Controller paradigm

as its base class and the *screen* class will be derived from *View*.

An important advantage of using the *MVC*-paradigm is that it allows the programmer to separate the problem-related code from the code needed to implement the (often intricate) details of interacting with the various input and output devices. Another advantage lies in the flexibility of the approach. One *model* object may be associated with arbitrary many different *view-controller* pairs, simply by adding another *view* object to the list of dependent objects that will be notified of a change. Since each *view* class specifies what it needs to know of the *model*, the *model* class itself will remain unaffected.

Although the *MVC*-paradigm was introduced in the Smalltalk-80 environment, similar interaction protocols have been used in user interface libraries for C++, for example the Interviews library (see Linton *et al.*, 1989). See also sections 7.3 and 11.4. From the perspective of design, the paradigm is attractive since it may be applied in a cookbook fashion to implement intricate user interfaces, often simply by reusing available code. See Krasner and Pope (1988) for a number of example recipes. In section 7.3 we will further explore the interaction protocol underlying the *MVC*-paradigm.

3.3   Contracts

To establish the interaction between objects in a more precise way, we need a notion of *contracts*, specifying the requirements a client must comply with when requesting a service from a server object. Our notion of contracts will be based on the notion of *types*.

In the universe of programming, *types* are above all a means to create order and regularity. Also, in an object-oriented approach, types may play an important role in organizing classes and their relationships. As observed in Halbert and O 'Brien (1987), the notion of types gives a natural criterion for *modularization*, perhaps not so much as a guideline to arrive at a particular object decomposition, but as a means to judge whether the modular structure of a system is consistently defined, that is technically well-typed. See slide 3-20.

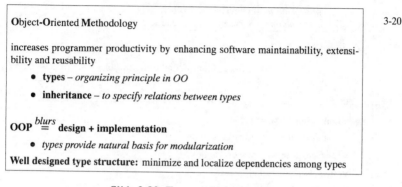

Slide 3-20: Types and inheritance

The meaning of a type must be understood as a formal characterization of the behavior of the elements belonging to the type. A type consists of a (possibly infinite) collection of elements which is characterized by the definition of the type. For example, a *class* defines such a collection, namely the instances of the class, whose behavior is constrained by the specification of the class.

Formal specification A formal specification of the behavior of an object may be given by defining a *pre-condition* and *post-condition* for each method. The pre-condition of a method specifies in a logical manner what restrictions the client invoking a particular method is obliged to comply with. When the client fails to meet these requirements the result of the method will be undefined. In effect, after the violation of a pre-condition anything can happen. Usually, this means that the computation may be aborted or that some other means of error-handling may be started. For instance, when the implementation language supports exceptions an exception handler may be invoked.

The post-condition of a method states what obligations the server object has when executing the method, provided that the client's request satisfies the method's precondition.

Apart from specifying a pre-condition and post-condition for each method publicly supported by the class, the designer of the class may also specify a *class invariant*, to define the invariant properties of the state of each instance of the class.

A class annotated with an invariant and pre- and post-conditions for the methods may be regarded as a *contract*, since it specifies precisely (in an abstract way) the behavioral conformance conditions of the object and the constraints imposed on the interactions between the object and its clients. See slide 3-21.

Intuitively, *contracts* have a clear analogy to our business affairs in everyday life. For instance, when buying audio equipment, as a client you wish to know what you get for the price you pay, whereas the dealer may require that you pay in cash. Following this metaphor through, we see that the supplier may actually benefit from imposing a (rea-

Slide 3-21: Contractual obligations

Slide 3-22: Formal specification of contracts

sonable) pre-condition and that the client has an interest in a well-stated post-condition. Most people are not willing to pay without knowing what they will get for their money.

The use of *contracts* was originally proposed by Meyer (1988), and is directly supported by the language Eiffel, which offers the keywords *require* (to indicate a pre-condition), *ensure* (to indicate a post-condition) and *invariant* (to indicate the invariance condition). See slide 3-22. The Eiffel environment has options to dynamically check any of the three kinds of assertions, even selectively per class. The assertions, except for the invariance condition, are directly embedded in the code. Although less elegant, the same functionality can be achieved in C++ by using the *assert* macro defined in `assert.h` as explained in section 2.2.3, which also introduced the *require* and *promise* macros for C++.

For dynamically checking the invariance condition, a test should be executed when evaluating the constructor and before and after each method invocation. While a method is being executed, the invariant need not necessarily hold, but it is the responsibility of a method to restore the invariant when it is disrupted. In case object methods are recursively applied, the invariant must be restored when returning to the original caller.

An alternative approach to incorporating assertions in a class description is presented in Cline and Lea (1990), which introduces an extension of C++ called Annotated C++. Instead of directly embedding assertions in the code, Annotated C++ requires the user to specify separately the axioms characterizing the functionality of the methods and their effect on the state of the object.

Important from a design perspective is that the specification, even without an implementation of the methods, may be understood as specifying a contract. In practice, they may only be stated as comments.

3.3.1   The notion of conformance

Having looked at a precise definition of contracts, we may well reflect (again) on the nature of object-oriented computation to draw implications with respect to system development. Each object, so to speak, carries a state and behavior. In principle, the state is not directly accessible but is encapsulated by a well-defined method interface. Computation in an object-oriented system, then, amounts to sending messages that may be dispatched by the dynamic binding mechanism to invoke the appropriate procedure. As a client of a server object, what you need to know is what you may expect as the result of invoking a method, irrespective of what actual procedure the message is dispatched to.

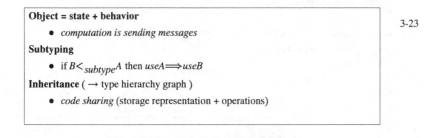

3-23

Slide 3-23: The substitutability requirement

In many cases it is sufficient to characterize the desired behavior in terms of (behavioral) *conformance*. Operationally, (the behavior of) an object B conforms to (the behavior of) an object A if the behavior of B is in some sense equivalent to the behavior of object A. More formally, this may be expressed in terms of the subtype relation, by saying that type B is a subtype of A if any object of type B may be used anywhere that an object of type A may be used. Behavioral conformance amounts to the requirement of substitutability. See slide 3-23. If we know what a type does, we may substitute any object that realizes the type as long as it does what it is expected to do. In other words, conformance to a type means that the behavior of the object respects the constraints imposed by the type.

A direct corollary of our notion of *conformance* is that instances of derived classes must conform to the type of their base classes. We will study how this affects the use of contracts to characterize the behavioral properties of a class.

System development From the perspective of system development, the notion of contracts has some interesting consequences. Most importantly, *contracts* may be used to document the method interface of a class. Pre- and post-conditions allow the class designer to specify in a concise manner the functional characteristics of a method, whereas the use of natural language often leads to lengthy (and imprecise) descriptions. Below, an example is given of a contract specifying an account.

The interface for the *account* class given in slide 3-24, specifies in an abstract way what the user expects of an account. From the perspective of design, the behavioral abstraction expressed by the axioms is exactly what we need, in principle. The implementation must guarantee that these constraints are met.

With regard to encapsulation, the obvious disadvantage of using assertions is that detailed knowledge of the class, including knowledge of the existence of private and pro-

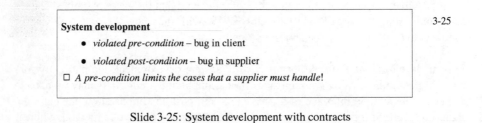

```
Contract – interface                                    [ account ]     3-24

        class account {
        public:
        account();
        // assert( invariant() );
        virtual float balance() { return _balance; }
        void deposit(float x);                        // to deposit money
        // require( x ≥ 0 );
        // promise( balance() == old_balance + x && invariant() );
        void withdraw(float x);                       // to withdraw money
        // require( x ≤ balance() );
        // promise( balance() == old_balance− x && invariant() );
        bool invariant() { return balance() ≥ 0; }
        protected:
        float _balance;
        };
```

Slide 3-24: The *account* contract

tected instance variables, is needed to be able to understand the meaning of these assertions. However, this may not be so odd as it appears, since we do regard an object as having a state and operations that possibly modify this state. From this point of view, encapsulation may be seen as merely prohibiting access to the state, not as a dictum not to look
at or reason about the state. Nevertheless, despite the advantages the use of assertions offers from a formal point of view, the cognitive complexity of logical assertions will usually necessitate additional comments (in natural language) for a user to be able to understand the functionality of an object and the services it offers.

```
System development                                               3-25

        • violated pre-condition – bug in client
        • violated post-condition – bug in supplier
     □ A pre-condition limits the cases that a supplier must handle!
```

Slide 3-25: System development with contracts

Assertions may be used to decide who is responsible for any erroneous behavior
of the system. See slide 3-25. For example, imagine that you are using a software library
to implement a system for financial transactions and that your company suffers a number of losses due to bugs in the system. How would you find out whether the loss is your
own fault or whether it is caused by some bug in the library?

Perhaps surprisingly, the use of assertions allows you to determine exactly whether
to sue the library vendor or not. Assume that the classes in the library are all annotated

with assertions that can be checked dynamically at runtime. Now, when you replay the examples that resulted in a loss for your company with the option for checking pre- and post-conditions on, it can easily be decided who is in error. In the case a pre-condition of a method signals violation, you, as a client of a library object, are in error. However, when no pre-condition violation is signaled, but instead a post-condition is violated, then the library object as the supplier of a service is in error; and you may proceed to go to court, or do something less dramatic as asking the software vendor to correct the bug.

Realization The contract specified in the class interface as given in slide 3-24 may actually be enforced in the code as illustrated in slide 3-26.

Realization   account   3-26

```
class account {
public:
account() { _balance = 0; assert(invariant()); }
virtual float balance() { return _balance; }
void deposit(float x) {
        require( x ≥ 0 );                    // check precondition
        hold();                              // to save the old state
        _balance += x;
        promise( balance() == old_balance + x );
        promise( invariant() );
        }
void withdraw(float x) {
        require( x ≤ _balance );              // check precondition
        hold();                              // to save the old state
        _balance -= x;
        promise( balance() == old_balance− x );
        promise( invariant() );
        }
virtual bool invariant() { return balance() ≥ 0; }
protected:
float _balance;
float old_balance;                           // additional variable
virtual void hold() { old_balance = _balance; }
};
```

Slide 3-26: The realization of the *account* contract

The additional variable *old_balance* is needed to compare the state preceding an operation with the state that results afterwards. The old state must explicitly be copied by calling *hold*. In this respect, Eiffel offers better support than C++.

Whenever *balance()* proves to be less than zero, the procedure sketched above can be used to determine whether the error is caused by an erroneous method invocation, for example when calling *withdraw(x)* with $x \geq balance()$, or whether the implementation code contains a bug.

For the developer of the software, pre-conditions offer a means to limit the number of cases that a method must be able to handle. Often, programmers tend to anticipate all possible uses. For instance, many programs or systems have options that may be learned only when inspecting the source code but are otherwise undocumented. Rather than providing all possible options, for now and the future, it is more sensible to delineate in a precise manner what input will be processed and what input is considered illegal. For the developer, this may significantly reduce the effort of producing the software. It is important that what is and what is not supported is in principle negotiable whenever the class interface explicitly states the requirements imposed on the user.

3.3.2 Realization versus refinement

Inheritance provides a convenient mechanism to factor out code and to use this code as basic building blocks from which the system may be composed. The difference between classes and procedures in this respect is the support offered by classes for encapsulation and modularization. In addition, inheritance is an important mechanism for structuring the design specification.

From the perspective of design, inheritance may be regarded as determining the type structure of the system. A type defines in an abstract way a collection of objects with similar behavior. This collection includes the collections of objects defined by its subtypes. A subtype may be regarded as imposing additional constraints and hence as corresponding to a generally smaller and more precisely delineated collection of objects.

Type = objects with similar behavior   3-27

- *partial types are designed to have subtypes*

Inheritance – *factor out code* (building blocks)

- *abstract interface* – implementation is left to subtypes
- *type hierarchy* – behavioral refinement and extension

Slide 3-27: Partial types

An important notion for understanding the use of types in an object oriented context is the notion of *partial types* as introduced in Halbert and O 'Brien (1987). See slide 3-27. Partial types are types designed to have subtypes! Other authors speak of abstract types or abstract classes (cf. Stroustrup, 1988; Meyer, 1988). A partial type (or abstract class) specifies the interface of an object (class), and hence of all its subtypes (subclasses), without necessarily providing a full implementation. The actual *realization* of the type is left to the object classes implementing a subtype.

As an example of a partial type, think of an interface specification of a *stack*. An abstract class may specify the interface to the stack and derived classes may specify a variety of implementations using, for example, fixed length arrays, linked lists or dynamic arrays. Another example of the use of partial types has already been given in section

2.2.2, when defining a collection of graphical shapes. The realization of the abstract class *shape* is left to the derived classes, such as *circle* and *rectangle*, which are sufficiently concrete to provide an implementation for the method *draw*.

Note that there is a significant difference between the two examples given. In the example of a *stack*, a realization amounts simply to providing an implementation. In the second example, however, the various realizations of the abstract graphical shape immediately correspond to a type hierarchy of graphical shapes. The concrete graphical shapes are refinements of the abstract class *shape*, and may further be refined into classes describing more specific graphical shapes. For instance, the class *rectangle* may be used as a base class for the class *square*. It is also possible that a derived class extends the interface of the base class, as has occurred for the *compound* shape class.

Issues – *delegation versus inheritance*   3-28

- *applicability* – how relevant to the type?

- *complexity* – how difficult to understand and implement?

- *reusability* – how (re)useful is the code?

- *implementation* – how dependent?

Slide 3-28: Delegation versus inheritance

A number of issues play a role in deciding where to put the functionality when constructing a (refinement) type hierarchy. See slide 3-28. First, it must be decided whether inheritance is the proper mechanism to use. Often, the reuse of code is more safely effected when using delegation or forwarding to an embedded object, instead of inheritance. See section 3.3.3. Inheritance should only be used when it can be shown that there is actually a (behavioral) refinement relation satisfying the constraints outlined below.

Whether particular code belongs to a type obviously depends upon whether the functionality expressed by the code is relevant to the type. Another criterion concerns the complexity of the resulting type structure, including both the cognitive complexity and the complexity of implementing it. In other words, how difficult is it to understand, respectively implement, the type hierarchy? More particularly, what tricks, such as explicit type conversions (casts) or the bypassing of encapsulation (friends), must be used to realize the desired functionality in code? Another important criterion is whether the type structure (and code) is easily reusable. How much effort is involved in adapting the structure to more specific needs? Admittedly, the solution to these issues will depend upon the application. However, the constraints that follow from extending the notion of contracts to include classes derived by inheritance do provide a (minimal) guideline for designing a well-behaved type structure.

Contracts and inheritance Contracts provide a means to specify the behavior of an object in a formal way by using logical assertions. In particular, a contract specifies the constraints involved in the interaction between a server object and a client invoking a method for that object. When developing a refinement subtype hierarchy we need to establish that the derived types satisfy the constraints imposed by the contract associated with the base type.

To establish that the contract of a derived class refines the contract of the base class it suffices to verify that the following rules are satisfied. See slide 3-29.

Refining a contract – *state responsibilities and obligations*   3-29

- *invariance* – the invariants of all the parents of a class apply to the class itself
- *methods* – services may be added or refined

Improving a service – *do only more than expected*

- accept weaker pre-conditions
- guarantee stronger post-conditions

Slide 3-29: Contracts and inheritance

First, the invariant of the base class must apply to all instances of the derived class. In other words, the invariance assertions of the derived class must be logically equal to or stronger than the assertions characterizing the invariant properties of the base class. This requirement may be verified by checking that the invariance properties of the base class can be logically derived from the statement asserting the invariance properties of the derived class. The intuition underlying this requirement is that the behavior of the derived class is more tightly defined and hence subject to stronger invariance conditions.

Secondly, each method occurring in the base class must occur in the derived class, possibly in a refined form. Note that from a type theoretical point of view it is perfectly all right to add methods but strictly forbidden to delete methods, since deleting a method would violate the requirement of behavioral conformance that adheres to the subtype relation. Apart from adding a method, we may also refine existing methods. Refining a method involves strengthening the post-condition and weakening the pre-condition. Suppose that we have a class C derived from a base class P, to verify that the method m_C refines the method m_P defined for the base class P, we must check, assuming that the signatures of m_C and m_P are compatible, that the post-condition of m_C is not weaker than the post-condition of m_P, and also that the pre-condition of m_C is not stronger than the pre-condition of m_P. See slide 3-30.

This rule may at first sight be surprising, because of the asymmetric way in which post-conditions and pre-conditions are treated. But reflecting on what it means to improve a service, the intuition underlying this rule, and in particular the contra-variant relation between the pre-conditions involved, is quite straightforward. To improve or refine a service, in our common sense notion of a service, means that the quality of the product or the result delivered becomes better. Alternatively, a service may be considered as improved when, even with the result remaining the same, the cost of the service is decreased. In other words, a service is improved if either the client may have higher expectations of the result or the requirements on the client becomes less stringent. The *or* is non-exclusive. A derived class may improve a service while at the same time imposing fewer constraints on the clients.

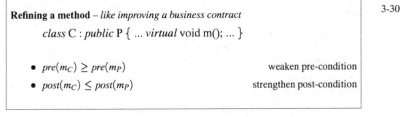

3-30

Refining a method – *like improving a business contract*

   class C : *public* P { ... *virtual* void m(); ... }

- $pre(m_C) \geq pre(m_P)$ weaken pre-condition
- $post(m_C) \leq post(m_P)$ strengthen post-condition

Slide 3-30: Refining a method

Example As an example of improving a contract, consider the refinement of the class *account* into a class *credit_account*, which allows a consumer to overdraw an account to a limit of some *maximum* amount. See slide 3-31.

As a first observation, we may note that the invariant of *account* immediately follows from the invariant of *credit_account*. Also, we may easily establish that the precondition of *withdraw* has (implicitly) been weakened, since we are allowed to overdraw the *credit_account* by the amount given by *credit*. Note, however, that this is implied by the virtual definition of *balance*(). To manage the *credit* given, the methods *credit* and *reduce* are supplied. This allows us to leave the methods *deposit* and *withdraw* unmodified.

3.3.3   Delegation or inheritance

Object-oriented languages offer a variety of constructs that may be used to implement a system. In particular, when developing a class, the designer has the choice between developing the class anew, deriving the class using inheritance, incorporating an (object of an) existing class to which messages may be delegated, or instantiating a given template class with an appropriate type parameter. The choice may be difficult, since there are a number of trade-offs involved. For instance, when using explicit delegation instead of inheritance, each indirection must be explicitly coded. When using inheritance, derived code can immediately be used, but the interface of the derived class may get too 'fat'.

The actual choice made will often be dependent on the functionality offered by the class libraries available. For example, only a few of the C++ libraries employ templates. See section 11.4. In the absence of template classes, the designer may be forced to use inheritance and type insecure casts to mimic generic data types such as lists.

In Halbert and O 'Brien (1987), guidelines are given on how and when to use inheritance. Their view is in accord with a design methodology centered around subtyping, that is the derivation of new object types within the constraints of behavioral conformance. See slide 3-32.

As we have seen previously, subtyping may be used to realize a partially defined (abstract) type, or as a means with which to add a specialization to a conceptual hierarchy. On a number of occasions, however, the need may arise to employ what Halbert and O 'Brien (1987) called *non-standard subtyping*, and which is also known as *non-strict inheritance*. An example of non-strict inheritance is a derivation that results in a *general-*

```
Refining the account contract                                    [C++]      3-31

    class credit_account : public account {
    public:
    credit_account(float x) { _maxcredit = x; _credit = 0; }
    float balance() { return _balance + _credit; }
    float credit(float x) {
        require( x + _credit ≤ _maxcredit );
        hold();
        _credit += x;
        promise( _credit = old_credit + x );
        promise( _balance = old_balance);
        promise( invariant() );
        }
    void reduce(float x) {
        require( 0 ≤ x && x ≤ _credit );
        hold();
        _credit -= x;
        promise( _credit = old_credit− x );
        promise( _balance = old_balance );
        promise( invariant() );
        }
    bool invariant() {
        return _credit ≤ _maxcredit && account::invariant();
        }
    protected:
    float _maxcredit, _credit;
    float old_credit;
    void hold() { old_credit = _credit; account::hold(); }
    };
```

Slide 3-31: Refining the *account* contract

ization, as occurs, for instance, when deriving a *colored window* class from a base class *window* (supporting only black and white). We speak of a *generalization* since the type associated with *colored windows* properly encompasses the collection of black and white windows. Yet from an implementation perspective, it may be convenient to simply extend the code written for black and white windows, instead of redesigning the class hierarchy.

Another example of non-strict inheritance is when the derivation results in what may be called a *variant* type, which occurs, for instance, when deriving a *pen* or *tablet* class from a class defining the behavior of a *mouse*. The proper course of action in such cases is to introduce an abstract class *pointing device* from which both the *mouse* and *tablet* classes may be derived (as proper subtypes).

Another, equally evident, violation of the subtyping regime occurs when restricting a given class to achieve the functionality belonging to the type of the derived class. A

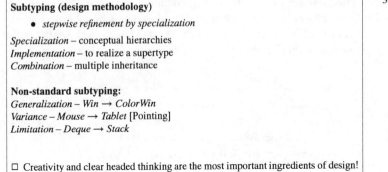

Subtyping (design methodology)

- *stepwise refinement by specialization*

Specialization – conceptual hierarchies
Implementation – to realize a supertype
Combination – multiple inheritance

Non-standard subtyping:
Generalization – Win → *ColorWin*
Variance – Mouse → *Tablet* [Pointing]
Limitation – Deque → *Stack*

☐ Creativity and clear headed thinking are the most important ingredients of design!

Slide 3-32: Design methodology

violation, since the requirement of behavioral conformance demands that either new behavior is added or already existing behavior is refined. Actual limitation of behavior results in a behaviorally incompatible class. The standard example of limitation, originally given in Snyder (1986), is the restriction of a *double ended queue* into a *stack*. A better, and from a type perspective, perfectly legal solution is to derive a stack from a double ended queue by using private inheritance. However, from a design perspective, the use of private inheritance must be considered ill-practice, since dependencies may be introduced in the object model that remain invisible in a more abstract (type oriented) description of the system. Delegation, as in the *handler/body* idiom described in section 2.3.2, is to be preferred in such cases since it makes the *uses* relation explicit and does not compromise the type system.

Example When developing a class structure, often the choice will arise as to whether to employ inheritance or explicit delegation as a means to utilize the functionality of a particular class.

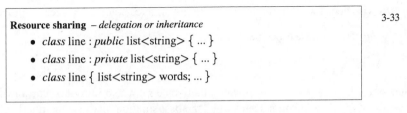

3-33

Resource sharing – *delegation or inheritance*
- *class* line : *public* list<string> { ... }
- *class* line : *private* list<string> { ... }
- *class* line { list<string> words; ... }

Slide 3-33: Sharing resources

The choices a designer may be confronted with when developing a system or a class library may be illustrated by a simple example. Suppose you must develop a system that produces a *kwicindex*. A *kwicindex* contains for each line of text all possible rotations, so that each word can be rapidly searched for, together with the context in which it occurs. The example is taken from Van Vliet (1993), who discusses a number of alternative solutions from the perspective of information hiding. An object-oriented solution appears to be surprisingly simple, in particular when a suitable library is available. The two classes that are of interest are, respectively, a class *line*, to represent each line of text, and a class *index* to represent the lines generated for the *kwicindex*.

3-34

```
class line {                                                          line
public:
line() { rot = 0; words.compare(lexicographic); }
bool operator< (line& l) { return words < l.words; }
operator void* () { return (void* ) ! ( rot >  length()); }
int length() { return words.count(); }
line& rotate() { rot++; words = words.rotate(); return * this; }
private:
list<string> words;
int rot;
friend ostream& operator≪(ostream& os, line& l);
};
```

Slide 3-34: Representing lines

The class *line* is simply a list of words (strings) that can be rotated. The actual implementation of a *line* is provided by an instantiation of a generic (template) class *list*, that is contained as a data member, to which the operations *insert* and *rotate* are delegated.

Instead of incorporating a member of type *list<string>*, the *line* class could have been made a descendant of the class *list<string>*, as indicated below

```
class line : public list<string> {
...
};
```

However, this would make the type *line* a subtype of *list<string>*, which does not seem to be a wise decision. Alternatively, private inheritance could have been employed as in

```
class line : private list<string> {
...
};
```

But, as we have noted before, private inheritance may also introduce unwanted dependencies. Explicit delegation seems to be the best solution, because the relation between a *line* object and a *list of strings* is best characterized as a *uses* relation.

For the *index* class, a similar argument as for the *line* class can be given as to why delegation is used instead of public or private inheritance.

Actually, the most difficult part of the code is the function defining how to compare two lines of text that is needed for sorting the *index*. Comparison is based on the lexicographical order as defined below.

3-35

```
class index {                                    | index |
line base;
list<line> lines;
public:
index(line& l) : base(l) {}
void generate() {
        line l;
        while ( l = base.rotate() ) lines.insert(l);
        lines = lines.sort();
        }
friend ostream& operator≪(ostream& os, index& t);
};
```

Slide 3-35: Generating the index

```
bool lexicographic(list<string>& a, list<string>& b) {
    if ( a.count() != b.count() ) return false;
    else {
    for ( int i = 0; i <  a.count() ; i++ ) {
        if ( b[i] <  a[i] ) return false;
        else if ( a[i] <  b[i] ) return true;
        }
    return false;
    }
}
```

The ease of implementing both the *line* and *index* classes depends largely upon the availability of a powerful *list* template class. In the example, we employed the functions *list* :: *rotate* to rotate the elements in the list, and *list* :: *sort* to sort the elements in the list. The function *list* :: *compare* was used to determine the $\leq$ relation between elements of the list. The actual library employed for this example is the *splash* library, which is discussed in section 11.4.

3.4   From specification to design

Designing an object-oriented system requires the identification of object classes and the characterization of their responsibilities, preferably by means of *contracts*.

In addition, one must establish the relationships between the object classes constituting the system and delineate the facilities the system offers to the user. Such facilities are usually derived from a requirements document and may be formally specified in terms of abstract operations on the system. See also section 11.3.1.

In this section we will look at the means we have available to express the properties of our object model, and we will study how we may employ abstract specifications of system operations to arrive at the integration of user actions and the object model underlying a system in a seamless way. The approach sketched may be characterized as event-centered.

3.4.1   Structural versus behavioral encapsulation

Object-oriented modeling has clearly been inspired by or, to be more careful, shows significant similarity to the method of *semantic modeling* that has become popular for developing information systems. In an amusing paper, King (1989) discusses how semantic modeling and object-oriented modeling are related. Apart from a difference in terminology, semantic modeling differs from object-oriented modeling primarily by its focus on *structural aspects*, whereas object-oriented modeling is more concerned with *behavioral* aspects, as characterized by the notion of *responsibilities*.

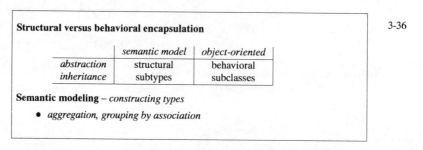

Structural versus behavioral encapsulation			3-36
	semantic model	*object-oriented*	
abstraction	structural	behavioral	
inheritance	subtypes	subclasses	

Semantic modeling – *constructing types*
- *aggregation, grouping by association*

Slide 3-36: Semantic modeling

Typically, semantic modeling techniques provide a richer repertoire for constructing types, including a variety of methods for aggregation and a notion of grouping by association. See slide 3-36. The object-oriented counterpart of aggregation may be characterized as the *has-a* or *part-of* relation, that is usually expressed by including the (part) object as a data member.

Associations between objects cannot be expressed directly in an object-oriented framework. On an implementation level, the association relation corresponds to membership of a common collection, or being stored in the same container. However, the absence of an explicit association relation makes it hard to express general *m-n relations*, as, for example, the relation between students and courses.

The influence of a semantic modeling background can be clearly felt in the OMT method. The object model of OMT is a rather direct generalization of the *entity-relationship* model. Entities in the *entity-relationship* model may only contain (non-object) data members, which are called attributes.

In contrast, *objects* (in the more general sense) usually hide object and non-object data members, and instead provide a method interface. Moreover, object-oriented modeling focuses on behavioral properties, whereas semantic modeling has been more concerned with (non-behavioral) data types and (in the presence of inheritance) data subtypes.

Relations, as may be expressed in the *entity-relationship* model, can partly be expressed directly in terms of the mechanisms supported by object-oriented languages. For

3-37

Object-oriented modeling

- *is-a* – inheritance
- *has-a, uses* – delegation
- *uses* – templates

Challenges

- *Clearly, the trend is for database researchers to view object-oriented models as having both structural and behavioral encapsulation facilities*

Slide 3-37: Relations between objects

instance, the *is-a* relation corresponds closely (although not completely) with the inheritance relation. See slide 3-37. Both the *has-a* and *uses* relation is usually implemented by including (a pointer to) an object as a data member. Another important relation is the *is-like* relation, which may exist between objects that are neither related by the inheritance relation nor by the subtype relation, but yet have a similar interface and hence may be regarded as being of analogous types. The *is-like* relation may be enforced by parametrized types that require the presence of particular methods, such as a *compare* operator in the case of a generic list supporting a *sort* method.

Due, partially, to what may be regarded as the natural dynamics of research (which includes financing), there seems to be a trend of convergence between the interests of the object-oriented community and the proponents of semantic modeling. The main challenge, from the perspective of object-oriented programming, is to provide efficient support for persistent objects and (explicit) support for aggregation and association relations. Within the community of database researchers, an interesting debate is going on about whether to extend the relational model with object-oriented notions or whether to start anew from fresh premises. The main challenge, from the perspective of database management systems, is clearly to provide efficient support for the behavioral aspects of objects. One approach is to extend the object model of object-oriented programming languages with *persistence* as proposed by the Object Database Management Group (ODMG) in Cattell (1994). See section 11.1.3. To meet the demands of future applications (featuring graphics and animation), support for persistence should include *active objects*, having activity of their own, as well.

From the perspective of object-oriented modeling, the main issue is to combine both structural and behavioral aspects in a coherent way.

3.4.2 Model-based specification

Several development methods, including Responsibility Driven Design and Fusion (see section 11.3.1), allow for the specification of user interactions in a semi-formal way by means of pre- and post-conditions. These approaches have been inspired by model-based specification methods such as VDM and Z, which offer a formal framework for specifying the requirements of a system. Model-based specification methods derive

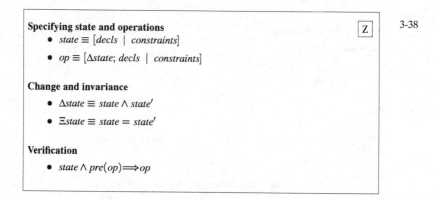

Specifying state and operations $\boxed{\text{Z}}$ 3-38
- $state \equiv [decls \mid constraints]$
- $op \equiv [\Delta state; decls \mid constraints]$

Change and invariance
- $\Delta state \equiv state \wedge state'$
- $\Xi state \equiv state = state'$

Verification
- $state \wedge pre(op) \Longrightarrow op$

Slide 3-38: Model-based specification

their name from the opportunity to specify a mathematical model capturing the relevant features of the system. Operations, which may correspond to user actions, can then be specified in a purely logical way.

In the following, an outline of the specification language Z will be given. More importantly, the specification of a simple library system will be discussed, illustrating how we may specify user actions in an abstract way. (The use of the Z specification language is in this respect only of subsidiary importance.) In the subsequent section, we will look at the realization of the library employing an abstract system of objects and events corresponding to the user actions, which reflects the characterization given in the formal specification.

The specification language Z is based on classical (two-valued) logic and set theory. It has been used in a number of industrial projects (Hayes, 1992) and to specify the architecture of complex intelligent systems (Craig, 1991). The central compositional unit of specification in Z is the *schema*. A schema may be used to specify both states and operations in a logical way. The logic employed in Z is a typed logic. The specification of a *schema* consists of a number of *declarations* followed by *constraints* specifying conditions on the variables introduced in the declarations. Declarations may include other schemas, as in the example specification of the operation *op*. The schema $\Delta state$ itself is a compound schema that results from the logical conjunction of the schema *state* and its primed version *state'*, which denotes *state* after applying *op*.

Both schema inclusion and schema conjunction are examples of the powerful schema calculus supported by Z, which enables the user to specify complex systems in Z.

Moreover, schemas may be decorated to specify the effects of an operation. Invariance may be specified as in $\Xi state$, which expresses that the *state* before applying the operation is the same as the state (denoted by *state'*) after applying the operation.

Because schemas are specified in a logical manner, both pre- and post-conditions are implicitly specified by the constraints included in the schema. Hence, to verify that an operation *op* is legal for a state it is merely required to verify that the conditions specified for *state* hold, and that, together with the pre-conditions (which are implicitly specified by the schema for *op*), they imply the logical formula characterizing *op*. See slide 3-38.

An important property of Z is that it allows for a graphical layout of schemas, as

Slide 3-39: The specification of a *Counter* in Z

illustrated in the specification of a *Counter* given in slide 3-39.

The state of a *Counter* is given by the *Counter* schema declaring an integer variable n, which is constrained by the condition $n \geq 0$. The operations *Incr* and *Decr* are specified by defining the state following the operation by, respectively, $n' = n + 1$ and $n' = n - 1$. Both operations require the declaration $\Delta Counter$ to indicate that the state specified by *Counter* will be modified. In addition, the operation *Decr* requires as a precondition that $n > 0$, needed to prevent the violation of the invariant, which would happen whenever n became less than zero.

An alternative specification of the *Counter* is given in slide 3-40.

To emphasize that we may regard the *Counter* as an object, the operations have been prefixed by *Counter* in a C++-like manner. This is only a syntactic device, however, carrying no formal meaning. In addition, both the operations *Incr* and *Decr* declare an integer variable v? which acts, by convention, as an input parameter. Similarly, the integer variable v! declared for the operation *value* acts, again by convention, as an output parameter.

Since Z allows the inclusion of other schemas in the declaration part of a schema, we may easily mimic inheritance as illustrated in the specification of *Bounded* :: *Counter*, which is a *Counter* with a maximum given by an integer constant *Max*.

```
┌─────────────────────────────────────────────────────────────────────┐
│ Counter                                                    ⌐Z¬   3-40 │
│                                                                       │
│     Counter ≘ [n : N | n ≥ 0]                                         │
│     Counter :: Incr ≘ [ΔCounter, v? : N | n' = n + v?]                │
│     Counter :: Decr ≘ [ΔCounter | n > 0; n' = n − 1]                  │
│     Counter :: Value ≘ [ΞCounter; v! : N | v! = n]                    │
│                                                                       │
│ Bounded counter                                                       │
│     Bounded :: Counter ≘ [Counter | n ≤ Max]                          │
│     Bounded :: Incr ≘ [Counter :: Incr | n < Max]                     │
│                                                                       │
└─────────────────────────────────────────────────────────────────────┘
```

Slide 3-40: An alternative specification of the *Counter*

Similarly, we may specify the operations for the *Bounded* :: *Counter* by including the corresponding operations specified for the *Counter*, adding conditions if required.

From a schema we may easily extract the pre-conditions for an operation by removing from the conditions the parts involving a primed variable. Clearly, the post-condition is then characterized by the conditions thus eliminated.

For example, the pre-condition of the *Counter* :: *Incr* operation is $v? \geq 0$, whereas the post-condition is $n' = n + v?$ which corresponds to the implementation requirement that the new value of the *Counter* is the old value plus the value of the argument $v?$. In a similar way, the pre-condition for applying the *Bounded* :: *Incr* operation is $n + v? \leq Max$. Note, however, that this pre-condition is stronger than the original pre-condition $v? \geq 0$, hence to conform with the rules for refinement we must specify what happens when $n + v? > Max$ as well. This is left as an exercise for the reader.

Clearly, although Z lacks a notion of objects or classes, it may conveniently be employed to specify the behavior of an object. In Stepney *et al.* (1992), a number of studies are collected which propose extending Z with a formal notion of classes and inheritance. The reader interested in these extensions is in particular invited to study Object-Z, OOZE and Z++. As an historical aside, we may note that Z has been of significant influence in the development of Eiffel (see Meyer, 1992b). Although the two approaches are quite divergent, they obviously still share a common interest in correctness.

In contrast to Eiffel, which offers only a semi-formal way in which to specify the behavior of object classes, Z allows for a precise formal specification of the requirements a system must meet. To have the specification reflect the object structure of the system more closely, one of the extensions of Z mentioned above may be used. An example of using (plain) Z to specify the functionality of a library system is given below.

The specification of a library Imagine that you must develop a program to manage a library, that is keep a record of the books that have been borrowed.

Before developing a detailed object model, you may well reflect on what user services the library must provide. These services include the borrowing of a book, returning a book and asking whether a person has borrowed any books, and if so which books.

```
State                                              Library (1)

    ┌─ Library ────────────────────────────────────────────
    │
    │  books : P Book
    │
    │  borrowed : Book ↦ Person
    │
    ├──────────────────────────────────────────────────────
    │
    │  dom borrowed ⊆ books
    │
    └──────────────────────────────────────────────────────
```

Slide 3-41: The specification of a *Library*

These operations are specified by the schemas *Borrow*, *Return* and *Has* in slide 3-42. (Don't be frightened of the mathematical notation in which these operations are specified. The notation is only of secondary importance and will be explained as we go along.)

Since we are only interested in the abstract relations between people and books, we may assume *Book* and *Person* to be primitive types. The specification given in slide 3-41 specifies an abstract state, which is actually a partial function delivering the person that borrowed the book if the function is defined for the book. The function is partial to allow for the situation where a book has not been borrowed, but still lies on the shelves. The invariant of the library system states that the domain of the function *borrowed* must be a subset of the books available in the library.

Given the specification of the state, and some mathematical intuition, the specification of the operations is quite straightforward.

When a *Borrow* action occurs, which has as input a book $b?$ and a person $p?$, the function $borrowed'$ is defined by extending *borrowed* with the association between $b?$ and $p?$, which is expressed as the mapping $b? \mapsto p?$. As a pre-condition for *Borrow*, we have that *borrowed* must not be defined for $b?$, otherwise some person would already have borrowed the book $b?$.

The *Return* action may be considered as the reverse of the *Borrow* action. Its precondition states that *borrowed* must be defined for $b?$ and the result of the operation is that the association between $b?$ and $p?$ is removed from $borrowed'$.

Finally, the operation *Has* allows us to query what books are in the possession of a person $p?$. The specification of *Has* employs the mathematical features of Z in a nice way. The output, which is stored in the output parameter $bks!$, consists of all the books related to the person $p?$. The set of books related to $p?$ is obtained by taking the relational image of the inversion of *borrowed* for the singleton set consisting of $p?$, that is, each book x for which an association $x \mapsto p?$ is in *borrowed* is included in the set $bks!$. Again, it is not the notation that is important here, but the fact that the specification defines all top-level user interactions.

Operations $\boxed{Library\ (2)}$ 3-42

Borrow

$\Delta Library;\ b?\ :\ Book;\ p?\ :\ Person$

$b?\ \notin\ \mathrm{dom}\ borrowed$

$b?\ \in\ books$

$borrowed' = borrowed \cup \{b? \mapsto p?\}$

Return

$\Delta Library;\ b?\ :\ Book;\ p?\ :\ Person$

$b?\ \in\ \mathrm{dom}\ borrowed$

$borrowed' = borrowed \setminus \{b? \mapsto p?\}$

Has

$\Xi Library;\ p?\ :\ Person;\ bks\ :\ \mathbb{P}\ Book$

$bks! = borrowed^{-1}(\!|\{p?\}|\!)$

Slide 3-42: The *Library* operations

3.4.3   Abstract systems and events

User actions may require complex interactions between the objects constituting the object model of a system. Such interactions are often of an *ad hoc* character in the sense that they embody one of the many possible ways in which the functionality of objects may be used. What we need is a methodology or paradigm that allows us to express these interactions in a concise yet pragmatically amenable way. In Henderson (1993), a notion of *abstract systems* is introduced that seems to meet our needs to a large extent. See slide 3-43.

Abstract systems extend the notion of abstract data types to capture the (possible) interactions between collections of objects.

The idea underlying the notion of an *abstract system* is to collect the commands available for the client or user of the *system*. The collection of commands comprising an abstract system are usually a (strict) subset of the commands available in the combined interface of the abstract data types involved. In other words, an abstract system provides a restricted interface, restricted to safeguard the user from breaking the protocol of interaction implicitly defined by the collection of abstract data types of which the system consists.

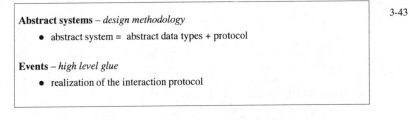

3-43

Abstract systems – *design methodology*
- abstract system = abstract data types + protocol

Events – *high level glue*
- realization of the interaction protocol

Slide 3-43: Abstract systems and events

An abstract system in itself merely provides a guideline on how a collection of objects is to be used, but does not offer a formal means to check whether a user plays by the rules. After presenting an example of an abstract system, we will look at how *events* may be used to protect the user against breaking the (implicit) laws governing the interaction.

Example – the library The abstract system comprising a library may be characterized as in slide 3-44. In essence, it provides an exemplary interface, that is, it lists the statements that are typically used by a client of the library software. We use typical identifiers to denote objects of the various types involved.

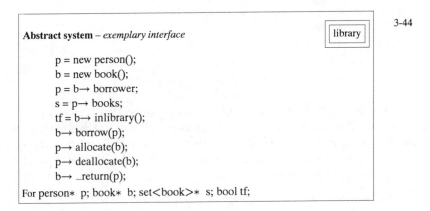

3-44

Abstract system – *exemplary interface*   library

```
        p = new person();
        b = new book();
        p = b→ borrower;
        s = p→ books;
        tf = b→ inlibrary();
        b→ borrow(p);
        p→ allocate(b);
        p→ deallocate(b);
        b→ _return(p);
For person∗ p; book∗ b; set<book>∗ s; bool tf;
```

Slide 3-44: The library system

The commands available to the user of the library software are constructors for a *person* and a *book*, an instruction to get access to the *borrower* of a particular book, an instruction to ask what books a particular person has borrowed, an instruction to query whether a particular book is in the library, and instructions for a person to *borrow* or *return* a book.

To realize the abstract system *library*, we evidently need the classes *book* and *person*. The class *book* may be defined as in slide 3-45.

It consists of a constructor, functions to *borrow* and *return* a book, a function to test whether the book is in the library and an instance variable containing the *borrower* of the book. Naturally, the class *book* may be improved with respect to encapsulation (by

```
class book {                                           book              3-45
public:
person* borrower;
book() {}
void borrow( person* p ) { borrower = p; }
void _return( person* p ) { borrower = 0; }
bool inlibrary() { return !borrower; }
};
```

Slide 3-45: The *book* class

providing a method to access the borrower) and may further be extended to store additional information, such as the title and publisher of the book.

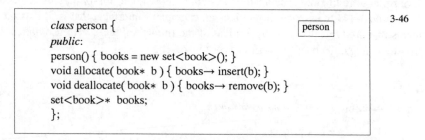

```
class person {                                         person            3-46
public:
person() { books = new set<book>(); }
void allocate( book* b ) { books→ insert(b); }
void deallocate( book* b ) { books→ remove(b); }
set<book>* books;
};
```

Slide 3-46: The *person* class

The next class involved in the *library* system is the class *person*, which is shown in slide 3-46. The class *person* offers a constructor, an instance variable to store the set of books borrowed by the person and the functions *allocate* and *deallocate* to respectively insert and remove the books from the person's collection. A typical example of using the library system is given below.

```
book* Stroustrup = new book();
book* ChandyMisra = new book();
book* Smalltalk80 = new book();

person* Hans = new person();
person* Cees = new person();

Stroustrup→ borrow(Hans);
Hans→ allocate(Stroustrup);
ChandyMisra→ borrow(Cees);
Cees→ allocate(ChandyMisra);
Smalltalk80→ borrow(Cees);
Cees→ allocate(Smalltalk80);
```

First, a number of books are defined, then a number of persons, and finally (some of) the books that are borrowed by (some of) the persons.

Note that lending a book involves both the invocation of *book* :: *borrow* and *person* :: *allocate*. This could easily be simplified by extending the function *book* :: *borrow* and *book* :: *_return* with the statements $p \rightarrow allocate(this)$ and $p \rightarrow deallocate(this)$ respectively. However, I would rather take the opportunity to illustrate the use of *events*, providing a generic solution to the interaction problem noted.

Events Henderson (1993) introduces *events* as a means by which to control the complexity of relating a user interface to the functionality provided by the classes comprising the library system. The idea underlying the use of events is that for every kind of interaction with the user a specific event class is defined that captures the details of the interaction between the user and the various object classes.   Abstractly, we may define an event as an entity with only two significant moments in its life-span, the moment of its *creation* (and initialization) and the moment of its *activation* (that is when it actually happens). As a class we may define an *event* as in slide 3-47.

3-47

class Event { | Event |

public:
virtual void *operator*()() = 0;
};

Slide 3-47: The *Event* class

The class *Event* is an abstract class, since the application operator that may be used to activate the event is defined as zero.

3-48

class Borrow : *public* Event { | Borrow |
public:
Borrow(person∗ _p, book∗ _b) { _b = b; _p = p; }
void *operator*()() {
    require(_b && _p);   // _b and _p exist
    _b→ borrow(p);
    _p→ allocate(b);
    }
private:
person∗ _p; book∗ _b;
};

Slide 3-48: The *Borrow* event class

For the *library* system defined above we may conceive of two actual events (that is, possible refinements of the *Event* class), namely a *Borrow* event and a *Return* event. See slides 3-48 and 3-49.

The *Borrow* event class provides a controlled way in which to effect the borrowing of a book. In a similar way, a *Return* event class may be defined as in slide 3-49.

3-49

```
class Return : public Event {                    Return
public:
Return( person* _p, book* _b ) { _b = b; _p = p; }
void operator()() {
    require( _b && _p );
    _b→ _return(p);
    _p→ deallocate(b);
    }
private:
person* _p; book* _b;
};
```

Slide 3-49: The *Return* event class

The operation *Has* specified in the previous section has an immediate counterpart in the *person :: books* data member and need not be implemented by a separate event.

Events are primarily used as intermediate between the user (interface) and the objects comprising the library system. For the application at hand, using events may seem to be somewhat of an overkill. However, as we will further illustrate in section 7.4, events not only give a precise characterization of the interactions involved but, equally as important, allow for extending the repertoire of interactions without disrupting the structure of the application simply by introducing additional event types.

Summary

This chapter presented an overview of the issues involved in the design of object-oriented software. The approach taken may be characterized as eclectic, in that various methods are referred to when illustrating design issues without commitment to a particular method or approach.

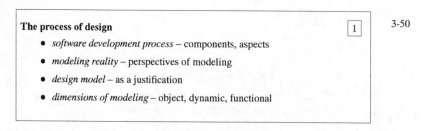

Slide 3-50: Section 3.1: The process of design

In section 1, we discussed the components or aspects of the software development process and characterized the perspectives of modeling associated with the various phases of development. We also looked at the various modeling dimensions distinguished in the OMT method.

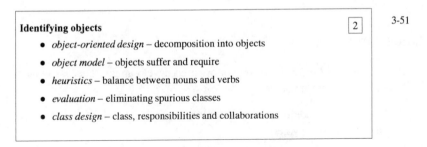

Slide 3-51: Section 3.2: Identifying objects

In section 2, we then discussed the issues that arise in defining an object model. We looked at heuristics for identifying objects, based on a linguistic analysis of the requirements document, and discussed the evaluation criteria that may be used for eliminating spurious classes. Also, the CRC method, which approaches class design by delineating responsibilities and collaborations, was illustrated with some examples.

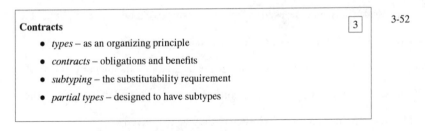

Slide 3-52: Section 3.3: Contracts

The object model resulting from an initial exploration may be formalized by employing types. In section 3, we discussed the notion of *contracts* as a means to characterize the behavioral aspects of types, specifying the restrictions and obligations of an object and its clients. We also looked at the requirements for subtype refinement and discussed the notion of partial types.

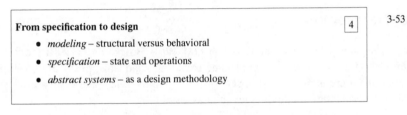
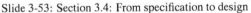

Slide 3-53: Section 3.4: From specification to design

In section 4, we discussed the distinction between structural and behavioral modeling. Also we looked at a model-based specification formalism and and discussed a design methodology employing *abstract systems* and events to realize the specification of user actions.

Questions

(1) Characterize the nature of object-oriented development. Discuss what aspects or components are involved.

(2) Describe the modeling activities that may occur in each of the various phases of the software life-cycle.

(3) What dimensions of modeling are distinguished in the OMT method? Give a short characterization.

(4) How would you characterize the differences between functional and object-oriented development methods?

(5) Give an outline of the steps required in object-oriented design.

(6) What heuristics can you think of for identifying objects?

(7) What criteria may be used to eliminate spurious classes from an initial object model?

(8) Explain the methods of CRC cards. Give an example.

(9) Explain how you may characterize the behavior of an object by means of a contract.

(10) What benefits may design by contract have for system developers? And for users?

(11) What are partial types? How may they be employed?

(12) Give a detailed account of the issues that arise in refining a contract.

(13) Characterize the differences between semantic modeling and object-oriented modeling.

(14) How would you characterize the notion of abstract systems?

(15) Explain how events may be employed to maintain system integrity.

Further reading

For further study, I recommend Booch (1994), Wirfs-Brock *et al.* (1990) and Rumbaugh *et al.* (1991). Also worthwhile are Henderson (1993) and Champeaux *et al.* (1993). Additional literature is mentioned in section 11.3. An overview and comparative study of design representation methods is given in Webster (1988).

4

Software engineering perspectives

The discipline of software engineering provides a number of techniques that aid the software developer (or development team) to construct reliable software. Testing, for example, is a technique to establish in an experimental way the reliability and robustness of software. Another way of validating a system is by means of correctness proofs, checking whether the program (design) meets its (formal) specification.

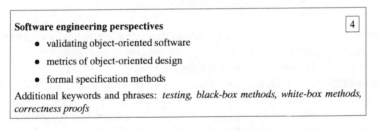

Software engineering perspectives   [4]

- validating object-oriented software
- metrics of object-oriented design
- formal specification methods

Additional keywords and phrases: *testing, black-box methods, white-box methods, correctness proofs*

Slide 4-1: Software engineering perspectives

Another area in which the discipline of software engineering has made a contribution is in measuring the structural complexity of software. Such measures may be used as indicators, for example to estimate the time needed to develop a system or the cost involved in maintenance. In this chapter, we will explore to what extent and how these techniques may be incorporated in an object-oriented approach. Also, the outline of a formal framework for developing object-oriented software will be sketched, merging the ideas developed when studying object-oriented design and the insights coming from a software engineering perspective.

4.1 Validating software

When validating a system a number of aspects play a role. First, it must be determined whether the software satisfies the original requirements and goals set by the user, as specified during analysis. Secondly, it must be established whether the system meets the specification laid down in the design document. The latter is usually referred to as 'verification'. Verification is only one of the aspects of validation, since validation is meant to establish whether the system is a *good* system in terms of user satisfaction, whereas the phrase verification is generally used to describe the process of establishing the correctness of software in a more formal sense. A third aspect of validation concerns the robustness of the system, that is the extent to which it can handle exceptional circumstances, such as excessive amounts of data and heavy workloads.

Software quality   4-2

- correctness – satisfies requirements and goals
- robustness – handles exceptional circumstances

Structural criteria

- maintenance – ease of adapting the software
- reuse – reusable components
- compatibility – plug-compatible components

Slide 4-2: Software quality

Validation is primarily concerned with the functional properties of a system. Questions that need to be answered are: Is the system capable of doing what it is expected to do? And, is the user satisfied with how the system does it?

In practice, the validation of a system is often restricted to functionality and user interface issues. However, other criteria, related to structural properties, are important as well. See slide 4-2. For example, a customer may want to know that the system may easily be adapted to changing circumstances or different platforms. Also, the customer may be interested in reusing components of the system to develop other applications. Actually, with the trend shifting from single applications to application frameworks and libraries, structural criteria are becoming increasingly important, since they determine the ease and reliability with which components may be used as building blocks for composing new applications. Correspondingly, the verification of the components constituting a system (or library) will become more important as well.

Testing is still the method most used for experimentally verifying the functional properties of a piece of software. In general, testing involves the execution of a program rather than formal methods of proof. In the sections that follow we will investigate what benefits we may expect from an object-oriented approach when it comes to testing.

4.1.1 Test methods

Testing is a relatively well-established discipline. It may be defined as *the process of judging experimentally whether a system or its components satisfy particular requirements*. The requirements are often laid down as a set of test data with which the system must comply.

Testing, essentially, is a way in which to expose errors. However, passing a test suite may simply indicate that the test suite is a feeble test.

Standard definitions of testing usually involve test cases and test procedures. Test cases define the input-output behavior of a program and test procedures specify how a program may be validated against a set of test data.

Smith and Robson (1990) note that the computation model of input-output transformations underlying traditional conceptions of testing is not entirely adequate for object-oriented systems. Instead, they propose to define the testing of object-oriented programs as *the process of exercising the routines provided by an object with the goal of uncovering errors in the implementation of the routines or the state of the object, or both.*

Three levels can be distinguished in the process of testing. A *strategic* level, which is primarily concerned with identifying the risks, that is the potentially dangerous components of a system that need to be validated with extra care. To decide which components involve high risks, metrics such as those described in section 4.3.1 may be of great value. Next, we have a *tactical* level, which for each component defines an appropriate test method and test set. And, finally, we have an *operational* level, consisting of the actual execution of the tests and evaluation of the test results. See slide 4-3.

4-3

Testing *– strategy, tactics, operational*

- the process of judging experimentally whether a system or component satisfies its specified requirements

Stop-criteria *– minimize effort, maximize confidence*

- after detecting N errors
- based on particular method
- if the ratio *errors/testtime* is sufficiently small

Paradigms

- demonstration, destruction, evaluation, prevention

Slide 4-3: Testing

As a rule, good testing practice is intended to minimize the effort in producing tests (in terms of time and costs), the number of tests and the effort of performing the tests, while maximizing the number of errors detected and (most importantly) the confidence in the software (in terms of the tests successfully passed).

One of the crucial moments in testing is to decide when to stop. Testing may halt either when the test results indicate that the system or component tested needs further improvement, or when the test results indicate that the system or component is sufficiently reliable. In principle, it is impossible to decide with absolute certainty that a piece of software is completely error-free. Usually, the particular method used will indicate when to stop testing. As a general stop-criterion, the ratio between errors and test time may be used. When the effort to detect another error reaches a certain limit, the system may be considered to be reliable. There is no need to say that there is a subjective moment involved in the decision to stop testing.

We can distinguish between four different paradigms of testing. We may consider it sufficient to demonstrate that the software behaves as required. However, this must be regarded as a very weak notion of testing. More appropriate, generally, is to construct tests with the actual intention of detecting errors. Although this may seem to be a rather destructive attitude towards software, it is the only way to gain confidence in the reliability of an actual system. However, already in the earlier stages of software development we may look for means to reduce potential errors by evaluation procedures such as are discussed in section 4.2.3. A step further in this direction would be to adopt a paradigm that actually prevents the occurrence of faults in the design and code. However, this requires a formal framework that for object-oriented programming has not yet been fully developed. See section 4.4.

Black-box versus white-box testing Traditionally, two approaches to testing can be distinguished. One approach is concerned only with the functionality, that is the input-output behavior of the component or system. The other approach takes into account the actual structure of the software as well. The first approach is known as *black-box testing*; the second as *white-box testing*, since the contents of the box may, as it were, be inspected. See slide 4-4.

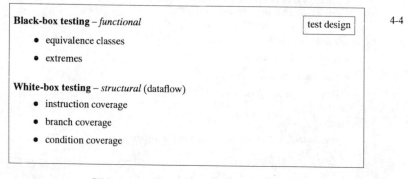

Slide 4-4: Black-box and white-box testing

To make black-box testing manageable, equivalent input is usually grouped in classes, from which a representative element is chosen when performing the actual test. In particular, attention needs to be paid to extremes, which may be regarded as equivalence classes with only a single element.

For example, when testing the function *sqrt* as specified in slide 4-5, a distinction may be made between input arguments greater than zero, precisely zero, and less than

4-5

Specification

- $r \equiv sqrt(x) \ \& \ x \geq 0 \Longleftrightarrow r^2 \equiv x$

Implementation

```
float sqrt( float x ) {
require( x ≥ 0 );
const float eps = 0.0001;
float guess = 1;
while( abs(x− guess ∗ guess )) > eps )
     guess = ( guess + x / guess ) / 2;
promise( guess ∗ guess− x ≤ eps );
return guess;
}
```

Slide 4-5: Specification and implementation

zero. This results in three cases that must be tested. For example, input values -2, 0 and 4 may be chosen. It could be argued, however, that the value 1 should be treated as another extremum, since *sqrt* behaves as the identity on 1.

As another example, imagine that we wish to test a function that sorts an array of integers, of maximal length say 1000. See slide 4-6. First, we need to select a number of different lengths, say 0, 1, 23 and 1000. For the latter two cases, we have the choice of filling the array with random-valued numbers, numbers in increasing order or numbers in decreasing order. For each of these distinct possibilities we need to select a number of test cases. The assumption underlying the use of equivalence classes is that one representative of a class is as good as any other. However, this works only when the assumptions on which our partition is based are sound. Moreover, our confidence will probably be stronger the more tests that are actually carried out.

White-box testing usually involves the notion of a computation graph, relating the different parts of the program by means of a flow-diagram. For white-box testing, criteria are used such as *instruction coverage* (showing that the test set executes each instruction at least once), *branch coverage* (showing that each possible branch in the program is taken at least once), or *condition coverage* (showing that the test set causes each condition to be true and false at least once).

These criteria impose increasingly stronger metrics on the flow-graph of the program and hence require more extensive testing to result in complete coverage. For example, when we consider the *bubble* sorting routine above, the array with values 5, 3 results in 100% instruction coverage, but not in 100% condition coverage since the condition r[j] > r[j+1] will never be false.

However, taking as input the array consisting of 5, 3, 7 we do have 100% condition coverage as well.

The test cycle Testing, as so many other things in software development, is usually an it-

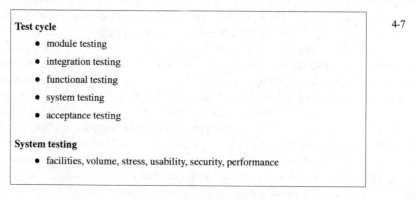

```
void bubble(int r[], int length) {          bubble          4-6
int k = length;
int sorted = 0;
while ( ( k > 0 ) && !sorted ) {
sorted = 1;
for( int j = 0; j < k ; j++ )
if ( r[j] > r[j+1] ) {
swap(r[j], r[j+1]);
sorted = 0;
}
k = k− 1;
}
}
```

Slide 4-6: The bubble function

erative process. A complete test cycle may be characterized as consisting of testing the functionality of each module, integration testing (to check whether the combination of modules has the desired effect), testing the system as a whole, and acceptance testing (in order to get user approval). See slide 4-7.

Test cycle   4-7

- module testing
- integration testing
- functional testing
- system testing
- acceptance testing

System testing

- facilities, volume, stress, usability, security, performance

Slide 4-7: The test cycle

System testing involves checking whether the system provides all the facilities required by the user and whether the user interface is satisfactory. Other aspects that may be of importance are the extent to which a system can cope with large volumes of data, whether it performs well on a heavily loaded network, whether it provides a sufficient level of security and whether the performance of the system is adequate in ordinary circumstances. For object-oriented software, the criteria of testing as well as the procedures of testing will virtually be the same. However, with respect to component testing (and to some extent, integration testing and functionality testing), we may expect significant differences.

4.1.2 Testing and inheritance

One of the most prominent claims made by adepts of an object-oriented approach is that code may easily and reliably be reused, even without access to the source code. This claim suggests that the inherited part of the code need not be re-tested. An example will be given, however, showing that this is only partially true. See slide 4-8. Like most such examples, it is a contrived one, but what it shows is that the correct behavior of a class can depend upon accidental properties of the class that may no longer hold when the code is being reused in a different context.

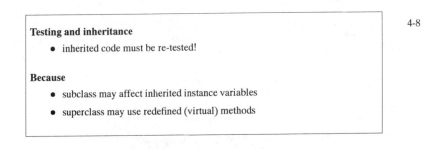

4-8

Testing and inheritance
- inherited code must be re-tested!

Because
- subclass may affect inherited instance variables
- superclass may use redefined (virtual) methods

Slide 4-8: Testing and inheritance

As a general rule, inherited code must be re-tested. One reason for this is that a subclass may affect inherited instance variables. This is a problem especially when using a language that does not provide encapsulation for derived classes, such as Eiffel. However, in Eiffel appropriate pre-conditions can save you from violation by derived classes. In contrast, C++ does allow such encapsulation (by means of the keyword *private*), but inherited instance variables may still be accessed when they are declared *protected* or when a method returns a (non const) reference. See section 2.5.1. Another reason not to assume that inherited code is reliable is that the inherited class may employ virtual functions which may be redefined by the derived class. Redefining a virtual function may violate the assumptions underlying the definition of the base class or may conflict with the accidental properties of the base class, resulting in erroneous behavior.

Example – violating the invariant The example shown in slide 4-9 illustrates that redefining a virtual function, even in a very minor way, may lead to a violation of the invariant of the base class. Actually, the invariant ($n \geq 0$) is an accidental property of the class, due to the fact that the square of both positive and negative numbers is always positive.

Testing instances of class A will not reveal that the invariant is based on incorrect assumptions, since whatever input is used, invoking *value*() will always result in a positive number. However, when an instance of B is created, invoking *strange*() will result in an error. See slide 4-10.

The example illustrates what happens when instances of a derived class (B) are behaviorally not conforming with their base class (A). The penalty of non-conformance is, as the example clearly shows, that functions defined for inputs of the base class no longer behave reliably, since instances of derived classes (although legally typed) may violate the assumptions pertaining to the base class.

```
class A {                              invariant A: n ≥ 0        4-9
public:
A() { n = 0; }
int value() { return next(n); }
void strange() { next(-3); }
protected:
virtual int next( int i ) { return n = n + i * i; }
int n;
};


class B : public A {                   not invariant A
public:
B() : A() { }
protected:
virtual int next( int i ) { return n = n + (n + 1) * i; }
};
```

Slide 4-9: Violating the invariant

```
Test cases                                                      4-10

      A* a = new A; a→ value(); a→ strange(); a→ value();   // ok
      A* b = new B; b→ value(); b→ strange(); b→ value(); // error


Dynamic binding

      int f(A* a) {
            a→ strange();
            return a→ value();
      }
```

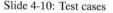

Slide 4-10: Test cases

As an aside, it should be noted that the problems illustrated above would not have occurred so easily if the invariant and the behavior of the base and derived classes had been made explicit by means of a *client-server contract*. Moreover, annotating the methods with the proper pre- and post-conditions would allow automatic monitoring of the runtime consistency of the objects.

4.2 A framework for testing object-oriented programs

Presently, we have no generally accepted framework for testing object-oriented systems. However, it seems likely that we can to some extent reuse the insights and methods coming from traditional testing practice. Further, it seems that we may gain great benefits from adopting a contract based design discipline. In the following, we will study what influence the architectural structure of object-oriented systems has on the practice of testing. In particular, we will look at ways in which to test that the actual behavior of an object conforms to our expectations.

Levels of testing Adopting an object-oriented approach will generally have a significant influence on the (architectural) structure of the program. Consequently, there will be a somewhat different distinction between levels of testing in comparison with a functional approach. The difference arises from the fact that in an object-oriented system the algorithm is distributed over a number of classes, involving multiple methods, whereas in a functional decomposition the components directly reflect the structure of the algorithm. Another difference comes from the fact that the notion of *module* in an object-oriented system encompasses both the concept of a *class* and the concept of a *cluster*, which is to be understood as a collection of (cooperating) classes. See slide 4-11.

Levels of testing   4-11

- algorithms – methods
- class – interaction between methods and instance variables
- cluster – interaction between groups of classes
- system – encompasses all classes

Influence of errors

- error is not executed
- error is executed but has no effect
- error results in legal state
- error results in illegal state

Slide 4-11: Levels of testing

When testing a system, a collection of objects, or an individual object, the effect that an error may not always be visible should be taken into account. It may be the case that erroneous code is simply not executed, or that the error is executed but without any effect on the results of the computation (as was the case for the instance of class *A* discussed previously). A further distinction must be made between errors that do have an effect on the computation, but nevertheless result in a legal (although erroneous) state, and errors that leave the computation in an illegal state. To understand what this means, however, we need to delineate more precisely the notion of *state*.

4.2.1   Testing the behavior of objects

To test the behavior of an object it is necessary to have some knowledge of the internal structure of the object, that is the state the object may be in at successive moments of the computation. For example, a *counter* object may be regarded as having two states, an initial state *zero* and a state in which the instance variable is greater than *zero*. On the other hand, for a *bounded counter*, bounded by *max*, three states must be distinguished: an initial state *zero*, a state characterized by $0 < n < max$ (where n is the instance variable of the bounded counter), and a state *max* that represents the terminal state of the counter, unless it can be reset to *zero*. Although many more states could have been distinguished, it suffices to consider only three states, since all the states (strictly) between *zero* and *max* may regarded as being equivalent. Since the actual parameters of a method may influence the transition from one object state to another object state, the values of these parameters must also be taken into account, in a similar way as when testing the extremum input values of a function. See slide 4-12.

Object test methods – *state transitions*   4-12

  • *equivalence classes* – distinct object states

  • *extrema testing* – includes parameters of methods

Errors – *wrong result, illegal state change*

  • *within object* – invariance

  • *involving multiple objects* – interaction protocols

Slide 4-12: Object test methods

The actual testing may occur with reference to a transition matrix displaying the effect of each method invocation.

Inspecting a transition matrix based on the internal state of the (instance variables of) the object may seem to be in contradiction with the principle of encapsulation encouraged in the chapter on design. However, providing a means to observe the state of an object is different from allowing clients unrestricted access to its instance variables.

As an example, consider the transition matrices for a *counter* and a *bounded counter* displayed in slide 4-13. Two states are distinguished for the counter, respectively (1) for the state $n = 0$ and (2) for the state $n > 0$, where we assume that the counter has an instance variable n to keep the actual count. For the *bounded counter* an additional state is added to allow for the possibility that $n = max$. Checking the behavior of these (admittedly very simple) objects may take place by a sequence of method calls followed by a check to determine whether the expected state changes have taken place.

For example, when incrementing a counter initialized to zero we must observe a state change from (1) to (2).

The important cases to test are the borderline cases. For instance, what happens when we decrement a newly created counter? With regard to the definition of the counter, as expressed by the pre- and post-conditions given in the transition matrix, this operation must be considered illegal since it will lead to an inconsistent state. What to do in such cases depends upon the policy taken when designing the object.

When what Meyer (1988) calls a *defensive programming* approach is followed, calling the method will be allowed but the illegal state change will not occur. When following the (preferred) method of *programming by contract* the method call results in a

4-13

Transition matrix – *counter*

function	(1) : $n = 0$	(2) : $0 < n$
inc(i)	2	2
dec(i)	–	1,2
value()	1	2

Transition matrix – *bounded counter*

function	(1) : $n = 0$	(2) : $0 < n < max$	(3) : $n = max$
inc()	2,3	2,3	3
dec()	–	1,2	2
value()	1	2	3

Slide 4-13: Transition matrix

failure due to the violation of a pre-condition, since the user did not conform to the protocol specified in the contract. We will consider this issue further when discussing runtime consistency checking in section 4.2.2.

Identity transitions Obviously, for other than very simple objects the number of states and the transitions to test for may become quite unwieldy. Hence, a state transition matrix enumerating all the interesting states in general seems not to be a practical solution. A better solution lies in looking for sequences of method calls that have an identical begin and end state. In slide 4-14, some of the identity transition sequences for the counter are given, but obviously there are many more.

One of the interesting features of identity transitions is that they may easily be checked by an automated test tool.

A tool employing identity transitions is discussed in Smith and Robson (1990). The tool generates arbitrarily many sequences of method calls resulting in an identity transition, and also generates the code to test these sequences, that is whether they actually leave the state of the object unaffected.

The idea of identity transitions ultimately derives from the axiomatic characterization of invariance properties of abstract data types. For example, when specifying the behavior of a *stack* algebraically, one of the axioms will be of the form $pop(push(s, x)) = s$, expressing that first pushing an element on the stack and then popping it results in an identical stack. (See section 8.2 for a more detailed discussion of abstract data types.) In contrast, we know that this property does not hold for a queue, unless the queue involved is the empty queue.

The advantage of the method of testing for identity transitions is that we need not explicitly specify the individual states and state transitions associated with each method. However, to use automated testing tools, the method requires that we are able to specify by what rules sequences of method calls resulting in identity transitions may be constructed. Moreover, we cannot be sure that we have tested all relevant properties of the

Identity transitions   4-14

>   counter c; int n1, n2;
>   n1 = c.value(); c.inc(1); c.dec(1); n2 = c.value();
>   n1 = c.value(); c.inc(1); c.inc(2); c.dec(3); n2 = c.value();

Abstract data types

- stack – $pop(push(s, x)) = s$
- queue – $remove(insert(q, x)) \neq q$

Interaction protocols

- tests all interesting interaction sequences

Slide 4-14: Identity transitions and interaction protocols

object, unless we can prove this from its formal specification.

Most difficult to detect, however, are errors that result from not complying to some (implicitly stated) protocol related to multiple objects. For an example, think of the *model-view* protocol outlined in section 3.2.3. When the initialization of the *model-view* pairs is not properly done, for instance when a *view* is not initialized with a *model*, an error will occur when updating the value of the *model*. Such requirements are hard if not impossible to specify by means of merely client/server contracts, since possibly multiple objects are involved along with a sequence of method invocations. We will look at formal methods providing support for these issues in section 10.5.

Another tool for testing sequences of method invocations is described in Doong and Frankl (1990). The approach relies on an algebraic specification of the properties of the object, and seems to be suitable primarily for testing associativity and commutativity properties of methods.

4.2.2   Runtime consistency checking

Debugging is a hopelessly time-consuming and unrewarding activity. Unless the testing process is guided by clearly specified criteria on what to test for, testing in the sense of looking for errors must be considered as ordinary debugging, that is running the system to see what will happen. Client/server contracts, as introduced in section 3.3 as a method for design, do offer such guidelines in that they enable the programmer to specify precisely the restrictions characterizing the legal states of the object, as well as the conditions that must be satisfied in order for legal state transitions to occur. See slide 4-15.

The Eiffel language is the first (object-oriented) language in which assertions were explicitly introduced as a means to develop software and to monitor the runtime consistency of a system.

Contracts as supported by Eiffel were primarily influenced by notions concerning the construction of correct programs. The unique contribution of Meyer (1988) consists

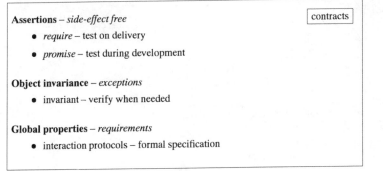

Slide 4-15: Runtime consistency checking

of showing that these notions may be employed operationally by specifying the pragmatic meaning of pre- and post-conditions defining the behavior of methods. To use assertions operationally, however, the assertion language must be restricted to side-effect free boolean expressions in the language being used.

Combined with a bottom-up approach to development, the notion of contracts gives rise to the following guidelines for testing. Post-conditions and invariance assertions should primarily be checked during development. When sufficient confidence is gained in the reliability of the object definitions, checking these assertions may be omitted in favor of efficiency. However, pre-conditions must be checked when delivering the system to ensure that the user complies with the protocol specified by the contract.

When delivering the system, it is a matter of contractual agreement between the deliverer and user whether pre- and/or post-conditions will be enabled. The safest option is to enable them both, since the violation of a pre-condition may be caused by an undetected violated post-condition.

In addition, the method of testing for identity transitions may be used to cover higher level invariants, involving multiple objects. To check whether the conditions with respect to complex interaction protocols are satisfied, explicit consistency checks need to be inserted by the programmer. See also section 10.5.

Example – robust programming As an example of how assertions may be applied to characterize the possible states of an object and to guard its runtime consistency, consider the doubly-bounded counter in slide 4-16.

The counter has both a lower and upper bound that are set when constructing the object. Both the functions *inc* and *dec* have pre-conditions, respectively stating that incrementing the counter is legal only when its value is less than its upper bound and, similarly, that decrementing a counter may be done only when its value is greater than its lower bound. This characterization is clearly equivalent to a characterization as given by the transition matrix for a bounded counter.

The implementation of the counter is robust, since it guards clients against possible misuse. The advantage of using assertions, apart from providing checks to test legal usage, is that they explicitly state the requirements imposed on the user.

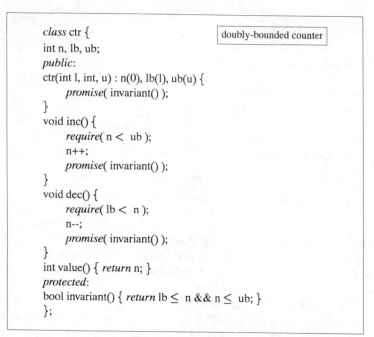

4-16

```
class ctr {                          doubly-bounded counter
int n, lb, ub;
public:
ctr(int l, int, u) : n(0), lb(l), ub(u) {
     promise( invariant() );
}
void inc() {
     require( n <  ub );
     n++;
     promise( invariant() );
}
void dec() {
     require( lb <  n );
     n--;
     promise( invariant() );
}
int value() { return n; }
protected:
bool invariant() { return lb ≤ n && n ≤ ub; }
};
```

Slide 4-16: Robust programming

Example – binary tree As a slightly less academic example (due to Meyer, 1992b), consider the implementation of a binary tree, consisting of nodes that are kept in a certain order. See slide 4-17.

How a node is actually inserted is not important; the only requirement imposed is simply that the inserted node does exist. However, we must guarantee that, in whatever way the node is inserted, the (ordered) structure of the tree is preserved. This requirement is expressed in the *invariant*, which states that whenever a child does exist, it points to the current object as its parent.

Now, when it comes to testing, we may wish to check more thoroughly whether the ordered structure of the tree is indeed preserved when inserting a node. This may be done in a non-intrusive way by refining the *tree* class as in slide 4-18.

Assume that we have defined a function *sorted*() to check whether the tree has the right order. Because the original tree invariant has been defined as a virtual function, we may rely on the dynamic binding mechanism to check the strengthened invariant when inserting a node. Thus, without much trouble, we have created a more robust version of the tree that may be used during testing and later be replaced by the original version.

4.2.3 Static testing

The test methods just described, whether organized around transition matrices or contracts, both involve the execution of the program and looking for errors. Either way, this

4-17

```
template< class T >                          binary tree
class tree {
public:
tree( tree<T>* p, T& n ) : parent(p) {
        left = right = 0;
        node = n;
        }
void insert( tree<T>* t ) {
        require( t != 0 );
        insert_node( t );
        promise( invariant() );
        }
virtual bool invariant() {
    return ( left == 0 || left→ parent == this ) &&
    ( right == 0 || right→ parent == this );
}
protected:
tree<T> * left, * right, * parent;
void insert_node(tree<T>* t);        // does the real work
T& node;
};
```

Slide 4-17: Checking invariants

is a laborious and time-consuming task. To avoid dynamic testing, several methods of
program validation have been proposed that do not require the program to run. These
methods may be referred to as *static testing*. One of the oldest, and perhaps most fruitful, methods is simply *careful reading*. Fiedler (1989) reports that in an experimental setting most errors were detected by carefully reading the relevant program text. The most
explicit proponent of this method is undoubtly Knuth (1992), who has proposed (and
demonstrated) the discipline of *literate programming*. Although tools supporting *literate*

4-18

```
template< class T >
class sortedtree : public tree<T> {          test version
public:
sortedtree( tree<T>* p, T& n ):tree<T>(p,n){}
protected:
bool invariant() {return sorted()&&tree<T>::invariant();}
int sorted();                        // check for order
};
```

Slide 4-18: Test version

programming in C++ are available (see section 11.3.3), no environment is as yet available that fully supports literate programming in an object-oriented style. See slide 4-19.

Methods for static testing   4-19

- careful reading – most successful (?)
- code inspection – looking for errors
- walkthrough – simulation game
- correctness proof – rigorous, but complex

Slide 4-19: Static testing

Another method of *static testing*, based on similar assumptions, is groupwise *code inspection*. This method may profitably be used by teams of programmers. Although the attention is primarily directed towards the detection of errors, the method has proved to be beneficial for improving the code. An additional advantage is that it provides a background for discussing terminological issues, programming practice and opportunities for code reuse.

More directed towards operational issues is the method of *walkthroughs*. A *walkthrough* is similar to the simulation game proposed for CRC cards (see section 3.2.2). The idea is that by simulating a computation, while reading the relevant parts of the code, errors will come to light. As for code inspection, walkthroughs are best performed in a group.

When employing groupwise code inspection it is advisable to have a small group of about four people, with a chairman to organize the meeting and with the author of the code as a silent observer. Each participant should receive the code and documentation a few days ahead, as well as a checklist with commonly occurring errors. As a goal, the actual meeting should result in a list of faults detected in the code.

A quite different method of *static testing*, which in contrast to the previous methods is *not* often used in practice, is to provide correctness proofs for the relevant parts of the program. Proving a program correct is by far the most rigorous of all methods discussed, but unfortunately quite complex and demanding with respect to the formal skills of the programmer. However, actually proving a program correct seems to be far more difficult than only annotating the program with appropriate invariants and pre- and postconditions. I believe that the notion of contracts provides a valuable means both to reason about the program and to check (dynamically) for the runtime consistency of a system, even without detailed correctness proofs.

Not as a means of static testing but as a way of increasing our belief in the reliability of software, it may be advisable to take recourse to bottom-up development. According to Meyer (1988), an object-oriented approach lends itself extremely well to bottom-up development. Instead of trying to grasp the functionality of a system as a whole, small well-understood building blocks may be constructed (preferably documented by *contracts*) which may be used for increasingly complex abstractions.

4.3   Guidelines for design

Computing is a relatively young discipline. Despite its short history, a number of styles and schools promoting a particular style have emerged. However, in contrast to other disciplines such as the fine arts (including architecture) and musical composition, there is no well-established tradition of what is to be considered as *good taste* with respect to software design. There is an on-going and somewhat pointless debate as to whether software design must be looked at as an *art* or must be promoted into a *science*. See, for example, Knuth (1992) and Gries (1981). The debate has certainly resulted in new technology but has not, I am afraid, resulted in universally valid design guidelines.

The notion of *good design* in the other disciplines is usually implicitly defined by a collection of examples of good design, as preserved in museums or (art or music) historical works. For software design, we are still a long way from anything like a museum, setting the standards of good design. Nevertheless, a compendium of examples of object-oriented applications such as Pinson and Wiener (1990) and Harmon and Tayler (1993), if perhaps not setting the standards for good design, may certainly be instructive.

Development process – *cognitive factors*
- model → realize → refine

Design criteria – natural, flexible, reusable
- abstraction – *types*
- modularity – *strong cohesion* (class)
- structure – *subtyping*
- information hiding – *narrow interfaces*
- complexity – *weak coupling*

4-20

Slide 4-20: Criteria for design

The software engineering literature abounds with advice and tools to measure the quality of good design. In slide 4-20, a number of the criteria commonly found in software engineering texts is listed. In software design, we evidently strive for a high level of abstraction (as enabled by a notion of types and a corresponding notion of *contracts*), a modular structure with strongly cohesive units (as supported by the class construct), with units interrelated in a precisely defined way (for instance by a client/server or subtype relation). Other desirable properties are a high degree of information hiding (that is narrowly defined and yet complete interfaces) and a low level of complexity (which may be achieved with units that have only weak coupling, as supported by the client/server model). An impressive list, indeed.

Design is a human process, in which *cognitive factors* play a critical role. The role of cognitive factors is reflected in the so-called *fractal design process model* introduced in Johnson and Foote (1988), which describes object-oriented development as a triangle with bases labeled by the phrases *model, realize* and *refine*. This triangle may be iterated at each of the bases, and so on. The iterative view of software development does justice to the importance of human understanding, since it allows for a simultaneous understanding of the problem domain and the mechanisms needed to model the domain and the system architecture.

Good design involves taste. My personal definition of good design would certainly also involve cognitive factors (*is the design understandable?*), including subjective criteria such as *is it pleasant to read or study the design?*

In contrast to the arts, however, software can be subjected to metrics measuring the cohesiveness and complexity of the system. In this section, we will look at a number of metrics which may, if well-established and supported by empirical evidence, be employed for managing software development projects. Also we will look at the *Law of Demeter*, which is actually not a law but which may act as a guideline for developing class interfaces. And finally, we will have a look at some guidelines for individual class design.

4.3.1   Metrics for object-oriented design

Object-oriented software development is a relatively new technology, still lacking empirical guidance and quantitative methods to measure progress and productivity. In Chidamber and Kemerer (1991), a suite of metrics is proposed that may aid in managing object-oriented software development projects, and, as the authors suggest, may be used also to establish to what extent an object-oriented approach has indeed been followed. See slide 4-21.

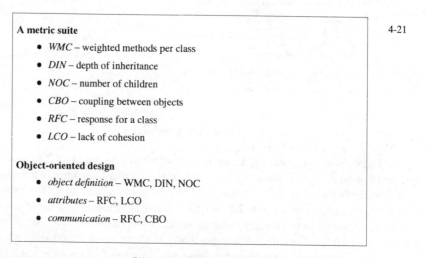

Slide 4-21: A metric suite

In general, quantitative measures of the size and complexity of software may aid in project planning and project evaluation, and may be instrumental in establishing the productivity of tools and techniques and in estimating the cost of both development and maintenance of a system.

The metrics proposed in Chidamber and Kemerer (1991) pertain to three distinct elements of object-oriented design, namely the definition of objects and their relation to other objects, the attributes and/or properties of objects, and the (potential) communication between objects. The authors motivate their proposal by remarking that existing metrics do no justice to the notions of classes, inheritance, encapsulation and message passing, since they were developed primarily from a function-oriented view, separating data and procedures.

Definitions To perform measurements on a program or design, we need to be able to describe the structure of a program or design in language-independent terms. As indicated below, the identifiers x, y and z will be used to name objects. Occasionally, we will use the term $class(x)$ to refer to the class of which object x is an instance. The term $iv(x)$ will be used to refer to the set of instance variables of the object x, and likewise $methods(x)$ will be used to refer to the set of methods that exists for x. Combined, the instance variables and methods of an object x are regarded as the *properties* of x. See slide 4-22.

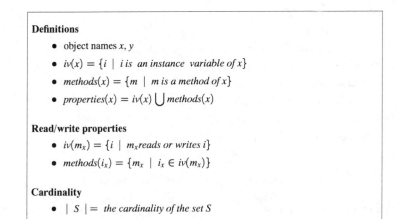

4-22

Definitions

- object names x, y
- $iv(x) = \{i \mid i \text{ is an instance variable of } x\}$
- $methods(x) = \{m \mid m \text{ is a method of } x\}$
- $properties(x) = iv(x) \bigcup methods(x)$

Read/write properties

- $iv(m_x) = \{i \mid m_x \text{reads or writes } i\}$
- $methods(i_x) = \{m_x \mid i_x \in iv(m_x)\}$

Cardinality

- $\mid S \mid = \text{the cardinality of the set } S$

Slide 4-22: Definitions

An important property for an instance variable is whether it is read or written by a method. The set of instance variables read or written by a particular method m_x will be referred to by the term $iv(m_x)$. Likewise, the set of methods that either read or write a particular instance variable is referred to by the term $methods(i_x)$.

A number of metrics are defined by taking the cardinality of some set. The cardinality of a set is simply the number of elements it contains. To refer to the cardinality of a set S, the notation $\mid S \mid$ will be used.

In addition, we need predicates to characterize the inheritance structure of a program or design. The term $root(x)$ will be used to refer to the root of the inheritance hierarchy of which $class(x)$ is a member. The term $descendants(x)$ will be used to refer to the set of classes of which $class(x)$ is a direct ancestor, and the term $distance(x, y)$ will be used to indicate the distance between $class(x)$ and $class(y)$ in the inheritance hierarchy. The distance will be one if y is a descendant of x and undefined if x and y are not related by inheritance.

To describe the potential communication between objects the term x *uses* y will be used to state that object x calls some method of y. The term x *calls* m_y is used to specify more precisely that x calls the method m_y.

Evaluation criteria Before discussing the individual metrics, we need to know by what criteria we may establish that a proposed metric is a valid instrument for measuring properties of a program. One means of validating a metric is gathering empirical evidence to determine whether a metric has predictive value, for instance with respect to the cost of maintaining software. Lacking empirical evidence, Chidamber and Kemerer (1991) establish the validity of their metrics with reference to criteria adapted from Weyuker (1988). See slide 4-23. The criteria proposed by Weyuker (1988) concern well-known complexity measures such as *cyclomatic number, programming effort, statement count* and *data flow complexity*.

Evaluation criteria   4-23

  (i) non-coarseness $-\exists x\exists y \bullet \mu(x) \neq \mu(y)$

 (ii) non-uniqueness $-\exists x\exists y \bullet \mu(x) = \mu(y)$

(iii) permutation $-\exists x\exists y \bullet y$ *is a permutation of* $x \wedge \mu(x) \neq \mu(y)$

(iv) implementation $-\forall x\forall y \bullet fun(x) = fun(y) \not\Rightarrow \mu(x) = \mu(y)$

 (v) monotonicity $-\forall x\forall y \bullet \mu(x) \leq \mu(x+y)$ & $\mu(y) \leq \mu(x+y)$

(vi) interaction $-\forall x\forall y\exists z \bullet \mu(x) = \mu(y) \wedge \mu(x+z) \neq \mu(y+z)$

(vii) combination $-\exists x\exists y \bullet \mu(x) + \mu(y) < \mu(x+y)$

Slide 4-23: Criteria for the evaluation of metrics

As a first criterion (i), it may be required that a metric has discriminating power, which means that there are at least two objects which give a different result. Another criterion (ii) is that the metric in question imposes some notion of equivalence, meaning that two distinct objects may deliver the same result for that particular metric.

As a third criterion (iii), one may require that a permutation (that is a different ordering of the elements) of an object gives a different result. None of the proposed metrics, however, satisfy this criterion. This may not be very surprising, considering that the method interface of an object embodies what Meyer (1988) calls a *shopping list*, which means that it contains all the services needed in an intrinsically unordered fashion.

The next criterion (iv) is that the actual implementation is of importance for the outcome of the metric. In other words, even though two objects perform the same function, the details of the implementation matter when determining the complexity of a system.

Another property that a metric must satisfy (v) is the property of *monotonicity*, which implies that a single object is always less complex than when it is in some way combined with another object. This seems to be a reasonable requirement, however for objects located in distinct branches of the inheritance graph this need not always be the case.

Another requirement that may be imposed on a metric (vi) is that it shows that two equivalent objects may behave differently when placed in a particular context. This requirement is not satisfied by one of the metrics (RFC), which may be an indication that the metric must be refined.

Finally, the last property (vii) requires that a metric must reflect that decomposition may reduce the complexity of design. Interestingly, none of the proposed methods satisfy this requirement. According to Chidamber and Kemerer (1991), this raises the issue *"that complexity could increase, not reduce as a design is broken into more objects"*.

To conclude, evidently more research, including empirical validation, is required before adopting any metric as a reliable measure for the complexity of a design. Nevertheless, the metrics discussed below provide an invaluable starting point for such an effort.

In the following sections, the individual metrics (WMC, DIN, NOC, CBO, RFC, LCO) will be characterized. For each metric, a formal definition will be given, and the notions underlying the definition characterized. Further, for each metric we will look at its implications for the practice of software development and establish (or disprove) the properties related to the evaluation criteria discussed previously.

Weighted methods per class The first metric we look at provides a measure for the complexity of a single object. The assumption underlying the metric is that both the number of methods as well as the complexity of each method (expressed by its weight) determines the total complexity of the object. See slide 4-24.

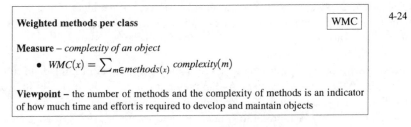

Slide 4-24: Weighted methods per class

The WMC measure pertains to the definition of an object. From a software engineering perspective, we may regard the measure as an indicator of how much time and effort is required to develop and maintain the object (class). In general, objects having many (complex) methods are not likely to be reusable, but must be assumed to be tied to a particular application.

To illustrate that property (vii) indeed does not hold for this metric, consider objects x and y with respectively n_x and n_y methods. Assume that x and y have δ methods in common. Then $n_x + n_y - \delta \leq n_x + n_y$, and hence $\mu(x + y) \leq \mu(x) + \mu(y)$, where $x + y$ denotes the combination of objects x and y.

Depth of inheritance The second metric (DIN) is a measure for the depth of the (class of the) object in the inheritance hierarchy. The measure is directly related to the scope of properties, since it indicates the number of classes from which the class inherits its functionality.

For design, the greater the depth of the class in the inheritance hierarchy the greater will be its expected complexity, since apart from the methods defined for the class itself

the methods inherited from classes higher in the hierarchy are also involved. The metric
may also be used as an indication for reuse, that is reuse by inheritance. See slide 4-25.

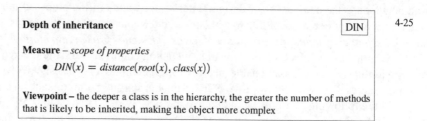

Slide 4-25: Depth of inheritance

Satisfaction of criteria (i), (ii) and (iv) is easily established. With respect to property (v), the monotonicity property, three cases must be distinguished. Recall that the
property states that for any object x it holds that $\mu(x) \leq \mu(x + y)$. Now assume that
y is a child of x and $\mu(x) = n$, then $\mu(y) = n + 1$. But combining x and y will give
$\mu(x + y) = n$ and $\mu(x + y) < \mu(y)$, hence property (v) is not satisfied. When x and y
are siblings, then $\mu(x) = \mu(y) = \mu(x + y) + 1$, hence property (v) is satisfied. Finally,
assume that x and y are not directly connected by inheritance and x and y are not siblings. Now if x and y are collapsed to the class lowest in the hierarchy, property (v) is
satisfied. However, this need not be the case. Just imagine that $class(x)$ is collapsed with
$root(x)$. Then, obviously, the monotonicity property is not satisfied.

Number of children The third metric (NOC) gives the number of immediate subclasses
of $class(x)$ in the class hierarchy. As the previous metric, it is related to the scope of
properties. It is also a measure of reuse, since it indicates how many subclasses inherit the
methods of $class(x)$. According to Chidamber and Kemerer (1991), it is generally better to have depth than breadth in the class hierarchy, since depth promotes reuse through
inheritance. Anyway, the number of descendants may be an indication of the influence
of the class on the design. Consequently, a class scoring high on this metric may require
more extensive testing. See slide 4-26.

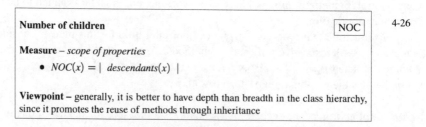

Slide 4-26: Number of children

The reader is invited to check that properties (i), (ii), (iv) and (v) are satisfied. Recall that property (vi) states that for some objects y and z, if $\mu(x) = \mu(y)$ then x might

behave differently when combined with z, that is $\mu(x + z) \neq \mu(y + z)$. Assume that $class(x)$ and $class(y)$ both have n children, that is $\mu(x) = \mu(y) = n$, and let $class(z)$ be a child of $class(x)$, and assume that $class(z)$ has r children. Then combining $class(x)$ and $class(z)$ will result in a class with $n - 1 + r$ children, whereas combining $class(y)$ and $class(z)$ will result in a class with $n + r$ children, which means that $\mu(x + z) \neq \mu(y + z)$ and hence that property (vi) is satisfied.

Coupling between objects The next metric (CBO) measures non-inheritance related connections with other classes. It is based on the notion that two objects are related if either one acts on the other, and as such is a measure of coupling, that is the degree of interdependence between objects.

As phrased in Chidamber and Kemerer (1991), *excessive coupling between objects outside of the inheritance hierarchy is detrimental to modular design and prevents reuse.* In other words, objects with a low degree of interdependence are generally more easily reused. Note that coupling, as expressed by the metric, is not transitive, that is, if x uses y and y uses z, then it is not necessarily the case that x also uses z. In fact, a famous style guideline discussed in section 4.3.2 is based on the intuition underlying this metric.

A high degree of coupling may indicate that testing the object may require a lot of effort, since other parts of the design are likely to be involved as well. As a general rule, a low degree of inter-object coupling should be strived for. See slide 4-27.

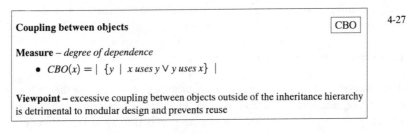

Slide 4-27: Coupling between objects

Establishing properties (i), (ii), (iv), (v) and (vi) is left to the (diligent) reader. However, we will prove property (vii) to be invalid. Recall that property (vii) states that there exist objects x and y for which $\mu(x) + \mu(y) \leq \mu(x + y)$, meaning that for those objects the complexity of x combined with y is higher than the total complexity of x and y in isolation. Just pick arbitrary objects x and y, and assume that x and y have $\delta \geq 0$ couplings in common, for example both use an object z. Now $\mu(x + y) = \mu(x) + \mu(y) - \delta$, and hence $\mu(x + y) \leq \mu(x) + \mu(y)$, contradicting property (vii). Strongly when $\delta > 0$.

Response for a class Our fifth metric (RFC) is based on the notion of *response set*. The *response set* of an object may be characterized as the set of methods it has available, consisting of the methods of its class and the methods of other objects that may be invoked by any of its own methods. This metric may be regarded as a measure of the communication that may occur between the object and other objects. If primarily (potential) extraneous method invocations are responsible for the size of the *response set*, it may be expected that testing the object will be difficult and will require a lot of knowledge of other parts of the design. See slide 4-28.

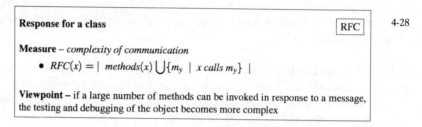

Slide 4-28: Response for a class

Establishing properties (i) and (iii) is left to the reader. To establish property (iv), stating that not only function but also implementation is important, it suffices to see that the actual implementation determines which and how many (extraneous) methods will be called. Property (v), monotonicity, follows from the observation that for any object y, it holds that $\mu(x + y) \geq max(\mu(x), \mu(y))$ and hence $\mu(x + y) \geq \mu(x)$. According to Chidamber and Kemerer (1991), property (vi) is not satisfied. To disprove property (vi) it must be shown that given a object x and an object y for which $\mu(x) = \mu(y)$, there is no object z that provides a context discriminating between x and y, in other words for which $\mu(x + z) \neq \mu(y + z)$. The proof given in Chidamber and Kemerer (1991) relies on the assumption that $\mu(x + y) = max(\mu(x), \mu(y))$, whereas one would expect $\mu(x + y) \geq max(\mu(x), \mu(y))$. However, assuming the latter, property (vi) indeed holds. Property (vii), nevertheless, may again be proven to be invalid.

Lack of cohesion The last metric (LCO) we will look at is based on the notion of *degree of similarity* of methods. If methods have no instance variables in common, their degree of similarity is zero. A low degree of similarity may indicate a lack of cohesion. As a measure for the lack of cohesion the number of disjoint sets partitioning the instance variables is taken. Cohesiveness of methods within a class is desirable, since it promotes encapsulation of objects. For design, lack of cohesion may indicate that the class is better split up into two or more distinct classes. See slide 4-29.

Establishing properties (i), (ii) and (iv) is left to the reader. To establish the monotonicity property (v), that is $\mu(x) \leq \mu(x + y)$ & $\mu(y) \leq \mu(x + y)$ for arbitrary y, consider that combining objects may actually reduce the number of different sets, that is $\mu(x + y) = \mu(x) + \mu(y) - \delta$ for some $\delta \geq 0$. The reduction δ, however, cannot be greater than the number of original sets, hence $\delta \leq \mu(x)$ and $\delta \leq \mu(y)$. Therefore, $\mu(x) + \mu(y) - \delta \geq \mu(x)$ and $\mu(x) + \mu(y) - \delta \geq \mu(y)$, establishing property (v). To establish property (vi), the interaction property, assume $\mu(x) = \mu(y)$ for some object y and let z be another object with $\mu(z) = r$. Now, $\mu(x + z) = n + r - \delta$ and $\mu(y + z) = n + r - \rho$, where δ and ρ are the reductions for, respectively, $x + z$ and $y + z$. Since neither δ nor ρ is dependent on n, they need not be equal, hence in general $\mu(x + z) \neq \mu(y + z)$, establishing property (vi). To disprove property (vii), consider that $\mu(x + y) = \mu(x) + \mu(y) - \delta$ for some $\delta \geq 0$, and hence $\mu(x + y) \leq \mu(x) + \mu(y)$. The violation of property (vii)

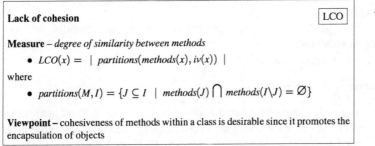

Slide 4-29: Lack of cohesion

seems to indicate that it may indeed be better sometimes to have a single non-cohesive object than multiple cohesive ones, implementing the same functionality.

4.3.2 An objective sense of style

The metrics discussed in the previous section clearly suggest principles for the design of object-oriented systems, but do not lead immediately to explicit guidelines for design. In contrast, Lieberherr and Holland (1989) present such guidelines, but they are less explicit in their formal approach. The guidelines they presented were among the first, and they still provide good advice with respect to designing class interfaces.

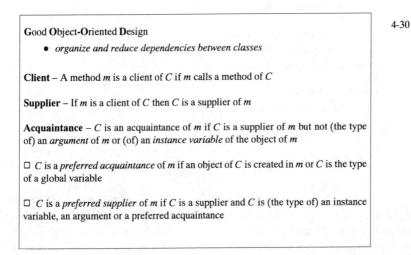

Slide 4-30: Clients, suppliers and acquaintances

In slide 4-30, an explicit definition of the dual notions of *client* and *supplier* has been given. It is important to note that not all of the potential suppliers for a class may be considered *safe*. Potentially *unsafe* suppliers are distinguished as *acquaintances*, of which those that are either created during a method call or stored in a global variable are to be preferred.

Although this may not be immediately obvious, this excludes *suppliers* that are accessed in some indirect way, for instance as the result of a method call to some *safe* supplier. As an example of using an unsafe supplier, consider the call

   screen→ cursor()→ move();

which instructs the cursor associated with the screen to move to its home position. Although *screen* may be assumed to be a safe supplier, the object delivered by *screen* → *cursor*() need not necessarily be a safe supplier. In contrast, the call

   screen→ move_cursor();

does not make use of an indirection introducing a potentially unsafe supplier.

The guideline concerning the use of *safe* suppliers is known as the *Law of Demeter*, of which the underlying intuition is that the programmer should not be bothered by knowledge that is not immediately apparent from the program text (that is the class interface) or founded in well-established conventions (as in the case of using special global variables). See slide 4-31.

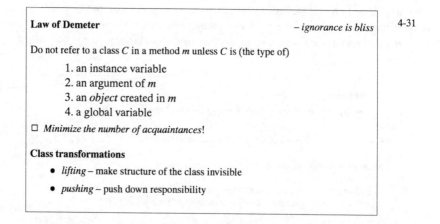

Slide 4-31: The Law of Demeter

To remedy the use of unsafe suppliers, two kinds of program transformation are suggested by Lieberherr and Holland (1989). First, the structure of a class should be made invisible for clients, to prohibit the use of a component as (an unsafe) supplier. This may require the *lifting* of primitive actions to the encompassing object, in order to make these primitives available to the client in a safe way. Secondly, the client should not be given the responsibility of performing (a sequence of) low-level actions. For example, moving the cursor should not be the responsibility of the client of the screen, but instead of the object representing the screen. In principle, the client need not be burdened with detailed knowledge of the cursor class.

The software engineering principles underlying the *Law of Demeter* may be characterized as representing a *compositional approach*, since *the law* enforces the use of immediate parts only. As additional benefits, conformance to *the law* results in hiding the component structure of classes, reduces the coupling of control and, moreover, promotes reuse by enforcing the use of localized (type) information.

4.3.3   Individual class design

We have nearly completed a first tour around the various landmarks of object-oriented design. Identifying objects, expressing the interaction between objects by means of client/server contracts and describing the collaboration between objects in terms of behavioral compositions belong to a craft that will only be learned in the practice of developing real systems.

A class should represent a faithful model of a single concept, and be a reusable, plug-compatible component that is robust, well-designed and extensible. In slide 4-32, we list a number of suggestions put forward by McGregor and Sykes (1992).

4-32

Class design – *guidelines*

- only methods public – *information hiding*
- do not expose implementation details
- public members available to all classes – *strong cohesion*
- as few dependencies as possible – *weak coupling*
- explicit information passing
- root class should be abstract model – *abstraction*

Slide 4-32: Individual class design

The first two guidelines enforce the principle of *information hiding,* advising that only methods public and all implementation details hidden. The third guideline states a principle of *strong cohesion* by requiring that classes implement a single protocol that is valid for all potential clients. A principle of *weak coupling* is enforced by requiring a class to have as few dependencies as possible, and to employ explicit information passing using messages instead of inheritance (except when inheritance may be used in a type consistent fashion). When using inheritance, the root class should be an abstract model of its derived classes, whether inheritance is used to realize a partial type or to define a specialization in a conceptual hierarchy.

The properties of classes, including their interfaces and relations with other classes, must be laid down in the design document. Ideally, the design document should present a complete and formal description of the structural, functional and dynamic aspects of the system, including an argument showing that the various models are consistent. However, in practice this will seldom be realized, partly, because object-oriented design techniques are as yet not sufficiently matured to allow a completely formal treatment, and partly because most designers will be satisfied with a non-formal rendering of the architecture of their system. Admittedly, the task of designing is already sufficiently complex, even without the additional complexity of a completely formal treatment. Nevertheless, studying the formal underpinnings of object-oriented modeling based on types and polymorphism is still worthwhile, since it will sharpen the intuition with respect to the notion of behavioral conformance and the refinement of contracts, which are both essential for developing reliable object models. And reliability is the key to reuse!

4.4   Towards a formal approach

Reliability is the cornerstone of reuse. Hence, object-oriented implementation, design and analysis must first and foremost support the development of reliable software, should the original claim to promote the reuse of software ever come true.

Validating software by means of testing alone is clearly insufficient. As argued in Backhouse (1986), the probability of finding an error is usually too small to view testing as a reliable method of detecting the error.

The fallacy of any empirical approach to validating software, which includes quantitative measurements based on software metrics, is that in the end we just have to wait and see what happens. In other words, it is useless as a design methodology.

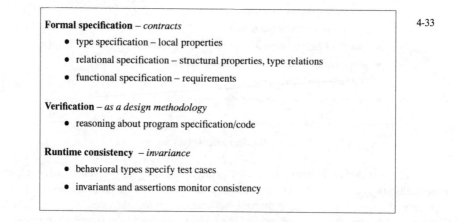

Formal specification – *contracts*   4-33

- type specification – local properties

- relational specification – structural properties, type relations

- functional specification – requirements

Verification – *as a design methodology*

- reasoning about program specification/code

Runtime consistency – *invariance*

- behavioral types specify test cases

- invariants and assertions monitor consistency

Slide 4-33: Formal specification and verification

Verification should be at the heart of any design method. In addition to allowing us to reason about the specification and the code, the design process should result in an architectural description of the system as well as in a proof that the system meets its requirements. Looking at the various approaches to the specification and verification of software, we can see that the notion of *invariance* plays a crucial role in developing provably correct solutions for a variety of problems (cf. Gries, 1981; Backhouse, 1986; Apt and Olderog, 1991; Dahl, 1992).

Invariance, as we observed when discussing object test methods, also play an important role in testing the runtime consistency of a system. Hence, from a pragmatic point of view, studying formal approaches may help us become aware of the properties that determine the runtime consistency of object-oriented systems.

In part III (chapter 10), we will explore what formal methods we have available for developing object-oriented software. Our starting point will be the foundations underlying the notion of *contracts* as introduced in Meyer (1988). We will take a closer look at the relation between *contracts* and the specification of the properties of abstract data types. Also, we will look at methods allowing us to specify structural and functional relations between types, as may occur in behavioral compositions of objects. More specifically, we will study the means available to relate an abstract specification of the properties of a data type to a concrete implementation. These studies are based on an analysis of the notion of abstract data types, and the relation between inheritance and subtyping. In particular, we will look at rules to determine whether a subclass derived by inheritance conforms to the subtype relation that we may define in a formal approach to object types.

However, before we delve into the formal foundations of object-oriented languages and develop a formal approach to object-oriented modeling, we will first explore the design space of object-oriented languages and system implementation techniques. These insights will enable us to establish to what extent we may capture a design in formal terms, and what heuristics are available to accomplish the tasks remaining in object-oriented development.

Summary

This chapter looked at system development from a software engineering perspective. How may we establish that software is reliable and to what extent can our experience be generalized to an object-oriented approach?

Validating software | 1 | 4-34

- *software quality* – structural criteria
- *testing* – strategy, tactics, operational
- *inheritance* – inherited code must be retested

Slide 4-34: Section 4.1: Validating software

We discussed the notions of software quality, including structural criteria, and testing, as an empirical way in which to validate software. An example has been given, illustrating that inherited code may need to be retested.

We developed (the beginnings of) a framework for testing object-oriented software, discussed the influence of errors and looked at object test methods directed at verifying state transitions. We also discussed how *contracts* may provide a guideline for testing, indicating state invariant interaction protocols. Testing may also be done by carefully reading the code, preferably with a group of colleagues.

A number of metrics for object-oriented design have been proposed. These metrics may be used to establish the complexity of object models. The metrics given are meant only as a starting point for further research and empirical validation. They cover

---

A framework for testing object-oriented programs   2   4-35

- *levels of testing* – influence of errors
- *object test methods* – state transitions
- *contracts* – interaction protocols
- *static testing* – careful reading

Slide 4-35: Section 4.2: A framework for testing object-oriented programs

---

Guidelines for design   3   4-36

- *metrics* – objects, attributes, communication
- *law of demeter* – class interfaces
- *reuse* – individual class design

Slide 4-36: Section 4.3: Guidelines for design

aspects such as the complexity of the relation between the definition and usage of attributes and the complexity of communication patterns between objects.

Related to the issues of complexity, we discussed the Law of Demeter which gives a guideline for good object-oriented design, including suggestions for class transformations to improve a particular design. Also we looked at some guidelines for individual class design.

Towards a formal approach   4   4-37

- *contracts* – formal specification
- *verification* – as a design methodology
- *runtime consistency* – invariance

Slide 4-37: Section 4.4: Towards a formal approach

Finally, we reflected on the possible contribution of formal methods to the software engineering of object-oriented systems, and concluded that the notion of *contracts* may play an invaluable role, both as a design methodology and as a means to establish the runtime consistency of a system.

Questions

(1) What aspects can you distinguish with respect to software quality?

(2) Give an example demonstrating how inheritance may affect tested code.

(3) Between what levels of testing can you distinguish? Discuss the influence of errors for each of these levels.

(4) Discuss the problems involved in testing the behavior of an object. What would be your approach?

(5) Discuss how contracts may be employed to test object behavior.

(6) What methods of static testing can you think of? Do you consider them relevant? Explain.

(7) What metrics can you think of for object-oriented design? What is the intuition underlying these metrics?

(8) What evaluation criteria for metrics can you think of? Are these sufficient for applying such metrics in actual software projects? Explain.

(9) Give a formal definition of the following metrics: WMC, DIT. NOC, CBO, RFC and LOC. Explain their meaning from a software engineering viewpoint.

(10) What would be your rendering of the Law of Demeter? Can you phrase its underlying intuition? Explain.

(11) Define the notions of client, supplier and acquaintance. What restrictions must be satisfied to speak of a preferred acquaintance and a preferred supplier?

(12) Characterize the elements that form part of a formal specification.

Further reading

There is a massive amount of literature on software validation and testing. A standard text is Myers (1979). As research papers, I recommend Doong and Frankl (1990) and Smith and Robson (1992). For a further study of the Law of Demeter look at Lieberherr and Holland (1989).

Part II

Object-Oriented Languages and Systems

5

Object-oriented programming languages

When developing an object-oriented system, at some time a choice has to be made for an actual programming language or environment. It goes without saying that the optimal environment will be one that is in accord with the method chosen for design. Naturally, other desiderata (involving efficiency, portability or client imposed constraints) may play an equally significant role.

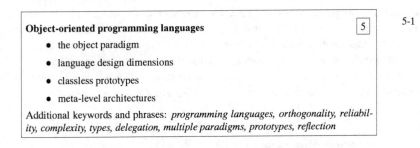

Object-oriented programming languages   5

- the object paradigm
- language design dimensions
- classless prototypes
- meta-level architectures

Additional keywords and phrases: *programming languages, orthogonality, reliability, complexity, types, delegation, multiple paradigms, prototypes, reflection*

5-1

Slide 5-1: Object-oriented programming languages

This chapter will present an overview of the numerous languages that exist for object-oriented development. A comparison of Smalltalk, Eiffel and C++ will be given, and we will look at the considerations underlying the design of the various object-oriented (extensions of) programming languages. Also, some possible modifications and alternatives to the traditional class-based object model will be discussed, including prototypes and meta-level architectures.

5.1   The object paradigm

The object paradigm is embodied in numerous programming languages. Saunders (1989) presents a survey of 88 object-oriented languages, of which 69 are *standalone* and 19 incorporated into either multi-paradigm or database systems. (A multi-paradigm system, in this context, means a system embedding an environment for window-programming or knowledge-based reasoning.)

In this section, we will first look at the classification of object-oriented languages (as given in Saunders, 1989). Most of the languages mentioned are based on a distinction between classes and objects. However, alternative object models (without classes) are also being employed. Finally, we will review a number of object extensions of the languages Lisp, C and Prolog.

On the notion of object Before our comparative study of object-oriented programming languages, we may well reflect on some issues of language design (specifically the motivations underlying the development of a programming language) and in particular on the notion of object underlying our conception of object oriented programming languages.

Language design is an intricate issue. The motivation to develop a programming language may come from the desire for experimentation (as it has been for the author, Eliëns (1992)), from governmental policy (in the case of Ada), corporate policy (as for PL-1), the wish to improve programming habits (which lies at the basis of Pascal and Modula, Wirth (1983)), the wish to provide more adequate programming constructs (as, for instance, C++ was originally meant to be a better C), or the efficient implementation of a theoretically interesting model of computing (as has been the case for Prolog).

Whatever motivation lies behind the development of a programming language, every language is meant to serve some purpose. Whether implicitly or explicitly stated, a programming language is characterized by its design goals and the applications it is intended to support. *A fortiori* this holds for object oriented programming languages.

The impetus to research in object oriented programming may be traced back to the development of Simula, which was originally intended for discrete event simulation. As observed in Taivalsaari (1993), Simula has since served as a valuable source of ideas in several research areas in computer science. See slide 5-2.

The notion of object *– Simula*   5-2

  • abstract data types *– software engineering*

  • frames *– artificial intelligence*

  • semantic data models *– database system development*

  • capability-based computing *– distributed systems*

Slide 5-2: The heritage of Simula

These areas include *abstract data types* (that play a prominent role in software engineering, Parnas (1972a,b); Liskov and Zilles 1974; Liskov and Zilles, 1975), *frames* in artificial intelligence (which have become an invaluable mechanism for knowledge representation, Fikes and Kehler (1985) and Minsky (1975)), *semantic data models*, (that are widely used to develop information systems, Hammer and McLeod (1978, 1981)), and *capability-based computing* (that plays a prominent role in distributed computer systems, Levy (1984)).

The research efforts in these areas in their turn have had a strong impact on our conception of object-oriented computing. With regard to object-oriented programming we may differentiate between three (partially distinct) viewpoints from which to characterize the notion of an object.

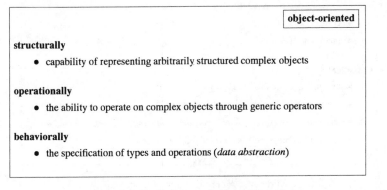

Slide 5-3: Perspectives of object orientation

From a *structural* viewpoint, object-oriented means the capability of representing arbitrarily complex objects. This viewpoint is of importance for implementing object-oriented languages and the development of adequate runtime models of object-oriented computing. From this perspective, an object is (in the end) a structure in memory.

From an *operational* viewpoint, object-oriented means the ability to operate on complex objects through generic operators. This viewpoint is closely related to the notion of semantic data models, and is of particular importance for conceptual modeling. From this perspective, in other words, an object represents (an element of) a conceptual model.

From a *behavioral* viewpoint, object-oriented means the support to specify abstract polymorphic types with associated operations. This viewpoint is primarily of importance for software engineering and the development of formal methods of specification and verification. From this perspective an object is like a module, to be used for data abstraction.

From the inception of Simula, there has been a close relation between object orientation and modeling, that is a tendency to regard a program as a physical model simulating the behavior of either a real or imaginary part of the world (see Knudsen and Madsen, 1988). However, as observed in Taivalsaari (1993), there seems to be a division between the European interpretation of object orientation (which remains close to the original notion of conceptual modeling) and the American interpretation (which is of a more pragmatic nature as it stresses the importance of data abstraction and the reusability of program components).

5.1.1   A classification of object-oriented languages

To be characterized as *object-oriented* a language must minimally support an *object creation* facility and a *message passing* facility (message-passing in the sense of method invocation). In addition, many languages provide a mechanism to define *classes* together with some form of *inheritance*. See slide 5-4.

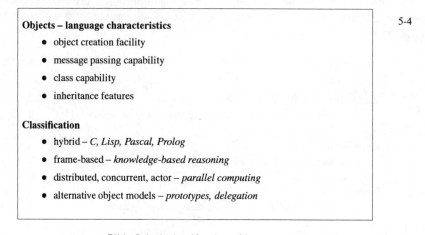

5-4

Objects – language characteristics
- object creation facility
- message passing capability
- class capability
- inheritance features

Classification
- hybrid – *C, Lisp, Pascal, Prolog*
- frame-based – *knowledge-based reasoning*
- distributed, concurrent, actor – *parallel computing*
- alternative object models – *prototypes, delegation*

Slide 5-4: A classification of languages

Actually, as we will see in section 5.3, there is a lively debate on the proper design dimensions of object-oriented programming languages. An important issue in this respect is what makes a language object-oriented as opposed to object-based. Other issues in this debate are whether an object-oriented language must support classes (in addition to a mechanism to create objects) and whether (static) inheritance should be preferred above (dynamic) delegation. This debate is reflected in a number of research efforts investigating alternative object models and object communication mechanisms. See section 5.4.

Of the 69 (standalone) object-oriented languages surveyed, 53 were research projects and only sixteen were commercial products. Of these, 14 were extensions of either Lisp (10) or C (4). Among the remaining languages, quite a number were derived from languages such as Pascal, Ada or Prolog.

There is a great diversity between the different object-oriented languages. However, following Saunders (1989), they may be divided among subcategories reflecting their origin or the area of application for which they were developed (as shown above).

Hybrid languages originating out of (an object-oriented extension of) an already existing language are likely to be applied in a similar area as their ancestor. In practice, this category of languages (which includes C++ and CLOS) seems to be quite important, partly because their implementation support is as good as the implementation support for their base languages and, more importantly, they allow potential software developers a smooth transition from a non object-oriented to an object-oriented approach.

Frame-based languages (in contrast to the previous category) were explicitly developed to deal with one particular application area, in particular knowledge-based reasoning. A *frame* is a structure consisting of *slots* that may either indicate a relation to other frames or contain the value of an attribute of the frame. In fact, the early frame-based languages such as FRL (see Bundy, 1986) and KRL (Bobrow and Winograd, 1977) may be considered as object-oriented *avant la lettre*, that is before object-orientation gained its popularity. Later frame-based systems, such as KEE (Kunz *et al.*, 1984) and LOOPS (Stefik and Bobrow, 1986), incorporated explicitly object-oriented notions such as classes and (multiple) inheritance.

Concurrent, distributed and actor languages To promote the use of parallel processing architectures a number of parallel object-oriented languages have been developed, among which are the language *Hybrid* (which supports active objects with their own thread of control, Nierstrasz (1987)), Concurrent Smalltalk (a concurrent extension of Smalltalk), Orient-K (a language for parallel knowledge processing) and POOL-T (which may be characterized as a simplified version of Ada). (See Yonezawa and Tokoro, 1987.)

POOL-T also supports the notion of *active objects*. Active objects have a body which allows them to execute their own activity in parallel with other active objects. To answer a request to execute a method, an active object must explicitly interrupt its activity (by means of an answer or *accept* statement as in Ada). POOL-T is interesting, primarily, because it is complemented by extensive theoretical research into the semantical foundations of parallel object-oriented computing. (See de Bakker *et al.*, 1990, and also section 10.3.)

The idea of simultaneously active objects leads in a natural way to the notion of distributed object-oriented languages that support objects which may be located on geographically distinct processors and which communicate by means of (actual) message passing. Examples of such languages are *Distributed Smalltalk* (a distributed extension of Smalltalk that introduces so-called *proxy objects* to deal with communication between objects residing on different processors, Bennett (1987)) and *Emerald* (that supports primitives to migrate objects across a processor network, Black and Hutchinson (1986)).

All parallel/distributed object-oriented languages introduced thus far are based on a traditional object model in so far as an object retains its identity during its lifetime. In contrast, the so-called *actor* languages support a notion of object whereby the parallel activity of an object is enabled by *self-replacement* of the object in response to a message. Self-replacement proceeds as follows. Each *actor* object has a mail-queue. When a message arrives for the *actor* object, the object invokes the appropriate method and subsequently creates a successor object (which basically is a copy of itself with some modifications that may depend upon the contents of the message). In other words, message handling occurs asynchronously. This scheme of asynchronous message passing enables an *actor* system to execute in parallel, since during the execution of a method the replacement object may proceed to handle other incoming messages.

In *actor* systems, object identity is replaced by what may be called mail-queue or address identity. From a theoretical viewpoint this allows us to treat *actor* objects as functions (in a mathematical sense) that deliver an effect and another object in response to a message. However, pragmatically this leads to a complicated and quite low-level object model which is hard to implement in a truly parallel way.

5.1.2 Alternative object models

Since the introduction of Smalltalk, the predominant notion of objects has been based on the distinction between classes and objects. Classes serve to describe the functionality and behavior of objects, while objects are instance of classes. In other words, classes serve as templates to create objects. Inheritance, then, may be regarded as a means by which to share (descriptions of) object behavior. It is generally defined on classes in terms of a derivation mechanism, that allows one to declare a class to be a subclass of another (super) class.

The distinction between classes and objects leads to a number of difficulties, both of a pragmatic and theoretical nature. (See also sections 5.3 and 5.5 for a discussion of the theoretical problems.) For example, the existence of *one-of-a-kind* classes, that is classes which have only one instance, is often considered unnatural. An example of a class-less language is the language *Self*. Self has a Smalltalk-like syntax, but in contrast to Smalltalk only supports *objects* (containing slots) and *messages*, and hence no classes. Slots may be designated to be parent-slots which means that messages that cannot be handled by the object itself are delegated to the parent object. In contrast to inheritance, which is static since the inherited functionality is computed at object creation time, delegation to parent objects as in Self is dynamic, since parent slots may be changed during the lifetime of an object.

Objects in Self may themselves be used to create other objects (as copies of the original object) in a similar way as classes may be used to create instances. However, the changes made to an object are propagated when cloning object copies. Single objects, from which copies are taken, may in other words be regarded as prototypes, approximating in a dynamic way the functionality of their offspring, whereas classes provide a more static, so to speak universal, description of their object instances. Self employs runtime compilation, which is claimed to result in an efficiency comparable to C. (See Ungar *et al.*, 1992.) In section 5.4 we will discuss the use of prototypes and the distinction between inheritance and delegation.

Alternative object models may also be encountered in object-oriented database managements systems and in systems embedding objects such as hypertext or hypermedia systems. See chapter 12.

5.1.3 Object extensions of Lisp, C and Prolog

The notion of object is to a certain extent orthogonal to, that is independent of, language constructs around which programming languages may be constructed, such as expressions, functions and procedures. Hence, it should come as no surprise that a number of (popular) object-oriented programming languages were originally developed as extensions of existing languages or language implementations. See slide 5-5.

The advantage of extending an existing language with object-oriented constructs, from the point of view of the user, is that the object-oriented approach can be gradually learned. However, at the same time this may be a disadvantage, since a hybrid approach to software development may give rise to sloppy design. Many proponents of an object-oriented approach, therefore, believe that learning to use object-oriented constructs is best done in an environment as offered by Smalltalk, where classes and objects are the sole means of developing an application.

Object extensions

- Lisp – LOOPS, FLAVORS, CLOS, FOOPS
- C – Objective C, C++
- Prolog – SPOOL, VULCAN, DLP

Commercial products – *languages*

- Smalltalk, Eiffel, C++, Objective C, Object Pascal

5-5

Slide 5-5: Object-oriented languages

It is noteworthy that, with the exception of Smalltalk and Eiffel, many commercially available languages are actually extensions of existing languages such as Lisp, C and (to some extent) Prolog.

Lisp-based extensions In Saunders (1989), ten Lisp-based object-oriented languages are mentioned, among which are LOOPS (introducing a variety of object-oriented constructs, see Stefik and Bobrow (1986)), Flavors (which extends Lisp by adding generic functions that operate on objects, see Moon (1986)), CLOS (which is actually a standardization effort of the ANSI X3J13 group to define the Common Lisp Object Standard). CLOS is a widely used system containing some nontrivial extensions to the object model and the way in which polymorphic methods may be defined.

C-based extensions Another very important class of object extensions is those of C-based object-oriented languages, of which the most well-known are Objective-C and C++.

The concepts underlying these two extensions are radically different. Objective-C introduces objects as an add-on to the constructs (including *struct*'s) available in C, whereas C++ realizes a close (and efficient) coupling between the *struct* (record) notion of C and the concept of a class.

In other words, in Objective-C there is a clear distinction between conventional C values and data types such as *int*, *float* and *struct* on the one hand, and objects on the other hand. Objects have a special data type (*id*) which allows them to be treated as first class elements. To define an object class, both an *interface* and *implementation* description must be given. These descriptions are preceded by a special sign to designate Objective-C specific code. Also, method declarations (in the interface description) and method definitions (that are to be put in the implementation section) must be preceded by a special sign to designate them as methods available for clients of object instances of that class.

The object model of Objective-C closely resembles the object model of Smalltalk. In contrast, C++ quite radically departs from this object model in order to achieve an as efficient as possible implementation of objects. The key to an efficient implementation lies in the integration of the *struct* (record) construct originally provided by C with the class concept, by allowing functions to be members of a *struct*.

As explained in Stroustrup (1991), the equivalences depicted in slide 5-6 hold.

Object structure – *efficient mapping* 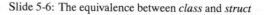   C++   5-6

- struct A { ... } ≡ *class* A { *public:* ... }
- *class* A { ... } ≡ struct A { *private:* ... }

Slide 5-6: The equivalence between *class* and *struct*

This interpretation allows an efficient mapping of object structures to the memory of a computer, provided that the compiler is clever enough.

Nevertheless, the efficiency of C++ comes at a price. C++ does support micro-efficiency but does not necessarily lead to the design of efficient code. In particular, hand-crafted memory management will not necessarily offer the most efficient solution when compared with built-in support, but is almost certainly detrimental to the quality of the code.

As argued in Ellis and Stroustrup (1990), the design of C++ is intended to allow an efficient compilation of C++ into C, that is efficient C code. Yet, the efficiency of C++ is not due to its being compiled into C, but comes from an efficient mapping of object (type) structures and class member functions to analogous C structures and functions that require a minimum of overhead.

In effect, C is increasingly being used as a target language for the compilation of high level languages. The reason for this is, however, primarily *portability*, and not efficiency. For example, Eiffel compilers (both under Unix and MS-DOS) produce C code and also allow Eiffel programs to interface with programs written in C. However, the overhead due to the exception handling primitives of Eiffel and the overhead in calling functions defined in C (still) results in quite inefficient code, despite the translation into C.

As portability is concerned, many authors optimistically claim the portability of their C++ code (across platforms and compilers). However, portability has not been realized for C++ as it has for ANSI-C. Currently available compilers (including AT&T 3.0 and those of Borland, GNU and Zortech) definitely disagree on the handling of, for instance, multiple inheritance, pure virtual functions, templates and overloading. Hopefully, the standardization efforts of the C++ ANSI committee will help to reduce these problems.

Prolog-based extensions A quite different class of object-oriented extensions, used primarily in research laboratories, consists of attempts to incorporate object-oriented features in (high level) logic-based languages, such as Prolog. Among these are languages such as SPOOL (developed in the context of the Japanese fifth-generation computing project, see Fukanaga (1986)), Vulcan (that provides a preprocessor giving syntactic support for embedding objects in concurrent logic programming languages, see Kahn *et al.* (1986)) and DLP (a language combining logic programming with object-oriented features and parallelism developed by the author, see appendix D). The list of research articles covering the subject of combining logic programming and object-oriented programming is quite extensive. An overview and discussion of the various approaches is given in Davison (1993) and also in Eliëns (1992).

5.2   Comparing Smalltalk, Eiffel and C++

The languages Smalltalk, Eiffel and C++ may be regarded as the three most important (and popular) representatives of classical object-oriented languages, classical in the sense of being based on a class/object distinction.

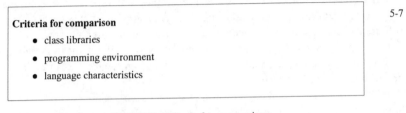

5-7

Slide 5-7: Criteria for comparison

In this section we will compare these languages with respect to what may be called their intrinsic language characteristics. Before that, however, we will indicate some other (more external) criteria for comparison such as the availability of class libraries and the existence of a programming environment. See slide 5-7. Our discussion is based on (but in some respects disagrees with) Blaschek *et al.* (1989).

5.2.1   Criteria for comparison

When choosing a particular programming language as a vehicle for program development a number of factors play a role, among which are the availability of a class library, the existence of a good programming environment, and, naturally, the characteristics of the language itself.

Class libraries An important criterion when selecting a class library may be the availability of sufficient class library support. A general class library, and preferably libraries suitable for the application domain one is working in, may drastically reduce development time. Another important benefit of using (well-tested) class libraries is an improvement of the reliability of the application.

Smalltalk (that is Smalltalk-80 of ParcPlace Systems) comes with a large collection of general purpose and graphics programming classes, that are identical for both MS-DOS and Unix platforms. Also Eiffel (albeit only on Unix platforms) comes with a standard collection of well-documented libraries containing common data structures, container classes and classes for graphics programming. For both Smalltalk and Eiffel, the accompanying classes may almost be considered to be part of the language definition, in the sense that they provide a standard means to solve particular problems.

In contrast, for C++ there is almost no standard library support (except for IO stream classes). Even worse, the various C++ compiler vendors disagree considerably in what functionality the standard class libraries of C++ must offer. Fortunately, however, there is an increasingly large number of third party libraries (commercially and non-commercially) available. These are more extensively described in section 11.4. The burden of choosing the appropriate libraries is, however, placed on the shoulders of a user or a company, which has the advantage that a more optimal solution may be obtained than possible within the confines of standard libraries.

Programming environments Another selection criterion in choosing a language is the existence of a good programming environment. What constitutes a *good* programming environment is not as simple as it may seem, since that depends to a large extent upon the experience and preferences of the user. For example, with respect to operating systems, many novice users favor a graphical interface as originally offered by the Apple Macintosh computers, while experienced users often feel constrained by the limitations imposed by such systems. In contrast, experienced users may delight in the terseness and flexibility of the command-based Unix operating system, which leads to outright bewilderment with many novice users.

Of the object-oriented programming languages we consider in this book, Smalltalk definitely offers the most comprehensive programming environment (including editors, browsers and debuggers). For Unix systems, Eiffel comes with a number of additional tools (such as a graphical browser, and a program documentation tool) to support program development (and maintenance). In contrast, C++ usually comes with nothing at all. However, increasingly many tools (including browsers and debuggers) have become available. See section 11.3.3.

Language characteristics Despite the commonality between Smalltalk, Eiffel and C++ (which may be characterized by saying that they all support *data abstraction, inheritance, polymorphism* and *dynamic binding*), these languages widely disagree on a number of other properties, such as those listed in slide 5-8.

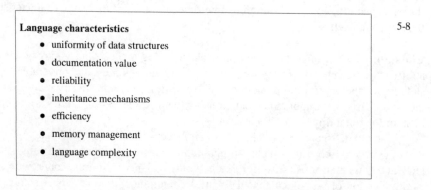

Slide 5-8: Language characteristics

These characteristics were used in Blaschek *et al.* (1989) to compare Smalltalk, Eiffel and C++ with the language Oberon, which offers what may be called a minimal (typed) object-oriented language. We will, however, discuss Oberon in section 5.3, and limit our discussion here to Smalltalk, Eiffel and C++.

5.2.2 Language characteristics

Smalltalk, Eiffel and C++ differ with respect to a number of language characteristics. An indication of the differences between these languages is given slide 5-9.

	Smalltalk	Eiffel	C++
uniformity	high	medium	low
documentation value	medium	high	medium
reliability	medium	medium	*low**
protected operations	no	no	yes
multiple inheritance	no	yes	yes
efficiency	low	medium	high
garbage collection	yes	yes	*no**
language complexity	*low**	medium	high

5-9

Slide 5-9: Comparing Smalltalk, Eiffel and C++

This characterization conforms to the one given in Blaschek *et al.* (1989), with which I think the majority of the object-oriented community will agree. It is further motivated below. However, the places indicated by an asterisk deserve some discussion. In particular, I wish to stress that I disagree with characterizing the reliability of C++ as *low*. (See below.)

Uniformity In Smalltalk, each data type is described by a class. This includes booleans, integers, real numbers and control constructs. In Eiffel there is a distinction between elementary data types (such as boolean, integer and real) and (user-defined) classes. However (in the later versions of Eiffel) the built-in elementary types behave as if declared by pre-declared classes. For C++, the elementary data types and simple data structures (as may be defined in C) do not behave as objects. To a certain extent, however, programmers may deal with this non-uniformity by some work-around, for example by overloading functions and operators or by embedding built-in types in a (wrapper) class.

Documentation value Smalltalk promotes a consistent style in writing programs, due to the assumption that *everything is an object*. One of perhaps the most important features of Eiffel is the use of special keywords for constructs to specify the correctness of programs and the behavioral properties that determine the external interface of objects. Moreover, Eiffel provides a tool to extract a description of the interface of the method classes (including pre- and post-conditions associated with a method) which may be used to document (a library of) classes. To my taste, however, the Eiffel syntax leads to somewhat verbose programs, at least in comparison with programs written in C++.

The issue of producing documentation from C++ is still open. A number of tools exist (including a WEB-like system for C++ and a tool to produce manual pages from C++ header files, see section 11.3.3) but no standard has yet emerged. Moreover, some people truly dislike the terseness of C/C++. Personally, I prefer the C/C++ syntax above the syntactical conventions of both Eiffel and Smalltalk, provided that it is used in a disciplined fashion.

Reliability Smalltalk is a dynamically typed language. In other words, type checking, other than detecting runtime errors, is completely absent. Eiffel is generally regarded as a language possessing all characteristics needed for writing reliable programs, such as static type checking and constructs for stating correctness assertions (that may be checked at runtime). In contrast, due to its heritage from C, the language C++ is still by many considered as unreliable. In contrast to C, however, C++ does provide full static type checking, including the signature of functions and external object interfaces as arise in independent compilation of module files. Nevertheless, C++ only weakly supports type checking across module boundaries.

In contrast to common belief, Eiffel's type system is demonstrably inconsistent, due to a feature that enables a user to dynamically define the type of a newly created object in a virtual way (see section 9.6). This does not necessarily lead to type-insecure programs though, since the Eiffel compiler employs a special algorithm to detect such cases.

In contrast, the type system of C++ is consistent and conforms to the notion of subtype as introduced informally in the previous part. Nevertheless, C++ allows the programmer to escape the rigor of the type system by employing casts.

An important feature of Eiffel is that it supports assertions that may be validated at runtime. In combinations with exceptions, this provides a powerful feature for the development of reliable programs.

At the price of some additional coding (for example, to save the current state to enable the use of the *old* value), such assertions may be expressed by using the assert macros provided for C++. A better way would probably be to employ exceptions, but these are supported by only a few C++ compilers.

In defense of C++, it is important to acknowledge that only C++ offers adequate protection mechanisms to shield classes derived by inheritance from the implementation details of their ancestor classes. Neither Smalltalk nor Eiffel offer such protection.

Inheritance Smalltalk offers only single inheritance. In contrast, both Eiffel and C++ offer multiple inheritance. For statically typed languages, compile-time optimizations may be applied that result in only a low overhead. In principle, multiple inheritance allows one to model particular aspects of the application domain in a flexible and natural way. See section 7.1.3 for a further discussion.

As far as the assertion mechanism offered by Eiffel is concerned, Meyer (1988) offers clear guidelines prescribing how to use assertions in derived classes. However, the Eiffel compiler offers no assistance in verifying whether these rules are followed. The same guidelines apply to the use of assertions in C++, naturally lacking compiler support as well.

Efficiency Smalltalk, being an interpreted language, is typically slower than conventionally compiled languages. Nevertheless, as discussed in section 5.4.2, interpreted object-based languages allow for significant optimizations, for example by employing runtime compilation techniques.

The compilation of Eiffel programs can result in programs having adequate execution speed. However, in Eiffel dynamic binding takes place in principle for all methods. Yet a clever compiler can significantly reduce the number of indirections needed to execute a method.

In contrast to C++, in Eiffel all objects are created on the heap. The garbage collection needed to remove these objects may affect the execution speed of programs.

As we have discussed in section 2.5, C++ has been designed with efficiency in mind. For instance, the availability of inline functions, and the possibility to allocate objects on the runtime stack (instead of on the heap), allow the programmer to squeeze out the last drop of efficiency. However, as a drawback, when higher level functionality is needed (as in automatic garbage collection) it must be explicitly programmed, and a similar price as when the functionality would have been provided by the system has to be paid. The only difference is that the programmer has a choice.

Language complexity Smalltalk may be regarded as having a low language complexity. Control is primarily effected by message passing, yet, many of the familiar conditional and iterative control constructs reappear in Smalltalk programs emulated by sending messages. This certainly has some elegance, but does not necessarily lead to easily comprehensible programs.

Eiffel contains few language elements that extend beyond object-oriented programming. In particular, Eiffel does not allow for overloading method names (according to signature) within a class. This may lead to unnecessarily elaborate method names. (The new version of Eiffel (Eiffel-3) does allow for overloading method names.)

Without doubt, C++ is generally regarded as a highly complex language. In particular, the rules governing the overloading of operators and functions are quite complicated. The confusion even extends to the various compiler suppliers, which is one of the reasons why C++ is still barely portable. Somewhat unfortunately, the rules for overloading and type conversion for C++ have to a large extent been determined by the need to remain compatible with C. Even experienced programmers need occasionally to experiment to find out what will happen.

According to Blaschek *et al.* (1989), C++ is too large and contains too much of the syntax and semantics inherited from C. However, their motto *small is beautiful* is not so obvious as it seems. The motivations underlying the introduction of the various features incorporated in C++ are quite well explained in Stroustrup (1994). The main problem, to my mind, in using C++ (or any of the object-oriented languages for that matter) lies in the area of design. We still have insufficient experience in using abstract data types to define a complete method and operator interface including its relation to other data types (that is its behavior under the various operators and type conversions that apply to a particular type). The problem is hence not only one of language design but of the design of abstract data types.

5.3   Design dimensions of object-oriented languages

Despite the widespread adoption of object-oriented terminology in the various areas of computer science and software development practice, there is considerable confusion about the precise meaning of the terms employed and the (true) nature of object-oriented computing. In an attempt to resolve this confusion, Wegner (1987) (in the landmark paper *Dimensions of object-based language design*) introduces the distinction between *object-based* and *object-oriented*. See slide 5-10. This distinction comes down to, roughly, the distinction between languages providing only encapsulation (object-based) or encapsulation plus inheritance (object-oriented). See section 5.3.1. Another issue in the debate about object orientation is the relation between *classes* and *types*. Wegner (1987) concludes that the notions of objects, classes and inheritance (that constitute the classical object model) are highly interrelated, and instead proposes an orthogonal approach by outlining the various dimensions along which to design an object-oriented language. These dimensions may be characterized by the phrases: *objects*, *types*, *delegation* and *abstraction*.

In this section we will look at the arguments presented in Wegner (1987) in somewhat more detail. Also, we will look at the viability of combining seemingly disparate paradigms (such as the logic programming paradigm) with the object-oriented language paradigm. In the sections that follow, we will discuss some alternatives and extensions to the object model.

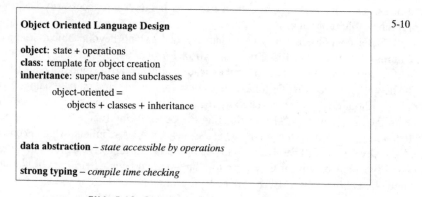

Slide 5-10: Object-based versus object-oriented

5.3.1 Object-based versus object-oriented

How would you characterize Ada83? See Barnes (1994). Is Ada object-oriented? And Modula-2? See Wirth (1983). The answer is no and no. And Ada9X and Modula-3? See Barnes (1994) and Cardelli *et al.* (1989). The answer is yes and yes. In the past there has been some confusion as to when to characterize a language as *object-oriented*. For example, Booch (1986) characterizes Ada as object-oriented and motivates this by saying that Ada can be used as an implementation language in an object-oriented approach to program development.

Clearly, Ada supports some notion of objects (which are defined as *packages*). However, although Ada supports objects and generic descriptions of objects (by generic packages), it does not support code sharing by inheritance. In a later work, Booch (1991) revises his original (faulty) opinion, in response to Wegner (1987), who proposed considering *inheritance* as an essential characteristic of *object orientation*.

Similarly, despite the support that Modula-2 offers for defining (object-like) abstract data types, consisting of an interface specification and an implementation (which may be hidden), Modula-2 does not support the creation of derived (sub)types that share the behavior of their base (super)type. See also section 8.3.

Classes versus types Another confusion that frequently arises is due to the ill-defined relationship between the notion of a class and the notion of a type.

The notion of *types* is already familiar from procedural programming languages such as Pascal and (in an ill-famed way) from C. The type of variables and functions may be profitably used to check for (syntactical) errors. Strong static type checking may prevent errors ranging from simple typos to using undefined (or wrongly defined) functions.

The notion of a class originally has a more operational meaning. Operationally, a class is a template for object creation. In other words, a *class* is a description of the collection of its instances, that is the objects that are created using the class description as a recipe.

Related to this notion of a class, *inheritance* was originally defined as a means to share (parts of) a description. Sharing by (inheritance) derivation is, pragmatically, very convenient. It provides a more controlled way of code sharing than, for example, the use of macros and file inclusion (as were popular in the C community).

Since Wegner (1987) published his original analysis of the dimensions of object-oriented language design, the phrase *object-oriented* has been commonly understood as involving *objects*, *classes* and *inheritance*. This is the traditional object model as embodied by Smalltalk and, to a large extent, by Eiffel and C++. However, unlike Smalltalk, both Eiffel and C++ have also been strongly influenced by the *abstract data type* approach to programming. Consequently, in Eiffel and C++ classes have been identified with types and derivation by inheritance with subtyping.

Unfortunately, derivation by inheritance need not necessarily result in the creation of proper subtypes, that is classes whose instances conform to the behavior specified by their base class. In effect, derived classes may be only distantly related to their base classes when inheritance is only used as a code sharing device. For example, a window manager class may inherit from a list container class (an idiom used in Meyer, 1988).

For those inclined to a more formal approach, the phrase *object-oriented* has gradually acquired the meaning of *abstract data types* and *polymorphism*. From the perspective of language design, however, this characterization merely serves as a constraint that (the application of) particular constructs must satisfy and as an invitation to explore language constructs that enable the use of abstractions and flexible behavioral specifications.

5.3.2   **Towards an orthogonal approach** – *type extensions*

According to Wegner (1987), much of the confusion around the various features of object-oriented programming languages arises from the fact that these features are largely interdependent, as for instance the notion of object and class on the one hand, and the notion of class and inheritance on the other.

To resolve this confusion, Wegner (1987) proposes a more orthogonal approach to characterize the various features of object-oriented languages, according to dimensions that are to a large extent independent. See slide 5-11.

The features that constitute an object-oriented programming language in an orthogonal way are, according to Wegner (1987): *objects*, *types*, *delegation* and *abstraction*.

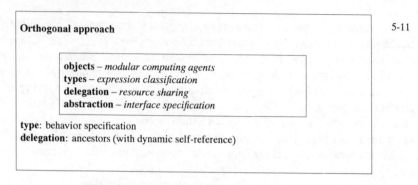

Orthogonal approach   5-11

> **objects** – *modular computing agents*
> **types** – *expression classification*
> **delegation** – *resource sharing*
> **abstraction** – *interface specification*
>
> **type**: behavior specification
> **delegation**: ancestors (with dynamic self-reference)

Slide 5-11: Orthogonal dimensions

Objects are in essence *modular computing agents*. They correspond to the need for encapsulation in design, that is the construction of modular units to which a principle of locality applies (due to combining data and operations).

Object-oriented languages may, however, differ in the degree to which they support encapsulation. For example, in a distributed environment a high degree of encapsulation must be offered, prohibiting attempts to alter global variables (from within an object) or local instance variables (from without). Moreover, the runtime object support system must allow for what may best be called *remote method invocation*.

As far as parallel activity is concerned, only a few languages provide constructs to define concurrently active objects. See chapter 6 for a more detailed discussion.

Whether objects support *reactiveness*, that is sufficient flexibility to respond safely to a message, depends largely upon (program) design. Meyer (1988), for instance, advocates a *shopping list approach* to designing the interface of an object, to allow for a high degree of (temporal) independence between method calls.

Types may be understood as a mechanism for *expression classification*. From this perspective, Smalltalk may be regarded as having a dynamic typing system: dynamic, in the sense that the inability to evaluate an expression will lead to a runtime error. The existence of types obviates the need to have classes, since a type may be considered as a more abstract description of the behavior of an object. Furthermore, subclasses (as may be derived through inheritance) are more safely defined as subtypes in a polymorphic type system. See section 9.3.

At the opposite side of the type dimension we find the statically typed languages, that allow us to determine the type of the designation of a variable at compile-time. In that case, the runtime support system need not carry any type information, except a dispatch table to locate virtual functions.

Delegation (in its most generic sense) is a mechanism for *resource sharing*. As has been shown in Lieberman (1986), delegation subsumes inheritance, since the resource sharing effected by inheritance may easily be mimicked by delegating messages to the object's ancestors by means of an appropriate dispatching mechanism.

In a narrower sense, delegation is usually understood as a more dynamic mechanism that allows the redirection of control dynamically. In addition, languages supporting dynamic delegation (such as Self, see section 5.4) do not sacrifice dynamic self-reference. This means that when the object executing a method refers to itself, the actual context will be the delegating object. See section 5.4 for a more detailed discussion.

In contrast, inheritance (as usually understood in the context of classes) is a far more static mechanism. Inheritance may be understood as (statically) copying the code from an ancestor class to the inheriting class (with perhaps some modifications), whereas delegation is truly dynamic in that messages are dispatched to objects that have a life-span independent of the dispatching object.

Abstraction (although to some extent related to types) is a mechanism that may be independently applied to provide an *interface specification* for an object. For example, in the presence of active objects (that may execute in parallel) we may need to be able to restrict dynamically the interface of an object as specified by its type in order to maintain the object in a consistent state. Also for purely sequential objects we may impose a particular protocol of interaction (as may, for example, be expressed by a *contract*) to be able to guarantee correct behavior.

Another important aspect of abstraction is *protection*. Object-oriented languages may provide (at least) two kinds of protection. First, a language may have facilities to protect the object from illegal access by a client (from without). This is effected by annotations such as *private* and *protected*. And secondly, a language may have facilities to protect the object (as it were from within) from illegal access through delegation (that is by instances of derived object classes). Most languages support the first kind of protection. Only few languages, however (among which are C++), support the second kind too.

The independence of abstraction and typing may further be argued by pointing out that languages supporting strong typing need not enforce the use of abstract data types having a well-defined behavior.

Discussion Currently there is no single language providing what in any sense can be called an ideal or optimal combination of features. At least there is no consensus as to whether Smalltalk, Eiffel, C++ or any of the other languages mentioned is the likely candidate for this position. A critique on many of these languages is that they contain too many features or try to serve too many goals. Think of Smalltalk's meta classes (see section 5.5), Eiffel's attempt to be satisfying both from a practical and formal point of view (which severely limits the power of the assertion mechanism) and the intricate type construction and coercion operators of C++ (which make it flexible, but complex). An interesting example of what may be called *minimal language design* is presented by the language Oberon that features so-called *type extensions* encompassing (in a *minimal* way) both the notion of object and class inheritance.

The Oberon language has been developed as the (object-oriented) successor of Modula-2. According to Blaschek *et al.* (1989), simplicity was the prime goal of its design. Oberon is a procedural language (like Modula-2) with strong static type checking. It provides only simple data types, arrays and records. A class concept is lacking.

Oberon, however, supports records that may contain (so-called *installed*) procedures. And, more importantly, records can be extended. Extension works like inheritance, in that a record type can be defined that includes all the components of the extended (read inherited) record type. In Oberon a record that is the result of extending a given record type is called *compatible* with the original record type, which means that it may be assigned to a variable holding a record of that (base) type. When such an assignment is made, the extended record is projected onto the original record (type), ignoring the fields that are added due to the extension.

In a similar way as Modula-2, Oberon supports separate compilation by requiring a definition part (containing an interface specification) and an implementation part. Modules may have private classes (that is records), just by omitting them from the interface specification. Oberon allows the dynamic creation of (record) objects. A garbage collector takes care of their elimination. As far as inheritance is concerned, Oberon only supports single inheritance. In other words, record extension only operates on a single (base) record. Moreover, inheritance in Oberon is strict, due to the restriction that no overriding is allowed. Viewed from the principle *small is beautiful*, Oberon indeed is a very nice language, containing a minimal set of features to support object-oriented programming. However, from a programming perspective, as a vehicle to implement concrete data types (see section 2.3) it leaves much to be desired. Not surprising, then, that even purported *object-oriented* extensions to Oberon have been proposed. See Blaschek *et al.* (1989) for a further discussion.

5.3.3 Multi-paradigm languages

Object-oriented programming has evolved as a new and strong *paradigm of programming*. Has it? Of the languages mentioned, only Smalltalk has what may be considered a radically new language design (and to some extent also the language Self, that we will discuss in the next section). Most of the other languages, including Eiffel, C++ (and for that matter also CLOS and Oberon), may be considered as object-oriented extensions of already existing languages, or to put it more broadly, language paradigms. Most popular are, evidently, object-oriented extensions based on procedural language paradigms, closely followed by the (Lisp-based) extensions of the functional language paradigm. Less well-known are extensions based on the logic programming paradigm, of which DLP is my favorite example.

In Wegner (1992), it is argued that the logic programming paradigm does not fit in with an object-oriented approach. I strongly disagree with this position. However, the arguments given in Wegner (1992) to defend it are worthwhile, in that they make explicit what desiderata we may impose on object-oriented languages.

Remaining within the confines of a classical object model, the basic ingredients for an object-oriented extension of any language (paradigm) are: *objects*, *classes* and *inheritance*. Although the exact meaning of these notions is open for discussion, language designers seem to have no difficulty in applying these concepts to extend (or design) a programming language.

According to Wegner (1992), the principle argument against combining logic programming and object-oriented programming is that such a combination does not support the development of open systems without compromising the logical nature of logic programming. Openness may be considered as one of the prime goals of object-orientation. See slide 5-12.

5-12

Open systems

- reactive – *flexible (dynamic) choice of actions*
- modular – *(static) scalability*

Dimensions of modularity

- encapsulation boundary – *interface to client*
- distribution boundary – *visibility from within objects*
- concurrency boundary – *threads per object, synchronization*

Slide 5-12: Dimensions of modularity

A software system is said to be *open* if its behavior can be easily modified and extended. Wegner (1992) distinguishes between two mechanisms to achieve openness; dynamically through *reactiveness*, and statically through *modularity*.

Reactiveness allows a program to choose dynamically between potential actions. For sequential object-oriented languages, *late binding* (that is, the dispatching mechanism underlying virtual function calls) is one of the mechanisms used to effect the dynamic selection of alternatives. Concurrent object-oriented languages usually offer an additional construct, in the form of a *guard* or *accept* statement, to determine dynamically which method call to answer. In both cases, the answer depends upon the nature of the object and (especially in the latter case) the state of the object (and its willingness to answer).

Openness through modularity means that a system can safely be extended by adding (statically) new components. The issue of openness in the latter sense is immediately related to the notion of *scalability*, that is the degree to which a particular component can be safely embedded in a larger environment and extended to include new functionality. At first sight, classes and inheritance strongly contribute to achieving such (static) openness. However, there is more to modularity than the encapsulation provided by classes only.

From a modeling perspective, encapsulation (as provided by objects and classes) is the basic mechanism to define the elements or entities of a model. The declarative nature of an object-oriented approach resides exactly in the opportunity to define such entities and their relations through inheritance. However, encapsulation (as typically understood in the context of a classical object model) only provides protection from illegal access from without. As such, it is a one-sided boundary.

The other side, the extent to which the outside world is visible for the object (from within), may be called the *distribution boundary*. Many languages, including Smalltalk and C++, violate the distribution boundary by allowing the use of (class-wide) global variables. (See also section 5.5.) Evidently, this may lead to problems when objects reside on distinct processors, as may be the case in distributed systems.

Typically, the message passing metaphor (commonly used to characterize the interaction between objects) contains the suggestion that objects may be physically distributed (across a network of processors). Also (because of the notion of encapsulation), objects are often regarded as autonomous entities, that in principle may have independent activity. However, most of the languages mentioned do not (immediately) fulfill the additional requirements needed for actual physical distribution or parallel (multi-threaded) activity. In section 6.2.3 we will look at these issues in more detail.

Object-oriented logic programming Logic programming is often characterized as *relational* programming, since it allows the exhaustive exploration of a search space defined by logical relations (for instance, by backtracking as in Prolog). The advantage of logic programming, from a modeling point of view, is that it allows us to specify in a logical manner (that is by logical clauses) the relations between the entities of a particular domain.

A number of efforts to combine logic programming with object-oriented features have been undertaken, among which is the development of the language Vulcan (that was mentioned in section 5.1.1). Vulcan is based on the Concurrent Prolog language and relies on a way of implementing objects as perpetual processes. Without going into detail, the idea (originally proposed in Shapiro and Takeuchi, 1983) is that an object may be implemented as a process defined by one or more (recursive) clauses. An object may accept messages in the form of a predicate call. The state of an object is maintained by parameters of the predicate, which are (possibly modified by the method call) passed to the recursive invocation of one of the clauses defining the object.

To communicate, an object (defined as a process) waits until a client asks for the execution of a method. The clauses defining the object are then evaluated to check which one is appropriate for that particular method call. If there are multiple candidate clauses, one is selected and evaluated. The other candidate clauses are discarded. Since the clauses defining an object are recursive, after the evaluation of a method the object is ready to accept another message.

The model of (object) interaction supported by Concurrent Prolog requires fine-grained concurrency, which is possible due to the side-effect free nature of logical clauses. However, to restrict the number of processes created during the evaluation of a goal, Concurrent Prolog enforces a *committed choice* between candidate clauses, thus throwing away alternative solutions.

Wegner (1992) observes, rightly I think, that the notion of committed choice is in conflict with the relational nature of logic programming. Indeed, Concurrent Prolog absolves logical completeness in the form of backtracking, to remain within the confines of the process model adopted. Wegner (1992), however, goes a step further and states that *reactiveness* and *backtracking* are irreconcilable features.

That these features may fruitfully be incorporated in a single language framework is demonstrated by the language DLP. However, to support backtracking and objects, a more elaborate process model is needed than the process model supported by Concurrent Prolog (which in a way identifies an object with a process). With such a model (that will be sketched in appendix D), there seems to be no reason to be against the marriage of logic programming and object orientation.

5.4   Prototypes – delegation versus inheritance

The classical object model (which is constituted by classes, objects and inheritance) not only has its theoretical weaknesses (as outlined in the previous section) but has also been criticized from a more pragmatic perspective because of its inflexibility when it comes to developing systems.

Code sharing has been mentioned as one of the advantages of inheritance (as it allows incremental development). However, alternative (read more flexible) forms of *sharing* have been proposed, employing prototypes and delegation instead of inheritance.

5.4.1 Alternative forms of sharing

A *class* provides a generic description of one or more objects, its instances. From a formal point of view, classes are related to types, and hence a class may be said to correspond to the set of instances that may be generated from it. This viewpoint leads to some anomalies, as in the case of *abstract* classes that at best correspond to partially defined sets. As another problem, in the context of inheritance, behavioral compatibility may be hard to arrive at, and hence the notion of *subtype* (which roughly corresponds with the subset relation) may be too restrictive. In practice, we may further encounter *one-of-a-kind* objects, for which it is simply cumbersome to construct an independent class.

In a by now classical paper, Lieberman (1986) proposes the use of *prototypes* instead of classes. The notion of prototypes (or *exemplars*) has been used in cognitive psychology to explain the incremental nature of concept learning. As Lieberman (1986) notes, the philosophical distinction between prototypes (which provide a representative example of an object) and classes (which characterize a set of similar objects) may have important pragmatical consequences as it concerns the incremental definition of (hierarchies of) related objects. First, it is (claims Lieberman, 1986) more natural to start from a concrete example than to start from an abstract characterization as given by a class. And secondly, sharing information between prototypes and clones (that is modified copies) thereof is far more flexible than the rather static means of sharing code as supported by the class inheritance mechanism.

Code sharing by inheritance may be characterized as *creation time* sharing, which in this respect is similar to creating a copy of the object by cloning. In addition, prototypes may also support *lifetime* resource sharing by means of delegation. In principle, delegation is nothing but the forwarding of a message. However, in contrast to the forwarding mechanism as described in sections 2.3 and 7.2, delegation in the context of prototypes does not change implicit self-reference to the forwarding object. In other words, when delegating a message to a *parent* object, the context of answering the message remains the same, as if the forwarding object answers the request directly. See slide 5-13.

Prototypes – *exemplars*
- cloning – *creation time sharing*
- delegation – *lifetime sharing*

5-13

Slide 5-13: Prototypes

An almost classical example used to illustrate *prototypical* programming is the example of a *turtle* object that delegates its request to move itself to a *pen* object (which has

x and y coordinate attributes and a *move* method). The flexibility of delegation becomes apparent when we define a number of *turtle* objects by cloning the *pen* object and adding an y coordinate private to each *turtle*. In contrast to derivation by inheritance, the x coordinate of the *pen* object is shared dynamically. When changing the value of x in one of the *turtle* objects, all the *turtle* objects will be affected. Evidently, this allows considerable (and sometimes unwished for) flexibility. However, for applications (such as multimedia systems) such flexibility may be desirable.

Design issues Strictly speaking, prototype-based delegation is not stronger than forwarding in languages supporting classes and inheritance. In Dony *et al.* (1992), a taxonomy of prototype-based languages is given. (This taxonomy has been partly implemented in Smalltalk. The implementation, however, employs so-called class-variables, which are not unproblematic themselves. See section 5.5.)

One of the principal advantages of prototype-based languages is that they offer a consistent yet simple model of programming, consisting of objects, cloning and delegation. Yet, when designing a prototype-based language, a number of design decisions must be made (as reflected in the taxonomy given in Dony *et al.*, 1992). These issues concern the representation of the state of an object, how objects are created and the way in which delegation is handled. See slide 5-14.

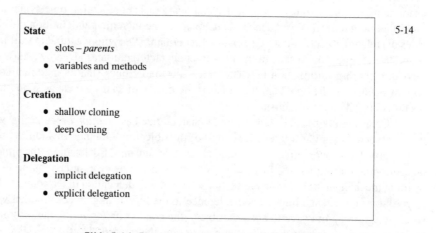

State   5-14

- slots – *parents*
- variables and methods

Creation

- shallow cloning
- deep cloning

Delegation

- implicit delegation
- explicit delegation

Slide 5-14: Prototypes – state, creation, delegation

The basic prototype model only features *slots* which may store either a value or a piece of code that may be executed as a method. Alternatively, a distinction may be made between variables and methods. In both cases, late binding must be employed to access a value. In contrast, instance variable bindings in class-based languages are usually resolved statically.

When creating a new object by cloning an existing object, we have the choice between deep copying and shallow copying. Only shallow copying, however, allows lifetime sharing (since deep copying results in a replica at creation time). Shallow copying is thus the obvious choice.

Finally, delegation is usually handled implicitly, for instance by means of a special *parent* slot, indicating the ancestor of the object (which may be changed dynamically). Alternatively, it may be required to indicate delegation explicitly for each method. This gives a programmer more flexibility since it allows an object to have multiple ancestors, but at the price of an increase in notational complexity. Explicit delegation, by the way, most closely resembles the use of forwarding in class-based systems.

One of the, as yet, unresolved problems of delegation-based computing is how to deal with what Dony *et al.* (1992) call *split* objects. An object may (internally) consist of a large number of (smaller) objects that are linked to each other by the delegation relation. It is not clear how to address such a complex object as a single entity. Also, the existence of a large number of small objects that communicate by message passing may impose severe performance penalties. To shed some light on the efficiency of object-oriented computing in general (and prototype-based computing in particular), we will have a brief look at the optimization techniques employed for the implementation of the language Self.

5.4.2   Implementation techniques – Self

A major concern of software developers is (often) the runtime efficiency of the system developed. An order of magnitude difference in execution speed may, indeed, mean the difference between acceptance and rejection.

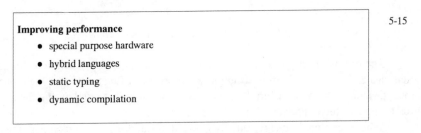

Slide 5-15: Improving performance

There are a number of ways in which to improve on the runtime efficiency of programs, including object-oriented programs. For example, Ungar *et al.* (1992) mention the reliance on special purpose hardware (which thus far has been rapidly overtaken by new general purpose processor technology), the use of hybrid languages (which is considered error-prone), static typing (which for object-oriented programming provides only a partial solution) and dynamic compilation (which has been successfully applied for Self). See slide 5-15.

As for the use of hybrid languages, of which C++ is an example, the apparent impurity of such an approach may (to my mind) even be beneficial in some cases. However, the programmer is required to deal more explicitly with the implementation features of the language than may be desirable.

In general, both with respect to reliability and efficiency, statically typed languages have a distinct advantage over dynamically typed (interpreted) languages. Yet, for the purpose of fast prototyping, interpreted languages (like Smalltalk) offer an advantage in terms of development time and flexibility. Moreover, the use of (polymorphic) virtual functions and dynamic binding necessitate additional dynamic runtime support (that is not needed in strictly procedural languages). Clever compilation reduces the overhead (even in the case of multiple inheritance) to one or two additional indirections.

Dynamic compilation The language Self, described in Ungar and Smith (1987), is at the time of writing one of the most popular prototype-based languages. It is quite pure and simple in design. It supports objects with *slots* (that may contain both values and code, representing methods), shallow cloning, and implicit delegation (via a designated *parent* slot). The developers of Self have introduced a number of techniques to improve the efficiency of prototype-based computing.

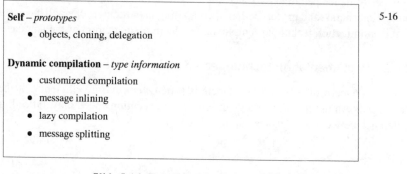

Slide 5-16: Dynamic compilation – Self

The optimization techniques are based on dynamic compilation, a technique that resembles the partial evaluation techniques employed in functional and logic programming. Dynamic compilation employs the type information gathered during the computation to improve the efficiency of message passing.

Whenever a method is repeatedly invoked, the address of the recipient object may be backpatched in the caller. In some cases, even the result may be inlined to replace the request. Both techniques make it appear that message passing takes place, but at a much lower price. More complicated techniques, involving lazy compilation (by delaying the compilation of infrequently visited code) and message splitting (involving a dataflow analysis and the reduction of redundancies) may be applied to achieve more optimal results.

Benchmark tests have indicated a significant improvement in execution speed (up to 60% of optimized C code) for cases where type information could be dynamically obtained. The reader is referred to Ungar *et al.* (1992) for further details.

5.5   Meta-level architectures

Another weakness of the classical object model (or perhaps one of its strengths) is that the concept of a class easily lends itself to being overloaded with additional meanings and features such as *class variables* and *metaclasses*. These notions lead to extensions to the original *class/instance* scheme that are hard to unify in a single elegant framework. In this section we will study a proposal based on a reflexive relation between classes and objects.

Dependent on one's perspective, a class may either be regarded as a kind of abstract data type (specifying the operational interface of its object instances) or, more pragmatically, as a template for object creation (that is a means to generate new instances).

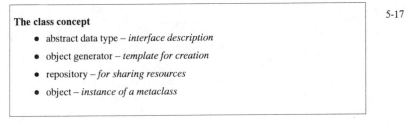

5-17

The class concept
- abstract data type – *interface description*
- object generator – *template for creation*
- repository – *for sharing resources*
- object – *instance of a metaclass*

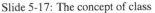

Slide 5-17: The concept of class

In addition, however, in a number of systems a class may be used as a repository for sharing class-wide resources. For example, the Smalltalk language allows the definition of *class variables* that are accessible to all instances of the class. See slide 5-17.

Class variables Clearly, the use of class variables violates what we have called the *distribution boundary* in section 5.3.3, since it allows objects to reach out of their encapsulation borders. Class variables may also be employed in C++ by defining data members as *static*. Apart from class variables, Smalltalk also supports the notion of *class methods*, which may be regarded as routines having the class and its instances as their scope. Class methods in Smalltalk are typically used for the creation and initialization of new instances of the class for which they are defined. In C++, creation and initialization is taken care of by the constructor(s) of a class, together with the (system supplied) *new* operator. Class methods, in C++, take the form of static member functions that are like ordinary functions (apart from their restricted scope and their calling syntax, which is of the form *class :: member(...)*).

Contrary to classes in C++, classes in Smalltalk have a functionality similar to that of objects. Classes in Smalltalk provide encapsulation (encompassing class variables and class methods) and message passing (for example for the creation and initialization of new instances). To account for this object-like behavior, the designers of Smalltalk have introduced the notion of *metaclass* of which a class is an instance.

Metaclasses In the classical object model, two relations play a role when describing the architectural properties of a system. The first relation is the *instance* relation to indicate that an object O is an instance of a class C. The second (equally important) relation is the *inheritance* relation, which indicates that a class C is a subclass (or derived from) a given (ancestor) class P. See slide 5-18.

When adopting the philosophy *everything is an object* together with the idea that *each object is an instance of a class* (as the developers of Smalltalk did), we evidently get into problems when we try to explain the nature (and existence) of a class.

To be an object, a class itself must be an instance of a class (which for convenience we will call a *metaclass*). Take, for example, the class *Point*. This class must be an instance of a (meta)class (say *Class*) which in its turn must be an instance of a (meta) class

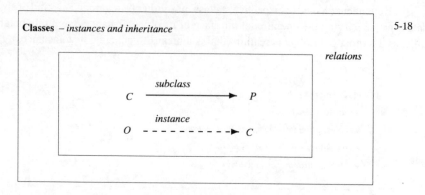

Slide 5-18: The *instance* and *inheritance* relation

(say *MetaClass*), and so on. Clearly, following the instance relation leads to an infinite regress. hence, we must postulate some system-defined *MetaClass* (at a certain level) from which to instantiate the (metaclasses of) actual classes such as *Point*. See slide 5-19.

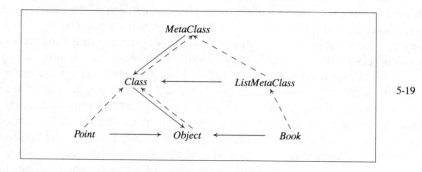

Slide 5-19: Meta architecture

The figure above is a (more or less) accurate rendering of the solution provided by Smalltalk. We may add additional flexibility by allowing user-defined metaclasses that may refine the behavior of the system-defined metaclass *Class*. (This is the solution chosen for Loops, see Stefik and Bobrow (1986).)

Thus far we have traced the instance relation which leads (following the reversed arrows) from top to bottom, from metaclasses to actual object instances. As pictured in the diagram above, the inheritance relation (followed in the same manner) goes in exactly the opposite direction, having the class *Object* at the root of the inheritance hierarchy. For example, the class *Point* (while being an instance of the metaclass *Class*) is derived by inheritance from the class *Object*. Similarly, the (meta)class *Class* itself inherits from the class *Object*, and in its turn the system-defined metaclass *MetaClass* inherits from *Class*. As for the user-defined metaclasses, these may be thought of as inheriting from the system-defined metaclass *Class*. Apart from being slightly confusing, the architecture presented above is rather inelegant due to the magic (that is system-defined) number of meta levels. In the following, we will study a means to overcome this inelegancy.

Reflection Cointe (1987) proposes an architecture that unifies the notions of object, class and metaclass, while allowing metaclasses to be defined at an arbitrary level. The key to this solution lies in the postulates characterizing the behavior of an object-oriented system given in slide 5-20.

5-20

Postulates – *class-based languages*

- everything is an object
- every object belongs to a class
- every class inherits from the class *Object*
- class variables of an object are instance variables of its class

---

Slide 5-20: Class-based languages – postulates

The first three postulates are quite straightforward. They agree with the assumptions underlying Smalltalk. The last postulate, however, stating that a class variable of an object must be an instance variable of the objects class (taken as an object), imposes a constraint of a self-recurrent or reflexive nature. This recurrence is pictured in the diagram below, which displays the object *Class* as an instance of itself (that is the class *Class*). See slide 5-21. In other respects, the diagram is similar to the diagram depicting the (meta) architecture of Smalltalk and Loops.

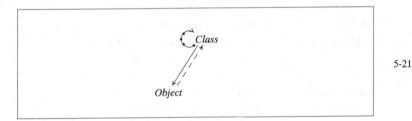

5-21

Slide 5-21: Reflective architecture

To indicate how such a reflective relation may be implemented, Cointe (1987) introduces a representation of objects involving the attributes *name* (to indicate the class of the object), *supers* (to indicate its ancestor(s)), *iv* (to list the instance variables of the object) and *methods* (to store the methods belonging to the object).

In this scheme of representation, the system-defined metaclass *Class* is precisely the object reflecting its own structure in the values of its attributes, as depicted above. Every instance of *Class* may assign values to its instance variables (contained in *iv*) that are appropriate to the instances that will be created from it. In general, a metaclass is an object having at least the attributes of *Class* (and possibly more). See slide 5-22.

Using this scheme, an arbitrary towering of metaclasses may be placed on top of concrete classes, thus allowing the software developer to squeeze out the last bit of differential programming. Elegant indeed, although it is doubtful whether many programmers

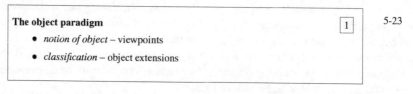

name	supers	iv	methods

Class (*Object*) (*name supers iv methods*) (*new ...*)

5-22

Slide 5-22: A reflective definition of *Class*

will endeavor upon such a route. A nice example of employing (customized) metaclasses, however, is given in Malenfant *et al.* (1989), where metaclasses are used to define the functionality of distribution and communication primitives employed by concrete classes.

Summary

This chapter presented an overview of object-oriented programming languages. We discussed the heritage of Simula and the various areas of research and development the ideas introduced by Simula has generated.

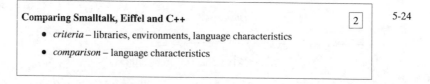

The object paradigm   1   5-23

- *notion of object* – viewpoints
- *classification* – object extensions

Slide 5-23: Section 5.1: The object paradigm

A classification and overview of existing object-oriented languages was given and we noted the prominence of hybrid languages derived from Lisp and C.

Comparing Smalltalk, Eiffel and C++   2   5-24

- *criteria* – libraries, environments, language characteristics
- *comparison* – language characteristics

Slide 5-24: Section 5.2: Comparing Smalltalk, Eiffel and C++

In section 2, we looked at a comparison of Smalltalk, Eiffel and C++, including criteria such as the availability of libraries, programming environments and language characteristics.

In section 3, we discussed the design dimensions of object-oriented languages and characterized an orthogonal set of dimensions consisting of objects, types, delegation and abstraction. We also discussed the notion of open systems and multi-paradigm languages combining logic programming with object-oriented features.

In section 4, we dealt with classless prototype-based languages, supporting dynamic delegation instead of inheritance.

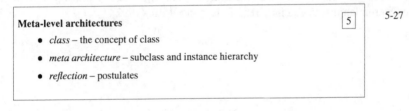

Design dimensions of object-oriented languages   [3]   5-25

- *object-oriented* – object-based + inheritance
- *orthogonal dimensions* – objects, types, delegation, abstraction
- *open systems* – dimensions of modularity

Slide 5-25: Section 5.3: Design dimensions of object-oriented languages

Prototypes – delegation versus inheritance   [4]   5-26

- *prototypes* – cloning and delegation
- *performance* – dynamic compilation

Slide 5-26: Section 5.4: Prototypes – delegation versus inheritance

We also discussed performance issues and observed that dynamic compilation based on runtime type information may achieve good results.

Meta-level architectures   [5]   5-27

- *class* – the concept of class
- *meta architecture* – subclass and instance hierarchy
- *reflection* – postulates

Slide 5-27: Section 5.5: Meta-level architectures

Finally, in section 5, we reflected on the concept of class and discussed a reflective architecture unifying the interpretation of a class as an object, capable of answering messages, and as a description of the properties of its instances.

Questions

(1) What are the basic characteristics of object-oriented languages?

(2) How would you classify object-oriented languages? Name a few representatives of each category.

(3) What do you consider to be the major characteristic of the object model supported by C++? Explain.

(4) How would you characterize Smalltalk, Eiffel and C++ with respect to reliability, efficiency and complexity? Explain.

(5) How would you characterize the difference between object-based and object-oriented?

(6) Along what orthogonal dimensions would you design an object-oriented language? Explain.

(7) How would you characterize prototype-based languages?

(8) What are the differences between inheritance and delegation?

(9) Does C++ support delegation? Explain.

(10) How would you characterize the concept of a class?

(11) Can you sketch the meta architecture of Smalltalk?

(12) How would you phrase the postulates underlying class-based languages? Can you give a reflective version of these postulates?

Further reading

A concise treatment of programming languages is given in Bal and Grune (1994). Further, you may want to consult Wegner (1987), which contains the original presentation of the discussion concerning the distinction between *object-based* and *object oriented*. For the Oberon language, you may read Reiser and Wirth (1992).

6

Distribution and concurrency

Many applications, for example in the area of telecomputing, banking and multimedia (but also in high performance computing and operating systems), require support for distribution and concurrency. Due to their complexity, these applications are likely candidates for an object-oriented approach. However, with regard to their distributed nature, some marriage between object-oriented computing and distributed/concurrent computing must be realized.

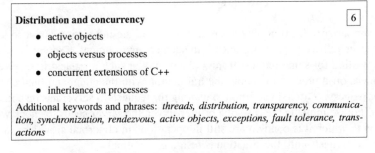

Slide 6-1: Distribution and concurrency

In this chapter, we will discuss a number of issues involved in combining objects and processes. First, we explore the notion of active objects, that is objects having (possibly multiple) process threads. Then, we look at some extensions of C++ supporting active objects, and investigate what problems are involved in synchronization and communication.

One of the (important) unresolved issues in combining processes with the traditional object model is how to employ inheritance to refine the behavior of active objects. To deal with this problem, we need to extend our notion of behavior to include aspects of synchronization.

Finally, we will discuss the infra-structure needed for distributed computing and how this affects the object model of a (distributed) object-oriented language.

6.1   A modeling perspective

Perhaps the most dominant metaphor in object-oriented design is what we have called the *client/server* model in sections 1.1.3 and 3.3. This model is supported by the notion of *contracts* as initially introduced for the language Eiffel. Not accidentally, the *client/server* model is also an important paradigm in distributed programming, and hence may serve as a good starting point from which to explore the possible contribution of object orientation to distributed and concurrent programming.

A *contract* (as introduced in section 3.3) describes the interface of an object and specifies the duties and benefits for a client in terms of (logical) pre- and post-conditions.

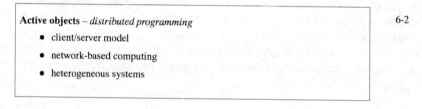

Active objects – *distributed programming*   6-2

- client/server model
- network-based computing
- heterogeneous systems

Slide 6-2: Active objects

A similar specification may be used to describe the interaction between a client and a server in a distributed environment. In such an environment, a server is generally a process waiting for some request from a client. When such a request is received, the server spawns off a process to handle the transaction with the client and then continues to wait for requests. Often, in addition to waiting for requests, a server has responsibility of its own. For example, in the case of a printer server, the server needs to check whether the printers to which it is coupled are still in operation. In abnormal situations, a server may hold the requests until the situation is restored to normal.

Despite the server's own activity, for a client a server is just an entity offering a collection of services. Hence, as observed in Meyer (1993), logically the distinction between *active* and *passive* objects need play no role.

Operationally, however, the distinction between passive and active objects should be clear. A passive object uses the processing resources of the caller to execute the method invoked, whereas an active object possesses its own processing resources to deal with the request. Consequently, the implementation language must provide constructs which allow the programmer to deal (either implicitly or explicitly) with the concurrency issues involved.

Which primitives are needed depends upon several factors, among which is the choice of a particular concurrency model (suiting the application domain in question).

Given the availability of wide and local area networks, it seems likely that complex systems will become increasingly distributed in nature and, hence, active objects will be the rule rather than an exception. An important consequence of the accessibility of networks, in conjunction with the growing size of systems, is that (large) systems will tend to become more and more heterogeneous. For example, multi-media systems are usually not built as a single monolithic program, but rather consist of a number of smaller cooperating components, that may in their turn rely on third party software to actually display the (multimedia) documents.

Concurrent problem solving From a modeling perspective, the availability of processes may lead to a more flexible, not to say natural, approach to problem solving. Having a notion of processes (or active objects) at one's disposal, may lead to employing the inherent concurrency characteristics of a problem domain to arrive at a more natural (that is intuitively suitable) model.

Problem solving – *concurrency*   6-3

- pipe-line concurrency

- divide and conquer

- cooperative problem solving

Slide 6-3: Concurrent problem solving

Traditionally, three patterns of concurrent problem solving can be distinguished, which may be characterized as *pipe-line concurrency*, *divide and conquer*, and *cooperative problem solving*. See slide 6-3.

Pipe-line concurrency may be used to apply a sequence of filters sorting out a good solution. A well-known example of this kind of concurrency is the implementation of the *sieve of Eratosthenes* as a (dynamically growing) sequence of communicating processes, each testing for divisibility by a prime number. As a remark, pipe-line concurrency is also a well-known composition mechanism of the Unix operating system, where it is used to connect programs that each perform a specific operation on a stream of (character-based) data.

Divide and conquer is an almost equally well-established technique of exploiting the parallelism inherent in a problem solution. The basic idea is to split a problem into relatively independent subproblems that may be solved in parallel. This subdivision may be repeated recursively. As an example of this approach, think of a parallel implementation of a sorting algorithm (for example *mergesort*) which consists of splitting the list to be sorted in two halves that may be sorted independently before being merged. Although this approach is straightforward, actual speedup may be hard to achieve.

The final pattern (or paradigm) may be characterized as *cooperative problem solving*. However, this characterization actually begs the question. In contrast to the two previous patterns, which employ a regular structure of processes (respectively a sequence for *pipe-lining* and a tree structure for *divide and conquer*), the process structure employed in *cooperative problem solving* may be arbitrarily complex. It is this kind of modeling we are interested in when discussing object-based concurrency. Actually, this kind of co-operation comes closer to a *peer-to-peer* relation than the *master-slave* relation characteristic for the *client/server* model. Hence, the notion of *client* and *server* must be taken in a relative sense, as reversible roles.

As an aside, as an area in which cooperative processes play an important role (as a modeling vehicle) we may mention *discrete event simulation*, which, historically, lies at the root of object-oriented programming.

6.2 Objects and processes

Parallel processing has an impressive history, both in a practical sense (one may say that processes existed before objects came into life) and in terms of the literature it has generated. (See, for example Andrews, 1991.) Yet the development of parallel (and distributed) programs is generally considered to be an expert's job, due to the inherent complexity of parallel solutions and the synchronization involved.

Not surprisingly, the object-oriented community has taken an interest in parallel computing, hoping that the intrinsic complexity of parallel processing could be better managed by an object-oriented approach.

In the following, we will first explore by what means we may introduce parallelism in an object-oriented system or language and, subsequently, what encapsulation is needed for processes and distribution in addition to the encapsulation already supported by the object model.

Language support The shift towards distributed systems, supporting concurrency and communication between (geographically) distinct objects requires support that is not found in the object-oriented languages we have discussed thus far.

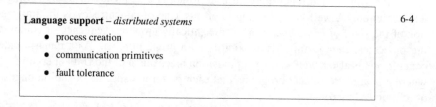

Slide 6-4: Language support

Usually, distributed applications rely on the primitives provided by the underlying operating system. However, the use of operating system primitives for process creation and communication is usually rather *ad hoc* and, consequently, error-prone and difficult to port across platforms.

Fortunately, the object model seems to lend itself in a quite straightforward way to a generalization supporting distribution and concurrency. In the sections that follow, we will take a closer look at the notion of processes and how it relates to our common notion of objects. Apart from processes, an object-oriented language supporting distributed/concurrent computing also needs to provide for synchronization and communication primitives that fit within the message passing model of object-oriented computing. See slide 6-4. Finally, to support truly distributed programming, issues of fault-tolerance need to be dealt with as well.

6.2.1 Object-based concurrency

When it comes to combining *objects* (the building blocks in an object-oriented approach) with *processes* (the building blocks in parallel computing), there are three distributed approaches conceivable. See slide 6-5.

Object-based concurrency

- add processes – *synchronization*
- multiple active objects – *rendezvous*
- asynchronous communication – *message buffers*

6-5

Slide 6-5: Objects and concurrency

One can simply add *processes* as an additional data type. Alternatively, one can introduce *active objects*, having activity of their own, or, one can employ *asynchronous communication*, allowing the client and server object to proceed independently.

Processes The first, most straightforward approach, is to simply add *processes* as a primitive data type, allowing the creation of independent threads of processing. An example is Distributed Smalltalk (see Bennett, 1987). The disadvantage of this somewhat naive approach, however, is that the programmer has full responsibility for the most difficult part of parallel programming, namely the synchronization between processes and the avoidance of common errors such as simultaneously assigning a value to a shared variable.

Despite the fact that the literature (see Andrews, 1991) abounds with primitives supporting synchronization (such as semaphores, conditional sections and monitors), such an approach is error-prone and means a heavy burden on the shoulders of the application developer.

Active objects A second, and in my view to be preferred, approach is to introduce explicitly a notion of *active objects*. Within this approach, parallelism is introduced by having multiple, simultaneously active objects. An example of a language supporting active objects is POOL (see America, 1987). Communication between active objects occurs by means of a (synchronous) rendezvous. To engage in a rendezvous, however, an active object must interrupt its own activity by means of an (Ada-like) *accept statement* (or *answer statement* as it is called in POOL), indicating that the object is willing to answer a message. The advantage of this approach is, clearly, that the encapsulation boundary of the object (its message interface) can conveniently be employed as a monitor-like mechanism to enforce mutual exclusion between method invocations.

Despite the elegance of this solution, however, unifying objects and processes in *active objects* is not without problems. First, one has to decide whether to make all objects active or allow both passive and active objects. Logically, passive objects may be regarded as active objects that are eternally willing to answer every message listed in the interface description of the object. However, this generalization is not without penalty in terms of runtime efficiency. Secondly, a much more serious problem is that the message answering semantics of active objects is distinctly different from the message answering semantics of passive objects with respect to self-invocation. Namely, to answer a message, an active object must interrupt its own activity. Yet, if an active object (in the middle of answering a message) sends a message to itself, we have a situation of *deadlock*. Direct self-invocation, of course, can be easily detected, but indirect self-invocations require an analysis of the complete method invocation graph, which is generally not feasible.

Asynchronous communication Deadlock comes about by synchronous (indirect) self-invocation. An immediate solution to this problem is provided by languages supporting asynchronous communication, which provide message buffers allowing the caller to proceed without waiting for an answer.

Asynchronous message passing, however, radically deviates from the (synchronous) message passing supported by the traditional (passive) object model. This has the following consequences. First, for the programmer, it becomes impossible to know when a message will be dealt with and, consequently, when to expect an answer. Secondly, for the language implementor, allocating resources for storing incoming messages and deciding when to deal with messages waiting in a message buffer becomes a responsibility for which it is hard to find a general, yet efficient, solution.

Active objects with asynchronous message passing constitute the so-called *actor* model, which has influenced several language designs. See Agha (1990).

6.2.2 Process-based encapsulation

In his seminal paper on the dimensions of object-oriented design, Wegner (1987) observes that various notions of encapsulation, as have become popular with object-oriented programming, already existed in one form or another in the distributed programming community. To establish what requirements an object-oriented system must meet to qualify as (potentially) distributed, we once more rely on the analytical work of Wegner (1987), delineating precisely the notions of processes, threads and distribution.

A *process*, according to Wegner (1987), consists of an *interface* (naming the possible transactions, that is operations, allowed) and one or more *threads* (that may be active or suspended). A *thread* is characterized by Wegner (1987) as consisting of a *locus of control* (in other words, a program counter) and an *execution state* (consisting of a runtime stack and possibly a heap for dynamically created data). See slide 6-6.

Dependent on the number of threads, we may characterize a process as either *sequential* (a single thread of control), *quasi-concurrent* (at most one active thread, arbitrarily many suspended) or (truly) *concurrent* (multiple active threads, arbitrarily many suspended).

When considering active objects, a distinction between *single threaded* objects and *multi-threaded* objects seems to be more appropriate. The most straightforward ap-

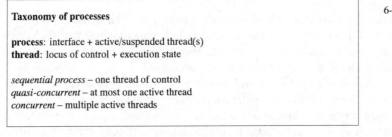

Taxonomy of processes   6-6

process: interface + active/suspended thread(s)
thread: locus of control + execution state

sequential process – one thread of control
quasi-concurrent – at most one active thread
concurrent – multiple active threads

Slide 6-6: Processes and threads

proach is to associate an object with a single thread of control, that may be divided between answering messages and the object's own activity.

The model of *communicating sequential processes* (corresponding to single threaded objects) was first advocated in Hoare (1978). It underlies programming languages such as CSP, occam and Ada, and is probably the best understood model of parallel processing that we have (see Andrews, 1991).

In combination with the assumption that objects share no variables, single threaded objects bear a close resemblance to what Wegner (1987) calls *distributed sequential processes*. However, with reference to the language DLP (which employs multi-threaded objects to support distributed backtracking), we must note that single-threaded objects are not the only means to implement active objects.

Distributed sequential processes, as characterized by Wegner (1987), provide a combination of characteristics that make them exemplary as a model for active objects. See slide 6-7.

Distributed sequential processes – *own address space*   6-7

Unit of modularity – user interface
Unit of concurrency – single thread
Unit of naming – name space

Slide 6-7: Sequential processes

Perhaps their most important characteristic is the absence of global data shared with other processes. As a consequence, they provide what may be called *strong encapsulation*, since in addition to the absence of global variables, the transaction interface of a process precisely delimits the functionality offered to potential clients.

In addition to the protection with regard to global variables, distributed processes must satisfy a number of other requirements to guarantee correct execution. These requirements will be dealt with in more detail in section 6.5.

6.2.3   On the notion of active objects

Active objects are objects with a thread of their own. This definition is minimal in the sense that it does not restrict active objects to having only one thread. Neither does it specify what communication primitives must be provided and how synchronization (to avoid simultaneous access to shared data) is effected.

As a starting point, we will present some examples of active objects, taken from Eliëns and Visser (1994). We will use these examples to illustrate some of the problems involved in combining objects and concurrency, and to discuss some of the criteria by which to compare the various language proposals dealing with concurrency and distribution.

The most straightforward, although somewhat naive, approach to supporting active objects (in C++) is to extend the constructor mechanism with a facility for process creation. Consequently, in addition to the initialization of an object, the constructor (of an active object) creates a thread that may be employed either for the object's own activity or to respond to a message.

As an example of a class specifying active objects, look at the definition of an active counter in slide 6-8

6-8

```
active class counter {                          Active C++
private:
  int val;
public:
active counter( int n )  {
  val = n;
  for(;;) accept (operator++ , operator() );
}
void operator++ ()   { val++; }
int operator() ()   { return val; }
};
```

Slide 6-8: Active objects in Active C++

In the example, the keyword *active* has been used to indicate that the class *counter* defines active objects and, in addition, to indicate that the constructor of the *counter* creates a process thread.

The *counter* class own activity presented is quite trivial. After initialization of the instance variable n, holding the actual value of the *counter*, a *counter* object enters a loop indicating its (eternal) willingness to execute either of the operators constituting the method interface. For the moment, we just assume that invoking a member function results in a *rendezvous* and provides complete mutual exclusion between member function calls, to guarantee the absence of simultaneous assignment to the instance variable n.

Interestingly, despite its simplicity, the example contains a number of problems for which a language designer (and implementor) must provide a solution.

The first, perhaps most fundamental, problem to note is that (taking the normal semantics of C++ constructors for granted) the constructor never terminates. One possible solution is to distinguish between the initialization of the object (for which naturally the constructor will be used) and the creation of a process (for example by a system-defined virtual function *main*()). However, an alternative solution would be to return a pointer to the object immediately, but to grant the constructor sufficiently high priority to guarantee that it finishes the initialization, until it blocks to wait for a request. As an aside, the latter solution would allow classes to inherit from classes defining active objects. See section 6.4.

Another problem, that is not of fundamental importance but which may highly influence the convenience with which the programmer may employ active objects (in combination with passive objects), is the extent to which the language constructs dealing with concurrency affect the programming style used to define (ordinary) passive objects.

There are two sides to this question. First, from the point of view of the client of an object, there should (ideally) be no distinction between dealing with a passive object and dealing with an active object. This includes the creation of an object and the invocation of member functions. However, in some circumstances the programmer may need to influence where the newly created object will be located and possibly with what priority it must run.

Secondly, to allow a gradual transition from a system consisting of passive objects to a system containing (some) active objects, the code defining the synchronization and communication properties of an active object should be as *non-interruptive* as possible. Naturally, whether a (collection of) language construct(s) must be regarded as *non-interruptive* is a highly qualitative judgement. It is merely used to stress the importance of a gradual transition from *passive* to *active* code, which seems to fit best within the incremental nature of object-oriented programming.

Communication by rendezvous Again, the most straightforward way to deal with member function invocation in a concurrent setting is to regard it as a *synchronous rendezvous* between (possibly remotely located) objects. Synchronizing the communication between objects may then be done by using *accept* statements, as illustrated in the *bounded buffer* example given in slide 6-9.

The acceptance of *put* and *get* is serialized to ensure that there is an item in the buffer when *get* is invoked. This buffer can be easily generalized to a bounded buffer containing a number of elements. Acceptance of requests then depends upon the internal state of the *buffer* object, that is whether the buffer is empty, full or somewhere in-between, as illustrated in the code slide 6-10.

The synchronous rendezvous provides a quite well-established parallel programming paradigm, familiar from Ada. However, it does not necessarily lead to the most optimal solution with respect to exploitation of the concurrency potentially available.

As another problem, and *a fortiori* this holds for C++ with its rather elaborate arsenal of data types, in a distributed environment provision needs to be made to transport arbitrarily complex data types across a network.

The examples looked at thus far are taken from an experimental language, Active C++, developed by the author's group as a vehicle for research in distributed/concurrent computing in C++. In the next section, we will look at a number of alternative proposals for extending C++ with concurrency and distribution.

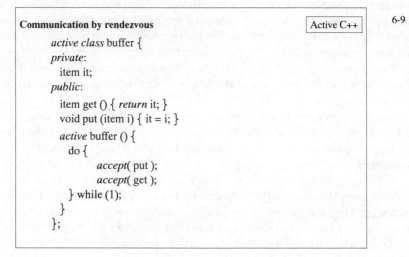

Slide 6-9: Communication by rendezvous

```
if (used <  size && used >  0) accept(put,get)
else if (used == 0) accept(put)
else accept(get);
```
6-10

Slide 6-10: Synchronization in Active C++

6.3   Concurrent extensions of C++

Extending C++ with facilities for concurrency and distribution has become a very active research area. The common motivation, learned from the reports describing this research, is that C++ was chosen because it is a very popular object-oriented language (which, very importantly, supports static type checking). The advantage of extending an existing language is that full use can be made of the tools and expertise already developed. Moreover, in many cases the transition to using the constructs introduced for distribution and concurrency can be done gradually, without adopting a completely different programming style.

In this section, we will look at a number of extensions of C++. These extensions include Concurrent C++ (that introduces *process* data types, see Gehani and Roome (1988)), ACT++ (which is based on the *actor* model, see Kafura and Lee (1990)), μC++ (which introduces a number of primitives for concurrent shared memory computing, see Buhr et al (1992)), Compositional C++ (that uses *write-once* variables to effect synchronization, see Chandy and Kesselman (1992)), Mentat (that utilizes data flow graphs for parallel computing, see Grimshaw and Liu (1987)) and P++ (that introduces primitives for remote object invocations, see Nolte (1991)). This list is certainly not complete, but each of the various languages discussed covers some of the important issues in the design of a parallel object-oriented language.

Design issues In slide 6-11 we have listed the design issues that occur when developing a parallel object-oriented language, either from scratch or by extending a given language such as C++.

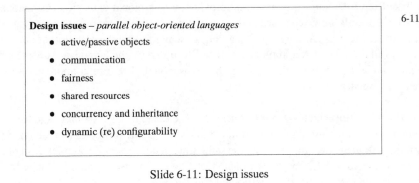

Slide 6-11: Design issues

An important choice is whether to distinguish between active and passive objects, or whether to support only one kind of object. Another important issue is how the activity of objects is to be defined. The choice we have is between providing an explicit *process data type* (as in Concurrent C++) or some merger between the process definition of an object and its class specification (as in ACT++). There is a wide choice of communication primitives, ranging from explicit constructs such as monitors and queues (as in µC++) to global *write-once* variables that allow for the suspension of processes reading uninitialized variables (as in Compositional C++). Global *write-once* variables also provide, in addition to a mechanism for synchronization, an excellent mechanism for sharing common resources. Other means to implement shared resources are based on the *client/server* model, and require the support for remote procedure call or synchronous rendezvous (as in Mentat). Transport across a network, moreover, requires suitable primitives (augmenting the type system of C++) to control the packaging of the data involved in the communication (as in P++).

Other issues in the design of a parallel object-oriented language have to do with the combination of concurrency and inheritance (that we will study in section 6.4) and the allocation of objects on a network of processes (which may be done statically or dynamically). The latter issue will be briefly dealt with in section 6.5

6.3.1   Encapsulating processes and transactions

Concurrent extensions of C++ may in principle be provided without disrupting the semantics of the original language constructs by employing libraries and the class inheritance mechanism. This approach has, for instance, been followed in Bershad *et al.* (1988). However, such an approach leaves the responsibility for process creation, process destruction, communication and synchronization entirely to the user. This is clearly not an optimal solution.

The alternative approach (which is viable only when the designers of an extension have access to the compiler or are willing to undertake the effort of developing a pre-processor) allows for more drastic modifications to be realized, modifications that may provide support for implicit synchronization protocols and high level concurrency abstractions.

Adopting this approach, we do again have a choice. We may leave the original semantics of the base language intact and provide an orthogonal extension (orthogonal in the sense that only new types are added) or we may introduce modifications that more deeply affect the original language by giving a (semantic) reinterpretation of constructs already available. The latter approach will be illustrated by the language ACT++, which extends C++ with constructs inspired by the *actor* model. The former approach is exemplified by Concurrent C++.

An orthogonal approach – Concurrent C++ The Concurrent C++ language has a history that is worth mentioning, since it illustrates some of the difficulties involved in programming language design. At about the same time that C++ was developed as an object-oriented extension of C, another extension of C was proposed, namely Concurrent C, which was intended for parallel distributed computing.

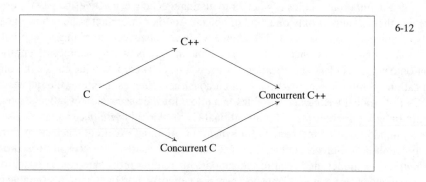

6-12

Slide 6-12: An orthogonal approach

Both C++ and Concurrent C may be regarded as orthogonal extensions of C, respectively as *C with classes* and *C with processes*. By combining these extensions, the developers of Concurrent C++ hoped to arrive at an orthogonal extension of both C++ and Concurrent C, which was also an orthogonal extension of C. See slide 6-12.

The Concurrent C language introduces the additional data type *process* in C, and supports a notion of *transaction*, which is a function belonging to a process type. (Actually, the phrase *transaction* is a misnomer, since it suggests the functionality of database transactions including properties such as atomicity. Transactions in the sense of Concurrent C are more like *entries* in Ada.) Process types are declared by means of a *process specification* that lists the transactions allowed and describes what parameters are needed for the creation of a process. An example of a process specification, declaring a consumer and producer process, is given in slide 6-13.

To define the actual meaning of a process, a *process body* must be defined. In addition to the primitives already mentioned, the language Concurrent C has an accept

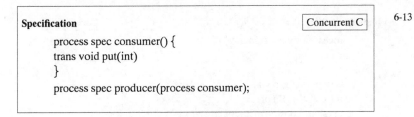

6-13

Slide 6-13: Process specification in Concurrent C

statement that may be employed to define the acceptance conditions of a particular transaction, as illustrated below.

The transaction *put* (which in the case of a multiple element buffer would have to be delayed if the buffer is full) results in assigning the parameter value to a local variable of the process. Following the acceptance of the transaction, the value is properly consumed and the consumer is again willing to engage in another transaction.

In comparison, the body of the producer process is very simple. It just sends the consumer the data taken from some external source. Note that the actual consumer must be given as a parameter to the producer at creation time, as illustrated in the code below.

```
void main() {
     create producer( create consumer() );
}
```

In Concurrent C, process types have a special status. They allow for checking whether the transactions invoked for a particular object are legal, as in the body of producer where the consumer transaction *put* is called. Also, they act as generic types that are used to pass process entities around, as in the creation of the producer process that takes a consumer as a parameter.

Obviously, the notion of process in Concurrent C provides interface description facilities analogous to the facilities provided by the class construct in C++. Yet, since encapsulation by processes leaves something to be desired, the designers of Concurrent C++ (justifiably) argue that proper encapsulation can only be offered by classes. Moreover, by encapsulating processes in classes, mechanisms such as inheritance may be employed as well. In slide 6-15, an example is given of how a process may be encapsulated in a class.

The example specifies a process *diskDriver* that is made a private data member of the class *disk*. Each transaction with the *diskDriver* process must now go through a member function of the class *disk*. The class disk now can offer high level disk access functions and hide the low level interactions with the actual *diskDriver* process from the user. For further details see Gehani and Roome (1988).

Concurrent C++ provides an example of a straightforward approach to combining object and processes. From a pragmatic point of view, supporting separate notions of classes and process types may lead to doubling the effort of defining suitable interfaces. However, some may consider that an advantage.

Implementation | Concurrent C | 6-14

```
      process body consumer() {
      int c;
      for(;;) {
       accept put(a) c = a;
       if ( c == EOF ) break;
       putchar( islower(c)?toupper(c):c );
       }
      }
      process body producer(process cons) {
      int c;
      do {
          cons.put( c = getchar() );
       } while ( c != EOF );
      }


      process body consumer() {
      int c;
      for(;;) {
          accept put(a) c = a;
          if ( c == EOF ) break;
          putchar( islower(c)?toupper(c):c );
          }
      }
      process body producer(process cons) {
      int c;
      do {
          cons.put( c = getchar() );
       } while ( c != EOF );
      }
```

Slide 6-14: Process implementation in Concurrent C

From a theoretical perspective, the solution chosen for Concurrent C++ is simply inadequate, as recognized in Gehani and Roome (1988). Given that a notion of *abstract data types* underlies both the notion of process types and classes, a unifying abstraction must be found that incorporates both notions in a common type system, while (preferably) retaining the possibility of defining passive (and also multi-threaded) object types. (To give the developers of Concurrent C++ credit, however, such a unifying abstraction is hard to arrive at, as we will see in the sections to follow.)

The actor model – ACT++ The actor model, as originally introduced in Hewitt (1977), is one of the earliest proposals to unify the notions of object and process. See slide 6-16.

An *actor* is an object whose functionality is characterized by a *behavioral descrip-*

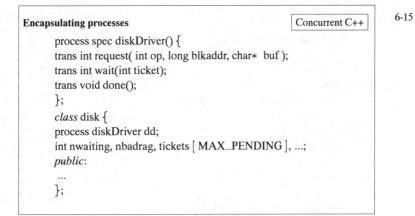

Slide 6-15: Encapsulating processes in Concurrent C++

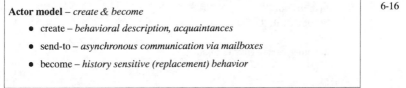

Slide 6-16: The actor model

tion, the actor's script. An actor may in addition have a number of *acquaintances,* which are other actors to which it may send messages. Each actor object has a *mailbox,* which so to speak is its address, and by which it is known to other actors. Communication, in the original actor model, is *asynchronous.* Actor objects repeatedly check their mailbox for incoming messages. If there is a message, it is handled and the actor continues its own behavior. At any time, an actor may decide to change its functionality by means of a *become* statement. The *become* statement results in changing the script of an actor (its behavioral description), and is a means to provide for *history sensitive behavior.* Although an actor may change its behavior, it cannot change its address. In other words, an actor may change its role but not its identity. In the actor model, an actor's mailbox may be regarded as the lifetime identity of the actor. The *become* statement, since it may affect the willingness of an actor to answer certain messages, may effectively be employed as a serialization technique to structure the computation. See Hewitt (1977).

The ACT++ language has been developed to explore whether the *actor* model would fit in a statically typed language such as C++. See Kafura and Lee (1990). The original idea underlying ACT++ is to employ the polymorphic type structure of class inheritance for specifying behavioral descriptions. In other words, classes are used both to create actor objects as well as to specify the change in behavior effected by a *become* statement.

For the user there is no difference in invoking a member function of an ordinary

```
Actors in C++                                    ACT++        6-17
        class bounded_buffer : actor {
        int buf[MAX];
        int in, out;
        public:
        bounded_buffer() { in=0; out=0; }
        int get() {
        reply buf[out++];
        out %= MAX;
        if (in == out)
         become( empty_buffer,in,out);
        else
         become( partial_buffer,in,out);
        }
        void put( int item ) {
        buf[in++] = item;
        in %= MAX;
        if (in == out )
         become( full_buffer,in,out);
        else
         become( partial_buffer,in,out);
        }
        };
```

Slide 6-17: Bounded buffer in ACT++

object or sending a message to an actor object. Actor objects, in ACT++, may immediately return a result to the user (by means of a *reply* statement) and continue to execute the function body in their own thread, invisible to the user.

Both for actor objects and ordinary objects, the public interface of the corresponding class determines what calls are legal. However, in addition to the static interface description given in the public section of the class, actor objects may restrict their interface dynamically by (explicitly) becoming an instance of a subtype of the original actor. For the example in slide 6-17, specifying a bounded buffer actor, this means either a *full buffer*, an *empty buffer* or a *partial buffer*, of which the specifications are given in slide 6-18.

The various subtypes of bounded buffer merely restrict the functionality of *bounded buffer* by offering a subset of the methods publicly available for the bounded buffer. With reference to our discussion of *behavioral compatibility* in section 3.3, this notion of subtype seems to be in conflict with the requirement of extending the range of behavior for subtypes. However, the semantics of message passing for actor objects (in ACT++) is such that requests that are legal with respect to static type checking are postponed until they are allowed by the dynamic interface specification as given by a *become* statement. Operationally, an actor object maintains a buffer of incoming messages from which it may select according to its state, which is determined by the successive *become*

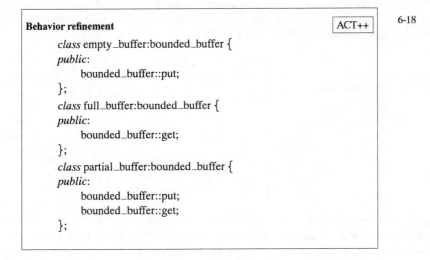

Slide 6-18: Refinement in ACT++

statements.

The language ACT++ realizes a close integration of the ordinary notion of a class and the notion of actors. However, this integration comes at the price of using class names to change the type of actor objects dynamically (which is hard to deal with, semantically, without reverting to higher order types). In section 6.4, we will discuss a different interpretation of the *become* statement in ACT++ which avoids using class names, and allows a more modular approach with respect to the inheritance of acceptance conditions by employing *behavioral abstractions*.

As a criticism, we may note that the concurrency model employed by ACT++ is quite limited. Actor objects derive their functionality by inheriting from a system defined *actor* class, and have only one (inherited) thread. This approach precludes the use of multiple inheritance to define the functionality of an actor as the combination of multiple actors. As we will discuss in section 6.4, multi-threaded active objects (composed by multiple inheritance) may be needed to fully employ an object-oriented approach in modeling concurrent systems.

6.3.2 Synchronization and communication

Concurrent programs tend to be expensive, due to the overhead involved in process creation and communication. In μC++ a number of constructs are offered that combine execution properties of concurrent processes in different ways, to allow the programmer the most optimal choice. A rather different approach is exemplified by Compositional C++, which provides constructs to write concurrent programs in a *compositional* manner, thus facilitating proofs of the correctness of a particular parallel solution.

Execution properties – μC++ The design goal of μC++ may be characterized as the intention to *provide features that allow maximum flexibility in accepting or subsequently* *postponing the servicing of requests*. The constructs offered in μC++ are motivated by an analysis of elementary execution properties, that are needed to extend the object model to obtain concurrency. See slide 6-19.

Slide 6-19: Execution properties

For concurrency, first we need a notion of *thread*. A thread may be considered as a virtual processor, in the sense that it may independently advance the computation. Secondly, we need a notion of *execution state*. An execution state contains the information needed to allow concurrent computation (such as a local state, the current routine invocations, etc.). An execution state may be independent of a thread, in the sense that a thread may continue with a particular execution state after an appropriate context switch. Finally, to guarantee the safety of a concurrent computation, we need constructs for *mutual exclusion*. A mechanism of mutual exclusion is needed to allow an action to be performed without being interrupted by another operation on the same resource. See Buhr et al (1992).

The execution properties mentioned above may be combined in a number of ways. For example, an ordinary class (in the traditional object model) may be characterized negatively as having no thread and no execution state of its own, since ordinary objects use the thread and execution state of their clients.

Coroutines, which provide a simple way in which to exploit (pseudo) concurrency, do have an execution state of their own, but (like classes) do not possess their own thread. Coroutines may be called as ordinary functions, but be interrupted by another call until an explicit resumption of the interrupted call is ordered, either by the client of the coroutine or a function of the coroutine itself.

Monitors provide a mechanism to effect synchronization. They do not possess a thread of their own, nor do they have an (independent) execution state. They may be used to queue processes that have to wait for a certain condition to hold. Storing processes in the monitor queue and releasing them must be explicitly done, using *wait* and *signal* statements respectively.

The most general construct to allow concurrency is the *task*, that provides not only a thread and an execution state but also implicit mutual exclusion by means of an accept statement. With respect to synchronization, tasks in μC++ behave like a generalized monitor. This analogy led the designers of μC++ to allow for postponing an already accepted call by means of a monitor-like *wait* statement (and to subsequently resume the call when an appropriate state change takes place).

The constructs developed in μC++ are restricted to shared memory parallelism. The assumption underlying the facilities offered for communication is, according to Buhr et al (1992), that communication takes place by means of ordinary (member) function call. Consequently, except for tasks (that allow an interpretation of function calls as a remote procedure call or rendezvous), additional synchronization primitives, such as a monitor construct, must be provided to support safe concurrent programming.

The μC++ extension is implemented as a pre-processor that defines additional *class-keys*, to indicate coroutine and task classes, and a special type specifier *mutex* to indicate that the concurrency class specified offers mutual exclusion. Buhr et al (1992) observe that the runtime efficiency of a concurrent program may significantly benefit from choosing a coroutine instead of a task. The overhead involved in communicating with a task almost doubles the overhead involved in the use of a coroutine. An obvious drawback of the approach embodied by μC++ is that it offers the programmer perhaps too rich a choice.

Write-once variables – Compositional C++ Among the concurrent extensions proposed for C++, Compositional C++ is exceptional in the sense that it is motivated by explicit proof-theoretical considerations with respect to the correctness of concurrent programs (see Chandy and Kesselman, 1992). Due to the non-deterministic nature of concurrent programs, the proof of the correctness of a component usually involves an explicit invariant stating the properties of all other components that are needed to ascertain the independence of that component from its environment. Compositional C++ intends to provide constructs that allow the programmer to develop components that are, to a high degree, independent, and may consequently be combined without danger of disrupting the integrity of the whole. See slide 6-20.

Write-once variables   Compositional C++   6-20

- compositional processes
- *sync* type modifier

Slide 6-20: Synchronization in Compositional C++

As stated in Chandy and Kesselman (1992), the idea in obtaining compositionality is that a process has private variables that cannot be referenced by other processes and shared variables that can be assigned values at most once.

The original contribution of Compositional C++ is the introduction of the *sync* type modifier. This modifier resembles the *const* type modifier (which may be used to indicate that a particular variable holds a constant value during its lifetime). In contrast to the *const* modifier (which may only be used for the initialization of an object at creation time), the *sync* modifier allows for an object to be initialized at an arbitrary point in the computation. However, a *sync* variable may be initialized only once. The *sync* variable provides a convenient mechanism both for synchronization and communication between concurrently executing threads. Moreover, it is an efficient mechanism as well. After being initialized, data pointed to by *sync* variables may be freely copied, since these data will not be changed thereafter. If a process tries to access data stored in a *sync* variable before initialization has taken place, it will be made to wait until the initialization is completed, that is until the *sync* variable is assigned a value by one of the processes sharing the variable.

As for the correctness of concurrent programs, according to Chandy and Kesselman (1992), a parallel composition is proper if all the variables shared by the processes being composed are *sync* variables.

The concurrency model adopted in Compositional C++ is rather limited, being restricted to processes that communicate by means of (global) shared variables. The advantage of such a restricted concurrency model, however, is that it allows a rigorous approach to proving the correctness of a concurrent program in C++. The notion of a *sync* (write-once) variable is certainly appealing, and may possibly be generalized to a truly distributed setting.

Data flow – Mentat/C++ A data flow approach (as exemplified by Petri nets, for example) is often used for the design of concurrent and distributed systems. A data flow diagram is a directed graph in which nodes represent computations and arcs represent the data dependence between nodes (see Grimshaw and Liu, 1987). Tokens carrying data and control information flow along the arcs from one node to another. See slide 6-21.

Data flow | Mentat/C++ | 6-21

  • persistent actors – to share data

  • futures – like a continuation

Slide 6-21: Continuations in Mentat/C++

In Grimshaw and Liu (1987), an extension of C++ called Mentat is proposed, that combines an object-oriented approach to concurrency with a data flow approach.

In the data flow model described in Grimshaw and Liu (1987), nodes are called *actors*, which are not to be confused with actors in the Actors model. In contrast to common data flow models, Mentat supports *persistent actors* that may carry a state. Persistent actors are active objects that behave like monitors. They may be used as resource managers, to share data.

In addition, the Mentat language offers so-called *futures* that may be used to determine the computation following a communication. Futures (which may be regarded as continuations, that is computations that are stored in a function that will be invoked somewhere in the future) correspond to subgraphs in the data flow model. The Mentat compiler provides support for implicitly generated futures, taking into account the persistent behavior of actor nodes. This allows for significant optimizations based on an analysis of the data flow between processes.

Mentat is implemented as a pre-compiler that generates actual actor objects inheriting from a system-defined class, defining a single threaded active object.

Despite the diversity between the extensions of C++ studied thus far, a common notion of active objects seems to emerge. In ACT++, μC++ and Mentat, active objects are single threaded objects which inherit their functionality from a system-defined base class. As we will see in the next section, this approach limits the opportunities for employing inheritance to characterize the functionality of active object classes in an incremental way.

As another issue we may note that none of the extensions discussed so far pays any (explicit) attention to the problems involved in (geographically) distributed objects. This will be the topic of section 6.5.

6.4 Inheritance on processes

Active objects provide a convenient way in which to employ concurrency in object-oriented systems. Unfortunately, active objects and inheritance do not easily sit side by side, as observed by a number of authors. See, for example, America (1987a), Briot and Yonezawa (1987) and Matsuoka and Yonezawa (1993). The objections to employing inheritance for active objects are based on semantical considerations, as well as on pragmatic reasons concerning the reuse of synchronization and acceptance conditions. The latter problems are commonly referred to as the *inheritance anomaly*. See Matsuoka and Yonezawa (1993) for an in-depth analysis. In this section we will analyze the nature of the incompatibility between active objects and inheritance and explore two solutions, namely the use of *behavioral abstractions* (as proposed for the actor model employed in ACT++) and the support for *multi-threaded active objects* (allowing the processes derived from ancestors to be combined).

6.4.1 Behavioral abstractions – *the inheritance anomaly*

Concurrency control for active objects is needed to indicate when the object is to interrupt its own activity and to determine which messages are eligible to be answered. See slide 6-22.

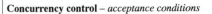

	6-22
Concurrency control – *acceptance conditions*	
• *centralized* – single *main process* routine	
• *decentralized* – per method	

Slide 6-22: Concurrency control

In many object-based languages supporting active objects, such as POOL-T (America, 1987a), concurrency control is centralized in a single *main process* routine of the object (called the *body* in POOL-T) by means of *accept* or *answer* statements listing the methods for which a request may be granted. As observed in America (1987a), when inheriting from an active object reuse does not apply to the *main process* routine, since in general synchronization and acceptance conditions will be quite dissimilar. (Which was a reason not to support inheritance in POOL-T.)

A quite different approach to concurrency control is to adopt a decentralized protocol, in which the synchronization and acceptance conditions are indicated per method. Such a protocol specifies what conditions hold after the method has been executed. Decentralized concurrency control is the mechanism chosen for ACT++. Each method in an actor object (in ACT++) issues a *become* statement to characterize its (replacement) behavior, that is its behavioral capabilities according to the dynamic interface specified by the (sub)type expression in the *become* statement.

Originally, behavioral transformations of this kind were specified in ACT++ by subclasses of the *actor* class. However, as observed in Kafura and Lee (1989), when adding a single method to an *actor* class by inheritance, the complete class structure characterizing the behavioral transformations of the original actor class must be rewritten to accommodate the newly added method. For example, when a method *get_rear* is (incrementally) added to a *bounded_buffer*, the synchronization conditions for *partial_buffer* and *full_buffer* must accordingly be changed. See slide 6-23.

Behavioral abstractions   ACT++   6-23

```
class bounded_buffer : actor {
int buf[MAX]; int in, out;
behavior:
empty_buffer = { put() };
full_buffer = { get() };
partial_buffer = {get(),put()};
public:
bounded_buffer() { in=0; out=0; }
int get() {
  reply buf[out++];
  out %= MAX;
  if (in == out)
    become empty_buffer;
  else
    become partial_buffer;
}
void put( int item ) {
  buf[in++] = item;
  in %= MAX;
  if (in == out )
    become full_buffer;
  else
    become partial_buffer;
}
};
```

Slide 6-23: Behavioral abstractions in ACT++

To remedy the inflexibility of their original approach, the designers of ACT++ proposed the use of *behavioral abstractions* (which are roughly sets of enabled methods) instead of (sub)classes to specify the behavioral capabilities of an object in a *become* statement.

As an example, in the *bounded_buffer* specified above, the *behavioral abstractions*, characterizing the various states an active object may be in with respect to synchronization, are specified in a separate *behavior* section of the actor object as subsets of the available methods (as listed in the public interface description). In a way similar to virtual member functions, behavioral abstractions may be redefined by a derived class, as illustrated in slide 6-24.

Behavioral extension   ACT++   6-24

```
class extended_buffer : bounded_buffer {
behavior:
full_buffer = {get(), get_rear()};
partial_buffer = {get(), get_rear(), put()};
public:

int get_rear() {
  reply buf[--in%MAX];
  out %= MAX;
  if (in == out) become empty_buffer;
  else
    become partial_buffer;
}
};
```

Slide 6-24: Behavioral extension in ACT++

The class *extended_buffer* adds a method *get_rear* and changes the behavioral abstractions *full_buffer* and *partial_buffer* accordingly.

Behavioral abstractions provide a way in which to specify synchronization conditions and concurrency control for active objects. First, behavioral abstractions characterize in a concise way the possible state transitions of an object, and thus allow reasoning about the correctness of the implementation on a high level of abstraction. Secondly, behavioral abstractions may serve to document the protocol of interaction a client must comply with, since they specify the dynamic interface, which determines which requests will be granted and which postponed.

In Neusius (1991), some refinements to decentralized concurrency control as employed for ACT++ are proposed. These refinements involve the possibility of specifying more detailed matching procedures to determine whether a particular method is available. In addition, Neusius (1991) gives some guidelines that must be followed to employ inheritance for active objects in an optimal way, for example: *when we redefine a method in a subclass we must be able to refine this within the concurrency control specified in the superclasses.* Evidently, active objects require careful design. As yet, no fully developed design method for active objects exists.

6.4.2 Multi-threaded active objects

Inheritance is a valuable mechanism for incremental process specification. In a similar way as for ordinary object classes, inheritance may be applied to processes (read active object classes) to achieve better conceptual modeling, and code reuse by factorization.

Stepwise refinement may be a helpful technique to structure the development of complex processes. In Thomsen (1987), an example is given of how multiple inheritance may be used to define distributed termination detection algorithms in a modular, incremental way.

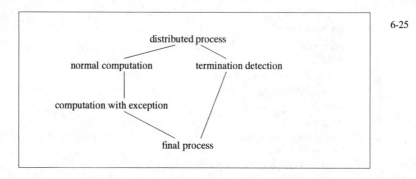

6-25

Slide 6-25: Distributed termination detection

The idea is to define the normal behavior of the (combined) process first and add exceptional behavior by means of a subclass. To complement the resulting process with termination detection, a separate process is defined for this task which is combined with the process specifying the actual computation by using multiple inheritance. A class that contains functionality pertaining to processes in general may be placed at the root of the inheritance graph, as shown in slide 6-25.

The problem of distributed termination detection is to determine whether all processes participating in the computation have terminated and that no messages are still waiting to be answered. The solution to distributed termination detection gives an interesting application of (multiple) inheritance on processes. We will, however, not go into details of the solution. Instead, we discuss the requirements the implementation language must meet to support the incremental development of distributed algorithms.

In Thomsen (1987) a sketch is given of an object-oriented language supporting the constructs needed to implement the design pictured above. Apart from the ordinary constructs for supporting object-oriented programming (such as classes and attributes), the language supports active objects that may contain multiple action parts and communication by means of CSP-like *send* statements.

Action parts inherited from ancestor classes result in processes that run in parallel with the process associated with the object itself. In other words, an active object may consist of multiple parallel (lightweight) threads. The priority with which a process runs decreases with the length of the inheritance chain. The process associated with the actual object itself has the highest priority. Ancestor processes run with a lower priority as they are higher up in the inheritance graph.

Communication between objects takes place in a CSP-like manner by asynchronous *send* and *receive* statements. A *receive* statement may be preceded by a *guard*. Each object must specify which messages it is willing to receive, by means of a non-deterministic *select* statement. Guards may be used to ensure that, on acceptance of a message, certain conditions are fulfilled.

The precise details of the language need not concern us here. However, we must note that any language supporting the incremental development of distributed algorithms must support both multi-threaded active objects and *guard* constructs that allow for the conditional acceptance of messages.

Inheriting behavior – Active C++ To inherit behavior in a concurrent context may imply the inheritance of processes defined by ancestor classes. Semantically, inheritance involving processes may be justified by observing that process inheritance results in (strictly) adding behavior. To finish this section, we will discuss the way in which class inheritance is dealt with in Active C++.

Active objects in Active C++ may have multiple threads. Multiple threads may arise either when deriving an active class from another active class or from specifying multiple active members.

An example of the latter situation is presented in the code fragment in slide 6-26.

6-26

```
active class P {
...
public:
    P() { ... }
    active m₁ () { ... }
    active m₂ () { ... }
};
```

Slide 6-26: Multi-threaded objects in Active C++

The constructor of this class is passive. The decision to allow ordinary member functions to be active is motivated by the consideration that constructors must take care of the initialization of an object and not necessarily of its activation.

Multiple threads may also arise from using inheritance. For example, assume an active class *bounded* (buffer) as defined in section 6.2.3, yet allowing for multiple elements. We will sketch the definition of an active class *special* (buffer) which allows elements to be taken from the rear. See slide 6-27.

6-27

```
active class special : public bounded {
public:
    special() : bounded() {
    for(;;) accept( rear:used> 0 );
    }
    int rear() { ... }
};
```

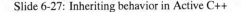

Slide 6-27: Inheriting behavior in Active C++

When creating a *special_buffer*, the constructor of *bounded_buffer* will be called, which results in a process willing to accept *put* and *get*. In addition, a process is created with a conditional accept statement, specifying that *get_rear* may be accepted whenever the instance variable *used* is greater than zero.

For this solution to work, we have to specify the body of the constructor of the *bounded_buffer* ancestor class as

for (;;) *accept*(put : used < size, get : used > 0);

employing accept expressions of the form *template* : *condition*, stating that acceptance is dependent on the function invoked as well as on the satisfaction of the condition. This is needed to enable the selection of incoming messages to be dependent on the actual value of the instance variable *used*.

To allow for the incremental specification of behavior we must impose the following restrictions on the semantics of the accept statement:

(1) The acceptance conditions of multiple accept statements (in multiple processes) must be combined to form a single set of acceptance conditions.

(2) While a rendezvous takes place, no other member call may interfere.

(3) The process containing the appropriate acceptance condition may proceed after the rendezvous is completed. (When there is ambiguity with respect to the identification of the process, the runtime system must make a choice).

With these restrictions we think to have provided a (partial) solution to the inheritance anomaly signaled in section 6.4.1. However, more research is needed to establish that the solution is valid in all conceivable circumstances.

6.5 Requirements for distribution

Object-oriented systems may be regarded as logically distributed systems. When properly designed, objects may be regarded as servers conforming to a locality principle enforcing strict encapsulation, forbidding access to global variables. However, as observed in Wegner (1992), physically distributed systems add another dimension of abstraction concerns. According to Wegner (1992), physically distributed systems supplement the logical autonomy requirements of object-oriented systems by requirements for *failure transparency* (robustness for hardware failures), *migration transparency* (to allow objects being moved), *replication transparency* (to allow objects being replicated) and *location transparency* (to ensure that objects function as they should irrespective of their location). See slide 6-28.

Transparency is a notion very similar to the abstraction concerns of object-oriented (component-based) software technology. According to Wegner (1992), both notions are likely to converge in future computing systems. In addition to the transparency concerns mentioned, distributed computing must (ideally) support *access transparency* (to allow access to both local and remote resources in an identical way), *concurrency transparency* (to abstract from the possible concurrent behavior of a server object), *performance transparency* (to allow for load balancing by means of dynamic reconfiguration) and *scaling transparency* (so as to be able to embed a system into another, larger system).

Transparency – *distributed abstraction*   6-28

- failure transparency – *hardware failure*
- access transparency – *local and remote resources*
- location transparency – *without knowledge of own location*
- concurrency transparency – *possibly concurrent*
- replication transparency – *multiple instances*
- migration transparency – *movement of objects*
- performance transparency – *reconfiguration, load balancing*
- scaling transparency – *embedded programs*

Slide 6-28: Distribution and transparency

Distribution transparency (encompassing the requirements listed above) is needed to ensure physical robustness, but significantly increases the design and implementation effort. In this section we will study the facilities needed to achieve distribution transparency in an object-oriented setting. These facilities include support for distributed objects, object identity, object migration, remote object method invocations and protocols for transport across a network.

Distributed object computing Remote object method invocation closely resembles *remote procedure call* (RPC), which is available on a variety of platforms.

In Mock (1993) an extension of the Open Software Foundation's Distributed Computing Environment (see OSF DCE, 1992) is described, offering support for fine-grained distributed objects, system-wide object identity, location-independent method call and dynamic object migration. See slide 6-29.

The unit of distribution supported by DCE++ consists of individual C++ objects, whereas for DCE the unit of distribution amounts to heavy-weight processes. Another improvement over DCE is the symmetry in communication between objects, which means in effect that there is no distinction necessary (as for DCE) between client and server processes. Communication between objects, whether remote or local, is by member call, which in the case of remote objects is automatically mapped onto the underlying DCE RPC mechanism.

To establish universally unique identifiers for objects, DCE++ relies on the name management services provided by DCE. This has as an additional advantage that applications may be integrated with any system conforming to the DCE standards.

Location-independence is implemented by providing a *proxy* for each distributed object. Requests to an object that is potentially located elsewhere are automatically addressed to the proxy that, in its turn, identifies the current location of the object and forwards the request.

In addition to the distributed name management and communication services, DCE offers supports for light-weight processes, security and the synchronization of distributed clocks. DCE defines a standard for which a number of implementations exist and

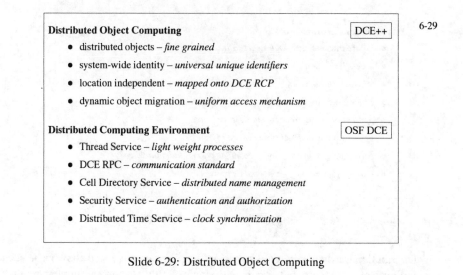

Slide 6-29: Distributed Object Computing

to which, for example, the Microsoft object linking and embedding facilities adhere. In contrast, DCE++ has only an experimental status. It offers support for employing DCE facilities more conveniently in an object-oriented setting.

Object replication Due to the communication overhead, remote object method invocations are considerably more expensive than local object invocations. As observed in Nolte (1991), even fast invocation protocols may not be sufficient when remote objects have to be accessed frequently. Therefore, replication techniques have to be considered to keep invocation overhead low.

In Nolte (1991), a novel object model for C++ (supporting so-called *dual objects*) is introduced to improve the efficiency of remote object invocations. (A similar model was originally introduced for the language Orca, in 1987 (Bal, 1991).) Dual objects consist of a *prototype* (which is the original object) and an arbitrary number of *extracts* (which are partial replicas, containing the public section of the original object). The model described in Nolte (1991) allows for temporary inconsistencies between the prototype and its extracts. However, vertical inconsistencies (that is, differences between the prototype and its replicas) are restored whenever the prototype is accessed directly. In a similar way, horizontal inconsistencies (that is, inconsistencies between various replicas) may be repaired by explicitly accessing the prototype.

The dual object model may significantly improve the efficiency of remote object invocations for *read-only* access. However, for *write access* the full price of remote invocation has to be paid if inconsistencies are to be prevented. To avoid simultaneous updates, communication with the prototype is governed by a so-called *clerk*, a light-weight process that controls access to the prototype.

Support for remote object invocations may be provided by means of annotations. Annotations (which are embedded in special C++ comments) are introduced in Nolte (1991), both for the invocation of methods of remote objects and to determine the actual

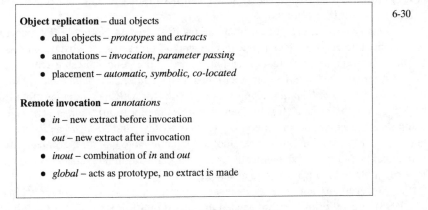

Slide 6-30: The dual object model

parameter passing mechanism to be used. See slide 6-30.

Invocation annotations are placed in the class defining the remote (prototype) object, in a similar way as *const* may be used in C++ to indicate that a method has no effect on the state of an object.

Methods may be annotated as *in* (to indicate that an extract must be made), as *out* (to indicate that a new extract must be made after invocation), as *inout* (which is a combination of *in* and *out*) and as *global* (to indicate that communication is to take place directly with the prototype).

A second category of annotations is needed to determine how parameter passing needs to be handled for remote invocations. In Nolte (1991), annotations are provided that support parameter passing mechanisms such as *call-by-value, call-by-result* and *call-by-value-result*, which determine whether to make a copy before, after or before and after execution of the method. The annotations for these are, similar to those for method invocations, respectively *in, out* and *inout*. We may note that, to support the full collection of data types offered by C++, these annotations need to be extended with type information to support the efficient marshaling (that is packing and unpacking) of the actual parameters of a remote method call. See also section 11.1.2, in which a more general approach to these problems is described.

In addition to these familiar mechanisms, a number of alternative parameter passing mechanisms may be thought of, mechanisms that provide support for object migration and (partial) replication. These include *call-by-share* (which is employed for the language Orca, see Bal (1991)), *call by unification* (which is the mechanism employed in DLP), and *call-by-move* and *call-by-visit* (which are supported by the language Emerald, Black and Hutchinson (1986)). These mechanisms, however, require a close interaction between the language runtime system and the underlying operating system. In particular, *call-by-share* is quite expensive, as it offers the choice between full copying (and maintaining consistency between the copies and the original) or passing by reference (which may result in expensive communication traffic).

As an intermediate between full copying and relying on remote references, Nolte

(1991) proposes a *call-by-likeness* mechanism that results in making extracts from the public section of the prototype.

Finally, a third category of annotations discussed in Nolte (1991) concerns the placement of objects on either a node in a network of processors, a separate address space on the same node, or a different execution context in the same address space.

Alternatives that have been mentioned include *automatic placement* (by some default strategy), *symbolic placement* (by using names for which a binding is provided separately), *direct placement* (that uniquely identifies the location), *scoped placement* (that determines placement dependent on a particular context) and *co-located placement* (that may be used to place an object near another object). Note that all placement directives may either be interpreted dynamically or statically. In addition, dynamic reconfiguration may be employed to improve load balancing.

However, annotations such as these help us only half-way. As observed in Lea *et al.* (1993), special primitives are needed to support multi-processor object configuration and remote object invocation in an efficient manner. The interested reader is referred to Lea *et al.* (1993) for further details.

Network infra-structure Remote object and method invocations require support from some communication system to access remote nodes and transport data across a network. These facilities need to be supplied by the operating system, and must in some way be embedded in the programming language, either in the form of a library or as built-in primitives.

Network programming has been an area of active development over the last decade. Rather than studying the research aimed at incorporating network facilities in object-oriented systems, we will look at what technology is (currently) available and what standards have been developed to implement distributed systems. The overview given in this section is based on Rieken (1992). In chapter 11.4 we will mention some of the libraries available for network programming in C++.

There are two connection metaphors underlying communication over a network such as the Internet: *mailing* and *phoning*. These mechanisms are supported by communication protocols that hide the particular hardware technology from the application.

The *mailing* metaphor is supported by the User Datagram Protocol (UDP), which is especially suited for delivering short messages periodically. See slide 6-31. For example, to establish whether nodes in a network are down, messages may be broadcast to the nodes. If a node does not respond in a fixed time, the server may assume that the node is down. To guarantee reliable communication using the User Datagram Protocol, the application has to take precautions against the loss of messages, receiving the messages in a different order and the possibility of duplicated messages.

Applications that require a continuous connection may make better use of the Transmission Control Protocol (TCP), which provides a virtual circuit connection with end-to-end reliability. See slide 6-31.

In addition, the Transmission Control Protocol guarantees delivery in the same order in which the data was sent (in other words, byte stream semantics, like reading or writing a file). This reliability, however, comes at the price of a three part handshake, consisting of the request for a connection, a reply and an acknowledgement to the reply.

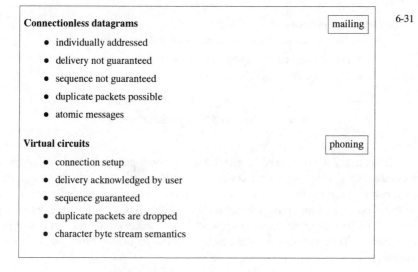

Slide 6-31: Communication metaphors

The communication facilities provided by the User Datagram Protocol and the Transmission Control Protocol underly a variety of higher level communication protocols such as remote procedure call (offering transparent access to remote procedures) and the Sun Network File System facility (offering transparent access to remote files).

For remote procedure calls, user level transparency is provided by so-called *stubs* that run on each host computer. (A *stub* may be considered as a representative that forwards the call to where the procedure actually resides.) One of the issues in remote procedure calls is reliability. Additional communication is needed to detect if a particular machine has crashed and to notify the user of failure of the request.

Summary

This chapter has given an introduction to the problems involved in extending the object paradigm with distribution and concurrency.

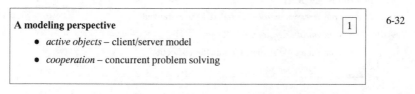

Slide 6-32: Section 6.1: A modeling perspective

In section 1, we looked at the client/server model and observed that the notion of active objects fits in naturally. We discussed concurrent problem solving and identified some common patterns of cooperation.

> **Objects and processes** $\boxed{2}$ 6-33
> - *language support* – processes, communication, fault-tolerance
> - *concurrency* – processes, active objects, asynchrony
> - *active objects* – sequential processes

Slide 6-33: Section 6.2: Objects and processes

In section 2 we discussed language support for concurrency and the notion of active objects. Language support for concurrency and distribution consists of adding processes, communication facilities and fault-tolerance. For concurrency, in particular, we have the choice of adding processes as additional data types, introducing active objects or employing asynchronous communication. Active objects unify the notions of objects and processes. They are analogous to communicating sequential processes as introduced in Hoare (1978).

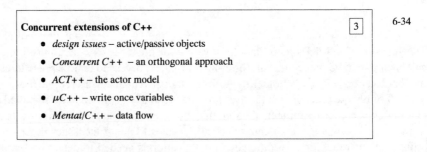

> **Concurrent extensions of C++** $\boxed{3}$ 6-34
> - *design issues* – active/passive objects
> - *Concurrent C++* – an orthogonal approach
> - *ACT++* – the actor model
> - *μC++* – write once variables
> - *Mentat/C++* – data flow

Slide 6-34: Section 6.3: Concurrent extensions of C++

In section 3, we looked at a number of concurrent extensions of C++, including Concurrent C++, ACT++, μC++, Compositional C++ and Mentat/C++, and we discussed their design rationale.

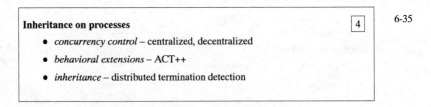

> **Inheritance on processes** $\boxed{4}$ 6-35
> - *concurrency control* – centralized, decentralized
> - *behavioral extensions* – ACT++
> - *inheritance* – distributed termination detection

Slide 6-35: Section 6.4: Inheritance on processes

Further, in section 4, we looked at the problems involved in combining processes and inheritance. An example was given demonstrating how inheritance and multi-threaded objects may be used to model distributed termination detection in a natural way.

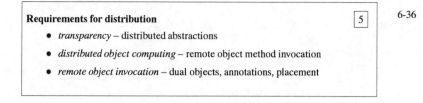

Slide 6-36: Section 6.5: Requirements for distribution

Finally, in section 5, we discussed a number of abstraction or transparency requirements and looked at an environment for distributed object computing. We also discussed the issues involved in replicating objects and and remote object method invocation. Finally, we looked at some network protocols.

Questions

(1) Explain why the *client/server* model may be regarded as a suitable metaphor for concurrent object-oriented computing.

(2) What ways can you think of to extend object-based languages with concurrency features?

(3) How would you characterize the notion of active objects?

(4) What do you consider the major design issues in extending C++ with concurrency?

(5) Discuss how Concurrent C++ extends C++ with concurrency?

(6) What are the features of the actor model? Describe how ACT++ realizes the actor model for C++.

(7) Characterize how μC++ extends C++ with concurrency. Do the same for Compositional C++.

(8) What problems arise with respect to concurrency control if you allow for inheritance?

(9) Can you think of an example where inheritance on processes is useful? What impacts does your solution have for the implementation language?

(10) What are the problems involved in remote object invocation? Characterize the model of dual objects. Do you consider this an adequate solution? Explain.

Further reading

For background reading on concurrency and distribution, consult Bal *et al.* (1989) or Andrews (1991). Research papers concerning concurrent object-oriented programming are collected in Yonezawa and Tokoro (1987) and Agha *et al.* (1993).

7

Composition mechanisms

No single language can offer the primitive constructs needed to solve all conceivable problems. Therefore, programmers need to develop techniques or idioms to express interactions at a sufficiently abstract level.

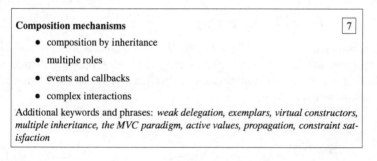

Composition mechanisms | 7 | 7-1

- composition by inheritance
- multiple roles
- events and callbacks
- complex interactions

Additional keywords and phrases: *weak delegation, exemplars, virtual constructors, multiple inheritance, the MVC paradigm, active values, propagation, constraint satisfaction*

Slide 7-1: Composition mechanisms

In this chapter, we will study a variety of composition mechanisms, including (multiple) inheritance, the definition of multiple roles by means of (weak) delegation, the use of callbacks and value propagation, and complex interaction schemes as embodied by the MVC-paradigm. Those composition mechanisms are not likely to be integrated at a language level, yet may become part of a framework supporting a methodical approach to software development if the consensus concerning their use is sufficiently well-established.

The program fragments discussed in this chapter may be regarded as *abstract schemas* or (in the terminology of Coplien, 1992) *idioms*. Coplien (1992) provides a very rich source of material and ideas (indispensable to the serious C++ programmer), including the emulation of functional, symbolic and prototype-based programming styles in C++. In this chapter we will focus primarily on the various ways in which we may organize the interaction between objects. The interested reader is referred to Coplien (1992) to study the other idioms.

7.1   Composition by inheritance

Inheritance is the composition mechanism par excellence for object-oriented programming. As argued before, inheritance allows for virtually unlimited factorization and hence reuse of code. Inheritance, however, is increasingly recognized as a mechanism that is difficult to control. Moreover, the programmer employing inheritance, when working with a statically typed language like Eiffel or C++, is faced with the problem of fitting the inheritance structure within the type system by designing an adequate type structure. In this section, we will look at the mechanisms available to develop hierarchic type structures and ways to check that derived classes meet the criterion of behavioral conformance as expressed in section 3.3. Brief examples will be presented to illustrate the problems and pitfalls of which the programmer must be aware. In particular, we will discuss the mechanism of explicit scoping, the difficulties involved in satisfying the invariant properties for derived classes, and the use of multiple inheritance with shared base classes (which results in structures having a *diamond* property).

7.1.1   Virtual functions and scoping

Scoping, when used in combination with recursive virtual functions, may lead to unexpected problems. In slide 7-2, an example is given illustrating a problem that may occur when defining a derived class that relies for its functionality on the original methods defined for the base class.

```
class P {                                                          P
public:
virtual int m(int i) {
  cout ≪ i; return i==0 ? i : m(i-1);
  }
};
class C : public P {                                               C
public:
virtual int m(int i) {
  cout ≪ "start"; return i< 0 ? 0 : P::m(i);
  }
};
```

7-2

Slide 7-2: Virtual functions – recursions

In the example, the derived class C is used to provide a better interface to the functionality P offers, by including an additional test in $C :: m$. This test prevents $P :: m$ from diverging. However, the statement

P* p = new C(); p→ m(k); $C :: m$

for any $k > 0$ will not result in printing the sequence 0..k backwards, since (inadvertently) the recursive call to m in $P :: m$ invokes $C :: m$ instead of $P :: m$.

Solution – *explicit scoping*   7-3

    class P { $\boxed{P'}$
    public:
    virtual int m(int i) {
      cout ≪ i; *return* i==0 ? i : P::m(i-1);
    }
    };

Slide 7-3: Explicit scoping

The solution, simple as it is, is to apply explicit scoping in the recursive call to m, as shown in slide 7-3. Beware, recursion is often indirect!

7.1.2 Inheritance and invariance

When developing complex systems or class libraries, reliability is of critical importance. As shown in section 2.2.3, assertions provide a means by which to check the runtime consistency of objects. In particular, assertions may be used to check that the requirements for behavioral conformance of derived classes are met.

Invariant properties – *algebraic laws*   7-4

    class employee {
    public:
    employee(int n = 0) : sal(n) { }
    employee* salary(int n) { sal = n; *return this*; }
    virtual long salary() { *return* sal; }
    protected:
    int sal;
    };
Invariant

    • $k \equiv (e \rightarrow salary(k)) \rightarrow salary()$

Slide 7-4: Invariant properties as algebraic laws

Invariant properties, however, are often conveniently expressed in the form of algebraic laws that must hold for an object. See section 4.1. Naturally, when extending a class by inheritance (to define a specialization or refinement) the invariants pertaining to the base class should not be disrupted. Although we cannot give a general guideline to prevent disruption, the example in slide 7-4 clearly suggests that *hidden features* should be carefully checked with respect to the invariance properties of the (derived) class. The example is taken from Bar-David (1992).

Below, we have defined a class *employee*. The main features of an *employee* are the (protected) attribute *sal* (storing the salary of an employee) and the methods to access and modify the salary attribute. For *employee* objects, the invariant (expressing that any amount k is equal to the salary of an employee whose salary has been set to k) clearly holds.

Now imagine that we distinguish between ordinary employees and managers by adding a permanent bonus when paying the salary of a manager, as shown in slide 7-5. The reader may judge whether this example is realistic or not.

Problem – *hidden bonus*   7-5

      class manager : *public* employee {
      public:
      long salary() { *return* sal + 1000; }
      };

Invariant

- $k \stackrel{?}{\equiv} (m \rightarrow salary(k)) \rightarrow salary()$

Slide 7-5: Violating the invariant

Then, perhaps somewhat to our surprise, we find that the invariant stated for employees no longer holds for managers. From the perspective of predictable object behavior this is definitely undesirable, since invariants are the cornerstone of reliable software (so to speak). The solution to this anomaly is to make the assignment of a bonus explicit, as shown in slide 7-6.

Solution – *explicit bonus*   7-6

      class manager : *public* employee {
      public:
      manager∗ bonus(int n) { sal += n; *return this*; }
      };

Invariant – *restored*

- $k + n \equiv ((m \rightarrow salary(k)) \rightarrow bonus(n)) \rightarrow salary()$

Slide 7-6: Restoring the invariant

Now, the invariant pertaining to managers may be strengthened by including the effects of assigning a bonus. As a consequence, the difference in salary no longer occurs as if by magic but is directly visible in the interaction with a manager object, as it should be.

7.1.3 **Multiple inheritance** – *the diamond structure*

Object-oriented programming languages provide the technology for a component-based approach to software development. Inheritance may be regarded as a means to extend components and to refine the functionality of a given component.

Usually, a component is taken to be identical to an object. However, the notion of a component may be extended to include multiple objects, each representing a sub-component responsible for some aspect of the component (such as, for example, its functional behavior or the display of its internal state in a window).

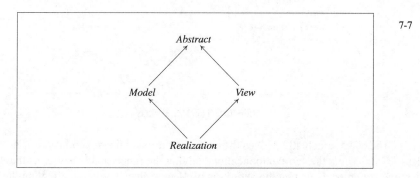

7-7

Slide 7-7: The diamond structure

Below, an (abstract) example will be given of how multiple inheritance may be used to organize the objects comprising the realization of a component in a flexible way. We employ in addition an abstract interface class, which is shared by the objects corresponding to the sub-components of a structure. We call the resulting structure a *diamond* structure for obvious reasons.

An abstract interface class is intended to provide an abstract interface to clients of the component. This interface will usually be the most stable part of the component. The actual realization is more likely to change.

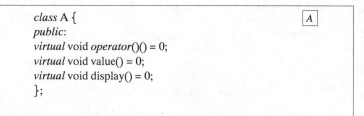

7-8

Slide 7-8: An abstract interface

The class A provides an apply operator (that is $operator()$), a method $value()$ (that delivers an integer value) and a method $display()$ (that displays the value). See slide 7-8. Note that this is just an example intended to illustrate the architecture of a diamond structure. In a more realistic example, the interface would no doubt offer numerous other services.

Next, to define a partial realization of the interface class A, we define a model class M. Since A is intended to be shared by other sub-components as well, we employ virtual inheritance here. See slide 7-9.

Model – *functional behavior*   7-9

    class M : *virtual public* A { $\boxed{M}$
    public:
    M(int k) : n(k) { }
    void *operator*()() { n++; }
    int value() { *return* n; }
    protected:
    int n;
    };

Slide 7-9: The *Model* class

The class M actually defines the apply operator and the method *value*. The model class M represents the sub-component embodying the functional behavior of the *AMVR* diamond structure. Note that the definition of M may change without affecting the interface provided by A, in other words without disturbing the clients of the component.

As the second sub-component providing a partial realization of the abstract class A, we need a class to display the value of the component (as realized by M). To this end we introduce the class V, as defined in slide 7-10.

View – *for display*   7-10

    class V : *virtual public* A { $\boxed{V}$
    public:
    V(int h, int w) : d(new Display(h,w)) { }
    void display() { d→ put(value()); }
    private:
    Display* d;
    };

Slide 7-10: The *View* class

A V object creates a new display, with a certain width and height, and puts the value on display when requested to do so. The display sub-component class V is likely to be the most volatile part of the structure. As observed in Guimaraes (1991), who introduced the technique discussed here, separating the window environment dependent aspects into a class allows for a relatively easy port to a variety of such environments.

We employ multiple inheritance to combine the functional sub-component and the display sub-component. In other words, the class R is a realization of the abstract interface class A, combining the partial realizations M and V. See slide 7-11.

Realization – *used for creation*   7-11

    class R : *public* M, *public* V { $\boxed{R}$

    public:

    R(int k=0, int h=10, int w=20) : M(k), V(h,w) {}

    };

Usage

    • A∗ a = new R(); (∗ a)(); a→ display();

Slide 7-11: The *Realization* class

Due to the use of virtual inheritance, instances of R have only one copy of A. If virtual inheritance had not been used then instances of R would contain two copies of A, one coming from M and one from V. Note that, whereas clients only need to know about the abstract interface class A, when an actual object realizing A must be created the realization type R must be explicitly used. Below, we will discuss a technique that allows us to hide the representation type during creation as well.

                                                           7-12

    class A { $\boxed{A}$

    public:

    A() { body = new R(); }

    virtual void *operator*()() { body→ *operator*()(); }

    virtual void value() { *return* body→ value(); }

    virtual void display() { *return* body→ display(); }

    protected:

    R∗ body;

    };

Slide 7-12: Hiding realizations

Hiding realizations Diamond structures provide a flexible means to develop portable and extensible code. However, a drawback of the approach described above is that the programmer needs to be aware of the structure of the realization of the component. Using the *handler/body* idiom introduced in section 2.3 this may easily be avoided, as shown in slide 7-12.

When creating an instance of A, an instance of R is (implicitly) created which is attached to the *body* pointer. All calls to instances of A will be delegated to the instances of the realization class R. Neither the creator nor the client of instances of A need to know about the existence of the realization class R.

Embedding the realization in the abstract interface works well if the realization class is stable and definite, meaning that it will not be changed and need not be refined by the programmer using the component. Note that the interface class is then no longer an abstract class in a technical sense, since it no longer employs pure virtual functions.

7.2   Interaction through delegation

The *handler/body* idiom (as introduced in Coplien, 1992, see section 2.3) is an elegant way in which to separate the implementation of a concrete data type (the body) from its interface (the handler). In the previous section, we looked at an example employing explicit weak delegation (forwarding) to redirect messages to the actual realization of some type. In this section, we will look at how we may use implicit (weak) delegation in C++, and as a related issue, how we may define *safe* or *smart* pointers in C++. Next, we will look at the use of delegation to regulate the processing of elements of various types within a single heterogeneous structure (employing tags). Finally, we will consider how we may implement dynamic types (allowing for multiple roles) using a combination of inheritance and (implicit) delegation.

7.2.1   Implicit delegation – *smart pointers*

Operator overloading is one of the most powerful features offered by C++. In particular, the possibility of overloading the de-reference operator offers vast opportunities for employing idioms deviating from the classical object-based approach, and (needless to say) for abuse. An interesting application of overloading the de-reference operator is the definition of smart pointers employing implicit forwarding.

As an example, assume that we have a class F defining functional behavior of some kind, as in slide 7-13.

7-13

```
class F {
public:
void a() { cout << "a"; }
void b() { cout << "b"; }
};
```

Slide 7-13: Functional behavior

Instead of accessing instances of F directly, we may define an interface class, say A and delegate the requests addressed to an instance of A to an instance of F embedded in the instance of A, as depicted in slide 7-14.

The interface class A also offers, apart from a constructor and the definition of *operator* $\rightarrow$, a member function *extra* (that is merely introduced to illustrate the differ-

```
Interface – access                                          7-14

    class A {                                    A
    public:
    A() { delegate = new F; }
    F* operator→ () { return delegate; }
    void extra() { cout ≪ "extra"; }
    private:
    F* delegate;
    };
```

Slide 7-14: An interface class

ence between invoking a method for *A* and using an instance of *A* to delegate a messages to the encapsulated instance of *F*).

A o; o.extra(); o→ a(); o→ b();

In the program fragment above, an object instance *o* of *A* is created, the method *extra* is invoked, and then *o* is used as if it were a pointer to an instance of *F*. The exact workings of de-referencing may seem a little tricky. For technical details the reader is referred to Ellis and Stroustrup (1990).

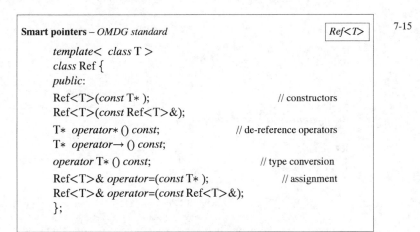

```
Smart pointers – OMDG standard                     Ref<T>    7-15

    template< class T >
    class Ref {
    public:
    Ref<T>(const T* );                        // constructors
    Ref<T>(const Ref<T>&);

    T* operator* () const;                    // de-reference operators
    T* operator→ () const;

    operator T* () const;                     // type conversion
    Ref<T>& operator=(const T* );             // assignment
    Ref<T>& operator=(const Ref<T>&);
    };
```

Slide 7-15: Smart pointers

Smart pointers Overloading the de-reference operator may be easily abused. Nevertheless, it is a powerful mechanism that may be used to implement *smart* (that is safe and flexible) pointers. Such pointers have been proposed as part of the Object Database Management Group (ODMG) standard C++ interface for object databases. See Strickland (1993). The interface proposed for such pointers is shown in slide 7-15.

The interface for the template class *Ref< T>* contains constructors, de-reference operators, a type conversion operator (to obtain a pointer to an instance of *T*) and assignment operators. The reader is invited to develop an implementation for this class. Instances of *Ref< T>* are used to access objects stored in the database. After retrieving objects from persistent storage (the object data base) into memory, ordinary pointers (obtained by one of the de-reference or type conversion operators) may be used as well. As described in Strickland (1993), additional data types (such as sets and lists) are needed to define a flexible interface to the object data base. In addition, a query language (à la SQL) may be needed to access the database.

7.2.2   Regulation – *heterogeneous types*

Many applications require heterogeneous structures, such as, for example, lists to store integers and strings (read from standard input) that must be processed afterwards. For the application programmer it is convenient in such cases to have a single consistent interface, hiding the actual realization.

The *handler/body idiom* (employing implicit delegation) is well-suited to this. In the following, we will look at an example of a heterogeneous structure (employing implicit delegation). Again, we distinguish between an abstract interface class and its realization(s). To avoid cluttering the code, we employ a general (abstract) realization class and refine this to obtain the actual element classes.

The interface class for our container may look as depicted in slide 7-16.

```
class R;                              // forward reference          7-16

class A {                                              A
public:
A(int n);                             // integer elements
A(char* s);                           // char* elements
~A() { delete rep; }
R* operator→ () { return rep; }
private:
R* rep;
};
```

Slide 7-16: The interface class

It contains two constructors, one that accepts an integer and one that takes a string. In addition, it provides a destructor and an overloaded de-reference operator, allowing implicit delegation.

The general (abstract) realization type may be defined as in slide 7-17.

The class *R* contains the functionality that is shared by each of the classes corresponding to the actual element types. Note that the function *action* is assigned zero, making *R* an abstract class. It is used by the function *process* to perform the action required for an element. The functions *insert* may be defined in a straightforward way. However, some trickery is needed to allow *insert* to be applied to the *next* pointer. Remember that

```
class R {                                             R           7-17
public:
R() { next = 0; }
virtual ~R() { if (next) delete next; }
void insert(A& r);
void process() { action(); if (next) (* next)→ process(); }
virtual void action() = 0;
protected:
A*  next;
};
R::insert(A& r) {                        // needs some trickery
      if (!next) next = &r;
      else (* next)→ insert(r);
      }
```

Slide 7-17: Abstract realization

the de-reference operator applies to objects of type A and delivers a pointer to an R object. Since R is an abstract class, the destructor for R must be declared virtual.

The function *process* amounts to printing the value of the elements (as defined by the function *action* of the element class). As an example of two realization types look at the classes N and S in slide 7-18.

```
Concrete realizations                                             7-18

          class N : public R {                        N
          public:
          N(int i) : n(i) { }
          void action() { cout ≪ n ≪ endl; }
          protected:
          int n;
          };
          A::A(int n) { rep = new N(n); }       // constructor for A


          class S : public R {                        S
          public:
          S(char*  p) : s(p) { }
          void action() { cout ≪ s ≪ endl; }
          protected:
          char*  s;
          };
          A::A(char*  s) { rep = new S(s); }    // constructor for A
```

Slide 7-18: Concrete realizations

Note that the creation of actual instances of N and S is hidden in the constructors of A. This technique is characterized in Coplien (1992) as the *virtual constructor* idiom, since the actual type of the body instance of A is determined dynamically. Since these are simple types, the destructor may safely be omitted.

As an example of using the heterogeneous container type A, look at the following fragment. First, an (integer) element is created (which becomes the first element of the chain) and then elements are appended to the chain

```
A e1(2),e2("hi"),e3(1);
e1→ insert(e2); e1→ insert(e3);
e1→ process();
```

In the solution presented we rely on the implicit dispatching of the virtual function mechanism to process the elements according to their types. An advantage of using classes (instead of tag fields) to define the various element types is that the collection of element types can be easily extended. Nevertheless, when adding a new element type the collection of constructors for the abstract interface A must still be extended.

7.2.3 Dynamic typing – *multiple roles*

An often heard criticism of statically typed object-oriented languages is that they do not allow for the flexibility necessary to characterize objects that change their type dynamically. Actually, few dynamically typed languages allow for changing the type of an object as well. However, the scheme employed to implement heterogeneous container types may be easily extended to allow for changing types (or *roles*) dynamically as well.

The construction relies (again) on the definition of an abstract interface comprising the interfaces of the (role) realization classes. In addition, we need a *control* class (containing a tag field) to switch between (realization) types dynamically.

Consider the abstract interface class A, shown in slide 7-19.

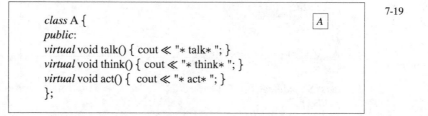

7-19

Slide 7-19: Abstract interface

The class A provides a so-called *fat* interface, combining all possible behaviors allowed by the role realization classes.

Next, we need a control class C, which distinguishes between the roles of a *PERSON* and a *STUDENT*. See slide 7-20.

Apart from a constructor and an overloaded de-reference operator, the class C contains a member function *role* (to switch between roles) and an array of roles (contain-

```
Control – dispatching                                          7-20
        class C : public A {                        [ C ]
        public:
        enum { PERSON = 0 , STUDENT };
        C() {
            roles[PERSON]=0;
            roles[STUDENT]=0;
            role(0);                          // default role
            }
        A* operator→ () { return roles[_role]; }
        void role( int r );                   // role switching
        protected:
        int _role;
        A* roles[2];
        };
```

Slide 7-20: Control

ing so to speak the repertoire of an instance of A). The default role is set to *PERSON* in the constructor.

The realization classes P (for *PERSON*) and S (for *STUDENT*) give the actual definition for the virtual member functions declared in the interface class A. See slide 7-21.

```
                                                              7-21
        class P : public A {                         [ P ]
        public:
        void talk() { cout ≪ "beach"; }
        void act() { cout ≪ "..."; }
        };


        class S : public A {                         [ S ]
        public:
        void talk() { cout ≪ "OOP"; }
        void think() { cout ≪ "Z"; }
        };
```

Slide 7-21: Realizations

Note that each of the role (realization) classes allows only for a strict subset of the behavior allowed by the abstract interface class A. See slide 7-22.

Switching between roles employs the technique of *virtual constructors*, which is introduced in Coplien (1992) as a means to enhance the functionality of the *envelope/letter* idiom. For each possible role, an instance of the role (realization) class is created, to which requests addressed to the instance of C (figuring as a representative for

7-22

```
void C::role( int r ) {                              C :: role
require( r == PERSON || r == STUDENT );
_role = r;
if (roles[_role] == 0) {
switch (r) {
case PERSON : roles[_role] = new P(); break;
case STUDENT : roles[_role] = new S(); break;
};
}
}
```

Slide 7-22: Switching between roles

each of the roles) are delegated. An example of using an instance of C is given below

```
C s;
s.role(S::STUDENT);
s→ think(); s→ talk(); s→ act();
s.role(S::PERSON);
s→ think(); s→ talk(); s→ act();
```

The disadvantage of the approach sketched here (and of *fat* interfaces in general) is that the compiler cannot ensure that only the functions relevant to a particular role are invoked. Obviously, the price that must be paid for flexibility of this kind is diminished compiler support and increased reliance on the programmer's discipline.

7.3 Indirect cooperation

The standard way in which to control computation is to call a function or create an object and invoke a member function.

However, in many situations such a model of direct control does not suffice. For example, in applications running in a window environment, control is delegated to the environment and user-defined classes must provide (callback) member functions that will be invoked whenever the window environment deems it appropriate. Callback functions are functions that are determined by convention or explicit declaration to be invoked at some point in the computation.

In the following, we will study indirect control via callback by looking at a number of skeleton fragments illustrating how control may be effected in a window environment. The first two examples are inspired by the InterViews C++ graphical interface library (see Linton *et al.*, 1989). The third example gives a simplified rendering of the *Model-View-Control* paradigm in C++. The MVC paradigm was originally introduced in Smalltalk-80 to facilitate the development of graphical user interfaces.

7.3.1 **Callbacks** – *resource management*

Our first example illustrates the use of callbacks to determine (dynamically) the resources a widget or gadget needs to be placed in a window. (The code below depicts in an abstract way how gadget resource allocation is handled by the InterViews library.) For those not familiar with window-based applications, a more comprehensive treatment of graphical user interface programming is given in section 12.2.

A gadget is an item (such as a button) that may figure in a graphical user interface. A gadget is displayed on the screen by some window object. An abstract simplified definition of a gadget may look as shown in slide 7-23.

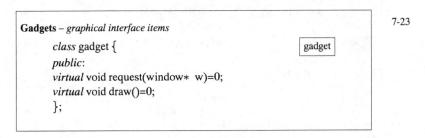

7-23

Gadgets – *graphical interface items*

```
class gadget {                                      gadget
public:
virtual void request(window* w)=0;
virtual void draw()=0;
};
```

Slide 7-23: A *gadget* class

A gadget (in our example) has only two member functions: the function *request* (to notify the window of its requirements, the space it needs to display itself), and the function *draw* (that is called to display the gadget on the screen).

For convenience, we associate a single gadget with a single window, although, as we will see in our next example, a window may contain an arbitrary number of gadgets.

The definition of a (simplified) window class is given in slide 7-24.

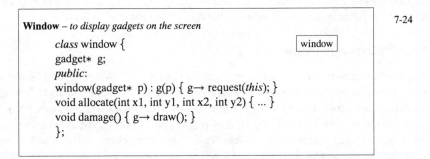

7-24

Window – *to display gadgets on the screen*

```
class window {                                      window
gadget* g;
public:
window(gadget* p) : g(p) { g→ request(this); }
void allocate(int x1, int y1, int x2, int y2) { ... }
void damage() { g→ draw(); }
};
```

Slide 7-24: A *window* class

The class *window* provides a constructor (taking a pointer to a gadget as an argument) and the function *damage*. By convention, gadgets are never directly drawn. When one or more gadgets needs to be (re)drawn this must be done by damaging the window containing the gadget. When the window constructor is evaluated, the gadget is requested (in an abstract fashion) to state its needs by invoking *gadget* :: *request*. In its turn, the gadget will allocate some portion of the screen layout by invoking *widget* :: *allocate*.

As an example of a gadget, look at the definition of a button in slide 7-25.

Items – *a button*   7-25

```
class button : public gadget {                          item
public:
button( int x, int y ) : _x(x), _y(y) {}
void request(window* w) {
    _w = w;
    w→ allocate(_x , _y, _x + 20, _y + 15);
    }
void draw() { w→ rectangle(_x , _y, _x + 20, _y + 15); }
private:
int _x; int _y;
window* _w;
};
```

Slide 7-25: A *button* class

Naturally, both the *request* and *draw* function of an actual gadget will in reality be somewhat more complex. However, the fragment below sufficiently illustrates how the *button* object is requested to state its requirements and to draw itself, in that order:

gadget* b = new button(100,200); window* w = new window(b); w→ damage();

The idea of callbacks is that an object (in this case a gadget) defines the functions that the controller object (in this case the window object) needs to get things right, that is displaying a gadget to the screen. In the following, we will extend this example to include more of the intricate details involved in handling windows and gadgets.

7.3.2 Window management – *events*

Applications running in a window environment (such as X-windows or MS-windows) may in general be characterized as having an event-based control structure. The reason for this is that most languages do not provide multi-threading. Otherwise, it would be quite natural to have a thread per window or gadget. Conceptually, event-based control amounts to having a main loop that checks for incoming events and dispatches control according to the type of the event. However, many window environments (for example, the X-window system) also provide facilities to associate one or more callback functions with a particular event for a particular window.

Moreover, an object-oriented architecture (such as the InterViews library) allows us to define these callbacks by means of virtual functions belonging to a gadget (instead of a window), as illustrated below. The example given here represents, in an abstract fashion, how a particular event handler (callback) function is selected in response to an event, mimicking features of the InterViews library.

```
Event – messages from the environment                              7-26

      class event {                              event
      int _info;
      public:
      event(int i) : _info(i) { }
      int info() { return _info; }
      };
```

Slide 7-26: An *event* class

We start by defining an abstract notion of *event*, as given by the class in slide 7-26. In general, an event is associated with some information that says why (and possibly where) the event occurred. For our example, it suffices to incorporate an (integer) *info* field and a method to extract this information.

Next, we define the class *handler*. The purpose of a handler object (which is created by a window in response to an event) is to check for which gadget the event is relevant. See slide 7-27.

The *gadget* class employed here, which is defined in slide 7-28, is an extension of the gadget class defined previously. For convenience, we assume that all event-related information is stored when the gadget is created.

```
Handler – interception                                             7-27

      class handler {                           handler
      event* e;
      public:
      handler(event* p) : e(p) { g = 0; }
      virtual ~handler() { delete e; }
      int info() { return e→ info(); }
      void set(gadget* p ) { g = p; }
      virtual void operator()() { if (g) g→ callback(); }
      protected:
      gadget* g;
      };
```

Slide 7-27: A *handler* class

In addition to a constructor and a method to deliver the event information, a handler object provides a method to associate a gadget with a handler. As we will see later, the window receiving the event will invoke the actual *callback* function which is defined by the gadget in question.

We also assume that a window may contain multiple gadgets. These gadgets are simply chained using the *next* field (as illustrated in the function *insert*). The most im-

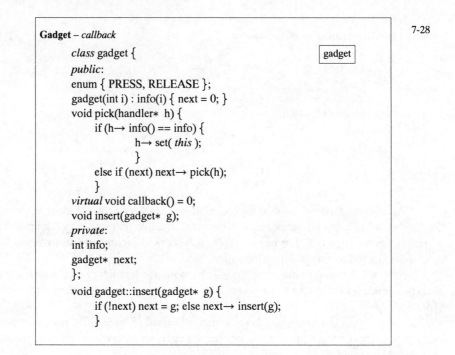

Gadget – *callback*   7-28

```
class gadget {                                           gadget
public:
enum { PRESS, RELEASE };
gadget(int i) : info(i) { next = 0; }
void pick(handler* h) {
    if (h→ info() == info) {
            h→ set( this );
            }
    else if (next) next→ pick(h);
    }
virtual void callback() = 0;
void insert(gadget* g);
private:
int info;
gadget* next;
};
void gadget::insert(gadget* g) {
    if (!next) next = g; else next→ insert(g);
    }
```

Slide 7-28: Another *gadget* class

portant member function of a gadget, in our example, is the function *pick*, used to determine whether an event is of relevance to the gadget. If the event is relevant to the gadget, which is checked by comparing the handler information with the gadget *info* field, then the gadget is associated with the handler by *handler* :: *set*. Otherwise, the next gadget in the chain is asked to check whether the event is relevant.

The class *gadget* is an abstract class, since it provides a pure virtual function *callback* (which is assumed to be defined by an actual gadget, as illustrated in the definition of the *button* class in slide 7-29).

```
class button : public gadget {                           button
public:
button() : gadget(PRESS) { }
void callback() { cout ≪ "..."; }
};
```

Slide 7-29: Another *button* class

Finally, we may define a window with a function *receive* that is invoked when there is an event for that window. See slide 7-30.

When an event is received, a handler for that event is created, the function *pick* is

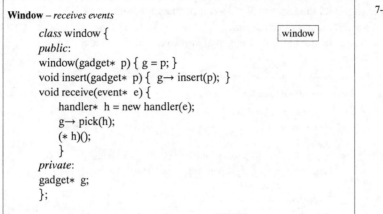

Slide 7-30: Another *window* class

invoked for the first gadget in the chain, and finally, the callback associated with the handler as a result of picking the chain is executed.

Discussion There is no need to say that in this example many of the details have been suppressed. However, note that the user is obliged only to define the function *callback* in the derived gadget class *button*. It should be noted that in the InterViews library, other forms of callback, including member functions of arbitrary objects, are allowed as well. However, these forms require the use of notationally quite complex pointers to member functions, which proved to be an obstacle for many student programmers. In section 12.2 we will look at an alternative approach to object-oriented window programming.

7.3.3 The MV(C) paradigm

The previous examples (describing the cooperation between gadgets, windows and events) illustrate how the complex details of the interactions involved may be hidden from the user, who merely has to define the appropriate (virtual) functions to specify the particularities of the application.

In a similar way, the interactions between user-defined objects may be specified by employing a collection of abstract classes, governing the overall structure of the process of cooperation.

As an example we will look at a skeleton implementation of the MVC-paradigm, which is an essential part of the graphical user interface development framework of the Smalltalk-80 system (see section 3.2.3). For convenience, we omit the controller (C) part (which is responsible for dealing with user input). However, in the next section we will discuss how we may employ events to deal with user input in an (even more) elegant way.

Omitting the *controller* class, the MV(C) structure consists of a *model* class (from which the class describing the functional behavior of the application will be derived), a *view* class (to display the state of the model to the user) which may be refined by the application to fit its particular needs, and one or more model realization classes defined by the user to model the functional behavior of the application.

An abstract model class may be defined as in slide 7-31. By employing a template class we have abstracted from the actual value type of the model.

```
Model – functional behavior                                           7-31

       template< class T >
       class model {                                          model
       public:
       void tell(view<T>* v) { dependent = v; }      // one view only
       void changed() { if (dependent) dependent→ update(); }
       virtual T value()=0;
       protected:
       view<T>* dependent;
       model() { dependent = 0; }                 // restricted creation
       };
```

Slide 7-31: A *model* class

The *model* class provides three public member functions. A function *tell* (to install a view object for the model), a function *changed* (to notify the view objects associated with the model of a change), and a function *value* (which is merely used to illustrate how the model object may give information concerning its state). For convenience, we assume that there is only one view object associated with a model object. (It is an easy exercise to extend the skeleton to associate multiple views with a model.) The view object is stored in the instance variable *dependent*. Also, the class *model* needs to have a virtual destructor, to reclaim the resources needed by its derived classes and their views.

Now look at the definition of the *view* class in slide 7-32. To allow for models supporting various value types, the class *view* must also be defined as a template class.

The *view* class provides a constructor which takes a pointer to a model object as its argument. Evaluating the constructor results in setting the *dependent* view pointer of the model to the view being created. When a view object receives the request *update*, the model associated with the view is consulted and the information delivered as a result is (in some way) displayed to the user.

As an example of a concrete model class, look at the *account* class defined in slide 7-33. It is derived from *model<int>* since the value type of the *account* class is simply *int*.

The *account* class introduces an integer instance variable, an operator to increment the instance variable (just like a counter), and (re)defines the function *value* (which merely returns the value of the integer instance variable). There is no need to redefine the view class, although this might have been easily done.

As an example of using the *account* class look at the fragment below:

    account a; view<int> v(&a); a++; a++;

An instance of *view<int>* must be created since *account* is derived from *model<int>*. Note that incrementing the account results in displaying the value automatically. This il-

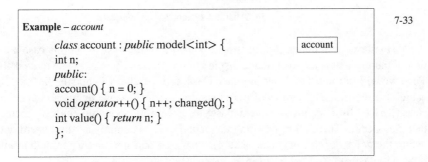

Slide 7-32: A *view* class

Slide 7-33: The *account* class

lustrates in a nutshell how the modification or access of a value may be propagated into a chain of arbitrarily complex (inter)actions. Yet, the abstract architecture of the MV(C) framework ensures that the interactions take place in a carefully controlled way.

However, there is a serious problem with using the MV(C) paradigm in C++. Despite its elegant appearance, it is hard to generalize the relation between model and view classes to include arbitrary interactions.

In the next section, we will elaborate on this by generalizing the notion of event-driven control to include user-defined events.

7.4   Event-driven control

How to model complex interactions is one of the (perhaps most important) issues that needs to be resolved to arrive at a (proper) discipline of object-oriented program design. In section 3.4.3 we looked at the notions of *abstract systems* (representing the combined interface of the object classes involved) and *events* (which are used to organize the interactions between the various objects living in the system).

To conclude this chapter about composition mechanisms, we will look at a somewhat more detailed example employing (user-defined) events to characterize and control the interaction between the objects representing the functional aspects of the application and the objects comprising the user interface (allowing the user to interact with the system). The example is taken from Henderson (1993).

Before describing the actual classes, we will first give an overview of the structure of the application. Our example involves the use of thermometers. The *abstract system* (see section 3.4.3) characterizing the functionality of our application may be characterized as in slide 7-34.

7-34

```
      th = new centigrade();
      th = new fahrenheit();
      th→ set(f);
      f = th→ get();
For thermometer* th, * th1; float f;
```

Slide 7-34: Abstract system – *thermometers*

First, we will define the functional behavior of the system (in this case a collection of thermometers that record and display temperature values, as characterized above). Then we will introduce the user interface classes, respectively to update the temperature value of a thermometer and to display its value. After that we define a concrete event class (derived form an abstract event class) for each of the possible kinds of interactions that may occur. Then, after installing the actual objects comprising the system, we will define the dependencies between (actual) events, so that we can guarantee that interactions with the user will not result in an inconsistent state.

Functional behavior A thermometer must provide the means to store a temperature value and allow for the changing and retrieving of this value. The temperature values are assumed to be stored in degrees Kelvin. See slide 7-35.

7-35

```
class thermometer {                          thermometer
public:
virtual void set(float v) { temp = v; }
virtual float get() { return temp; }
protected:
float temp;
thermometer( float v ) : temp(v) { }
};
```

Slide 7-35: The *thermometer* class

Since only derived classes can use the protected constructor, no direct instances of *thermometer* exist, so the class is abstract. Moreover, both the member functions *set* and *get* are defined as virtual.

We will distinguish between two kinds of thermometers, measuring temperatures respectively in centigrade and fahrenheit. See slides 7-36 and 7-37.

7-36

```
class centigrade : public thermometer {              centigrade
public:
centigrade() : thermometer(0) { }
void set(float v) { temp = v + 273; }
float get() { return temp− 273; }
};
```

Slide 7-36: The *centigrade* class

The class *centigrade* redefines the methods *get* and *set* according to the measurement in centigrade, and in a similar way we may define the class *fahrenheit*.

7-37

```
class fahrenheit : public thermometer {              fahrenheit
public:
fahrenheit() : thermometer(0) { }
void set(float v) { temp = (v− 32) ∗ 5/9 + 273; }
float get() { return temp ∗ 9/5 + 32− 273; }
};
```

Slide 7-37: The *fahrenheit* class

Both the thermometer realization classes take care of performing the conversions necessary to store and retrieve the absolute temperature value.

User interface We will define two simple interface classes, of which we omit the implementation details. First, we define the interface of the *displayer* class, needed to *put* values to the screen as shown in slide 7-38.

7-38

```
class displayer : public window {              displayer
public:
displayer();
void put(char∗ s);
void put(float f);
};
```

Slide 7-38: The *displayer* class

And secondly, we define a *prompter* class, which defines (in an abstract way) how we may get a value from the user (or some other component of the system). See slide 7-39.

7-39

```
class prompter : public window {          prompter
public:
prompter(char* text);
float get();
char* gets();
};
```

Slide 7-39: The *prompter* class

Together, the classes *displayer* and *prompter* define a rudimentary interface which is sufficient to take care of many of the interactions between the user and the system.

Events To define the interactions with the user (and their possible consequences) we will employ *events*, that is instances of realizations of the abstract event class, defined in slide 7-40.

7-40

Events – *to define interactions*

```
class event {                              event
public:
void dependent(event* e);
void process();
virtual void operator()() = 0;
private:
set<event>* dep;
};
```

Slide 7-40: The *event* class

Since a simple event (for example, the modification of a value) may result in a series of events (needed to keep the system in a consistent state), an event object maintains a set of dependent events, which may be activated using the function *event :: process*. Further, each class derived from *event* is assumed to define the application operator, that is the actual actions resulting from activating the event.

The first realization of the abstract event class is the *update* event class, which corresponds to retrieving a new temperature value from the user. See slide 7-41.

An update involves a thermometer and a prompter, which are stored when creating the update event object. Activating an update event instance results in retrieving a value from the prompter, setting the thermometer to this value and activating the dependent events.

7-41

```
class update : public event {                    update
public:
update(thermometer* th, prompter* p) : _th(th), _p(p) {}
void operator()() {
    _th→ set( _p→ get() );
    event::process();
    }
protected:
thermometer* _th; prompter* _p;
};
```

Slide 7-41: The *update* class

In a similar way, we define the second realization of the abstract event class, the *show* event class, which corresponds to displaying the value of a thermometer. See slide 7-42.

7-42

```
class show : public event {                    show
public:
show(thermometer* th, displayer* d) : _th(th), -d(d) {}
void operator()() {
    _d→ put( _th→ get() );
    event::process();
    }
protected:
thermometer* _th; displayer* _d;
};
```

Slide 7-42: The *show* class

Activating a show event instance results in retrieving a value from the thermometer, putting that value on display and activating the events associated with this event.

The installation The next step we must take is to install the application, that is to create the objects comprising the functional behavior of the system, the user interface objects and (finally) the various event objects. See slide 7-43.

Having created the objects, we are almost done. The most important and perhaps difficult part is to define the appropriate dependencies between the respective event objects. See slide 7-44.

As shown above, we declare the event of showing the value of the centigrade thermometer (and also of the fahrenheit thermometer) to be dependent upon the event of updating the value of the centigrade thermometer. And we repeat this declaration for the event of updating the value of the fahrenheit thermometer.

```
        thermometer* c = new centigrade();                        7-43
        thermometer* f = new fahrenheit();

        displayer* cd = new displayer("centigrade");
        displayer* fd = new displayer("fahrenheit");

        prompter* cp = new prompter("enter centigrade value");
        prompter* fp = new prompter("enter fahrenheit value");

        show* sc = new show(c,cd);
        show* sf = new show(f,fd);

        update* uc = new update(c,cp);
        update* uf = new update(f,fp);
```

Slide 7-43: Installing the objects

```
Dependencies – to interconnect events                             7-44
        uc→ dependent(sc);
        uc→ dependent(sf);
        uf→ dependent(sc);
        uf→ dependent(sf);
```

Slide 7-44: Assigning dependencies

We may now allow the user the choice between updating the centigrade or fahrenheit thermometer temperature value, for example by inserting these events in a menu, as indicated below

```
menu→ insert(uc);
menu→ insert(uf);
```

The reader is urged to do some mental processing to check that updating the value of one thermometer actually results in changing the value displayed for the other thermometer as well.

Discussion Organizing interactions with the user (and the other components of the system as well) by means of events provides a powerful way in which to control the consequences of one particular (kind of) interaction. The advantage of such an approach is that the repertoire of possible interactions can easily be extended or modified without affecting the other parts of the system (the parts realizing the functional behavior of the system and the particularities of the user interface). From the perspective of design, it is (in my view) the best approximation we have of defining *behavioral compositions* (and its corresponding protocol of interaction) in a formal way. See also section 10.5.

Summary

This chapter explored techniques that may be used to structure object-oriented programs. These techniques may be regarded as idioms or guidelines augmenting the mechanisms provided by object-oriented languages.

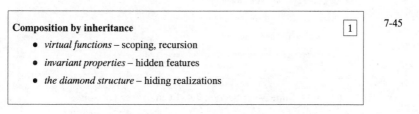

Slide 7-45: Section 7.1: Composition by inheritance

In section 1, we looked at the problems that may occur when employing virtual functions and explicit scoping, in particular in the presence of recursion, how to maintain invariance when using inheritance, and we discussed the diamond structure for the realization of compound objects.

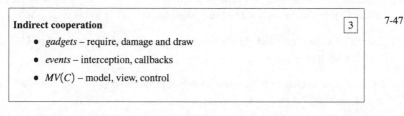

Slide 7-46: Section 7.2: Interaction through delegation

In section 2, an example was given demonstrating implicit delegation in C++. Also, we looked at the notion of *smart pointers*. Delegation underlies the envelope/letter idiom which allows for separating the interface of a data type from its realization. We also discussed an example of dynamic role switching, employing explicit delegation.

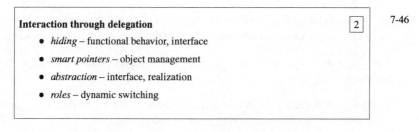

Slide 7-47: Section 7.3: Indirect cooperation

In section 3, we looked at some patterns of cooperation between objects. The examples were inspired by solutions employed in the Interviews user interface development library. Also, a schematic implementation of the Smalltalk MV(C) paradigm was given.

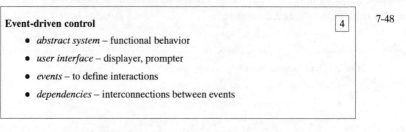

Slide 7-48: Section 7.4: Event-driven control

Finally, in section 4, we looked at an example demonstrating event-driven control. Events provide a powerful abstraction to define the interaction of objects in response to a user action.

Questions

(1) Discuss the interplay between scoping and recursion for virtual functions.

(2) How would you express the invariant behavior of an *employee* class? Explain what problems may occur when adding a bonus to the *salary* of a derived *manager* class.

(3) Explain how compound objects may be constructed by employing the diamond structure.

(4) Explain how the functionality of a class may be made accessible through an arbitrary interface class by employing implicit delegation.

(5) What are smart pointers? Why are they useful? How would you implement them?

(6) Sketch how you would implement dynamic role switching in C++.

(7) What is a gadget? Give an example showing the interaction between a gadget and a window.

(8) Characterize the notion of *event* in a window environment. Characterize also the interaction between events and the gadget to which the event is directed.

(9) Sketch how the Smalltalk MV(C) paradigm may be implemented in C++. Give a simple example of its use.

(10) Explain how events may be used to regulate the effects of user actions. Why are events needed?

Further reading

An invaluable source with respect to idioms and advanced usage of C++ is Coplien (1992). Further, you may consult Krasner and Pope (1988) for examples of applying the MVC paradigm, and Henderson (1993) for examples of employing events. Henderson (1993) also proposes a canonical mapping from a formal specification language to an implementation in C++.

Part III

Foundations of Object-Oriented Modeling

8

Abstract data types

The history of programming languages may be characterized as the genesis of increasingly powerful abstractions to aid the development of reliable programs.

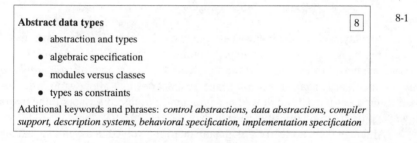

8-1

Slide 8-1: Chapter 8: Abstract data types

In this chapter we will look at the notion of *abstract data types*, which may be regarded as an essential constituent of object-oriented modeling. In particular, we will study the notion of data abstraction from a foundational perspective, that is based on a mathematical description of types. We start this chapter by discussing the notion of *types as constraints*. Then, we look at the (first order) algebraic specification of abstract data types, and we explore the trade-offs between the traditional implementation of abstract data types by employing modules and the object-oriented approach employing classes. We conclude this chapter by exploring the distinction between classes and types, as a preparation for the treatment of (higher order) polymorphic type theories for object types and inheritance in the next chapter.

8.1 Abstraction and types

The concern for abstraction may be regarded as the driving force behind the development of programming languages (of which there are astoundingly many). In the following we will discuss the role of abstraction in programming, and especially the importance of types. We then briefly look at what mathematical means we have available to describe types from a foundational perspective and what we may (and may not) expect from types in object-oriented programming.

8.1.1 Abstraction in programming languages

In Shaw (1984), an overview is given of how increasingly powerful abstraction mechanisms have shaped the programming languages we use today. See slide 8-2.

Abstraction – *programming methodology*   8-2

- control abstractions – *structured programming*

- data abstraction – *information hiding*

The kind of abstraction provided by ADTs can be supported by any language with
a procedure call mechanism (given that appropriate *protocols* are developed and observed by the programmer). Danforth and Tomlinson (1988)

Slide 8-2: Abstraction and programming languages

Roughly, we may distinguish between two categories of abstractions: abstractions that aid in specifying *control* (including subroutines, procedures, *if-then-else* constructs, *while*-constructs, in short the constructs promoted by the school of *structured programming* in their battle against the *goto*); and abstractions that allow us to hide the actual representation of the data employed in a program (introduced to support the *information hiding* approach, originally advocated in Parnas (1972a)).

Although there is clearly a pragmatic interest involved in developing and employing such abstractions, the concern with abstraction (and consequently types) is ultimately motivated by a concern with programming methodology and, as observed in Danforth and Tomlinson (1988), the need for reliable and maintainable software. However, the introduction of language features is also often motivated by programmers' desires for ease of coding and naturalness of expression.

In the same vein, although types were originally considered as a convenient means to assist the compiler in producing efficient code, types have rapidly been recognized as a way in which to capture the meaning of a program in an implementation independent way. In particular, the notion of abstract data types (which has, so to speak, grown out of data abstraction) has become a powerful device (and guideline) to structure large software systems.

In practice, as the quotation from Danforth and Tomlinson (1988) in slide 8-2 indicates, we may employ the tools developed for structured programming to realize abstract data types in a program, but with the obvious disadvantage that we must rely on conventions with regard to the reliability of these realizations. Support for abstract data types (support in the sense as discussed in section 1.3) is offered (to some extent) by languages such as Modula-2 and Ada by means of a syntactic module or package construct, and (to a larger extent) by object-oriented languages in the form of object classes. However, both realizations are of a rather *ad hoc* and pragmatic nature, relying in the latter case on the metaphor of encapsulation and message passing. The challenge to computer science in this area is to develop a notion of types capturing the power of abstract data types in a form that is adequate both from a pragmatic point of view (in the sense of allowing efficient language support) and from a theoretical perspective (laying the foundation for a truly declarative object-oriented approach to programming).

8.1.2   A foundational perspective – *types as constraints*

Object-oriented programming may be regarded as a *declarative* method of programming, in the sense that it provides a computation model (expressed by the metaphor of encapsulation and message passing) that is independent of a particular implementation model. In particular, the inheritance subtype relation may be regarded as a pure description of the relations between the entities represented by the classes. Moreover, an object-oriented approach favors the development of an object model that bears close resemblance to the entities and their relations living in the application domain. However, the object-oriented programming model is rarely introduced with the mathematical precision characteristic of descriptions of the other declarative styles, for example the functional and logic programming model. Criticizing, Danforth and Tomlinson (1988) remark that *OOP is generally expressed in philosophical terms, resulting in a proliferation of opinions concerning what OOP really is.*

From a type theoretical perspective, our interest is to identify abstract data types as elements of some *semantic* (read mathematical) domain and to characterize their properties in an unambiguous fashion. See slide 8-3.

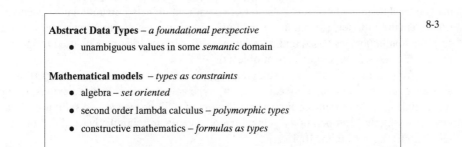

Abstract Data Types – *a foundational perspective*   8-3

  - unambiguous values in some *semantic* domain

Mathematical models – *types as constraints*

  - algebra – *set oriented*
  - second order lambda calculus – *polymorphic types*
  - constructive mathematics – *formulas as types*

Slide 8-3: Mathematical models for types

There seems to be almost no limit to the variety and sophistication of the mathematical models proposed to characterize abstract data types and inheritance. We may make a distinction between first order approaches (based on ordinary set theory) and higher order approaches (involving typed lambda calculus and constructive logic).

The algebraic approach is a quite well-established method for the formal specification of abstract data types. A type (or sort) in an algebra corresponds to a set of elements upon which the operations of the algebra are defined. In the next section, we will look at how equations may be used to characterize the behavioral aspects of an abstract data type modeled by an algebra.

Second order lambda calculus has been used to model information hiding and the polymorphism supported by inheritance and templates. In the next chapter we will study this approach in more detail.

In both approaches, the meaning of a type is (ultimately) a set of elements satisfying certain restrictions. However, in a more abstract fashion, we may regard a type as specifying a constraint. The better we specify the constraint, the more tightly the corresponding set of elements will be defined (and hence the smaller the set). A natural consequence of the idea of *types as constraints* is to characterize types by means of logical formulas. This is the approach taken by type theories based on constructive logic, in which the notion of *formulas as types* plays an important role. Although we will not study type theories based on constructive logic explicitly, our point of view is essentially to regard types as constraints, ranging from purely syntactical constraints (as expressed in a signature) to semantic constraints (as may be expressed in contracts).

From the perspective of types as constraints, a typing system may contribute to a language framework guiding a system designer's conceptualization and supporting the verification (based on the formal properties of the types employed) of the consistency of the descriptive information provided by the program. Such an approach is to be preferred (both from a pragmatic and theoretical point of view) to an *ad hoc* approach employing special annotations and support mechanisms, since these may become quite complicated and easily lead to unexpected interactions.

Formal models There is a wide variety of formal models available in the literature. These include algebraic models (to characterize the meaning of abstract data types), models based on the lambda-calculus and its extensions (that are primarily used for a type theoretical analysis of object-oriented language constructs), algebraic process calculi (that may be used to characterize the behavior of concurrent objects), operational and denotational semantic models (to capture behavioral and properties of programs), and various specification languages based on first or higher-order logics (that may be used to specify the desired behavior of collections of objects).

We will limit ourselves to studying algebraic models capturing the properties of abstract data types and objects (section 8.2.4), type calculi based on typed extensions of the lambda calculus capturing the various flavors of polymorphism and subtyping (sections 9.3–9.6), and an operational semantic model characterizing the behavior of objects sending messages (section 10.3).

Both the algebraic and type theoretical models are primarily intended to clarify the means we have to express the desired behavior of objects and the restrictions that must be adhered to when defining objects and their relations. The operational characterization of object behavior, on the other hand, is intended to give a more precise characterization of the notion of state and state changes underlying the verification of object behavior by means of assertion logics.

Despite the numerous models introduced there are still numerous approaches not covered here. One approach worth mentioning is the work based on the *pi-calculus*. The *pi-calculus* is an extension of algebraic process calculi that allow for communication via named channels. Moreover, the *pi-calculus* allows for a notion of migration and the creation and renaming of channels. A semantics of object-based languages based on the *pi-calculus* is given in Walker (1990). However, this semantics does not cover inheritance or subtyping. A higher-order object-oriented programming language based on the *pi-calculus* is presented in Pierce at al. (1993).

Another approach of interest, also based on process calculi, is the object calculus (OC) described in Nierstrasz (1993). OC allows for modeling the operational semantics of concurrent objects. It merges the notions of agents, as used in process calculi, with the notion of functions, as present in the lambda calculus.

For alternative models the reader may look in the `comp.theory` newsgroup to which information concerning formal calculi for OOP is posted by Tom Mens of the Free University, Brussels.

8.1.3 Objectives of typed OOP

Before loosing ourselves in the details of mathematical models of types, we must reflect on what we may expect from a type system and what not (at least not currently).

From a theoretical perspective our ideal is, in the words of Danforth and Tomlinson (1988), to arrive at a simple type theory that provides a consistent and flexible framework for *system descriptions* (in order to provide the programmer with sufficient descriptive power and to aid the construction of useful and understandable software, while allowing the efficient utilization of the underlying hardware).

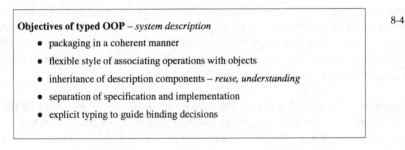

8-4

Objectives of typed OOP – *system description*

- packaging in a coherent manner
- flexible style of associating operations with objects
- inheritance of description components – *reuse, understanding*
- separation of specification and implementation
- explicit typing to guide binding decisions

Slide 8-4: Object orientation and types

The question now is, what support does a typing system provide in this respect. In slide 8-4, a list is given of aspects in which a typing system may be of help.

One important benefit of regarding ADTs as real types is that realizations of ADTs become so-called *first class citizens,* which means that they may be treated as any other value in the language, for instance being passed as a parameter. In contrast, syntactic solutions (such as the module of Modula-2 and the package of Ada) do not allow this.

Pragmatically, the objective of a type system is (and has been) the prevention of errors. However, if the type system lacks expressivity, adequate control for errors may result in becoming over-restrictive.   In general, the more expressive the type system the better the support that the compiler may offer. In this respect, associating constructors with types may help in relieving the programmer from dealing with simple but necessary tasks such as the initialization of complex structures. Objects, in contrast to modules or packages, allow for the automatic (compiler supported) initializations of instances of (abstract) data types, providing the programmer with relief from an error-prone routine.

Another area in which a type system may make the life of a programmer easier concerns the association of operations with objects. A polymorphic type system is needed to understand the automatic dispatching for virtual functions and the opportunity of overloading functions, which are useful mechanisms to control the complexity of a program, provided they are well-understood.

Reuse and understanding are promoted by allowing inheritance and refinement of description components. (As remarked earlier, inheritance and refinement may be regarded as the essential contribution of object-oriented programming to the practice of software development.) It goes without saying that such reuse needs a firm semantical basis in order to achieve the goal of reliable and maintainable software.

Another important issue for which a powerful type system can provide support is the separation of specification and implementation. Naturally, we expect our type system to support type safe separate compilation. But in addition, we may think of allowing multiple implementations of a single (abstract type) specification. Explicit typing may then be of help in choosing the right binding when the program is actually executed. For instance in a parallel environment, behavior may be realized in a number of ways, that differ in the degree to which they affect locality of access and how they affect, for example, load balancing. With an eye to the future, these are problems that may be solved with a good type system (and accompanying compiler).

One of the desiderata for a future type system for OOP, laid down in Danforth and Tomlinson (1988), is the separation of a *behavioral hierarchy* (specifying the behavior of a type in an abstract sense) and an *implementation hierarchy* (specifying the actual realization of that behavior). Separation is needed to accommodate the need for multiple realizations and to resolve the tension between subtyping and inheritance (a tension we have already noted in sections 1.1.3 and 3.3).

Remark In these chapters we cannot hope to do more than get acquainted with the material needed to understand the problems involved in developing a type system for object-oriented programming. For an alternative approach, see Palsberg and Schwartzback (1994).

8.2   Algebraic specification

Algebraic specification techniques have been developed as a means to specify the design of complex software systems in a formal way. The algebraic approach has been motivated by the notion of *information hiding* put forward in Parnas (1972a) and the ideas concerning *abstraction* expressed in Hoare (1972). Historically, the ADJ-group (see Goguen *et al.*, 1978) provided a significant impetus to the algebraic approach by showing that abstract data types may be interpreted as (many sorted) algebras. (In the context of algebraic specifications the notion of *sorts* has the same meaning as *types*. We will, however, generally speak of *types*.)

As an example of an algebraic specification, look at the module defining the data type *Bool*, as given in slide 8-5.

Algebraic specification – *ADT* | *Bool* | 8-5

    adt *bool* is
    functions
     true : *bool*
     false : *bool*
      and , *or* : *bool* × *bool* → *bool*
     not : *bool* → *bool*
    axioms
     [B1] *and* $(true, x) = x$
     [B2] *and* $(false, x) = false$
     [B3] *not*$(true) = false$
     [B4] *not*$(false) = true$
     [B5] $or(x, y) = not($ *and* $(not(x), not(y)))$
    end

Slide 8-5: The ADT *Bool*

In this specification two constants are introduced (the zero-ary functions *true* and *false*), three functions (respectively *and, or* and *not*). The *or* function is defined by employing *not* and *and*, according to a well-known logical law. These functions may all be considered to be (strictly) related to the type *bool*. Equations are used to specify the desired characteristics of elements of type *bool*. Obviously, this specification may mathematically be interpreted as (simply) a boolean algebra.

Mathematical models The mathematical framework of algebras allows for a direct characterization of the behavioral aspects of abstract data types by means of equations, provided the specification is consistent. Operationally, this allows for the execution of such specifications by means of term rewriting, provided that some (technical) constraints are met. The model-theoretic semantics of algebraic specifications centers around the notion of *initial algebras*, which gives us the preferred model of a specification.

To characterize the behavior of *objects* (that may modify their state) in an algebraic way, we need to extend the basic framework of initial algebra models either by allowing so-called *multiple world* semantics or by making a distinction between hidden and observable sorts (resulting in the notion of an object as an *abstract machine*). As a remark, in our treatment we obviously cannot avoid the use of some logico-mathematical formalism. If needed, the concepts introduced will be explained on the fly. Where this does not suffice, the interested reader is referred to any standard textbook on mathematical logic for further details.

8.2.1 **Signatures** – *generators and observers*

Abstract data types may be considered as modules specifying the values and functions belonging to the type. In Dahl (1992), a type T is characterized as a tuple specifying the set of elements constituting the type T and the collection of functions related to the type T. Since constants may be regarded as zero-ary functions (having no arguments), we will speak of a *signature* Σ or Σ_T defining a particular type T. Also, in accord with common parlance, we will speak of the sorts $s \in \Sigma$, which are the sorts (or types) occurring in the declaration of the functions in Σ. See slide 8-6.

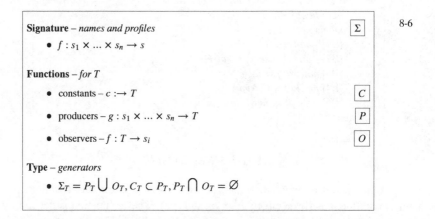

8-6

Signature – *names and profiles* $\boxed{\Sigma}$

- $f : s_1 \times \ldots \times s_n \to s$

Functions – *for T*

- constants – $c :\to T$ $\boxed{C}$
- producers – $g : s_1 \times \ldots \times s_n \to T$ $\boxed{P}$
- observers – $f : T \to s_i$ $\boxed{O}$

Type – *generators*

- $\Sigma_T = P_T \bigcup O_T, C_T \subset P_T, P_T \bigcap O_T = \varnothing$

Slide 8-6: Algebraic specification

A *signature* specifies the names and (function) profiles of the constants and functions of a data type. In general, the profile of a function is specified as

- $f : s_1 \times \ldots \times s_n \to s$

where s_i $(i = 1..n)$ are the sorts defining the domain (that is the types of the arguments) of the function f, and s is the sort defining the codomain (or result type) of f. In the case $n = 0$ the function f may be regarded as a constant. More generally, when $s_1, ..., s_n$ are all unrelated to the type T being defined, we may regard f as a relative constant. Relative constants are values that are assumed to be defined in the context where the specification is being employed.

The functions related to a data type T may be discriminated according to their role in defining T. We distinguish between *producers* $g \in P_T$, that have the type T under definition as their result type, and *observers* $f \in O_T$, that have T as their argument type and deliver a result of a type different from T. In other words, producer functions define how elements of T may be constructed. (In the literature one often speaks of *constructors*, but we avoid this term because it already has a precisely defined meaning in the object-oriented programming language C++.) In contrast, observer functions do not produce values of T, but give instead information on some particular aspect of T.

The signature Σ_T of a type T is uniquely defined by the union of producer functions P_T and observer functions O_T. Constants of type T are regarded as a subset of the producer functions P_T defining T. Further, we require that the collection of producers is disjoint from the collection of observers for T, that is $P_T \cap O_T = \varnothing$.

Generators The producer functions actually defining the values of a data type T are called the *generator basis* of T, or generators of T. The generators of T may be used to enumerate the elements of T, resulting in the collection of T values that is called the *generator universe* in Dahl (1992). See slide 8-7.

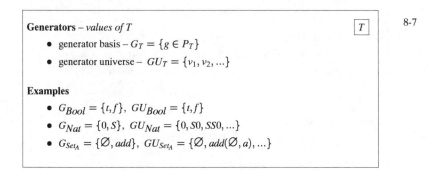

Generators – *values of* T $\boxed{T}$ 8-7

- generator basis – $G_T = \{g \in P_T\}$
- generator universe – $GU_T = \{v_1, v_2, ...\}$

Examples

- $G_{Bool} = \{t, f\}$, $GU_{Bool} = \{t, f\}$
- $G_{Nat} = \{0, S\}$, $GU_{Nat} = \{0, S0, SS0, ...\}$
- $G_{Set_A} = \{\varnothing, add\}$, $GU_{Set_A} = \{\varnothing, add(\varnothing, a), ...\}$

Slide 8-7: Generators – *basis* and *universe*

The generator universe of a type T consists of the closed (that is variable-free) terms that may be constructed using either constants or producer functions of T. As an example, consider the data type *Bool* with generators t and f. Obviously, the value domain of *Bool*, the generator universe GU_{Bool} consists only of the values t and f.

As another example, consider the data type *Nat* (representing the natural numbers) with generator basis $G_{Nat} = \{0, S\}$, consisting of the constant 0 and the successor function $S : Nat \rightarrow Nat$ (that delivers the successor of its argument). The terms that may be constructed by G_{Nat} is the set $GU_{Nat} = \{0, S0, SS0, ...\}$, which uniquely corresponds to the natural numbers $\{0, 1, 2, ...\}$. (More precisely, the natural numbers are isomorphic with GU_{Nat}.)

In contrast, given a type A with element a, b, ..., the generators of Set_A result in a universe that contains terms such as $add(\varnothing, a)$ and $add(add(\varnothing, a), a)$ which we would like to identify, based on our conception of a set as containing only one exemplar of a particular value. To effect this we need additional equations imposing constraints expressing what we consider as the desired shape (or *normal form*) of the values contained in the universe of T. However, before we look at how to extend a signature Σ defining T with equations defining the (behavioral) properties of T we will look at another example illustrating how the choice of a generator basis may affect the structure of the value domain of a data type.

In the example presented in slide 8-8, the profiles are given of the functions that may occur in the signature specifying sequences. (The notation _ is used to indicate parameter positions.)

Dependent on which producer functions are selected to generate the universe of T, the correspondence between the generated universe and the intended domain is either

---

Sequences $\boxed{Seq}$ 8-8

    $\varepsilon : seqT$ empty

    $\_ \triangleright \_ : seqT \times T \to seqT$ right append

    $\_ \triangleleft \_ : T \times seqT \to seqT$ left append

    $\_ \cdot \_ : seqT \times seqT \to seqT$ concatenation

    $\langle \_ \rangle : T \to seqT$ lifting

    $\langle \_, ..., \_ \rangle : T^n \to seqT$ multiple arguments

Generator basis *– preferably one-to-one*

- $G_{seqT} = \{\varepsilon, \triangleright\}$, $GU_{seqT} = \{\varepsilon, \varepsilon \triangleright a, \varepsilon \triangleright b, ..., \varepsilon \triangleright a \triangleright b, ...\}$
- $G'_{seqT} = \{\varepsilon, \triangleleft\}$, $GU'_{seqT} = \{\varepsilon, a \triangleleft \varepsilon, b \triangleleft \varepsilon, ..., b \triangleleft a \triangleleft \varepsilon, ...\}$
- $G''_{seqT} = \{\varepsilon, \cdot, \langle \_ \rangle\}$, $GU''_{seqT} = \{\varepsilon, \langle a \rangle, \langle b \rangle, , ..., \varepsilon \cdot \varepsilon, ..., \varepsilon \cdot \langle a \rangle, ...\}$

Infinite generator basis

- $G'''_{seqT} = \{\varepsilon, \langle \_ \rangle, \langle \_, \_ \rangle, ...\}$, $GU'''_{seqT} = \{\varepsilon, \langle a \rangle, \langle b \rangle, , ..., \langle a, a \rangle, ...\}$

Slide 8-8: The ADT *Seq*

one-to-one (as for G and G') or *many-to-one* (as for G''). Since we require our specification to be first-order and finite, infinite generator bases (such as G''') must be disallowed, even if they result in a one-to-one correspondence. See Dahl (1992) for further details.

8.2.2 Equations – *specifying constraints*

The specification of the signature of a type (which lists the *syntactic constraints* to which a specification must comply) is in general not sufficient to characterize the properties of the values of the type. In addition, we need to impose *semantic constraints* (in the form of equations) to define the meaning of the observer functions and (very importantly) to identify the elements of the type domain that are considered equivalent (based on the intuitions one has of that particular type).

     Mathematically, the equality predicate may be characterized by the properties listed above, including *reflexivity* (stating that an element is equal to itself), *symmetry* (stating that the orientation of the formula is not important) and *transitivity* (stating that if one element is equal to another and that element is equal to yet another, then the first element is also equal to the latter). In addition, we have the property that, given that two elements are equal, the results of the function applied to them (separately) are also equal. (Technically, the latter property makes a *congruence* of the equality relation, lifting equality between elements to the function level.) See slide 8-9.

     Given a suitable set of equations, in addition to a signature, we may identify the elements that can be proved identical by applying the equality relation. In other words, given an equational theory (of which the properties stated above must be a part), we can divide the generator universe of a type T into one or more subsets, each consisting of el-

---

The equivalence relation – *congruence*   8-9

- $x = x$ reflexivity
- $x = y \Longrightarrow y = x$ symmetry
- $x = y \land y = z \Longrightarrow x = z$ transitivity
- $x = y \Longrightarrow f(...,x,...) = f(...,y,...)$

Equivalence classes – *representatives*

- abstract elements – $GU_T / \sim$

Slide 8-9: Equivalence

ements that are equal according to our theory. The subsets of $GU/ \sim$, that is GU factored with respect to equivalence, may be regarded as the abstract elements constituting the type T, and from each subset we may choose a concrete element acting as a *representative* for the subset which is the equivalence class of the element.

Operationally, equations may be regarded as *rewrite rules* (oriented from left to right), that allow us to transform a term in which a term t_1 occurs as a subterm into a term in which t_1 is replaced by t_2 if $t_1 = t_2$. For this procedure to be terminating, some technical restrictions must be met, amounting (intuitively) to the requirement that the right-hand side must in some sense be simpler than the left-hand side.

Also, when defining an observer function, we must specify for each possible generator case an appropriate rewriting rule. That is, each observer must be able to give a result for each generator. The example of the natural numbers, given below, will make this clear. Identifying spurious elements by rewriting a term into a canonical form is somewhat more complex, as we will see for the example of sets.

Equational theories To illustrate the notions introduced above, we will look at specifications of some familiar types, namely the natural numbers and sets.

In slide 8-10, an algebraic specification is given of the natural numbers (as first axiomatized by Peano).

In addition to the constant 0 and successor function S we also introduce a function *mul* for multiplication and a function *plus* for addition. (The notation Sy stands for application by juxtaposition; its meaning is simply $S(y)$.) The reader who does not immediately accept the specification in slide 8-10 as an adequate axiomatization of the natural numbers must try to unravel the computation depicted in slide 8-11.

Admittedly, not an easy way to compute with natural numbers, but fortunately term rewriting may, to a large extent, be automated (and actual calculations may be mimicked by semantics preserving primitives).

Using the equational theory expressing the properties of natural numbers, we may eliminate the occurrences of the functions *mul* and *prod* to arrive (through symbolic evaluation) at something of the form $S^n 0$ (where n corresponds to the magnitude of the natural number denoted by the term).

The opportunity of symbolic evaluation by term rewriting is exactly what has

Slide 8-10: The ADT *Nat*

8-10

```
Natural numbers                                    Nat
    functions
    0 : Nat
    S : Nat → Nat
    mul : Nat × Nat → Nat
    plus : Nat × Nat → Nat
    axioms
    [1] plus(x,0) = x
    [2] plus(x,Sy) = S(plus(x,y))
    [3] mul(x,0) = 0
    [4] mul(x,Sy) = plus(mul(x,y),x)
    end
```

Slide 8-10: The ADT *Nat*

8-11

$$mul(plus(S0,S0),S0) \xrightarrow{2}$$
$$mul(S(plus(S0,0)),S0) \xrightarrow{1}$$
$$mul(SS0,S0) \xrightarrow{4}$$
$$plus(mul(SS0,0),S0) \xrightarrow{3} SS0$$

Slide 8-11: Symbolic evaluation

made the algebraic approach so popular for the specification of software, since it allows (under some restrictions) for executable specifications.

Since they do not reappear in what may be considered the *normal forms* of terms denoting the naturals (that are obtained by applying the evaluations induced by the equality theory), the functions *plus* and *mul* may be regarded as *secondary* producers. They are not part of the generator basis of the type *Nat*.

Since we may consider *mul* and *plus* as secondary producers at best, we can easily see that when we define *mul* and *plus* for the case 0 and *Sx* for arbitrary x, that we have covered all possible (generator) cases. Technically, this allows us to prove properties of these functions by using structural induction on the possible generator cases. The proof obligation (in the case of the naturals) then is to prove that the property holds for the function applied to 0 and assuming that the property holds for applying the function to x, it also holds for *Sx*.

As our next example, consider the algebraic specification of the type Set_A in slide 8-12.

In the case of sets we have the problem that we do not start with a one-to-one generator base as we had with the natural numbers. Instead, we have a many-to-one generator base, so we need equality axioms to eliminate spurious elements from the (generator) universe of sets.

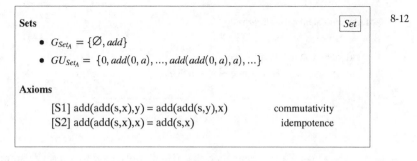

8-12

Sets $\boxed{Set}$

- $G_{Set_A} = \{\varnothing, add\}$
- $GU_{Set_A} = \{0, add(0, a), ..., add(add(0, a), a), ...\}$

Axioms

    [S1] add(add(s,x),y) = add(add(s,y),x)   commutativity
    [S2] add(add(s,x),x) = add(s,x)   idempotence

Slide 8-12: The ADT *Set*

8-13

$\{\varnothing\}$

$\{add(0, a), add(add(0, a), a), ...\}$

...

$\{add(add(0, a), b), add(add(0, b), a), ...\}$

Slide 8-13: Equivalence classes for *Set*

The equivalence classes of $GU_{Set_A} / \sim$ (which is GU_{Set_A} factored by the equivalence relation), each have multiple elements (except the class representing the empty set). To select an appropriate representative from each of these classes (representing the abstract elements of the type Set_A) we need an ordering on terms, so that we can take the smaller term as its canonical representation. See slide 8-13.

8.2.3 Initial algebra semantics

In the previous section we have given a rather operational characterization of the equivalence relation induced by the equational theory and the process of term rewriting that enables us to purge the generator universe of a type, by eliminating redundant elements. However, what we actually strive for is a mathematical model that captures the meaning of an algebraic specification. Such a model is provided (or rather a class of such models) by the mathematical structures known as (not surprisingly) algebras.

A *single sorted* algebra $\mathcal{A}$ is a structure (A, Σ) where A is a set of values, and Σ specifies the signature of the functions operating on A. A *multi-sorted* algebra is a structure $\mathcal{A} = (\{A_s\}_{s \in S}, \Sigma)$ where S is a set of sort names and A_s the set of values belonging to the sort s. The set S may be ordered (in which case the ordering indicates the subtyping relationships between the sorts). We call the (multi-sorted) structure $\mathcal{A}$ a Σ-algebra.

Having a notion of algebras, we need to have a way in which to relate an algebraic specification to such a structure. To this end we define an interpretation *eval* : $T_\Sigma \rightarrow \mathcal{A}$ which maps closed terms formed by following the rules given in the specification to elements of the structure $\mathcal{A}$. We may extend the interpretation *eval* to include variables as well (which we write as *eval* : $T_\Sigma(X) \rightarrow \mathcal{A}$), but then we also need to assume that an as-

---

Mathematical model – *algebra*   8-14

- Σ-algebra – $\mathcal{A} = (\{A_s\}_{s \in S}, \Sigma)$
- interpretation – $eval : T_\Sigma \to \mathcal{A}$
- adequacy – $\mathcal{A} \models t_1 = t_2 \Longleftrightarrow E \vdash t_1 = t_2$

Slide 8-14: Interpretations and models

signment $\theta : X \to T_\Sigma(X)$ is given, such that when applying θ to a term t the result is free of variables, otherwise no interpretation in $\mathcal{A}$ exists. See slide 8-14.

Interpretations As an example, consider the interpretations of the specification of *Bool* and the specification of *Nat*, given in slide 8-15.

Booleans   8-15

- $\mathcal{B} = (\{tt, ff\}, \{\neg, \wedge, \vee\})$
- $eval_{\mathcal{B}} : T_{Bool} \to \mathcal{B} = \{or \mapsto \vee, \quad and \quad \mapsto \wedge, not \mapsto \neg\}$

Natural numbers

- $\mathcal{N} = (\mathbb{N}, \{++, +, ^*\})$
- $eval_{\mathcal{N}} : T_{Nat} \to \mathcal{N} = \{S \mapsto ++, mul \mapsto ^*, plus \mapsto +\}$

Slide 8-15: Interpretations of *Bool* and *Nat*

The structure $\mathcal{B}$ given above is simply a boolean algebra, with the operators $\neg$, $\wedge$ and $\vee$. The functions *not*, *and* and *or* naturally map to their semantic counterparts. In addition, we assume that the constants *true* and *false* map to the elements *tt* and *ff*.

As another example, look at the structure $\mathcal{N}$ and the interpretation $eval_{\mathcal{N}}$, which maps the functions S, *mul* and *plus* specified in *Nat* in a natural way. However, since we have also given equations for *Nat* (specifying how to eliminate the functions *mul* and *plus*) we must take precautions such that the requirement

$$\mathcal{N} \models eval_{\mathcal{N}}(t_1) =_{\mathcal{N}} eval_{\mathcal{N}}(t_2) \Longleftrightarrow E_{Nat} \vdash t_1 = t_2$$

is satisfied if the structure $\mathcal{N}$ is to count as an adequate model of *Nat*. The requirement above states that whenever equality holds for two interpreted terms (in $\mathcal{N}$) then these terms must also be provably equal (by using the equations given in the specification of *Nat*), and vice versa.

As we will see illustrated later, many models may exist for a single specification, all satisfying the requirement of adequacy. The question is, do we have a means to select one of these models as (in a certain sense) the best model. The answer is yes. These are the models called *initial models*.

Initial models A model (in a mathematical sense) represents the meaning of a specification in a precise way. A model may be regarded as stating a commitment with respect to the interpretation of the specification. An initial model is intuitively the least committing model, least committing in the sense that it imposes only identifications made necessary by the equational theory of a specification. Technically, an initial model is a model from which every other model can be derived by an algebraic mapping which is a homomorphism.

8-16

Initial algebra

- ΣE-algebra – $\mathcal{M} = (T_\Sigma / \sim, \Sigma / \sim)$

Properties

- *no junk* – $\forall a : T_\Sigma / \sim \exists t \bullet eval_\mathcal{M}(t) = a$
- *no confusion* – $\mathcal{M} \models t_1 = t_2 \iff E \vdash t_1 = t_2$

Slide 8-16: Initial models

The starting point for the construction of an initial model for a given specification with signature Σ is to construct a term algebra T_Σ with the terms that may be generated from the signature Σ as elements. The next step is then to factor the universe of generated terms into equivalence classes, such that two terms belong to the same class if they can be proven equivalent with respect to the equational theory of the specification. We will denote the representative of the equivalence class to which a term t belongs by $[t]$. Hence $t_1 = t_2$ (in the model) *iff* $[t_1] = [t_2]$.

So assume that we have constructed a structure $\mathcal{M} = (T_\Sigma / \sim, \Sigma)$ then; finally, we must define an interpretation, say $eval_\mathcal{M} : T_\Sigma \to \mathcal{M}$, that assigns closed terms to appropriate terms in the term model (namely the representatives of the equivalence class of that term). Hence, the interpretation of a function f in the structure $\mathcal{M}$ is such that

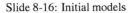

$$f_\mathcal{M}([t_1], ..., [t_n]) = [f(t_1, ..., t_n)]$$

where $f_\mathcal{M}$ is the interpretation of f in $\mathcal{M}$. In other words, the result of applying f to terms $t_1, ..., t_n$ belongs to the same equivalence class as the result of applying $f_\mathcal{M}$ to the representatives of the equivalence classes of $t_1, ..., t_n$. See slide 8-16.

An initial algebra model has two important properties, known respectively as the *no junk* and *no confusion* properties. The *no junk* property states that for each element of the model there is some term for which the interpretation in $\mathcal{M}$ is equal to that element. (For the $T_\Sigma / \sim$ model this is simply a representative of the equivalence class corresponding with the element.) The *no confusion* property states that if equality of two terms can be proven in the equational theory of the specification, then the equality also holds (semantically) in the model, and vice versa. The *no confusion* property means, in other words, that sufficiently many identifications are made (namely those that may be proven to hold), but no more than that (that is, no other than those for which a proof exists). The latter property is why we may speak of an initial model as the least committing model; it simply gives no more meaning than is strictly needed.

The initial model constructed from the term algebra of a signature Σ is intuitively a very natural model since it corresponds directly with (a subset of) the generator universe of Σ. Given such a model, other models may be derived from it simply by specifying an appropriate interpretation. For example, when we construct a model for the natural numbers (as specified by *Nat*) consisting of the generator universe $\{0, S0, SS0, ...\}$ and the operators $\{++, +, {}^*\}$ (which are defined as $S^n++ = S^{n+1}$, $S^n * S^m = S^{n*m}$ and $S^n + S^m = S^{n+m}$) we may simply derive from this model the structure $(\{0, 1, 2, ...\}, \{++, +, {}^*\})$ for which the operations have their standard arithmetical meaning. Actually, this structure is also an initial model for *Nat*, since we may also make the inverse transformation.

More generally, when defining an initial model only the structural aspects (characterizing the behavior of the operators) are important, not the actual contents. Technically, this means that initial models are defined up to isomorphism, that is a mapping to equivalent models with perhaps different contents but an identical structure. Not in all cases is a structure derived from an initial model itself also an initial model, as shown in the example below.

Example Consider the specification of *Bool* as given before. For this specification we have given the structure $\mathcal{B}$ and the interpretation *eval*$_\mathcal{B}$ which defines an initial model for *Bool*. (Check this!)

Structure – $\mathcal{B} = (\{tt, ff\}, \{\neg, \wedge, \vee\})$ $\boxed{\mathcal{B}}$ 8-17

- *eval*$_\mathcal{B}$: $T_{\Sigma_{Bool}} \to \mathcal{B} = \{or \mapsto \vee, not \mapsto \neg\}$

- *eval*$_\mathcal{B}$: $T_{\Sigma_{Nat}} \to \mathcal{B} = \{S \mapsto \neg, mul \mapsto \wedge, plus \mapsto xor\}$

Slide 8-17: Structure and interpretation

We may, however, also use the structure $\mathcal{B}$ to define an interpretation of *Nat*. See slide 8-17. The interpretation *eval*$_\mathcal{B}$: $T_{Nat} \to \mathcal{B}$ is such that $eval_\mathcal{B}(0) = ff$, $eval_\mathcal{B}(Sx) = \neg eval_\mathcal{B}(x)$, $eval_\mathcal{B}(mul(x, y)) = eval_\mathcal{B}(x) \wedge eval_\mathcal{B}(y)$ and $eval_\mathcal{B}(plus(x, y)) = xor(eval_\mathcal{B}(x), eval_\mathcal{B}(y))$, where $xor(p, q) = (p \vee q) \wedge (\neg(p \wedge q))$. The reader may wish to ponder on what this interpretation effects. The answer is that it interprets *Nat* as specifying the naturals modulo 2, which discriminates only between odd and even numbers. Clearly, this interpretation defines not an initial model, since it identifies all odd numbers with *ff* and all even numbers with *tt*. Even if we replace *ff* by 0 and *tt* by 1, this is not what we generally would like to commit ourselves to when we speak about the natural numbers, simply because it assigns too much meaning.

8.2.4 Objects as algebras

The types for which we have thus far seen algebraic specifications (including *Bool*, *Seq*, *Set* and *Nat*) are all types of a mathematical kind, which (by virtue of being mathematical) define operations without side-effects. Dynamic state changes, that is side-effects, are often mentioned as determining the characteristics of objects in general. In the following we will explore how we may deal with assigning meaning to dynamic state changes in an algebraic framework.

Let us look first at the abstract data type *stack*. The type *stack* may be considered as one of the 'real life' types in the world of programming. See slide 8-18.

8-18

Abstract Data Type – *applicative*   stack

    functions
      new : stack;
      push : element × stack) → stack;
      empty : stack → boolean;
      pop : stack → stack;
      top : stack → element;
    axioms
      empty(new) = *true*
      empty(push(x,s)) = *false*
      top(push(x,s)) = x
      pop(push(x,s)) = s
    preconditions
      pre: pop(s : stack) = *not* empty(s)
      pre: top(s : stack) = *not* empty(s)
    end

Slide 8-18: The ADT *Stack*

Above, a stack has been specified by giving a signature (consisting of the functions *new*, *push*, *empty*, *pop* and *top*). In addition to the axioms characterizing the behavior of the stack, we have included two pre-conditions to test whether the stack is empty in case *pop* or *top* is applied. The pre-conditions result in conditional axioms for the operations *pop* and *top*. Conditional axioms, however, do preserve the initial algebra semantics.

The specification given above is a maximally abstract description of the behavior of a stack. Adding more implementation detail would disrupt its nice applicative structure, without necessarily resulting in different behavior (from a sufficiently abstract perspective).

The behavior of elements of abstract data types and objects is characterized by state changes. State changes may affect the value delivered by observers or methods. Many state changes (such as the growing or shrinking of a set, sequence or stack) really are nothing but applicative transformations that may mathematically be described by the input-output behavior of an appropriate function.

An example in which the value of an object on some attribute is dependent on the history of the operations applied to the object, instead of the structure of the object itself (as in the case of a stack) is the object *account*, as specified in slide 8-19. The example is taken from Goguen and Meseguer (1986).

An *account* object has one attribute function (called *bal*) that delivers the amount of money that is (still) in the account. In addition, there are two method functions, *credit* and *debit* that may respectively be used to add or withdraw money from the account. Finally,

```
Dynamic state changes – objects                          account        8-19
         object account is
         functions
           bal : account → money
         methods
           credit : account × money → account
           debit : account × money → account
         error
           overdraw : money → money
         axioms
           bal(new(A)) = 0
           bal(credit(A,M)) = bal(A) + M
           bal(debit(A,M)) = bal(A)− M if bal(A) ≥ M
         error-axioms
           bal(debit(A,M)) = overdraw(M) if bal(A) < M
         end
```

Slide 8-19: The algebraic specification of an *account*

there is one special error function, *overdraw*, that is used to define the result of *balance* when there is not enough money left to grant a *debit* request. Error axioms are needed whenever the proper axioms are stated conditionally, that is contain an *if* expression. The conditional parts of the axioms, including the error axioms, must cover all possible cases.

Now, first look at the form of the axioms. The axioms are specified as

$$fn \ (method(Object, Args)) = expr$$

where *fn* specifies an attribute function (*bal* in the case of account) and *method* a method (either *new*, which is used to create new accounts, *credit* or *debit*). By convention, we assume that *method*(*Object, ...*) = *Object*, that is that a method function returns its first argument. Applying a method thus results in redefining the value of the function *fn*. For example, invoking the method *credit*(*acc*, 10) for the account *acc* results in modifying the function *bal* to deliver the value *bal*(*acc*) + 10 instead of simply *bal*(*acc*). In the example above, the axioms define the meaning of the function *bal* with respect to the possible method applications. It is not difficult to see that these operations are of a non-applicative nature, non-applicative in the sense that each time a method is invoked the actual definition of *bal* is changed. The change is necessary because, in contrast to, for example, the functions employed in a boolean algebra, the actual value of the account may change in time in a completely arbitrary way. A first order framework of (multi sorted) algebras is not sufficiently strong to define the meaning of such changes. What we need may be characterized as a *multiple world semantics*, where each world corresponds to a possible state of the account. As an alternative semantics we will also discuss the interpretation of an object as an *abstract machine*, which resembles an (initial) algebra with hidden sorts.

Multiple world semantics From a semantic perspective, an object that changes its state may be regarded as moving from one world to another, when we see a world as representing a particular state of affairs. Take for example an arbitrary (say John's) account, which has a balance of 500. We may express this as *balance(accountJohn)* = 500. Now, when we invoke the method *credit*, as in *credit(accountJohn,* 200), then we expect the balance of the account to be raised to 700. In the language of the specification, this is expressed as

$$bal(credit(accountJohn, 200)) = bal(accountJohn) + 200$$

Semantically, the result is a state of affairs in which *bal(accountJohn)* = 700.

In Goguen and Meseguer (1986) an operational interpretation is given of a multiple world semantics by introducing a database D (that stores the values of the attribute functions of objects as first order terms) which is transformed as the result of invoking a method, into a new database D' (that has an updated value for the attribute function modified by the method). The meaning of each database (or world) may be characterized by an algebra and an interpretation as before.

The rules according to which transformations on a database take place may be formulated as in slide 8-20.

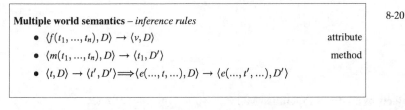

Multiple world semantics – *inference rules*   8-20

* $\langle f(t_1, ..., t_n), D \rangle \rightarrow \langle v, D \rangle$ attribute
* $\langle m(t_1, ..., t_n), D \rangle \rightarrow \langle t_1, D' \rangle$ method
* $\langle t, D \rangle \rightarrow \langle t', D' \rangle \Longrightarrow \langle e(..., t, ...), D \rangle \rightarrow \langle e(..., t', ...), D' \rangle$

Slide 8-20: The interpretation of change

The first rule (*attribute*) describes how attribute functions are evaluated. Whenever a function f with arguments $t_1, ..., t_n$ evaluates to a value (or expression) v, then the term $f(t_1, ..., t_n)$ may be replaced by v without affecting the database D. (We have simplified the treatment by omitting all aspects having to do with matching and substitutions, since such details are not needed to understand the process of symbolic evaluation in a multiple world context.) The next rule (*method*) describes the result of evaluating a method. We assume that invoking the method changes the database D into D'. Recall that, by convention, a method returns its first argument. Finally, the last rule (*composition*) describes how we may glue all this together.

No doubt, the reader needs an example to get a picture of how this machinery actually works.

In slide 8-21, we have specified a simple object *ctr* with an attribute function *value* (delivering the value of the counter) and a method function *incr* (that may be used to increment the value of the counter).

The end result of the evaluation depicted in slide 8-22 is the value 2 and a context (or database) in which the value of the counter C is (also) 2. The database is modified in each step in which the method *incr* is applied. When the attribute function *value* is evaluated the database remains unchanged, since it is merely consulted.

8-21

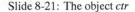

$object$ ctr is

function n : ctr $\rightarrow$ nat

method incr : ctr $\rightarrow$ ctr

axioms

   n(new(C)) = 0

   n(incr(C)) = n(C) + 1

end

Slide 8-21: The object ctr

8-22

Abstract evaluation

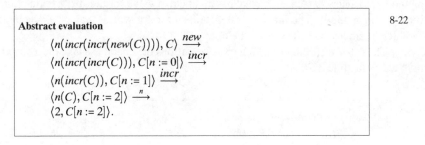

$$\langle n(incr(incr(new(C)))), C\rangle \xrightarrow{new}$$
$$\langle n(incr(incr(C))), C[n := 0]\rangle \xrightarrow{incr}$$
$$\langle n(incr(C)), C[n := 1]\rangle \xrightarrow{incr}$$
$$\langle n(C), C[n := 2]\rangle \xrightarrow{n}$$
$$\langle 2, C[n := 2]\rangle.$$

Slide 8-22: An example of abstract evaluation

Objects as abstract machines Multiple world semantics provide a very powerful framework in which to define the meaning of object specifications. Yet, as illustrated above, the reasoning involved has a very operational flavor and lacks the appealing simplicity of the initial algebra semantics given for abstract data types. As an alternative, Goguen and Meseguer (1986) propose an interpretation of objects (with dynamic state changes) as *abstract machines*.

Recall that an initial algebra semantics defines a model in which the elements are equivalence classes representing the abstract values of the data type. In effect, initial models are defined only up to isomorphism (that is, structural equivalence with similar models). In essence, the framework of initial algebra semantics allows us to abstract from the particular representation of a data type, when assigning meaning to a specification. From this perspective it does not matter, for example, whether integers are represented in binary or decimal notation.

The notion of *abstract machines* generalizes the notion of initial algebras in that it loosens the requirement of (structural) isomorphism, to allow for what we may call *behavioral equivalence*. The idea underlying the notion of behavioral equivalence is to make a distinction between *visible* sorts and *hidden* sorts and to look only at the visible sorts to determine whether two algebras A and B are behaviorally equivalent. According to Goguen and Meseguer (1986), two algebras A and B are behaviorally equivalent if and only if the result of evaluating any expression of a visible sort in A is the same as the result of evaluating that expression in B.

Now, an *abstract machine* (in the sense of Goguen and Meseguer, 1986) is simply the equivalence class of behaviorally equivalent algebras, or in other words the maximally abstract characterization of the visible behavior of an abstract data type with (hidden) states.

The notion of abstract machines is of particular relevance as a formal framework to characterize the (implementation) refinement relation between objects. For example, it is easy to determine that the behavior of a stack implemented as a list is equivalent to the behavior of a stack implemented by a pointer array, whereas these objects are clearly not equivalent from a structural point of view. Moreover, the behavior of both conform (in an abstract sense) with the behavior specified in an algebraic way. Together, the notions of abstract machine and behavioral equivalence provide a formalization of the notion of *information hiding* in an algebraic setting. In the chapters that follow we will look at alternative formalisms to explain information hiding, polymorphism and behavioral refinement.

8.3   Decomposition *– modules versus objects*

Abstract data types allow the programmer to define a complex data structure and an associated collection of functions, operating on that structure, in a consistent way. Historically, the idea of data abstraction was originally not type-oriented but arose from a more pragmatic concern with information hiding and representation abstraction (see Parnas, 1972b). The first realization of the idea of data abstraction was in the form of modules grouping a collection of functions and allowing the actual representation of the data structures underlying the values of the (abstract) type domain to be hidden (see also Parnas, 1972a).

In Cook (1990), a comparison is made between the way in which abstract data types are realized traditionally (as modules) and the way abstract data types may be realized using object-oriented programming techniques. According to Cook (1990), these approaches must be regarded as being orthogonal to one another and, being to some extent complementary, deserve to be integrated in a common framework.

After presenting an example highlighting the differences between the two approaches, we will further explore these differences and study the trade-offs with respect to possible extensions and reuse of code.

Recall that abstract data types may be completely characterized by a finite collection of generators and a number of observer functions that are defined with respect to each possible generator. Following this idea, we may approach the specification of a data abstraction by constructing a *matrix* listing the generators column-wise and the observers row-wise, that for each *observer/generator* pair specifies the value of the observer for that particular generator. Incidentally, the definition of such a matrix allows us to check in an easy way whether we have given a complete characterization of the data type. Above, an example is given of the specification of a *list*, with generators *nil* and *cons*, and observers *empty*, *head* and *tail*. (Note that we group the secondary producer *tail* with the observers.)

Now, the traditional way of realizing abstract data types as modules may be characterized as *operation oriented*, in the sense that the module realization of the type is organized around the observers, resulting in a horizontal decomposition of the matrix.

On the other hand, an object-oriented approach may be characterized as *data oriented*, since the object realization of a type is based on specifying a method interface for

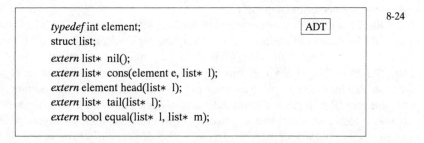

Slide 8-23: Decomposition and data abstraction

each possible generator (sub)type, resulting in a vertical decomposition of the matrix. See slide 8-23.

Note, however, that in practice, different generators need not necessarily correspond to different (sub)classes. Behavior may be subsumed in variables, as an object cannot change its class/type. See section 7.2.3.

8.3.1 Abstract interfaces

When choosing for the module realization of the data abstraction *list* in C style, we are likely to have an abstract functional interface as specified in slide 8-24.

```
                                                      8-24
    typedef int element;              ADT
    struct list;

    extern list* nil();
    extern list* cons(element e, list* l);
    extern element head(list* l);
    extern list* tail(list* l);
    extern bool equal(list* l, list* m);
```

Slide 8-24: Modules – a functional interface

For convenience, the *list* has been restricted to contain integer elements only. However, at the expense of additional notation, we could also easily define a generic list by employing template functions as provided by C++. This is left as an exercise for the reader.

The interface of the abstract class *list* given in slide 8-25 has been defined generically by employing templates.

8-25

```
template< class E >                                    OOP
class list {
public:
list() { }
virtual ~list() { }
virtual bool empty() = 0;
virtual E head() = 0;
virtual list<E>* tail() = 0;
virtual bool operator==(list<E>* m) = 0;
};
```

Slide 8-25: Objects – a method interface

Note that the *equal* function in the ADT interface takes two arguments, whereas the *operator==* function in the OOP interface takes only one, since the other is implicitly provided by the object itself.

8.3.2 Representation and implementation

The realization of abstract data types as modules with functions requires additional means to hide the representation of the *list* type. In contrast, with an object-oriented approach, data hiding is effected by employing the encapsulation facilities of classes.

Modules – representation hiding Modules provide a syntactic means to group related pieces of code and to hide particular aspects of that code. In slide 8-26 an example is given of the representation and the generator functions for a list of integers.

For implementing the *list* as a collection of functions (ADT style), we employ a *struct* with an explicit tag field, indicating whether the list corresponds to *nil* or a *cons*.

The functions corresponding with the generators create a new structure and initialize the tag field. In addition, the *cons* operator sets the *element* and *next* field of the structure to the arguments of *cons*.

The implementation of the *observers* is given in slide 8-27.

To determine whether the list is *empty* it suffices to check whether the tag of the list is equal to *NIL*. For both *head* and *tail* the pre-condition is that the list given as an argument is not empty. If the pre-condition holds, the appropriate field of the *list* structure is returned.

The equality operator, finally, performs an explicit switch on the tag field, stating for each case under what conditions the lists are equal.

Below, a program fragment is given that illustrates the use of the list

```
list* r = cons(1,cons(2,nil()));
while (!empty(r)) {
    cout << head(r) << endl;
    r = tail(r);
    }
```

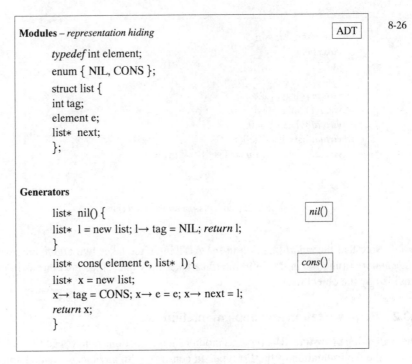

Slide 8-26: Data abstraction and modules

Note that both the generator functions *nil* and *cons* take care of creating a new *list* structure. Writing a function to destroy a list is left as an exercise for the reader.

Objects – method interface The idea underlying an object-oriented decomposition of the specification matrix of an abstract type is to make a distinction between the (syntactic) subtypes of the data type (corresponding with its generators) and to specify for each subtype the value of all possible observer functions. (We speak of *syntactic* subtypes, following Dahl (1992), since these subtypes correspond to the generators defining the value domain of the data type. See Dahl (1992) for a more extensive treatment.)

In the object realization in slide 8-28, each subtype element is defined as a class inheriting from the *list* class. For both generator types *nil* and *cons* the observer functions are defined in a straightforward way. Note that, in contrast to the ADT realization, the distinction between the various cases is implicit in the member function definitions of the generator classes.

As an example of using the *list* classes consider the program fragment below

```
list<int>* r = new cons<int>(1, new cons<int>(2, new nil<int> ));
while (! r→ empty()) {
    cout ≪ r→ head() ≪ endl;
    r = r→ tail();
}
delete r;
```

```
Modules – observers                                          ADT      8-27
        int empty(list* lst) { return !lst || lst→ tag == NIL; }
        element head(list* l) {                              // head
        require( ! empty(l) );
        return l→ e;
        }
        list* tail(list* l) {                                // tail
        require( ! empty(l) );
        return l→ next;
        }
        bool equal(list* l, list* m) {                       // equal
        switch( l→ tag) {
          case NIL: return empty(m);
          case CONS: return !empty(m) &&
                  head(l) == head(m) &&
                  tail(l) == tail(m);
          }
        }
```

Slide 8-27: Modules – observers

For deleting a list we may employ the (virtual) destructor of *list*, which recursively destroys the tail of a list.

8.3.3 Adding new generators

Abstract data types were developed with correctness and security in mind, and not so much from a concern with extensibility and reuse. Nevertheless, it is interesting to compare the traditional approach of realizing abstract data types (employing modules) and the object-oriented approach (employing objects as generator subtypes) with regard to the ease with which a specification may be extended, either by adding new generators or by adding new observers.

Let us first look at what happens when we add a new generator to a data type, such as an interval list subtype, containing the integers in the interval between two given integers.

For the module realization of the list, adding an *interval*(x, y) generator will result in an extension of the (hidden) representation types with an additional representation tag type *INTERVAL* and the definition of a suitable generator function.

To represent the *interval* list type, we employ a union to select between the *next* field, which is used by the *cons* generator, and the z field, which indicates the end of the interval.

Also, we need to modify the observer functions by adding an appropriate case for the new interval representation type, as pictured in slide 8-30.

Clearly, unless special constructs are provided, the addition of a new generator

---

Method interface – *list*   OOP   8-28

```
        template< class E >
        class nil : public list<E> {                        nil<E>
        public:
        nil() {}
        bool empty() { return 1; }
        E head() { require( false ); return E(); }
        list<E>∗ tail() { require( 0 ); return 0; }
        bool operator==(list<E>∗ m) { return m→ empty(); }
        };
        template< class E >
        class cons : public list<E> {                       cons<E>
        public:
        cons(E e, list<E>∗ l) : _e(e), next(l) {}
        ∼cons() { delete next; }
        bool empty() { return 0; }
        E head() { return _e; }
        list<E>∗ tail() { return next; }
        bool operator==(list<E>∗ m);
        protected:
        E _e;
        list<E>∗ next;
        };
```

Slide 8-28: Data abstraction and objects

case requires disrupting the code implementing the given data type manually, to extend the definition of the observers with the new case.

In contrast, not surprisingly, when we wish to add a new generator case to the object realization of the list, we do not need to disrupt the given code, but we may simply add the definition of the generator subtype as given in slide 8-31.

Adding a new generator subtype corresponds to defining the realization for an abstract interface class, which gives a method interface that its subclasses must respect. In section 3.3, we have characterized this as the realization of a partial type.

Observe, however, that we cannot exploit the fact that a list is defined by an interval when testing equality, since we cannot inspect the type of the list as for the ADT implementation.

8.3.4 Adding new observers

Now, for the complementary case, what happens when we add new observers to the specification of a data type. Somewhat surprisingly, the object-oriented approach now seems to be at a disadvantage.

Since in a module realization of an abstract data type the code is organized around

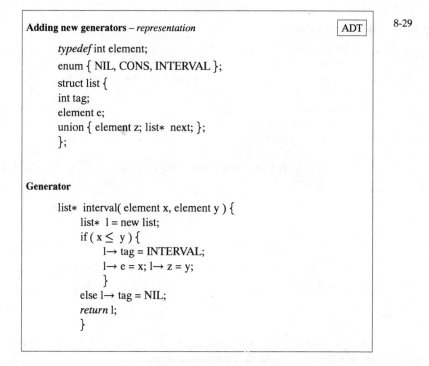

Slide 8-29: Modules and generators

observers, adding a new observer function amounts simply to adding a new operation with a case for each of the possible generator types, as shown in slide 8-32.

When we look at how we may extend a given object realization of an abstract data type with a new observer we are facing a problem.

The obvious solution is to modify the source code and add the *length* function to the *list* interface class and each of the generator classes. This is, however, against the spirit of object orientation and may not always be feasible.

Another, rather awkward solution, is to extend the collection of possible generator subtypes with a number of new generator subtypes that explicitly incorporate the new observer function. However, this also means redefining the *tail* function since it must deliver an instance of a *list with length* class. (This solution does not compile with the AT&T 3.0 compiler, which does not allow one to change the result type of virtual function, but it will be accepted by compilers conforming to the ANSI/ISO standard.)

As a workaround, one may define a function *length* and an extended version of the *list* template class supporting only the *length* (observer) member function as depicted in slide 8-33.

A program fragment illustrating the use of the *listWL* class is given below

```
list<int>* r = new cons<int>(1, new cons<int>(2, new interval(3,7) ));
while (! r→ empty()) {
    cout ≪ ((listWL<int>* )r)→ length() ≪ endl;
```

```
Modifying the observers                                    ADT      8-30
        element head(list* l) {                        // head
        require( ! empty(l) );
        return l→ e;                    // for both CONS and INTERVAL
        }
        list*  tail(list* l) {                         // tail
        require( ! empty(l) );
        switch( l→ tag ) {
            case CONS: return l→ next;
            case INTERVAL: return interval((l→ e)+1,l→ z);
            }
        }
```

Slide 8-30: Modifying the observers

```
        r = r→ tail();
        }
    delete r;
```

Evidently, we need to employ a cast whenever we wish to apply the *length* observer function. Hence, this seems not to be the right solution.

Alternatively, we may use the function *length* directly. However, we are then forced to mix method syntax of the form $ref \rightarrow op(args)$ with function syntax of the form $fun(ref, args)$, which may easily lead to confusion.

Discussion We may wonder why an object-oriented approach, that is supposed to support extensibility, is at a disadvantage here when compared to a more traditional module-based approach.

As observed in Cook (1990), the problem lies in the fact that neither of the two approaches reflect the full potential and flexibility of the matrix specification of an abstract data type. Each of the approaches represents a particular choice with respect to the decomposition of the matrix, into either an *operations oriented* (horizontal) decomposition or a *data oriented* (vertical) decomposition.

The apparent misbehavior of an object realization with respect to extending the specification with observer functions explains why in some cases we prefer the use of overloaded functions rather than methods, since overloaded functions allow for implicit dispatching to take place on multiple arguments, whereas method dispatching behavior is determined only by the type of the object.

However, it must be noted that the dispatching behavior of overloaded functions in C++ is of a purely syntactic nature. This means that we cannot exploit the information specific for a class type as we can when using virtual functions. Hence, to employ this information we would be required to write as many variants of overloaded functions as there are combinations of argument types.

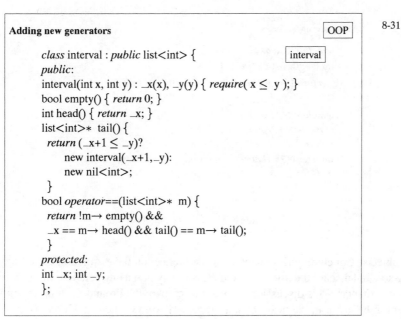

Slide 8-31: Objects and generators

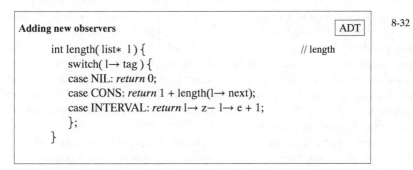

Slide 8-32: Modules and observers

Dynamic dispatching on multiple arguments is supported by *multi-methods* in CLOS (see Paepcke, 1993). According to Cook (1990), the need for such methods might be taken as a hint that objects only partially realize the true potential of *data abstraction*.

8.4 Types versus classes

Types are primarily an aid in arriving at a consistent system description. Most (typed) object-oriented programming languages offer support for types by employing classes as a device to define the functionality of objects. Classes, however, have originated from a far more pragmatic concern, namely as a construct to enable the definition and creation

```
Adding new observers                                      OOP    8-33

    template< class E >
    int length(list<E>* l) {                             length()
      return l→ empty() ? 0 : 1 + length( l→ tail() );
    }
    template< class E >
    class listWL : public list<E> {                      listWL<E>
    public:
    int length() { return ::length( this ); }
    };
```

Slide 8-33: Objects and observers

of objects. Concluding this chapter, we will reflect on the distinction between types and classes, and discuss the role types and classes play in reusing software through derivation by inheritance. This discussion is meant to prepare the ground for a more formal treatment to be given in the next chapter. It closely follows the exposition given in Wegner and Zdonik (1988).

Types must primarily be understood as predicates to guide the process of type checking, whereas classes have come into being originally as templates for object creation.

It is interesting to note how (and how easily) this distinction may be obscured. In practice, when compiling a program in C++, the compiler will notify the user of an error when a member function is called that is not listed in the public interface of the objects class. As another example, the runtime system of Smalltalk will raise an exception, notifying the user of a dynamic type error, when a method is invoked that is not defined in the objects class or any of its superclasses. Both kinds of errors have the flavor of a typing error, yet they rely on different notions of typing and are based on a radically different interpretation of classes as types.

To put types into perspective, we must ask ourselves what means we have to indicate the type of an expression, including expressions that somehow reference a class description.

In Wegner and Zdonik (1988), three attitudes towards typing are distinguished: (1) typing may be regarded as an administrative aid to check for simple typos and other administrative errors, (2) typing may be regarded as the ultimate solution to defining the behavior of a system, or (3) typing may (pragmatically) be regarded as a consequence of defining the behavior of an object. See slide 8-34. Before continuing, the reader is invited to sort the various programming languages discussed into the three slots mentioned.

Typing as an administrative aid is typically a task for which we rely on a compiler to check for possible errors. Evidently, the notion of typing that a compiler employs is of a rather syntactic nature. Provided we have specified a signature correctly, we may trust a compiler with the routine of checking for errors. As a language that supports signature type checking we may (obviously) mention C++.

Evidently, we cannot trust the compiler to detect conceptual errors, that is incom-

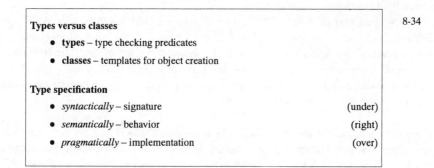

Slide 8-34: Types and classes

plete or ill-conceived definitions of the functionality of an object or collections of objects. Yet, ultimately we want to be able to specify the behavior of an object in a formal way and to check mechanically for the adequacy of this definition. This ideal of *semantic types* underlies the design of Eiffel, not so much the Eiffel type system as supported by the Eiffel compiler, but the integration of assertions in the Eiffel language and the notion of *contracts* as a design principle. Pragmatically, we need to rely on runtime (consistency) checks to detect erroneous behavior, since there are (theoretically rather severe) limits on the extent to which we may verify behavioral properties in advance. (Nevertheless, see section 10.4 for some attempts in this direction.)

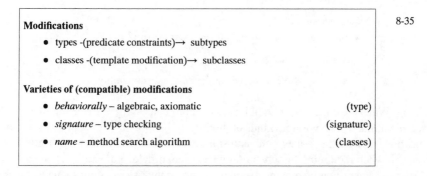

Slide 8-35: Type modifications

Finally, we can take a far more pragmatic view towards typing, by regarding the actual specification of a class as an implicit characterization of the type of the instances of the class. Actually, this is the way (not surprisingly, I would say) types are dealt with in Smalltalk. Each object in Smalltalk is typed, by virtue of being an instance of a class. Yet, a typing error may only be detected dynamically, as the result of not responding to a message.

A distinction between perspectives on types (respectively syntactic, behavioral and pragmatic) may seem rather academic at first sight. However, the differences are, so to speak, amplified when studied in the context of type modifications, as for example effected by inheritance.

Wegner and Zdonik (1988) make a distinction between three notions of *compatible modifications*, corresponding to the three perspectives on types, respectively *signature compatible modifications* (which require the preservation of the static signature), *behaviorally compatible modification* (which rely on a mathematical notion of definability for a type) and *name compatible modifications* (that rely on an operationally defined method search algorithm). See slide 8-35.

Signature compatible modifications The assumption underlying the notion of *types as signatures* is that behavior is approximated by a (static) signature. Now the question is: to what extent can we define semantics preserving extensions to a given class or object?

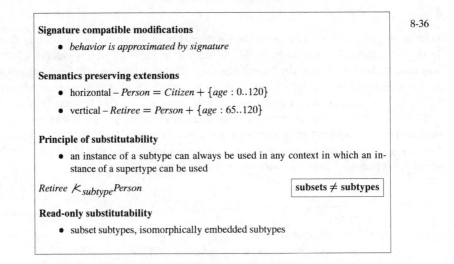

8-36

Signature compatible modifications

- *behavior is approximated by signature*

Semantics preserving extensions

- horizontal – *Person* = *Citizen* + {*age* : 0..120}
- vertical – *Retiree* = *Person* + {*age* : 65..120}

Principle of substitutability

- an instance of a subtype can always be used in any context in which an instance of a supertype can be used

Retiree $K_{subtype}$*Person*   subsets ≠ subtypes

Read-only substitutability

- subset subtypes, isomorphically embedded subtypes

Slide 8-36: The principle of substitutability

When we conceive of an object as a record consisting of (data and method) fields, we may think of two possible kinds of modifications. We may think of a *horizontal* modification when adding a new field, and similarly we may think of a modification as being *vertical* when redefining or constraining a particular field. For example, when we define *Citizen* as an entity with a name, we may define (at the risk of being somewhat awkward) a *Person* as a *Citizen* with an age and a *Retiree* as a *Person* with an age that is restricted to the range 65..120.

The principle by which we may judge these extensions valid (or not) may be characterized as the *principle of substitutability*, which may be phrased as: *an instance of a subtype can always be used in any context in which an instance of a supertype can be used.*

Unfortunately, for the extension given here we have an easy counterexample, showing that syntactic signature compatibility is not sufficient. Clearly, a *Person* is a supertype of *Retiree* (we will demonstrate this more precisely in section 9.2). Assume that we have a function

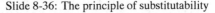

set_age : *Person* × *Integer* → *Void*

that is defined as $set\_age(p, n)\{p.age = n; \}$. Now consider the following fragment of code:

```
Person*  p = r;                    // assuming r refers to some Retiree
p→ set_age(40);
```

where we employ object reference notation when calling set_age. Since we have assigned r (which is referring to a *Retiree*) to p, we know that p now points to a *Retiree*, and since a *Retiree* is a person we may apply the function set_age. However, set_age sets the *age* of the *Retiree* to 40, which gives (by common standards) a semantic error. The lesson that we may draw from this is that being a subset is no guarantee for being a subtype as defined by the principle of substitutability. However, we may characterize the relation between a *Retiree* and a *Person* as being of a weaker kind, namely *read-only substitutability*, expressing that the (value of) the subtype may be used safely everywhere an instance of the supertype is expected, as long as it is not modified. Read-only substitutability holds for a type that stands in a subset relation to another type or is embeddable (as a subset) into that type. See slide 8-36.

Behaviorally compatible modifications If the subset relation is not a sufficient condition for being in a subtype relation, what is? To establish whether the (stronger) substitutability relation holds we must take the possible functions associated with the types into consideration as well. First, let us consider what relations may exist between types. Recall that semantically a type corresponds to a set together with a collection of operations that are defined for the set and that the subtype relation corresponds to the subset relation in the sense that (taking a type as a constraint) the definition of a subtype involves adding a constraint and, consequently, a narrowing of the set of elements corresponding to the supertype.

Complete compatibility is what we achieve when the principle of substitutability holds. Theoretically, complete compatibility may be assured when the behavior of the subtype fully complies with the behavior of the supertype. Behavioral compatibility, however, is a quite demanding notion. We will deal with it more extensively in chapter 10, when discussing *behavioral refinement*. Unfortunately, in practice we must often rely on the theoretically much weaker notion of *name compatibility*.

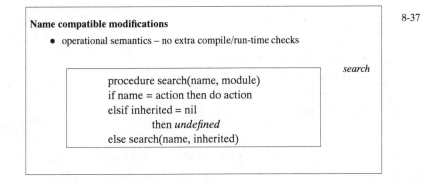

Name compatible modifications   8-37

   • operational semantics – no extra compile/run-time checks

                                                       search

        procedure search(name, module)
        if name = action then do action
        elsif inherited = nil
            then *undefined*
        else search(name, inherited)

Slide 8-37: The inheritance search algorithm

Name compatible modifications Name compatible modifications approximate behaviorally compatible modifications in the sense that substitutability is guaranteed, albeit not in a semantically verifiable way.

Operationally, substitutability can be enforced by requiring that each subclass (that we may characterize as a pragmatic subtype) provides at least the operations of its super classes (while giving a sensible result on all argument types allowed by its superclasses). Actually, name compatibility is an immediate consequence of the overriding semantics of derivation by inheritance, as reflected in the search algorithm underlying method lookup. See slide 8-37. Although name compatible modifications are by far the most flexible, from a theoretical point of view they are the least satisfying since they do not allow for any theory formation concerning the (desired) behavior of (the components of) the system under development.

Summary

This chapter has presented an introduction to the theoretical foundations of abstract data types. In particular, a characterization was given of *types as constraints*.

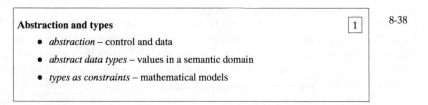

Slide 8-38: Section 8.1: Abstraction and types

In section 1, we discussed the notion of abstraction in programming languages and distinguished between control and data abstractions. Abstract data types were characterized as values in some domain, and we looked at the various ways in which to define mathematical models for types.

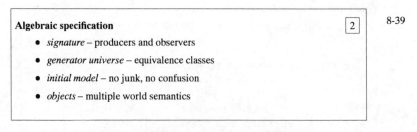

Slide 8-39: Section 8.2: Algebraic specification

In section 2, we studied the algebraic specification of abstract data types by means of a signature characterizing producers and observers. We discussed the notions of equivalence classes and initial models, which consist of precisely the equivalence classes that are needed.

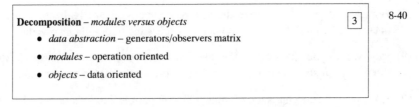

Slide 8-40: Section 8.3: Decomposition – *modules versus objects*

Also, we looked at the interpretation of objects as algebras, and we discussed a multiple world semantics allowing for dynamic state changes.

In section 3, we looked at the various ways we may realize data abstractions and we distinguished between a modular approach, defining a collection of operations, and a data oriented approach, employing objects.

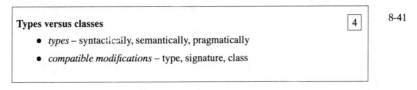

Slide 8-41: Section 8.4: Types versus classes

Finally, in section 4, we discussed the differences between a syntactic, semantic and operational interpretation of types, and how these viewpoints affect our notion of refinement or compatible modification.

Questions

(1) Characterize the differences between control abstractions and data abstractions. Explain how these two kinds of abstractions may be embodied in programming language constructs.

(2) How can you model the meaning of abstract data types in a mathematical way? Do you know any alternative ways?

(3) Explain how types may affect object-oriented programming.

(4) What is a signature? What distinction can you make between the various functions specified in a signature?

(5) What is an initial model? What properties does such a model satisfy?

(6) How would you characterize the meaning of an object with dynamic state changes in an algebraic fashion?

(7) Explain how you may characterize an abstract data type by means of a matrix with generator columns and observer rows. What benefits does such an organization have?

(8) How would you characterize the differences between the realization of abstract data types by modules and by objects? Discuss the trade-offs involved.

(9) How would you characterize the distinction between types and classes? Mention three ways of specifying types. How are these kinds related to each other?

(10) How would you characterize signature compatible modifications? Explain its weaknesses. What alternatives can you think of?

Further reading

There is a vast amount of literature on the algebraic specification of abstract data types. You may consult, for example, Dahl (1992).

9

Polymorphism

From a theoretical perspective object orientation may be characterized as combining *abstract data types* and *polymorphism*.

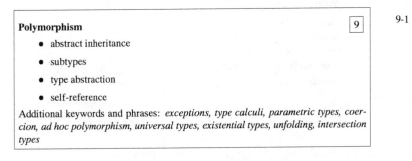

Polymorphism　　　　　　　　　　　　　　　　　　　　9

- abstract inheritance
- subtypes
- type abstraction
- self-reference

Additional keywords and phrases: *exceptions, type calculi, parametric types, coercion, ad hoc polymorphism, universal types, existential types, unfolding, intersection types*

Slide 9-1: Polymorphism

In this chapter we will study the notion of polymorphism. We start our exploration by looking at the role of inheritance in knowledge representation. Then we will formally characterize the (signature) subtype relation and explain the *contravariance* rule for function subtypes. To better understand polymorphism and its relation to inheritance, we will develop a type calculus, allowing us to define abstract types using universally and existentially quantified type expressions. In a similar way, we will look at polymorphism due to overloading and generic type definitions. Finally, we will look at the role of self-reference in typing object descriptions derived by inheritance. Together with developing the calculi, examples will be given that illustrate the properties of the C++ and Eiffel type systems.

9.1   Abstract inheritance

Inheritance hierarchies play a role both in knowledge representation systems and object-oriented programming languages (see Lenzerini *et al., 1990*). In effect, historically, the notions of *frames* and *is-a hierarchies* (that play a role in knowledge representation) and the notions of *classes* and *inheritance* (that have primarily been developed in a programming language context) have mutually influenced each other.

In object-oriented programming languages, classes and inheritance are strongly related to types and polymorphism, and directed towards the construction of reliable programming artifacts. In contrast, the goal of knowledge representation is to develop a semantically consistent description of some real world domain, which allows us to reason about the properties of the elements in that domain.

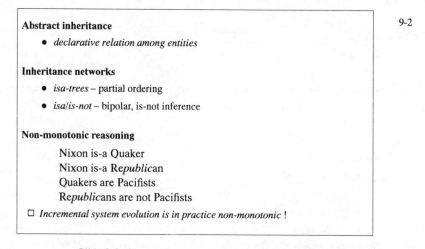

Slide 9-2: Knowledge representation and inheritance

One of the first formal analyses of the declarative aspects of inheritance systems was given in Touretzky (1986). The theoretical framework developed in Touretzky (1986) covers the inheritance formalisms found in frame systems such as FRL, KRL, KLONE and NETL, but also to some extent the inheritance mechanisms of Simula, Smalltalk, Flavors and Loops. The focus of Touretzky (1986), however, is to develop a formal theory of inheritance networks including defaults and exceptions. The values of attributes play a far more important role in such networks than in a programming context. In particular, to determine whether the relationships expressed in an inheritance graph are consistent, we must be able to reason about the values of these attributes. In contrast, the use of inheritance in programming languages is primarily focused on sharing instance variables and overriding (virtual) member functions, and is not so much concerned with the actual values of instance variables.

Inheritance networks in knowledge representation systems are often *non-monotonic* as a result of having *is-not* relations in addition to *is-a* relations and also because properties (for example *can-fly*) can be deleted. Perhaps the most famous example of an inconsistency that may arise due to non-monotonic reasoning in an inheritance network is expressed by the so-called *Nixon-diamond*, which leaves us in doubt whether Nixon was or was not a pacifist. See slide 9-3.

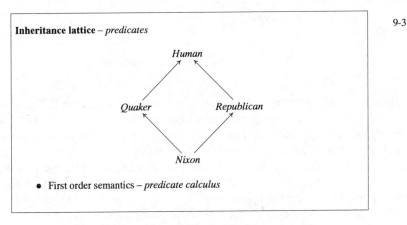

Slide 9-3: Non-monotonicity in inheritance networks

Monotonicity is basically the requirement that all properties are preserved, which is the case for strict inheritance satisfying the substitution principle. It is a requirement that should be adhered to at the risk of jeopardizing the integrity of the system. Nevertheless, strict inheritance may be regarded as too inflexible to express real world properties in a knowledge representation system.

The meaning of *is-a* and *is-not* relations in a knowledge representation inheritance graph may equivalently be expressed as predicate logic statements. For example, the statements

$$\forall x.Quaker(x) \rightarrow Human(x)$$

$$\forall x.Republican(x) \rightarrow Human(x)$$

express the relation between, respectively, the predicates *Quaker* and *Republican* to the predicate *Human* in the graph above. In addition, the statements

$$\forall x.Quaker(x) \rightarrow Pacifist(x)$$

$$\forall x.Republican(x) \rightarrow \neg Pacifist(x)$$

introduce the predicate *Pacifist* that leads to the observed inconsistency.

Some other examples of statements expressing relations between entities in a taxonomic structure are given in slide 9-4.

The latter is often used as an example of non-monotonicity that may occur when using defaults (in this case the assumption that *all birds can fly*).

The mathematical semantics for declarative taxonomic hierarchies given in Touretzky (1986) are based on the notion of constructible lattices of predicates, expressing a partial order between the predicates involved in a taxonomy (such as, for example, *Quaker*

Taxonomic structure 9-4

$\forall x.Elephant(x) \rightarrow Mammal(x)$

$\forall x.Elephant(x) \rightarrow color(x) = gray$

$\forall x.Penguin(x) \rightarrow Bird(x) \land \neg CanFly(x)$

Slide 9-4: Taxonomies and predicate logic

and *Human*). A substantial part of the analysis presented in Touretzky (1986), however, is concerned with employing the graph representation of inheritance structures to improve on the efficiency of reasoning about the entities populating the graph. In the presence of multiple inheritance and non-monotonicity due to exceptions and defaults, care must be taken to follow the right path through the inheritance graph when searching for the value of a particular attribute. Operationally, the solution presented by Touretzky (1986) involves an ordering of inference paths (working upwards) according to the number of intermediate nodes. Intuitively, this corresponds to the distance between the node using an attribute and the node defining the value of the attribute. In strictly monotonic situations such a measure plays no role, however!

9.2 The subtype relation

In this section, we will study the subtype relation in a more formal manner. First we investigate the notion of subtypes in relation to the interpretation of *types as sets*, and then we characterize the subtype relation for a number of constructs occurring in programming languages (such as ranges, functions and records). Finally, we will characterize objects as records and correspondingly define the subtype relation for simple record (object) types. These characterizations may be regarded as a preliminary to the type calculi to be developed in subsequent sections.

9.2.1 Types as sets

A type, basically, denotes a set of elements. A type may be defined either extensionally, by listing all the elements constituting the type, or descriptively, as a constraint that must be satisfied by an individual to be classified as an element of the type.

Formally, we may define the value set of a type with subtypes as an isomorphism of the form

$$V \approx Int \cup ... \cup V \times V \cup V \rightarrow V$$

which expresses that the collection of values V consists of (the union of) basic types (such as Int) and compound types (of which V itself may be a component) such as record types (denoted by the product $V \times V$) and function types (being part of the function space $V \rightarrow V$).

Within this value space V, subtypes correspond to subsets that are ordered by set inclusion. Technically, the subsets corresponding to the subtypes must be *ideals*, which

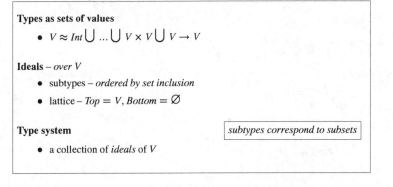

Types as sets of values

- $V \approx Int \bigcup \ldots \bigcup V \times V \bigcup V \to V$

Ideals – *over V*
  - subtypes – *ordered by set inclusion*
  - lattice – *Top* $= V$, *Bottom* $= \emptyset$

Type system   subtypes correspond to subsets
  - a collection of *ideals* of V

Slide 9-5: The interpretation of types as sets

comes down to the requirement that any two types have a maximal type containing both (in the set inclusion sense).

Intuitively, the subtype relation may be characterized as a refinement relation, constraining the set of individuals belonging to a type. The subtype refinement relation may best be understood in terms of improving our knowledge with respect to (the elements of) the type. For a similar view, see Ghelli and Orsini (1990). In case we have no knowledge of a particular element we simply (must) assume that it belongs to the value set V. Having no knowledge is represented by the maximal element of the lattice *Top*, which denotes the complete set V. Whenever we improve our knowledge, we may be more specific about the type of the element, since fewer elements will satisfy the constraints implied by our information. The bottom element *Bottom* of our type lattice denotes the type with no elements, and may be taken to consist of the elements for which we have contradictory information. See slide 9-5.

Mathematically, a type system is nothing but a collection with ideals within some lattice V. In our subsequent treatment, however, we will primarily look at the refinement relation between two elements, rather than the set inclusion relation between their corresponding types.

9.2.2   The subtype refinement relation

In determining whether a given type is a subtype of another type, we must make a distinction between simple (or basic) types built into the language and compound (or user-defined) types explicitly declared by the programmer. Compound types, such as *integer subranges*, *functions*, *records* and *variant records*, themselves make use of other (basic or compound) types. Basic types are (in principle) only a subtype of themselves, although many languages allow for an implicit subtyping relation between for example integers and reals. The rules given in slide 9-6 characterize the subtyping relation for the compound types mentioned.

We use the relation symbol $\leq$ to denote the subtype relation. Types (both basic and compound) are denoted by σ and τ. For subranges, a given (integer) subrange σ is a subtype of another subrange τ if σ is (strictly) included in τ as a subset. In other words,

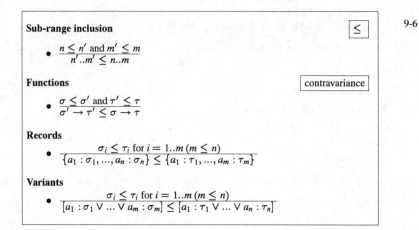

Sub-range inclusion $\leq$ 9-6

- $$\frac{n \leq n' \text{ and } m' \leq m}{n'..m' \leq n..m}$$

Functions   contravariance

- $$\frac{\sigma \leq \sigma' \text{ and } \tau' \leq \tau}{\sigma' \to \tau' \leq \sigma \to \tau}$$

Records

- $$\frac{\sigma_i \leq \tau_i \text{ for } i = 1..m \, (m \leq n)}{\{a_1 : \sigma_1, ..., a_n : \sigma_n\} \leq \{a_1 : \tau_1, ..., a_m : \tau_m\}}$$

Variants

- $$\frac{\sigma_i \leq \tau_i \text{ for } i = 1..m \, (m \leq n)}{[a_1 : \sigma_1 \vee ... \vee a_m : \sigma_m] \leq [a_1 : \tau_1 \vee ... \vee a_n : \tau_n]}$$

Slide 9-6: The subtype refinement relation

if $\sigma = n'..m'$ and $\tau = n..m$ then the subtyping condition is $n \leq n'$ and $m' \leq m$. We may also write $n'..m' \subseteq n..m$ in this case.

For functions we have a somewhat similar rule, a function $f' : \sigma' \to \tau'$ (with domain σ' and range or codomain τ') is a subtype of a function $f : \sigma \to \tau$ (with domain σ and codomain τ) if the subtype condition $\sigma \leq \sigma'$ and $\tau' \leq \tau$ is satisfied. Note that the relation between the domains is contravariant, whereas the relation between the ranges is covariant. We will discuss this phenomenon of contravariance below.

Records may be regarded as a collection of labels (the record fields) that may have values of a particular type. The subtyping rule for records expresses that a given record (type) may be extended to a (record) subtype by adding new labels, provided that the types for labels which occur in both records are refined in the subtype. The intuition underlying this rule is that by extending a record we add, so to speak, more information concerning the individuals described by such a record, and hence we constrain the set of possible elements belonging to that (sub)type.

Variants are (a kind of) record that leave the choice between a (finite) number of possible values, each represented by a label. The subtyping rules for variants states that we may create a subtype of a given variant record if we reduce the choice by eliminating one or more possibilities. This is in accord with our notion of refinement as improving our knowledge, since by reducing the choice we constrain the set of possible individuals described by the variant record.

The subtyping rules given above specify what checks to perform in order to determine whether a given (compound) type is a subtype of another type. In the following we will look in more detail at the justification underlying these rules, and also hint at some of the restrictions and problems implied. However, let us first look at some examples. See slide 9-7.

As a first example, when we define a function $f' : 8..12 \to 3..5$ and a function $f : 9..11 \to 2..6$ then, according to our rules, we have $f' \leq f$. Recall that we required subtypes to be compatible with their supertypes, compatible in the sense that an instance

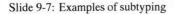

Examples $\boxed{\text{subtyping}}$

- $8..12 \rightarrow 3..5 \leq 9..11 \rightarrow 2..6$
- $\{age : int, speed : int, fuel : int\} \leq \{age : int, speed : int\}$
- $[yellow \vee blue] < [yellow \vee blue \vee green]$

Slide 9-7: Examples of subtyping

of the subtype may be used at all places where an instance of the supertype may be used. With regard to its signature, obviously, f' may be used everywhere where f may be used, since f' will deliver a result that falls within the range of the results expected from f and, further, any valid argument for f will also be accepted by f' (since the domain of f' is larger, due contravariance, than the domain of f).

As another example, look at the relation between the record types $\{age : int, speed : int, fuel : int\}$ and $\{age : int, speed : int\}$. Since the former has an additional field *fuel* it delimits so to speak the possible entities falling under its description and hence may be regarded as a subtype of the latter.

Finally, look at the relation between the variant records $[yellow : color \vee blue : color]$ and $[yellow : color \vee blue : color \vee green : color]$. The former leaves us the choice between the colors *yellow* and *blue*, whereas the latter also allows for *green* objects and, hence, encompasses the set associated with $[yellow : color \vee blue : color]$.

Contravariance rule The subtyping rules given above are all rather intuitive, except possibly for the *function* subtyping rule. Actually, the *contravariance* expressed in the function subtyping rule is somewhat of an embarrassment since it reduces the opportunities for specializing functions to particular types. See slide 9-8.

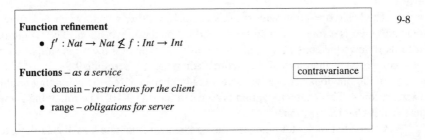

Function refinement

- $f' : Nat \rightarrow Nat \nleq f : Int \rightarrow Int$

Functions – *as a service* $\boxed{\text{contravariance}}$

- domain – *restrictions for the client*
- range – *obligations for server*

Slide 9-8: The function subtype relation

Consider, for example, that we have a function $f : Int \rightarrow Int$, then it seems quite natural to specialize this function into a function $f' : Nat \rightarrow Nat$ (which may make use of the fact that *Nat* only contains the positive elements of *Int*). However, according to our subtyping rule $f' \nleq f$, since the domain of f' is smaller than the domain of f.

For an intuitive understanding of the function subtyping rule, it may be helpful to regard a function as a *service*. The domain of the function may then be interpreted as characterizing the restrictions imposed on the client of the service (the caller of the function) and the codomain of the function as somehow expressing the benefits for the client and the obligations for the (implementor of the) function. Now, as we have already indicated, to refine or improve on a service means to relax the restrictions imposed on the client and to strengthen the obligations of the server. This, albeit in a syntactic way, is precisely what is expressed by the contravariance rule for function subtyping.

9.2.3   Objects as records

Our interest in the subtype relation is primarily directed towards objects. However, since real objects involve self-reference and possibly recursively defined methods, we will first study the subtyping relation for objects as (simple) records. Our notion of *objects as records* is based on the views expressed in Cardelli (1984).

Objects may be regarded as records (where a record is understood as a finite association of values to labels), provided we allow functions to occur as the value of a record field.

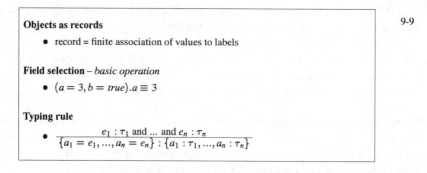

Slide 9-9: The object subtype relation

The basic operation with records is *field selection* which, when the value of the field accessed is a function, may be applied for method invocation. The typing rule for records follows the construction of the record: the type of a record is simply the record type composed of the types of the record's components. See slide 9-9.

In the previous section we have already characterized the subtyping relation between records. This characterization is repeated in slide 9-10. The following is meant to justify this characterization.

Let us first look at a number of examples that illustrate how the subtype relation fits into the mechanism of derivation by inheritance.

Suppose we define the type *any* as the record type having no fields. In our view of *types as constraints*, the empty record may be regarded as imposing no constraints. This is in agreement with our formal characterization of subtyping, since according to the record subtyping rule the record type *any* is a supertype of any other record type.

Subtyping in the sense of refinement means adding constraints, that is information that constrains the set of possible elements associated with the type. The record type *entity*, which assumes a field *age*, is a subtype of *any*, adding the information that *age* is

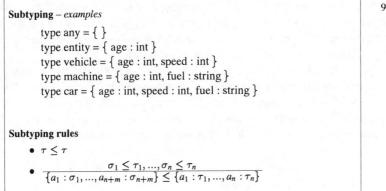

Slide 9-10: Examples of object subtyping

a relevant property for an entity. Following the same line of reasoning, we may regard the types *vehicle* and *machine* as subtypes of the type *entity*.

Clearly, we may have derived the respective types by applying inheritance. For example, we may derive *vehicle* from *entity* by adding the field *speed*, and *machine* from *entity* by adding the field *fuel*. Similarly, we may apply multiple inheritance to derive the type *car* from *vehicle* and *machine*, where we assume that the common field *age* (ultimately inherited from *entity*) only occurs once. Obviously, the type *car* is a subtype of both *vehicle* and *machine*.

Each of the successive types listed above adds information that constrains the possible applicability of the type as a descriptive device. The other way around, however, we may regard each object of a particular (sub)type to be an instance of its supertype simply by ignoring the information that specifically belongs to the subtype. Mathematically, we may explain this as a projection onto the fields of the supertype. Put differently, a subtype allows us to make finer distinctions. For example, from the perspective of the supertype two entities are the same whenever they have identical ages but they may be different when regarded as vehicles (by allowing different speeds).

Conformance The importance of subtyping for practical software development comes from the *conformance* requirement (or substitutability property) stating that any instance of a subtype may be used when an instance of a supertype is expected. This property allows the programmer to express the functionality of a program in a maximally abstract way, while simultaneously allowing for the refinement of these abstract types needed to arrive at an acceptable implementation.

For objects as records, the refinement relation concerns both attributes and functions (as members of the object record). For attributes, refinement means providing more information. Syntactically, with respect to the (signature) type of the attribute, this means a restriction of its range. In other words, the possible values an attribute may take may only be restricted. Alternatively, the refinement relation may be characterized as restricting the non-determinism contained in the specification of the supertype, by making a more specific choice. For example, if we specify the speed range of a *vehicle* initially as 0..300.000 then we may restrict the speed range of a *car* safely to 0..300. However, to stay within the regime of subtyping we may not subsequently enlarge this range by defining a subtype *racing car* with a speed range of 0..400. Intuitively, subtyping means enforcing determinism, the restriction of possible choices.

Our (syntactic) characterization of the subtyping relation between object types does not yet allow for data hiding, generics or self-reference. These issues will be treated in sections 9.5 and 9.6. However, before that, let us look at the characterization of the subtyping relation between object types as defined (for example) for the language Emerald. The characterization given in slide 9-11 is taken from Danforth and Tomlinson (1988).

Subtyping in Emerald – *S conforms to T*   9-11

- *S* provides at least the operations of *T*
- for each operation in *T*, the corresponding operation in *S* has the same number of arguments
- the type of the result of operations of *S* conform to those of the operations of *T*
- the types of arguments of operations of *T* conform to those of the operations of *S*

Slide 9-11: The subtype relation in Emerald

The object subtyping relation in Emerald is characterized in terms of *conformance*. The rules given above specify when an object type S conforms to an object (super) type T. These rules are in agreement with the subtyping rules given previously, including the contravariance required for the argument types of operations. Taken as a guideline, the rules specify what restrictions to obey (minimally) when specifying a subtype by inheritance. However, as we will discuss in the next section, polymorphism and subtyping is not restricted to object types only. Nor are the restrictions mentioned a sufficient criterion for a semantically safe use of inheritance.

9.3 Flavors of polymorphism

Polymorphism is not a feature exclusive to object-oriented languages. For example the ML language is a prime example of a non object-oriented language supporting a polymorphic type system (see Milner *et al.*, 1990). Also, most languages, including Fortran and Pascal, support implicit conversion between integers and floats, and backwards from floats to integers, and (in Pacal) from integer subranges to integers. Polymorphism (including such conversions) is a means to relieve the programmer from the rigidity imposed by typing. Put differently, it's a way in which to increase the expressivity of the type system.

Typing, as we have argued before, is important as a means to protect against errors. We must distinguish between *static typing* (which means that type checking takes place at compile time) and *strong typing* (which means that each expression must be type consistent). In other words, strong typing allows illegal operations to be recognized and rejected. Object-oriented languages (such as Eiffel, and to a certain extent C++) provide

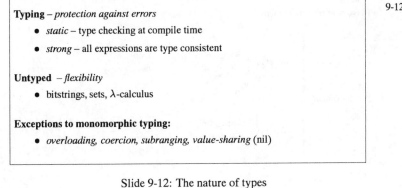

Typing – *protection against errors*   9-12

  • *static* – type checking at compile time

  • *strong* – all expressions are type consistent

Untyped – *flexibility*

  • bitstrings, sets, λ-calculus

Exceptions to monomorphic typing:

  • *overloading, coercion, subranging, value-sharing* (nil)

Slide 9-12: The nature of types

strong typing which is a mixture of static typing and runtime checks to effect the dynamic binding of method invocations. See slide 9-12.

Typed languages impose rather severe constraints on the programmer. It may require considerable effort to arrive at a consistently typed system and to deal with the additional notational complexity of defining the appropriate types. In practice, many programmers and mathematicians seem to have a preference for working in an untyped formalism, like bitstrings, (untyped) sets or (untyped) lambda calculus. We may further note that languages such as Lisp, Prolog and Smalltalk are popular precisely because of the flexibility due to the absence of static type checking.

For reliable software development, working in an untyped setting is often considered as not satisfactory. However, to make typing practical, we need to relieve the typing regime by supporting well-understood exceptions to monomorphic typing, such as overloaded functions, coercion between data types and value sharing between types (as provided by a generic nil value). More importantly, however, we must provide for controlled forms of polymorphism.

In Cardelli and Wegner (1985), a distinction is made between *ad hoc* polymorphism (which characterizes the mechanisms mentioned as common exceptions to monomorphic typing) and *universal* polymorphism (which allows for theoretically well-founded means of polymorphism). Universal polymorphism may take the form of *inclusion polymorphism* (which is a consequence of derivation by inheritance) or *parametric polymorphism* (which supports generic types, as the template mechanism offered by C++). See slide 9-13. The term *inclusion polymorphism* may be understood by regarding inheritance as a means to define the properties of a (sub)type incrementally, and thus (by adding information) delimiting a subset of the elements corresponding to the supertype. When overloading is done in a systematic fashion we may speak of *intersection* types, which allows for polymorphism based on a finite enumeration of types. See section 9.4.1.

9.3.1 Inheritance as incremental modification

The notion of inheritance as incremental modification was originally introduced in Wegner and Zdonik (1988). Abstractly, we may characterize derivation by inheritance in a formula

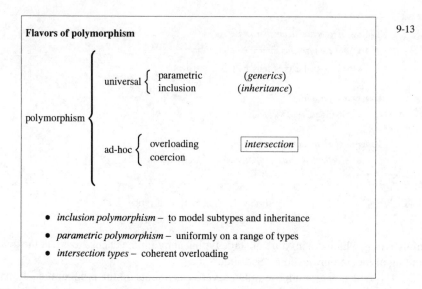

Slide 9-13: Flavors of polymorphism

as $R = P + M$, where R is the result obtained by modifying the parent P by (modifier) M. See slide 9-14. In C++ this might have been expressed as something like *class R : P{M}*.

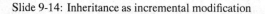

Slide 9-14: Inheritance as incremental modification

For example, we may define the record consisting of attributes $a_1 \ldots a_n$ by adding $\{a_2, a_3\}$ to the parent $\{a_1, a_2\}$. Clearly, we must make a distinction between *independent* attributes (that occur in either P or M) and *overlapping* attributes (that occur in both P and M and are taken to be overruled by the definition given in M).

An important property of objects, not taken into account in our interpretation of *object as records* given before, is that objects (as supported by object-oriented languages) may be referring to themselves. For example, both in the parent and the modifier methods may be defined that refer to a variable *this* or *self* (denoting the object itself). It is important to note that the variable *self* is dynamically bound to the object and not (statically) to the textual module in which the variable *self* occurs. Wegner and Zdonik (1988) make a distinction between attributes that are redefined in M, *virtual* attributes (that need to be defined in M) and *recursive* attributes (that are defined in P). Each of these attributes may represent methods which (implicitly) reference *self*. (In many object-oriented languages, the variable *self* or *this* is implicitly assumed whenever a method defined within the scope of the object is invoked.) Self-reference (implicit or explicit) underlies dynamic binding and hence is where the power of inheritance comes from. Without self-reference method calls would reduce to statically bound function invocation.

9.3.2   Generic abstract data types

Our goal is to arrive at a type theory with sufficient power to define generic (polymorphic) abstract data types. In the following section, we will develop a number of type calculi (following Pierce, 1993) that enable us to define polymorphic types by employing *type abstraction*.

Type abstraction may be used to define generic types, data hiding and (inheritance) subtypes. The idea is that we may characterize generic types by quantifying over a type variable. For example, we may define the identity function *id* generically as $\forall\, T.id(x : T) = x$, stating that for arbitrary type T and element x of type T, the result of applying *id* to x is x. Evidently this holds for any T.

In a similar way, we may employ type parameters to define generic abstract data types. Further, we may improve on our notion of *objects as records* by defining a packaging construct that allows for data hiding by requiring merely that there exists a particular type implementing the hidden component.

Also, we may characterize the (inheritance) subtyping relation in terms of bounded quantification, that is quantification over a restricted collection of types (restricted by imposing constraints with respect to the syntactic structure of the type instantiating the type parameter).

9.4   Type abstraction

In this section we will study type calculi that allow us to express the various forms of polymorphism, including *inclusion polymorphism* (due to inheritance), *parametric polymorphism* (due to generics) and *intersection types* (due to overloading), in a syntactic way, by means of appropriate *type expressions*.

The type calculi are based on the typed lambda calculus originally introduced in Cardelli (1984) to study the semantics of multiple inheritance. We will first study some simple extensions to the typed lambda calculus and then discuss examples involving universal quantification (defining parametric types), existential quantification (hiding implementation details) and bounded quantification (modeling subtypes derived by inheritance). For those not familiar with the lambda calculus, a very elementary introduction is given below. For each calculus, examples will be given to relate the insights developed to properties of the C++ type system.

The lambda calculus   The lambda calculus provides a very concise, yet powerful formalism to reason about computational abstraction. The introduction given here has been taken from Barendrecht (1984), which is a standard reference on this subject.

Lambda calculus – *very informal* $\boxed{\lambda}$ 9-15

- variables, abstractor λ, punctuation (,)

Lambda terms – Λ

- $x \in \Lambda$ variables
- $M \in \Lambda \Longrightarrow \lambda x.M \in \Lambda$ abstraction
- $M \in \Lambda$ *and* $N \in \Lambda \Longrightarrow MN \in \Lambda$ application

---

Slide 9-15: The lambda calculus – terms

Syntactically, lambda terms are built from a very simple syntax, figuring variables, the abstractor λ (that is used to bind variables in an expression), and punctuation symbols. Abstractors may be used to abstract a lambda term M into a function $\lambda x.M$ with parameter x. The expression $\lambda x.M$ must be read as denoting the function with body M and formal parameter x. The variable x is called the bound variable, since it is bound by the abstractor λ. In addition to function abstraction, we also have (function) application, which is written as the juxtaposition of two lambda terms. See slide 9-15.

Behaviorally, lambda terms have a number of properties, as expressed in the laws given in slide 9-16.

Laws   9-16

- $(\lambda x.M)N = M[x := N]$ beta conversion
- $M = N \Longrightarrow MZ = NZ$ *and* $ZM = ZN$
- $M = N \Longrightarrow \lambda x.M = \lambda x.N$

Slide 9-16: The lambda calculus – laws

The most important rule is the *beta conversion* rule, which describes in a manner of speaking how parameter passing is handled. In other words function call, that is the application $(\lambda x.M)N$, results in the function body M in which N is substituted for x. Two other laws are the so-called extensionality axioms, which express how equality of lambda terms is propagated into application and function abstraction. These laws impose constraints upon the models characterizing the meaning of lambda terms.

Substitution is defined by induction on the structure of lambda terms. A variable y is replaced by N (for a substitution $[x := N]$) if y is x and remains y otherwise. A substitution $[x := N]$ performed on an abstraction $\lambda y.M$ results in substituting N for x in M if x is not y. If x is identical to y, then y must first be replaced by a fresh variable (not occurring in M). A substitution performed on an application simply results in applying the substitution to both components of the application. See slide 9-17.

Some examples of *beta conversion* are given in slide 9-18. In the examples, for simplicity we employ ordinary arithmetical values and operators. This does not perturb

9-17

Substitution

- $x[x := N] \equiv N$
- $y[x := N] \equiv y$ if $x \neq y$
- $(\lambda y.M)[x := N] \equiv \lambda y.(M[x := N])$
- $(M_1 M_2)[x := N] \equiv (M_1[x : N])(M_2[x := N])$

Slide 9-17: The lambda calculus – substitution

the underlying λ-theory, since both values and operations may be expressed as proper λ-terms.

9-18

Examples

$$(\lambda x.x)1 = x[x := 1] = 1$$
$$(\lambda x.x + 1)2 = (x + 1)[x := 2] = 2 + 1$$
$$(\lambda x.x + y + 1)3 = (x + y + 1)[x := 3] = 3 + y + 1$$
$$(\lambda y.(\lambda x.x + y + 1)3)4) =$$
$$((\lambda x.x + y + 1)3)[y := 4] = 3 + 4 + 1$$

Slide 9-18: Beta conversion – examples

Note that the result of a substitution may still contain free variables (as in the third example) that may be bound in the surrounding environment (as in the fourth example).

Lambda calculus may be used to state properties of functions (and other programming constructs) in a general way.

9-19

Properties

- $\forall M (\lambda x.x)M = M$ identity
- $\forall F \exists X.FX = X$ fixed point

Proof: take $W = \lambda x.F(xx)$ and $X = WW$, then

$$X = WW = (\lambda x.F(xx))W = F(WW) = FX$$

Slide 9-19: The lambda calculus – properties

Consider, for example, the statement that the identity function works for each lambda term as expected. The quantification with respect to M indicates that in each possible model for the lambda calculus (that respects the extensionality axioms given above) the identity $(\lambda x.x)M = M$ holds. See slide 9-19.

As another example, consider the statement that each function F has a fixed point, that is a value X for which $FX = X$. The proof given above, however, does not give us any information concerning the actual contents of the fixed point, but merely proves its existence. In the following (see section 9.6) we will write $\mathbf{Y}\,(F)$ for the fixed point of a function F.

In Barendrecht (1984), an extensive account is given of how to construct mathematical models for the lambda calculus. A semantics of our type calculus may be given in terms of such models; however we will not pursue this any further here.

9.4.1   A simple type calculus

In our first version of a type calculus we will restrict ourselves to a given set of basic types (indicated by the letter ρ) and function types (written $\sigma \rightarrow \tau$, where σ stands for the domain and τ for the range or codomain). This version of the typed lambda calculus (with subtyping) is called $\lambda_{\leq}$ in Pierce (1993) from which most of the material is taken. The $\lambda_{\leq}$ calculus is a first order calculus, since it does not involve quantification over types. See slide 9-20.

The structure of type expressions is given by the definition

$$\tau ::= \rho \mid \tau_1 \rightarrow \tau_2$$

where we use τ as a type identifier and ρ as a meta variable for basic types. The expressions of our language, that we indicate with the letter e, are similar to lambda terms, except for the typing of the abstraction variable in $\lambda x : \tau.e$.

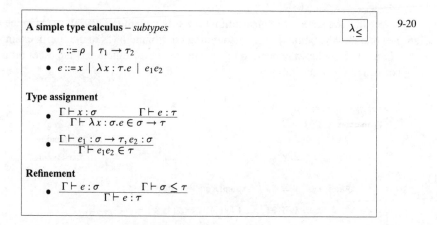

Slide 9-20: The subtype calculus

To determine whether an expression e is correctly typed (with some type expression τ) we need type assignment rules, as given above. Typing is usually based on a collection of assumptions Γ, that contains the typing of expressions occurring in the expression for which we are determining the type. In the type assignment rules and the (subtyping) refinement rules, the phrase $\Gamma \vdash e : \tau$ means that the expression e has type τ, under the assumption that the type assignments in Γ are valid. When Γ is empty, as in $\vdash e : \tau$, the type assignment holds unconditionally. Occasionally, we write $\Gamma \vdash e \in \tau$ instead of $\Gamma \vdash e : \tau$ for readability. These two expressions have identical meaning.

The premises of a type assignment rule are given above the line. The type assignment given below the line states the assignment that may be made on the basis of these premises.

For example, the first type assignment rule states that, assuming $\Gamma \vdash x : \sigma$ (x has type σ) and $\Gamma \vdash e : \tau$ (e has type τ) then $\Gamma \vdash \lambda x : \sigma.e \in \sigma \to \tau$, in other words the abstraction $\lambda x : \sigma.e$ may be validly typed as τ.

Similarly, the second type assignment rule states that applying a function $e_1 : \sigma \to \tau$ to an expression e_2 of type σ results in an (application) expression $e_1 e_2$ of type τ.

We may assume the basic types denoted by ρ to include (integer) subranges, records and variants. As a consequence, we may employ the subtyping rules given in section 9.2 to determine the subtyping relation between these types. The (subtyping) refinement rule repeated here expresses the substitutability property of subtypes, which allows us to consider an expression e of type σ, with $\sigma \leq \tau$, as being of type τ.

In slide 9-21, some examples are given illustrating the assignment of types to expressions. Type assignment may to a certain extent be done automatically, by type inference, as for example in ML (Milner *et al.*, 1990). However, in general, typing is not decidable when we include the more powerful type expressions treated later. In those cases the programmer is required to provide sufficient type information to enable the type checker to determine the types.

9-21

Examples

- $S = \lambda x : Int.x + 1$
  $S : Int \to Int$

- $twice = \lambda f : Int \to Int. \lambda y : Int.f(f(y))$
  $twice : (Int \to Int) \to Int \to Int$

Application

- $S0 = 1 \in Int$

- $twice(S) = \lambda x.SSx \in Int \to Int$

Slide 9-21: Subtypes – examples

When we define the successor function S as $\lambda x : Int.x + 1$ then we may type S straightforwardly as being of type $Int \to Int$. Similarly, we may type the (higher order) function *twice* as being of type $(Int \to Int) \to Int \to Int$. Note that the first argument to *twice* must be a function. Applying *twice* to a function argument only results in a function. When applied to S it results in a function of type $Int \to Int$ that results in applying S twice to its (integer) argument. The subtyping rules (partly imported from section 9.2) work as expected. We may define, for example, a function $+ : Real \times Real \to Int$ as a subtype of $+ : Int \times Int \to Int$ (according to the contra-variant subtyping rule for functions).

Subtyping in C++ Subtyping is supported in C++ only to a very limited extent. Function subtypes are completely absent. However, class subtypes due to derivation by inheritance may be employed. Also, built-in conversions are provided, some of which are in accordance with the subtyping requirements, and some of which, unfortunately, violate the subtyping requirements. Built-in conversions exist, for example, between *double* and *int*, in both ways. However, whereas the conversion from *int* to *double* is safe, the other way around may cause loss of information by truncation.

The type system sketched in slide 9-20 is quite easily mapped to a C++ context. For example, we may mimic the functions S and *twice* as given in slide 9-21 in C++ as:

```
int S(int x) { return x+1; }
int twice(int f(int), int y) { return f(f(y)); }
int twice_S(int y) { return twice(S,y); }
```

Nevertheless, the type system of C++ imposes some severe restrictions. For example, functions may not be returned as a value from functions. (Although we may provide a workaround, when we employ the *operator*() function for objects.)

The absence of function subtyping becomes clear when, for example, we call the function *twice* with the function *SD*, which is defined as:

```
int SD(double x) { return x+1; }
```

According to the subtyping rules and in accordance with the substitutability requirement, we employ *SD* whenever we may employ S. But not so in C++.

We run into similar limitations when we try to refine an object class descriptions following the object subtype refinement rules.

Suppose we have a parent class P which offers the member functions *self* and *attach*, as in slide 9-22. The meaning of the function *self* is that it de-references the _*self* variable if it is non-zero and delivers *this* otherwise. (See section 12.2 for an example of its use.) The function *attach* may be used to connect an instance of C to the _*self* variable.

The class C in its turn inherits from P and redefines *self* and *attach*. Syntactically, both refinements are allowed, due to the function subtype refinements rules. The function *self* is redefined to deliver a more tightly specified result, and the *attach* function is allowed to take a wider range of arguments.

In the AT&T 3.0 version of C++, both redefinitions are considered illegal. However, in the ANSI/ISO standard of C++, redefining a member function to deliver a subtype (that is, derived class) pointer will be allowed. Redefining *attach*, as has been done for C is probably not a wise thing to do, since it changes the semantics of *attach* as defined for the parent class P. In effect, it allows us to write $c \rightarrow attach(p)$ instead of $p \rightarrow attach(c \rightarrow self())$, for $P * p$ and $C * c$. Nevertheless, from a type theoretical perspective, there seem to be no grounds for forbidding it.

9.4.2 Intersection types

We define our second version of the typed lambda calculus $(\lambda_\wedge)$ as an extension of the first version $(\lambda_\le)$, an extension which provides facilities for (*ad hoc*) overloading polymorphism. Our extension consists of adding a type expression $\bigwedge[\tau_1, ..., \tau_n]$ which denotes a finite conjunction of types. Such a conjunction of types, that we will also write as $\tau_1 \wedge ... \wedge \tau_n$ is called an intersection type. The idea is that an expression e of type

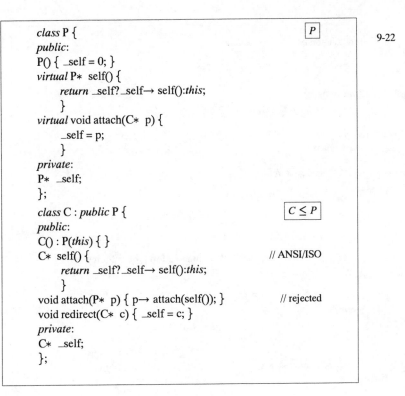

Slide 9-22: Subtyping in C++

$\bigwedge[\tau_1, ..., \tau_n]$ is correctly typed if $e : \tau_i$ for some i in $1..n$. This is expressed in the type assignment rule given in slide 9-23.

The subtyping rule for intersection types states that any subtype of a type occurring in the intersection type $\bigwedge[\tau_1, ..., \tau_n]$ is itself a subtype of the intersection type.

In addition we have two subtyping rules without premises, the first of which says that the intersection type itself may be regarded as a subtype of any of its components. In other words, from a typing perspective an intersection type is equal (hence may be replaced by) any of its component types.

Also, we may refine a function, with domain σ, which has an intersection type $\bigwedge[\tau_1, ..., \tau_n]$ as its range into an intersection type consisting of functions $\sigma \rightarrow \tau_i$ for $i = 1..n$.

Intersection types allow us to express a limited form of overloading, by enumerating a finite collection of possible types. Since the collection of types comprising an intersection type is finite, we do not need a higher order calculus here, although we might have used type abstraction to characterize intersection types.

A typical example of an intersection type is presented by the addition operator, overloaded for integers and reals, which we may define as

$$+ : \bigwedge[Int \times Int \rightarrow Int, Real \times Real \rightarrow Real]$$

Intersection types – *overloading* $\lambda_\wedge$ 9-23

- $\tau ::= \rho \mid \tau_1 \rightarrow \tau_2 \mid \bigwedge[\tau_1..\tau_n]$

Type assignment

- $\dfrac{\Gamma \vdash e : \tau_i \ (i \in 1..n)}{\Gamma \vdash e : \bigwedge[\tau_1..\tau_n]}$

Refinement

- $\dfrac{\Gamma \vdash \sigma \leq \tau_i \ (i \in 1..n)}{\Gamma \vdash \sigma \leq \bigwedge[\tau_1..\tau_n]}$

- $\bigwedge[\tau_1..\tau_n] \leq \tau_i$

- $\Gamma \vdash \bigwedge[\sigma \rightarrow \tau_1..\sigma \rightarrow \tau_n] \leq \sigma \rightarrow \bigwedge[\tau_1..\tau_n]$

Slide 9-23: The intersection type calculus

Examples   9-24

-  $+ : \bigwedge[Int \times Int \rightarrow Int, Real \times Real \rightarrow Real]$

- $Int \rightarrow Int \leq \bigwedge[Int \rightarrow Int, Real \rightarrow Real]$

- 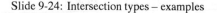 $Msg \rightarrow Obj_1 \wedge Msg \rightarrow Obj_2 \leq Msg \rightarrow \bigwedge[Obj_1, Obj_2]$

Slide 9-24: Intersection types – examples

According to our refinement rule, we may specialize an intersection type into any of its components. For example, when we have an intersection type defining a mapping for integers and a mapping for reals, we may choose the one that fits our purposes best. This example illustrates that intersection types may be an important tool for realizing optimizations that depend upon (dynamic) typing.

Similarly, we may refine a generic function working on objects into a collection of (specialized) functions by dividing out the range type. See slide 9-24. The resulting intersection type itself may subsequently be specialized into one of the component functions. In Castagna *et al.* (1993), a similar kind of type is used to model the overloading of methods in objects, that may but need not necessarily be related by inheritance. The idea is to regard message passing to objects as calling a polymorphic function that dispatches on its first argument. When the type of the first argument is compatible with multiple functions (which may happen for methods that are refined in the inheritance hierarchy) the most specific function component is chosen, that is the method with the minimal object type. A similar idea is encountered in CLOS, which allows for the definition of *multi-methods* for which dynamic dispatching takes place for all arguments. (A problem that occurs in modeling methods as overloaded functions is that the subtyping relation between methods no longer holds, due to the domain contravariance requirement. See Castagna *et al.* (1993) for a possible solution.)

Overloading in C++ Although C++ does not provide support for subtyping, it does provide extensive support for function overloading. Given a collection of functions (overloading a particular function name) C++ employs a *system of matches* to select the function that is most appropriate for a particular call.

Overloaded function selection rules $\boxed{C++}$ 9-25

1 no or unavoidable conversions – *array* → *pointer, T* → *const T*

2 integral promotion – *char* → *int, short* → *int, float* → *double*

3 standard conversions – *int* → *double, double* → *int, derived* → *base**

4 user-defined conversions – *constructors and operators*

5 ellipsis in function declaration – ...

Multiple arguments – *intersect rule*

● better match for at least one argument and at least as good a match for every
other argument

Slide 9-25: Overloading in C++

Matches may involve built-in or user-defined conversions. The general rule underlying the application of conversions is that *conversions that are considered less error-prone and surprising are to be preferred over the others*. This rule is reflected in the ordering of the C++ overloading selection rules depicted in slide 9-25.

According to the rules, the absence of conversions is to be preferred. For compatibility, with C, *array* to *pointer* conversions are applied automatically, and also *T* to *const T* conversions are considered as unproblematic. Next, we have the integral promotion rules, allowing for the conversion of *char* to *int* and *short* to *int*, for example. These conversions are also directly inherited from C, and are safe in the sense that no information loss occurs. Further, we have the standard conversions such as *int* to *double* and *derived** to *base**, user-defined conversions (as determined by the definition of one-argument constructors and conversion operators), and the ... ellipsis notation, which allows us to avoid type-checking in an arbitrary manner.

For selecting the proper function from a collection of overloaded functions with multiple arguments, the so-called *intersect* rule is used, which states that the function is selected with a better match for at least one argument and at least as good a match for every other argument. In the case that no *winner* can be found because there are multiple candidate functions with an equally good match, the compiler issues an error, as in the example below

```
void f(int, double);
void f(double, int);

f(1,2.0);                                        // f(int, double);
f(2.0,1);                                        // f(double,int);
f(1,1);                                          // error: ambiguous
```

The reason that C++ employs a system of matches based on declarations and actual parameters of functions is that the graph of built-in conversions (as inherited from C) contains cycles. For example, implicit conversions exist from *int* to *double* and *double* to *int* (although in the latter case the C++ compiler gives a warning). Theoretically, however, the selection of the best function according to the subtype relation would be preferable. However, the notion of *best* is not unproblematic in itself. For example, consider the definition of the overloaded function *f* and the classes *P* and *C* in slide 9-26.

```
class P;
class C;
void f(P* p) { cout ≪ "f(P* )"; }                // (1)
void f(C* c) { cout ≪ "f(C* )"; }                // (2)
class P {
public:
virtual void f() { cout ≪ "P::f"; }              // (3)
};
class C : public P {
public:
virtual void f() { cout ≪ "C::f"; }              // (4)
};
```

9-26

Slide 9-26: Static versus dynamic selection

What must be considered the best function *f*, given a choice between (1), (2), (3) and (4)?

```
P*  p = new P;                    // static and dynamic P*
C*  c = new C;                    // static and dynamic C*
P*  pc = new C;                   // static P*, dynamic C*

f(p);                            // f(P*)
f(c);                            // f(C*)
f(pc);                           // f(P*)

p→ f();                          // P::f
c→ f();                          // C::f
pc→ f();                         // C::f
```

In the example given above, we see that for the functions *f* (corresponding to (1) and (2)) the choice is determined by the static type of the argument, whereas for the member functions *f* (corresponding to (3) and (4)) the choice is determined by the dynamic type.

We have a dilemma. When we base the choice of functions on the dynamic type of the argument, the function subtype refinement rule is violated. On the other hand, adhering to the domain contravariance property seems to lead to ignoring the potentially useful information captured by the dynamic type of the argument.

9.4.3 Bounded polymorphism

Our next extension, which we call $F_{\leq}$, involves (bounded) universal quantification. For technical reasons we need to introduce a primitive type *Top*, which may be considered as the supertype of all types (including itself). Also we need type abstraction variables, that we will write as α and β. Our notation for a universally quantified (bounded) type is $\forall \alpha \leq \sigma.\tau$, which denotes the type τ with the type variable α replaced by any subtype σ' of σ. In a number of cases, we will simply write $\forall \alpha.\tau$, which must be read as $\forall \alpha \leq Top.\tau$. Recall that any type is a subtype of *Top*. Observe that, in contrast to $\lambda_{\leq}$ and $\lambda_{\wedge}$, the calculus $F_{\leq}$ is second order (due to the quantification over types).

In addition to the (value) expressions found in the two previous calculi, $F_{\leq}$ introduces a *type abstraction* expression of the form $\Lambda \alpha \leq \tau.e$ and a *type instantiation* expression of the form $e[\tau]$. The type abstraction expression $\Lambda \alpha \leq \tau.e$ is used in a similar way as the function abstraction expression, although the abstraction involves types and not values. Similar to the corresponding type expression, we write $\Lambda \alpha.e$ as an abbreviation for $\Lambda \alpha \leq Top.e$. The (complementary) type instantiation statement is written as $e[\tau]$, which denotes the expression e in which the type identifier τ is substituted for the type variable bound by the first type abstractor.

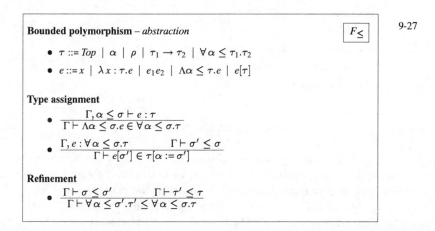

Bounded polymorphism – *abstraction*　　　　　　　　　　　　　$\boxed{F_{\leq}}$　　9-27

- $\tau ::= Top \mid \alpha \mid \rho \mid \tau_1 \rightarrow \tau_2 \mid \forall \alpha \leq \tau_1.\tau_2$
- $e ::= x \mid \lambda x : \tau.e \mid e_1 e_2 \mid \Lambda \alpha \leq \tau.e \mid e[\tau]$

Type assignment

- $$\frac{\Gamma, \alpha \leq \sigma \vdash e : \tau}{\Gamma \vdash \Lambda \alpha \leq \sigma.e \in \forall \alpha \leq \sigma.\tau}$$

- $$\frac{\Gamma, e : \forall \alpha \leq \sigma.\tau \qquad \Gamma \vdash \sigma' \leq \sigma}{\Gamma \vdash e[\sigma'] \in \tau[\alpha := \sigma']}$$

Refinement

- $$\frac{\Gamma \vdash \sigma \leq \sigma' \qquad \Gamma \vdash \tau' \leq \tau}{\Gamma \vdash \forall \alpha \leq \sigma'.\tau' \leq \forall \alpha \leq \sigma.\tau}$$

Slide 9-27: The bounded type calculus

The type assignment rule for type abstraction states that, when we may type an expression ε as being of type τ (under the assumption that $\alpha \leq \sigma$), then we may type $\Lambda \alpha \leq \sigma.e$ as being of type $\forall \alpha \leq \sigma.\tau$.

The type assignment rule for type instantiation characterizes the relation between type instantiation and substitution (which is notationally very similar). When we have an expression e of type $\forall \alpha \leq \sigma$ and we have that $\sigma' \leq \sigma$, then $e[\sigma']$ is of type $\tau[\alpha := \sigma']$, which is τ with σ' substituted for α. See slide 9-27.

The refinement rule for bounded types states the subtyping relation between two bounded types. We have that $\forall \alpha \leq \sigma'.\tau'$ is a subtype of $\forall \alpha \leq \sigma.\tau$ whenever $\sigma \leq \sigma'$ and $\tau' \leq \tau$. Notice that the relation is contravariant with respect to the types bounding the abstraction, similar as for the domains of function subtypes in the function subtyping rule.

In contrast to the polymorphism due to object type extensions and overloading, bounded polymorphism (employing type quantifiers) is an example of what we have called parametric polymorphism. In effect, this means that we must explicitly give a type parameter to instantiate an object or function of a bounded (parametric) type, similar to when we use a template in C++.

The examples given in slide 9-28 illustrate how we may define and subsequently type parametric functions. In these examples, we employ the convention that in the absence of a bounding type we assume *Top* as an upper limit. The examples are taken from Cardelli and Wegner (1985).

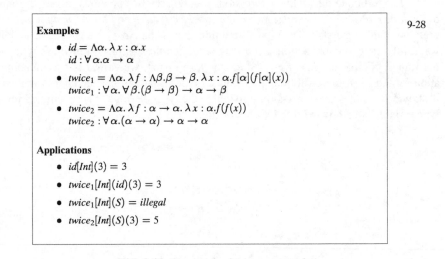

Examples

- $id = \Lambda\alpha.\,\lambda x : \alpha.x$
  $id : \forall\alpha.\alpha \rightarrow \alpha$

- $twice_1 = \Lambda\alpha.\,\lambda f : \Lambda\beta.\beta \rightarrow \beta.\,\lambda x : \alpha.f[\alpha](f[\alpha](x))$
  $twice_1 : \forall\alpha.\forall\beta.(\beta \rightarrow \beta) \rightarrow \alpha \rightarrow \beta$

- $twice_2 = \Lambda\alpha.\,\lambda f : \alpha \rightarrow \alpha.\,\lambda x : \alpha.f(f(x))$
  $twice_2 : \forall\alpha.(\alpha \rightarrow \alpha) \rightarrow \alpha \rightarrow \alpha$

Applications

- $id[Int](3) = 3$

- $twice_1[Int](id)(3) = 3$

- $twice_1[Int](S) = illegal$

- $twice_2[Int](S)(3) = 5$

Slide 9-28: Parametrized types – examples

The (generic) identity function *id* is defined as $\Lambda\alpha.\,\lambda x : \alpha.x$, which states that when we supply a particular type, say *Int*, then we obtain the function $\lambda x : Int.x$. Since the actual type used to instantiate *id* is not important, we may type *id* as being of type $\forall\alpha.\alpha \rightarrow \alpha$. In a similar way, we may define and type the two (generic) variants of the function *twice*. Notice the difference between the two definitions of *twice*. The first variant requires the function argument itself to be of a generic type, and fails (is incorrectly typed) for the successor function S which is (non generic) of type $Int \rightarrow Int$. In contrast, the second variant accepts S, and we may rely on the automatic conversion of $id : \forall\alpha.\alpha \rightarrow \alpha$ to $id[Int] : Int \rightarrow Int$ (based on the second type assignment rule) to accept *id* as well.

The interplay between *parametric* and *inclusion* polymorphism is illustrated in the examples presented in slide 9-29. Recall that inclusion polymorphism is based on the subtyping relation between records (which states that refinement of a record type involves the addition of components and/or refinement of components that already belong to the super type).

The first example defines a function g that works on a record with at least one component *one* and delivers as a result the value of the component *one* of the argument record. The function g' is a generalized version of g that abstracts from the particular type of the *one* component. Notice that both g and g' may be applied to any record that con-

---

Bounded quantification

- $g = \Lambda\alpha \leq \{one : Int\}. \lambda x : \alpha.(x.one)$
  $g : \forall \alpha \leq \{one : int\}.\alpha \rightarrow Int$
- $g' = \Lambda\beta.\Lambda\alpha \leq \{one : \beta\}. \lambda x : \alpha.(x.one)$
  $g' : \forall \beta.\forall \alpha \leq \{one : \beta\}.\alpha \rightarrow \beta$
- $move = \Lambda\alpha \leq Point. \lambda p : \alpha. \lambda d : Int.(p.x := p.x + d); p$
  $move : \forall \alpha \leq Point. \alpha \rightarrow Int \rightarrow \alpha$

Application

- $g'[Int][\{one : Int, two : Bool\}](\{one = 3, two = true\}) = 3$
- $move[\{x : Int, y : Int\}](\{x = 0, y = 0\})(1) = \{x = 1, y = 0\}$

Slide 9-29: Bounded quantification – examples

forms to the requirement stated in the bound, such as the record $\{one = 3, two = true\}$.

As another example of employing bounds to impose requirements, look at the function *move* that is defined for subtypes of *Point* (that we assume to be a record containing x and y coordinates). It expects a record (that is similar to or extends *Point*) and an (integer) distance, and as a result delivers the modified record.

Discussion Parametric polymorphism is an important means to incorporate subtyping in a coherent fashion. Apart from Pierce (1993), from which we have taken most of the material presented here, we may mention Plotkin and Abadi (1993) as a reference for further study. In Pierce (1993) a calculus $F_\wedge$ is also introduced in which intersection polymorphism is expressed by means of an explicit type variable. The resulting type may be written as $\forall \alpha \in \{...\}$, where $\{...\}$ denotes a finite collection of types. As already mentioned, intersection types may also be used to model inclusion polymorphism (see Castagna *et al.*, 1993).

It is an interesting research issue to explore the relation between parametric polymorphism and inclusion polymorphism further along this line. However, we will not pursue this line here. Instead, in the next section we will look at another application of parametric polymorphism, namely existential types that allow us to abstract from hidden component types. This treatment is based on Cardelli and Wegner (1985). In the last section of this chapter, we will look in more detail at the role of self-reference in defining (recursive) object types, following Cook *et al.* (1990). We will conclude this chapter with some observations concerning the relevance of such type theories for actual programming languages. In particular, we will show that Eiffel is not type consistent.

Type abstraction in C++ As shown in section 2.4 (which discussed generic types), type abstraction in C++ may occur in various guises. One important means of type abstraction is to employ what we have called polymorphic base class hierarchies. For example, the function *move*, which was somewhat loosely characterized in slide 9-29, may be defined in C++ as follows:

```
Point* move(Point* p, int d);                              // require int Point :: x
Point* move(Point* p, int d) { p.x += d; return p; }
```

In effect, the function *move* accepts a pointer to an instance of *Point*, or any class derived from *Point*, satisfying the requirement that it has a public integer data member x.

Similar restrictions generally hold when instantiating a template class, but in contrast to base class subtyping requirements, these restrictions will only be verified at link time.

9-30

```
template< class T >                         // requires T::value()
class P {
public:
P(T& r) : t(r) {}
int operator==( P<T>& p) {
    return t.value() == p.t.value();
    }
private:
T& t;
};
```

Slide 9-30: Type abstraction in C++

Consider the template class definition given in slide 9-30. Evidently, for the comparison function to operate properly, each instantiation type substituted for the type parameter T must satisfy the requirement that it has a public member function *value*.

9-31

```
template< class T >
class A {                                        A<T>
public:
virtual T value() = 0;
};
class Int : public A<int> {                 Int ≤ A<int>
public:
Int(int n = 0) : _n(n) {}
int value() { return _n; }
private:
int _n;
};
```

Slide 9-31: Type instantiation

Such a requirement may also be expressed by defining an abstract class A defining a pure virtual member function *value*. See slide 9-31. The restrictions on instantiating P may then be stated informally as the requirement that each instantiation type T

must be a subtype of $A<X>$ for arbitrary type X. The class *Int* is an example of a type complying with the implicit requirements imposed by the definition of P. An example of using P is given below

```
Int i1, i2;
P<Int> p1(i1), p2(i2);
if ( p1 == p2 ) cout ≪ "OK" ≪ endl;                    // OK
```

Note, however, that the derivation of $A<int>$ is by no means necessary or in any way enforced by C++.

9.5   Existential types – *hiding*

Existential types were introduced in Cardelli and Wegner (1985) to model aspects of data abstraction and hiding. The language introduced in Cardelli and Wegner (1985) is essentially a variant of the typed lambda calculi we have looked at previously.

Our new calculus, that we call $F_\exists$, is an extension of $F_\le$ with type expressions of the form $\exists \alpha \le \sigma.\tau$ (to denote existential types) and expressions of the form $pack[\alpha = \sigma\ in\ \tau]$ (to denote values with hidden types). Intuitively, the meaning of the expression $pack[\alpha = \sigma\ in\ \tau]$ is that we represent the abstract type α occurring in the type expression τ by the actual type σ (in order to realize the value e). Following the type assignment rule, we may actually provide an instance of a subtype of the bounding type as the realization of a hidden type. See slide 9-32.

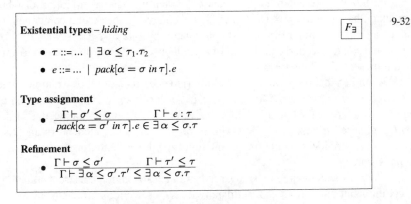

Slide 9-32: The existential type calculus

The subtyping refinement rule is similar to the refinement rule for universally quantified types. Notice also here the contravariance relation between the bounding types.

More interesting is what bounding types allow us to express. (As before, we will write $\exists\alpha.\tau$ to denote $\exists\alpha \le Top.\tau$.) First, existential types allow us to indicate that the realization of a particular type exists, even if we do not indicate how. The declaration $e : \exists\alpha.\tau$ tells us that there must be some type σ such that e of type τ can be realized. Apart from claiming that a particular type exists, we may also provide information concerning its structure, while leaving its actual type undetermined.

Structure – *undeterminacy*   9-33

- $Top = \exists\,\alpha.\alpha$ *(the biggest type)*
- $AnyPair = \exists\,\alpha\,\exists\,\beta.\alpha \times \beta$ *(any pair)*
- $(3,4) : \exists\,\alpha.\alpha$ – *does not provide sufficient structure!*
- $(3,4) : \exists\,\alpha.\alpha \times \alpha$

Information hiding

- $\exists\,\alpha.\alpha \times (\alpha \rightarrow Int)$ *object, operation*
- $x : \exists\,\alpha.\alpha \times (\alpha \rightarrow Int)$ $\rightsquigarrow snd(x)(fst(x))$

Slide 9-33: Existential types – examples

For example, the type $\exists\,\alpha.\alpha$ (which may clearly be realized by any type) carries no information whatsoever, hence it may considered to be equal to the type *Top*. More information, for example, is provided by the type $\exists\,\alpha\,\exists\,\beta.\alpha \times \beta$ which defines the product type consisting of two (possibly distinct) types. (A product may be regarded as an unlabeled record.) The type $\exists\,\alpha.\alpha \times \alpha$ gives even more information concerning the structure of a product type, namely that the two components are of the same type. Hence, for the actual product $(3,4)$ the latter is the best choice. See slide 9-33.

Existential types may be used to impose structure on the contents of a value, while hiding its actual representation. For example, when we have a variable x of which we know that it has type $\exists\,\alpha.\alpha \times (\alpha \rightarrow Int)$ then we may use the second component of x to produce an integer value from its first component, by $snd(x)(fst(x))$, where *fst* extracts the first and *snd* the second component of a product. Clearly, we do not need to know the actual representation type for α.

A similar idea may be employed for (labeled) records. For example, when we have a record x of type $\exists\,\alpha.\{val : \alpha, op : \alpha \rightarrow Int\}$ then we may use the expression $x.op(x.val)$ to apply the operation *op* to the value *val*. Again, no knowledge of the type of *val* is required in this case. However, to be able to use an element of an existential type we must provide an actual representation type, by instantiating the type parameter in a *pack* statement.

The *pack* statement may be regarded as an encapsulation construct, allowing us to protect the inner parts of an abstract data type. When we look more closely at the *pack* statement, we can see three components. First, we have an *interface* specification corresponding to the existential type associated with the *pack* expression. Secondly, we need to provide an actual representation of the hidden type, *Int* in the example above. And finally, we need to provide the actual contents of the structure. See slide 9-34.

In combination with the notion of *objects as records*, existential types provide us with a model of abstract data types. Real objects, however, require a notion of *self-reference* that we have not captured yet. In the next section we will conclude our exploration of type theories by discussing the F_μ calculus that supports recursive (object) types and inheritance.

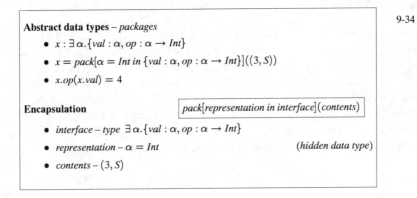

9-34

Abstract data types – *packages*

- $x : \exists \alpha.\{val : \alpha, op : \alpha \rightarrow Int\}$
- $x = pack[\alpha = Int \ in \ \{val : \alpha, op : \alpha \rightarrow Int\}]((3, S))$
- $x.op(x.val) = 4$

Encapsulation $pack[representation \ in \ interface](contents)$

- *interface – type* $\exists \alpha.\{val : \alpha, op : \alpha \rightarrow Int\}$
- *representation –* $\alpha = Int$ *(hidden data type)*
- *contents –* $(3, S)$

Slide 9-34: Packages – examples

Hiding in C++ Naturally, the classical way of data hiding in C++ is to employ *private* or *protected* access protection. Nevertheless, an equally important means is to employ an abstract interface class in combination with forwarding, as discussed in section 7.2.

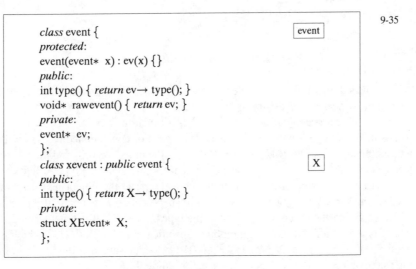

9-35

```
class event {                                    event
protected:
event(event* x) : ev(x) {}
public:
int type() { return ev→ type(); }
void* rawevent() { return ev; }
private:
event* ev;
};
class xevent : public event {                    X
public:
int type() { return X→ type(); }
private:
struct XEvent* X;
};
```

Slide 9-35: Hiding in C++

For example, as depicted in slide 9-35, we may offer the user a class *event* which records information concerning events occurring in a window environment, while hiding completely the underlying implementation. The actual *xevent* class realizing the type *event* may itself need access to other structures, as for example those provided by the X window environment. Yet, the *xevent* class itself may remain entirely hidden from the user, since events are not something created directly (note the protected constructor) but only indirectly, generally by the system in response to some action by the user.

9.6 Self-reference

Recursive types are compound types in which the type itself occurs as the type of one of its components. Self-reference in objects clearly involves recursive types since the expression *self* denotes the object itself, and hence has the type of the object. In F_μ, our extension of $F_\le$ taken from Cook *et al.* (1990), recursive types are written as $\mu\,\alpha.\tau[\alpha]$, where μ is the recursion abstractor and α a type variable. The dependence of τ on α is made explicit by writing $\tau[\alpha]$. We will use the type expressions $\mu\,\alpha.\tau[\alpha]$ to type object specifications of the form $\lambda(self).\{a_1 = e_1, ..., a_n = e_n\}$ as indicated by the type assignment rule below. Object specifications may be regarded as class descriptions in C++ or Eiffel.

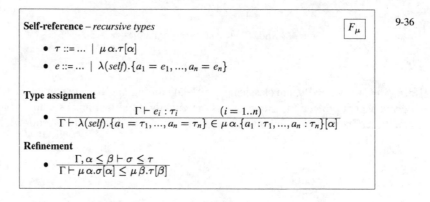

Self-reference – *recursive types* $\boxed{F_\mu}$ 9-36

- $\tau ::= ... \mid \mu\,\alpha.\tau[\alpha]$
- $e ::= ... \mid \lambda(self).\{a_1 = e_1, ..., a_n = e_n\}$

Type assignment

$$\cdot\ \frac{\Gamma \vdash e_i : \tau_i \qquad (i = 1..n)}{\Gamma \vdash \lambda(self).\{a_1 = \tau_1, ..., a_n = \tau_n\} \in \mu\,\alpha.\{a_1 : \tau_1, ..., a_n : \tau_n\}[\alpha]}$$

Refinement

$$\cdot\ \frac{\Gamma, \alpha \le \beta \vdash \sigma \le \tau}{\Gamma \vdash \mu\,\alpha.\sigma[\alpha] \le \mu\,\beta.\tau[\beta]}$$

Slide 9-36: A calculus for recursive types

The subtype refinement rule for recursive types states that $\mu\,\alpha.\sigma[\alpha] \le \mu\,\beta.\tau[\beta]$ if we can prove that $\sigma \le \tau$ assuming that $\alpha \le \beta$.

An object specification $\lambda(self).\{...\}$ is a function with the type of the actual object as its domain and (naturally) also as its range. For convenience we will write an object specification as $\lambda(self).F$, where F denotes the object record, and the type of an object specification as $\mu\,\alpha.F[\alpha]$, where $F[\alpha]$ denotes the (abstract) type of the record F.

To obtain from an object specification $\lambda(self).F$ the object that it specifies, we need to find some type σ that types the record specification F as being of type σ precisely when we assign the expression *self* in F the type σ. Technically, this means that the object of type σ is a fixed point of the object specification $\lambda(self).F(self)$ which is of type $\sigma \to \sigma$. We write this as $\mathbf{Y}\,(\lambda(self).F(self)) : \sigma$, which says that the object corresponding to the object specification is of type σ. See slide 9-36.

Finding the fixed point of an object specification involves technically a procedure known as *unrolling*, which allows us to rewrite the type $\mu\,\alpha.F[\alpha]$ as $F[\mu\,\alpha.F[\alpha]]$. Notice that unrolling is valid, precisely because of the fixed point property. Namely, the object type σ is equal to $\mu\,\alpha.F[\alpha]$, due to the type assignment rule, and we have that $\sigma = F[\sigma]$. See slide 9-37.

Unrolling allows us to reason on the level of types and to determine the subtyping relation between recursive subtypes. Consider, for example, the type declarations T and T_i $(i = 1..3)$ above. Based on the refinement rules for object records, functions

---

Object semantics *– fixed point* $\sigma = F[\sigma]$

9-37

- $\mathbf{Y}\,(\lambda(\textit{self}).F(\textit{self})) : \sigma$

Unrolling *– unraveling the meaning of a type*

- $\mu\alpha.F[\alpha] = F[\mu\alpha.F[\alpha]]$

Example

$$T = \mu\alpha.\{a : int, c : \alpha, b : \alpha \to \alpha\}$$
$$T_1 = \{a : int, c : T, b : T \to T, d : bool\}$$
$$T_2 = \mu\alpha.\{a : int, c : \alpha, b : T \to T, d : bool\}$$
$$T_3 = \mu\alpha.\{a : int, c : \alpha, b : \alpha \to \alpha, d : bool\}$$

$T_1, T_2 \leq T, T_3 \not\leq T$ (contravariance)

Slide 9-37: Recursive types – examples

and recursive types, we may establish that $T_1 \leq T$, $T_2 \leq T$ but $T_3 \not\leq T$. To see that $T_1 \leq T$, it suffices to substitute T for α in F, where $F = \{a : Int, c : \alpha, b : \alpha \to \alpha\}$. Since $F[T] = \{a : Int, c : T, b : T \to T\}$ we immediately see that T_1 only extends T with the field $d : Bool$, hence $T_1 \leq T$. A similar line of reasoning is involved to determine that $T_2 \leq T$, only we need to unroll T_2 as well. We must then establish that $c : T_2 \leq c : T$, which follows from an application of the refinement rule.

To show that $T_3 \not\leq T$, let $G[\beta] = \{a : Int, c : \beta, b : \beta \to \beta, d : Bool\}$ and $T_3 = \mu\beta.G[\beta]$. Then, by unrolling, $T_3 = G[T_3] = \{a : Int, c : T_3, b : T_3 \to T_3, d : Bool\}$. Now, suppose that $T_3 \leq T$, then $G[T_3] \leq F[T_3]$ and consequently $b : T_3 \to T_3$ must refine $b : T \to T$. But from the latter requirement it follows that $T_3 \leq T$ and that $T \leq T_3$ (by the contravariance rule for function subtyping). However, this leads to a contradiction since T is clearly not equal to T_3 because T_3 contains a field $d : Bool$ that does not occur in T.

Although analyses of this kind are to some extent satisfactory in themselves, the reader may wonder where this all leads to. In the following we will apply these techniques to show the necessity of dynamic binding and to illustrate that inheritance may easily violate the subtyping requirements.

Inheritance In section 9.3 we have characterized inheritance as an incremental modification mechanism, which involves a dynamic interpretation of the expression *self*. In the recursive type calculus F_μ we may characterize this more precisely, by regarding a derived object specification C as the result of applying the modifier M to the object specification P. We employ the notation $C = \lambda(\textit{self}).P(\textit{self})$ with $\{a_1' = e_1', ..., a_k' = e_k'\}$ to characterize derivation by inheritance, and we assume the modifier M corresponding with $\{a_1' = e_1', ..., a_k' = e_k'\}$ to extend the record associated with P in the usual sense. See slide 9-38.

The meaning of an object specification C is again a fixed point $\mathbf{Y}\,(C)$, that is $\mathbf{Y}\,(\lambda(\textit{self}).M(\textit{self})(P(\textit{self})))$. Now when we assume that the object specification is of type $\tau \to \tau$ (and hence $\mathbf{Y}\,(P)$ of type τ), and that C is of type $\sigma \to \sigma$ (and hence $\mathbf{Y}\,(C)$

Inheritance $- C = P + M$ 9-38

- $P = \lambda(self).\{a_1 = e_1, ..., a_n = e_n\}$
- $C = \lambda(self).P(self)$ **with** $\{a'_1 = e'_1, ..., a'_k = e'_k\}$

Semantics $-$ $\mathbf{Y}(C) = \mathbf{Y}(\lambda(self).M(self)(P(self)))$

- $P : \sigma \to \sigma \Longrightarrow \mathbf{Y}(P) : \sigma$
- $C = \lambda(s).M(s)(P(s)) : \tau \to \tau \Longrightarrow \mathbf{Y}(C) : \tau$

Slide 9-38: Inheritance semantics – self-reference

of type σ), then we must require that $\sigma \le \tau$ to obtain a properly typed derivation. We write $C \le P$ whenever $\sigma \le \tau$.

A first question that arises when we characterize inheritance as incremental modification is how we obtain the meaning of the composition of two object specifications.

$P = \lambda(self).\{i = 5, id = self\}$ 9-39
$C = \lambda(self).P(self)$ **with** $\{b = true\}$

$\mathbf{Y}(P) : \tau$ where $\tau = \mu\alpha.\{i : int, id : \alpha\}$ and $P : \tau \to \tau$
Simple typing $-$ $\mathbf{Y}(C) : \sigma = \{i : int, id : \tau, b : bool\}$
Delayed $-$ $\mathbf{Y}(C) : \sigma' = \mu\alpha.\{i : int, id : \alpha, b : bool\}$

We have $\sigma' \le \sigma$ 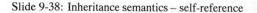 (more information)

Slide 9-39: Object inheritance – dynamic binding

Let (parent) P and (child) C be defined as above. Now, if we know that the type of $\mathbf{Y}(P)$ is τ then we may simply characterize $\mathbf{Y}(C)$ as being of type $\sigma = \{i : Bool, id : \tau, b : Bool\}$. However, when we delay the typing of the P component (by first composing the record specifications before abstracting from *self*) then we may obtain $\sigma' = \mu\alpha.\{i : Int, id : \alpha, b : Bool\}$ as the type of $\mathbf{Y}(C)$. By employing the refinement rule and unrolling we can show that $\sigma' \le \sigma$. Hence, delayed typing clearly provides more information and must be considered as the best choice. Note, however, that both $\sigma' \le \tau$ and $\sigma \le \tau$ hold. See slide 9-39.

A second, important question that emerges with respect to inheritance is how self-reference affects the subtyping relation between object specifications related by inheritance.

Consider the object specifications P and C given in slide 9-40. In the (derived) specification C, the method *eq* is redefined to include an equality test for the b component. However, when we determine the object types corresponding to the specifications P and C we observe that $C \not\le P$.

The reasoning is as follows. For $\mathbf{Y}(P) : \tau$ and $\mathbf{Y}(C) : \sigma$, we have that $\sigma = \mu\beta.\{i : Int, id : \beta \to Bool, b : Bool\}$ which is (by unrolling) equal to $\{i : Int, id : \sigma \to Bool, b : Bool\}$. Now suppose that $\sigma \le \tau$, then we have that

9-40

$$P = \lambda(self).\{i = 5, eq = \lambda(o).(o.i = self.i)\}$$
$$\quad C = \lambda(self).P(self) \textbf{ with } \{b = true,$$
$$\quad\quad eq = \lambda(o).(o.i = self.i \;\; and$$
$$\quad\quad o.b = self.b)$$
$$\quad \}$$
$$\mathbf{Y}(P) : \tau \text{ where } \tau = \mu\alpha.\{i : int, eq : \alpha \rightarrow bool\}$$
$$\mathbf{Y}(C) : \sigma \text{ where } \sigma = \mu\alpha.\{i : int, id : \alpha \rightarrow bool, b : bool\}$$

However $\sigma \nleq \tau$ **(subtyping error)**

Slide 9-40: Object inheritance – contravariance

$\{i : Int, eq : \sigma \rightarrow Bool, b : Bool\}$ is a subtype of $\{i : Int, eq : \tau \rightarrow Bool\}$ which is true when $eq : \sigma \rightarrow Bool \leq eq : \tau \rightarrow Bool$ and hence (by contravariance) when $\sigma \leq \tau$. Clearly, this is impossible. Hence $\sigma \nleq \tau$.

We have a problem here, since the fact that $C \nleq P$ means that the type checker will not be able to accept the derivation of C from P, although C is clearly dependent on P. The solution to our problem lies in making the type dependency involved in deriving C from P explicit. Notice, in this respect, that in the example above we have omitted the type of the abstraction variable in the definition of eq, which would have to be written as $\lambda x : \mathbf{Y}(P).x.i = self.i$ (and in a similar way for C) to do it properly.

Type dependency The expression *self* is essentially of a polymorphic nature. To make the dependency of object specification on *self* explicit, we will employ an explicit type variable similar as in $F_\leq$.

Let $F[\alpha]$ stand for $\{a_1 : \tau_1, ..., a_n : \tau\}$ as before. We may regard $F[\alpha]$ as a type function, in the sense that for some type τ the expression $F[\tau]$ results in a type. To determine the type of an object specification we must find a type σ that satisfies both $\sigma \leq F[\sigma]$ and $F[\sigma] \leq \sigma$.

9-41

Type dependency – *self* is polymorphic

- Let $F[\alpha] = \{m_1 : \sigma_1, ..., m_j : \sigma_j\}$ (type function)
- $P : \forall \alpha \leq F[\alpha].t \rightarrow F[\alpha]$
- $P = \Lambda\alpha \leq F[\alpha]. \lambda(self : \alpha).\{m_1 : e_1, ..., m_j : e_j\}$

F-bounded constraint $\alpha \leq F[\alpha]$
Object instantiation: $\mathbf{Y}(P[\sigma])$ for $\sigma = \mu t.F[t]$
We have $P[\sigma] : \sigma \rightarrow F[\sigma]$ because $F[\sigma] = \sigma$

Slide 9-41: Bounded type constraints

We may write an object specification as $\Lambda\alpha \leq F[\alpha]. \lambda(self : \alpha).\{a_1 = e_1, ..., a_n = e_n\}$, which is typed as $\forall \alpha \leq F[\alpha].\alpha \rightarrow F[\alpha]$. The constraint that $\alpha \leq F[\alpha]$, which is called an *F-bounded constraint*, requires that the subtype substituted for α is a (structural) refinement of the record type $F[\alpha]$. As before, we have that $\mathbf{Y}(P[\sigma]) = \sigma$

with $\sigma = \mu\,\alpha.F[\alpha]$, which differs from our previous definition only by making the type dependency in P explicit. See slide 9-41.

Now, when applying this extended notion of object specification to the characterization of inheritance, we may relax our requirement that $\mathbf{Y}(C)$ must be a subtype of $\mathbf{Y}(P)$ into the requirement that $G[\alpha] \leq F[\alpha]$ for any α, where F is the record specification of P and G the record specification of C.

Inheritance   9-42

$$P = \Lambda\alpha \leq F[\alpha].\,\lambda(self : \alpha).\{...\}$$
$$C = \Lambda\alpha \leq G[\alpha].\,\lambda(self : \alpha).P[\alpha](self) \text{ with } \{...\}$$

with recursive types

$F[\alpha] = \{i : int, id : \alpha \to bool\}$
$G[\alpha] = \{i : int, id : \alpha \to bool, b : bool\}$

Valid, because $G[\alpha] \leq F[\alpha]$
However $\mathbf{Y}(C[\sigma]) \not\leq_{subtype} \mathbf{Y}(P[\tau])$ (see discussion)

Slide 9-42: Inheritance and constraints

For example, when we declare $F[\alpha]$ and $G[\alpha]$ as in slide 9-42, we have that $G[\alpha] \leq F[\alpha]$ for every value for α. However, when we find types σ and τ such that $\mathbf{Y}(C[\sigma]) : \sigma$ and $\mathbf{Y}(P[\tau]) : \tau$ we (still) have that $\sigma \not\leq \tau$. Conclusion, inheritance allows more than subtyping. In other words, our type checker may guard the structural application of inheritance, yet will not guarantee that the resulting object types behaviorally satisfy the subtype relation.

Discussion – Eiffel is not type consistent We have limited our exploration of the recursive structure of objects to (polymorphic) object variables. Self-reference, however, may also occur to *class variables*. The interested reader is referred to Cook *et al.* (1990). The question that interests us more at this particular point is what benefits we may have from the techniques employed here and what lessons we may draw from applying them.

One lesson, which should not come as a surprise, is that a language may allow us to write programs that are accepted by the compiler yet are behaviorally incorrect. However, if we can determine syntactically that the subtyping relations between classes is violated we may at least expect a warning from the compiler. So one benefit, possibly, is that we may improve our compilers on the basis of the type theory presented in this chapter. Another potential benefit is that we may better understand the trade-offs between the particular forms of polymorphism offered by our language of choice.

The analysis given in Cook *et al.* (1990) indeed leads to a rather surprising result. Contrary to the claims made by its developer, Cook *et al.* (1990) demonstrate that Eiffel is *not* type consistent. The argument runs as follows. Suppose we define a class C with a method *eq* that takes an argument of a type similar to the type of the object itself (which may be written in Eiffel as *like Current*). We further assume that the class P is defined in a similar way, but with an integer field i and a method *eq* that tests only on i. See slide 9-43.

We may then declare variables v and p of type P. Now suppose that we have an

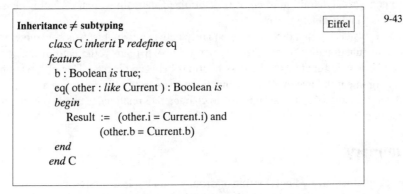

Slide 9-43: Inheritance and subtyping in Eiffel

object c of type C, then we may assign c to v and invoke the method eq for v, asking whether p is equal to v, as in

```
p,v:P, c:C

v := c;
v.eq(p);                                    // error p has no b
```

Since v is associated with an instance of C, but syntactically declared as being of type P, the compiler accepts the call. Nevertheless, when p is associated with an instance of P trouble will arise, since (due to dynamic binding) the method eq defined for C will be invoked while p not necessarily has a field b.

When we compare the definition of C in Eiffel with how we may define C in C++, then we are immediately confronted with the restriction that we do not have such a dynamic typing mechanism as *like Current* in C++. Instead, we may use overloading, as shown in slide 9-44.

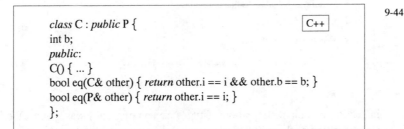

Slide 9-44: Inheritance and subtyping in C++

When we would have omitted the P variant of eq, the compiler complains about hiding a virtual function. However, the same problem arises when we define eq to be virtual in P, unless we take care to explicitly cast p into either a C or P reference. (Overloading is also used in Liskov (1993) to solve a similar problem.) In the case we choose for a non virtual definition of *eq*, it is determined statically which variant is chosen and (obviously) no problem occurs.

Considering that determining equality between two objects is somehow orthogonal to the functionality of the object proper, we may perhaps better employ externally defined overloaded functions to express relations between objects. This observation could be an argument to have overloaded functions apart from objects, not as a means to support a hybrid approach but as a means to characterize relations between objects in a type consistent (polymorphic) fashion.

Summary

This chapter has treated polymorphism from a foundational perspective.

In section 1, we looked at abstract inheritance as employed in knowledge representation.

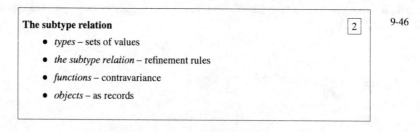

Abstract inheritance |1| 9-45
- *abstract inheritance* – declarative relation
- *inheritance networks* – non-monotonic reasoning
- *taxonomic structure* – predicate calculus

Slide 9-45: Section 9.1: Abstract inheritance

We discussed the non-monotonic aspects of inheritance networks and looked at a first order logic interpretation of taxonomic structures.

The subtype relation |2| 9-46
- *types* – sets of values
- *the subtype relation* – refinement rules
- *functions* – contravariance
- *objects* – as records

Slide 9-46: Section 9.2: The subtype relation

In section 2, a characterization of types as sets of values was given. We looked at a formal definition of the subtype relation and discussed the refinement rules for functions and objects.

In section 3, we discussed types as a means to prevent errors, and distinguished between various flavors of polymorphism, including parametric polymorphism, inclusion polymorphism, overloading and coercion. Inheritance was characterized as an incremental modification mechanism, resulting in inclusion polymorphism.

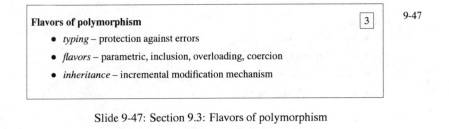

Slide 9-47: Section 9.3: Flavors of polymorphism

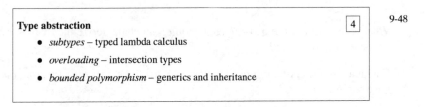

Slide 9-48: Section 9.4: Type abstraction

In section 4, some formal type calculi were presented, based on the typed lambda calculus. These included a calculus for simple subtyping, a calculus for overloading, employing intersection types, and a calculus for bounded polymorphism, employing type abstraction. Examples were discussed illustrating the (lack of) features of the C++ type system.

Slide 9-49: Section 9.5: Existential types

In section 5, we looked at a calculus employing existential types, modeling abstract data types and hiding by means of packages and type abstraction.

Finally, in section 6, we discussed self-reference and looked at a calculus employing recursive types. It was shown how object semantics may be determined by unrolling, and we studied the semantic interpretation of dynamic binding. Concluding this chapter, an example was given showing an inconsistency in the Eiffel type system.

Questions

(1) How would you characterize inheritance as applied in knowledge representation? Discuss the problems that arise due to non-monotony.

(2) How would you render the meaning of an inheritance lattice? Give some examples.

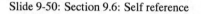

Self reference $\boxed{6}$ 9-50

- *self-reference* – recursive types
- *object semantics* – unrolling
- *inheritance* – dynamic binding
- *subtyping* – inconsistencies

Slide 9-50: Section 9.6: Self reference

(3) What is the meaning of a type? How would you characterize the relation between a type and its subtypes?

(4) Characterize the subtyping rules for ranges, functions, records and variant records. Give some example.

(5) What is the intuition underlying the function subtyping rule?

(6) What is understood by the notion of *objects as records*? Explain the subtyping rule for objects.

(7) Discuss the relative merits of typed formalisms and untyped formalisms.

(8) What flavors of polymorphism can you think of? Explain how the various flavors are related to programming language constructs.

(9) Discuss how inheritance may be understood as an incremental modification mechanism.

(10) Characterize the simple type calculus $\lambda_{\leq}$, that is the syntax, type assignment and refinement rules. Do the same for $F_\wedge$ and $F_\leq$.

(11) Type the following expressions: (a) $\{a = 1, f = \lambda\,x : Int.x+1\}$, (b) $\lambda\,x : Int.x * x$, and (c) $\lambda\,x : \{b : Bool, f : \{a : Bool\}\} \to Int.x.f(x)$

(12) Verify whether: (a) $f' : 2..5 \to Int \leq f : 1..4 \to Int$, (b) $\{a : Bool, f : Bool \to Int\} \leq$ (c) $\{a : Int, f : Int \to Int\}$, and (d) $\lambda\,x : \{a : Bool\} \to Int \leq \lambda\,x : \{a : Bool, f : Bool \to Int\} \to Int$.

(13) Explain how you may model abstract data types as existential types.

(14) What realizations of the type $\exists\,\alpha.\{a : \alpha, f : \alpha \to Bool\}$ can you think of? Give at least two examples.

(15) Prove that $\mu\,\alpha.\{c : \alpha, b : \alpha \to \alpha\} \not\leq \mu\,\alpha.\{b : \alpha \to \alpha\}$.

(16) Prove that $\mu\,\alpha.\{c : \alpha, b : \tau \to \alpha\} \leq \tau$, for $\tau = \mu\,\alpha.\{b : \alpha \to \alpha\}$.

Further reading

As further reading I recommend Cardelli and Wegner (1985) and Pierce (1993). Additional papers on the lambda calculus approach may be found at `ftp.dcs.ed.ac.uk:pub/bcp`. See appendix G. This collection includes a paper containing exercises and solutions, employing a tool *fomega*. As another source of material and exercises consult Palsberg and Schwartzback (1994).

10

Behavioral refinement

Ultimately, types are meant to specify behavior in an abstract way. To capture behavioral properties, we will generalize our notion of *types as constraints* to include behavioral descriptions in the form of logical assertions.

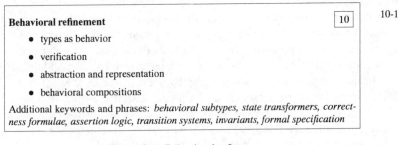

Slide 10-1: Behavioral refinement

In this chapter we will explore the notion of behavioral (sub)types. First we characterize the trade-offs between statically imposed (typing) constraints and dynamic constraints resulting from the specification of behavioral properties. We will provide a brief introduction to the assertion logic underlying the verification of behavioral constraints. Also, we look at how we may characterize the behavior of object-based systems in a mathematical way. Then we will describe the duality between abstraction and representation in defining behavioral subtypes that define concrete realizations of abstract specifications. In particular, we specify the correspondence requirements for behavioral subtypes. We will conclude this chapter by discussing the problems involved in specifying behavioral compositions, and explore what specification techniques are available to model the behavior of object-based systems.

10.1   Types as behavior

In the previous chapter we have developed a formal definition of types and the subtyping relation. However, we have restricted ourselves to (syntactic) signatures only, omitting (semantic) behavioral properties associated with function and object types.

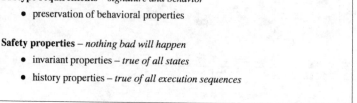

Slide 10-2: Subtyping and behavior

From a behavioral perspective, the subtype requirements (implied by the substitutability property) may be stated abstractly as *the preservation of behavioral properties*. According to Liskov (1993), behavioral properties encompass *safety properties* (which express that nothing bad will happen) and *liveness properties* (which express that eventually something good will happen). For safety properties we may further make a distinction between *invariant properties* (which must be satisfied in all possible states) and *history properties* (that hold for all possible execution sequences). See slide 10-2.

Behavioral properties (that are generally not captured by the signature only) may be important for the correct execution of a program. For example, when we replace a *stack* by a *queue* (which both have the same signature if we rename *push* and *insert* into *put*, and *pop* and *retrieve* into *get*) then we will get incorrect results when our program depends upon the *LIFO* (*last-in first-out*) behavior of the stack.

As another example, consider the relation between a type *FatSet* (which supports the methods *insert*, *select* and *size*) and a type *IntSet* (which supports the methods *insert*, *delete*, *select* and *size*). See slide 10-3.

With respect to its signature, *IntSet* merely extends *FatSet* with a *delete* method and hence could be regarded as a subtype of *FatSet*. However, consider the history property stated above, which says that for any (*FatSet*) s, when an integer x is an element of s in state ϕ then x will also be an element of s in any state ψ that comes after ϕ. This property holds since instances of *FatSet* do not have a method *delete* by which elements can be removed. Now if we take this property into account, *IntSet* may not be regarded as a subtype of *FatSet*, since instances of *IntSet* may grow and shrink and hence do not respect the *FatSet* history property.

This observation raises two questions. Firstly, how can we characterize the behavior of an object or function and, more importantly, how can we extend our notion of types to include a behavioral description? And secondly, assuming that we have the means to

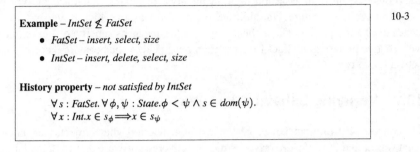

Example – *IntSet* $\not\le$ *FatSet*

- *FatSet* – insert, select, size
- *IntSet* – insert, delete, select, size

History property – *not satisfied by IntSet*

$\forall s : FatSet. \forall \phi, \psi : State. \phi < \psi \land s \in dom(\psi).$
$\forall x : Int.x \in s_{\phi} \Longrightarrow x \in s_{\psi}$

Slide 10-3: History properties – example

characterize the behavior of a function or object type, how can we verify that a subtype respects the behavioral constraints imposed by the supertype?

The answer to the first question is suggested by the observation that we may also express the constraints imposed by the signature by means of logical formulae that state the constraints as assertions which must be satisfied.

Types as behavior – *constraints*   10-4

- $x : 9..11 \Longleftrightarrow x : Int \land 9 \le x \le 11$

Behavioral constraints – *signature versus assertions*

- $f(x : 9..11) : 3..5\{...\}$

```
int f(int x) {
require( 9 ≤  x  && x ≤  11 );
...
promise( 3 ≤  result && result ≤  5);
return result;
}
```

Slide 10-4: Types and behavioral constraints

For example, we may express the requirement imposed by typing a variable as an element of an integer subrange also by stating that the variable is an integer variable that respects the bounds of the subrange. Similarly, we can express the typing constraints on the domain and range of a function by means of pre- and post-conditions asserting these constraints. See slide 10-4.

More generally, we may characterize the behavior of a function type by means of pre- and post-conditions and the behavior of an object type by means of pre- and post-conditions for its methods and an invariant clause expressing the invariant properties of its state and behavior. Recall that this is precisely what is captured in our notion of *contract*, as discussed in section 3.3.

With regard to the second question, to verify behavioral properties (expressed as assertions) we need an assertion logic in the style of Hoare. Such a logic will be discussed in the next section. In addition, we need a way in which to verify that (an instance of) a subtype respects the behavioral properties of its supertype. In section 10.4.2 we will give precise guidelines for a programmer to check the behavioral correspondence between two types.

10.2   Verifying behavioral properties

The concern with program correctness stems from a period when projects were haunted by what was called the *software crisis*. Projects delivered software that contained numerous bugs and large programs seemed to become unmanageable, that is never error-free. One of the most radical ideas proposed to counteract the software crisis was to require that programs should formally be proven correct before acceptance. The charm of the idea, I find personally, is that programming in a way becomes imbued with the flavor of mathematics, which may in itself be one of the reasons that the method never became very popular.

10.2.1   State transformers

Proving the correctness of (imperative) programs is based on the notion of *states* and the interpretation of programs as *state transformers*. A *state*, in a mathematical sense, is simply a function that records a value for each variable in the program. For example, having a program S in which the (integer) variable i occurs, and a state ϕ, we may have $\phi(i) = 3$. States may be modified by actions that result from executing the program, such as by an assignment of a value to a variable. We employ *substitutions* to modify a state. As before, substitutions may be defined by an equation, as given in slide 10-5.

$$\phi[x := v](y) = \begin{cases} v & \text{if } x = y \\ \phi(y) & \text{otherwise} \end{cases}$$

10-5

Slide 10-5: Substitution

A substitution $\phi[x := v](y)$ states that modifying ϕ by assigning the value v to the variable x then, for a variable y, the state ϕ will deliver v whenever y is identical to x and $\phi(y)$ otherwise.

When we have, for example, an assignment $i = 5$ then we have as the corresponding transition

$$\phi \xrightarrow{i=5} \phi'$$

where $\phi' = \phi[i := 5]$, that is ϕ' is like ϕ except for the variable i for which the value 5 will now be delivered.

Whenever we have a sequence of actions $a_1, ..., a_n$ then, starting from a state ϕ_0 we have corresponding state transformations resulting in states $\phi_1, ..., \phi_{n-1}$ as intermediary states and ϕ_n as the final state. Often the states ϕ_0 and ϕ_n are referred to as respectively the *input* and *output* state and the program that results in the actions $a_1, ..., a_n$ as the *state transformer* modifying ϕ_0 into ϕ_n.

10-6

Program state $- \phi$

- $\phi \in \Sigma : Var \rightarrow Value$

State transformations $-$ *operations* $a_1, a_2, ..., a_n$

- $\phi_0 \xrightarrow{a_1} \phi_1... \xrightarrow{a_n} \phi_n$

Correctness formulae $-$ *Hoare logic*

- $\{P\}S\{Q\}$

Verification

- $\phi_i \xrightarrow{a} \phi_j \wedge \phi_i \models P \Longrightarrow \phi_j \models Q$

Slide 10-6: The verification of state transformations

To characterize the actions that result from executing a program, we need an operational semantics that relates the programming constructs to the dynamic behavior of a program. We will study such a semantics in section 10.3.

The requirements a program (fragment) has to meet may be expressed by using predicates characterizing certain properties of a program state. Then, all we need to do is check whether the final state of a computation satisfies these requirements.

Predicates characterizing the properties of a state before and after executing a program (fragment) may be conveniently stated by correctness formulae of the form

$$\{P\}S\{Q\}$$

where S denotes a program (fragment) and P and Q respectively the pre-condition and post-condition associated with S.

A formula of the form $\{P\}S\{Q\}$ is true if, for every initial state ϕ that satisfies P and for which the computation characterized by S terminates, the final state ϕ' satisfies Q. This interpretation of $\{P\}S\{Q\}$ characterizes *partial correctness*, partial since the truth of the formula is dependent on the termination of S (which may, for example, for a *while statement*, not always be guaranteed). When termination can be guaranteed, then we may use the stronger notion of *total correctness*, which makes the truth of $\{P\}S\{Q\}$ no longer dependent on the termination of S.

Pre- and post-conditions may also be used to check invariance properties. As an example, consider the following correctness formula:

$$\{s = i * (i + 1)/2\}i = i + 1; s = s + i; \{s = i * (i + 1)/2\}$$

It states that the begin and end state of the computation characterized by $i = i + 1; s = s + i$ is invariant with respect to the condition $s = i * (i + 1)/2$. As an exercise, try to establish the correctness of this formula!

To verify whether for a particular program fragment S and (initial) state ϕ_i satisfying P the correctness formula $\{P\}S\{Q\}$ holds, we need to compute the (final) state ϕ_j and check that Q is true for ϕ_j. In general, for example in the case of non-deterministic programs, there may be multiple (final) states resulting from the execution of S. For each of these states we have to establish that it satisfies (the post-condition) Q. We call the collection of possible computation sequences of a program fragment S the *traces* of S. Traces characterize the (operational) behavior of a program.

10.2.2 Assertion logic

Reasoning about program states based on the traces of a program may be quite cumbersome. Moreover, a disadvantage is that it relies to a great extent on our operational intuition of the effect of a program on a state. Instead, Hoare (1969) has proposed using an axiomatic characterization of the correctness properties of programming constructs. An axiomatic definition allows us to prove the correctness of a program with respect to the conditions stating its requirements by applying the appropriate inference rules.

Axioms   10-7

- assignment – $\{Q[x := e]\}x = e\{Q\}$
- composition – $\{P\}S_1\{R\} \land \{R\}S_2\{Q\} \Longrightarrow \{P\}S_1; S_2\{Q\}$
- conditional – $\{P \land b\}S\{Q\} \Longrightarrow \{P\}$ *if* $(b)S\{Q\}$
- iteration – $\{I \land b\}S\{I\} \Longrightarrow \{I\}while(b)S\{I \land \neg b\}$

Consequence rules

- $P \rightarrow R \land \{R\}S\{Q\} \Longrightarrow \{P\}S\{Q\}$
- $R \rightarrow Q \land \{P\}S\{R\} \Longrightarrow \{P\}S\{Q\}$

Procedural abstraction

- $m(x) \mapsto S(x) \land \{P\}S(e)\{Q\} \Longrightarrow \{P\}m(e)\{Q\}$

Slide 10-7: The correctness calculus

In slide 10-7 correctness axioms have been given for *assignment, sequential composition, conditional statements* and *iteration*. These axioms rely on the side-effect free nature of expressions in the programming language. Also, they assume convertibility between programming language expressions and the expressions used in the assertion language.

The *assignment* axiom states that for any post-condition Q we can derive the (weakest) pre-condition by substituting the value e assigned to the variable x for x in Q. This axiom is related to the weakest pre-condition calculus introduced by Dijkstra (1976). It is perhaps the most basic axiom in the correctness calculus for imperative programs. As an example, consider the assignment $x = 3$ and the requirement $\{P\}\,x = 3\,\{y = x\}$. Applying the assignment axiom we have $\{y = 3\}\,x = 3\,\{y = x\}$. Consequently, when we are able to prove that P implies $y = 3$, we have, by virtue of the first *consequence* rule, proved that $\{P\}\ x = 3\ \{x = y\}$.

The next rule, for *sequential composition*, allows us to break a program (fragment) into parts. For convenience, the correctness formulae for multiple program fragments that are composed in sequential order are often organized as a so-called proof outline of the form $\{P\}\ S_1\ \{R\}\ S_2\ \{Q\}$. When sufficiently detailed, proof outlines may be regarded as a proof. For example, the proof outline

$$\{s = i*(i+1)/2\}\, i = i+1;\ \{s+i = i*(i+1)/2\}\, s = s+i;\ \{s = i*(i+1)/2\}$$

constitutes a proof for the invariance property discussed earlier. Clearly, the correctness formula for the two individual components can be proved by applying the assignment axiom. Using the sequential composition rule, these components can now be easily glued together.

As a third rule, we have a rule for conditional statements of the form *if* $(b)\ S$. As an example, consider the correctness formula

$$\{\textit{true}\}\quad \textit{if}\ (x > y)\ z = x;\ \{z > y\}$$

All we need to prove, by virtue of the inference rule for conditional statements, is that $\{x > y\}\ z = x\ \{z > y\}$ which (again) immediately follows from the assignment axiom.

As the last rule for proving correctness, we present here the inference rule for iterative (*while*) statements. The rule states that whenever we can prove that a certain invariant I is maintained when executing the body of the *while* statement (provided that the condition b is satisfied) then, when terminating the loop, we know that both I and $\neg b$ hold. As an example, the formula

$$\{\textit{true}\}\ \text{while}\ (i>0)\ i\text{--};\ \{i \leq 0\}$$

trivially follows from the *while* rule by taking I to be *true*.

Actually, the *while* rule plays a crucial role in constructing verifiable algorithms in a structured way. The central idea, advocated among others by Gries (1981), is to develop the algorithm around a well-chosen invariant. Several heuristics may be applied to find the proper invariant starting from the requirements expressed in the (output) predicate stating the post-condition.

In addition to the assignment axiom and the basic inference rules related to the major constructs of imperative programming languages, we may use so-called *structural* rules to facilitate the actual proof of a correctness formula. The first structural (*consequence*) rule states that we may replace a particular pre-condition for which we can prove a correctness formula (pertaining to a program fragment S) by any pre-condition of which the original pre-condition is a consequence, in other words which is stronger than the original pre-condition. Similarly, we may replace a post-condition for which we know a correctness formula to hold by any post-condition that is weaker than the original post-condition. As an example, suppose that we have proved the formula

$$\{x \geq 0\}\ S\ \{x < 0\}$$

then we may, by simultaneously applying the two consequence rules, derive the formula

$$\{x > 0\}\ S\ \{x \leq 0\}$$

which amounts to strengthening the pre-condition and weakening the post-condition. The intuition justifying this derivation is that we can safely *promise less and require more*, as it were.

Finally, the rule most important to us in the present context is the inference rule characterizing correctness under *procedural abstraction*. Assuming that we have a function m with formal parameter x (for convenience we assume we have only one parameter, but this can easily be generalized to multiple parameters), of which the (function) body consists of $S(x)$. Now, moreover, assume that we can prove for an arbitrary expression e the correctness formula $\{P\}\ S(e)\ \{Q\}$, with e substituted for the formal parameter x in both the conditions and the function body, then we also have that $\{P\}\ m(e)\ \{Q\}$, provided that P and Q do not contain references to local variables of the function m.

In other words, we may abstract from a complex program fragment by defining a function or procedure and use the original (local) correctness proof by properly substituting actual parameters for formal parameters. The *procedural abstraction* rule, which allows us to employ functions to perform correct operations, may be regarded as the basic construct needed to verify that an object embodies a (client/server) *contract*.

10.3   On the notion of behavior

The assertion logic presented in the previous section allows us to reason about the behavior of a system without explicitly generating the possible sequences of states resulting from the execution of the program. However, underlying the inference rules of our assertion logic we need a mathematical model for the operational behavior of a system.

An operational model is needed to prove the soundness of the inference rules. Further, an operational model may aid in understanding the meaning of particular language constructs and their associated correctness rules. In the following we will sketch the construction of a *transition system* modeling the behavior of an object-based program. Studying the formal semantics is relevant to understanding object orientation only in so far as it provides a means with which to characterize the desired behavior of object creation and message passing in an unambiguous manner.

Transition system A transition system for a program is a collection of rules that collectively describe the effect of executing the statements of the program. A labeled transition system is one that enables us to label the transition from one state to another by some label indicating the observable behavior of a program step.

In the transition system defined below, we will employ states ϕ, which may be decorated by object identifiers α, as in ϕ^α. Object identifiers are created when creating a new instance of an object type τ. We assume newly created object identifiers to be unique.

We assume that each object type τ has a constructor (which is a, possibly empty, statement that we write as S_τ) and an arbitrary number of methods m. Each method m is assumed to be defined by some statement, that we write as $S_m(e)$, for method calls of the form $m(e)$. Also we allow an object α of type τ to have attributes or instance variables v that may be accessed (read-only) as $\alpha.v$ for an object identifier α or $x.v$ for an object variable x (which must have α as its value).

To determine the visible behavior of a program, we will employ labels of the form α (to denote the creation of an object α) and m_α (to indicate the invocation of a method m for object α). We allow transitions to be labeled by sequences of labels that we write as λ and which are concatenated in the usual way.

We will define a transition system for a simple language of which the syntax is defined in slide 10-8.

Expressions syntax   10-8

- $e ::= v \mid x.v$

Elementary statements

- $s ::= v = e \mid x = new\,\tau \mid x.m(e)$

Compound statement

- $S ::= \varepsilon \mid s \mid S_1; S_2 \mid \quad if \;\; (b)\,S \mid while\,(b)\,S$

Slide 10-8: The syntax of a simple OO language

Expressions are either local variables v or object instance variables that we write as $x.v$, where x is an object variable. As elementary statements we have $v = e$ (indicating the assignment of (the value of) an expression e to a local variable v), $x = new\,\tau$ (which stands for the creation of a new object of type τ), and $x.m(e)$ (which calls a method m with arguments e for object x). The object variable x is associated with an object identifier α by the state ϕ in which the statement in which x occurs is executed. As compound statements we have an empty statement ε (that is needed for technical reasons), an elementary statement s (as defined above), a sequential composition statement, a conditional statement and an iteration statement, similar to that in the previous section.

The transition rules for elementary statements are given in slide 10-9.

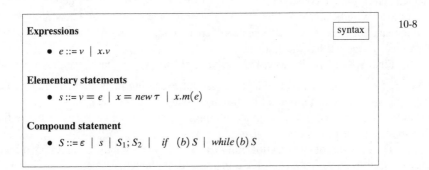

Slide 10-9: Transition system – rules

The *assignment* rule states that the assignment of (the value of) an expression e to a (local) variable v in state ϕ decorated by an object identifier α results in the empty statement and the state ϕ modified by assigning the value of e in ϕ (which is written as e_ϕ) to the instance variable v of object α. Hence, decorations allow us to work in the local environment of the object indicated by the decoration.

The *object creation* rule states that if we assume a transition $\langle S_\tau, \phi^\alpha \rangle \xrightarrow{\lambda} \langle \varepsilon, \phi' \rangle$ (which states that the constructor for type τ executed in state ϕ decorated by α results in the state ϕ' with behavior λ) then we may interpret the creation of a new τ object to result in behavior $\alpha \cdot \lambda$ (where α is the newly created object identifier) and state ϕ' in which the object variable x has the value α.

Finally, in a similar way, the *method call* rule states that if we assume a transition $\langle S_m(e), \phi^\alpha \rangle \xrightarrow{\lambda} \langle \varepsilon, \phi' \rangle$ (which states that executing the statement $S_m(e)$, that is the code associated with method m and arguments e, for object α in state ϕ, results in behavior λ and state ϕ') then we may interpret the method call $x.m(e)$ in ϕ as a transition to state ϕ' displaying behavior $m_\alpha \cdot \lambda$.

The rules for object creation and method call already indicate that transition rules may be used to construct a complex transition from elementary steps. In other words, a transition system defines a collection of proof rules that allow us to derive (state) transitions and to characterize the behavior that may be observed. To obtain a full derivation, we need in addition to the rules for elementary statements the rules for compound statements listed in slide 10-10.

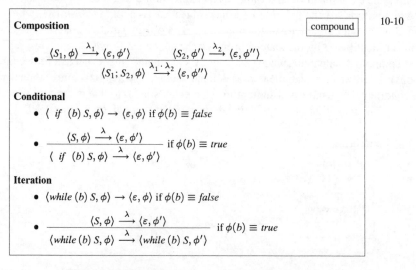

Composition | compound | 10-10

$$\frac{\langle S_1, \phi \rangle \xrightarrow{\lambda_1} \langle \varepsilon, \phi' \rangle \qquad \langle S_2, \phi' \rangle \xrightarrow{\lambda_2} \langle \varepsilon, \phi'' \rangle}{\langle S_1; S_2, \phi \rangle \xrightarrow{\lambda_1 \cdot \lambda_2} \langle \varepsilon, \phi'' \rangle}$$

Conditional

- $\langle \; if \; (b) \; S, \phi \rangle \rightarrow \langle \varepsilon, \phi \rangle$ if $\phi(b) \equiv false$

- $\dfrac{\langle S, \phi \rangle \xrightarrow{\lambda} \langle \varepsilon, \phi' \rangle}{\langle \; if \; (b) \; S, \phi \rangle \xrightarrow{\lambda} \langle \varepsilon, \phi' \rangle}$ if $\phi(b) \equiv true$

Iteration

- $\langle while \; (b) \; S, \phi \rangle \rightarrow \langle \varepsilon, \phi \rangle$ if $\phi(b) \equiv false$

- $\dfrac{\langle S, \phi \rangle \xrightarrow{\lambda} \langle \varepsilon, \phi' \rangle}{\langle while \; (b) \; S, \phi \rangle \xrightarrow{\lambda} \langle while \; (b) \; S, \phi' \rangle}$ if $\phi(b) \equiv true$

Slide 10-10: Transition system – compound statement

The *composition* rule states that if a statement S_1 transforms ϕ into ϕ' with behavior λ_1 and S_2 transforms ϕ' into ϕ'' with behavior λ_2 then the compound statement $S_1; S_2$ transforms ϕ into ϕ'' with behavior $\lambda_1 \cdot \lambda_2$.

The *conditional* rules state that, dependent on the value of the boolean b, the statement *if* (b) S has either no effect or results in a state ϕ' assuming that S transforms ϕ into ϕ' with behavior λ.

The *iteration* rules state that dependent on the value of the boolean b the statement *while* (b) S has either no effect or results in a state ϕ' assuming that S transforms ϕ into ϕ' with behavior λ. In contrast to the conditional, an iteration statement is repeated when b is true, in accordance with our operational understanding of iteration.

Example In our rules we have made a distinction between unadorned states ϕ and states ϕ^α decorated with an object identifier α. This reflects the distinction between the execution of a program fragment in a global context and a local context, within the confines of a particular object α.

Assume, for example, that we have defined a counter type *ctr* with a method *inc* that adds one to an instance variable n. In slide 10-11, a derivation is given of the behavior resulting from a program fragment consisting of the creation of an instance of *ctr*, a method call to *inc* and the assignment of the value of the attribute n of the counter to a variable v.

10-11

Program

- $x = new\ ctr; x.inc(); v = x.n$

Transitions

- $\langle x = new\ ctr, \phi_1 \rangle \xrightarrow{ctr_1} \langle \varepsilon, \phi_1[x := ctr_1] \rangle$ [1]
- $\langle n = n + 1, \phi_2^\alpha \rangle \rightarrow \langle \varepsilon, \phi_2[\alpha.n = \alpha.n + 1] \rangle$ [2]
- $\langle x.inc(), \phi_2 \rangle \xrightarrow{inc_\alpha} \langle \varepsilon, \phi_2[\phi_2(x).n := \phi_2(x).n] \rangle$ [2']
- $\langle v = x.n, \phi_3 \rangle \rightarrow \langle \varepsilon, \phi_3[v := \phi_3(x).n] \rangle$ [3]

Trace

- $\phi \xrightarrow{\lambda} \phi'$ with $\phi = \phi_1$, $\phi' = \phi_3$ and $\lambda = ctr_1 \cdot inc_\alpha$

Slide 10-11: Transitions – example

To derive the transition $\phi \xrightarrow{\lambda} \phi'$ corresponding with the program fragment $x = new\ ctr; x.inc(); v = x.n$ we must dissect the fragment and construct transitions for each of its (elementary) statements as shown in [1], [2] and [3]. The second statement, the method call $x.inc()$, needs two transitions [2] and [2'], of which the first represents the execution of the body of *inc* in the local context of the object created in [1] and the second represents the effect of the method call from a global perspective. For the first statement, we have assumed that the constructor for *ctr* is empty and may hence be omitted. Notice that the object identifier α (introduced in [1]) is assumed in [2] to effect the appropriate local changes to n.

After constructing the transitions for the individual statements we may compose these transitions by applying the composition rule and, in this case, identifying ϕ_2 with $\phi_1[x := \alpha]$ and ϕ_3 with $\phi_2[\alpha.n := \alpha.n + 1]$. As observable behavior we obtain $ctr_1 \cdot inc_\alpha$

(where $ctr_1 = \alpha$), which represents the creation of a counter and its subsequent modification by *inc*.

Discussion Transition systems, such as the one given above, were originally introduced as a means to model the behavior of CSP. They have been extensively used to model the operational semantics of programming languages, including concurrent and object-oriented languages. See, for example, America *et al.* (1989) and Eliëns (1992).

In Apt and Olderog (1991), transition systems have been used as a model to prove the soundness and completeness of correctness rules for concurrent programming constructs. Also in America and de Boer (1993), transition systems are used to demonstrate the validity of a proof system for a parallel object-oriented programming language. The interested reader is invited to explore the sources mentioned for further study.

10.4 Objects as behavioral types

A syntax directed correctness calculus as presented in section 10.2 provides, in principle, excellent support for a problem-oriented approach to program development, provided that the requirements a program has to meet can be made explicit in a mathematical, logical framework.

When specifying requirements, we are primarily interested in the abstract properties of a program, as may be expressed in some mathematical domain. However, when actually implementing the program (and verifying its correctness) we mostly need to take recourse to details we do not wish to bother with when reasoning on an abstract level. In this section we will discuss how we may verify that an abstract type is correctly implemented by a behavioral (implementation) subtype, following America (1990). Also, we will define precise guidelines for determining whether two (behavioral) types satisfy the (behavioral) subtype relation, following Liskov (1993).

10.4.1 Abstraction and representation

In America (1990) a proposal is sketched to define the functionality of objects by means of *behavioral types*. Behavioral types characterize the behavioral properties of objects in terms of (possible) modifications of an abstract state. So as to be able to ignore the details of an implementation when reasoning about the properties of a particular program, we may employ a *representation abstraction function* which maps the concrete data structures and operations to their counterparts in the abstract domain.

The diagram in slide 10-12 pictures the reasoning involved in proving that a particular implementation is correct with respect to a specification in some abstract mathematical domain. Assume that we have, in the concrete domain, an action a that corresponds with a state transformation function ξ. Now assume that we have a similar operation in the abstract domain, that we will write as $\alpha(a)$, with a corresponding state transformation function $\alpha(\xi)$. To prove that the concrete operation a correctly implements the abstract operation $\alpha(a)$, we must prove that the concrete state modification ξ resulting from a corresponds with the modification that occurs in the abstract domain. Technically speaking, we must prove that the diagram above commutes, that is, that $\xi(\phi) = \phi' \Longleftrightarrow \alpha(\xi)(\alpha(\phi)) = \alpha(\phi')$ whenever we have that $\phi \xrightarrow{a} \phi'$.

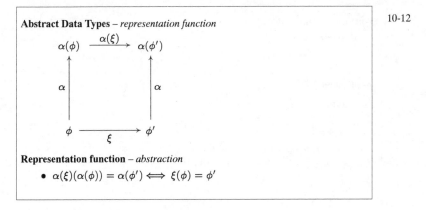

Slide 10-12: Abstraction and representation

To prove that a particular implementation a respects the abstract operation $\alpha(a)$, for which we assume that it has abstract pre- and post-conditions $\alpha(P)$ and $\alpha(Q)$, we must find a representation invariant I and (concrete) pre- and post-conditions P and Q for which we can prove that $\alpha(P) \wedge I \Longrightarrow P$ and that $\alpha(Q) \wedge I \Longrightarrow Q$. Furthermore, the representation invariant I must hold before and after the concrete operation a.

The proof strategy outlined above is of particular relevance for object-oriented program development, since the behavior of objects may, as we have already seen, be adequately captured by *contracts*. As an additional advantage, however, the method outlined enables us to specify the behavior of an object in a more abstract way than allowed by contracts as supported by Eiffel.

Realization As an example, consider the specification of a generic *stack* as given in slide 10-13. The specification of the stack is based on the (mathematically) well-known notion of *sequences*. We distinguish between empty sequences, that we write as $\langle \rangle$, and non-empty (finite) sequences, that we write as $\langle x_1, ..., x_n \rangle$. Further, we assume to have a concatenation operator for which we define $s \cdot \langle \rangle = \langle \rangle \cdot s = s$ and $\langle x_1, ..., x_n \rangle \cdot \langle y_1, ..., y_m \rangle = \langle x_1, ..., x_n, y_1, ..., y_m \rangle$. A sequence is employed to represent the state of the stack.

The operations *push* and *pop* may conveniently be defined with reference to the sequence representing the (abstract) state of the stack. We use s and s' to represent the state respectively before and after the operation. The operations themselves are completely specified by their respective pre- and post-conditions. Pushing an element e results in concatenating the one-element sequence $\langle e \rangle$ to the stacks state. For the operation *pop* we require that the state of the stack must be non-empty. The post-condition specifies that the resulting state s' is a prefix of the original state, that is the original state with the last element (that is returned as a result) removed.

To prove that a particular implementation of the *stack* is conformant with the type definition given above we must prove that

$$\{I \wedge pre(\alpha(m(e)))\}\, m(e)\, \{I' \wedge post(\alpha(m(e)))\}$$

for both methods *push* and *pop*. These proofs involve both an abstraction function α and

---

Sequences – *abstract domain*   10-13

- empty sequence – $\langle \rangle$
- concatenation – $\langle x_1, .., x_n \rangle \cdot \langle y_1, .., y_m \rangle = \langle x_1, .., x_n, y_1, .., y_m \rangle$

Specification

    type stack T {
    $s : seq\,T$;
    axioms:
    $\{true\}push(t : T)\{s' = s \cdot \langle t \rangle\}$
    $\{s \neq \langle \rangle\}pop()\{s = s' \cdot \langle result \rangle\}$
    };

Slide 10-13: The specification of a stack

a representation invariant I, relating the abstract state of the stack to the concrete state of the implementation.

Now consider an implementation of the generic stack in C++, as given in slide 10-14.

---

template< class T > | implementation | 10-14

class as {
int t;
T a[MAX];
public:
as() { t = 0; }
void push(T e) { *require*(t< MAX-1); a[t++] = e; }
T pop() { *require*(t> 0); *return* a[--t]; }
invariant: $0 \leq t \;\&\&\; t < MAX$;
};

Slide 10-14: The realization of a stack

To prove that this implementation may be regarded as an element of the (abstract) type *stack*, we must find a representation (abstraction) function to map the concrete implementation to the abstract domain, and further we must specify a *representation invariant* that allows us to relate the abstract properties to the properties of the implementation.

For the implementation in slide 10-14, the abstraction function α simply creates the sequence of length t, with elements $a[0], ..., a[t-1]$. The representation invariant, moreover, gives an explicit definition of this relation. See slide 10-15.

In order to verify that our implementation of the abstract data type *stack* is correct (that is as long as the bound *MAX* is not exceeded), we must show, given that the representation invariant holds, that the pre-conditions of the concrete operations imply

Abstraction function

- $\alpha(a, t) = \; <a[0], ..., a[t]>$

Representation invariant

- $I(a, t, s) \equiv t = length(s) \wedge t \geq 0 \wedge s = \alpha(a, t)$

10-15

Slide 10-15: Abstraction function and representation invariant

the pre-conditions of the corresponding abstract operations, and, similarly, that the post-conditions of the abstract operations imply the post-conditions of the concrete operations.

First, we show that for the operation *push* the post-condition of the abstract type specification is indeed stronger than the (implicit) post-condition of the implementation. This is expressed by the following formula.

$$s' = s \cdot < e > \wedge I(a', t', s') \Longrightarrow t' = t + 1 \wedge a'[t'] = e$$

Since we know that $I(a', t', s')$, we may derive that $t' = t + 1$ and $a'[t'] = e$.

To establish the correctness of the operation *pop*, we must prove that the pre-condition specified for the abstract operation is indeed stronger than the pre-condition specified for the concrete operation, as expressed by the formula

$$I(a, t, s) \wedge s \neq <> \Longrightarrow t > 0$$

It is easy to see that $t > 0$ immediately follows from the requirement that the sequence is non-empty.

Finally, to prove that the operator *pop* leaves the stack in a correct state, we must prove that

$$s = s' \cdot < result > \wedge I(a', t', s') \Longrightarrow result = a'[t] \wedge t' = t - 1$$

which is done in a similar manner as for *push*.

10.4.2 Correspondence

Behavioral refinement is not restricted to the realization of abstract specifications. We will now look at a definition of behavioral refinement, following Liskov (1993), that may serve as a guideline for programmers to define behavioral subtypes, both abstract and concrete, including subtypes extending the behavioral repertoire of their supertypes.

In Liskov (1993) the relation between behavioral types is explained by means of a so-called *correspondence mapping*, that relates a subtype to its (abstract) supertype.

A *correspondence mapping* is a triple consisting of an *abstraction* function α (that projects the values of the subtype on the value domain of the supertype), a *renaming* ρ (that defines the relation between methods defined in both types) and an *extension* map ξ (that defines the meaning of additional methods). See slide 10-16. Technically, the function α must be *onto*, that is each value of the supertype domain must be representable

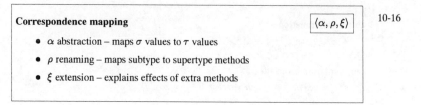

Slide 10-16: The subtype correspondence mapping

by one or more values of the subtype domain. Generally, when applying the abstraction function, we loose information (which is irrelevant from the perspective of the supertype), for example the specific ordering of items in a container.

To determine whether a type σ is a (behavioral) subtype of a type τ, one has to define a correspondence mapping $\langle \alpha, \rho, \xi \rangle$ and check the issues listed in slide 10-17.

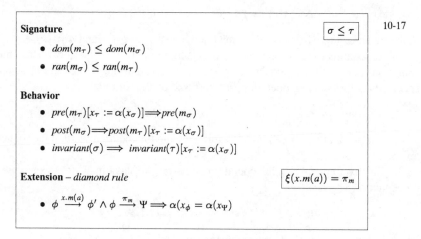

Slide 10-17: Behavioral subtyping constraints

First, syntactically, we must check that the signature of σ and τ satisfy the (signature) subtyping relation defined in the previous chapter. In other words, for each method m associated with the object type τ (which we call m_τ), and corresponding method m_σ (which is determined by applying the renaming ρ) we must check the (contravariant) function subtyping rule, that is $dom(m_\tau) \leq dom(m_\sigma)$ and $ran(m_\sigma) \leq ran(m_\tau)$, where ran is the range or result type of m.

Secondly, we must check that the behavioral properties of σ respect those of τ. In other words, for each method m occurring in τ we must check that $pre(m_\tau)[x_\tau := \alpha(x_\sigma)] \Longrightarrow pre(m_\sigma)$ and that $post(m_\sigma) \Longrightarrow post(m_\tau)[x_\tau := \alpha(x_\sigma)]$. Moreover, the invariant characterizing σ must respect the invariant characterizing τ, that is $invariant(\sigma) \Longrightarrow invariant(\tau)[x_\tau := \alpha(x_\sigma)]$. The substitutions $[x_\tau := \alpha(x_\sigma)]$ occurring in the behavioral rules are meant to indicate that each variable of type τ must be replaced by a corresponding variable of type σ to which the abstraction function is applied (in order to obtain a value in the (abstract) domain of τ).

And thirdly, in the final place, it must be shown that the extension map ξ is well-defined. The extension map must be defined in such a way that each method call for an object x of type σ, which we write as $x.m(a)$ where a represents the arguments to the call, is mapped to a program π_m in which only calls appear to methods shared by σ and τ (modulo renaming) or external function or method calls. In addition the *diamond rule* must be satisfied, which means that the states ϕ' and ψ resulting from applying respectively $x.m(a)$ and π_m in state ϕ must deliver identical values for x from the perspective of τ, that is after applying the abstraction function. In other words, extension maps allow us to understand the effect of adding new methods and to establish whether they endanger behavioral compatibility.

In Liskov (1993) a distinction is made between *constructors* (by which objects are created), *mutators* (that modify the state or value of an object) and *observers* (that leave the state of an object unaffected). Extension maps are only needed for mutator methods. Clearly, for *observer* methods the result of ξ is empty, and *constructors* are taken care of by the abstraction function.

Behavioral subtypes The behavioral subtyping rules defined above are applicable to arbitrary (sub)types, and not only to (sub)types defined by inheritance. As an example, we will sketch (still following Liskov (1993)) that a *stack* may be defined as a behavioral subtype of the type *bag*. Recall that a *bag* is a *set* allowing duplicates. See slide 10-18.

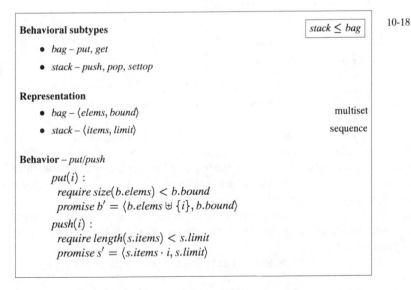

Slide 10-18: Behavioral subtypes – example

Let the type *bag* support the methods $put(i : Int)$ and $get() : Int$ and assume that the type *stack* supports the methods $push(i : Int)$, $pop() : Int$ and in addition a method $settop(i : Int)$ that replaces the top element of the stack with its argument. Now, assume that a *bag* is represented by a pair ⟨*elems, bound*⟩, where *elems* is a multiset (which is a set which may contain multiple elements of the same value) and *bound* is an integer indicating the maximal number of elements that may be in the *bag*. Further, we assume that a *stack* is represented as a pair ⟨*items, limit*⟩, where *items* is a sequence and *limit* is a the maximal length of the sequence. For example ⟨{1, 2, 7, 1}, 12⟩ is a legal value of *bag* and ⟨1 · 2 · 7 · 1, 12⟩ is a legal value of *stack*.

The behavioral constraints for respectively the method *put* for *bag* and *push* for *stack* are given as pre- and post-conditions in slide 10-18. To apply *put*, we require that the size of the multiset is strictly smaller than the bound and we ensure that the element *i* is inserted when that pre-condition is satisfied. The multi-set union operator ⊎ is employed to add the new element to the bag. Similarly, for *push* we require the length of the sequence to be smaller than the limit of the stack and we then ensure that the element is appended to the sequence. As before, we use the primed variables *b'* and *s'* to denote the value of respectively the bag *b* and the stack *s* after applying the operations, respectively *put* and *push*.

Proceeding from the characterization of *bag* and *stack* we may define the correspondence mapping ⟨α, ρ, ξ⟩ as in slide 10-19.

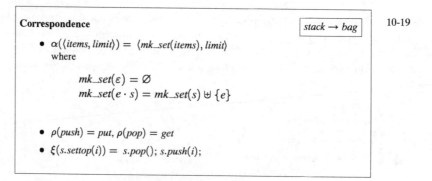

Slide 10-19: Behavioral subtypes – correspondence

To map the representation of a stack to the bag representation we use the function *mk_set* (which is inductively defined to map the empty sequence to the empty set and to transform a non-empty sequence into the union of the one-element multiset of its first element and the result of applying *mk_set* to the remaining part). The stack *limit* is left unchanged, since it directly corresponds with the bound of the bag.

The renaming function ρ maps *push* to *put* and *pop* to *get*, straightforwardly. And, the extension map describes the result of *settop(i)* as the application of (subsequently) *pop()* and *push(i)*.

With respect to the behavioral definitions given for *push* and *put* we have to verify that

$$pre(put(i))[b := \alpha(s)] \Longrightarrow pre(push(i))$$

and that

$$post(push(i)) \Longrightarrow post(put(i))[b := \alpha(s)].$$

Proof obligations – *push/put*

- $size(\alpha(s).elems) < \alpha(s).bound$
  $\Longrightarrow$
  $length(s.items) < s.limit$
- $s' = \langle s.items \cdot i, s.limit \rangle$
  $\Longrightarrow$
  $\alpha(s') = \langle \alpha(s).elems \uplus \{i\}, \alpha(s).bound \rangle$

Slide 10-20: Behavioral subtypes – proof obligations

These conditions, written out fully in slide 10-20, are easy to verify.

Generally, a formal proof is not really necessary to check that two types satisfy the behavioral subtype relation. As argued in Liskov (1993), the definition of the appropriate behavioral constraints and the formulation of a correspondence mapping is already a significant step towards verifying that the types have the desired behavioral properties.

10.5　Specifying behavioral compositions

The notion of *behavioral types* may be regarded as the formal underpinning of the notion of *contracts* specifying the interaction between a client and server (object). Cf. Meyer (1993). Due to the limited power of the (boolean) assertion language, contracts as supported by Eiffel are more limited in what may be specified than (a general notion of) behavioral types. However, some of the limitations are due, not to limitations on the assertion language, but to the local nature of specifying object behavior by means of contracts. See also Meyer (1993).

To conclude this chapter, we will look at an example illustrating the need to specify global invariants. Further we will briefly look at alternative formalisms for specifying the behavior of collections of objects, and in particular we will explore the interpretation of *contracts* as behavioral compositions.

Global invariants Invariants specify the constraints on the state of a system that must be met for the system to be consistent. Clearly, as elementary logic teaches us, an inconsistent system is totally unreliable.

Some inconsistencies cannot be detected locally, within the scope of an object, since they may be caused by actions that do not involve the object directly. An example of a situation in which an externally caused inconsistent object state may occur is given in slide 10-21. (The example is taken from Meyer (1993), but rephrased in C++.)

When creating an instance of A, the *forward* pointer to an instance of B is still empty. Hence, after creation, the invariant of the object is satisfied. Similarly when, after creating an instance of B, this instance is attached to the *forward* pointer, and as a consequence the object itself is attached to the *backward* pointer of the instance of B. After this, the invariant is still satisfied. However, when a second instance of A is created, for which the same instance of B is attached to the *forward* pointer, the invariant for this ob-

---

Problem – *dynamic aliasing*   10-21

```
class A {
public:
A() { forward = 0; }
attach(B* b) { forward = b; b→ attach(this); }
bool invariant() {
  return !forward || forward→ backward == this;
}
private:
B* forward;
};
class B {
public:
B() { backward = 0; }
attach(A* a) { backward = a; }
bool invariant() {
  return !backward || backward→ forward == this;
}
private:
A* backward;
};
```

Slide 10-21: Establishing global invariants

ject will hold, but as a result the invariance for the first instance of A will become violated. See below.

```
A a1, a2; B b;
a1.attach(b);
a2.attach(b);                                       // violates invariant a1
```

This violation cannot be detected by the object itself, since it is not involved in any activity. Of course, it is possible to check externally for the objects not directly involved whether their invariants are still satisfied. However, the cost of exhaustive checking will in general be prohibitive. Selective checking is feasible only when guided by an adequate specification of the possible interferences between object states.

Specifying interaction Elementary logic and set-theory provide a powerful vehicle for specifying the behavior of a system, including the interaction between its components. However, taking into account that many software developers prefer a more operational mode of thinking when dealing with the intricacies of complex interactions, we will briefly look at formalisms that allow a more explicit specification of the operational aspects of interaction and communication, yet support to some extent to reason about such specifications. See slide 10-22.

In Helm *et al.* (1990), a notion of *behavioral contracts* is introduced that allows for characterizing the behavior of compositions of objects. Behavioral contracts fit quite

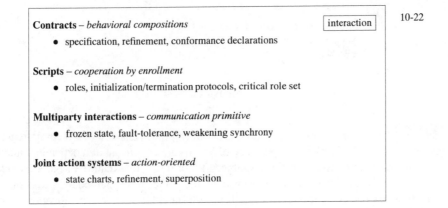

Contracts – *behavioral compositions* | interaction | 10-22
- specification, refinement, conformance declarations

Scripts – *cooperation by enrollment*
- roles, initialization/termination protocols, critical role set

Multiparty interactions – *communication primitive*
- frozen state, fault-tolerance, weakening synchrony

Joint action systems – *action-oriented*
- state charts, refinement, superposition

Slide 10-22: Specifying interactions

naturally in the object oriented paradigm, since they allow both refinement and (type) conformance declarations. See below. Somewhat unclear, yet, is what specification language the *behavioral contracts* formalism is intended to support. On the other hand, from an implementation perspective the interactions captured by behavioral contracts seem to be expressible also within the confines of a class system supporting generic classes and inheritance.

A similar criticism seems to be applicable to the formalism of (role) *scripts* as proposed in Francez *et al.* (1989). Role scripts allow the developer to specify the behavior of a system as a set of roles and the interaction between objects as subscribing to a role. In contrast to behavioral contracts, the script formalism may also be applied to describe the behavior of concurrently active objects. In particular, the script formalism allows for the specification of predefined initialization and termination policies and for the designation of a so-called *critical role set*, specifying the number and kind of participants minimally required for a successful computation.

Also directed towards the specification of concurrent systems is the *multi-party interactions* formalism proposed in Evangelist *et al.* (1989), which is centered around a (synchronous) communication primitive allowing multiple objects to interact simultaneously. The notion of *frozen state* (that may be understood as an invariance requirement that holds during the interaction) may be useful in particular for the specification of fault-tolerant systems. An interesting research issue in this respect is to what extent the assumption of synchrony may be weakened in favor of efficiency.

A rather different orientation towards specifying the interaction between collections of concurrently active objects is embodied by the *joint action systems* approach described in Kurki-Suonio and Jarvinen (1989). Instead of relying on the direct communication between objects *joint action systems* proceed from the assumption that there exists some global decision procedure that decides which actions (and interactions) are appropriate.

An example of an *action* specification is given in slide 10-23. Whether the *service* is performed depends upon the state of both the client and the server object selected

```
action service() by client c; server s is          10-23
when c.requesting && s.free do
<body>
```

Slide 10-23: Specifying actions – example

by the action manager. Kurki-Suonio and Jarvinen (1989) characterize their approach as *action-oriented* to stress the importance of specifying actions in an independent manner (as entities separate from classes and objects). An interesting feature of the *joint action systems* approach is that the behavior of individual objects is specified by means of *state charts*, a visual specification formalism based on Harel (1987). The specification formalism adopted gives rise to interesting variants on the object oriented repertoire, such as inheritance and refinement by superposition. From a pragmatic viewpoint, the assumption of a global manager seems to impose high demands on system resources. Yet, as a specification technique, the concept of *actions* may turn out to be surprisingly powerful.

In summary, this brief survey of specification formalisms demonstrates that there is a wide variety of potentially useful constructs that all bear some relevance to object oriented modeling, and as such may enrich the repertoire of (object oriented) system developers.

Contracts as protocols of interaction Contracts as supported by Eiffel and Annotated C++ are a very powerful means of characterizing the interaction between a server object and a client object. However, with software becoming increasingly complex, what we need is a mechanism to characterize the behavior of collections or compositions of objects as embodied in the notion of *behavioral contracts* as introduced in Helm *et al.* (1990).

A *contract* (in the extended sense) lists the objects that participate in the task and characterizes the dependencies and constraints imposed on their mutual interaction. For example, the contract *model-view*, shown below (in a slightly different notation than the original presentation in Helm *et al.* (1990)), introduces the object *model* and a collection of *view* objects. Also, it characterizes the minimal assumptions with respect to the functionality these objects must support and it gives an abstract characterization of the effect of each of the supported operations.

To indicate the type of variables, the notation $v : type$ is used expressing that variable v is typed as *type*. The object *subject* of type *model* has an instance variable *state* of type V that represents (in an abstract fashion) the value of the *model* object. Methods are defined using the notation

method $\mapsto$ action

Actions may consist either of other method calls or conditions that are considered to be satisfied after calling the method. Quantification as for example in

$\forall v \in$ views • v.update()

is used to express that the method *update()* is to be called for all elements in *views*.

10-24

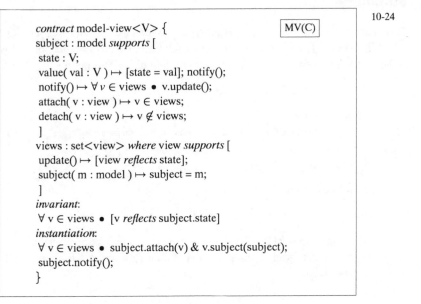

Slide 10-24: The Model-View contract

The *model-view* contract specifies in more formal terms the MV part of the MVC paradigm discussed in section 3.2.3. Recall, that the idea of a *model-view* pair is to distinguish between the actual information (which is contained in the *model* object) and the presentation of that information, which is taken care of by possibly multiple *view* objects.

The actual protocol of interaction between a *model* and its *view* objects is quite straightforward. Each *view* object may be considered as a handler that must minimally have a method to install a model and a method *update* which is invoked, as the result of the *model* object calling *notify*, whenever the information contained in the model changes. The effect of calling *notify*() is abstractly characterized as a universal quantification over the collection of *view* object. Calling *notify*() for *subject* results in calling *update*() for each *view*. The meaning of *update*() is abstractly represented as

update() ↦ [view *reflects* state];

which tells us that the *state* of the *subject* is adequately reflected by the *view* object.

The invariant clause of the *model-view* contract states that every change of the (state of the) *model* will be reflected by each *view*. The instantiation clause describes, in a rather operational way, how to initialize each object participating in the contract.

In order to instantiate such a contract, we need to define appropriate classes realizing the abstract entities participating in the contract, and further we need to define how these classes are related to their abstract counterparts in the contract by means of what we may call, following Helm *et al.* (1990), *conformance declarations*. Conformance declarations specify, in other words, how concrete classes embody an abstract role, similar as in the realization of a partial type by means of inheritance.

Summary

This chapter extended the notion of subtyping to include behavioral properties.

In section 1, we discussed the interpretation of types as behavior and we looked at the issues involved in preserving invariance and history properties.

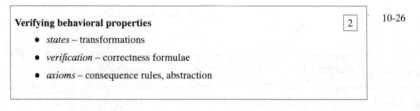

Types as behavior	1	10-25

- *subtype requirements* – preservation of behavioral properties
- *behavioral properties* – invariance, history
- *duality* – static versus dynamic constraints

Slide 10-25: Section 10.1: Types as behavior

Also, we discussed the duality between static and dynamic type constraints.

In section 2, a brief characterization of an assertion logic for verifying behavioral properties was given.

Verifying behavioral properties	2	10-26

- *states* – transformations
- *verification* – correctness formulae
- *axioms* – consequence rules, abstraction

Slide 10-26: Section 10.2: Verifying behavioral properties

We looked at a formal characterization of states and state transitions and correctness formulae were introduced as a means to verify the correctness of transitions.

We also looked at an axiomatic characterization of the correctness properties of programming language constructs.

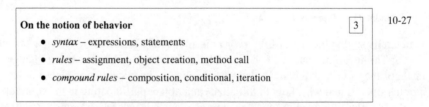

On the notion of behavior	3	10-27

- *syntax* – expressions, statements
- *rules* – assignment, object creation, method call
- *compound rules* – composition, conditional, iteration

Slide 10-27: Section 10.3: On the notion of behavior

In section 3, we looked at how the behavior of an object may be defined in a formal way by means of a transition system. A transition system for an object-based language specifies the rules for assignment, object creation and method call, as well as the computation steps resulting from the evaluation of compound statements.

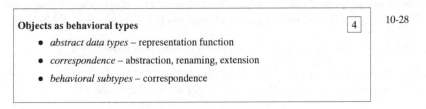

Slide 10-28: Section 10.4: Objects as behavioral types

In section 4, it was shown how actual objects may be related to abstract types by means of a representation abstraction function. Further, we discussed explicit guidelines for defining a subtype correspondence relation between behavioral types.

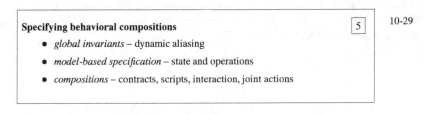

Slide 10-29: Section 10.5: Specifying behavioral compositions

Finally, in section 5, we looked at the problems involved in determining global invariants and we discussed what formal means we have available to specify behavioral properties of a collection of objects.

Questions

(1) How would you characterize the conformance requirements for subtyping? Explain what properties are involved.

(2) Give an example of signature compatible types not satisfying the history property.

(3) Explain the duality between imposing constraints statically and dynamically.

(4) How would you formally characterize program states and state transformations?

(5) Explain how you may verify the behavior of a program by means of correctness formulae.

(6) Characterize how the behavior of objects may be modeled by means of a transition system and specify a transition system for a simple object-oriented language.

(7) How would you characterize the relation between an abstract data type and its realizations?

(8) Give an example of an abstract specification of a *stack*. Define a realization and show that the realization is correct with respect to its abstract specification.

(9) Explain the notion of correspondence for behavioral subtypes.

(10) Show that a *stack* is a behavioral subtype of a *bag* by defining an appropriate correspondence relation. What proof obligations must be met?

(11) Discuss the problems involved in satisfying global invariance properties.

(12) What formal methods do you know that deal with specifying the behavior of collections of objects?

Further reading

As further reading with respect to the verification of programs, I recommend Apt and Olderog (1991) and Dahl (1992). An assertion logic for a parallel object-oriented language is presented in America and de Boer (1993).

Part IV

Object-Oriented Application Frameworks

11

Libraries and environments

Adopting an object-oriented approach is ultimately motivated by the need to develop applications. The advantage of an object-oriented approach lies in the opportunities for reuse, maintainability and interoperability of distinct software components.

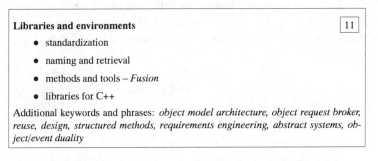

Libraries and environments	11

- standardization
- naming and retrieval
- methods and tools – *Fusion*
- libraries for C++

Additional keywords and phrases: *object model architecture, object request broker, reuse, design, structured methods, requirements engineering, abstract systems, object/event duality*

Slide 11-1: Chapter 11: Libraries and environments

From a pragmatic point of view, object-oriented technology supports a component-based approach. In this chapter, we will look at the standardization efforts undertaken by the OMG (Object Management Group) that are directed towards the interoperability of independent software components. Also, we will look at the design issues involved in developing library components by discussing the lessons drawn from the development of the Eiffel libraries. Further, we will discuss a number of the methods and tools available for object-oriented software development. We discuss the Fusion method in greater detail, then look at a number of libraries for C++. In particular, we will discuss the criteria by which such libraries may be evaluated before deciding to use them in an actual software development project.

11.1   Application integration – *standards*

The potential of an object-oriented approach, obviously, lies in the opportunities for *reuse*, both of code and design. However, reuse requires a common understanding of the basic principles underlying the technology and its application. More particularly, the reuse of code requires (a much more strict) agreement with respect to the components from which an application will be constructed and the language constructs used to implement them.

In this section, we will look at the object linking and embedding facilities offered by Microsoft OLE, and the standardization efforts undertaken by the OMG (Object Management Group) directed towards the interoperability of object components. In addition, we will look at the efforts of the ODMG (Object Database Management Group) undertaken to develop a standard for persistent objects. And, finally we will discuss the duality between object and events, which both play an important role in the design and realization of component-based systems.

11.1.1   Object linking and embedding

Reuse is not necessarily code sharing. In effect, there seems to be a trend towards sharing components at a higher level of granularity, as possibly independent applications. This approach has, for example, been taken by the Microsoft object linking and embedding facility (OLE), which offers support for embedding (a copy) of a component in a (container) component, for including a link to another component, and for storing compound objects. See slide 11-2.

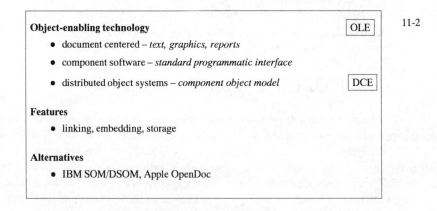

Slide 11-2: Object-enabling technology – OLE

The OLE technology is characterized by its developers as *object-enabling* technology, to contrast it with a more classical language-dependent object oriented approach relying on inheritance.

The object linking technology allows the user to maintain a link from one application to another, so that for example a text processor may directly employ the results of a spreadsheet. Moreover, object linking is dynamic and allows to reflect any updates in the spreadsheet application directly in the outcome of the text processor. In contrast, object embedding works more as the traditional *cut and paste* techniques in that it results in including only a copy of the material. To be embedded or linked, applications must satisfy a standard programmatic interface. In effect, the interface must provide facilities to request an update of the display of the information contained in the application. In this respect, the OLE technology may be characterized as *document-centered*.

The component object model underlying OLE allows for distribution along the DCE standard discussed in section 6.5. The commercial competitors are currently the Apple OpenDoc framework and the IBM SOM/DSOM realization of the OMG CORBA standard. It is interesting to note that future releases of OLE are also promised to be compatible with the CORBA standard.

11.1.2 Distribution – *OMG*

The ultimate goal of object technology may be phrased as the development of plug-compatible software that allows one to construct a particular application from off-the-shelf components. To achieve this goal, it is necessary to develop standards with respect to object interaction and communication interfaces that support *information sharing* between distinct components. Such standards are (being) developed by the OMG (the Object Management Group, in which the leading vendors of software systems participate, including Digital Equipment Corporation, Hewlett-Packard Company, HyperDesk Corporation, NCR Corporation, Object Design Inc. and Sunsoft Inc.). The OMG aims at defining standards for information sharing in widely distributed, heterogeneous (multi-vendor) networks to support the reusability and portability of commercially available components, and more generally, to develop the technology and guidelines that allow the interoperability of applications. See slide 11-3.

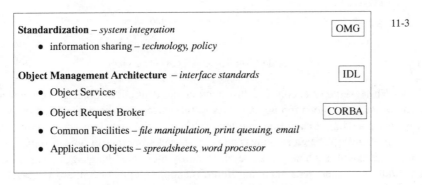

Slide 11-3: The OMG standardization effort

The OMG proceeds from the assumption that object technology (including encapsulation, polymorphism and inheritance) provides the mechanism necessary for language-, platform- and vendor-independent, *system integration*. The OMG has proposed an *abstract object model* and discusses technical and political objectives in the OMA Guide (Object Management Architecture Guide). The architecture specified in OMA provides a generic description of the components that constitute a system and defines the interface standards to which the components must comply.

An important aspect of OMA is the *interface description language* (IDL) that is introduced as a standard to describe object interfaces in a language independent manner.

According to OMA, a system must support a number of *Object Services* (dealing with the lifecycle of objects, persistence, naming an event notification), and a so-called *Object Request Broker* (which is an intermediary between the object providing a service and the client requesting a service). Also a system will need, generally, *Common Facilities* (such as file manipulation and print queuing), and in addition will contain a number of *Application Objects* (such as a spreadsheet or word-processor) that constitute the proper application.

The OMG is primarily concerned with the adoption of technology by the producers and vendors of common facilities and application objects. Its contribution in this respect is the definition of a set of common object services and a standard interface to invoke such services by means of an object request broker. This standard has been adopted in CORBA (the Common Object Request Broker Architecture) which allows for the interaction between an application and distinct object request brokers.

The *object services* envisioned in OMA are intended to deal with objects in a language- and platform-independent manner. See slide 11-4.

Object Services   11-4

- life cycle – *creation and deletion*
- persistence – *management of object storage*
- naming – *mapping names to references*
- event notification – *registration of events*

Future

- transactions, concurrency, relationships,...,time

Slide 11-4: The OMG Object Services

These services encompass the creation and deletion of objects, the management of object storage, the mapping of names to references and the registration of events as triggers for actions. In addition, services will be defined that allow transactions, concurrency, relationships between objects and time-based properties of objects to be specified. To a large extent, such services are provided by individual languages (such as C++ or Smalltalk) with their accompanying libraries and development frameworks (such as the X-window environment or the Unix operating system). However, the efforts of the OMG are directed towards (the ambitious goal of) providing such services in a generic fashion, independent of a particular language or environment.

11.1.3 Persistent objects – *ODMG*

In a similar vein as the OMG, a number of vendors of object database management systems (including SunSoft, Object Design, Ontos, O_2 Technology, Versant, Objectivity, Hewlett Packard, POET Software, Itasca, Intellitic, Digital Equipment Corporation, Servio, Texas Instruments) have participated in the ODMG (Object Database Management systems Group) to develop a standard for the definition and manipulation of persistent objects.

The standards proposal of the ODMG encompasses an object definition language ODL, which is intended as an extension of the OMG/IDL standard, an object manipulation language, OML and an object query language, OQL, that provides SQL-like facilities for the retrieval of information.

The advantage of employing an object database system over employing a relational database system is that, in principle, the application programmer may work within a unified type system, encompassing both persistent and transient objects. See slide 11-5.

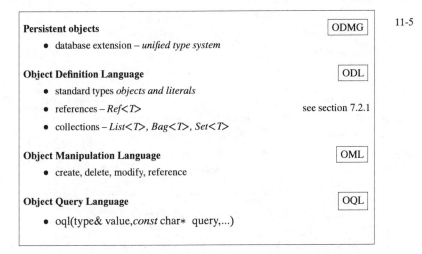

Slide 11-5: The ODMG-93 standardization efforts

The extensions to the various languages, which currently include only C++ and Smalltalk, involve the definition of persistent objects, the creation and use of objects and facilities to pose queries concerning their attributes and relations. These extensions are proposed as language-specific bindings for respectively ODL, OML and OQL.

The object model proposed by the ODMG supports *objects* (which may have attributes and methods), *literals* (which may be considered as primitive values), *relationships between objects* (including $m - n$ relations), *extents* (which contain the collection of instances of a particular type), and *named objects* (to facilitate retrieval).

To define objects and literals, the programmer may employ the standard types offered by the language, as well as a number of additional parametrized types to define references and collections. For references the ODMG-93 proposal employs the *Ref<T>* construct discussed in section 7.2.1. For dealing with collections a number of generic collection classes such as *List<T>*, *Bag<T>* and *Set<T>* must be provided by a standard library. (To provide a binding for Smalltalk, which does not have a type system, type annotations must be employed to define the properties of persistent objects.)

The manipulation of persistent objects conforms with the manipulation of ordinary objects as far as attribute access and method invocation are concerned. However, the language-specific OML bindings must take precautions for the creation, deletion and modification of objects. In particular, when employing a reference to a persistent object, the implementation must check whether the referenced object has been modified.

The C++ binding for the object query language OQL in the ODMG-93 proposal is quite simple. It consists merely of a function that allows the programmer to pass an extended SQL-like query as a string. The query may contain symbolic variables that are bound in a similar way as allowed by the C *printf* function.

The design principle guiding the ODMG effort has been to promote that *the programmer feels that there is one language.* However, there are a number of difficulties that arise when defining a particular language binding for the ODMG object model, as for example for C++. See slide 11-6.

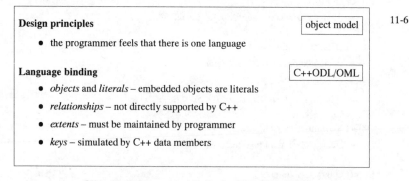

Slide 11-6: Language binding – C++ ODL/OML

Embedded objects which are defined in C++ as object data members, must be taken as literals in the ODMG object model, whereas embedded references to objects are to be taken as objects.

Relationships are not directly supported in C++. In the ODMG-93 proposal, the programmer is required to employ an explicit data structure for updating and traversing a relation.

Extents, which contain the collection of instances of a type, must explicitly be maintained by the programmer. Extents may conveniently be stored in a collection that is associated with a static data member of the class.

Keys, which are needed for efficient retrieval must be simulated by C++ data members. Support for indexing and retrieval by key requires additional compiler support, for which no provision is made in the ODMG-93 proposal.

Other problems that arise in defining a binding to C++ involve the naming of objects, the restriction that C++ allows for only one implementation of a particular type and the duality between arrays and pointers.

Discussion Both the OMG and ODMG standardization efforts aim at the portability of software. The ODMG proposal not only entails the portability of design and source code, but also includes object code, in the form of persistent objects.

The ODMG-93 proposal is inadequate due, partially, to the self-imposed restrictions with respect to the compiler support required.

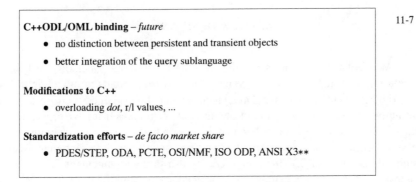

Slide 11-7: Future standardization efforts

The future C++ODL/OML binding will probably no longer distinguish between references to persistent and transient objects, and will provide a better integration of the query language OQL. To realize these goals, however, extended compiler support is needed and perhaps also modifications of C++ to allow the incorporation of code for integrity checking.

It is worth noting that there are a number of additional efforts at defining a standard object model. See slide 11-7. The ODMG proposal is explicitly meant as a superset of the object model proposed by the OMG, in order to become what they aptly phrase as a standard enforced by a *de facto market share*.

11.1.4 The object/event duality

One of the major problems in software engineering that must be resolved for each software development project is to obtain a proper modular decomposition of a system. Object orientation, supporting a component-based approach, is a big step, as it provides the mechanisms necessary to address this problem. However, as argued in our historical aside below, it provides only part of the solution. What is still lacking, somehow, is a proper solution to the problem of characterizing the interaction between collections of objects. A (partial) solution to this problem, however, is suggested by employing events to define the interaction between objects. See also sections 3.4.3 and 7.4.

In the OOPSLA'92 panel, with the title *The heresy of event-orientation in a world of objects*, several speakers observed a discomfort with respect to the notion of *events* in the object-oriented community. A reason for this discomfort is the tension between objects and events, a tension which is known as the *object/event duality*. Traditionally, events are actions operating on passive entities, whereas objects are meant explicitly to integrate data and operations thereupon.

Events – *actions involving objects*   11-8

- requirements – *user actions*
- design – *object compositions*
- implementation – *action callbacks*

Slide 11-8: Objects and events

Why not abolish events altogether, then? The title of the panel, obviously indicates the reluctance of many software developers to part from events in modeling the behavior of (object-oriented) systems. This reluctance may be explained (partly) as a drive for continuity, a natural opposition to throwing away techniques that have proven to be beneficial in the past. (This is probably also the reason that event-based techniques also occur in modernized, read object-oriented, versions of structured development methods, as examined in section 11.3.) However, there are also strong arguments in favor of the position that *events* (which are extraneous to objects) are an essential ingredient (in modeling the behavior) of object-oriented systems. See also sections 3.1.2 and 7.4.

The notion of events may play a role in requirements analysis, as well as in design and implementation. As for requirements analysis, the first author of Jacobson *et al.* (1992), who was one of the speakers of the panel, observed that *use case analysis* (which is part of Objectory) in essence comes down to listing all possible events occurring in the interaction with the user. Such an analysis specifies the functional properties of a system whose behavior will be realized by an appropriate object model.

As for design, we may note that events may be used to characterize the interaction between objects in a generic fashion. In section 7.4, we discussed an example demonstrating the use of *event-driven control* as a means to manage the complexity of object compositions.

Event-driven control also underlies the implementation of many window-based systems. An event coming from the user or window manager may trigger an action that is defined as a callback function associated with the event. See slide 11-8. In the next chapter we will look in more detail at the way in which control is handled by objects in response to events occurring in a window-based system.

Some history In sections 1.1 and 8.1, we have sketched the history underlying the development of object-oriented programming languages, as directed towards increasingly powerful abstractions and constructs for developing reliable software.

In short, we may characterize the genesis of *structured programming* as the outcome of the war against the *goto* and its associated *spaghetti code*. The subsequent development of object-oriented programming may then be understood as the realization that *data* is as important as *control*. Ironically, the disciplined use of encapsulation and inheritance (as mechanisms for data abstraction) may lead to another proliferation of control, threatening the integrity and manageability of object-oriented code.

One part of the control problem of object orientation is known as *ravioli code*, which expresses depictively the existence of a large number of (small) objects with well-

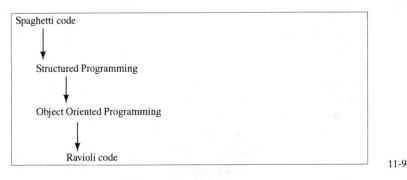

Slide 11-9: Some history

defined interfaces, which interact in a complex way. See slide 11-9. The other part of the control problem is known as the *yo-yo problem*, which characterizes the difficulty of locating control in a class hierarchy with virtual functions. These problems are notoriously hard to solve, yet lie at the core of good library design. As a partial solution to the problem of structuring the interaction between objects we have discussed the notion of *events* to define generic interactions. However, essential to a successful component-based approach, we need sufficiently high-level components to start with.

11.2   Library design

One of the great promises of object orientation is what has been called the *industrial reuse of software* in Meyer (1990). The idea of objects as reusable components was originally put forward in Cox (1986), who coined the phrase *software IC* to indicate the analogy with building electronic circuits from *off-the-shelf components*.

Software reuse is certainly not an exclusive interest of object-oriented developers, as testified for instance in Biggerstaff and Perlis (1989). However, object orientation holds strong cards, as the mechanisms of encapsulation and inheritance directly support the reuse of software. Encapsulation may be used to define *wrapper classes* for existing software, and inheritance may be used to refine existing classes to meet specific requirements. Essentially, a well-designed class library may act as a repository of reusable components. The *unit of reuse* is, however, generally not a single class but rather a collection of classes providing a framework for application development. In this section, we will look at the design decisions underlying the Eiffel libraries, and discuss the development of template classes for abstract data structures in C++.

11.2.1   **Taxonomic classification** – *the Eiffel libraries*

A good example of a well-designed and well-documented collection of class libraries is given in Meyer (1990), who describes the design and implementation of the standard Eiffel libraries. (See also Meyer, 1994.)

The Eiffel libraries include *kernel* classes (for arrays, strings and io), *support* classes (for browsing, persistent storage and debugging), *data structures* (such as lists,

---

Library design – *industrial reuse of software*   11-10

- *unit of reuse* – class/cluster

The Eiffel libraries – *contracts*

- *Kernel* – basic system needs, array, strings, io ...
- *Support* – browsing, persistent storage, debugging
- *Data Structures* – lists, trees, stacks,...
- *Lexical/Parsing* – scanners and parsers
- *Graphics* – windows, mouse handling, figures

Slide 11-10: The Eiffel libraries

trees and stacks), classes for *lexical analysis* and *parsing*, and *graphics* classes (for windows, mouse handling and figures). See slide 11-10.

Consistency – *support tools*   11-11

obsolete

> *The great Tempter of Perfection exhorts: "Correct it here and now, before it is to late." But, here the Guardian Angel of the Installed Base is really a frontman for the hideous Devil of Eternal Compatibility with the Horrors of the Past, whose nefarious influence is also visible in Computer Science.*   Meyer (1990)

Slide 11-11: The problem of consistency

The Eiffel libraries may serve as an example of rational and consistent library design. Each class interface is described by a *contract* stating the class invariant and the pre- and post-conditions for the services provided. An interesting feature of the Eiffel libraries is that the class interface documentation has been extracted automatically from the class implementations, thus guaranteeing consistency between the actual library classes and their description.

Like any software system, libraries tend to evolve over time. As the quotation taken from Meyer (1990) in slide 11-11 indicates, the developer is faced with the dilemma of keeping the library clean and consistent or satisfying the user of earlier versions by maintaining the original class interfaces. As an intermediate solution, the Eiffel language provides the keyword *obsolete* which may be used to indicate that particular methods may eventually be removed from the class interface. The user acquiring a new version of the library is then urged to adapt the code without being confronted with a non-functioning system.

Good library design is aimed at the development of a stable collection of classes with stable interfaces. Stable interfaces mean that the user of the library need not worry about any changes in the implementation of the library, since as long as class interfaces remain the same user code is not affected.

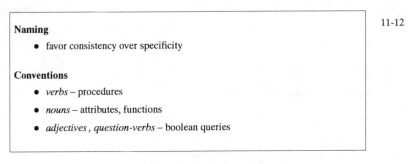

11-12

Naming

- favor consistency over specificity

Conventions

- *verbs* – procedures
- *nouns* – attributes, functions
- *adjectives , question-verbs* – boolean queries

Slide 11-12: Naming conventions

An important aspect of developing library classes is to arrive at a consistent and understandable (read predictable) naming scheme for the methods listed in the class interface. The advice given in Meyer (1990) is to use *verbs* for (state modifying) procedures, *nouns* for (non-modifying) functions and attributes, and *adjectives* or *question verbs* for boolean queries. Note that this advice is not without ambiguity, since words such as *empty* and *count* may be used both as nouns and verbs. In addition, rather than adhering to specific method names that are conventionally used (such as *push* and *pop* for stacks and *insert* and *extract* for queues), Meyer (1990) advises resorting to standard feature or method names that apply to all classes of a particular category. See slide 11-12.

11-13

Standard feature names   containers

item – access operation
count – number of items
has – membership test
put – insert or replace item
force – like put
remove – remove an item
wipe_out – remove all items
empty – absence of items
full – no more space

Slide 11-13: Feature names for containers

As an example, consider the development of a collection of container classes. Our aim, obviously, is to arrive at an inheritance hierarchy representing a classification of container types that allows us to choose the kind of container that most closely fits our needs with respect to *access, traversal* and *storage requirements*.

The advantage of using standard feature names for the complete collection instead of the specific names conventionally used for the different kinds of containers is that essentially no code has to be changed when replacing one kind of container with another. The standard feature names for container classes in the Eiffel library are listed in slide 11-13, with a short explanation of their meaning.

Underlying the implementation of container classes in the Eiffel libraries is a taxonomy of data structures, and a taxonomy of access and traversal methods, that may be combined in a variety of ways using multiple inheritance. From a user's point of view, access methods are the most important attributes of containers, as they determine the order of insertion and retrieval.

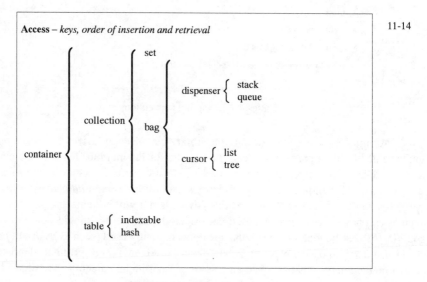

Slide 11-14: Access taxonomy

The hierarchy associated with access methods most closely corresponds with the traditional classification of containers according to their (mathematical) type. See slide 11-14. For example, a *stack* may be regarded as a refinement of a *bag*, imposing additional order. See section 10. Somewhat peculiar in the hierarchy shown above is that the container type *set* is not a refinement of *bag*, which would mathematically be more appropriate.

In addition to the hierarchy corresponding to access methods, we also have a hierarchy corresponding to traversal methods (which are either hierarchical or linear) and a hierarchy representing the options for storage requirements.

As an example of the possible interplay between access methods and traversal methods, look at the *tree* container in the access hierarchy. Similar to a *list*, a *tree* may be accessed by means of a *cursor*, which is a pointer to a particular element in the structure. Dependent on the traversal method, the *cursor* points to the respective elements of the tree either in a linear (that is sorted) order or hierarchically (corresponding with the levels of the nodes).

With respect to the storage requirements, we have the choice between finite structures or potentially infinite structures (that must be implemented in a *lazy*, that is demand-

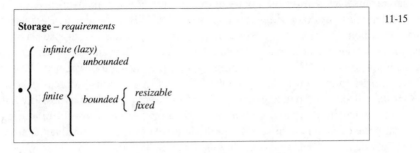

Slide 11-15: Storage taxonomy

driven, fashion). Bounded structures such as arrays may again be subdivided into fixed or resizable structures. See slide 11-15.

The hierarchies corresponding to access and traversal methods and storage requirements may be regarded as the dimensions along which a variety of container types may be constructed. The properties chosen with respect to these dimensions may be used as type annotations serving as an index for retrieval.

Indexing and retrieval To support the retrieval of classes from a repository (a database of software components), the Eiffel language provides the keyword *index* by which attributes associated with a class may be defined. For instance, a container class may be given the attributes *fifo* (first-in first-out) or *lifo* (last-in first-out) that characterize respectively the access behavior of a queue and a stack. See slide 11-16. The Eiffel system itself, however, does not provide for a software repository facility.

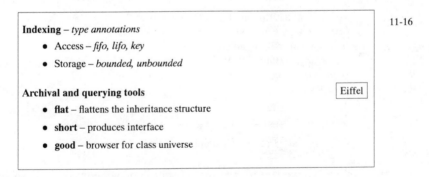

Slide 11-16: Indexing and retrieval

The retrieval of classes (and software components in general) is one of the unresolved problems in software reuse. Clearly, a *browser* allowing traversal of the class universe does not suffice. As an anecdote, Alan Kay (the spiritual father of Smalltalk) once remarked that after an absence of a few months in which the class structure of the Smalltalk library had been changed he had considerable difficulty in locating the appropriate classes. The anecdote indicates that browsers are only helpful to refresh our memory, but not to familiarize ourselves with a class library or to select previously unknown classes for reuse.

The class browser *good* that comes with the Eiffel system is a graphical class browser which sets (apart from its speed) an example for a general purpose class browser, as it allows a graphical display of both inheritance relations and client-server relations. In addition to a class browser, the Eiffel system provides a tool *flat* that allows one to flatten a class to include all features inherited from its ancestors. Moreover, it provides a tool *short* that allows one to extract an interface description from a (possibly flattened) class implementation. A tool such as *short* is an invaluable means for producing automatically the documentation specifying the interface of a class. Invaluable, since reuse ultimately depends upon understanding the functionality offered by a library.

11.2.2   Template classes – *bags and sets*

Numerous C++ libraries offering data structures for containers are available. Yet, many programmers choose to develop such a library themselves. The reasons for this may vary from matters of taste to considerations with respect to the formal properties of the types offered.

```
template< class T >
class bag {                                        bag<T>
public:
bag() { s = new list<T>; }
bag(const bag<T>& b) { s = b.s; }
~bag() { delete s; }
bag<T>& operator=(const bag<T>& b) {
    s = b.s; return * this;
    }
virtual void insert(const T& e) { s→ insert(e); }
operator iter<T>() const { return * s; }
int count(const T& e) const;
void map(T f(const T& e));
protected:
list<T>* s;                          // see section 2.4.2
};
```

11-17

Slide 11-17: The implementation of a bag

In the following, we will look at some issues in defining generic classes for the mathematical data types *bag*, *set* and *powerset*. Such data types must, for example, be provided in a library meant to support the use of formal methods as outlined in section 3.4. Naturally, in developing real industrial-strength libraries many more issues play a role. See, for example, Booch and Vilot (1990).

In slide 11-17, a generic definition for the type *bag* is given. Mathematically, a *bag* or *multi-set* is a *set* which may contain multiple instances of a particular value. (With respect to the subtype refinement relation, however, a *set* may be considered as a subtype of *bag*.)

The template class *bag< T>* offers a default constructor, a copy constructor and a member function for assignment, as required by the canonical class idiom presented in section 2.3. An instance of the (generic) *list< T>* class, developed in section 2.4, is used to store the elements of the *bag*. The destructor of *bag* simply deletes the the protected data member *s*.

To insert an element, *bag< T>* :: *insert* forwards the call to *list< T>* :: *insert* and, similarly, when an iterator is requested the list pointer is converted appropriately.

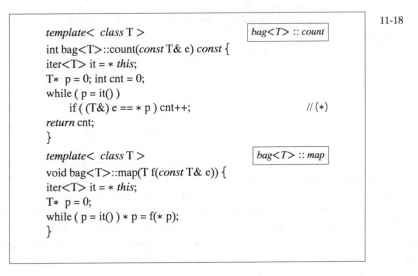

11-18

```
template< class T >                          bag<T> :: count
int bag<T>::count(const T& e) const {
iter<T> it = * this;
T*  p = 0; int cnt = 0;
while ( p = it() )
      if ( ( (T&) e == * p ) cnt++;                    // (*)
return cnt;
}
template< class T >                          bag<T> :: map
void bag<T>::map(T f(const T& e)) {
iter<T> it = * this;
T*  p = 0;
while ( p = it() ) * p = f(* p);
}
```

Slide 11-18: Bag operations

The function *bag< T>* :: *count* and *bag< T>* :: *map* are defined in slide 11-18. The *count* function tells how many instances of a particular element are in the *bag*. It employs an iterator to traverse the list and compares its contents with the element given as an argument.

The function *map* may be used to modify the contents of the *bag* applying some mapping function to each element:

```
int S(const int& x) { return x+1; }

bag<int> b;
b.insert(1); b.insert(2); b.insert(1);
b.map(S);
iter<int> it = b;                            // get the iterator
int* p = 0;                                  // start
while ( p = it() ) {
      cout << "item;" << * p << endl;        // take the value
      }
```

In the example above, the function *S* is defined as the successor function for integers. Also, a bag *b* of integers is declared, into which the (integer) elements 1,2 and 1 are inserted. As a consequence *b.count*(1) will deliver 2 and *b.count*(2) will deliver 1 as a result.

The *bag< T>* :: *map* function is used to apply the successor function S to each element of the *bag*. Then, an iterator is obtained, simply by assignment with an implicit conversion, and the contents of the *bag* are written to standard output.

```
template< class T >                                    set<T>
class set : public bag<T> {
public:
void insert(const T& e) {
    if (!member(e)) bag<T>::insert(e);
    }
bool member(const T& e) {
    return count(e) == 1;
    }
};
```
11-19

Slide 11-19: Deriving a set class

Evidently, the class *bag< T>* lacks many of the features required for the mathematical notion of a *bag*, such as operators for bag union and bag intersection. Nevertheless, *bag< T>* may conveniently be used to define the class *set< T>* as a derived class.

The *set< T>* class given in slide 11-19 defines an additional function *member* and redefines *insert* to check that the element is not already a member of the set (since, in contrast to a bag, a set may not contain multiple instances of a value). The function *member* delivers *true* when the number of occurrences of an element is precisely one, otherwise it returns *false*.

```
template< class T >              set<T> ≡ set<T>
int operator==(const set<T>& s, const set<T>& b) {
iter<T> it = s;
T* p = 0; int eq = 1;
while ( eq && (p = it()) )
    if ( s.count(* p) != b.count(* p) ) eq = false;
return eq;
}
```
11-20

Slide 11-20: Equality for sets

Equality between sets may be defined as in slide 11-20. Set equality amounts to element-wise correspondence, irrespective of the order in which the elements occur. The definition given in slide 11-20 is somewhat more general than necessary, in that it also applies to bags. The requirement *!member*(*$*p$) would have been sufficient.

The definition of equality for sets is necessary in order to be able to define instances of set having a set-valued instantiation parameter, such as the class *power< T>*

defined in slide 11-22, which is derived from *set*<*set*<*T* > >. When instantiating *set*<*set*<*T* > > for some type *T*, equality is required for *set*<*T*> by the line (∗) in the function *bag*<*T*> :: *count* defined in slide 11-18.

```
template< class T >                        operator<<
ostream& operator≪(ostream& os, const set<T>& s) {
iter<T> it = s;
T∗ p = 0;
while ( p = it() ) {
    cout ≪ ∗ p ≪ endl;
    }
return os;
}
```
11-21

Slide 11-21: Writing a set to a stream

In slide 11-21, a generic operator is defined to write an arbitrary set to a stream, by overloading `operator<<` for *const set*<*T*> & . To traverse the elements of the set it employs an iterator, obtained by assigning the set reference to an *iter*<*T*> instance.

```
template< class T >
class power : public set< set<T>> > {        power<T>

};
```
11-22

Slide 11-22: The *powerset* class

To define the class *power*<*T*> it suffices to derive the class from *set*<*set*<*T* > >. However, according to the rules given for the canonical class idiom, both *power*<*T*> and *set*<*T*> should be augmented with a default and copy constructor, and an assignment operator and destructor as well.

Note that the *map* function as defined for *bag*<*T*> is potentially unsafe for both *set*<*T*> and *power*<*T*> instances. For example, the function given to *map* may result in identical values for different arguments. As a consequence, the restriction that the set does not contain multiple instances of the same value may be violated.

```
set<int> s1;
s1.insert(1); s1.insert(2);
set<int> s2;
s2.insert(2); s2.insert(3);
cout ≪ s1;
power<int> b;
b.insert(s1); b.insert(s2);
cout ≪ (set< set<int> > &) b;                // cast is necessary
```

An example of employing the powerset is given above. First, two instances of *set<int>* are created, which are then inserted in an instance of *power<int>*. The operator<< function (defined for *set<T>* in slide 11-21) may be used to write the powerset to standard output. For each (set-valued) element of the powerset, the operator<< function instantiated for *set<int>* is called to write the individual elements to standard output.

11.3   Methods and tools

Object-oriented software development is a relatively new technology. Consequently, ideas with respect to methodologies supporting an object-oriented approach are still in flux. Nevertheless, a plethora of methods and tools does exist supporting object-oriented analysis and design. See slide 11-23.

		11-23
Methods		
• OOA/D – *incremental*	[Coad and Yourdon (1991b)]	
• Objectory – *use-case analysis*	[Jacobson *et al.* (1992)]	
• OOSA – *model-driven*	[Kurtz *et al.* (1990)]	
• OOSD – *structured*	[Wasserman (1989)]	
• CRC – *cards*	[Beck and Cunningham (1989)]	
• RDD – *responsibility-driven*	[Wirfs-Brock (1989)]	
• OMT – *object modeling*	[Rumbaugh *et al.* (1991)]	
• OOD – *development*	[Booch (1991)]	
• Fusion – *lifecycle*	[Coleman *et al.* (1994)]	

Slide 11-23: Software development methods

In the list above, we have collected a number of development methods. With the exception of OOSA (which proposes a model-driven approach to analysis), OOSD (which introduces a structured design representation method) and Fusion (which presents a promising synthesis of ideas found in a number of other methods, such as CRC, RDD and OMT) we have encountered these methods previously in chapters 1 and 3.

We have based our discussion of the object-oriented lifecycle in section 1.2 on the OOA/D method proposed in Coad and Yourdon (1991a) and Coad and Yourdon (1991b), which stresses the gradual transition from the analysis to the design and implementation phase. In section 3.1 we have briefly discussed the Objectory method, which proposes employing a *use case analysis* to arrive at a model specifying system requirements. In section 3.1 and 3.3, we have discussed the responsibility-driven approach proposed in Wirfs-Brock (1989), and the various modeling perspectives suggested by Rumbaugh *et al.* (1991). Our discussion of object-oriented development in section 3.2 has been based on Booch (1986, 1991, 1994).

Some of these methods (and corresponding tools) directly stem from a more conventional approach to software development. Others are more radical and propose new tools to support the decomposition principles underlying object-oriented technology.

Naturally, those who wish to make a gradual shift from conventional technology to adopting an object-oriented approach may benefit from methods that adapt familiar techniques to the new concepts.

In this section we will look at a variety of existing methods and the tools they offer. We do not discuss the tools and diagram techniques used in any detail. However, we will discuss the Fusion method in some detail. Fusion is a strongly systematic approach to object-oriented software development that integrates various concepts and modeling techniques from the other methods, notably OMT, Booch OOD and CRC. We will discuss the process view underlying Fusion and sketch the models it supports in relation to the other methods. For the reader this section may supply an overview and references needed for a more detailed study of a particular method or tool.

Structured methods Initially, structured methods (which were developed the beginning of the 1970s) were primarily concerned with modeling processes in a modular way. Based on software engineering principles such as *module coupling* and *cohesion,* tools were developed to represent the structure of a design (within what we have previously called the procedural or modular paradigm). See, for example, Yourdon and Constantine (1979). Apart from diagrams to describe the modular architecture of a system (such as *structure charts* and *process specifications*), structured methods also employ *data flow diagrams* to depict processes and the flow of data between them, and *hierarchy diagrams* to model the structure of the data involved. See slide 11-24.

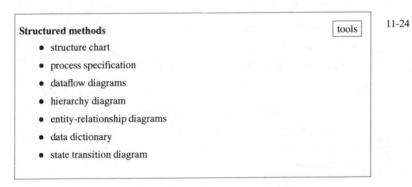

Slide 11-24: Tools for a structured approach

Later, structured methods were extended to encompass analysis, and the focus shifted to modeling the data by means of *entity-relationship diagrams* and *data dictionaries.* Also, *state transition diagrams* were employed to represent the behavioral aspects of a system.

As observed in Fichman and Kemerer (1992), *in the late 1970s and early 1980s, planning and modeling of data began to take on a more central role in system development, culminating in data oriented methodologies, such as information engineering* (which may be regarded as precursors to object-oriented methods). Information engineering, however, is primarily concerned with analysis and strategic planning. In addition to the modeling techniques mentioned, tools were developed to model the information needs of an enterprise and to perform risk analysis. Also, extensions to the *data dictionary* were proposed in order to have an integrated repository, serving all phases of the development. Currently, repository-based techniques are again of interest since, in combination with modern hypermedia technology, they may serve as the organizational basis for reuse.

11.3.1   Requirements engineering – *Fusion*

The Fusion method is presented in Coleman *et al.* (1994) as a second generation object-oriented method. The phrase *second generation* is meant to indicate the method transcends and incorporates the ideas and techniques that were employed in the early object-oriented methods.

Above all, the Fusion method focuses on a strongly systematic approach to object-oriented software development, with an emphasis on the *process* of development and the validation of the consistency between the models delivered in the various phases of a project.

The software lifecycle model underlying Fusion is the traditional waterfall model, consisting of the subsequent phases of analysis, design and implementation. Each phase results in a number of models describing particular aspects of the system. See slide 11-25. A *data dictionary* is to be kept as a means to unify the terminology employed in the various phases.

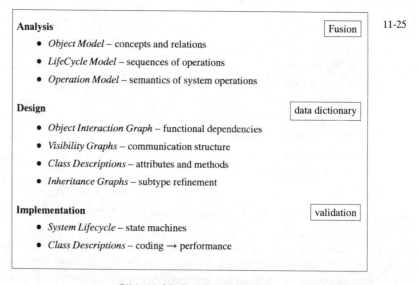

Slide 11-25: The Fusion method

The models produced as the result of analysis, design and implementation serve to document the decisions made during the development.

Each of the phases covers different aspects of the system. Analysis serves to document the system requirements from a user perspective. The Fusion method describes how to construct an *Object Model* that captures the basic concepts of the application domain. These concepts are represented as entities or objects and are connected by relations, similar to *entity-relationship* diagrams employed in semantic modeling. Analysis also results in an *Operation Model*, describing the semantics of the operations that may be performed by a user by means of pre- and post-conditions, in a formal manner. In addition, Fusion defines a *Lifecycle Model* that describes, by means of regular expressions, which sequences of operations are allowed, as in the JSD method.

Design may be considered as the transition between analysis and implementation. During design, decisions are made with respect to the realization of the system operations identified during analysis. Design according to the Fusion method results in an *Object Interaction Graph*, that for each system operation describes which objects are involved and which methods are invoked. Fusion also allows one to label the arrows representing method calls in the interaction diagram with sequencing information. In addition, design involves the construction of *Visibility Graphs*, indicating the attribute and method interface for each object, *Class Descriptions*, defining the attributes and methods of objects, and *Inheritance Graphs*, specifying the subtype refinement relation between classes.

Implementation is considered in the Fusion method as a phase in which to work out the details of the decisions taken during analysis and design. It results in a *System Lifecycle* description for each object identified in the *Object Model*, in the form of a finite state machine, and precise *Class Descriptions*, in the form of (preferably) efficient code.

Validation An important aspect of the Fusion method is the validation of the completeness and consistency of the collection of models. Completeness, obviously, is a relative matter and can only be established with respect to explicitly stated user requirements. However, the models developed in a particular phase impose additional requirements upon the efforts engaged in the later phases and in the end maintenance. Consistency involves verifying whether the various models are not contradictory. For both development and validation, the data dictionary plays an important role, as a common point of reference.

11.3.2 Tools for analysis and design – *a comparative study*

In Fichman and Kemerer (1992) a comparative review of a selected number of object-oriented analysis and design methods is given. Criteria for selection were the availability of documentation and acceptance in the object-oriented community, measured in terms of refereed articles.

Paraphrasing Fichman and Kemerer (1992) again: *As with traditional analysis, the primary goal of object-oriented analysis is the development of an accurate and complete description of the problem domain.*

The three analysis models described in Fichman and Kemerer (1992) share a number of diagram techniques with both structured methods and methods for object-oriented design. However, in particular the method proposed in Shlaer and Mellor (1988) reflects the domain oriented focus of analysis.

A similar focus on domain requirements and analysis may be found in the Objectory method. See slide 11-26. Objectory is one of the methods that has inspired Fusion, in particular because it presents a systematic approach to the process of software development. The Objectory method centers around *use case* analysis. Use case analysis involves a precise description of the interaction between the user of a system and the components representing domain-specific functionality. The Objectory method gives precise guidelines on how to proceed from the identification of *use cases*, which include user interface aspects, to their realization in the subsequent phases of design and implementation. Objects are called blocks in Objectory. Use case analysis corresponds in a loose way with the identification of system operations in Fusion.

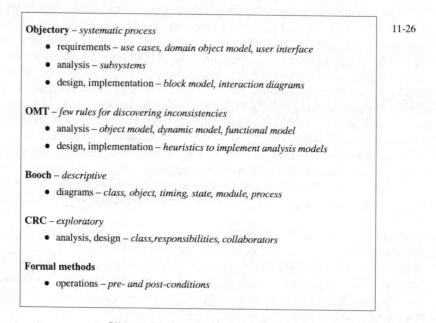

Objectory – *systematic process*   11-26

- requirements – *use cases, domain object model, user interface*
- analysis – *subsystems*
- design, implementation – *block model, interaction diagrams*

OMT – *few rules for discovering inconsistencies*

- analysis – *object model, dynamic model, functional model*
- design, implementation – *heuristics to implement analysis models*

Booch – *descriptive*

- diagrams – *class, object, timing, state, module, process*

CRC – *exploratory*

- analysis, design – *class, responsibilities, collaborators*

Formal methods

- operations – *pre- and post-conditions*

Slide 11-26: Comparison of methods (1)

There is a close correspondence between the OMT object model and the analysis object model of Fusion. Both OMT and Fusion employ extended entity-relationship diagrams. Also, the dynamic model of OMT reoccurs in the Fusion method, albeit in a later phase. The functional model of OMT, which has the form of a dataflow diagram, is generally considered to be inappropriate for object-oriented analysis. Instead, Fusion employs a model in which the semantics of system operations are captured by means of formal pre- and post-conditions. In Coleman *et al.* (1994), OMT is characterized as a very loose method, giving few rules for discovering inconsistencies between the various models and lacking a clear view with respect to the process of development. OMT is strongly focused on analysis, giving nothing but heuristics to implement the models that result from analysis. However, what is called the *light-weight Fusion method* almost coincides with OMT.

A lack of detailed guidelines for the process of software development is also characteristic for the Booch OOD method. Booch offers a wealth of descriptive diagrams, giving detailed information on the various aspects of a system, but offers merely heuristics for the actual process of development.

The CRC method must be regarded primarily as a means to explore the interaction between the various objects of a domain. It is powerful in generating ideas, but offers poor support for documenting the decisions with respect to the objects and how they interact.

Formal methods have been another important source of inspiration for the Fusion method. The description of system operations during analysis employs a characterization of the functionality of operations that is directly related to the specification of operations in model-based specification methods such as VDM and Z. See section 10.5.

The Fusion method may be regarded as being composed of elements of the methods mentioned above. It shares its object model with OMT, its approach to the characterization of system operations with formal methods, its focus on object interaction with CRC and its explicit description of classes and their relations with Booch. See slide 11-27.

11-27

Comparison – *as a systematic approach*					Fusion
	Objectory	OMT	Booch	CRC	Fusion
development	+	±	−	⊕	+
maintenance	+	±	+	−	+
structure	±	±	+	+	+
management	+	±	±	−	+
tool support	±	±	±	−	+

Slide 11-27: Comparison of methods (2)

In comparison with these methods, however, it provides a much more systematic approach to the process of development and, moreover, is explicitly concerned with issues of validation and consistency between models. In addition, Coleman *et al.* (1994) claim to provide explicit semantics for their various models, whereas the other methods fail to do so. However, it must be remarked that the Fusion method remains somewhat obscure about the nature of system operations. System operations are characterized as *asynchronous*. Yet, if they are to be taken as methods, such operations may return a result, which is quite hard to reconcile with their asynchronous nature. The claim that the models have a precise semantics, which is essential for tool support, must be substantiated by providing an explicit semantics in a formal manner!

With regard to the process of development, both Objectory and Fusion provide precise guidelines. The CRC method may be valuable as an additional exploratory device. For maintenance, the extent to which a method enforces the documentation of design decisions is of the utmost importance. Both the Objectory and Booch method satisfys this criterion, as does the Fusion method. OMT is lacking in this respect, and CRC is clearly inadequate.

Whether a method leads to a *good* object-oriented design of the system architecture, depends to a large extent upon the ability and experience of the development team. Apart from Fusion, both the Booch method and CRC may be characterized as purely object-oriented, whereas Objectory and OMT are considered to be impure.

A strongly systematic approach to the process of development is important in particular from the point of view of project management. Project management support entails a precise definition of the deliverables associated with each phase, as well as an indication of the timing of their deliverance and validation. Both the OMT method and Booch are lacking in this respect, since they primarily provide techniques to develop descriptive models. Clearly, CRC lacks any support for project management.

Tool support is dependent on the existence of a well-defined semantics for the models employed. For both Objectory and OMT commercial tools are available, despite their loosely specified semantics. The Fusion diagraming techniques are also supported, for example by Paradigm Plus, which also supports the diagraming techniques of OMT. See section 11.3.3. For CRC, tool support is considered to be useless. The success of the method depends upon flexibility, the ease with which new ideas can be tried, a flexibility which even hypertext cannot offer, according its authors.

An important question, when considering methods for software development, is what means we wish to have to represent the decisions taken during design.

Design representation As phrased in Fichman and Kemerer (1992), *design is the process of mapping system requirements defined during analysis to an abstract representation of a specific system-based implementation meeting cost and performance constraints.* In other words, design is concerned with architectural issues, whereas analysis is concerned with requirements and constraints. Although different in objective, in an object-oriented approach analysis and design may share a common object model. Both in the method proposed by Coad and Yourdon (1991b) and the method proposed in Booch (1991), the difference between analysis and design lies primarily in the level of detail in which the respective components of the system are specified. Many of the diagram techniques employed, however, have no clear semantics, and rely on an informal description of common cases only. In slide 11-28 a number of the diagram types proposed in Booch (1991) are listed.

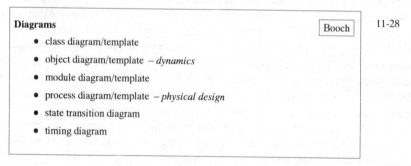

Slide 11-28: Diagrams for design

Apart from *class diagrams* and *templates* to describe the functionality of classes and their (static) relations to other classes, the methods also uses *object diagrams* (and templates) to characterize the dynamic behavior of (collections of) objects. Moreover, the method provides for *module diagrams* to depict the relations between modules and to describe the physical architecture of distributed systems. As additional techniques to describe the behavioral characteristics of object, Booch (1991) employs *state-transition diagrams* and *timing diagrams* (expressing constraints on the order in which methods may be invoked).

These diagram techniques have as a common objective to represent the important properties and aspects of a design. Along the dimensions by which we may classify design representation technologies, *expressiveness* and *formality*, object-oriented technology may be ranked as being midway between non-formal, highly expressive techniques such as hypertext, and highly formal (logic-based) techniques which require a lot of expertise to express relationships and properties. However, object-oriented techniques cover a broad range. For example, *collaboration graphs* (Wirfs-Brock *et al.*, 1990) and *contracts* (Meyer (1988)) offer (in principle) a high degree of formality, whereas many of the diagram techniques seem to be amenable to an extension with hypertext features to support browsing and the retrieval of information. See Coad and Yourdon (1991b), Bigelow (1988) and Webster (1988).

A major problem that is still not satisfactorily solved by any of the existing methods is to support what may be called the *harvesting of reuse*, that is the actual exploitation of the reuse potential that is intrinsic to object-oriented technology. Both at the level of analysis and design, a repository-based approach to managing reuse (in combination with appropriate retrieval techniques) seems to be the most promising. Another issue about which opinions diverge is by what principles objects should be clustered, and what techniques must be provided to support system partitioning. Perhaps the solution to these problems is not strictly a matter of technology, but instead requires us to wait for appropriate conventions and styles to emerge within each particular application domain.

11.3.3   Program development environments – *OODBMS*

A method provides guidelines with respect to the development of a system, possibly including maintenance and project management. We speak of a CASE (Computer Aided Software Engineering) tool, when the tool supports a method in its various aspects. Support may even include the generation of code. Usually, a distinction is made between Upper CASE tools, supporting the first phases of software development, and Lower CASE tools, providing support primarily for the later phases, include code generation. At the lower end of the spectrum of tools we have program development environments. A program development environment is a collection of more or less well-integrated software tools that support the various activities that arise in the course of realizing the project aims in actual software. Program development environments may include configuration management facilities, a graphical interface builder, various browsers (for example for the class inheritance structure, cross referencing and source code module dependencies), and facilities for interactive debugging.

An example of a CASE tool is the tool accompanying the Objectory method. Paradigm Plus may be characterized as a meta CASE tool, in that it supports multiple diagraming techniques, including those of OMT and Fusion. See slide 11-29.

HP/Softbench may be characterized as a broad spectrum tool. It supports a variety of diagram techniques (via third party Softbench-compatible tools, such as Protosoft's Paradigm Plus), among which are the techniques employed in the HP Fusion method. Moreover, it provides a C++ workbench, including editors, browsers, profilers as well as additional libraries with utilities.

A veritable programming environment is CenterLine's ObjectCenter. ObjectCenter is a descendant of SaberC++. It includes a variety of browsers, a configuration management facility and quite impressive interactive debugging facilities. An interesting feature of ObjectCenter is that it supports both interpreted and compiled code, thus facilitating rapid incremental development. Apart from the latter facility, which is quite a unique

```
┌─────────────────────────────────────────────────────────────────────┐
│  CASE tools                                           ┌─────┐  11-29  │
│                                                       │ C++ │         │
│    •  Paradigm Plus – OMT, Fusion          sales@protosoft.com        │
│    •  HP/Softbench – Fusion                                           │
│                                                                       │
│  Program development environments                                     │
│    •  ObjectCenter – SaberC++                         CenterLine      │
│    •  Objectworks/C++                                                 │
│    •  Microsoft Visual C++ – Foundation Classes                       │
│    •  Sniff                                     info@takefive.co.at   │
│                                                                       │
│  Public domain                                                        │
│    •  ET++PE                               iamsun.unibe.ch:/C++       │
│    •  Cweb                            labrea.stanford.edu:/pub/cweb   │
└─────────────────────────────────────────────────────────────────────┘
```

Slide 11-29: Program development environments

feature, ObjectCenter provides a rather shallow interface to standard Unix facilities. Beware, using ObjectCenter requires a powerful workstation with lots of memory. For an evaluation of ObjectCenter, consult Leggett and Franklin (1994).

Another example of a program development environment is Objectworks/C++, which provides a functionality similar to Objectworks/Smalltalk, including class hierarchy browsers, editors and debugging facilities.

Not really a program development, but rather a graphical user interface development tool, is provided by Microsoft Visual C++. Visual C++, together with the Microsoft Foundation Classes, allows one to develop an application, including the graphical user interface interactively. The advantage of such an approach is that it relieves the programmer of coding the graphical layout and organizing the code related to the window-based events.

Sniff is another interactive program development environment with a visual flavor. It supports a repository-based approach and allows for browsing and editing in a unified fashion. Information may be obtained by email from `info@takefive.co.at`.

In the public domain, we have, for example, ET++PE, which is closely coupled with a C++ library for the development of graphical interfaces. See section 11.4.

An essential ingredient of any CASE tool is documentation support. Some even go so far as to denounce CASE tools altogether by stating that these tools do *produce nothing but PostScript (documentation)*. As a package that in principle may valuably be incorporated in a program development tool, the Cweb package may be mentioned which may be used for producing literate C++ code. See section 4.2.3. Documentation tools are also part of the OSE library that is mentioned in section 11.4.

OODBMS Many applications require data storage facilities as offered by (object) data base systems. The list of systems in slide 11-30 is taken from Harmon and Tayler (1993).

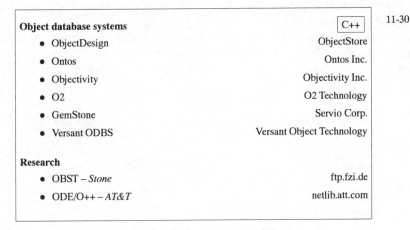

Slide 11-30: Object database systems

Above, we have listed some of the popular object database systems with an interface to C++. These include ObjectDesign, Ontos, Objectivity, O2, GemStone and Versant ODBS. As packages available for research we may mention OBST (which is the result of an ESPRIT research project) and ODE/O++ which provides an extension of C++ with persistent objects and transactions.

11.4 Libraries for C++

The employment of appropriate libraries may be crucial to the success of a software development project.

Libraries show a great variety with respect to the features offered, the reliability of the code and the level and quality of documentation. In this section we will discuss the criteria by which to evaluate (C++) libraries. We restrict ourselves largely to a discussion of public domain libraries, but also a number of commercially available libraries will be mentioned.

A trend that is worth mentioning is the publication of books including (source code) software, usually pertaining to a particular domain. For C/C++ books are available including software for *graphics* (e.g. Ammeraal, 1992), *mathematics* (e.g. Reverchon and Duchamp, 1993), *discrete event simulation* (e.g. Watkins, 1993), *neural networks* (e.g. Blum, 1992), *data structures* (e.g. Gorlen *et al.*, 1990), *modeling* (e.g. Henderson, 1993) and *programming* (e.g. Coad and Nicola, 1993). Obviously, the advantage of this format is the availability of (in principle) carefully written documentation.

The number and quality of libraries becoming available for C++ is increasing rapidly. Prices for these libraries vary widely. The starting point for most users will be what price they are willing to pay and what platform and compiler they have at their disposal. Often, especially for IBM-compatible PCs, a compiler comes with a number of libraries. For example, the Borland C++ compiler includes a powerful graphics library that has become quite popular (measured by the number of books about graphics programming in Borland C++).

An easily overlooked aspect of libraries is what requirements they impose with respect to additional hardware or software. However, with the development of standards (such as the multimedia standard for PCs) this is less likely to become a problem.

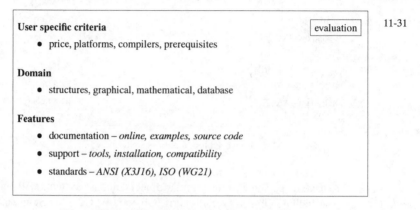

User specific criteria   evaluation   11-31

 • price, platforms, compilers, prerequisites

Domain

 • structures, graphical, mathematical, database

Features

 • documentation – *online, examples, source code*

 • support – *tools, installation, compatibility*

 • standards – *ANSI (X3J16), ISO (WG21)*

Slide 11-31: Libraries – evaluation criteria

Naturally, an important criterion for choosing a library is the domain of application it covers. Possible domains include data structures, graphical programming, mathematical programming, database applications and also business and financial applications.

Important features that must be paid attention to when selecting a particular library are the *documentation* (which preferably includes online help and a collection of tutorial examples), the *support* offered (for example browsing tools, the ease of installation and the compatibility with other libraries and environments). Also important is whether the library conforms to the standards being developed by ANSI and ISO, and more recently by the OMG. As for the use of C++ language features, the standard reference to which both ANSI and ISO adhere is Ellis and Stroustrup (1990). In the near future, moreover, libraries will probably be required to be CORBA-compliant. See section 11.1.2.

With respect to the documentation requirements, we may observe that many library vendors have been forced to include the source code to compensate for insufficient documentation. In addition, frequent changes to the source code are needed to permit effective derivation by inheritance. Only when conventions emerge that are commonly subscribed to will this no longer be necessary.

For each of the domains mentioned in slide 11-31, we may list a number of functional requirements that must be minimally satisfied.

For example, we may expect a library for *data structures* to support strings, lists, stacks, bags and sets, and preferably also maps (such as hashtables) and trees and graphs. Also, we may expect a *mathematics* library to support matrices, complex numbers, statistical functions and algebraic features. And we may expect a *simulation* library to support resources, processes, events, random number generation and histograms. Particular attention should be paid to how the various structures supported by a library may inter-

---

Requirements – *interaction*   11-32

- data structures – *string, list, stack, tree, bag, set, map, graph*
- mathematics – *matrix, complex, statistics, algebra*
- simulation – *resource, process, events, random, histogram*

Requirements for GUI class libraries – *events*

- control – *buttons, entry, listbox, menu, slider*
- dialogs – *message, file selector, online help*
- graphics – *point, line, box, rectangle, circle, bitmap*
- platform – *window manager, drag and drop*
- tools – *interface builder*

Slide 11-32: Libraries – functionality requirements

act. For example, can we define a tree search for strings and can we manipulate matrices of complex numbers?

Similar requirements may be stated for libraries supporting the development of graphical user interfaces. Minimally, such a library should contain *control* features (such as buttons, entry widgets, listboxes and menus), *dialog* features (such as messages, file selectors and facilities to create online help) and a collection of *graphics* items (including points, lines, boxes, rectangles, circles and bitmaps). See slide 11-32.

Generally, GUI libraries are platform dependent. However, platform independent GUI libraries do exist, although they do not usually offer the full functionality supported by a particular platform (which may include *drag and drop* facilities and interaction with the window manager). Finally, some GUI libraries come with additional tools such as an *interface builder*, which provides a fast way for developing interface prototypes.

In the next chapter, we will discuss the issues involved in developing a hypermedia framework, including the design of a user interface development library.

In the following we will briefly discuss a number of the C++ libraries that are currently available. Most of the libraries mentioned are in the public domain with the exception of those that are explicitly indicated as commercial. For the public domain libraries we indicate where they may be obtained via anonymous ftp (for those having access to the Internet). For most libraries there will be other ftp sites as well from which the software may be retrieved.

The quality and extent of the libraries varies considerably. Hence, the reader is urged to perform a preliminary evaluation before incorporating any of these libraries in an actual software project.

Structures The general purpose libraries, offering data structures and utilities, show considerable variation in size and organization. See slide 11-33. No standard data structures library for C++ does yet exist. However, it is one of the goals of the ANSI committee to arrive at such a standard.

Structures	11-33
• NIHCL – *Smalltalk-like utilities*	alw.nih.gov:/pub/NIHCL
• OATH – *type hierarchy*	cs.utexas.edu:/pub/OATH
• COOL – *structures*	cs.utexas.edu:/pub/COOL
• LEDA – *algorithms*	iamsun.unibe.ch:C++
• OSE – *templates*	iamsun.unibe.ch:C++
• Splash – *perl utilities*	iamsun.unibe.ch:C++
• Libg++ – *utilities*	aeneas.mit.edu:/pub/gnu
Commercial	
• Classix – *container classes*	BSO/Tasking
• Tools.h++	Rogue Wave
• Booch C++ Components	(Booch and Vilot, 1990

Slide 11-33: Libraries for (data) structures

One of the first and most well-known libraries with data structures and utilities is the National Institute of Health class library NIHCL. See Gorlen *et al.* (1990). NIHCL offers (apart from common data structures such as lists, strings and arbitrary length numbers) *meta-level functionality* in a Smalltalk-like fashion, which enables the user for example to ask for the class (type) of a particular object and for the methods supported by that class. The library is organized as a single inheritance hierarchy, with a type *Object* at the root. The NIHCL library was developed before templates were generally available, and may be regarded in general as somewhat cumbersome to use.

The OATH library is organized as a forest. It offers an abstract definition of data structures such as lists, bags, sets and a collection of number types. A quite noteworthy characteristic of the OATH library is that a distinction is made between a type hierarchy underlying the type definition of the data structures and an implementation hierarchy containing the actual class implementations. A disadvantage of the OATH library is that it imposes a rather complicated protocol for usage and refinement.

COOL stands for *Common Object Oriented Library*. It offers a very extensive collection of classes and a large number of data types. Similar to the NIHCL library and the OATH library, it stems from a pre-template era. Moreover, it requires the use of a pre-processor.

The LEDA library also offers, in addition to a number of data structures, algorithms for combinatorial computing and computational geometry. It is free for research and education, but requires a license for commercial applications.

A quite extensive library of general purpose classes, including facilities for memory management and operating system utilities, is offered by the OSE library. In contrast to the libraries previously discussed, OSE supports (standard C++) template classes. In addition, OSE provides a number of tools to facilitate maintenance and documentation, such as a tool to convert .h include files to manual pages. OSE is claimed by its developers to work for a wide spectrum of compilers and platforms.

Unlike the other libraries, the Splash library is a fairly small library offering a few, rather powerful constructs such as strings (including pattern matching methods), lists (in the form of standard C++ template classes) and associative arrays. The Splash library has been developed to make perl-like string manipulation and list processing facilities available in C++.

The Libg++ library (a library with data structures and utilities that comes with GNU C++) comes closest to a standard library for C++. However, it is currently only available for GNU C++.

Commercially available, we have the Classix library (which offers a number of general purpose data structures and facilities for meta-level programming), the Rogue Wave Tools.h libraries (offering a variety of data structures). Further, the Booch C++ Components offer a variety of structures as originally developed for Ada. The library supports multi-tasking and a non-standard template facility.

Mathematics Similar as for the general purpose data structure libraries, there is a variety of (mutually incompatible) mathematical libraries for C++. See slide 11-34.

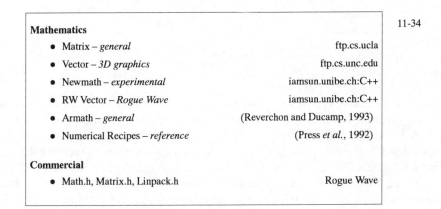

11-34

Mathematics

- Matrix – *general*   ftp.cs.ucla
- Vector – *3D graphics*   ftp.cs.unc.edu
- Newmath – *experimental*   iamsun.unibe.ch:C++
- RW Vector – *Rogue Wave*   iamsun.unibe.ch:C++
- Armath – *general*   (Reverchon and Ducamp, 1993)
- Numerical Recipes – *reference*   (Press *et al.*, 1992)

Commercial

- Math.h, Matrix.h, Linpack.h   Rogue Wave

Slide 11-34: Libraries for mathematics

General (medium-sized) matrix manipulation facilities are offered by the Matrix library. The Vector library, in contrast, is dedicated to 3 and 4 elements matrix and vector classes, suitable for 3D graphical work. The Newmath library is an experimental matrix and vector manipulation library which (as a special feature) also offers an interface to the functions provided by Numerical Recipes. A (to some extent) more standard approach is taken in the RW Vector library, which offers (as a public domain library) the facilities for matrix manipulation and linear algebra that are provided in the (commercial) Rogue Wave Math.h, Matrix.h and Linpack.h libraries (for PC platforms). Apart from portability, this has the advantage that one may obtain proper documentation with respect to the usage and functionality of the facilities offered.

Another interesting collection of classes for mathematical programming is provided by the Armath library described in Reverchon and Ducamp (1993), which includes the software. As an important reference and code source for numerical programming in C we may mention Press *et al.* (1992).

As a remark, a disadvantage of all the libraries mentioned is that when they do offer template classes, they offer them as (non-standard) macro-defined templates. Again, standardization (of both the language and the compilers) is of utmost importance to arrive at well-established conventions for doing mathematics in C++.

Discrete event simulation Despite the fact that object-oriented programming languages are historically related to discrete event simulation, additional functionality is needed to write simulation programs in C++.

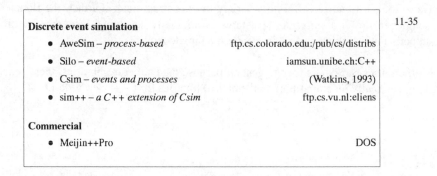

Discrete event simulation	11-35
● AweSim – *process-based*	ftp.cs.colorado.edu:/pub/cs/distribs
● Silo – *event-based*	iamsun.unibe.ch:C++
● Csim – *events and processes*	(Watkins, 1993)
● sim++ – *a C++ extension of Csim*	ftp.cs.vu.nl:eliens
Commercial	
● Meijin++Pro	DOS

Slide 11-35: Libraries for discrete event simulation

A process-based package for simulation is provided by AweSim, which includes some statistical features, queues and processes. It requires GNU C++ and may be regarded as an extension of Libg++, including features for discrete simulation. Also based on Libg++ is the Silo packages which provides a C++ version of the event-based approach described in MacDougall (1987), which was originally implemented in C.

In Watkins (1993) an approach to discrete event simulation is described that encompasses both event-based and process-based simulation. Software, written in C, is included. It provides an excellent introduction to the problems of discrete event simulation and discusses a variety of applications. An C++ extension of the Csim software, including a number of examples, is available at `ftp.cs.vu.nl:eliens`.

As a commercial library for simulation, we may mention Meijin++Pro (which, however, only operates under DOS).

User interface development The two most popular window environments nowadays are X-windows (which operates under Unix) and MS-windows (which provides a window environment on top of DOS). Although both environments provide a C interface (as a collection of low-level library functions), most application developers prefer a library that provides higher-level functionality and pre-defined widgets.

The credo of the consortium supporting X-windows may be expressed as the wish to offer *mechanism instead of policy*. Two standards have been developed which do support *policy* (that is, conventions with respect to the graphical layout of user interfaces) as

well, namely the Motif standard (that is adhered to by many X-window library vendors)
and the Openlook standard.

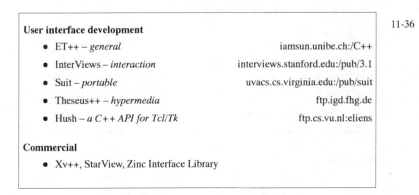

Slide 11-36: Libraries for GUI development

One of the earliest graphic user interface development libraries for C++ is ET++.
See Weinand *et al.* (1988). Originally developed for SunView, ET++ is now also available for X-windows. It is part of a programming environment PE++, which includes program support tools such as browsers and editors. See slide 11-36.

Another important library for developing user interfaces (under X-windows) in
C++ is the InterViews library. See Linton *et al.* (1989). Intended as a research vehicle, the
InterViews library provides an important example of designing an object-oriented library.
In particular, it supports object interaction mechanisms related to the MVC-paradigm discussed in section 7.3. It includes a library (Unidraw) for structured graphics and even provides a user interface builder. Experience in students' assignment, however, shows that the
library is not very easy to use, which is partly due to the absence of proper documentation.

A library for window programming in C, which is interesting primarily because it
is available for both X-windows and MS-windows, is the SUIT library.

The Theseus++ library provides a collection of classes for developing hypermedia
systems. I cannot report any experience, but the approach seems promising.

Lastly, I mention the *hush* library, which provides a C++ interface to the Tcl/Tk
toolkit operating under X-windows. See Ousterhout (1991). As we will discuss in the next
chapter, the design of hush has been inspired by the InterViews library. However, it provides a considerably simplified class structure, yet offers the full functionality of the underlying Tcl/Tk toolkit. See section 12.2. Both the InterViews library and the Tcl/Tk toolkit
(and as a consequence the hush library) comply (optionally) with the Motif standard.

For the commercial libraries a distinction may be made between the libraries that
claim to be platform-independent and the libraries associated with a particular platform or
environment. An example of a platform-dependent library is Xv++, which provides an interface to XView. The platform-independent libraries (such as StarView and the Zinc Interface Library) provide an interface that is portable across X-windows and MS-windows
environments. For example, StarView even supports OS/2, MS-Windows, OSF/Motif,
OPENLOOK and the MacIntosh window system.

Distribution and persistence In comparison with the libraries encountered in the previous domains, the C++ libraries available for distribution, communication and persistence are of a fairly experimental nature. See slide 11-37.

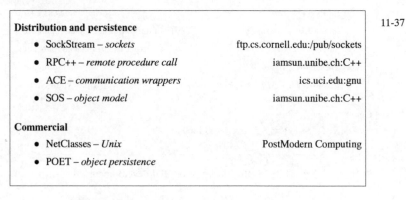

Distribution and persistence	11-37
• SockStream – *sockets*	ftp.cs.cornell.edu:/pub/sockets
• RPC++ – *remote procedure call*	iamsun.unibe.ch:C++
• ACE – *communication wrappers*	ics.uci.edu:gnu
• SOS – *object model*	iamsun.unibe.ch:C++
Commercial	
• NetClasses – *Unix*	PostModern Computing
• POET – *object persistence*	

Slide 11-37: Libraries for distribution and persistence

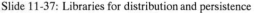

The SockStream library provides a collection of stream-like classes for communications via sockets and the select statement. The RPC++ library provides a C++ interface to the Sun remote procedure call package.

A rather large collection of communication features is offered by the ACE library. Included in the ACE library are classes for event-based processing and inter-application communication. See Schmidt (1993).

Persistence is supported by the SOS library. SOS consists of an object description compiler and associated support classes. It is the result of a project aimed at developing the Obst multi-paradigm object database system. See section 11.3.3.

A commercial package supporting communication and object transport over a network is NetClasses, from PostModern Computing technologies Inc. As a commercial library supporting object persistence in C++ we may mention POET.

Summary

This chapter has dealt with the implications an object-oriented approach has for practical application development.

In section 1, the Microsoft object linking and embedding facility and the OMG proposal for the integration of disparate components, which involves an interface description language (IDL), general object services and an object request broker (ORB), were discussed. We also looked at the ODMG standard for persistent objects, which extends the OMG proposal with object storage facilities. Further, we discussed the duality between objects and events, which plays a role in analysis, design and implementation.

In section 2, we looked at the issues that arise in the design of reusable software libraries, and we discussed the conventions and support tools that were developed for the

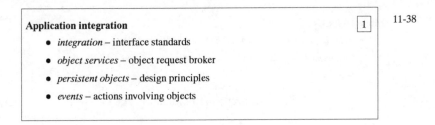

Slide 11-38: Section 11.1: Application development

Eiffel libraries. We also looked at the realization of template classes for the abstract data structures *bag* and *set* in C++.

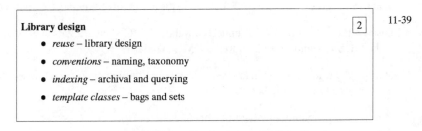

Slide 11-39: Section 11.2: Library design

In section 3, when considering methods and tools for object-oriented application development, we discussed the heritage from structured approaches and looked at the Fusion method as an example of a strongly systematic approach to the process of development. The Fusion method has been compared with a number of other methods, including Objectory, OMT, Booch OOD and CRC. Further, we looked at some CASE tools and programming environments, as well as some of the object database systems for C++.

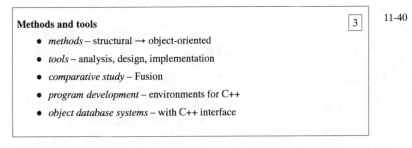

Slide 11-40: Section 11.3: Methods and tools

We concluded, in section 4, with an overview of the libraries for C++. In particular, we looked at the criteria guiding the choice for a particular library, including user-specific criteria, domain-specific criteria and features concerning documentation and support.

Libraries for C++   [4]   11-41

- *criteria for libraries* – user specific, domain, features
- *requirements* – data structures, mathematics, simulation, GUI

Slide 11-41: Section 11.4: Libraries for C++

Questions

(1) Discuss the problems involved in developing large applications. What solutions can you think of?

(2) Discuss the standardization efforts initiated by the OMG. What are they aimed at? What solutions are proposed? What problems are involved in realizing these aims?

(3) Discuss the design principles underlying the ODMG standardization efforts. How is the ODMG standard related to the OMG standard?

(4) Discuss the role of events in analysis, design and implementation. How would you characterize the relation between objects and events?

(5) Discuss the problems involved in library design. How would you solve the problem of maintaining consistency between different releases?

(6) What are your preferences with regard to naming conventions for object methods? Discuss the pros and cons of your approach.

(7) What tools can you think of to support reuse in practice?

(8) Give an overview of the methods available for object-oriented development. Indicate what part of the software lifecycle they cover.

(9) Describe the Fusion method. What do you consider as its most characteristic feature?

(10) How would you compare the Fusion method with the following methods: Objectory, OMT, Booch OOD, CRC? Explain.

(11) What criteria can you think of for evaluating software libraries?

(12) What do you consider to be the minimal functionality requirements for a library of data structures? And for mathematics? Discuss also what classes you expect to find in a GUI library.

Further reading

As further reading I recommend Pinson and Wiener (1990) and Harmon and Tayler (1993), describing object oriented applications. When you are looking for a practical method, I recommend the study of Coleman *et al.* (1994), which describes Fusion. You may also consult OMG (1991) and Cattell (1994) and, naturally, the conference proceedings of OOPSLA, ECOOP and TOOLS. For an overview of libraries for C++ consult Locke (1994). See also appendix G.

12

Hypermedia frameworks

Object-oriented technology is essentially a technology in search of applications. Applications range over business information modeling, distributed systems programming, knowledge-based problem solving and hypermedia systems.

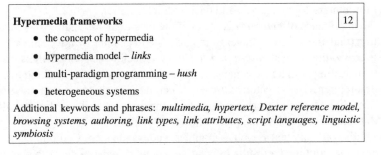

12-1

Slide 12-1: Chapter 12: Hypermedia frameworks

In this chapter, we will conclude our study of object-oriented technology by looking at the design and implementation issues that arise in developing hypermedia systems.

First, we will introduce the concept of hypermedia from a user perspective. In particular, we will discuss the problems of presentation and navigation. Then we will discuss a hypermedia model supporting multimedia presentation channels and timing constraints. We explore the nature of (hyper) links and discuss the notion of *active documents*, and we will look at how a multi-paradigm approach to hypermedia programming may be realized by discussing the design underlying *hush* (the *hyper utility shell* library for C++). Finally, we will discuss the software engineering issues involved in developing hypermedia systems. In particular, we will look at the contribution of object-oriented technology to the development of heterogeneous systems, and simultaneously (concluding this chapter and book) at the possible future of object orientation.

12.1   The concept of hypermedia

Due to the rapidly evolving software and hardware technology, including the mass storage provided by CD-ROM, hypermedia have become accessible to the general public. Hypermedia provide the technology to manage large amounts of information of various kinds by means of the computer.

From a historical perspective, hypermedia may be understood as the combination of hypertext and (interactive) multimedia. Hypertext was conceived shortly after the second world war as a means by which to support mechanically the storage and retrieval of large amounts of information. Interactive multimedia have been developed as the result of integrating computing with media (notably audio and video display).

12.1.1   Nodes and links – *presentation and navigation*

The basic model underlying hypertext may be characterized as (text) *nodes* and *links* between nodes or components thereof. For the user, the conception of *text* as consisting of nodes and links results in what may be called *non-linear text*. According to Bush (1945), who was the first to put the idea into print, the interpretation of text as a network is a natural way for humans to think about and deal with information.

The importance of *hypertext* is thus not the idea of an associative organization of information (that allows one to travel from one node to another by traversing a link), but rather the realization of *machine-supported links*. Machine-supported links give great flexibility in dealing with text as a network. For example, instead of walking to a library to consult a reference on infections diseases when reading about a virus, one may simply traverse a link by clicking on an item to have the material available for consultation.

Multimedia comes into the picture when we, once more, generalize the notion of *text* to comprise ordinary text as well as graphics, audio and video. Combining the notions of hypertext and multimedia results in what we know as *hypermedia*, allowing the user flexible access to a variety of information. Underlying the notion of hypermedia, however, is the assumption that the information is somehow available in electronic form, and that this information may be managed by means of computation. Hypermedia systems, in other words, require *programmable media*. The restriction to plain text of the earlier systems may be explained by the observation that text processing and display technology is relatively easy and cheap. Graphics, and in particular audio and video, require considerably more extensive resources for storage and computation.

A hypermedia system may, in a general way, be conceived of as consisting of a collection of stored *components* (containing text, graphics, audio or video fragments), a collection of *links* (which allow the user to retrieve components in an associative manner) and *presentation facilities* (to enable a structured display of the components selected by the user).

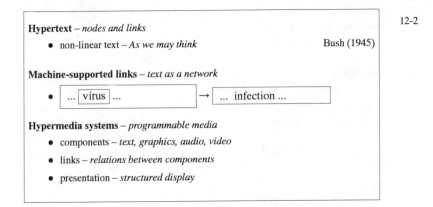

Slide 12-2: The concept of hypermedia

The ease of use of a hypermedia system depends to a great extent upon the organization of the material (components) and the presentation of the associative relations (links) between the components. In particular, a powerful user interface is required to allow the user to navigate through the information without losing orientation.

Direct manipulation interfaces Graphical user interfaces with buttons and menus, and windows for the display of text and graphics, have become the standard for a variety of applications, including text processing, spreadsheets and CAD systems. Originally menu-based, user interfaces have developed into what are often called *object-oriented* user interfaces, or more appropriately *direct manipulation* interfaces.

Direct manipulation interfaces allow for the association of actions with the items displayed. For example, clicking on an icon may result in opening the window associated with that icon. Conversely, clicking on a specific part of the window may result in iconifying the window into a small graphical item on the screen. The reason for calling such interfaces *object-oriented*, obviously, is the analogy with sending a message or command to an object considered as the target. However, direct manipulation interfaces need not necessarily be implemented or designed in an object-oriented way, although in my opinion they had better be.

Hypermedia systems may be used for browsing or authoring, or a combination of both. Browsing hypertext requires an interface resembling the interface of a WYSIWYG (*What You See Is What You Get*) text processor, in that it must support a readable display of the material and the facility to open and close documents. In addition, it must enable the selection of specific parts of the document, which may be blocks or single words, to activate links that lead to another block. See slide 12-3. Often, as in the Intermedia system described in Meyrowitz (1986), the user is allowed to copy parts into a private notebook, containing the material selected while browsing the system. See slide 12-4. Naturally, the display facilities of hypermedia as opposed to hypertext systems must be far more encompassing. These facilities and the issues involved in authoring will be discussed in section 12.1.3.

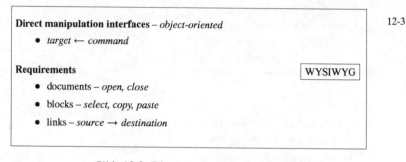

Slide 12-3: Direct manipulation interfaces

Navigation One of the major problems in hypermedia interface design is the support for navigation. Experiments indicate that users have considerable trouble in maintaining a sense of orientation, and often rely on using a keyword index or the traditional hierarchical structure of the document instead of the associative access allowed by following links. See McKnight *et al.* (1991).

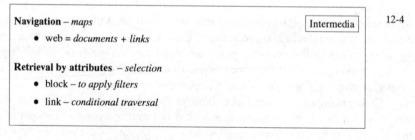

Slide 12-4: Navigation and retrieval

To support navigation based on content characteristics or personal preference, the Intermedia system allows for the creation of *webs*. A *web* is a particular collection of documents and links, which is a subset of the total collection satisfying user-specific criteria, such as field of interest or level of aptitude. Moreover, the Intermedia system supports the graphical display of the structure of a web by means of maps, showing the blocks and the links between them. An example of a web is the private notebook mentioned above, which contains the blocks and links satisfying the condition *selected*.

To support the selection of (parts of) documents and links, the Intermedia system maintains attributes for both blocks and links. The value of block attributes determine whether a particular block is selected or filtered out, and the value of link attributes determine whether activating a link results in traversal or not.

The latter facilities, by the way, suggest that hypermedia offer significantly more than merely user interface gadgets. My opinion in this respect, following Woodhead (1990), is that hypermedia technology may be regarded as a *unifying paradigm* allowing the integration of disparate elements in a common presentation framework.

12.1.2 Hypermedia applications

Hypermedia technology may best be thought of as technology that may be embedded in a variety of applications. This is reflected in the classification of hypertext and hypermedia systems given in Conklin (1987), pictured in slide 12-5.

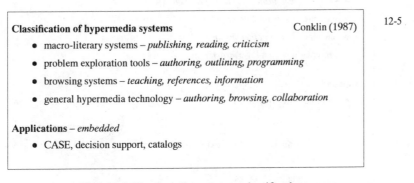

Slide 12-5: Hypermedia systems – classification

Conklin (1987) makes a distinction between *macro-literary systems* which support publishing, reading and criticism and may serve as online annotated libraries, *problem exploration tools* which support authoring, outlining and programming and may be characterized as *idea processors*, *browsing systems* which support the display and content-based retrieval of information and may be used for teaching, reference or online help, and systems that explore general hypermedia technology which offer a combination of authoring, browsing and collaboration facilities (of which the Intermedia system is an example). In general, for systems that primarily support browsing, the presentation facilities will be most important, whereas for authoring systems the functional or programming capabilities will count most.

Applications for which hypermedia technology is an essential ingredient encompass CASE tools, decision support systems and product catalogs. All these applications have in common that a large amount of material, that may come in various media formats, needs to be related, to allow the user flexible access both in a structured and associative manner. Despite the differences due to the particular application domains, we may discern a common hypermedia model underlying the associative structure of these applications.

It is interesting to note that when looking at successful applications of object-oriented programming, such as those reported in Harmon and Tayler (1993), these almost invariably include an embedded hypermedia component, as well as functionality that is derived from a rule-based reasoning facility.

12.1.3 Structure versus presentation – *hypermedia reference models*

Hypermedia technology supports the organization of a variety of material into an associative structure. In addition, hierarchical structuring facilities may be supported.

The basic notions underlying the structuring facilities of hypertext have been expressed in the Dexter hypertext model. See Halasz and Schwartz (1994).

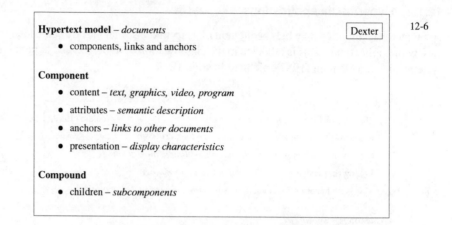

Slide 12-6: The Dexter hypertext reference model

The Dexter model explains the structure of hypertext documents in terms of *components*, *links* and *anchors*. The notion of anchors is introduced to explain how to attach a link to either a source or destination component. An *anchor* is the indication of a particular spot in the document, or rather a component thereof, usually identified by some coordinate.

The Dexter model distinguishes between three layers in a hypertext system, namely the *document* layer (defining the content and structure of documents), a *storage* layer (handling the storage and retrieval of components and links) and a *presentation* layer (handling the display of documents and the interaction with the user).

A *component*, which is a part of a document is characterized by the following features: *content* (which may be text, graphics, audio, video or even a program), *attributes* (which give a semantic description that may be used for retrieval or selective display), *anchors* (which identify the places to which a link is attached), and *presentation* characteristics (which determine the display of the component). In addition, for compound components, a feature *children* may be defined, for storing the list of subcomponents.

Multimedia The original Dexter hypertext model is strongly oriented towards *text*, despite the provision for multimedia content. Multimedia, in particular audio and video, are intrinsically time-based and require temporal primitives to synchronize the presentation of material from different sources.

In the CMIF multimedia model described in Hardman *et al.* (1994), *channels* (which are abstract output devices) are introduced to allow for the specification of abstract timing constraints by means of synchronization arcs between channels.

The notion of *channels* provides the abstraction needed to separate the contents of a presentation from the actual display characteristics. For example, text may be output through a text channel while, simultaneously, video may be output through a video channel. The screen layout and allocation of these channels may be determined independently.

The actual presentation is determined by *events*, that may either arise as the result of a user action or as the result of the activation of a synchronization arc. For example,

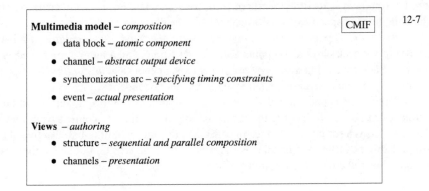

Slide 12-7: The CMIF multimedia model

a synchronization constraint may specify that an audio fragment containing speech must be started 10 seconds after the beginning of a video sequence. Then, after 10 seconds, the video channel will issue an event that causes the audio channel to start presenting its contents.

The CMIF model has been developed to allow for portable multimedia documents. In particular, the notion of channels allows for a platform-independent characterization of presentation characteristics and timing constraints. An important characteristic of the model, from an authoring perspective, is that it supports a compositional approach to authoring, since it allows us to compose a channel (specifying a sequential composition of components) with arbitrary many other channels, in parallel.

In Hardman *et al.* (1994), an extension of the CMIF multimedia model is developed to incorporate the associative structuring facilities defined by the Dexter hypertext model.

Slide 12-8: A hypermedia reference model

In the combined model, a single component consists of *contents* containing the actual data blocks of the component, *attributes* that specify semantic information, a list of *anchors* (each specifying a symbolic name and a value, which in the case of an audio or video fragment is its time measured from the start), and *presentation* characteristics, which include the specification of a channel and the duration of the component.

As in the Dexter model, *compound* components may have *children* attributes, specifying for each child a component and its start-time, and a number of *synchronization arcs*, each specifying a *source* (component and anchor) and *destination* (component and anchor). Synchronization arcs may cross channel boundaries.

The reader is encouraged to specify a more detailed object model, based on the outline given above. Evidently, the incorporation of a variety of content types and display channels is a serious challenge. In particular, the notion of time-based active objects will probably be difficult to handle. For an abstract characterization of active time-based (media) object, the reader is referred to Nierstrasz (1987).

12.1.4   On the notion of links – *active documents*

Hypermedia documents are often referred to as *hyperdocuments*, because of their associative structure imposed by (hyper) links. Links, in general, may be characterized as a possibly conditional connection between a source anchor and destination anchor. There has been an ongoing discussion as to whether links must lead from byte to byte or whether they must be defined at some higher level. On closer inspection, there appear to be a number of choices with respect to the kind of links that may be supported. See, for example, Halasz (1988, 1991).

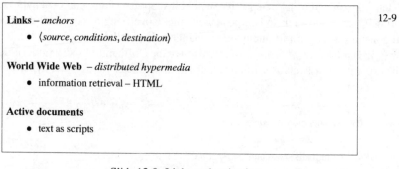

Links – *anchors*
- ⟨*source, conditions, destination*⟩

World Wide Web – *distributed hypermedia*
- information retrieval – HTML

Active documents
- text as scripts

12-9

Slide 12-9: Links and activation

Perhaps the most important distinction is that between hard-wired links that act as a *goto* in programming languages and what may be called *virtual* links, the destination of which is computed when activating the source anchor.

This distinction is exemplified in the World Wide Web (WWW) distributed hypermedia system, which was initiated by CERN (Switzerland). The World Wide Web supports HTML (HyperText Markup Language), a semi-official hypermedia markup language in the SGML tradition. The World Wide Web allows the user to locate and retrieve documents worldwide across the Internet. However, a document may either be stored physically somewhere on a node in the network or may be generated on the fly by some information retrieval server producing HTML output.

The production of HTML documents by some external program as the result of accessing a link somehow blurs the distinction between programs and documents. One step further in this direction is to allow documents, whether stored or generated, to contain embedded code that is executed when the document is viewed. Such documents may be characterized as *active documents*. Active documents are, for example, proposed as an extension to the MIME (Multipurpose Internet Mail) standard, to allow for 'live mail'. Embedding code in documents would allow for synchronization facilities that are currently beyond the scope of HTML and MIME. However, a standard (in development) that provides features for synchronization is the HyTime markup language, which is another offspring of the SGML family.

Summarizing, active documents are documents that result in programmed actions by being displayed. From a systems programming point of view, we may regard active documents as program scripts that are executed by a (hypermedia) interpreter. (A well-know example of a script-based hypermedia programming language is HyperTalk.) Hypermedia programming, using scripts, relies intrinsically on an event-driven control mechanism. In the following section, we will explore how we may combine script-based (event-driven) programming with (more traditional) object-oriented development (in C++).

12.2   Multi-paradigm programming

Hypermedia programming is by its nature complex, partly because of the variety of content that must be dealt with, and partly because the graphical user interface forms an essential part of the hypermedia application.

In this section, we will look at an approach to graphical interface programming that may best be characterized as *multi-paradigm programming*. Our approach, embodied in the *hush* library (Eliens, 1994), combines the use of C++ and the script language Tcl. The advantage of using C++ is its robustness. The advantage of using scripts is, clearly, flexibility. A multi-paradigm approach offers the best of both worlds. Or the worst, for that matter.

The *hush* library offers an interface to the Tcl/Tk (window programming) toolkit, and a number of multimedia devices, including real-time synthesized audio and MPEG (Motion Pictures Experts Group) software video.

The principal contribution of the approach embodied in *hush* is that it offers a type-secure solution for connecting script code with C++ (and vice versa). In particular, it allows one to associate events with actions by means of *handler* objects. In addition, the *hush* library allows the programmer to employ inheritance for the development of possibly compound widgets.

Hush stands for *hyper utility shell*. The standard interpreter associated with the *hush* library is a shell, called *hush*, including a number of the available extensions of Tcl/Tk and widgets developed by ourselves. The *hush* library offers a C++ interface to the Tcl/Tk toolkit and its extensions. Moreover, a program created with *hush* is itself an interpreter extending the *hush* interpreter.

Tcl/Tk The language Tcl was first presented in Ousterhout (1990). Tcl was announced as a flexible cshell-like language, intended to be used for developing an X11-based toolkit. A year later, the Tk toolkit (based on Tcl) was presented in Ousterhout (1991). From the start Tcl/Tk has received a lot of attention, since it provides a flexible and convenient way in which to develop quite powerful window applications.

The Tcl language offers variables, assignment and a procedure construct. Also it provides a number of control constructs, facilities for manipulating strings and built-in primitives giving access to the underlying operating system. The basic Tcl language may easily be extended by associating a function written in C with a command name. Arguments given to the command are passed as strings to the function defining the command.

The Tk toolkit is an extension of Tcl with commands to create and configure widgets for displaying text and graphics, and providing facilities for window management. The Tk toolkit, and the *wish* interpreter based on Tk, provides a convenient way to program X-window based applications.

Example | *wish* | 12-10

┌─────────────────┐
│ [X] hello   [꣰] │
├─────────────────┤
│ **Hello, world** │
└─────────────────┘

Scripts – *hello world*

```
button .b -text "Hello, world" -command {
    puts stdout "hello world"
    }
pack .b
```

Slide 12-10: A Wish example

The *wish* program is an interpreter for executing Tcl/Tk scripts. As an example of a *wish* script, look at the *hello world* program in slide 12-10. The *hello world* script defines a button that displays *Hello, world*, and prints *hello world* to standard output when it is activated by pressing the left mouse button. The language used to write this script is simply Tcl with the commands defined by Tk, such as the *button* command (needed to create a button) and the *pack* command (that is used to map the button to the screen).

The *wish* program actually provides an example of a simple application based on Tcl/Tk. It may easily be extended to include, for example, 3D-graphics by linking the appropriate C libraries and defining the functions making this functionality available as (new) Tcl commands.

To define Tcl commands in C, the programmer has to define a command function and declare the function to be a command in Tcl by invoking the *Tcl_CreateCommand* function.

Creating a command is done with reference to an interpreter, which accounts for the first argument of *Tcl_CreateCommand*. The name of the command, as may be used in a Tcl script must be given as a second argument, and the C/C++ function defining the command as a third argument. Finally, when declaring a command, the address of a structure containing client data may be stored, which may be (the address of) the root window, for example.

When the function is invoked as the result of executing the Tcl command, the client data stored at declaration time is passed as the first argument to the function. Since the type *ClientData* is actually defined to be *void*∗, the function must first cast the client data argument to an appropriate type. Evidently, casting is error-prone.

Another problem with command functions as used in the Tcl C API is that permanent data are possible only in the form of client data, global variables or static local variables. Both client data and global variables are unsafe by being too visible and static local data are simply inelegant.

12.2.1 Program structure

The *hush* library is intended to provide a convenient way to program window-based applications in C++. Basically, there are two considerations that may lead you to employ the *hush* library. When you are familiar with Tcl/Tk and you need to combine Tcl scripts with C++ code, you may use *handler* classes to do so in a relatively type-secure way. On the other hand, when you want to program graphical user interfaces in C++, you may employ the *hush* widget classes. In the latter case, you may choose to remain ignorant of the underlying Tcl/Tk implementation or exploit the Tcl script facility to the extent you wish.

In this section, a brief overview will be given of the classes offered by the *hush* library. Further, it will be shown how to construct the *hush* interpreter referred to in the introduction. In addition, we will take a closer look at the classes *kit* and *session*, which are needed to communicate with the embedded Tcl interpreter and to initialize the main event loop.

The hush class library The *hush* C++ library consists of three kinds of classes, namely (a) the widget classes, which mimic the functionality of Tk, (b) the handler classes, which are involved in the handling of events and the binding of C++ code to Tcl commands, and (c) the classes *kit* and *session*, which encapsulate the embedded interpreter and the window management system,

In the widget class hierarchy depicted in slide 12-11 (a), the *widget* class represents an abstract widget, defining the commands that are valid for each of the descendant concrete widget classes. The *widget* class, however, is not an abstract class in C++ terms. It may be used for creating pointers to widgets defined in Tcl. In contrast, employing the constructor of one of the concrete widget classes results in actually creating a widget. A more detailed example showing the functionality offered by the widget classes will be given in section 12.2.3. A description of the individual widget classes is included in appendix E.

The class hierarchy depicted in slide 12-11 (b) depicts the *handler* class as a subclass of client. The reason for this will become clear in section 12.2.2. The *handler* class may also be considered an abstract class, in the sense that it is intended to be used as the ancestor of a user-defined handler class. The *handler* class has two pre-defined descendant classes, namely the *widget* class and the *item* class. This implies, indeed, that both the *widget* and the *item* classes (the latter of which is discussed in section 12.2.4) may also be used as ancestor handler classes. The reason for this is that any descendant of a

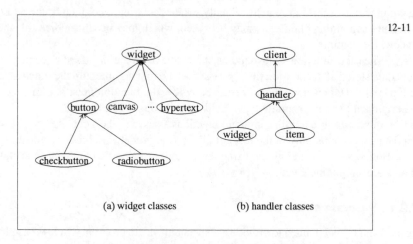

(a) widget classes   (b) handler classes

Slide 12-11: An overview of the hush library

widget or *item* class may declare itself to be its own handler and define the actions that are invoked in response to particular events. This will be illustrated and discussed in sections 12.2.2 and 12.2.3.

The hush interpreter In the introduction, *hush* was announced as both a C++ library and as an interpreter extending the *wish* interpreter. The program shown in slide 12-12 substantiates this claim, albeit in a perhaps disappointingly simple way.

The structure of the program is characteristic for *hush*-based applications.   Part [1] consists merely of including the hush.h header file and may possibly define additional functionality.   Part [2] consists of an application class, derived from *session*, defining how the *hush* interpreter deals with command-line arguments (a and d) and the initialization that takes place when the main event loop is started (c). To understand (a) and (d) it is enough to know that the *hush* library provides a hypertext widget and that the -x option treats the next argument as the name of a hypertext file. In section 12.2.4, an example will be given that involves the hypertext widget. In (b) the hush.tcl file is declared to be the initialization file. It contains the Tcl code for installing the extensions loaded in (c). In (e), a predefined button .quit is packed to the root widget. Part [3] is needed to initialize the application and start the main event loop.

The *hush* interpreter defined by the program extends the *wish* interpreter by loading some extensions to Tcl and by allowing for the display of a hypertext file. The interpreter accepts any command-line argument accepted by the *wish* interpreter, in addition to the -x hypertext option.

The *kit* class *Hush* is meant to provide a parsimonious C++ interface to Tcl/Tk. Nevertheless, as with many a toolkit, some kind of API shock seems to be unavoidable. This is especially true for the *widget* class (covered in section 12.2.3) and the class *kit* defining the C++ interface with the embedded Tcl interpreter. The functionality of *kit* can only be completely understood after reading this section. However, since an instance of *kit* is

```
#include "hush.h"                                              [1]

class application : public session {                          [2]
public:
application(int argc, char* argv[]) : session(argc,argv) {
   hyper = 0;
   if ( (argc == 3) && !strcmp( argv[1],"-x") ) {            // a
         hyper = 1;
         strcpy(hyperfile,argv[2]);
         }
   init("/usr/prac/se/hush/lib/hush/hush.tcl");              // b
}
void main(kit* tk, int argc, char* argv[] ) {
   init_expect(tk); init_itcl(tk); init_dp(tk);              // c
   if (hyper) {
      hypertext* h = new hypertext(".help");                 // d
      h→ file(hyperfile);
      h→ geometry(330,250);
      h→ pack();
      tk→ pack(".quit");                                     // e
      }
}
private:
char hyperfile[BUFSIZ];
int hyper;
};
int main (int argc, char* argv[]) {                          [3]
session* s = new application(argc,argv);
s→ run();
}
```

Slide 12-12: The *hush* interpreter

used in almost any other object (class), it is presented here first. See slide 12-13. The reader will undoubtly gradually learn the functionality of *kit* by studying the examples.

To understand why a *kit* class is needed, recall that each *hush* program contains an embedded Tcl interpreter. The *kit* class encapsulates this interpreter and provides a collection of member functions to interact with the embedded interpreter.

The first group of functions (*eval, result, evaluate* and *source*) may be used to execute commands in the Tcl scripting language directly. A Tcl command is simply a string conforming to certain syntactic requirements. The function *eval* evaluates a Tcl command. The function *result*() may be used to fetch the result of the last Tcl command. In contrast, the function *result*(*char**) may be used to set the result of a Tcl command, when this command is defined in C++ (as may be done with *kit* :: *action*). The function *evaluate* provides a shorthand for combining *eval* and *result*(). The function *source* may be used to read in a file containing a Tcl script.

Also, we have the *kit* :: *action* function that may be used to associate a Tcl command with a handler object. In section 12.2.2, alternative ways of defining an action are discussed.

The next group of functions is related to widgets and events that may occur to widgets. The *event* function delivers the latest event. It may only be used in a command that is bound to some particular event. See section 12.2.2. When other events occur before accessing the event object, the information it contains may be obsolete.

12-13

```
interface kit {                                        kit

int eval(char* cmd);              // to evaluate script command
char* result();                   // to fetch the result of eval
void result(char* s);             // to set the result of eval
char* evaluate(char* cmd)         // combines eval and result
int source(char* f);              // to load a script from file
action& action(char* name, handler* h);

class event event();                        // returns the last event

widget* root();                   // returns toplevel (root) widget
widget* pack(widget* w, char* options = "");
widget* pack(char* wp, char* options = "";

char* selection(char* options="");          // X environment

void after(int msecs, char* cmd);
void after(int n, handler* h);

void update(char* options="");

char* send(char* it, char* cmd);

void trace(int level = 1);
void notrace();
void quit()                                 // to terminate the session
};
```

Slide 12-13: The *kit* class

The function *root* gives access to the toplevel root widget associated with that particular instance of the *kit*. The function *pack* may be used to append widgets to the root widget, in order to map them to the screen. Widgets may be identified either by a pointer to a *widget* object or by their *path name*, which is a string. See section 12.2.3.

Next, we have a group of functions related to the X environment. The function *selection* delivers the current X selection. The function *after* may be used to set a timer callback for a handler. Setting a timer callback means that the handler object will be invoked after the number of milliseconds given as the first argument to *after*.

The function *update* may be used to ensure that all pending events are processed. For example, when moving items on a canvas, an update may be needed to make the changes visible. Also, we have a *send* function that may be used to communicate with other Tcl/Tk applications. The first argument of *send* must be the name of an application, which may be set when creating a session.

Further, we have the functions *trace*() and *notrace*(), which may be used to turn on, respectively off, tracing. The level indicates at what detail information will be given. Trace level zero is equivalent to notrace(). Finally, the function *quit* may be used to terminate the main event loop.

The *session* class Each program written with *hush* may contain only one embedded interpreter. To initialize the *kit* object wrapping the interpreter and to start the main event loop, an instance of the class *session* must be created. See slide 12-14.

The preferred way of doing this is by defining a descendant class of the *session* class, redefining the virtual function *session* :: *main* to specify what needs to be done before starting the main loop. In addition, the constructor of the newly defined class may be used to check command line arguments and to initialize application specific data, as illustrated in slide 12-12.

12-14

```
interface session {                                    session
    session(int argc, char* * argv, char* name = 0);
    void init(char* fname);
    virtual void prelude(kit* tk, int argc, char* argv[] );
    virtual void main(kit* tk, int argc, char* argv[] );
    int run( );
};
```

Slide 12-14: The *session* class

When creating a *session* object, the *name* of the application may be given as the last parameter. Under this name, the application is known to other Tk applications, which may communicate with each other by means of the *send* command.

The function *init* may be used to specify a different initialization script. This script must include the default *hush* initialization script, which is an adapted version of the original *wish* initialization script.

Apart from the function *main*, a function *prelude* may also be defined. When the program is used as an interpreter (by giving −f *file* as command line arguments) only the *prelude* function will be executed, otherwise *prelude* will be executed before *main*. In interpreter mode, the *main* function will also be executed when the script contains the command *go-back*. Finally, the function *run* must be called to actually initialize the program and start the main loop.

12.2.2 Binding actions to events

Handler objects may be bound to Tcl commands or events. Events are generated by the (X) window environment in response to actions of the user. These actions include pressing a mouse button, releasing a mouse button, moving the mouse, etc. Instead of explicitly dealing with all incoming events, applications delegate control to the environment by associating a callback function with each event that is relevant for a particular widget.

This mechanism frees the programmer from the responsibility of deciding to which widget the event belongs and what action to take.

Nevertheless, from the perspective of program design, the proper organization of the callback functions is not a trivial matter. Common practice is to write only a limited number of callback functions and perform explicit dispatching according to the type of event.

An object-oriented approach may be advantageous as a means to organize a collection of callback functions as member functions of a single class. One way of doing this is to define an abstract event handler class which provides a virtual member function for each of the most commonly occurring events. In effect, such a handler class hides the dispatching according to the type of the event. A concrete handler class may then be defined simply by overriding the member functions corresponding to the events of interest.

Before studying the abstract *handler* class in more detail, we will briefly look at the definition of the *event* class.

Events Events always belong to a particular widget. To which widget events are actually directed depends upon whether the programmer has defined a binding for the event type. When such a binding exists for a widget and the (toolkit) environment decides that the event belongs to that widget, then the callback associated with that event is executed. Information concerning the event may be retrieved by asking the kit for the latest event.

12-15

```
interface event {
    int type();                          // X event type
    char* name();                        // type as string

    int x();
    int y();

    int button(int i = 0);               // ButtonPress
    int buttonup(int i = 0);             // ButtonRelease
    int motion();                        // MotionNotify

    int keyevent();                      // KeyPress or KeyRelease
    int buttonevent(int i = 0);          // ButtonPress or Release

    int keycode();

    void trace();                        // prints event information

    void* rawevent();                    // delivers raw X event
};
```

event

Slide 12-15: The *event* class

Event objects represent the events generated by the X-window system. Each event has a type. The type of the event can be inspected with *type*() which returns an integer value or *name*() which returns a string representation of the type. For some of the common event types, such as *ButtonPress, ButtonRelease* and *MotionNotify*, member functions are provided to facilitate testing. If an integer argument (1, 2 or 3) is given to *button, buttonup* or *buttonevent*, it is checked whether the event has occurred for the corresponding button.

The functions x and y deliver the widget coordinates of the event, if appropriate.

Calling *trace* for the event results in printing the type and coordinate information for the event. When setting the *kit* :: *trace* level to 2 this information is automatically printed.

Programmers not satisfied with this interface can check the type and access the underlying XEvent at their own risk.

Handlers Handler objects provide a type secure way in which to deal with local data and global resources needed when responding to an event. A handler object may store the information it needs in instance variables, when its constructor is called. See slide 12-16.

12-16

```
interface handler : client {                            handler
    virtual int dispatch(kit* _tk, int _argc, char* _argv[]);
    virtual int operator()();
    virtual void press( event& ) { }
    virtual void release( event& ) { }
    virtual void keypress( event& ) { }
    virtual void keyrelease( event& ) { }
    virtual void motion( event& ) { }
    virtual void enter( event& ) { }
    virtual void leave( event& ) { }
    virtual void other( event& ) { }
protected:
    int argc;
    char* * argv;
    kit* tk;
};
```

Slide 12-16: The *handler* class

Activating a handler object in response to an event or a Tcl command occurs by calling the *dispatch* function of the handler. The system takes care of this, provided that the user has bound the handler object to a Tcl command or event.

The *dispatch* function, in its turn, calls the *operator*() function, after storing the *kit*, *argc* and *argv* arguments in the corresponding instance variables. See slide 12-17. The *handler* :: *operator*() function fetches the latest event from the *kit* object and selects one of the predefined member functions (*press, motion, release,* etc.) according to the type of the event. The original handler class knows only virtual functions. Each of these function, including the *dispatch* and *operator*() function, may be redefined. The two-step indirection, via the *dispatch* and *operator*() functions, is introduced to facilitate derivation by inheritance, directly from the *handler* or from classes that are themselves derived from the *handler* class, such as the widget classes.

Actions Handler objects will be activated only when a binding has been defined, by using *kit* :: *action* or implicitly by employing *widget* :: *bind* or *widget* :: *handler*. Such bind-

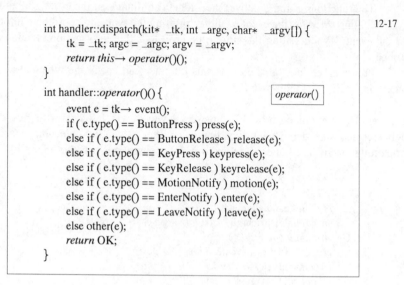

Slide 12-17: The *dispatch* and *operator*( ) function

ings may also be defined by *kit* :: *after* or *item* :: *bind* and *item* :: *handler*. Implicit binding results in the creation of an anonymous action.

Actions, as characterized by the class *action*, provide the actual means with which to bind C++ code to Tcl commands. Actions may be defined either trivially by a Tcl command, by a C/C++ *command* function or by *handler* objects. In effect, defining an action by means of a handler object amounts, implicitly, to defining a command function with a privileged client for which, by convention, the *dispatch* function is invoked.

```
Client                                                    client      12-18

        class client {  };                        // empty class


Command                                                   command

        typedef command(client* , kit* , int argc, char*  argv[]);
```

Slide 12-18: The *client* class

Data passed to a *command* function must be of the type *client*, which is defined by an empty class introduced only to please the compiler. In slide 12-18 the type definition of *command* is given. Apart from the *client** parameter, a command function must also declare a *kit** parameter and an *argc* and *argv* parameter, similar to that for *main*. The *client** data of a command (and similarly for the *clientdata* parameter of a *tclcommand*) can be any kind of class. However, it is to be preferred that such classes are made a subclass of *client*. The *client* data pointer is declared when creating an action and passed to the command function when the actual call is made. The other parameters (*argc* and *argv*) depend on the actual call. The use of *argc* and *argv* comes from the original C interface of Tcl. It proves to be a very flexible way of communicating data, especially in string-oriented applications.

```
interface action {                                    action
    action(char* name);

    action(char* name, handler* h);
    action(char* name, command f, client* data = 0);
    action(char* name, tcl_command f, ClientData data = 0);

    action( handler* h);                          // anonymous
    action( command f, client* data = 0);
    action( tcl_command f, ClientData data = 0);

    char* name();                    // returns the name of an action
};
```

12-19

Slide 12-19: The *action* class

The class *action* offers no less than seven constructors. The first constructor, which takes a (*char**) string as a parameter, is merely for convenience. It may be used to convert the name of a Tcl script command into an *action*. The following three constructors differ from the last three constructors only by their first string parameter, which serves to define the name under which the action will be known by the Tcl script interpreter. The last three constructors, in contrast, create anonymous actions, of which the user, however, can ask the name by invoking the function *name*.

The preferred form of creating an action is by giving it (apart from a name) a *handler* as a parameter. As already noted, handler objects offer a type-secure way of dealing with client information. In contrast, the second constructor of this group, which takes a *command* function and possibly a pointer to *client* data as parameters, may make (type-insecure) conversions of the client data necessary.

The constructor taking a *tcl_command* and *ClientData* as parameters is incorporated for compatibility reasons only.

When using any of the last six constructors, as a side-effect an association is created between the *name* of the action and a Tcl command. If such a Tcl command already exists, the previous association will be overwritten. This is also the case if it has been defined as a Tcl script command.

12.2.3 User interface widgets

The Tk toolkit offers numerous built-in widgets. The Tk widgets conform to the look-and-feel of the OSF/Motif standard. The *hush* C++ interface for Tk provides for each Tk widget a class of the same name which supports the creation of a widget and allows the user to access and modify it. In addition to the standard Tk widgets, the *hush* library includes a number of other widgets, such as a *barchart*, *hypertext* and *photo* widget (created by other Tk adepts). Also, widgets of our own making are offered, such as a *filechooser* and MPEG video widget.

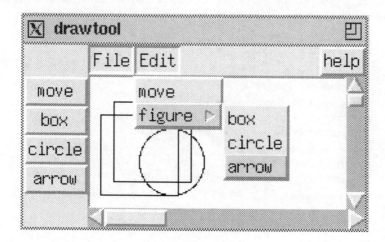

Slide 12-20: The *drawtool* interface

In this section we will look at the realization of simple drawing tool. The example illustrates how to use the *hush* library widgets, and serves to illustrate in particular how handlers may be attached to widgets, either by declaration or by inheritance, and how to construct compound widgets.

Our approach may be considered object-oriented, in the sense that each component of the user interface is defined by a class derived from a widget class. It must be pointed out beforehand that the main difficulty in defining compound or mega widgets is not the construction of the components themselves, but delegating the configuration and binding instructions to the appropriate components. Section 12.2.3 shows how a compound widget defined in C++ may be made to correspond to a widget command that may be used in a Tcl script. Ideally, defining a new widget includes both the definition of a C++ class interface and the definition of the corresponding Tcl command.

Our drawing tool consists of a *tablet*, which is a canvas with scrollbars to allow for a large size canvas of which only a part is displayed, a *menu_bar*, having a *File* and an *Edit* menu, and a *toolbox*, which is a collection of buttons for selecting from among the drawing facilities. In addition, a help facility is offered. See slide 12-20.

In slide 12-21 the application class for *drawtool* is depicted. Before the main event loop is started, the components of the drawing tool are created and packed to the root widget. In addition to the *tablet, menu_bar* and *toolbox*, a *frame* widget is created to pack the menubar and tablet together. This is needed to ensure that the geometrical layout of the widget comes out right. Each of the component widgets is given a pointer to the root widget. In addition, a pointer to the tablet is given to the *toolbox* and a pointer to the *toolbox* is given to the *menu_bar*. The reason for this will become clear when dis-

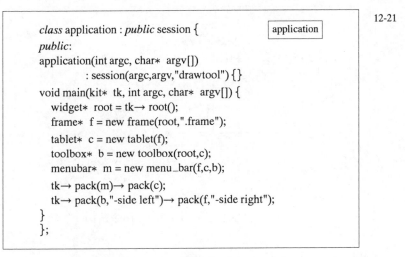

Slide 12-21: The drawing tool

cussing the *toolbox* and *menu_bar* in sections 12.2.3 and 12.2.3, respectively. In the example, no attention will be paid to memory management.

Configuring widgets Widgets are the elements from which a GUI is made. They appear as windows on the screen to display text or graphics and may respond to events such as motioning the mouse or pressing a key by calling an action associated with that event.

Usually, the various widgets constituting the user interface are (hierarchically) related to each other, such as in the *drawtool* application which contains a canvas to display graphic elements, a button toolbox for selecting the graphic items and a menubar offering various options such as saving the drawing in a file.

Widgets in Tk are identified by a *path name*. The path name of a widget reflects its possible subordination to another widget. See slide 12-22.

Pathnames consist of strings separated by dots. The first character of a path must be a dot. The first letter of a path must be lower case. The format of a path name may be expressed in BNF form as

$$<path> ::= '.' \mid '.'<string> \mid < path>'.'<string>$$

For example '.' is the path name of the root widget, whereas '.quit' is the path name of a widget subordinate to the root widget. A widget subordinate to another widget must have the path name of that widget as part of its own path name. For example, the widget '.f.m ' may have a widget '.f.m.h ' as a subordinate widget. Note that the widget hierarchy induced by the path names is completely orthogonal to the widget class inheritance hierarchy depicted in slide 12-11 (a) and slide E-1. With respect to the path name hierarchy, when speaking of ancestors we simply mean superordinate widgets.

Pathnames are treated somewhat more liberally in *hush*. For example, widget path names may simply be defined or extended by a string. The missing dot is then automatically inserted.

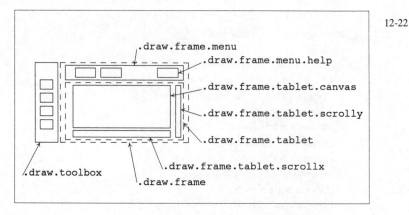

Slide 12-22: The *drawtool* widget hierarchy

Calling the constructor *widget* as in

widget* w = new widget(".awry");

does not result in creating an actual widget but only defines a pointer to the widget with that particular name. (It is not an abstract class, technically, since it does not contain any pure virtual functions, see section 2.2.2.) If a widget with that name exists, it may be treated as an ordinary widget object, otherwise an error will occur. The constructor *widget*(*widget* * *w*, *char* * *path*) creates a widget by appending the path name *path* to the path name of the argument widget *w*.

The function *path* delivers the path name of a widget object. Each widget created by Tk actually defines a Tcl command associated with the path name of the widget. In other words, an actual widget may be regarded as an object which can be asked to evaluate commands. For example a widget '.b ' may be asked to change its background color by a Tcl command like

.b configure -background blue

The functions *eval, result* and *evaluate* enable the programmer to apply Tcl commands to the widget directly, as does the *configure* command. The function *geometry* sets the width and height of the widget.

Naming widgets in a hierarchical fashion does not imply that the widgets behave accordingly. The widget class interface offers two *pack* functions. The function *widget* :: *pack*(*char*) applies to individual widgets. As options one may specify, for example, −side *X*, where *X* is either top, bottom, left or right, to pack the widget to the appropriate side of the cavity specified by the ancestor widget. Other options are −fill x or −fill y, to fill up the space in the appropriate dimensions, or −padx *N* or −pady *N*, for some integer *N*, to surround the widget with some extra space.

Alternatively, the function *widget* :: *pack*(*widget**, *char**) may be used, which allows for the same options but applies packing to the widget parameter. This function is convenient when packing widgets in a *frame* or *toplevel* widget. As a remark, the *kit* :: *pack* function may only be used to pack widgets to the root window.

```
interface widget : handler {                          widget

widget(char* p);
widget(widget& w, char* p);

char* type();                        // returns type of the widget
char* path();                        // returns path of the widget

int eval(char* cmd);                 // invokes "thepath() cmd"
char* result();                      // returns the result of eval
char* evaluate(char* cmd)            // combines eval and result()

virtual void configure(char* cmd);         // uses 'path()'
virtual void geometry(int xs, int ys);     // width x height

widget* pack(char* options = "" );
widget* pack(widget* w, char* options = "" );

bind(char * b, handler* h, char* args = "" );
bind(char * b, action& ac, char* args = "" );

handler(class handler* h, char* args = "" );
handler(action& ac, char* args = "" );

void xscroll(scrollbar* s);          // to attach scrollbars
void yscroll(scrollbar* s);

void focus(char* options="");
void grab(char* options="");

void destroy();                      // removes widget from the screen

void* tkwin();                       // gives access to Tk window

widget* self();                      // for constructing mega widgets
void redirect(widget* w);
protected:
char* thepath();                     // delivers the virtual path
virtual install(action&,char* args="");
};
```

Slide 12-23: The *widget* class

Binding events Widgets may respond to events. To associate an event with an action, an explicit binding must be specified for that particular widget. Some widgets provide default bindings. These may, however, be overruled.

The function *bind* is used to associate handlers or actions with events. The first string parameter of *bind* may be used to specify the event type. Common event types are, for example, *ButtonPress*, *ButtonRelease* and *Motion*, which are the default events for canvas widgets. Also keystrokes may be defined as events, for example *Return*, which is the default event for the *entry* widget.

The function *widget* :: *handler* may be used to associate a handler object or action with the default bindings for the widget. Concrete widgets may not override the *handler* function itself, but must define the protected virtual function *install*. Typically, the install function consists of calls to *bind* for each of the event types that is relevant to the widget.

For both the *bind* and *handler* functions, the optional *args* parameter may be used to specify the arguments that will be passed to the handler or action when it is invoked. For the *button* widget, for example, the default *install* function supplies the text of the button as an additional argument for its handler.

In addition, the widget class offers four functions that may be used when defining compound or mega widgets. The function *redirect(w)* must by used to delegate the invocation of the *eval, configure, bind* and *handler* functions to the widget *w*. The function *self( )* gives access to the widget to which the commands are redirected. After invoking *redirect,* the function *thepath* will deliver the path that is determined by *self( )* → *path( )*. In contrast, the function *path* will still deliver the path name of the outer widget. Calling *redirect* when creating the compound widget class suffices for most situations. However, when the default events must be changed or the declaration of a handler must take effect for several component widgets, the virtual function *install* must be redefined to handle the delegation explicitly. How *redirect* and *install* actually work will become clear in the examples.

Handlers A note on terminology is in place here. The reader may be a little astonished by the fact that we have both a *handler* class and a *handler* function, which is more properly written as *widget* :: *handler*. The situation may even seem more confusing when realizing that the *widget* class itself is a descendant of the *handler* class. Schematically, we have the situation as depicted in slide 12-24.

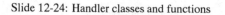

```
class widget : public handler {                          12-24
public:
...
void handler(class handler* h) { ... }
...
};
```

Slide 12-24: Handler classes and functions

Note that there is no ambiguity here. A *handler* object is an object that may be invoked in response to a Tcl command or an event. The *handler* function declares a *handler* object to be responsible for dealing with the events that are of interest to the widget. Note that since a widget is a *handler* instance, it may declare itself as a handler for the incoming events.

Buttons As the first component of the drawing tool, we will look at the *toolbox*. The *toolbox* is a collection of buttons packed in a frame. See slide 12-25.

Each button is an instance of the class *toolbutton*. When a toolbutton is created (a), the actual button is given the name of the button as its path. Next, (b) the button is given the name as its text, the ancestor widget *w* is declared to be the handler for the button and the button is packed. The function *text* is a member function of the class *button*, whereas both *handler* and *pack* are common widget functions. Note that the parameter

```
    class toolbutton : public button {              toolbutton
    public:
    toolbutton(widget* w, char* name)
                  : button(w,name) {                    // (a)
        text(name); handler(w,name); pack();            // (b)
        }
    };
    class toolbox : public frame {                   toolbox
    public:
    toolbox(widget* w, tablet* t)
                  : c(t), frame(w,"toolbox") {          // (c)
      button* b1 = new toolbutton(this,"move");
      button* b2 = new toolbutton(this,"box");
      button* b3 = new toolbutton(this,"circle");
      button* b4 = new toolbutton(this,"arrow");
      }
    int operator()() {                                  // (d)
        c→ mode(argv[1]);
        return OK;
        }
    private:
    tablet* c;
    };
```

12-25

Slide 12-25: The *toolbox*

name is used as a path name, as the text to display, and as an argument for the handler, that will be passed as a parameter when invoking the handler object.

The *toolbox* class inherits from the *frame* widget class, and creates a frame widget with a path relative to the widget parameter provided by the constructor (c). The constructor further creates the four toolbuttons.

The *toolbox* is both the superordinate widget and handler for each *toolbutton*. When the *operator()* function of the *toolbox* is invoked in response to pressing a button, the call is delegated to the *mode* function of the *tablet* (d). The argument given to *mode* corresponds to the name of the button pressed.

The definition of the *toolbutton* and *toolbox* illustrates that a widget need not necessarily be its own handler. The decision, whether to define a subclass which is made its own handler or to install an external handler depends upon what is considered the most convenient way in which to access the resources needed. As a guideline, exploit the regularity of the application.

Menus The second component of our drawing tool is the *menubar*. The class *menu_bar*, depicted in slide 12-26 is derived from the *hush* widget *menubar*. Its constructor requires an ancestor widget, a *tablet* and a *toolbox*. The tablet is passed as a parameter to the

```
class menu_bar : public menubar {                    menu_bar          12-26
public:
menu_bar(widget* w, tablet* t, toolbox* b)
                : menubar(w,"bar") {
    configure("-relief sunken");
    menubutton* b1 = new file_menu(this,t);
    menubutton* b2 = new edit_menu(this,b);
    button* b3 = new help_button(this);
}
};
```

Slide 12-26: The *menu_bar*

file_menu, and the *toolbox* to the *edit_menu*. In addition, a *help_button* is created, which provides online help in a hypertext format when pressed. The help facility will be discussed in section 12.2.4.

A menubar consists of menubuttons to which actual menus are attached. Each menu consists of a number of entries, which may possibly lead to cascaded menus.

The *file_menu* class, depicted in slide 12-27, defines a menu, but is derived from *menubutton* in order to attach the menu to its *menubar* ancestor (a). Its constructor defines the appearance of the button and creates a *file_handler* (b). It then defines the actual menu (c). The menu must explicitly be attached to the menubutton by invoking the *menubar* member function *menu*. For creating the menu, the keyword *class* is needed to disambiguate between the creation of an instance of the class menu and the call of the *menubar* :: *menu* function.

Before defining the various entries of the menu, the *file_menu* instance is declared as the handler for the menu entries (d). However, except for the entry *Quit*, which is handled by calling the *kit* :: *quit* function (e), the calls are delegated to the previously created *file_handler*.

The second button of the *menu_bar* is defined by the *edit_menu*. The *edit_menu* requires a *toolbox* and creates a menubutton. It configures the button and defines a menu containing two entries, one of which is a cascaded menu. Both the main menu and the cascaded menu are given the *toolbox* as a handler. This makes sense only because for our simple application, the functionality offered by the *toolbox* and *edit_menu* coincide.

Defining actions The most important component of our *drawtool* application is defined by the *tablet* widget class depicted in slide 12-28.

The various modes supported by the drawing tool are enumerated in a separate class *drawmode*. The *tablet* class itself inherits from the *canvas* widget class. This has the advantage that it offers the full functionality of a canvas. In addition to the constructor and *operator*() function, which delegates the incoming event to the appropriate handler according to the *_mode* variable, it offers a function *mode*, which sets the mode of the canvas as indicated by its string argument, and a function *init* that determines the creation

```
class file_menu : public menubutton {          file_menu

public:
file_menu(widget* w, tablet* t)
        : c(t), menubutton(w,"file") {                      // (a)
    configure("-relief sunken");
    text("File");
    pack("-side left");
    f = new file_handler(c);                                // (b)
                                                            // (c)

    class menu* m = new class menu(this,"menu");
    this→ menu(m);              // declares it for the menubutton
    m→ handler(this);                                       // (d)

    m→ entry("Open");
    m→ entry("Save");
    m→ entry("Quit");
}
int operator()() {
    if (!strcmp(argv[1],"Quit")) tk→ quit();               // (e)
    else f→ dispatch(tk,argc,argv);
    return OK;
}
protected:
tablet* c;
file_handler* f;
};
```

Slide 12-27: The *file_menu*

and geometrical layout of the component widgets. As instance variables, it contains an integer _mode variable and an array of handlers that contains the handlers corresponding to the modes supported. See section 12.2.4 for an example of a typical canvas handler.

Dispatching Although the *tablet* must act as a canvas, the actual *tablet* widget is nothing but a *frame* that contains a canvas widget as one of its components. See slide 12-29.

This is reflected in the invocation of the canvas constructor (a). By convention, when the options parameter is 0 instead of the empty string, no actual widget is created but only an abstract widget, as happens when calling the *widget* class constructor. Instead of creating a canvas right away, the *tablet* constructor creates a top frame, initializes the actual component widgets, and redirects the *eval, configure, bind* and *handler* invocations to the subordinate *canvas* widget (b). It then declares itself to be its own handler, which results in declaring itself to be the handler for the canvas component (c). Note that reversing the order of calling *redirect* and *handler* would be disastrous. After that it creates the handlers for the various modes and sets the initial mode to *move*.

The *operator*() function takes care of dispatching calls to the appropriate handler.

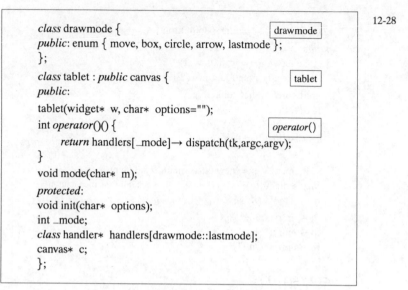

Slide 12-28: The *tablet*

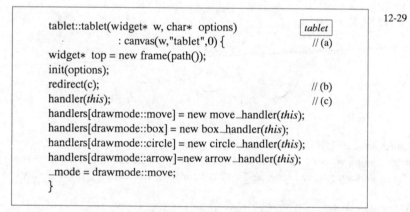

Slide 12-29: Installing the handlers

The *dispatch* function must be called to pass the *tk, argc* and *argv* parameters.

Creating new widgets Having taken care of the basic components of the drawing tool, that is the *toolbox, menu_bar* and *tablet* widgets, all that remains to be done is to define a suitable *file_handler*, appropriate handlers for the various drawing modes and a *help_handler*. We will skip the *file_handler*, but look at the latter two issues in sections 12.2.4 and 12.2.4, respectively. However, before that it will be shown how we may grant the *drawtool* the status of a veritable Tk widget, by defining a *drawtool* handler class and

```
class drawtool : public canvas {                            drawtool           12-30
public:
drawtool() : canvas() { }                                              // (I)
drawtool(char* p, char* opts="") : canvas(p,0) {
  init(opts);
  redirect(c);
}
int operator()(){                                                      // (II)
  if ( !strcmp( "drawtool" ,* argv) )
         create(--argc,++argv);
  else if (!strcmp("self",argv[1]) )
          tk→ result(self()→ path());
  else self()→ eval( flatten(--argc,++argv) );
  return OK;
}
protected:
tablet* c;

void init(char* options);
void create(int argc, char* argv[]) {                                  // (III)
  char* name = * argv;
  char* args = flatten(--argc,++argv);
  handler* h = new drawtool(name, args );
  tk→ action(name,h);
}
};
```

Slide 12-30: The *drawtool* widget command

a corresponding *drawtool* widget command. See slide 12-30.

Defining a widget command involves three steps: (I) the declaration of the binding between a command and a handler, (II) the definition of the *operator()* action function, which actually defines a mini-interpreter, and (III) the definition of the actual creation of the widget and its declaration as a Tcl/Tk command.

Step (I) is straightforward. We need to define an empty handler, which will be associated with the *drawtool* command when starting the application. See slide 12-31 (a). The functionality offered by the interpreter defined by the *operator()* function in (II) is kept quite simple, but may easily be extended. When the first argument of the call is *drawtool*, a new *drawtool* widget is created as specified in (III), except when the second argument is *self*. In that case, the virtual path of the widget is returned, which is actually the path of the *tablet*'s canvas. It is the responsibility of the writer of the script that the *self* command is not addressed to the empty handler. If neither of these cases apply, the function *widget :: eval* is invoked for *self()*, with the remaining arguments flattened to a string. This allows for using the drawtool almost as an ordinary canvas. See the example hypertext script shown in section 12.2.4.

The creation of the actual widget and declaration of the corresponding Tcl command, according to the Tk convention, is somewhat more involved (III).

Recall that each Tk widget is identified by its path, which simultaneously defines a command that may be used to configure the widget or, as for a canvas, to draw figures on the screen. Hence, the function *create* must create a new widget and declare the widget to be the handler of the command corresponding to its path name.

```
class application : public session {                    ┌──────────┐         12-31
public:                                                 │ drawtool │
application(int argc, char* argv[])                     └──────────┘
              : session(argc,argv,"drawtool") { }
void prelude( kit* tk, int, char* argv[] ) {
    tk→ action("drawtool", new drawtool());                    // (a)
}
void main( kit* tk, int, char* argv[] ) {
    drawtool* d = new drawtool(".draw");
    tk→ action("drawtool",d);                                  // (b)
    d→ rectangle(30,30,80,80,"-fill red");
    d→ pack();
}
};
```

Slide 12-31: The drawtool application

The *application* class depicted in slide 12-31 will by now look familiar, except for the function *prelude*. In the body of the *prelude* function, the Tcl command *drawtool* is declared, with an instance of *drawtool* as its handler (a).

In this way, the *drawtool* widget is made available as a command when the program is used as an interpreter. However, in the *main* function this declaration is overridden (b). Instead, the actual *drawtool* widget is made the handler of the command, to allow for a script to address the *drawtool* by calling *drawtool self*.

Delegation You may by now have lost track of how delegation within a compound widget takes place. Perhaps a brief look at the implementation will clarify this.

Each *eval, configure* or *bind* function call for a widget results in a command addressed to the path of the widget. By redirecting the command to a different path, the instructions may be delegated to the appropriate (component) widget. Delegation occurs, in other words, by directing the commands to the widget's virtual path, which is obtained by the protected function *thepath()*. In contrast, the function *path()* delivers the path of the widget's outer component. Indirection takes place by invoking the function *self()*, which relies on an instance variable _self that may be set by the *redirect* function.

The implementation of *thepath()* and *self()* is simply:

```
char* thepath() { return self()→ path(); }
widget* self() { return _self? _self→ self():this; }
```

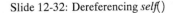

Slide 12-32: Dereferencing *self*( )

Hence, resolving a compound widget's primary inner component relies on simple pointer chasing, which may be applied recursively to an arbitrary depth at acceptable costs.

12.2.4 Graphics and hypertext

The Tk toolkit offers powerful facilities for graphics and (hyper)text (see Ousterhout, 1993). In this section we will discuss only the *canvas* widget offered by Tk. Instead of looking at the *text* widget provided by Tk, we will (briefly) look at the *hypertext* widget, which presents an alternative approach to defining hyperstructures.

```
interface item {                                    item     12-33
operator int();                     // returns item index
void configure(char* cmd);             // uses canvas
void tag(char* s);                      // sets tag for item
char* tags();               // delivers tags set for the item
void move(int x, int y);
bind(char * b, handler* h, char* args = "" );
bind(char * b, action& ac, char* args = "" );
handler(class handler* h, char* args = "" );
handler(action& ac, char* args = "" );
protected:
virtual install(action&,char* args="");
};
```

Slide 12-33: The *item* class

The *item* class The canvas widget allows the programmer to create a number of built-in graphic items. Items are given a numerical index when created and, in addition, they may be given a (string) tag. Tags allow items to be manipulated in a group-wise fashion. To deal with items in a C++ context, the *hush* library contains a class *item* of which the functionality is shown in slide 12-33.

Instances of *item* may not be created directly by the user, but instead are created by the canvas widget. For an item, its index may be obtained by casting the item to *int*. If the index does not identify an existing item, it will be zero. Existing items may be moved, in a relative way, by the *move* function.

In a similar way as for widgets, items may be associated with events, either explicitly by using *item* :: *bind*, or implicitly by using *item* :: *handler*. The default bindings for *items* are identical to the default bindings for the canvas widget, but these may be overridden by descendant classes.

Similar to the *widget* class, the *item* class is derived from the *handler* class. This allows the user to define possibly compound shapes defining their own handler.

The *canvas* widget The Tk canvas widget offers a powerful means for creating structured graphics. The *hush* class *canvas* provides merely a simplified interface to the corresponding Tk widget.

```
class move_handler : public handler {            [ move_handler ]           12-34
public:
move_handler( canvas*  cv ) : c(cv) { dragging = 0; }
void press( event& e ) {
        x = e.x(); y = e.y();
        id = c→ overlapping(x, y);
        if (id) dragging = 1;
}
void motion( event& e ) {
if (dragging) {
        id.move( e.x()− x, e.y()− y );
        x = e.x(); y = e.y();
        }
}
void release( event&  ) { dragging = 0; }
protected:
canvas*  c; int dragging; item id; int x,y;
};
```

Slide 12-34: The *move_handler* class

As an example of the use of a canvas, consider the definition of the *move_handler* class in slide 12-34. The *move_handler* class is derived from the class *handler*. It makes use of the *dispatch* and *operator*() function defined for *handler*, but redefines the (virtual) functions *press*, *motion* and *release*.

When creating an instance of *move_handler*, a pointer to the canvas must be given to the constructor. In addition, the class has data members to record position coordinates and whether a particular item is being moved. Actually, moving an item occurs by pressing the (left) mouse button on an item and dragging the item along. When the mouse button is released, moving stops. To identify the item, the function *overlapping* is used. The movement is determined by the distance between the last recorded position and the current position of the cursor.

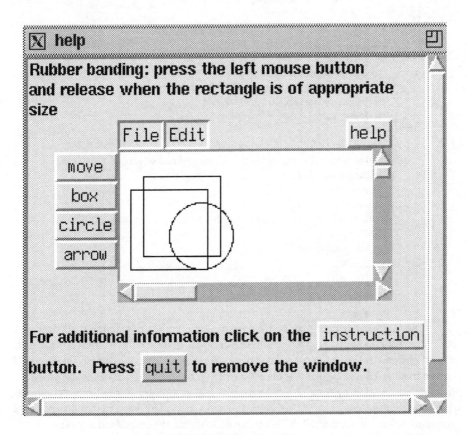

Slide 12-35: Hypertext help

In an analogous manner, a *box_handler* may be defined. The *box_handler* sets dragging to true when the button is pressed and creates a rectangle of zero width and height. Each time the function *motion* is called, the item created in the previous round is deleted and a new rectangle is created by calling

   c→ rectangle(x,y,e.x(),e.y());

where c is a pointer to the canvas and x and y the button pointer coordinates stored when dragging began. For circles and lines, it suffices to replace the call to rectangle with a call to the appropriate figure creation function.

The *hypertext* **widget** Both the Tk canvas and text widget allow the binding of actions to particular items and hence defining dynamically what we may call *hyperstructures*.

A different, in a way more static, approach is offered by the *hypertext* widget originally developed by George Howlett.

12-36

Rubber banding: press the left mouse button
and release when the rectangle is of appropriate
size
   %%
drawtool $*this*.draw
$*this* append $*this*.draw
$*this*.draw create rectangle 20 20 80 80
$*this*.draw create rectangle 10 30 70 90
$*this*.draw create oval 40 40 90 90
$*this* append $*this*.draw
%%
For additional information click on the %%
button $*this*.goto -text instruction -command end-of-text
$*this* append $*this*.goto
%%
button. Press %%
button $*this*.quit -command { destroy . } -text quit -bg pink
$*this* append quit
%% to remove the window.

Slide 12-36: A hypertext help file

The *hypertext* widget may be used to display text files containing embedded Tcl code. The Tcl code must be placed between escapes, that take the form of %% for both the start and end of the code. A screen shot of a fragment of the online help for *drawtool* is given in slide 12-35. Notice that the online help provides a replica of the *drawtool* application, surrounded by text. When looking at (again a fragment of) the hypertext file specifying the contents of the online help, given in slide 12-36, you see that the *drawtool* command defined in section 12.2.3 is employed to create the embedded widget.

When specifying the hypertext file, widgets may be given a pathname relative to the pathname of the hypertext widget by using the variable *this*. In addition, the hypertext widget offers the variables *thisline* and *thisfile* to identify the current line number and current file name.

Any of the widgets and commands offered by Tcl/Tk or supported by *hush* may be included in a hypertext file, including the ones defined by the program itself.

12.3 Heterogeneous systems

Hypermedia require the connection of (a large number of) *hybrid* components. Moreover, as we have seen in the previous section, a multi-paradigm approach seems to be best suited to cope with the variety of aspects (both computational and presentational) involved in the application of hypermedia technology.

The problem of achieving a *symbiosis* of hybrid components bears a close analogy to the problems addressed by object-oriented technology.

12-37

Hypermedia technology

- hybrid components – *symbiosis*

Heterogeneous systems

- wrapping – *encapsulation and refinement*
- embeddable interpreters – *multi-paradigm approach*
- distribution – *active objects, communication*

Slide 12-37: Heterogeneous systems

Object orientation is about program organization, and not about programming *per se*. This was the characterization given at the beginning of the first chapter. Subsequently, we have dealt with modeling, validation, programming language constructs (including constructs for distribution and concurrency), programming techniques, theoretical foundations, libraries and system development support. Our discussion of distribution and system support (as proposed by the OMG and Microsoft OLE) paved the way, so to speak, for the viewpoint that object-oriented technology intrinsically supports the development of heterogeneous systems.

In particular, the techniques of *wrapping* (employing encapsulation and refinement) and *distribution* (for example, by employing object request brokers) are invaluable in realizing heterogeneous systems as the integration of multiple (hybrid) components. Wrapping allows us to incorporate old (procedural) code by defining a clean object interface, whereas distribution supports the incorporation of distinct *active* components.

The motivation for employing *wrapping* as a technique for reuse may be that the code involved cannot be rewritten, due to a lack of resources or expertise. Wrapping, despite its *ad hoc* nature, may in practice be a good substitute for (object-oriented) redesign.

The motivation for distribution may simply be the need to have applications operating on a local or wide area network. Another aspect of distribution of course is reuse, not on a component level but on the level of applications (employing other applications, such as a text editor, as a functional component).

One aspect of heterogeneous systems that has not been adequately dealt with thus far (except to some extent by the OMG CORBA proposal, see section 11.1.2) is that different components of an application may require a different (application) programming language. To a certain extent, this problem has also been dealt with by 4GL application generators, but only in a very limited, application-dependent manner.

As may be observed in a number of research projects, there seems to be a trend towards the development of *embeddable interpreters*, and the combinations of interpreted languages (such as Tcl or Perl) with system implementation languages (such as C, C++, Lisp and Prolog). Moreover, in many cases a widget binding (to Tk widgets, Athena or Motif widgets) is offered in both languages, similar to that described in the previous section. However, thus far, language embeddings have only been realized on the level of functions and procedures and not on the level of objects, providing a mapping between object interfaces instead of single functions. This is exactly the problem addressed by the

OMG proposal. However, there seems to be no generally accepted solution thus far.

This brings us to our final question. What will be the future of OOP? Is it worth investing in, and where will it lead us?

The future of OOP Object orientation is here to stay., as object-oriented programming, as well as in the form of object-oriented modeling and design.

Object orientation is commercially viable, as testified in Harmon and Tayler (1993). Moreover, it is the method of choice for many of large companies (including HP, Sun and Microsoft) and, increasingly, many smaller ones.

To have an indication of where object orientation will lead us, we conclude by reflecting on the meaning of the phrases encountered in project and research proposals.

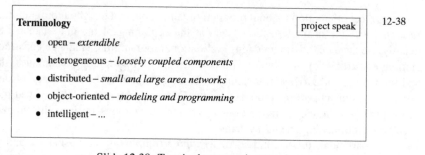

Slide 12-38: Terminology – project speak

The phrase *open* is mostly used to indicate that the result will not be a closed system, but may be extended to include extraneous functionality. By their very nature, objects are extensible by means of refinement by inheritance (provided they are well-designed).

The phrase *heterogeneous* is often meant to indicate that the result is dependent on extraneous components, that will be obtained from some external source. Given the complexity of many systems (including information systems, management support systems or systems for scientific visualization), this is only natural. The difference with earlier times lies primarily in the way in which such extraneous components are being (re)used. Object-oriented technology in principle makes it possible to reuse components in a clean way, without requiring access to the source code.

The phrase *distributed* is often motivated by the wish to support the interaction of geographically distinct components or to achieve speed-up by means of parallel/distributed processing. However, parallel/distributed programming is intrinsically difficult. Distribution seems to be an area in which the technology has not (yet) outgrown the level of systems programming. Also here, object orientation appears to be gaining ground.

The phrase *object orientation* itself has in the past often be abused. See King (1989) and Stroustrup (1988). However, now the technology is maturing, the standards with respect to what may be called object-oriented are becoming more solid, and object orientation is increasingly recognized as being valuable both in modeling and programming, and not merely as a trend.

Finally, the phrase *intelligent*, encountered in a variety of situations, may be taken to mean either *adaptable*, *tunable* to user needs, augmented with *reasoning* capabilities, or simply superior. In a more neutral way, it may be taken to mean the incorporation of logic-based, declarative (programming) formalisms to specify the functionality of a system in a knowledge-based manner.

On the one hand, there lies a challenge to incorporate (and actually employ) object-oriented technology in, for example, expert systems, but also hypermedia and (intelligent) information systems. On the other hand, I am convinced, that logic-based programming and specification techniques may be fruitfully applied in object-oriented system development.

That was the good news. And now for the bad news. One potential danger that haunts the field of object orientation is the diversification of programming languages, programming techniques, analysis and design methods and development frameworks. Even for a single language like C++ there already exist a number of mutually incompatible compilers. The only way to resolve the problems of proliferation is *standardization*.

Standardization involves not only the adherence to a single language reference manual but also an agreement on the terminology employed. Moreover it requires the adoption of appropriate conventions concerning issues of design and the utilization of object-oriented techniques. This book has been written from the conviction that an understanding of the theoretical foundations of object-oriented programming is a prerequisite to the development of a consensus concerning these issues, if not interesting for its own sake. In summary, the future of object orientation lies in stabilization and consolidation.

Summary

This chapter discussed the application of object-oriented technology to the area of hypermedia. Hypermedia has been defined as the combination of hypertext and multimedia.

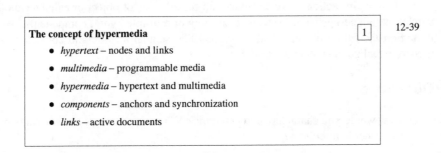

The concept of hypermedia   1   12-39

- *hypertext* – nodes and links
- *multimedia* – programmable media
- *hypermedia* – hypertext and multimedia
- *components* – anchors and synchronization
- *links* – active documents

Slide 12-39: Section 12.1: The concept of hypermedia

Hypertext consists of document nodes and machine-supported links between these nodes. Multimedia, in the context of hypermedia, as been characterized as *programmable media*. We looked at the requirements for hypermedia user interfaces and discussed a number of applications of hypermedia technology.

A hypermedia model has been presented, that combines the Dexter hypertext reference model and a multimedia model supporting channels and synchronization. We also reflected on the nature of links, and discussed the notion of *active documents*.

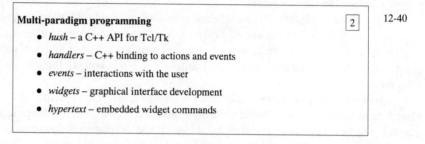

Slide 12-40: Section 12.2: Multi-paradigm programming

In section 2, we looked at the multi-paradigm *hush* toolkit for developing hypermedia interfaces. The *hush* toolkit provides a large number of widgets and graphics features, and supports the combination of the scripts written in Tcl/Tk with handler objects defined in C++.

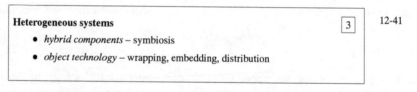

Slide 12-41: Section 12.3: Heterogeneous systems

Finally, in section 3, we discussed the contribution of object-oriented technology in relation to heterogeneous systems, consisting of multiple hybrid components. We reflected on the future of OOP, and concluded that standardization and consolidation is needed to realize the potential of OOP.

Questions

(1) How would you characterize hypermedia? What requirements can you think of for hypermedia interfaces?

(2) Discuss the problem of navigation in hypermedia systems. Think of some solutions.

(3) How would you classify hypermedia systems? Discuss some examples.

(4) Give an outline of an integrated hypermedia model. What problems do you expect in the realization of your model?

(5) Discuss the nature of links. How are links related to active objects?

(6) What is your opinion on combining C++ with scripts written in an interpreted language? Explain your point of view.

(7) Discuss the problems involved in realizing heterogeneous systems? How does object technology contribute to the solution of these problems?

(8) What do you consider the contribution of OOP to the practice of software development?

Further reading

As further reading, I recommend Conklin (1987) and Woodhead (1990). For a study of hypermedia models, consult Halasz and Schwartz (1994) and Hardman *et al.* (1994). Another interesting paper in this respect is Nierstrasz (1987). As a source of information on multimedia, I recommend Burger (1993).

Appendix

A

The language Smalltalk

Smalltalk has been, without doubt, the most influential of all object-oriented programming languages. Originally meant as an *easy-to-use* programming language for the *Dynabook* (a laptop *avant-la-lettre* developed in 1972 at Xerox Parc), it has developed into a powerful general purpose programming language (which has stabilized in Smalltalk-80) that runs on many platforms. From the start, an interactive programming environment has been an integral part of the language implementation. Later implementations also include support for the interactive construction of user interfaces.

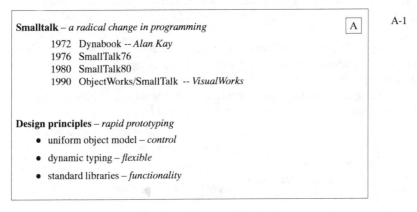

Slide A-1: The language Smalltalk

Influenced by the ideas of objects and classes embodied in Simula, the design philosophy underlying Smalltalk clearly reflects the desire to effect nothing less than a radical change in programming practice. Characteristic for the design of Smalltalk is a *uniform object model* (which is even used to support common control constructs), *dynamic typing* (which accounts for much of the flexibility of Smalltalk) and a sizable collection of *standard library classes* (providing the functionality necessary to build complex applications). Smalltalk has successfully been used, in particular for rapid prototyping.

Terminology The introduction of Smalltalk came along with an, at the time, astounding terminology. See slide A-2.

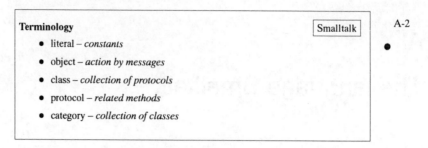

Slide A-2: Smalltalk – terminology

Most important is the notion of *object*, which is something that acts in response to messages (by executing a *method* procedure). In Smalltalk, everything is an object. Moreover, every object is an instance of a class. A *class* is the description of a collection of objects which share the same structure and applicable methods. The methods of both objects and classes (considered as an object) are grouped in so-called *protocols*. Related collections of classes may be grouped in so-called *categories*. Both *protocols* and *categories* are merely syntactic add-ons, meant to facilitate programming.

Expressions The syntax of Smalltalk needs some time to get used to. Since everything is an object, expressions may be regarded as being composed of constants, variables and method expressions.

There is a large variety of literal constants (including numbers, characters, strings, symbols, byte arrays and literal arrays), as depicted in slide A-3.

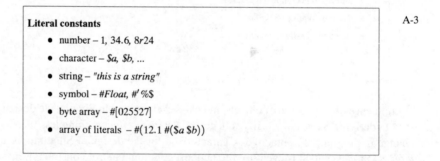

Slide A-3: Smalltalk – expressions (1)

Expressions may be assigned to variables. Usually, variables are given a name that betrays their expected type, as for example *anInteger*. (In Smalltalk, class names start with an upper case and variables with a lower case letter.)

We distinguish between *temporary variables* (having a method procedure scope), *instance variables* (having an object scope), *class variables* (having as their scope the collection of instances of the class), *pool variables* (that have a category as their scope) and *global variables* (that are visible everywhere). See slide A-4.

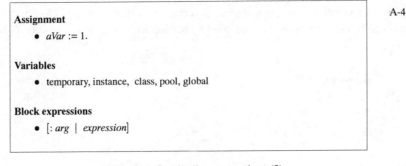

Slide A-4: Smalltalk – expressions (2)

A special kind of expression is the *block expression* that consists of a program fragment, possibly parametrized with an argument. Block expressions are used to define control structures employing message expressions. Block expressions correspond to function literals (lambda-expressions) in languages such as Lisp and Smalltalk.

Message expressions may be characterized as either *unary*, *binary* or *keyword* messages. See slide A-5.

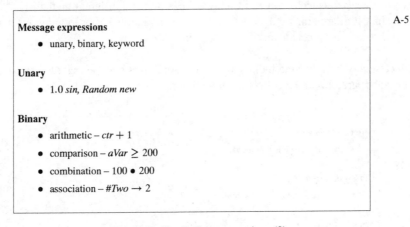

Slide A-5: Smalltalk – expressions (3)

Unary messages consist of a single method name addressed at an expression denoting an object, for example a constant or a class.

As binary method expressions, we have the familiar arithmetic and comparison expressions as well as the less familiar combination expression (used for graphics coordinates) and association expression (used to define associative maps). All binary (infix) message selectors have the same precedence and bind to the left. Despite their common appearance, these are all true message expressions (which may lead to surprises, for example in the case of a non-commutative definition of the arithmetic operations). Examples of keyword message selectors are given in slide A-6.

Control Smalltalk has no control structures except message passing. However, familiar control structures are defined as methods on *booleans* and *integers*. See slide A-6.

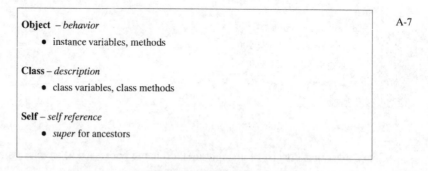

Slide A-6: Smalltalk – control

For example, an *if-statement* may be obtained by defining the method *ifTrue: if-False:* on booleans. (Despite the use of keywords, parameter passing in Smalltalk is positional. Each sequence of keywords may be regarded as a different method.)

In a similar vein, we may define iteration and looping. For looping, we may employ the parameter mechanism of blocks, as indicated above.

Objects Everything in Smalltalk is an object. An *object* may be regarded as consisting of instance variables and a collection of methods.

<table>
<tr><td>

Object *– behavior*
- instance variables, methods

Class *– description*
- class variables, class methods

Self *– self reference*
- *super* for ancestors

</td><td>A-7</td></tr>
</table>

Slide A-7: Smalltalk – objects (1)

A *class* is the description of a collection of objects, its instances. Considered as an object, a class may be said to have class variables and class methods.

For self-reference the special expression *self* may be used. To invoke methods from the parent class the expression *super* may be be used.

An example of an object class description is given in slide A-8. The class *Ctr* is defined as a subclass of the class *behavior*. It supports an *initialization* protocol (containing the method *initialize*), a protocol for modification (containing the method *add*), and an *inspection* protocol (containing the method *value*).

Example – *class*   A-8

    Behavior *subclass*: #Ctr
    instanceVariableNames: 'value'
    Ctr methodsFor: 'initialization'
     initialize
       value := 0.
    Ctr methodsFor: 'modifications'
     add: Avalue
       value := value + aValue.
    Ctr methodsFor: 'inspection'
     value
       ^value

Slide A-8: Smalltalk – objects (2)

Note that *value* occurs both as an instance variable and as a method. Only the method is accessible by the user.

In addition, we need a class description defining the object functionality of Ctr, which consists of an *instance creation* protocol defining the class method *new*. See slide A-9. This class description is (implicitly) an instance of a meta class generated by the Smalltalk system. See section 5.5.

Class description – *meta class*   A-9

    Ctr *class*
    instanceVariableNames: ''
    Ctr *class* methodsFor: 'instance creation'
     new
       ^super new initialize

Slide A-9: Smalltalk – objects (3)

Inheritance Each class in the Smalltalk library is (ultimately) a subclass of the class *Object*. See slide A-10.

Smalltalk supports only single inheritance. Above, the ancestor classes of the class *Integer* are depicted as a branch of the inheritance tree.

Techniques Inheritance, in combination with message passing, allows for powerful programming techniques. As an example, an illustration is given of the cooperation between

```
Inheritance                                            A-10
        Object
          Magnitude
            ArithmeticValue
              Number
                Integer
```

Slide A-10: Smalltalk – inheritance

two objects employing the *Model/View* paradigm. The *model* class *Ctr*, depicted in slide A-11, may be regarded as embodying the proper functionality of the application.

```
Model subclass: #Ctr                          Model      A-11
   ...
   initialize
     value :=  0.
     TV open: self.
   ...
   add: anInt
     value :=  value + anInt.
     self changed: #value.
```

Slide A-11: Smalltalk – techniques (1)

```
View subclass: #TV                              View      A-12
instanceVariableNames: ''
TV methodsFor: 'updating'
update: aValue
    Transcript show: 'ok'; cr .
TV class
instanceVariableNames: ''
TV class methodsFor: 'instance creation'
    open: aCtr
      self new model: aCtr
```

Slide A-12: Smalltalk – techniques (2)

A *view* class defines an object that may be used to monitor the behavior of the *model* instance in a non-intrusive way. To support monitoring, the model class *Ctr* needs to install one or more view objects during initialization, and further, it must notify its view object(s) whenever its contents have been modified, as in *add*. See slide A-12.

The view class *TV* defines a class method *open* to create a new view object for an instance of the *Ctr* class. It must further define a method *update* (that will automatically be invoked when the *Ctr* instance signals a change) to display some message, for example the value of the *Ctr* object monitored.

The Smalltalk programming environment forms an integral part of the Smalltalk system. The code depicted above (which clearly reflects the object nature of classes) is usually not the result of text editing, but is generated by the system. The Smalltalk programming system, in particular the standard library, however, will take some time to get familiar with.

Summary

This section presented a brief introduction to the programming language Smalltalk.

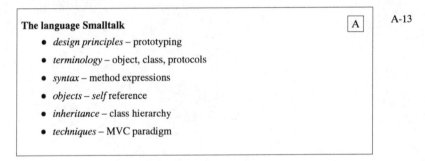

Slide A-13: Smalltalk – summary

It discussed the design principles underlying Smalltalk and the terminology originally associated with Smalltalk. It further covered the basic syntactic constructs and characterized object behavior and inheritance using examples. Also, an illustration was given of the use of the MVC paradigm.

B

The language Eiffel

The language Eiffel has been designed with a clear concern for correctness and validation. It supports a bottom-up development approach, centered around the design of robust classes. Along with the language, Meyer (1988) introduces the notion of *contracts* as a means to specify the mutual obligations between the user of an object and the object in terms of a *client/server* relation.

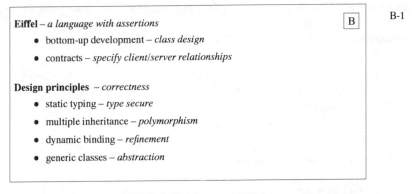

B-1

Slide B-1: The language Eiffel

Eiffel is a (type secure) *statically typed* language, providing *multiple inheritance* and generic classes. Recently, Eiffel-3 has been introduced, supporting a number of features (such as overloading) inspired by C++. See Meyer (1992a).

Terminology The design of Eiffel also reflects a concern with the software engineering issues involved in the development and maintenance of class libraries. (See also section 11.2.) The language is built around a number of keywords, which accounts for an easy to read, albeit somewhat verbose, layout of programs.

The keyword *class* precedes a class definition, which in the terminology of Meyer (1988) may be considered as a model for a collection of objects. The keyword *feature* precedes the attributes, functions and procedures defined by a class. The keyword *export* precedes the list of visible features, in other words the interface declaration of the class. The keyword *inherit* precedes the list of inherited classes, specifying class inclusion and

443

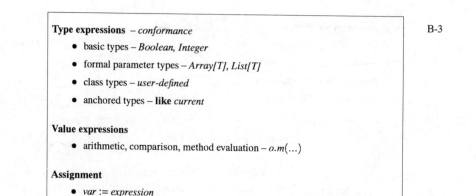

> **The language Eiffel** – *keywords*   B-2
>
> *class* – a model for a set of objects
> *feature* – attribute, function, procedure
> *export* – interface declaration
> *inherit* – class inclusion and subtyping (!)
> *redefine, rename* – to change inherited features
> *deferred* – to postpone the implementation
> *require, ensure, invariant* – assertions

Slide B-2: Eiffel – terminology

the subtyping relationships. The keywords *rename* and *redefine* are used to change inherited features. The keyword *deferred* may be used to indicate that a feature will be implemented (in the future) in an inherited class, and the keyword *obsolete* may be used to indicate that a feature will not be supported in a future release. Finally, the keywords *require, ensure* and *invariant* indicate assertions that specify respectively the pre- and postconditions for a (method) feature and the class invariant.

> **Type expressions** – *conformance*   B-3
>
> • basic types – *Boolean, Integer*
>
> • formal parameter types – *Array[T], List[T]*
>
> • class types – *user-defined*
>
> • anchored types – **like** *current*
>
> **Value expressions**
>
> • arithmetic, comparison, method evaluation – *o.m(...)*
>
> **Assignment**
>
> • *var* := *expression*

Slide B-3: Eiffel – type expressions

Expressions Eiffel is a strongly typed language. In Eiffel, variables must be explicitly typed by means of a declaration involving type expressions. Type expressions range over *basic types* (such as *Boolean* and *Integer*), *formal type parameters* of generic types (as the T in $Array[T]$, which stands for the type of the elements of the array), *class types* (that are defined by the user) and *anchored types*, for instance *like current* (which results in the type of the *current* object, or *self* in Smalltalk terminology). Anchored types present some problems for the type safety of Eiffel programs. See section 9.6 for a discussion.

In Meyer (1988) *conformance* rules are specified which are used to determine whether a given type is a subtype of another type. See section 9.2 for an extensive discussion of the subtyping relationship.

Value expressions in Eiffel comprise the familiar arithmetical and comparison operations, as well as the message expressions of the form $o.m(...)$ that result in the evaluation of the method m by the object o. Parameter passing in Eiffel is positional. See slide B-3.

Control structures Control in Eiffel is meant to be effected primarily by defining (and redefining) the appropriate classes. However, control constructs both for branching and iteration are provided. See slide B-4.

Control – *method refinement*   B-4

   ● branching – *if ... then ... elsif ... else ... end*

   ● iterations – *from ... until ... loop ... end*

Slide B-4: Eiffel – control

The *if-statement* has a classical form, as in Pascal. The *iteration-statement* may be used in a variety of ways, as a *for-loop* and as a *while-statement* (by omitting the *from*) part).

Objects Objects in Eiffel are defined by classes. A typical class definition is given in slide B-5.

The class *counter* exports the features *inc* and *val*. The feature *count* is hence private to an instance of *counter*, since it does not appear in the interface defined by the *export* part.

---

   class counter *export* inc val *feature*   B-5
   count : Integer
   create *is do* count := 0 *end*
   inc(n : Integer) *is*
      require n > 0 *do*
      count := count + n
      ensure count = *old* count + n
      end
   val : Integer *is do Result* := count *end*
   invariant count $\geq$ 0
   end -- class counter

Slide B-5: Eiffel – objects

The *create* feature is automatically exported, and is used to create an instance of *counter* by the statement x.*create* for a variable x of type *counter*. The reserved word *Result* is used to return a value from a function feature. The method feature *inc* specifies both a pre-condition and a post-condition. The reserved word *old* is used to access the value of the instance variable *count* before evaluating *inc*. Finally, the invariance states the constraint that a *counter* instance never has a value below zero.

Inheritance Eiffel supports multiple inheritance. As an example, look at the class *FixedList* in slide B-6, that is implemented as a combination (by inheritance) of a generic *List* and a generic *Array*.

```
Multiple inheritance                                            B-6

     class Fixed_List[T] export ...
     inherit
          List[T]
          Array[T]
     feature
          ...
     end
```

Slide B-6: Eiffel – inheritance

Using (multiple) inheritance implies that a *FixedList* may be regarded as a sub-type of both *Array* and *List*. However, the *export* list in the end determines what interface is provided and hence what type the class embodies.

Techniques Developing programs in Eiffel is meant to be primarily a matter of modeling, that is designing classes and the (inheritance) relations between classes. An essential ingredient of class development is the design of appropriate interfaces.

```
Rename and/or redefine                                         B-7

     class C export ... inherit
     A rename m as m1 redefine p
     B rename m as m2 redefine q
     feature
          ...
     end
```

Slide B-7: Eiffel – techniques

To define a class as (derived from) a combination of classes, Eiffel allows both the renaming and redefinition of inherited features. See slide B-7. In Meyer (1988), many practical hints are given and numerous examples employing these mechanisms.

Summary

This section has given an introduction to the Eiffel language. It discussed the design principles underlying Eiffel, which may be characterized as being focused on static typing and support for the development of reliable programs.

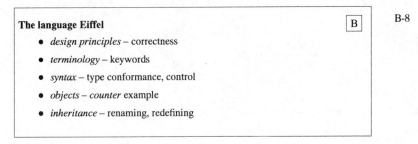

Slide B-8: Eiffel – summary

Further, it presented an overview of the keywords related to the constructs offered, and discussed type expressions, value expressions and control statements. An example was given to illustrate the features offered. Finally, we looked at the mechanisms of renaming and redefining, which are needed to avoid name clashes when using multiple inheritance.

C

The language C++

C++ is often disparaged because of its C heritage. Nevertheless, not only is C++ in many respects better than C, it also offers much more. From its conception, C++ has reflected a strong concern with static typing. As such it has influenced the ANSI C standard accepted in 1985. Thus far there have been three releases of the AT&T C++ compiler (which may be considered as a semi-official standard), implementing a successively larger subset of the language as described in the Annotated Reference Manual (ARM). See Ellis and Stroustrup (1990).

C++ *– is much more than a better C* $\boxed{\text{C}}$ C-1

    1972 C *Kernigan and Ritchi* (Unix)
    1983 C++ (*Simula 1976*)
    1985 ANSI/ISO C
    1985 Release 1.0
    1990 Release 2.0
    1992 Release 3.0 *-- templates*

Design principles *– the benefits of efficiency*

- superset of C *– supporting OOP*

- static typing *– with user-defined exceptions*

- explicit *– no default virtual functions*

- extensible *– libraries in C and C++*

Slide C-1: The language C++

    The leading design principle underlying C++ is to support object-oriented programming, yet allow the programmer and user the benefits of (runtime) efficiency. It has been designed as (almost) a superset of C, to allow the integration of C code in a seamless way. It provides strong static typing, yet allows the programmer to escape the rigidity of typing if absolutely necessary. C++ is designed to be extensible. This means that no assumptions are made with regard to a programming environment or standard library classes.

The C language was originally introduced as a (Unix) systems programming language, and is gradually being replaced by C++ for this purpose. However, C++ lends itself to many other applications, including mathematical programming and business applications.

Terminology The C++ language is without doubt a large and complex language. Fortunately, an increasing number of textbooks have become available which provide an appropriate introduction to C++ and its use for the realization of abstract data types, including Headington and Riley (1994) and Weiss (1993).

Among the additional keywords introduced in C++ (extending C) we have the keyword *const* (that may be used to define constants), the keyword *inline* (that may be used to define inline expanded functions, that for C have to be defined using macros), the keyword *new* (to dynamically create objects on the heap), the keyword *delete* (to destroy dynamically created objects) and, finally, the keywords *private, public* and *protected* (to indicate access restrictions for the instances of an object class). See slide C-2.

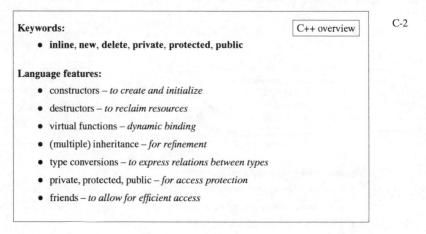

Slide C-2: C++ – terminology (1)

The language features offered by C++ supporting object-oriented programming include *constructors* (that are defined for each class to create and initialize instances), *destructors* (that may be used to reclaim resources), *virtual functions* (that must be used to effect dynamic binding), *multiple inheritance* (to specify behavioral refinement), *type conversions* (that allow the user to define coercion relations between, both system-defined and user-defined, data types), and *friend declarations* (that may be used to grant efficient access to selected functions or classes).

The annotated reference manual (ARM) is not a book to be used to learn the language, but provides an excellent source of detailed technical explanations and the motivations underlying particular design decisions.

To get an idea of the full set of features offered by C++, look at the meaning of a name in C++ (as described in the ARM). See slide C-3. A *name* can either denote an object, a function, a set of functions, an enumerator, a type (including classes, structs and

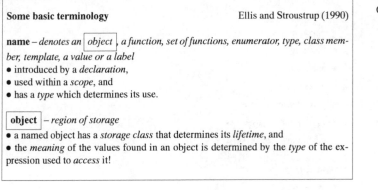

Slide C-3: C++ – terminology (2)

unions), a class member, a template (class or function), a value or a label. A name is typically introduced by a declaration, and is used within a scope. Moreover, each name has a type which determines its use. An *object* in C++ is nothing but a *region of storage*, with a lifetime determined by its storage class (that is, whether it is created on the stack or on the heap). Meaning is given to an object by the type used to access it, which is determined during compile time. The only information needed at runtime in C++ is concerned with virtual functions (which require a virtual function dispatch table for dynamic binding).

Expressions Again due to its C heritage, C++ supports many *basic types* (including *int*, *char* and *float*) and *compound types* (including arrays, functions, pointer types, reference types, and user-defined class, union or struct types). See slide C-4.

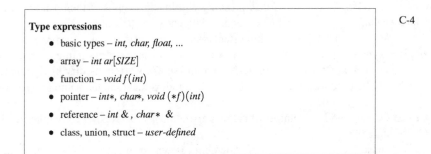

Slide C-4: C++ – expressions (1)

Pointer types encompass pointers to basic types and pointers to user-defined types, such as functions and classes. The difference between *object*, *reference* and *pointer types* may be succinctly characterized as the difference between the actual thing, an alias (that looks like the actual thing but isn't) and an address of the actual thing (where you have to go to get it).

Value expressions may be created using arithmetic and comparison operators (in-

C-5

Expressions

- operators $- +, -, ..., <, \leq, ..., ==, \, ! =, ..., \&\&, \|$
- indexing $- o[e]$
- application $- o(...)$
- access $- o.m(...)$
- dereference $- p \rightarrow m(...)$
- in/decrement $-$ o++, o--
- conditional $- b \, ? \, e_1 : e_2$

Assignment

- $var = expression$
- modifying $- + =. - =, ...$

Slide C-5: C++ – expressions (2)

cluding == for equality and ! = for inequality). As logical operators, C++ includes conjunction (&&) and disjunction (||), as well as a number of bitwise logical operators. Also, we have an *indexing* operator (which may be defined for arbitrary types), an *application* operator (that may also be defined for arbitrary types), an *access* operator (that is as a standard used for member function invocation or method calls), a *dereference* operator (that is used to invoke member functions through a pointer to an object) and *in-* and *decrement* operations (that, again, may be defined for arbitrary types). Needless to say, user-defined operators must be applied with care. Also, we have a conditional expression of the form $b \, ? \, e_1 : e_2$ testing the condition b to deliver e_1 when it evaluates to true and e_2 otherwise. Also, C++ allows for sequencing within expressions of the form $(e_1, ..., e_n)$, which evaluates $e_1, ..., e_n$ in that order and delivers e_n as its value.

Assignments in C++, it is important to note, are written as *var = expression*, with a single = symbol. This convention is known to cause mistakes by programmers raised with languages such as Pascal or Modula-2. In addition, C++ offers modifying assignments, which may be used as, for example, in n += 1, which is identical in meaning to n = n + 1.

Control C++ provides a number of elementary control structures, directly inherited from C. See slide C-6.

These include a *conditional* statement (of which the else part may be omitted), a *selection* statement (that allows for a default branch), an *iteration* statement (which is also offered in a reversed form to allow a repeat), a *loop* statement (consisting of an initialization part, a part to test for termination, and a repetition part to increase the loop variable) and, finally, *jumps* (including the so much despised *goto*).

Objects Despite the (at first sight) overwhelming possibilities of defining values and control, the essence of programming in C++ must be the development of the abstract data types. To illustrate the difference between C and C++, let us first look at the realization

C-6

Control

- conditional – *if* (*b*) S_1;   *else* S_2;
- selection – *switch*(*n*){*case* n_1 : S_1; *break*; ...*default* : ...}
- iteration – *while* (*b*) *S*
- looping – *for* (*int i* = 1; *i* ≤ *MAX*; *i* + +) *S*
- jumps – *return, break, continue, goto*

Slide C-6: C++ – control

of abstract data type in a procedural way in a C style (employing references), and then at the realization in C++ employing the class construct. Note that in plain C, pointers must be used instead of references.

C-7

ADT in C style

        struct ctr { int n; }
        void ctr_init(ctr& c) { c.n = 0; }
        void ctr_add(ctr& c, int i = 1) { c.n = c.n + i; }
        int ctr_val(ctr& c) { *return* c.n; }

Usage

        ctr c; ctr_init(c); ctr_add(c,1); cout ≪ ctr_val(c);
        ctr∗ p = new ctr; ctr_init(∗ p); ctr_add(∗ p);

Slide C-7: C++ – objects (1)

The *ctr* type defined in slide C-7 may be regarded as a standard realization of abstract data types in a procedural language. It defines a data structure *ctr*, an initialization function *ctr_init*, a function *ctr_add* to modify the value or state of an element of the (abstract) type and an observation function *ctr_val* that informs us about its value. We may either declare a *ctr* object or a pointer to a *ctr* instance and invoke the functions as indicated.

In contrast, to define (the realization of) an abstract data type in C++, we employ the class construct and define member functions (or methods) that operate on the data encapsulated by instances of the class. See slide C-8.

Inheritance Not only is C++ an efficient language, but it also offers features lacking in Smalltalk and Eiffel. In particular, it allows us to make a distinction between (private) members of a class that are inaccessible to everybody (including descendants), (protected) members that are inaccessible to ordinary clients (but not to descendants), and (public) members that are accessible to everybody.

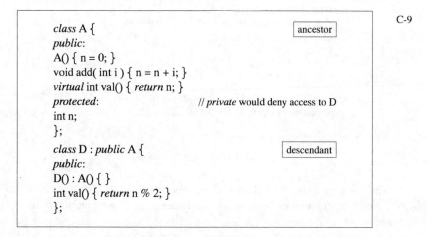

```
ADT in C++                                                            C-8
      class ctr {
      public:
            ctr() { n = 0; }                                 // constructor
            ~ctr() { cout ≪ "bye"; };                        // destructor
            void add( int i = 1) { n = n + i; }
            int val( ) { return n; }
      private:
      int n;
      };


Usage

      ctr c; c.add(1);  cout ≪ c.val();
      ctr∗  p = new ctr();  c→ add(1);  cout ≪ c→ val();
```

Slide C-8: C++ – objects (2)

```
                                                                     C-9
      class A {                                         ┌──────────┐
      public:                                           │ ancestor │
      A() { n = 0; }                                    └──────────┘
      void add( int i ) { n = n + i; }
      virtual int val() { return n; }
      protected:              // private would deny access to D
      int n;
      };
      class D : public A {                              ┌────────────┐
      public:                                           │ descendant │
      D() : A() { }                                     └────────────┘
      int val() { return n % 2; }
      };
```

Slide C-9: C++ – inheritance

In the example in slide C-9, using *private* instead of protected would deny access to the instance variable *n* of *A*. The example also illustrates the use of virtual functions (to refine the observation *val* to deliver the value of the object modulo two) and the invocation of constructors of ancestor classes (which need not be explicitly specified by the user).

Allowing descendants full access to the instance variables defined by ancestors, however, increases the dependency on the actual implementation of these ancestors, with the risk of a total collapse when the implementation of an ancestor changes. See chapter 7 for a discussion of techniques to avoid such risks.

Techniques In addition to the elements introduced thus far, C++ offers a number of other features that may profitably be used in the development of libraries and programs. See slide C-10.

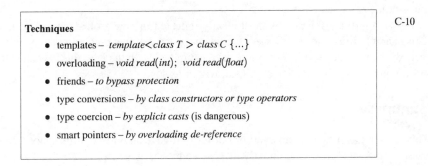

Slide C-10: C++ – techniques (1)

For instance, C++ offers *templates* (to define generic classes and functions), *overloading* (to define a single function for multiple types), *friends* (to bypass protection). *type conversion* (that may be defined by class constructors or type operators), *type coercions* (or casts, that may be used to resolve ambiguity or to escape a too rigid typing regime), and *smart pointers* (obtained by overloading the dereference operator). In section 7.2, examples are given of how these features may be used.

To get some of the flavor of using C++, look at the definition of the *ctr* class in slide C-11 employing multiple constructors, operators, default arguments and type conversion.

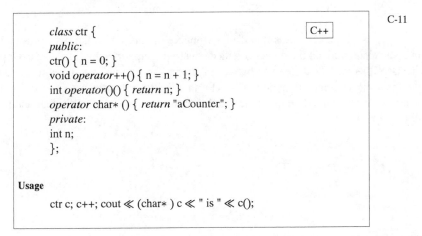

Slide C-11: C++ - techniques (2)

The *ctr* provides two constructors, one with an integer argument (which is by default set to zero, if omitted) and one with a string argument (that expects a valid coding of an integer as a string). The increment operator is used to define the function *add* (which also has a default argument to increment by one), and the application operator is used instead of *val*. Also, a type conversion operator is defined to deliver the value of the *ctr* instance anywhere where an integer is expected. In addition, a type conversion operator (employing a conversion function from integers to (*char*∗) strings) is used to return the value of the *ctr* instance as a string.

Again, the difference is most clearly reflected in how an instance of *ctr* is used. This example illustrates that C++ offers many of the features that allow us to define objects which may be used in a (more or less) natural way. In the end, this is what software development is about, to please the user, within reason.

Summary

This section has presented an overview of C++. It gave an outline of its history, and discussed the design principles underlying C++ and its heritage from C.

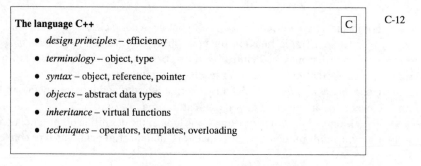

Slide C-12: C++ – summary

It listed the keywords that C++ introduces in addition to the keywords employed in C and characterized the object-oriented constructs supported by C++. An example was given to illustrate the difference between realizing an abstract data type in C and realizing the same abstract data type in C++. Further, it illustrated the use of virtual functions when deriving classes by inheritance, and discussed a number of additional features supported by C++.

D

The language DLP

Apart from what may be considered the mainstream languages Smalltalk, Eiffel and C++, there are numerous other (experimental) languages incorporating the object paradigm in one way or another. See section 5.1.1 and, for example, Davison (1993) for an overview. Of particular interest is the combination of the logic programming paradigm with object orientation, of which the language DLP is an example.

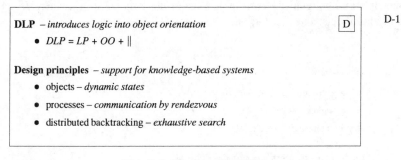

DLP *– introduces logic into object orientation*

- *DLP = LP + OO + ‖*

Design principles *– support for knowledge-based systems*

- objects *– dynamic states*
- processes *– communication by rendezvous*
- distributed backtracking *– exhaustive search*

Slide D-1: The language DLP

The DLP language combines logic programming (*LP*) with object orientation (*OO*) and parallelism (‖). DLP is a (very) high-level language, meant to support the development of knowledge-based systems. In addition to the logic programming features, it provides *objects* (that may change their state dynamically), *processes* (such as active objects, that communicate by rendezvous), and it allows for *distributed backtracking* (to enable exhaustive search in a logic programming style). See Eliëns (1992) for a full treatment.

Terminology Syntactically, DLP may be regarded as an extension of Prolog with constructs for parallel object-oriented programming. However, in addition to the familiar Prolog constructs it offers objects as well.

An object definition or object in DLP is a (labeled) collection of (Prolog) clauses that define the methods supported by the object, and which in addition may contain non-logical variables that are private to each instance. Active objects also contain one or more constructor clauses that define the objects's own activity. See slide D-2.

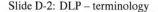

Slide D-2: DLP – terminology

Expressions The expressiveness of DLP is derived to a large extent from its heritage from Prolog. The basic syntactic units in Prolog are *terms*, which are either *constants* (such as characters, integers, strings, or the empty list $[]$), *variables* (which by convention start with a capital or underscore), or *compound terms* (which may be written as a function symbol with argument terms or as a list of the form $[H \mid T]$, where H stands for the head of the list and T for its tail). See slide D-3.

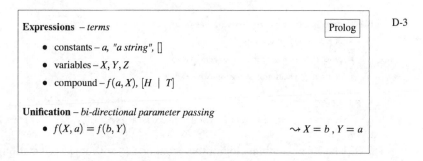

Slide D-3: DLP – expressions

Terms allow for what is called *unification*, which is an extended form of pattern matching. Unification results in binding variables to terms, in such a way that the two unified terms become syntactically equal. As an example, unifying $f(X, a)$ with $f(b, Y)$ results in binding X to a and Y to b. Unification is the primary mechanism of parameter passing in Prolog. It is essentially bi-directional and satisfies the *one-assignment-only* property, which means that evaluating a goal must result in a consistent binding, otherwise the goal fails.

Control The computation mechanism employed by Prolog may be characterized as goal reduction with unification and backtracking. As an example, look at the Prolog program in slide D-4, consisting of a number of clauses and facts.

When we pose our query, it is first attempted to resolve the goal $p(X, Y)$ with the first clause for p (which fails because $r(Z)$ cannot be resolved). Then the second clause is tried, which leads to binding Y to 2 (since $q(2)$ is a fact), and gives us two possible bindings for X, due to the facts $a(1)$ and $b(0)$. (Variables are local to clauses and will

```
Prolog                                                        D-4

     p(X,Y) :–  r(Z), b(X).                     clauses
     p(X,Y) :–  q(Y), b(X).
     b(X) :–  a(X).
     b(0).                                      facts
     a(1).
     q(2).
Query

     ?- p(X,Y).        results in (X = 1, Y = 2) and (X = 0, Y = 2)
```

Slide D-4: DLP – control (1)

be renamed automatically to avoid clashes.) Hence, the evaluation of the goal $p(X, Y)$ leads to two consistent bindings, that may successively be obtained by backtracking.

As an example of somewhat more realistic clauses, look at the list processing predicates *member* and *append* in slide D-5.

```
List processing – backtracking                               D-5

     member(X,[ X | _ ]).
     member(X,[ _ | T ]) :–  member(X,T).
     append([],L,L).
     append([ H | T ],L,[ H | R ]) :–  append(T,L,R).
```

Slide D-5: DLP – control (2)

Both predicates are specified in an inductive manner, taking care of all possible cases. For example, the first clause for *member* states as a fact that an element is contained in a list when it is the first element. The second clause prescribes the recursive application of member to the tail of the list if this is not the case. Similarly, the clauses for *append* distiguish between the case of appending a list to an empty list, and the case of appending a list to a non-empty list.

This manner of specification closely adheres to standard practice in mathematical logic and has proven to be a powerful means to develop knowledge-based systems (such as expert systems) that rely on logical reasoning.

Objects The language DLP supports active objects with a state (expressed as the value of non-logical instance variables) and communication by rendezvous (which realizes message passing for active objects). See slide D-6.

To support these features we need, in addition to terms and clauses, statements to assign terms to non-logical variables, a statement to create new active instances of an object (class), a statement to call a method for an object (which is essentially the invocation

```
┌─────────────────────────────────────────────────────────────┐
│ Additional statements                            ┌─────┐      │  D-6
│                                                  │ DLP │      │
│    • v := t - to assign to non-logical variables └─────┘      │
│    • O = new(c(t)) - to create an active instance of the      │
│      object c                                                 │
│    • O!m(t) - to call the method m(t) for the object O        │
│    • accept(m₁, ..., mₙ) - to accept method requests          │
└─────────────────────────────────────────────────────────────┘
```

Slide D-6: DLP – objects (1)

of a goal), and an *accept* statement that allows an active object to interrupt its own activity and accept the request to execute a method. When binding terms to logical variables or assigning terms to non-logical variables simple rewriting rules are applied. Rewriting includes arithmetic simplification and string manipulation.

```
┌─────────────────────────────────────────────────────────────┐
│ Computation model – distributed logic                        │  D-7
│                                                              │
│ objects – state + methods                                    │
│ processes – to evaluate goals                                │
│ communication – backtrackable rendezvous                     │
└─────────────────────────────────────────────────────────────┘
```

Slide D-7: DLP – objects (2)

The computation model underlying DLP is a model that supports distributed logic, and may be seen as a combination of the models underlying logic programming and parallel object-oriented languages. See slide D-7.

The DLP support system provides, in addition to a Prolog-like evaluation mechanism, support for *objects* (having a state, and methods defined by clauses), *processes* (to realize the object's own activity as well as to evaluate method calls or goals for the object), and a *communication* mechanism (that allows for a backtrackable rendezvous).

As an example of an object in DLP, look at the *travel* agency defined in slide D-8, which has a non-logical instance variable *cities* (containing a number of destinations), a constructor *travel* (which defines the object's own activity) and two methods, *reachable* and *add*.

The *reachable* method may be used to ask whether a particular destination exists or to ask for all possible destinations (which are actually obtained by backtracking). The *add* method may be used to add new destinations to the list of *cities*.

The *travel* constructor merely consists of a (tail-recursive) loop allowing to accept any request, one at a time. By specifying which requests may be accepted at a particular point in the lifetime of the object, the message interface of the object may be dynamically specified. In addition, an explicit *accept* statement is needed to guarantee mutual exclusion between method calls.

Inheritance DLP supports static inheritance, by code sharing, as do Smalltalk, Eiffel and

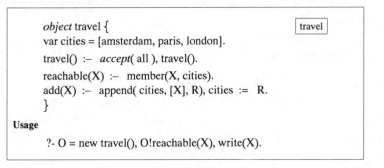

Slide D-8: DLP – objects (3)

C++. For a discussion of dynamic inheritance, by delegation, see section 5.4. As an example of inheritance in DLP, look at the refinement of the *travel* object into a veritable *agency*. See slide D-9.

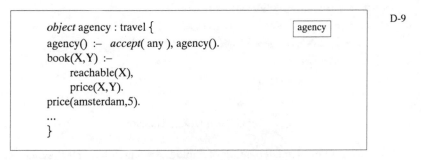

Slide D-9: DLP – inheritance

An *agency* offers the user, in addition to the functionality offered by *travel*, the opportunity to *book* for a particular destination and be informed of its price.

Inheritance in DLP conforms to the subsumption relation for logical theories, in that it extends the functionality of a given object in a strict manner. DLP allows for multiple inheritance and even checks for cycles to protect the user from repetitions or cycles in the inheritance chain.

Techniques Logic programming offers a wealth of techniques. In particular, the meta programming facilities (which are essentially based on the interpretation of programs as data) allow for very powerful programming techniques. See, for example, Bratko (1990).

By virtue of being an extension of Prolog, DLP inherits these facilities. In addition, DLP provides the constructs necessary to define what may be called (active) *intelligent agents*, of which the functionality can be specified in a declarative, logic-based fashion. DLP, in other words, is an example of a fruitful combination of paradigms, merging logic with object orientation.

Techniques – *logic*   D-10
- meta programming
- active intelligent objects

Slide D-10: DLP – techniques

Summary

This section has presented an overview of the DLP language. It discussed the design principles underlying DLP and characterized its principal application area as the development of knowledge-based systems.

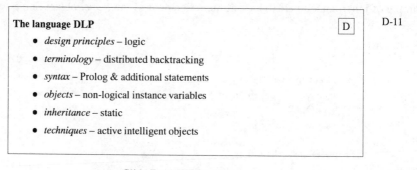

The language DLP   D   D-11
- *design principles* – logic
- *terminology* – distributed backtracking
- *syntax* – Prolog & additional statements
- *objects* – non-logical instance variables
- *inheritance* – static
- *techniques* – active intelligent objects

Slide D-11: DLP – summary

It gave a brief characterization of Prolog, explained how DLP syntactically extends Prolog with constructs for parallel object-oriented programming, and characterized the computation model of DLP. Some examples were given to illustrate the definition of objects and the use of inheritance.

E

The hush widget classes

The *hush* widget class library encapsulates the standard Tk widgets. In addition, a hypertext widget is offered. The widget classes are organized as a tree, with the class *widget* at the root.

E-1

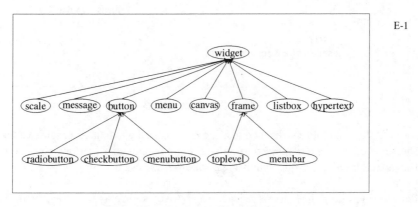

Slide E-1: The *hush* widget classes

Each concrete widget class offers the functionality supported by the (abstract) *widget* class and may in addition define functions specific to the particular widget class. The member functions for a widget class have usually a straightforward correspondence with the command interface defined by the Tcl/Tk toolkit. See Ousterhout (1994) for the most recent description.

Each function listed in the class interface is *public* unless it is explicitly indicated as *protected*. The interface descriptions start with the pseudo-keyword *interface*. This is merely done to avoid the explicit indication of *public* for both the ancestor and the member functions of the class.

Each widget class specifies two constructors, one with only a path and one which allows both for a widget and a path. In the latter case, the actual path consists of the concatenation of the path of the widget and the path specified by the string parameter. For the concrete widget classes, no widget will be created when the *options* parameter is zero. This convention is adopted to allow composite widgets to inherit from the standard widgets, yet define their own components.

In addition, each widget class has a destructor, which is omitted for brevity. The destructor may be used to reclaim the storage for a widget object. To remove a widget from the screen, the function *widget* :: *destroy* must be used.

The *scale* **class** The *scale* widget may be used to obtain numerical input from the user.

E-2

```
interface scale : widget {                                    scale
scale(char* p, char* options = "");
scale(widget* w, char* p, char* options = "");
void text(char* s);                        // text to display
void from(int n);                          // begin value
void to(int n);                            // end value
int get();                                 // gets the value
void set(int v);                           // sets the value
protected:
install(action&, char* args);
};
```

Slide E-2: The *scale* class

When a handler is attached to a *scale* it is called when the user releases the slider. The value of the *scale* is passed as an additional parameter when invoking the handler. The default binding for the scale is the *ButtonRelease* event.

The *message* **class** The *message* widget may be used to display a message on the screen.

E-3

```
interface message : widget {                            message
message(char* p, char* options = "" );
message(widget* w, char* p, char* options = "" );
void text(char* s);
};
```

Slide E-3: The *message* class

The *message* class does not define default bindings, but the user is free to associate events to a message widget by employing *widget* :: *bind*.

The *button* **class** Buttons come in a number of varieties, such as ordinary (push) buttons, that simply invoke an action, checkbuttons, that toggle between an on and off state, and radiobuttons, that may be used to constrain buttons to allow the selection of only a single alternative. Checkbuttons and radiobuttons are implemented as subclasses of the class *button*, and will not be discussed further here.

E-4

```
interface button : widget {                          button
button(char* p, char* options = "");
button(widget* w, char* p, char* options = "");
void text(char* s);                    // to display text
void bitmap(char* s);                  // to display a bitmap
void state(char * s);                  // to change the buttons state
void flash();
char* invoke();
protected:
install(action&,char* args);
};
```

Slide E-4: The *button* class

In addition to the constructors, which have the same format for each widget class, the *button* class offers the function *text* to define the text displayed by the button and the function *bitmap*, which takes as its argument the name of a file containing a bitmap, to have a bitmap displayed instead. The function *state* may be used to change the state of the button. Legal arguments are either *normal*, *active* or *disabled*. Further, the *button* class defines the functions *flash* and *invoke* that result, respectively, in flashing the button and in invoking the action associated with the button by means of the *widget* :: *handler* function. (Note that *button* :: *install* is defined, albeit protected.)

The *menubutton* class The *menubutton* is a specialization of the *button* widgets. It allows for attaching a menu that will be displayed when pressing the button. The *menubutton* must be used to pack menus in a *menubar*.

E-5

```
interface menubutton : button {                      menubutton
menubutton(char* p, char* options = "");
menubutton(widget* w, char* p, char* options = "");
void menu(char* s);                    // to attach menu
void menu(class menu* m);
};
```

Slide E-5: The *menubutton* widget

The *menu* class A menu consists of a number of button-like entries, each associated with an action. A menu entry may also consist of another menu, that pops up whenever the entry is selected.

```
interface menu : widget {                          [ menu ]        E-6
menu(char* p, char* options = "");
menu(widget* w, char* p, char* options = "");
menu* add(char* s, char* options = "");
menu* entry(char* s,char* args ="", char* opts="");
menu* entry(char* ,action&, char* ="", char* ="");
menu* cascade(char* s, char* m, char* opts = "");
menu* cascade(char* s, menu* m, char* opts = "");
char* entryconfigure(int i, char* options);
int index(char * s);
int active();                                // returns active index
void del(int i);                             // delete entry with index i
void del(char* s);                                     // delete entry
char* invoke(int i);                         // invoke entry with index i
char* invoke(char * s );                                      // invoke
void post(int x = 500, int y = 500);
void unpost();
protected:
install(action&, char* args);
};
```

Slide E-6: The *menu* class

The *add* function is included to allow arbitrary entries (as defined by Tk) to be added. We restrict ourselves to simple command and cascade entries.

The *entry* function (used for adding simple command entries) may explicitly be given an *action* to be associated with the entry. Alternatively, if no action is specified, the default handler action installed by invoking *widget :: handler* will be used. The string used as a label for the entries (the first parameter of *entry*) will be given as a parameter to the action invoked when selecting the entry. The string given in the *args* parameter will be added to the actual parameters for the action invoked.

The *cascade* function may either be given a *menu* or a string, containing the pathname of the menu. In any case, the cascaded menu must be a descendant of the original menu.

The function *index* returns the integer index associated with the string describing the entry. The function *active* may be used to ask which entry has been selected.

Entries may be deleted using the function *del* and invoked by using *invoke*. For both functions, the entry may be indicated by its numerical index or a string. Menus are top level widgets; they are mapped to the screen either by invoking the function *post*, or by pressing the *menubutton* to which the menu is attached.

The *canvas* class Apart from the two standard constructors, it offers the functions *tag*, *tags* and *move* that merely repeat the functions offered by the *item* class, except that *move*

E-7

```
interface canvas : widget {                    canvas
canvas(char * p, char* options="");
canvas(widget* w, char * p, char* options="");

void tag(int id, char* tag);
char* tags(int id);

void move(int id, int x, int y);
void move(char* id, int x, int y);

item bitmap(int x1, int y1, char* bm, char* opts="");
item line(int x1, int y1, int x2, int y2, char* opts ="");
item line(char* linespec, char* opts ="");
item circle(int x1, int y1, int rad, char* opts ="");
item oval(int x1, int y1, int x2, int y2, char* opts ="");
item polygon(char* linespec, char* opts ="");
item rectangle(int x1,int y1,int ,int ,char* opts ="");
item text(int x1, int y1, char* txt, char* opts="");
item window(int x1, int y1, char* w, char* opts="");

item current();
item overlapping(int x, int y);

itemconfigure(int it, char* options);
itemconfigure(char* tag, char* options);
itembind(int it, char* s, action&, char* args = "" );
itembind(char* tg,char* s,action&, char* args = "" );

void postscript(char* file, char* options="");
};
```

Slide E-7: The *canvas* class

may also be given a tag to identify the items to be moved.

Currently, the graphic items *bitmap, line, oval, polygon* and *rectangle* may be created and, in addition, *text* items and *window* items consisting of a widget. The function *overlapping* may be used to retrieve the item overlapping a particular position.

In addition, the *canvas* class has auxiliary functions which are needed to support the functionality provided by the *item* class. The canvas may be written as Postscript to a file with the function *canvas :: postscript*.

The *frame* **class** Frame widgets may used to combine widgets. A frame has no functionality or bindings of its own.

The frame widget class has the *toplevel* and *menubar* as subclasses.

The *toplevel* widget is used when the widget must be independently mapped to the screen.

The *menubar* widget is used as a special frame to collect *menubutton* and button widgets.

The *scrollbar* **class** The *scrollbar* allows the user to scroll through widgets that are only

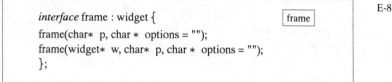

E-8

```
interface frame : widget {                    frame
frame(char* p, char * options = "");
frame(widget* w, char* p, char * options = "");
};
```

Slide E-8: The *frame* class

E-9

```
interface scrollbar : widget {                    scrollbar
scrollbar(char* p, char* options = "");
scrollbar(widget* w, char* p, char* options = "");
void orient(char* opts="vertical");
xview(widget* w);                    // install widget to scroll
yview(widget* w);                    // install widget to scroll
};
```

Slide E-9: The *scrollbar* class

partly displayed.

The default orientation of a *scrollbar* is vertical. A scrollbar must be explicitly attached to a widget w by calling the *scrollbar* :: *yview* functions for vertical scrollbars and *scrollbar* :: *xview* for horizontal scrollbars. To obtain the proper geometrical layout, the scrollbar and the widget it controls must usually be packed in a frame.

The *listbox* **class** The *listbox* widget is used to allow the user to select an item from a list of alternatives.

E-10

```
interface listbox : widget {                    listbox
listbox(char* p, char* options = "");
listbox(widget* w, char* p, char* options = "");
void insert(char* s);
char* get(int d);                    // entry with index d, starts from 0
void singleselect();
protected:
install(action&, char* args);
};
```

Slide E-10: The *listbox* class

The *listbox* may be filled by using *insert*. When a handler is attached to the widget, it is activated when the user double clicks on an item. The selected entry is passed as an additional parameter to the handler. The entry may also be obtained by either *kit* :: *selection* or *listbox* :: *get*.

The *entry* **class** An *entry* widget may be used to display text or allow the user to type a short text.

E-11

> *interface* entry : widget { | entry |
>
> entry(char∗ p, char∗ options = "");
> entry(widget∗ w,char∗ p, char∗ options = "");
>
> void insert(char∗ s);   // insert text
> char∗ get();   // to get the text
> *protected*:
> install(action&, char∗ args);
> };

Slide E-11: The *entry* class

When a handler is attached to the entry widget it is activated whenever the user double clicks on the widget or presses the return key. The contents of the entry are added as an argument when calling the handler.

The *hypertext* **class** The *hypertext* widget may be used to display text with embedded Tcl code.

E-12

> *interface* hypertext : widget { | hypertext |
> hypertext(char∗ p, char∗ options = "");
> hypertext(widget∗ w, char∗ p, char∗ options = "");
> void file(char∗ f);   // to read in hypertext file
> };

Slide E-12: The *hypertext* class

Apart from the standard constructors, it offers the function *file* to read in a hypertext file. Such a hypertext file allows one to embed widgets in the text by inserting them in escape sequences.

F

Programming projects

An object-oriented approach to software development requires an attitute that must be formed by experience with a practical programming task, employing object-oriented technolgy. In slide F-1, a number of projects are listed that have served as programming assignments at the Vrije Universiteit, Amsterdam.

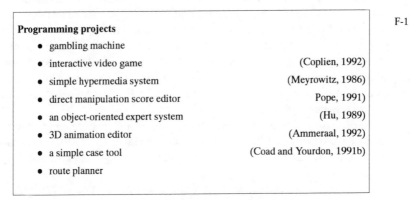

F-1

Programming projects

- gambling machine
- interactive video game   (Coplien, 1992)
- simple hypermedia system   (Meyrowitz, 1986)
- direct manipulation score editor   Pope, 1991)
- an object-oriented expert system   (Hu, 1989)
- 3D animation editor   (Ammeraal, 1992)
- a simple case tool   (Coad and Yourdon, 1991b)
- route planner

Slide F-1: Programming projects

The programming language (mandatorily) employed was C++. The *hush* library, sketched in section 12.2, was used for developing graphical user interfaces. Students were allowed to work in groups of two. Before starting a project, students were required to write a synopsis giving a global outline of the intended functionality of their system.

The minimal design documentation required was a description of each class interface in the style of CRC cards. Students were encouraged to make documentation and help available online, preferably in a hypertext format.

The programming projects are based on suggestions found in the literature, with the exception of the *gambling machine* and the *routeplanner*. The *gambling machine* seemed nice to allow students to animate with animation techniques.

The projects A typical example of a *gambling machine* is a *one armed bandit* with three columns of fruit. It is important to offer a realistic interface. Further, one must employ stochastic techniques to determine the chance of winning.

An example of an *interactive video game* is a volley or tennis game for one or two players. One must allow for an option to determine the speed of the ball and an option for replay. See Coplien (1992).

A *simple hypermedia* system must be capable of presenting text and graphics and must allow for the traversal of links between such items. An important aspect of this project is the development of an adequate object model for the items supported, including links. See Meyrowitz (1986) and Conklin (1987).

A *direct manipulation score editor* allows for editing musical fragments interactively. Some musical knowledge is required for such a project. The layout of music notation appears to be a difficult issue, because it is essentially two-dimensional and involves many special symbols. See Pope (1991).

The notion of an *object-oriented expert system* is quite open-ended. An approach one may take is to implement a traditional rule-based expert system in an object-oriented way, using C++. Take care to include an example knowledge-base to test the functionality of the system. See Hu (1989). A more general approach to employimg object-oriented technology for the development of knowledge-based systems is described in Eliëns (1992).

A *3D animation editor* supports the creation of (simple) 3D figures and must minimally allow for some basic manipulations in 3D space, such as rotations and translations. As an additional requirement, there must be a facility to replay a series of manipulations. See Ammeraal (1992).

A *simple case tool* allows for the interactive development of a simple object model, including the description of attributes of objects and the inheritance relations between object types. For an example of such tools, see Coad and Yourdon (1991b) and Rumbaugh *et al.* (1991).

A *routeplanner* allows the user to indicate a starting location and an end location. The system then calculates an appropriate route, for example the fastest or cheapest. As an additional requirement, the system must allow for the user to ask additional information about the route and the intermediate locations situated along the selected route. This information should preferably be in multimedia format.

Comments The *routeplanner* has successfully been used as an assignment as part of a CS2 Software Engineering course. Students, indeed, took the opportunity to experiment with the multimedia facilities of *hush*. Some of the other project assignments, such as the *score editor* and the *3D editor*, have led to quite remarkable results. For example, the *3D editor* project led students to develop a system to wander in 3D virtual space. Somewhat disappointingly, however, the *object-oriented expert system* project has not been chosen thus far. Perhaps it is regarded as too difficult or as not interesting enough.

Since the assignments were meant primarily as a means to gain experience with practical aspects of object-oriented programming, students were left free to choose a particular design method. The use of CRC-style documentation, however, was mandatory. Quite often, students developed a design employing OMT notation, which did not necessarily lead to a better result.

To gain experience with object-oriented design and analysis, a practical course focusing on modeling and requirements analysis is advisable. Any of the assignments above may be used in such a course. Other suggestions may be found in Coleman *et al.* (1994) and Sanden (1994) (which may be obtained by anonymous ftp at `isse.gmu.edu:/pub/techrep`).

G

Internet addresses

The Internet is increasingly becoming a rich source for a variety of information. Below, a number of addresses are given, from which to obtain programs, software libraries or technical papers. These addresses are partly taken from Locke (1994).

G-1

Email

- `ftpmail@decwrl.dec.com` – subject: *help*
- `netlib@research.att.com` – *send index*
- `omg@omg.org` – OMG

Slide G-1: Internet – email facilities

For those who have only an email facility at their disposal, software may be obtained by sending email to `ftpmail@decwrl.dec.com` (put *help* in the subject field) or `ftpmail@decwrl.dec.com` (write *send index* in the message body). Information concerning the activities of the OMG may be obtained by sending email to `omg@omg.org`. See slide G-1.

G-2

Newsgroups

- `comp.lang.c++`
- `comp.lang.eiffel`
- `comp.lang.smalltalk`
- `comp.databases.object`

Slide G-2: Internet – newsgroups

Another valuable source of information and programs are the Internet news-groups `comp.lang.c++`, `comp.lang.eiffel`, `comp.lang.smalltalk` and `comp.databases.object`. See slide G-2.

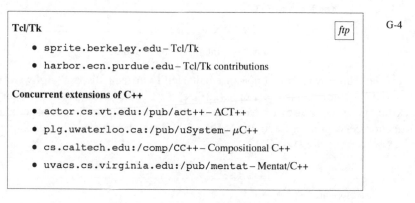

Slide G-3: Internet – ftp sites

For those that may use *ftp*, source code posted to either one of the news-groups may be obtained by anonymous ftp from `ftp.uu.net`. Other valu-able ftp sites are those mentioned in sections 11.3.3 and 11.4, among which `research.att.com`,`sunsite.unc.edu` and `iamsun.unibe.ch`. See slide G-3.

Slide G-4: Internet – miscellaneous

Further, two sites are listed from which Tcl/Tk and contributed software may be obtained, as well as the addresses from which to obtain the concurrent extensions to C++ discussed in section 6.3. See slide G-4.

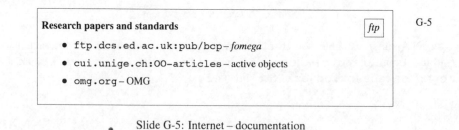

Slide G-5: Internet – documentation

A valuable collection of research papers may be obtained from `ftp.dcs.ed.ac.uk:pub/bcp`, among which is an introductory paper on type theoretical aspects of OOP which comes with a collection of exercises and an accompanying tool *fomega*. Other research papers may be found at `cui.unige.ch:OO-articles`.

Also available via anonymous ftp are the writings of the OMG, which may be collected at `omg.org`. See slide G-5.

World Wide Web Apart from email, news and ftp, you may access the Internet by means of dedicated information retrieval programs, such as the Mosaic browser for the World Wide Web. See Berners-Lee *et al.* (1992).

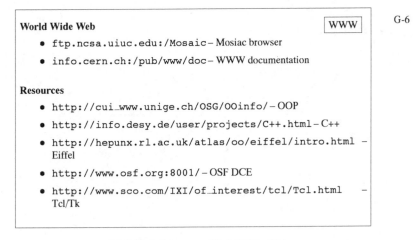

Slide G-6: Internet – World Wide Web

The World Wide Web is an initiative from CERN (the European Library for Particle Physics, Switzerland), intended to make a variety of material available in a common hypermedia format (HTML, see section 12.1.3). The Mosaic browser provides a graphical interface to the World Wide Web. It is available for X-windows, MS-windows and the Macintosh by anonymous ftp from `ftp.ncsa.uiuc.edu:/Mosaic`, where you can also find documentation. More information concerning the World Wide Web initiative may be obtained from `info.cern.ch:/pub/www/doc`.

The addresses listed in slide G-6 are HTML information resource identifiers, which provide you with a starting point for a journey in cyberspace documents on OOP.

H

Answers to Questions

Chapter 1

(1) Object-oriented programming stands for an approach to structure programs by employing encapsulation and inheritance. See slide 1-2. It is motivated by the need to manage the complexity of software. See slide 1-19.

(2) Slides 1-5 and 1-6 give an exhaustive overview. The most important features are, obviously, data abstraction and polymorphism due to inheritance.

(3) An object-oriented approach blurs the distinction between analysis, design and implementation. See slide 1-16. Moreover, it allows for different software development models, such as prototyping. See slide 1-18. What is your opinion?

(4) Aspects of software quality include correctness, robustness and extendibility. See slide 1-23. In particular, with regard to the cost of maintenance, a valid criterion would be *maintainabiliy*. OOP contributes to maintainability by supporting a strong notion of *locality*.

(5) See slide 1-25.

(6) From a historical perspective, OOP is a paradigm of programming. See slide 1-27. However, from a software engineering perspective, OOP is increasingly becoming important for design and analysis as well. See slide 1-11.

(7) Those include imperative languages, functional languages and logic programming languages. The essential features of OOP encapsulation and inheritance. These may be realized in a variety of language settings.

Chapter 2

(1) The complexity referred to is not the structural complexity of the computation, that is the space and time needed to solve a problem, but the conceptual complexity of programming, the organization of the software. See slide 2-3.

(2) Constructors describe what needs to be done when an instance of the class is created. Leaving the initialization of an object to the user may lead to many errors that are easily avoided by defining appropriate constructors. Destructors play a complementary role, by taking care of cleaning up before the object is destroyed.

(3) The type modifier *const* is used to declare a variable referring to a constant of a particular type. See slide 2-6. In addition *const* may be used to indicate that a member function does not affect the instance variables of an object.

(4) Automatic type conversion from a source to a target type may take place, when (a) the target type has a constructor with the source type as a single argument, or when (b) the source type defines a type operator of the target type. Type conversions may be enforced by using a cast. See slide 2-7.

(5) Friends may be classes or functions. They are allowed access to the private parts of an object. They may be necessary for reasons of efficiency. Friends are a relatively safe feature, since they must explicitly be declared by the class itself. They are not inherited. Neither is it possible for a class or function to declare itself as a friend of a class. Nevertheless, friends may jeopardize the integrity of an object. Treat friends with care.

(6) Generic types allow the programmer to define functionality in a general way, with respect to a variety of types. For instance, a generic container may contain items of arbitrary type. C++ supports generic types by means of inheritance and template classes. See slides 2-23 and 2-24 for some examples.

(7) A canonical class is a class realizing a concrete data type, that is defined to behave as a built-in type. It must include the definition of a default constructor, a copy or reference constructor, a destructor and assignment. An example is given in slide 2-18.

(8) The handler/body idiom describes how to separate the interface of an object class from its implementation. An example is given in slides 2-19 and 2-20.

(9) When derived classes have unlimited access to instance variables of ancestor classes, the class hierarchy defined by the inheritance relation may collapse when the implementation of an ancestor class is changed. The solution is to distinguish between private instance variables that are invisible even to derived classes and protected variables that are invisible only for external clients.

(10) This is the sneaky reference example given in slide 2-31.

(11) Inheritance allows for an elegant conceptual organization of the class types employed in a library or program. Some potential disadvantages are listed in slide 2-32.

(12) The most important extensions are meta classes, which support runtime type information, persistence, to allow for the storage of objects, and active objects, to allow for concurrency. See slide 2-37.

Chapter 3

(1) Object-oriented development centers around the decomposition of a system into objects. See slide 3-2. Aspects of the process of development include the definition of an object model, the choice of a method guiding the process of development, the management of the process of development and the actual design, capturing the essential architectural properties of the system.

(2) Modeling may be used to capture the requirements of a system, to define a conceptual model of the domain in analysis, to describe the system architecture during design and to realize the implementation objects. See slide 3-4.

(3) The OMT method distinguishes between an object model, a dynamic model and a functional model. See slide 3-5.

(4) A functional approach describes the global steps of a computation, whereas an object-oriented approach is of a more distributed nature, describing the objects participating in the computation. Advantages of an object-oriented approach are support for localized changes and support to introduce concurrency in the form of active objects. See slides 3-7 and 3-8.

(5) See slide 3-10.

(6) Most of the heuristics are based on a linguistic analysis of the requirements document. See slide 3-11.

(7) Criteria to eliminate spurious classes essentially come down to avoiding classes that provide no information. See slide 3-13.

(8) The CRC method consists of defining, for each class, its responsibilities and its collaborators, that is the classes that are needed to function properly. See slide 3-14.

(9) A contract defines the behavior of an object by means of an invariant and assertions characterizing the pre- and post-conditions of the methods supported by an object. See slide 3-21.

(10) Contracts may help to decide who is responsible for software failures. See slide 3-25.

(11) Partial types are types designed to have subtypes. By refinement through inheritance, partial types may be given a concrete realization. See slide 3-27.

(12) Refining a contract amounts to strengthening the invariant and, for each method, weakening the pre-conditions and strengthening the post-conditions. Also, methods may be added. See slide 3-29.

(13) Semantic modeling is mostly concerned with defining the attributes of objects and the relation between object classes. Object-oriented modeling, in contrast, is more concerned with characterizing the behavioral properties of objects. However, the two approaches are converging.

(14) Abstract systems may be regarded as the characterization of the functionality offered by a collection of abstract data types. It specifies the repertoire of methods available to the user of such a collection.

(15) Classes corresponding to actual events specify the interactions which must occur between objects. The resources which are needed when the event occurs are specified when creating the event. Protection is offered by hiding the interaction between the objects in the definition of the event activation operator.

Chapter 4

(1) Software quality may be characterized with respect to external characteristics, such as correctness and robustness. However, also structural characteristics, which determine maintenance, reuse and compatibility may be considered important as well. See slide 4-2.

(2) An example is given in slides 4-9 and 4-10. Inherited code may need to be retested because a subclass may affect inherited instance variables and because a superclass may use virtual methods that are redefined in a subclass.

(3) Within an object-oriented approach, we may distinguish between the levels of individual methods, objects, a collection of objects and the system level. See slide 4-11.

(4) Testing the behavior of objects involves checking whether invoking methods results in appropriate object state transitions. A more abstract approach to testing consists of checking sequences of operations resulting in identity transitions. See slide 4-14.

(5) Contracts may be used to establish runtime consistency characteristics. Testing runtime consistency amounts to checking object invariants and method pre- and post-conditions.

(6) See slide 4-19.

(7) A number of metrics are listed in slide 4-21. These metrics pertain to the definition of object classes and the relation between classes.

(8) A number of criteria are listed in slide 4-23. Some of these criteria give counter-intuitive results with respect to common opinions concerning object oriented design. Empirical validation is needed before applying any metric in actual development project.

(9) See slides 4-24 – 4-29.

(10) See slide 4-31. The intuition underlying the Law of Demeter is essentially that ignorance of how a class is implemented is beneficial for understanding and maintenance.

(11) See slide 4-30.

(12) A formal specification must characterize the requirements of a system and must also provide guidelines for its validation. Contracts may be used to specify invariant consistency properties that may be tested at runtime. See slide 4-33.

Chapter 5

(1) Object-oriented languages generally offer a facility for creating objects, the capability of message passing, classes and inheritance. See slide 5-4.

(2) A classification of object-oriented languages may distinguish between hybrid languages, frame-based languages as employed in Artificial Intelligence, parallel/distributed languages and languages supporting prototypes. See slide 5-4.

(3) Characteristic for the object model supported by C++ is the unification of classes with the *struct* record type. See slide 5-6.

(4) Object-based implies support for encapsulation, whereas object-oriented implies support for encapsulation and inheritance. See slide 5-10.

(5) As orthogonal dimensions along which to describe the design of object-oriented languages you may distinguish between objects, types, delegation and abstraction. See slide 5-11.

(6) Prototype-based languages support an object model based on exemplars. Their most characteristic feature is support for dynamic delegation.

(7) Inheritance is static; it amounts to creation-time sharing, whereas delegation supports lifetime sharing. See slide 5-13.

(8) The C++ language supports the forwarding of member function calls. Forwarding does not, however, allow for binding self-reference to the forwarding object.

(9) In classical object-oriented languages, the notion of class stands for object generator and interface description. A class may further be a repository for sharing resources and act as an object capable of answering (class) methods. See slide 5-17.

(10) The first three postulates given in slide 5-20 pertain to Smalltalk. With some minor modifications, these postulates hold for other classical languages. The fourth postulate of slide 5-20 specifies the constraint that must be met by a reflective architecture: class variables of an object must be instance variables of the class of the object (when considering the class as an object).

Chapter 6

(1) The object-oriented community has originally adopted the client/server metaphor from the distributed computing community. The client/server model intrinsically supports concurrency and active objects. See slide 6-2.

(2) There are three ways to extend an object-oriented language with concurrency: add processes as an orthogonal concept; introduce active objects; or allow for asynchronous communication. See slide 6-4.

(3) Active objects unify the characteristics of objects and processes. To communicate with active objects, message passing must be extended to communication by rendezvous. See section 6.2.3.

(4) Issues in developing a concurrent extension of C++ are: the combination of objects and processes; how to resolve communication and synchronization; and whether to support inheritance. See slide 6-11.

(5) Concurrent C++ is meant as an orthogonal extension of both C++ and Concurrent C. See slide 6-12. It offers processes in addition to objects, yet allows for encapsulating processes in objects. See slide 6-15.

(6) The original actor model supports active objects, of which the behavior is defined by scripts, asynchronous communication between actors via mailboxes and behavioral replacement, that allows for an actor to change its behavior after responding to a message. The actor model supported by ACT++ is considerably simpler. It supports only synchronous communication and defines behavior replacement through refinement by inheritance. See slides 6-16 and 6-18.

(7) μC++ extends C++ with a variety of concurrency and synchronization features, including monitors and tasks supporting communication by rendezvous. See slide 6-19. Compositional C++ allows for the creation of processes and supports synchronization by write-once variables. See slide 6-20.

(8) The problem is known as the *inheritance anomaly*, which amounts to the observation that the object's own activity and synchronization aspects must usually be redefined when inheriting from an active object. See slide 6-22.

(9) An example of employing inheritance for processes is given in slide 6-25. The solution given, however, requires multi-threaded active objects.

(10) An important problem is fault-tolerance. See slide 6-28. Another issue that must be dealt with is the inefficiency of remote invocations. One may think of replication strategies to reduce the traffic of data involved. See slide 6-30.

Chapter 7

(1) See the discussion in section 7.1.1.

(2) See the discussion in section 7.1.2.

(3) The diamond structure allows for separating the specification of an abstract interface of a compound object, its functional behavior, the way it is displayed and its actual realization. See section 7.1.3.

(4) Overloading the de-reference operator allows one to bypass type checking on the level of the interface class. Dereferencing results in applying the function called to the de-referenced object. See slides 7-13 and 7-14.

(5) Smart pointers may be introduced by overloading the de-reference operator. They are employed, for example, in the ODMG-93 standard to implement transparent references to both transitory and persistent objects. (The implementation is left as an exercise.)

(6) Dynamic role switching may be realized by introducing a so-called fat abstract interface class and employing a switch to invoke a function for the realization that matches the actual role. See section 7.2.3.

(7) A gadget is an item that may be found in a graphical user interface. The interaction between gadgets and windows takes place by callback functions. See section 7.3.1.

(8) An event is the result of a user action, such as clicking a mouse button. A gadget that has been declared sensitive to a particular user action must be notified if the corresponding event occurs. It may then respond with an appropriate action, if it considers the event of relevance. See section 7.3.2.

(9) See section 7.3.3.

(10) Event-driven control is not exclusive to window management systems. It may also be fruitfully applied to realize the actions occurring in response to operations of the user. User-defined events allow for the combination of system operations and the declaration of dependent events. As such, they provide an elegant means to maintain the integrity of a system. See section 7.4.

Chapter 8

(1) Control abstractions primarily affect the flow of control. Control abstractions were introduced to support a structured approach to algorithm design. A structured approach avoids the use of goto's, and instead employs if-statements and explicit while-statements. In contrast, data abstraction pertains to data structures and information hiding. Abstract data types may be realized as a collection of functions. Object-oriented languages, however, provide far better support for data abstraction. See slide 8-2.

(2) Types contribute primarily to the reliability of systems. See slide 8-4.

(3) The most obvious interpretation of objects (as algebras) is to regard each object state as an algebra. A state change for the object, then, results in a different algebra. Mathematically, the object may then be considered to live in a different world. See slide 8-28.

(4) A data abstraction matrix, as shown in slide 8-23, provides a powerful way to specify the properties of an abstract data type. Its realization by modules or objects reflects a choice for a particular decomposition, sacrificing the generality of the original matrix.

(5) The realization of an abstract data type as a module results in organizing the functionality of the type around the observers. For each observer, the result for the various generators is specified as a separate case. In contracts, objects may be regarded as specifying for each generator the value for the observer operation. As trade-offs we have that objects behave comparatively better when extending the abstract data type with new generators, whereas the reverse seems to hold for extending an abstract data type with new observers.

(6) Types have a formal interpretation as the specification of constraints, whereas classes may be taken as templates for object creation, which is a far more pragmatic interpretation.

(7) Types may be specified in a syntactic way, semantically or purely pragmatically. In the latter case, the notion of types coincides with the notion of classes. Classes, clearly, may be regarded as an over-specification of the properties of a type. When regarded from a syntactic point of view, types specify too little. However, a purely syntactic specification allows for rigid type checking. The behavioral specification of types must be regarded as an ideal. Contracts as supported by Eiffel are one possible approximation of this ideal. See slides 8-34 and 8-35.

(8) Behaviorally compatible modifications are refinements that fully meet the substitutability requirement. Alternatives are signature compatible modifications, that are constrained only by syntactic requirements, and name compatible modifications that rely only on the method search algorithm employed, imposing even weaker constraints.

Chapter 9

(1) In knowledge representation, inheritance is primarily applied to describe taxonomic structures in a declarative way. Employing exceptions in inheritance networks leads to non-monotony. Non-monotonic inheritance networks may give rise to inconsistencies. See slide 9-2.

(2) The meaning of an inheritance lattice may be expressed as a first order logic formula. An example is given in slide 9-4

(3) A type denotes a set of individuals. The subtyping relation is essentially the set inclusion relation, with some additional constraints. However, the subtype relation is best defined by means of subtype refinement rules.

(4) See slide 9-6.

(5) The contravariant nature of the function subtype refinement rule may be explained by relying on the business service metaphor: refining a service means better work for less money. Or, put differently, refining a function means imposing less constraints on the client, yet delivering a result that is more tightly defined. See slide 9-8.

(6) The notion of *objects as records* is introduced simply to justify the interpretation of objects as records or tuples of values and functions. Again employing a business metaphor, regarding an object as a collection of services, improving such a collection means offering more, and possibly better, services. See slide 9-9.

(7) Typed formalisms provide protection against errors. Yet, untyped formalisms are generally more flexible. In the practice of computer science and mathematics, untyped formalisms are surprisingly popular.

(8) A first distinction may be made between universal polymorphism and *ad hoc* polymorphism, which accounts for overloading and coercion. Universal polymorphism may be subdivided into parametric polymorphism, which covers template classes, and inclusion polymorphism, that results from derivation by inheritance. See slide 9-13.

(9) Inheritance allows for the incremental development of object descriptions. A child class may be regarded as modifying the parent base class, as it may include additional attributes and methods and may refine inherited attributes or methods.

(10) See slides 9-20, 9-23 and 9-27.

(11) (a) $\{a : Int, f : Int \rightarrow Int\}$, (b) $Int \rightarrow Int$, (c) $\{a : Bool, f : Bool \rightarrow Int\} \rightarrow Int$.

(12) (a) No, since $1..4 \not\leq 2..5$. (b) No, since $f : Bool \rightarrow Int \not\leq f : Int \rightarrow Int$, because $Int \not\leq Bool$. (c) Yes, since $\{a : Bool, f : Bool \rightarrow Int\} \leq \{a : Bool\}$.

(13) To give an example, if you have a record x of type $\exists \alpha.\{val : \alpha.op : \alpha \rightarrow Int\}$ then you do not need to know the precise nature of the (hidden) type α to be able to type the expression $x.op(x.val)$ as Int. See slide 9-34.

(14) A possible realization is given by the record $\{a = 0, f = \lambda x.E\}$, for $E =$ *if even(x) then true else false*. The corresponding package is given by the expression $pack[\alpha = Int \ in \{a : \alpha, f : \alpha \rightarrow Bool\}](0, \lambda x.E)$. Another realization is given by the record type $\{a : R, f : R \rightarrow Bool\}$ where R stands for $\{x : Int, y : Int\}$.

(15) The proof involves unrolling. Let $T_1 = \mu \alpha.\{c : \alpha, b : \alpha \rightarrow \alpha\}$ and $T_2 = \mu \alpha.\{b : \alpha \rightarrow \alpha\}$. Now suppose that $T_1 \leq T_2$ then, by unrolling, we would have that $\{c : T_1, b : T_1 \rightarrow T_1\} \leq \{b : T_2 \rightarrow T_2\}$, and hence, by the function subtyping rule, that $T_2 \leq T_1$ and $T_1 \leq T_2$. This would only hold if $T_1 = T_2$, which is obviously not the case.

(16) Let $\sigma = \mu \alpha.\{c : \alpha, b : \tau \rightarrow \alpha\}$ and assume that $\sigma \leq \tau$, then by unrolling we have that $\{c : \sigma, b : \tau \rightarrow \sigma\} \leq \{b : \tau \rightarrow \tau\}$ which clearly holds since $b : \tau \rightarrow \sigma \leq b : \tau \rightarrow \tau$. And, by applying the refinement rule for recursive types (given in slide 9-36), we indeed have that $\sigma \leq \tau$.

Chapter 10

(1) Conformance not only involves syntactic properties, but behavioral properties as well. Behavioral properties include invariant properties and history properties. See slide 10-2.

(2) See slide 10-3.

(3) Static constraints may be expressed directly in the signature, but also by means of pre- and post-conditions. To a certain, but definitely lesser, extent, the reverse is also true. See slide 10-4.

(4) States may be modeled as functions and state transformations as function modifications. See slides 10-6 and 10-5.

(5) There are two ways to verify the behavior of a program: (a) prove for each possible transition that the formula holds; and (b) employ the correctness calculus given in slide 10-7.

(6) For each syntactical kind of statement allowed by the language, a transition system specifies a corresponding execution step, or series of such steps, by means of a transition derivation rule. An example transition system for a simple object-based language, supporting object creation and message passing, is given in section 10.3.

(7) To prove that a realization is correct with respect to its abstract specification, one must prove that each concrete operation satisfies the constraints imposed on the abstract level. See slide 10-12.

(8) See slides 10-13, 10-14 and 10-15.

(9) Correspondence between subtypes involves syntactic constraints, defined by the subtyping rules given in chapter 9, behavioral constraints, as characterized by the refinement relation for pre- and post-conditions and invariants, and constraints for the extensions, as expressed by the diamond rule. See slides 10-16 and 10-17.

(10) See slides 10-18, 10-19 and 10-20.

(11) Invariance properties of objects cannot completely be checked locally, within the confines of a single object. See slide 10-21. Checking invariants explicitly for each object, however, is likely to be too expensive.

(12) Formal methods to specify the interaction between objects include model-based specification methods, the specification of contracts as behavioral compositions, the specification of cooperating actors by means of scripts, the specification of multiparty interactions, and the specification of joint action systems. See slide 10-22.

Chapter 11

(1) Large applications need to be decomposed into components of a manageable size. Prefarably off-the-shelf components. To combine components, possibly obtained from various vendors, standardization is necessary.

(2) The OMG aims at defining a standard allowing for the combination of components in a distributed environment. The goal is to define standards allowing for application integration in a language-, platform- and vendor-independent manner. The OMG proposed an Object Management Architecture offering an interface description language (IDL) and standards for Object Services. To realize these aims, many technical problems need to be solved. See slide 11-4. But perhaps more importantly, issues of terminology and policy need to be sorted out as well.

(3) The ODMG standardization effort aims at introducing object persistence as an extension to object-oriented languages, within a unified type system. See slide 11-5. The ODMG standard is intended to be compatible with the OMG standard. The object interface description language ODL may be regarded as an extension of IDL.

(4) See slide 11-8 for a discussion of the role of events in analysis, design and implementation. Clearly, objects and events are in a way complementary entities. Complementary, in the sense that events may be said to occur to objects, whereas objects may be regarded as being susceptible to events. On the other hand, events may be regarded as objects themselves.

(5) The main problem of library design is to arrive at a simple, comprehensible class structure, offering the functionality needed in an easy to use manner. Backward compatibility is a difficult issue. Annotating methods that are outdated as *obsolete* seems to be a reasonable compromise. See slide 11-11.

(6) See slide 11-12 for the conventions used in the Eiffel libraries. Just think of something to rationalize your own approach.

(7) What we need are tools for archiving and retrieval. One can think of an object repository for storing objects and annotations to allow for the retrieval of objects by index attributes. One of the unsolved problems, still, is what indexes or annotations need to be provided. A promising technology for retrieval from software repositories is offered by hypermedia.

(8) An overview of development methods is given in slide 11-23. More details for a selected number of methods can be found in slide 11-26 Some methods, such as OMT and CRC, primarily cover analysis. But most methods also cover design. The Booch method offers numerous diagram techniques, which also apply to the implementation phase.

(9) See slide 11-25 for an overview of the Fusion method. Characteristic for the Fusion method is that it offers a systematic approach to the process of software development.

(10) See slide 11-27.

(11) See slide 11-31. Often cost factors will be an important criterion. A criterion easily overlooked is adherence to (emerging) standards.

(12) What may be regarded as the minimal functionality for these libraries is listed in slides 11-33, 11-34 and 11-36. If you find these lacking, add the functionality that you consider essential.

Chapter 12

(1) Hypermedia is a combination of hypertext and multimedia. See slide 12-2. Hypermedia interfaces are usually direct manipulation interfaces. They must support the display of a variety of media components and the anchors embedded in

documents. Also, they must allow for following links in response to the activation of an anchor. See slide 12-3.

(2) See slide 12-4. Support for navigation may be offered by selective traversal, based on attributes, content listings, indexes and, in a graphical manner, by maps displaying the information components and their connections.

(3) See slide 12-5.

(4) Such a model is essentially based on the Dexter hypertext reference model. Important for hypermedia is the support for time-based documents and the synchronization between components. See slide 12-8.

(5) A link is a, possibly conditional, connection between a source anchor and a target anchor. An important distinction is that between structural links, which determine the hierarchical organization of the hyperdocument, and referential links, that may impose an arbitrary associative structure upon the document. Both anchors and links may be defined in a virtual way. The actual meaning of virtual links is computed when reading the document. Active documents are scripts that require computation to display their contents. Following links usually is the result of executing a procedure in response to an event or an action of the user.

(6) Just think of the time you have spent waiting for your program to compile.

(7) The problem of heterogeneous systems is essentially to combine multiple hybrid components in a seamless way. An object-oriented approach allows for employing techniques such as encapsulation by wrapping, refinement by inheritance and distributed application integration along the lines sketched in the OMG proposal. See slide 12-37.

(8) Answer this question with some caution. You may want to write a paper about it.

References

Agha G. (1990) The structure and semantics of actor languages. In de Bakker *et al.* (1990), pp. 1-59

Agha G., Wegner P. and Yonezawa A., eds. (1993) *Research directions in concurrent object-oriented programming.* MIT Press

Agrawal R. and Gehani N.H. (1989) Ode (Object database and environment): The language and the data model. In *Proc. ACM-SIGMOD 1989 Int. Conf. of Data*, Portland, Oregon, pp. 36-45

Akscyn R., McCracken D. and Yoder E. (1988) KMS: a distributed hypermedia system for managing knowledge in organizations. *CACM* 31(7), pp. 820-835

America P. (1987) POOL-T: a parallel object-oriented language. In *Object-oriented concurrent systems* (Yonezawa A. and Tokoro M., eds.), MIT Press, pp. 199-220

America P. (1987a) Inheritance and subtyping in a parallel object-oriented language. In *Proc. ECOOP 87*, Paris, Springer LNCS 276, pp. 234-242

America P., de Bakker J.W., Kok J.N. and Rutten J.J.N.N. (1989) Denotational semantics of a Parallel Object-Oriented Language. *Information and Computation*, 83 (2) pp. 152-205

America P. (1990) A behavioral approach to subtyping in object-oriented programming languages. In Lenzerini *et al.* (1990), pp. 173-190

America P. and de Boer F. (1993) Reasoning about dynamically evolving process structures. *Formal aspects of computing* 3, pp. 1-53

Ammeraal L. (1992) *Programming principles in computer graphics.* Wiley, 2nd edn.

Andrews G.R. (1991) *Concurrent programming – principles and practice.* Benjamin/Cummings

Apt K.R. and Olderog E-R. (1991) *Verification of sequential and concurrent programs.* Springer

Back R.J.R. and Kurki-Suonio R. (1988) Distributed cooperation with action systems. *ACM TOPLAS* 10(4), pp. 513-514

Backhouse R. (1986) *Program construction and verification.* Prentice-Hall

de Bakker J.W., de Roever W.P. and Rozenberg G., eds. (1990) *Foundations of Object-Oriented Languages.* Springer LNCS 489

de Bakker J.W., de Roever W.P. and Rozenberg G., eds. (1992) *Semantics: Foundations and Applications.* Springer LNCS 666

Bal H., Steiner J. and Tanenbaum A. (1989) Programming languages for distributed systems. *ACM Computing Surveys* 21(3), pp. 262-322

Bal H. (1991) *Programming distributed systems.* Prentice Hall

Bal H.E. and Grune D. (1994) *Programming language essentials.* Addison-Wesley

Bar-David T. (1992) Practical consequences of formal definitions of inheritance. *JOOP* July/August 1992, pp. 43-49

Barendrecht H.P. (1984) *The lambda calculus – Its syntax and semantics.* North-Holland, rev. edn.

Barnes J.G.P. (1994) *Programming in Ada, Plus an overview of Ada 9X.* Addison-Wesley, 4th edn.

Beck K. and Cunningham W. (1989) A laboratory for teaching object-oriented thinking. In *Proc. OOPSLA '89*, ACM Sigplan Notices 17(4), pp. 1-6

Beck B. (1990) Shared-memory parallel programming in C++. *IEEE Software* 7(7), pp. 38-48

Bennett J.K. (1987) The design and implementation of Distributed Smalltalk. In *Proc. OOPSLA'87*, pp. 318-330

Bergin J. (1994) *Data abstraction – The object-oriented approach using C++.* McGraw-Hill

Berners-Lee T.J., Cailliau R., Groff J-F. and Pollermann B. (1992) World Wide Web: The Information Universe . *Electronic Networking: Research, Applications and Policy* 2(1), Meckler Publishing, pp. 52-58

Bershad B.N., Lazowska E.D., and Levy H.M. (1988) Presto: a system for object-oriented parallel programming. *Software – Practice and Experience* 18(8), pp. 713-732

Bersoff E.H. and Davis A.M. (1991) Impacts of life cycle models on software configuration management. *CACM* 34(8), pp. 105-117

Bezem M. and Grootte J.F., eds. (1993) *Typed lambda calculi and applications. Proc. Int. Conf. on typed lambda calculi and applications, TCLA'93*, Springer LNCS 664

Bigelow J. (1988) Hypertext and CASE. *IEEE Software*, March 1988, pp. 23-26

Biggerstaff T.J. and Perlis A.J., eds. (1989) *Software reusability, Volume I: Concepts and Models, Volume II: Applications and Experience.* Addison-Wesley

Black A. and Hutchinson N. (1986) Object structure in the Emerald system. In *Proc. OOPSLA'86*, pp. 78-86

Blaschek G., Pomberger G. and Stritzinger A. (1989) A comparison of object-oriented programming languages. *Structured Programming* 10(4), pp. 187-197

Blum A. (1992) *Neural networks in C++ – An object-oriented framework for building connectionist systems.* Wiley

Bobrow D.G. and Winograd T. (1977) An overview of KRL – a knowledge representation language. Technical Report R76/581 Stanford University

Booch G. (1986) Object-oriented development. *IEEE Transactions on Software Engineering* 12(2), pp. 211-221

Booch G. and Vilot M. (1990) The design of the C++ Booch components. In *Proc. ECOOP/OOPSLA '90*, pp. 1-11

Booch G. (1991) *Object-oriented design with applications.* Benjamin Cummings

Booch G. (1994) *Object-oriented analysis and design with applications.* Benjamin Cummings, 2nd edn.

Bratko I. (1990) *Prolog Programming for Artificial Intelligence.* Addison-Wesley, 2nd edn.

Briot J. and Yonezawa A. (1987) Inheritance and synchronization in concurrent OOP. In *Proc. ECOOP '87*, Springer LNCS 276, pp. 32-40

Budd T. (1991) *An introduction to object-oriented programming.* Addison-Wesley

Budd T. (1994) *Classic data structures in C++.* Addison-Wesley

Buhr P.A., Ditchfield G., Stroobosscher R.A., Younger B.M., and Zarnke C.R. (1992) µC++ : Concurrency in the object-oriented language C++. *Software – Practice and Experience* 22(2), pp. 137-172

Buhr P.A. and MacDonald H.I. (1992) Synchronous and asynchronous handling of abnormal events in the µSystem. *Software – Practice and Experience* 22(9), pp. 735-776

Bush V. (1945) As we may think. *Atlantic Monthly*, August 1945, pp. 101-108

Bundy A., ed. (1990) *Catalogue of Artificial Intelligence tools.* Springer, 3rd edn.

Burger J. (1993) *The desktop multimedia bible.* Addison-Wesley

Cardelli L. (1984) A semantics of multiple inheritance. In *Semantics of Data Types*, Springer LNCS 173, pp. 51-68

Cardelli L. and Wegner P. (1985) On understanding types, data abstraction and polymorphism. *ACM Computing Surveys* 17(4), pp. 472-522

Cardelli L., Donahue J., Jordan M. Kalsow B. and Neslon G. (1989) The Modula-3 Type System. In *Proc. ACM Symposium on Principles of Programming Languages*, Austin, Texas, pp. 202-212

Carroll M. and Ellis M.A. (1994) *Designing and implementing reusable C++.* Addison-Wesley

Castagna G., Ghelli G. and Longo G. (1993) A semantics for λ &-*early*: a calculus with overloading and early binding. In Bezem en Grootte (1993), pp. 107-123

Cattell R., ed. (1994) *The object database standard: ODMG-93.* Morgan-Kaufmann

Champeaux D., Lea D. and Faure P. (1993) *Object-oriented system development.* Addison-Wesley

Chandy K.M. and Misra J. (1989) *Parallel program design – A foundation.* Addison-Wesley

Chandy K.M. and Kesselman C. (1992) Compositional C++: compositional parallel programming. In *Proc. of the Workshop on Parallel Computing and Compilers*, Springer

Chidamber S.K. and Kemerer C.F. (1991) Towards a metric suite for object-oriented design. In *Proc. OOPSLA'91*, pp. 197-211

Cline M. and Lea D. (1990) The behavior of C++ classes. In *Proc. Symp. on Object-Oriented Programming*, Marist College

Coad P. and Nicola J. (1993) *Object-oriented programming.* Yourdon Press

Coad P. and Yourdon E. (1991a) *Object-oriented analysis.* Prentice Hall, 2nd edn.

Coad P. and Yourdon E. (1991b) *Object-oriented design.* Prentice Hall

Cointe P. (1987) Metaclasses are first class: the ObjVLisp Model. In *Proc. OOPSLA'87, ACM Sigplan Notices* 22(12), pp. 156-167

Coleman D., Arnold P., Bodoff S., Dollin C., Gilchrist H., Hayes F. and Jeremaes P., (1994) *Object-oriented development – The Fusion method.* Prentice Hall

Conklin J. (1987) Hypertext: An Introduction and Survey. *IEEE Computer* 20(9), pp. 17-41

Cook W.R. (1990) Object-oriented programming versus abstract data types. In de Bakker *et al.* (1990), pp. 151-178

Cook W. and Palsberg J. (1989) A denotational semantics of inheritance and its correctness. In *Proc. OOPSLA 1989*, pp. 433-434

Cook W., Hill W. and Canning P. (1990) Inheritance is not subtyping. In *Proc. ACM Symp. on Principles of Programming Languages*

Coplien J. (1992) *Advanced C++ Programming Styles and Idioms.* Addison-Wesley

Cox B.J. (1986) *Object-Oriented Programming – An evolutionary approach.* Addison-Wesley

Craig I. (1991) *The formal specification of advanced AI architectures.* Ellis Horwood

Dahl O-J. and Nygaard K. (1966) Simula – an algol-based simulation language. *CACM* 9, pp. 671-678

Dahl O-J. (1992) *Verifiable Programming.* Prentice Hall

Danforth S. and Tomlinson C. (1988) Type theories and object-oriented programming. *ACM Computing Surveys* 20(1), pp. 30-72

Davis A.M., Bersoff E.H. and Comer E.R. (1988) A strategy for comparing alternative software development life cycle models. *IEEE Trans. on Software Engineering* 14(10), pp. 1453-1461

Davison A. (1993) A survey of logic programming based object-oriented languages. In Agha *et al.* (1993), pp. 43-106

Detlefs D.L., Herlihy M.P. and Wing J.M. (1988) Inheritance of synchronization and recovery properties in Avalon/C++. *IEEE Computer* 21(12), pp. 57-69

Diller A. (1990) *Z: An Introduction to Formal Methods.* Wiley

Dixon G.N., Parrington G.D., Shrivastava S.K. and Wheater S.M. (1989) The treatment of persistent objects in Arjuna. In *Proc. ECOOP '89*, Cambridge University Press, pp. 169-189

Dony C., Malenfant J. and Cointe P. (1992) Prototype-based languages: From a new taxonomy to constructive proposals and their validation. In *Proc. OOPSLA'92*, pp. 201-217

Doong R.K. and Frankl P. (1990) Tools for testing object-oriented programs. In *Proc. Pacific NorthWest Conf. on Software Quality*, pp. 309-324

Doong R.K. and Frankl P. (1991) Case studies in testing object-oriented programs. In *Proc. of The Testing, Analysis and Verification Symposium, ACM*, pp. 165-177

Ducournau R. and Habib M. (1988) On some algorithms for multiple inheritance in object-oriented programming. In *Proc. ECOOP 1987*, Springer LNCS 276, pp. 243-252

Duff C.B. (1986) Designing an efficient language. *Byte*, August 1986, pp. 133-139

Dijkstra E.W. (1968) Goto statement considered harmful. *CACM* 11, pp. 147-148

Dijkstra E.W. (1976) *A discipline of programming.* Prentice Hall

Eliëns A. (1991) Distributed Logic Programming for Artificial Intelligence. *AI Communications* Vol. 4 No. 1, pp. 11-21

Eliëns A. (1992) *DLP – A language for distributed logic programming.* Wiley

Eliëns A. (1992b) An object-oriented approach to distributed problem solving. In *Research and Development in Expert Systems IX, Proc. ES92*, (Bramer M. and Milne R., eds), pp. 285-300, Cambridge University Press

Eliëns A. and de Vink E.P. (1992) Asynchronous rendez-vous in distributed logic programming. In de Bakker *et al.* (1992), pp. 174-203

Eliëns A. and Visser C. (1994) Active C++, active classes and communication by rendezvous. Technical Report IR-299 Vrije Universiteit, Amsterdam

Eliëns A. (1994) Hush - a C++ API for Tcl/Tk. Report Vrije Universiteit

Ellis M. and Stroustrup B. (1990) *The annotated C++ reference manual.* Addison-Wesley

Evangelist M., Francez N. and Katz S. (1989) Multiparty interactions for interprocess communication and synchronization. *IEEE Trans. on Software Engineering* 15(11), pp. 1417-1426

Fekete J-D. (1992) WWL – A Widget Wrapper Library for C++. Technical report LRI France

Fichman R.G. and Kemerer C.F. (1992) Object-oriented and conventional analysis and design methodologies. *IEEE Computer* 25(10), pp. 22-39

Fiedler S.P. (1989) Object-oriented unit testing. Hewlett-Packard Journal, April 1989, pp. 69-74

Fikes R. and Kehler T. (1985) The role of frame-based representation in reasoning. *CACM* 28, pp. 904-920

Francez N., Hailpern B. and Taubenfeld (1989) Script: a communication abstraction mechanism and its verification. *Science of Computer Programming* 6(1), pp. 35-88

Fukanaga K. (1986) An experience with a Prolog-based object-oriented language. In *Proc. OOPSLA'86*, pp. 224-234

Gehani N.H. and Roome W.D. (1988) Concurrent C++ : Concurrent programming with classes. *Software – Practice and Experience* 18(12), pp. 1157-1177

Ghelli G. and Orsini R. (1990) Types and subtypes as partial equivalence relations. In Lenzerini *et al.* (1990), pp. 191-209

Gibbs S. (1991) Composite multimedia and active objects. In *Proc. OOPSLA'91*, pp. 97-112

Goguen J.A., Thatcher J.W. and Wagner E.G. (1978) An initial algebra approach to the specification, correctness and implementation of abstract data types. In *Current trends in programming methodology*, Vol. 4, Yeh R.T. (ed.), Prentice Hall, pp. 80-149

Goguen J.A. and Meseguer J. (1986) Extensions and foundations of object-oriented programming. *ACM SIGPLAN Notices*, Oct. 1986, pp. 153-162

Goldberg A. and Robson D. (1983) *Smalltalk-80: The language and its implementation.* Addison-Wesley

Gorlen K. (1987) An object-oriented class library for C++ programs. *Software – Practice and Experience* 17(12), pp. 899-922

Gorlen K., Orlow S. and Plexico P. (1990) *Data abstraction and object-oriented programming in C++.* Wiley

Graham I. (1991) *Object-oriented methods.* Addison-Wesley

Gries D. (1981) *The science of programming.* Springer

Grimshaw A.S. and Liu J.W.S. (1987) Mentat: an object-oriented macro data flow system. In *Proc. OOPSLA '87, ACM SIGPLAN Notices* 22(12), pp. 35-47

Guimaraes N. (1991) Building generic interface tools: an experience with multiple inheritance. In *Proc. OOPSLA'91*, pp. 89-96

Guttag J.V. and Horning J.J. (1978) The algebraic specification of data types. *Acta Informatica* 10, pp. 27-52

Halasz F. (1988) Reflections on NoteCards: seven issues for the next generation of hypermedia systems. *CACM* 31(7), pp. 836-852

Halasz F. (1991) Seven issues revisited. Invited lecture ACM Hypertext 91

Halasz F. and Schwartz M. (1994) The Dexter Hypertext reference model. *CACM* 37(2), pp. 30-39

Halbert D. and O 'Brien P. (1987) Using types and inheritance in Object-Oriented Programming. *IEEE Software* 4(5), pp. 71-79

Hammer M. and McLeod D. (1978) The semantic data model: a modeling mechanism for database applications. In *Proc. ACM SIGMOD Int. Conf. on Management of Data*, pp. 26-35

Hammer M. and McLeod D. (1981) Database description with SDM: A semantic database model. *ACM Trans. Data Syst.* 6, pp. 351-386

Hardman L., Bulterman D.C.A. and van Rossum G. (1993) The   Amsterdam hypermedia model: extending hypertext to real multimedia. *Hypermedia* 5(1), pp. 47-69

Hardman L., Bulterman D.C.A. and van Rossum G. (1994) The   Amsterdam hypermedia model: adding time and context to the Dexter model. *CACM* 37(2), pp. 50-62

Harel D. (1987) Statecharts: a visual formalism for complex systems. *Science of Computer Programming* 8, pp. 231-274

Harmon P. and Taylor D.A. (1993) *Objects in action – Commercial applications of object-oriented technologies.* Addison-Wesley

Hayes F. and Coleman D. (1991) Coherent models for object-oriented analysis. In *Proc. OOPSLA'91, ACM Sigplan Notices* 26(4), pp. 171-183

Hayes I. (1992) *Specification Case Studies.* Prentice Hall, 2nd edn

Headington M.R. and Riley D.D. (1994) *Data abstraction and structures using C++.* D.C. Heath and Company

Helm R., Holland I.M. and Gangopadhyay D. (1990) Contracts: Specifying behavioral compositions in object-oriented systems. In *Proc. ECOOP/OOPSLA'90*, pp. 169-180

Henderson-Sellers B. and Edwards J.M. (1990) The object-oriented systems life cycle. *CACM* 33(9), pp. 143-159

Henderson-Sellers B. (1992) *A book of object-oriented knowledge.* Prentice-Hall

Henderson P. (1993) *Object-oriented specification and design with C++.* McGraw-Hill

Hewitt C. (1977) Viewing Control Structures as Patterns of Passing Messages. *Artificial Intelligence* 8, pp. 323-364

Hoare C.A.R. (1969) An axiomatic basis for computer programming. *CACM* 12, pp. 576-580, 583

Hoare C.A.R. (1972) Proof of correctness of data representation. *Acta Informatica* 1, pp. 271-281

Hoare C.A.R. (1978) Communicating Sequential Processes. *CACM* 21(8), pp. 666-677

Hoare C.A.R. (1987) An overview of some formal methods for program design. *IEEE Computer* (September 1987), pp. 85-91

Holland I.M. (1992) Specifying reusable components using contracts. In *Proc. ECOOP'92* (Lehrmann Madsen O., ed.), Springer, pp. 287-308

Hopcroft J.E. (1997) *Introduction to automata theory, languages and computation.* Addison-Wesley

Howell G. (1992) *Building Hypermedia Applications – A Software Developer Guide.* McGraw-Hill

Hu D. (1989) *C/C++ for expert systems.* MIS Press

Ince D. (1991) *Object-oriented software engineering with C++.* McGraw-Hill

Ishikawa Y., Tokuda H. and Mercer C.W. (1992) An object-oriented real time programming language. *IEEE Computer* 25(10), pp. 66-73

Jacobson I., Christeron M., Jonsson P. and Övergaard G. (1992) *Object-oriented software engineering – A use case driven approach.* Addison-Wesley

Jarvinen H., Kurki-Suoni R., Sakkinen M. and Systa K. (1990) Object-oriented specification of reactive systems. In *Proc. Int. Conf. on Software Engineering*, Nice, France, pp. 63-71

Johnson R.E. and Foote B. (1988) Designing reusable classes. *JOOP* 1(2), pp. 22-35

Jones C.B. (1991) *Systematic software development using VDM.* Prentice Hall, 2d edn.

Jones G.W. (1990) *Software Engineering.* Wiley

Kafura D. and Lee K. (1989) Inheritance in actor based concurrent object-oriented languages. In *Proc. ECOOP '89*, Cambridge University Press, pp. 131-145

Kafura D. and Lee K. (1990) ACT++ : building a concurrent C++ with actors. *JOOP* 3(1), May/June 1990, pp. 25-37

Kahn K., Tribble E.D., Miller M.S. and Bobrow D.G. (1986) Objects in concurrent logic programming languages. In *Proc. OOPSLA'86*, pp. 242-257

Kim W. and Lochovsky F.,eds. (1989) *Object-oriented concepts, databases and applications.* Addison-Wesley

King R. (1989) My cat is object-oriented. In Kim and Lochovsky (1989), pp. 23-30

Knudsen J.L. and Madsen O.L. (1988) Teaching object-oriented programming is more than teaching object-oriented programming languages. In *Proc. ECOOP'88*, Springer LNCS 276, pp. 21-40

Knuth D. (1992) *Literate Programming.* CSLI Lecture Notes 27, Stanford

Krasner G. (1984) *Smalltalk-80: Bits of history, words of advice.* Addison-Wesley

Krasner G.E. and Pope S.T. (1988) A cookbook for using the Model-View-Controller user interface paradigm in Smalltalk-80. *JOOP*, August 1988, pp. 26-49

Kunz J.C., Kehler T.P. and Williams M.D. (1984) Applications development using a hybrid AI development system. *AI Magazine*, September 1984, pp. 41-54

Kurki-Suonio R. and Jarvinen H.M. (1989) Action system approach to the specification and design of distributed systems. In *Proc. 5th Int. Workshop on Software Specification and Design, ACM Software Engineering Notes* 14(3), pp. 34-40

Kurtz B., Woodfield S.N. and Embley D.W. (1990) *Object-oriented system analysis – a model-driven approach.* Prentice Hall

Lalonde W. and Pugh J. (1991) Subclassing ≠ Subtyping ≠ Is-a. *JOOP* 1991, pp. 57-63

Lea R., Jacquemot C. and Pillevesse E. (1993) COOL: System support for distributed programming. *CACM* 36(9), pp. 34-46

LeJacq J.P. (1991) Function preconditions in object-oriented software. *ACM Sigplan Notices* 26(10), pp. 13-18

Leggett B. and Franklin D. (1994) ObjectCenter 2.0 for SunSparc. Product Review C++Report Febr 1994, pp. 66-71

Open Software Foundation (1992) *Introduction to DCE.* Prentice Hall

Lenzerini M., Nardi D. and Simi M. (eds.) (1990) *Inheritance hierarchies in knowledge representation and programming languages.* Wiley

Levy H.M. (1984) *Capability-based computer systems.* Digital Press, Bedford Massachusetts

Lieberherr K. and Holland I. (1989) Assuring good style for object-oriented programs. *IEEE Software* 6(5), pp. 38-48 (1989)

Lieberman H. (1986) Using prototypical objects to implement shared behavior in object-oriented systems. In *Proc. OOPSLA'86*, pp. 214-223

Linton M., Vlissides J. and Calder P. (1989) Composing user interfaces with Interviews. *IEEE Computer* 22(2), pp. 8-22

Lippman S. (1991) *A C++ Primer.* Addison-Wesley, 2nd edn.

Liskov B.H. and Zilles S.N. (1974) Programming with abstract data types. *ACM Sigplan Notices* 9, pp. 50-59

Liskov B.H. and Zilles S.N. (1975) Specification techniques for data abstraction. *IEEE Trans. on Software Engineering* 1, pp. 7-19

Liskov B. and Wing J.L. (1993) A new definition of the subtype relation. In *Proc. ECOOP'93*, Springer LNCS 707, pp. 119-141

Locke N. (1994) C++ FTP libraries. *C++Report* 6(2), pp. 61-65

London R. and Duisberg R. (1985) Animating programs using Smalltalk. *IEEE Computer* 18(8), pp. 61-71

MacDougall M.H. (1987) *Simulating computer systems – techniques and tools.* MIT Press

Malenfant J., Lapalme G. and Vaucher J. (1989) ObjVProlog: Metaclasses in Logic. In *Proc. ECOOP'89*, Cambridge University Press, pp. 257-269

Matsuoka S. and Yonezawa A. (1993) Analysis of inheritance anomaly in object-oriented concurrent programming languages. In Agha *et al.* (1993), pp. 107-150

McCue D.L. (1992) Developing a class hierarchy for object-oriented transaction processing. In *Proc. ECOOP '92*, Springer LNCS 615, pp. 413-426

McGregor J. and Sykes D. (1992) *Object-oriented software development: engineering software for reuse.* Van Nostrand Reinhold

McKnight C., Dillon A. and Richardson J. (1992) *Hypertext in Context.* Cambridge University Press

Meyer B. (1988) *Object-oriented software construction.* Prentice Hall

Meyer B. (1990) Tools for the new culture: Lessons from the design of the Eiffel libraries. *CACM* 33(9), pp. 69-88

Meyer B. (1992a) *Eiffel: the Language.* Prentice Hall

Meyer B. (1992b) Applying Design by Contract. *IEEE Computer* 25(10), pp. 40-51

Meyer B. (1993) Systematic concurrent object-oriented programming. *CACM* 36(9), pp. 56-80

Meyer B. and Nerson J-M., eds. (1993) *Object-oriented applications.* Prentice Hall

Meyer B. (1994) *Reusable software – The base object-oriented component libraries.* Prentice Hall

Meyrowitz N. (1986) Intermedia: The Architecture and Construction of an Object-Oriented Hypermedia System and Applications Framework. In *Proc. OOPSLA '86*, pp. 186-201

Milner R. (1983) *Communication and concurrency.* Prentice Hall

Milner R., Tofte M. and Harper R. (1990) *The definition of Standard ML.* MIT Press

Minsky M. (1975) A framework for representing knowledge. In *The psychology of computer vision*, Winston P. (ed.), McGraw-Hill, New York, pp. 211-277

Mock M.U. (1993) DCE++: Distributed C++ Objects using OSF DCE. In *DCE – The OSF Distributed Computing Environment*, Schill A. (ed.), Springer LNCS 731, pp. 242-255

Moon D.A. (1986) Object-oriented programming with Flavors. In *Proc. OOPSLA'86*, pp. 1-8

Mullin M. (1989) *Object-oriented program design with examples in C++.* Addison-Wesley

Myers G.J. (1979) *The art of software testing.* Wiley

Nelson M. (1991) Concurrency and object-oriented programming. *ACM Sigplan Notices* 26(10), pp. 63-72

Neusius C. (1991) Synchronizing actions. In *Proc. ECOOP '91*, Springer LNCS 512, Springer, pp. 118-132

Nierstrasz O. (1987) Active objects in Hybrid. In *Proc. OOPSLA'87*, pp. 243-253

Nierstrasz O. and Papathomas M. (1990) Towards a type theory of active objects. In: *OOPS Messenger, April '91*, ACM, pp. 89-93

Nierstrasz O., Gibbs S. and Tsichritzis D. (1992) Component oriented software development. *CACM* 35(9), pp. 160-166

Nierstrasz O. (1993) Composing active objects – the next 700 concurrent object-oriented languages. In Agha *et al.* (1993)

Nolte J. (1991) Language-level support for remote object invocations. GMD FIRST Report, German National Research Center for Computer Science (1991)

Nyce J.M. and Kahn P., eds. (1991) *From Memex to Hypertext: Vannevar Bush and the Mind's Machine.* Academic Press

OMG (1991) *The Common Object Request Broker : Architecture and Specification.* Revision 1.1, Object Management Group

Ousterhout J.K. (1990) Tcl: an embeddable command language. In *Proc. USENIX Winter Conference*, pp. 133-146

Ousterhout J.K. (1991) An X11 Toolkit based on the Tcl language. In *Proc. USENIX Winter Conference*, pp. 105-115

Ousterhout J.K. (1993) Hypergraphics and hypertext in Tk. *The X resource* 5, pp. 113-127

Ousterhout J.K. (1994) *Tcl and the Tk toolkit.* Addison-Wesley

Paepcke A., ed. (1993) *Object-oriented programming – The CLOS perspective.* MIT Press

Palsberg J. and Schwartzback M.I. (1994) *Object-oriented type systems.* Wiley

Parnas D.L. (1972a) A technique for software module specification. *CACM* 15, pp. 330-336

Parnas D.L. (1972b) On the criteria to be used in decomposing systems into modules. *CACM* 15, pp. 1052-1058

Parrington G. and Shrivastava S. (1988) Implementing concurrency control in reliable distributed object-oriented systems. In *Proc. ECOOP '88*, Springer LNCS 322, pp. 233-249

Parsaye K., Chignell M., Koshafian S. and Wong H. (1989) *Intelligent databases: Object-oriented, deductive and hypermedia technologies.* Wiley

Pierce B.C. (1993) Intersection types and bounded polymorphism. In Bezem en Grootte (1993), pp. 346-359

Pierce B.C., Remy D. and Turner D.N. (1993) A typed higher-order programming language based onthe pi-calculus. Report University of Edinburgh (available at `ftp.dcs.ed.ac.uk:pub/bcp/pilang.ps`)

Pinson L. and Wiener R., eds. (1990) *Applications of Object Oriented Programming.* Addison-Wesley

Plotkin G.D. (1983) An operational semantics for CSP. In *Formal Description of Programming Concepts II*, D.Bjorner (ed.), North Holland, pp. 199-223

Plotkin G.D. and Abadi M. (1993) A logic for parametric polymorphism. In Bezem en Grootte (1993), pp. 361-375

Pohl I. (1989) *C++ for C programmers.* Benjamin Cummings

Pokkunuri B. (1989) Object Oriented Programming. *ACM Sigplan Notices* 24(11), pp. 96-101

Pope S. (1991) *The Well-Tempered Object: Musical applications of Object-Oriented Software Technology.* MIT Press

Potter B., Sinclair J. and Till D. (1991) An introduction to formal specification and Z. Prentice Hall

Press W.H., Teukolsky S.A., Vetterling W.T. and Flannery B.P. (1992) *Numerical Recipes in C – The art of scientific computing.* Cambridge University Press, 2nd edn

Rabin M.O. (1974) The computational complexity of Artificial Intelligence. IEEE Symposium

Reiser M. and Wirth N. (1992) *Programming in Oberon: Steps beyond Pascal and Modula.* Addison-Wesley

Reiss S.P. (1990a) Interacting with the FIELD environment. *IEEE Software – Practice and Experience* 20(1), pp. 89-115

Reiss S.P. (1990b) Connecting tools using message passing in the FIELD program development environment. *IEEE Software – Practice and Experience* 20(1)

Reverchon A. and Ducampl M. (1993) *Mathematical software tools in C++.* Wiley

Rieken B., Weiman L. (1992) *Adventures in Unix network applications programming.* Wiley

Ross P. (1988) Object-oriented techniques in AI. In *Proc. Object Oriented Computing Systems* (Randell B., ed.) University of NewCastle upon Tyne, England

Rumbaugh J., Blaha M., Premerlani W., Eddi F. and Lorensen W. (1991) *Object-oriented modeling and design.* Prentice Hall

Sakkinen M. (1989) Disciplined inheritance. In *Proc. ECOOP'89* (Cook S., ed.), Cambridge University Press, pp. 35-56

Sanden B. (1994) A graduate course in object-oriented analysis based on student-generated projects. Technical Report ISSE-TR-94-102, George Mason University, Fairfax, USA

Saunders J. (1989) A survey of object-oriented programming languages. *JOOP* March/April 1989, pp. 5-11

Schindler M. (1987) Expert system fits with conventional software. *Electronic design* 14, pp. 87

Schmidt D.C. (1993) The object-oriented design and implementation of the Reactor. *C++Report*, Sept. 1993, pp. 33-43

Sedgewick R. (1992) *Algorithms in C++.* Addison-Wesley

Shapiro E. and Takeuchi A. (1983) Object-oriented programming in Concurrent Prolog. *New Generation Computing* 1(2), pp. 5-48

Shapiro M., Gautron P. and Mosseri L. (1989) Persistence and migration for C++ objects. In *Proc. ECOOP '89*, Cambridge University Press, pp. 191-204

Shaw M. (1984) Abstraction techniques in modern programming languages. *IEEE Software*, October 1984, pp. 10-26

Shlaer S. and Mellor S.J. (1988) *Object-oriented analysis: modeling the world in data.* Yourdon Press, Englewood Cliffs, N.J.

Shlaer S. and Mellor S.J. (1992) *Object life cycles: modeling the world in states.* Yourdon Press, Englewood Cliffs, N.J.

Shriver B. and Wegner P. (1987) *Research directions in object-oriented programming.* MIT Press

Smith M.D. and Robson D.J. (1990) Object-oriented programming – the problem of validation. In *Proc. of the 6th Int. Conf. on Software Maintenance*, IEEE, pp. 272-282

Smith M.D. and Robson D.J. (1992) A framework for testing object-oriented programs. *JOOP* 5(3), pp. 45-53

Snyder A. (1986) Encapsulation and inheritance in object-oriented programming languages. In *Proc. OOPSLA 1986*, pp. 31-45 (extended verion in: Shriver and Wegner (1987), pp. 165-188)

Stasko J. (1990) Tango – A framework and system for algorithm animation. PhD thesis, Brown University

Stepney S., Barden R. and Cooper D. (eds.) (1992) *Object orientation in Z.* Springer

Strickland H. (1993) ODMG-93 – The object database standard for C++. *C++Report*, October, pp. 45-48, 70

Stroustrup B. (1986) *The C++ Programming Language.* Addison-Wesley, 1986

Stroustrup B. (1988) What is "Object-Oriented Programming"?. *IEEE Software* 5(3), pp. 10-20

Stroustrup B. (1991) *The C++ Programming Language.* Addison-Wesley, 2nd edn

Stroustrup B. (1994) *The Design and Evolution of C++.* Addison-Wesley

Stefik M. and Bobrow D.G. (1986) Object-oriented programming: themes and variations. *AI Magazine*, December 1986, pp. 40-62

Stubbs D. and Webre N. (1987) *Data structures with abstract data types and Modula-2.* Brooks and Cole

Taivalsaari A. (1993) On the notion of object. *J. Systems Software* 21, pp. 3-16

Tello E.R. (1989) *Object-oriented programming for Artificial Intelligence.* Addison-Wesley

Thomsen K.S. (1987) Inheritance on processes, exemplified on distributed termination detection. *Int. Journal for Parallel Computing* 16(1), pp. 17-52

Touretsky S. (1986) *The mathematics of inheritance systems.* Pitman London

Ungar D. and Smith R.B. (1987) Self: The power of simplicity. In *Proc. OOPSLA'87*, *ACM Sigplan Notices* 4(8), pp. 227-242

Ungar D., Smith B.S., Chambers C. and Hölze U. (1992) Object, message and performance: How they coexist in Self. *IEEE Computer* 25(10), pp. 53-63

van Vliet J.C. (1993) *Software Engineering.* Wiley

Walker D. (1990) Pi-calculus semantics of object-oriented programming languages. Report ECS-LFCS-90-122, University of Edinburgh

Wasserman A., Pircher P. and Muller R.J. (1989) An object-oriented structured design method for code generation. *Software Engineering Notes* 14(1), pp. 32-55

Waterworth J. and Chignell M. (1989) A manifesto for hypermedia usability research. *Hypermedia* 1(3), pp. 205-234

Watkins K. (1993) *Discrete event simulation in C.* McGraw-Hill

Webster D. (1988) Mapping the Design Information Representation Domain. *IEEE Computer*, December 1988, pp. 8-23

Wegner P. (1987) Dimensions of object-based language design. *ACM Sigplan Notices* 23(11), pp. 168-182

Wegner P. (1992) Dimensions of object-oriented modeling. *IEEE Computer* 25(10), pp. 12-19

Wegner P. and S. Zdonik S. (1988) Inheritance as an Incremental Modification Mechanisms or what Like Is and Isn't Like. In *Proc. ECOOP'88*, Springer, pp. 56-77

Weinand A., Gamma E. and Marty R. (1988) ET++, an object-oriented application framework in C++. In *Proc. OOPSLA'88*, pp.46-57

Weiss M.A. (1993) *Data structures and algorithm analysis in C++.* Addison-Wesley

Weyuker E.J. (1988) Evaluating software complexity measures. *IEEE Trans. on Software Engineering* 14(9), pp. 1357-1365

Wiener R. and Pinson L. (1988) *An introduction to object-oriented programming and C++.* Addison-Wesley

Wilkie G. (1993) *Object-oriented software engineering – The professional developers guide.* Addison-Wesley

Winblad A., Edwards S. and King D. (1990) *Object-oriented software.* Addison-Wesley

Wirfs-Brock R. (1989) Object-oriented design: a responsibility-driven approach. In *Proc. OOPSLA'89*, pp. 71-75

Wirfs-Brock R., Wilkerson B. and Wiener L. (1990) *Designing object-oriented software.* Prentice Hall

Wirth N. (1983) *Programming in Modula-2.* Springer

Woodhead N. (1990) *Hypertext and hypermedia.* Addison-Wesley

Wyatt B.R., Kavi K. and Hufnagel S. (1992) Parallelism in object-oriented languages: A survey. *IEEE Computer* 9(6), pp. 56-66

Yonezawa A. and Tokoro M., eds. (1987) *Object-oriented concurrent systems.* MIT Press

Yourdon E. and Constantine L. (1979) *Structured Design: Fundamentals of a discipline of computer programming and design.* Prentice Hall

Yourdon E. (1989) *Modern structured analysis.* Yourdon Press, Englewood Cliffs, N.J.

Zdonik S. and Maier D. (1990) *Readings in object-oriented database systems.* Morgan Kaufmann

Index